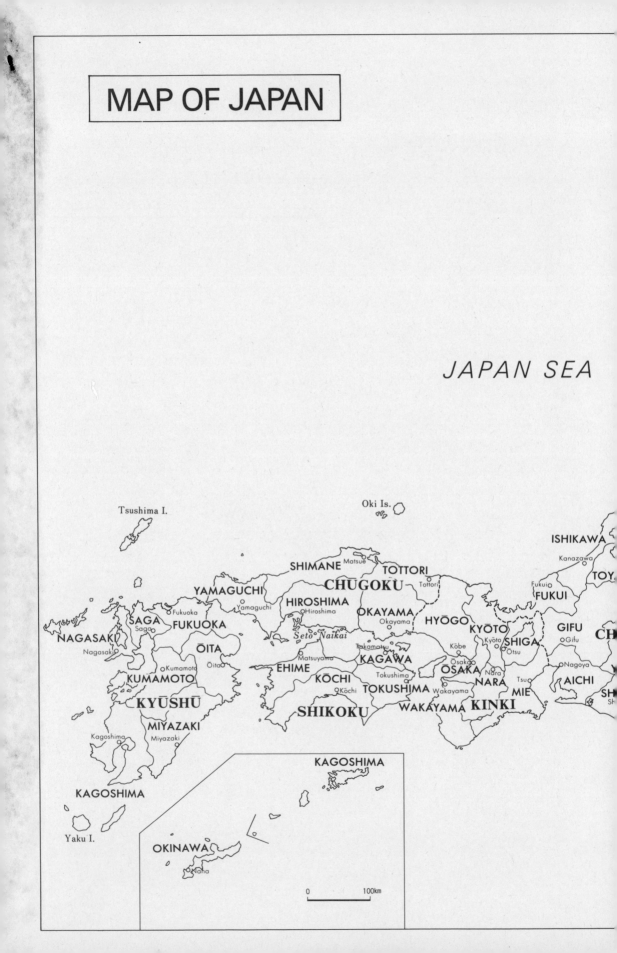

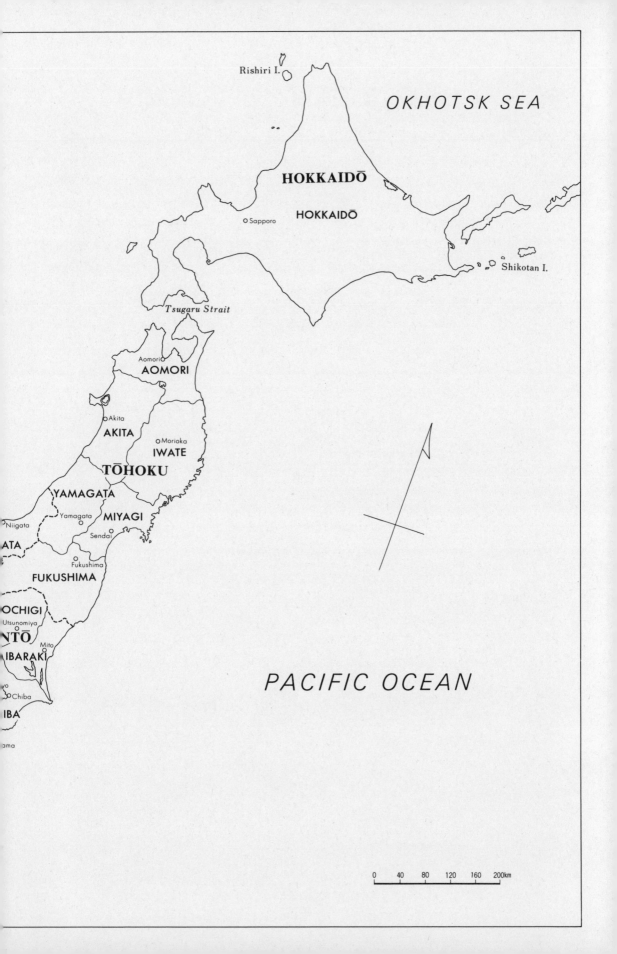

Rishiri I.

OKHOTSK SEA

HOKKAIDŌ

HOKKAIDŌ

○ Sapporo

Shikotan I.

Tsugaru Strait

Aomori○
AOMORI

○Akita
AKITA

○Morioka
IWATE

TŌHOKU

YAMAGATA

○Niigata

Yamagata○
MIYAGI

Sendai○

○Fukushima
FUKUSHIMA

ATA

OCHIGI

Utsunomiya○

NTŌ

Mito○
IBARAKI

○Chiba

IBA

ama

PACIFIC OCEAN

0   40   80   120   160   200km

JAPANESE FOR BUSY PEOPLE

II

JAPANESE FOR BUSY PEOPLE

II

Association for Japanese-Language Teaching

KODANSHA INTERNATIONAL
Tokyo and New York

Distributed in the United States by Kodansha International/USA Ltd., 114 Fifth Avenue, New York, New York 10011. Published by Kodansha International Ltd., 2-2 Otowa 1-chome, Bunkyo-ku, Tokyo 112 and Kodansha International/USA Ltd., 114 Fifth Avenue, New York, New York 10011. Copyright © 1989 by the Association for Japanese-Language Teaching. All rights reserved. Printed in Japan.

ISBN 4-7700-1419-8 (in Japan)

First edition, 1990

Library of Congress Cataloging in Publication Data
Japanese for busy people II
  Includes index.
  1. Japanese language—Textbooks for foreign speakers—English. I. Kokusai Nihongo Fukyū Kyōkai (Japan)
PL539.5.E5J36 1989   495.6'83421   88-46049
ISBN 0-87011-919-2

CONTENTS

INTRODUCTION

This text carries on from where our previous work, *Japanese for Busy People I*, leaves off, and, as before, the main focus is on having adult students acquire a working knowledge of the spoken language in everyday life. Written Japanese, including Sino-Japanese characters, is also included. Aside from minor changes necessary to accommodate the greater length and complexity of the material, the format is the same as in the introductory volume.

Key factors in the development of these texts have been a thorough evaluation of existing teaching materials and a reassessment of the ability and objectives of students. It has generally been assumed that businessmen, diplomats, technicians or scholars for whom Japanese is a second language can use it in their work only after having reached an advanced level. However, both the spoken and written languages encountered in science or business, being specialized and adapted to a particular field, are more explicit than the language found in literature or even informal conversation. Moreover, having professional knowledge of a subject area contributes to comprehension, which is understandably more difficult if one is on unfamiliar ground. As a consequence it is possible for motivated learners to go on to specialized programs of their choice after finishing the basic level, that is, a level which can be reached at the end of this volume by applied study.

As before, the vocabulary and situations dealt with are slanted slightly towards business people, but there is no technical language or jargon, and the material is general enough to give students of college age or above an orientation to daily life in Japan and its customs and traditions. Speech of varied levels of politeness and formality and elliptical and contracted forms and expressions occur as appropriate.

Arrangement of the Book

The forty lessons in this volume, divided into parts I and II, require approximately two hundred hours of classroom time. In this main text, all the Japanese is written in Japanese. The Supplement to the Text gives all the romanized Japanese for the twenty lessons in part I. Also in the supplement are the answers to the quizzes and the opening passages of each lesson in the format they would ordinarily be written in in Japanese.

A new feature in this volume is the gradual introduction of kanji in the opening dialogues and reading sections. The first occurrence of a kanji in each lesson is in *furigana*, the contextual reading of the character being given in hiragana just below the kanji itself. Guidance on how to write each character (stroke order and the number of strokes), a few additional readings and, from lesson 21 on, compound words for recognition are given in the section after lesson 40.

As noted above, in other respects the arrangement of this book is the same as the earlier one.

To the Reader

This text presupposes familiarity with the grammar and vocabulary in *volume I*; any student who has difficulty with the first lessons in this book should review the beginning text before proceeding to this more advanced material.

Mastery of hiragana and katakana was recommended in the introduction to the first volume, since reliance on romanized Japanese tends to have a negative effect on pronunciation. Another reason for learning the Japanese writing systems as early as possible is that romanized Japanese has only very limited applications, the only publications printed in this script being basic texts for Japanese as a second language.

It is a good idea to learn kanji when they first occur, as a knowledge of Sino-Japanese characters is an absolute must for advanced study of the language. Knowing these characters makes learning faster and more effective, and students already able to read them should take advantage of the vertically written Japanese passages in the supplement, using them as their main text, or at least for reference.

Other students will find this normally written Japanese of value both for studying kanji and for getting used to the conventions of ordinary Japanese writing. After a lesson has been studied, its opening dialogue or reading passage in the supplement can be compared with the same section in the main text.

Linguistic Differences

Students who have completed the first volume or its equivalent are probably already aware of at least a few of the ways in which Japanese and English differ and know that at times translating from one language into the other can be challenging.

In these volumes we have taken the position that each language should be as natural and unforced as is possible in a book of instruction. In those cases where literal translation into English is inadvisable, the situation is taken into account, appropriate English is used, and sometimes this is followed by a literal translation to give a better idea of the meanings of Japanese words and other expressions. The vocabulary lists have been compiled in a similar way. The contextual meanings of words are given first, then, if the literal meaning is different, that is given too. When a term has other common additional meanings, these are given too, to the extent possible. This should help the student to avoid forming the habit of thinking a word is always translated into English in exactly the same way, whereas in fact with a great many vocabulary items a certain amount of flexibility is needed.

Another important aspect of linguistic differences is grammar. It has been our intention to incorporate in these lessons grammar patterns that are typical and essential, while at the same time not allowing the explanations of grammar to become too technical. Although English grammar terms appear in the descriptions of Japanese grammar, they should be regarded as expedients only, used for the sake of understandability. In discussing grammar, attaining a working knowledge takes priority over theoretical understanding.

ACKNOWLEDGMENTS

Four AJALT teachers have written this textbook. They are Ms. Miyako Iwami, Ms. Shigeko Miyazaki, Ms. Masako Nagai and Ms. Kimiko Yamamato. They were assisted by two other teachers, Ms. Kumiko Endo and Ms. Chikako Ogura.

For background information, many sources were consulted. The authors would particularly like to thank the Japan Sumo Association for making it possible to write lesson 14, the Meteorological Agency for material included in lesson 20 and the Agency for Cultural Affairs for information used in lesson 39. They also wish to express their appreciation to their editors at Kodansha International for assistance with translating and rewriting, as well as the more usual editorial tasks.

ABBREVIATIONS
aff.   affirmative
neg.   negative
A*a*:   answer, affirmative
A*n*:   answer, negative
ex.   example
-i adj.   **-i** adjective
-na adj.   **-na** adjective
† Indicates a word or expression that is not found in contemporary Japanese.

PART

1

LESSON 1 RUSH HOUR

Mr. Chang tells Mr. Smith about taking a rush hour train for the first time.

チャン：けさ、はじめて でんしゃで 会社に 来ました。とても こんでいま
　　　　した。えきの 人が じょうきゃくの せなかを おして、中に おし
　　　　こんでいました。すごかったですよ。

スミス：でも でんしゃの ほうが くるまより はやいですよ。
　　　　みちも こんでいますから。

チャン：スミスさんは なんで つうきんしていますか。

スミス：わたしは 行きも かえりも ちかてつです。とうきょうの こうつう
　　　　きかんの 中で ちかてつが いちばん べんりですよ。

チャン：ちかてつは あさも ゆうがたも こんでいますか。

スミス：ええ、でも ゆうがたは あさほど こんでいません。
　　　　あさの 8時はんごろが ピークですから、わたしは まいあさ 7時
　　　　に うちを でます。

チャン：その じかんは すいていますか。

スミス：ええ、7時ごろは 8時ごろより すいていますよ。わたしは まいあ
　　　　さ ちかてつの 中で 日本語を べんきょうしています。カセットテ
　　　　ープを ききながら、テキストを よんでいます。

チャン：へえ、そうですか。

Chang: This morning I came to work by train for the first time. It was awfully crowded. The station people were pushing on passengers' backs and squeezing them inside (the trains). It was terrible.

Smith: Trains are faster than cars, though. The roads are crowded too.

Chang: How do you commute?

Smith: I come and go back by subway. The subway is the most convenient of all transportation systems in Tokyo.

Chang: I suppose the subway is crowded morning and evening.

Smith: Yes. But evenings are not so crowded as mornings. Around 8:30 (A.M) is the peak of the rush hour, so every morning I leave home at seven.

Chang: Is it emptier at that time?

Smith: Oh, yes. (Around) 7 o'clock is less crowded than (around) 8 o'clock. I study Japanese on the subway every morning. I read the text while listening to the cassette tape.

Chang: Oh, really?

Vocabulary			

けさ	**kesa**, this morning	こうつう	**kōtsū**, transportation
はじめて	**hajimete**, for the first time	きかん	**kikan**, system
じょうきゃく	**jōkyaku**, passenger	~の なかで	**no naka de**, of all, among
せなか	**senaka**, back	いちばん	**ichiban**, most, number one
おしこんでいました	**oshikonde imashita**, squeezing	~ほど…ません	**hodo . . . masen**, not so . . . as
おしこみます（おしこむ）	**oshikomimasu (oshikomu)**, squeeze	ピーク	**pīku**, peak
すごい	**sugoi**, terrible, wonderful	その じかん	**sono jikan**, that time
でも	**demo**, though	すいています	**suite imasu**, be empty
~の ほうが	**no hō ga**, = -er/more/less	すきます（すく）	**sukimasu (suku)**, be/become empty/ uncrowded
ほう	**hō**, more (*lit.* side)		
~より	**yori**, than	カセットテープ	**kasetto tēpu**, cassette tape
はやい	**hayai**, fast		
みち	**michi**, road, street	ききながら	**kikinagara**, while listening
つうきんしています	**tsūkin shite imasu**, commute	~ながら	**-nagara**, while——ing, at the same time
つうきん	**tsūkin**, commuting		
~も~も	**mo . . . mo**, both . . . and	へえ	**hē**, oh

GRAMMAR & LESSON OBJECTIVES

• Comparisons

. . . no hō ga . . . yori

Densha no hō ga kuruma yori hayai desu. The word order can be reversed: **Kuruma yori densha no hō ga hayai desu.**

To compare two things the question pattern is: **. . . to . . . to dochira/dotchi ga . . . desu/ -masu ka.**

ex. **Yokohama to Tōkyō to dochira ga ōkii desu ka.** "Which is bigger, Yokohama or Tokyo?"

The response, "Tokyo is bigger than Yokohama," can be any of the following:

ex. **Yokohama yori Tōkyō no hō ga ōkii desu.**

Tōkyō no hō ga Yokohama yori ōkii desu.

Tōkyō no hō ga ōkii desu.

Tōkyō wa Yokohama yori ōkii desu is a statement with the same meaning. The dialogue sentence **7-ji goro wa . . .** is of this type.

. . . no naka de . . . ichiban

Tōkyō no kōtsū kikan no naka de chikatetsu ga ichiban benri desu.

Ichiban, "number one, the first," before adjectives expresses the superlative degree of comparison—**ichiban suki**, "most likeable, best liked"; **ichiban kirei**, "prettiest," and so on. Note how the subject marker **ga** discriminates the subject exclusively from other possibilities. The example above implies that neither taxis nor buses nor trains but subways are the most convenient.

ex. **Nihon no toshi no naka de Tōkyō ga ichiban ōkii desu.** "Among Japanese cities, Tokyo is the biggest."

Kudamono no naka de ringo ga ichiban suki desu. "Of all fruits, (I) like apples best."

To compare three or more things, the question pattern is: **. . . no naka de nani/dore/dare/ itsu/doko ga ichiban . . . desu/-masu ka.**

ex. **Nihon no toshi no naka de doko ga ichiban ōkii desu ka.** "Which among Japanese cities is the biggest?"

. . . hodo . . . masen

Yūgata wa asa hodo konde imasen.

A **wa** B **hodo** with negative verbs and adjectives means A is not so . . . as B.

ex. **Ōsaka wa Tōkyō hodo ōkikunai desu.**

● **-nagara**

Kasetto tēpu o kikinagara tekisuto o yonde imasu.

This is made with the stem of the **-masu** form and **-nagara**, and then the main clause is added. It is used when the subject of the sentences, always animate, is doing two things at the same time. The primary activity is designated in the main clause.

NOTES

1. **Watashi wa iki mo kaeri mo chikatetsu desu.**
   Chikatetsu wa asa mo yūgata mo konde imasu.
   Mo, repeated to mean "both . . . and . . . ," is used in negative sentences too to express "neither . . . nor . . ." Words like **iki** and **kaeri** (the **-masu** stems of the verbs **ikimasu** and **kaerimasu**) are at times employed in a way similar to English gerunds (here *coming* and *going* back).

2. **Sono jikan**
   Chang is referring to Smith's preceding sentence, "I leave home at seven." **Ko, so, a, do** words are not limited to things immediately at hand. They may, like *this* and *that*, refer to intangibles, abstractions or previous phrases or statements. (*See also* p. 132.)

3. **Nihon-go o benkyō shite imasu**
   Both **benkyō o shimasu** and **benkyō shimasu** are correct but when, as here, there is a direct object followed by **o, benkyō shimasu** is the inevitable choice.
   ex. **Denwa (o) shimasu.** "I'll telephone."
   Sōdan (o) shimasu. "I'll consult (her)."

PRACTICE

KEY SENTENCES

1. とうきょうは おおさかより おおきいです。
2. とうきょうと おおさかと どちらが おおきいですか。
   とうきょうの ほうが おおきいです。
3. 3がつは 1がつほど さむくないです。
4. ［わたしは］ スポーツの なかで テニスが いちばん すきです。
5. スミスさんは コーヒーを のみながら、テレビを みています。

1. Tokyo is bigger than Osaka.
2. Which is bigger, Tokyo or Osaka?
   Tokyo is bigger.
3. March is not so cold as January.

4. I like tennis best of all sports.
5. Mr. Smith is drinking coffee while watching TV.

Vocabulary

～と～と   **to ... to,** (particle for   スポーツ   **supōtsu,** sports
                 comparisons)
どちら   **dochira,** which

EXERCISES

Make dialogues by changing the underlined parts as in the examples given.

A. *ex.* **Q**：ちきゅうは　つきより　おおきいですか。
     A：ええ、つきより　おおきいです。

       1. とうきょうの　じんこう、ロンドンの　じんこう、おおいです
       2. みず、あぶら、おもいです
       3. はやしさん、かとうさん、としが　うえです
       4. フランスの　パリ、にほんの　さっぽろ、きたに　あります

B. *ex.* **Q**：とりにくと　ぎゅうにくと　どちら/どっち　が　やすいですか。
     A：とりにくの　ほうが　やすいです。

       1. ファクシミリ、てがみ、べんりです
       2. はやしさん、かとうさん、えいごが　じょうずです
       3. あさ、ゆうがた、こんでいます
       4. かとうさん、すずきさん、たくさん　おさけを　のみます

C. *ex.* **Q**：のみものは　コーヒーと　こうちゃと　どちら/どっち　が　いいですか。
     A：コーヒーの　ほうが　いいです。

       1. りょうり、　てんぷら、　しゃぶしゃぶ
       2. じかん、　ごぜん、　ごご
       3. デザート、　アイスクリーム、くだもの
       4. パーティー、　きんようび、　どようび

D. *ex.* **Q**：スポーツの　なかで　なにが　いちばん　すきですか。
     A：テニスが　いちばん　すきです。

       1. ししゃ、　どこ、　おおきいです、　ニューヨーク
       2. ごきょうだい、　どなた、　せが　たかいです、　おとうと
       3. いちにち、　いつ、　こんでいます、　あさ　8じごろ

4. かいしゃ、　だれ、　よく　はたらきます、　しゃちょう

E. *ex.* **A**：りょうりが　じょうずですね。
　　B：いいえ、[わたしは]　リンダさんほど　じょうずでは　ありません。

　　1. テニス、　はやしさん
　　2. スキー、　スミスさん
　　3. にほんご、　ブラウンさん

F. *ex.* **A**：おおさかは　おおきいですね。
　　B：ええ、でも　とうきょうほど　おおきくないです。

　　1. しんかんせん、　たかいです、　ひこうき
　　2. とうきょう、　あついです、　ホンコン
　　3. でんわ、　べんりです、　ファクシミリ

G. *ex.* **Q**：かとうさんは　なにを　していますか。
　　A：ラジオを　ききながら　しんぶんを　よんでいます。

　　1. コーヒーを　のみます、　しごとを　します
　　2. たばこを　すいます、　てがみを　かきます
　　3. はなしを　します、　バスを　まちます
　　4. イヤホーンで　おんがくを　ききます、　べんきょうします

Vocabulary			
ちきゅう	**chikyū**, earth, globe	きた	**kita**, north
つき	**tsuki**, moon	どっち	**dotch**, which
じんこう	**jinkō**, population	ファクシミリ	**fakushimiri**, facsimile
ロンドン	**Rondon**, London	てんぷら	**tempura**, tempura
おおい	**ōi**, many, much	ニューヨーク	**Nyūyōku**, New York
あぶら	**abura**, oil, grease	せが　たかい	**se ga takai**, tall
おもい	**omoi**, heavy	せ	**se**, height, back
としが　うえ	**toshi ga ue**, older, senior	はたらきます	**hatarakimasu (hataraku)**,
とし	**toshi**, age	（はたらく）	work
うえ	**ue**, upper, above	しゃちょう	**shachō**, president
パリ	**Pari**, Paris	ホンコン	**Honkon**, Hong Kong
さっぽろ	**Sapporo** (city)		

SHORT DIALOGUES

1. **A**：ちょっと　はなしが　あります。しょくじを　しながら、はなしませんか。
　B：そう　しましょう。

A：きょうは　わたしが　ごちそうします。

B：そうですか。じゃ、ごちそうに　なります。

A: There are (some things I'd like to) talk (with you) about briefly. Shall we have a talk while having a meal?
B: Let's do (that).
A: Today will be my treat.
B: Really? Well, thank you (*lit.* I'm going to be treated!).

2. **A**：コーヒーと　こうちゃと　どちらが　すきですか。

B：りょうほう　すきです。

A: Which do you like better, coffee or tea?
B: I like both.

Vocabulary

はなします **hanashimasu (hanasu)**,
　（はなす）　　talk, speak, tell
ごちそうします **go-chisō shimasu**, treat
　ごちそう **go-chisō**, treat, banquet, entertainment

ごちそうに　な **go-chisō ni narimasu**,
　ります　　be treated/entertained
りょうほう **ryōhō**, both

QUIZ

I　Read this lesson's opening dialogue and answer the following questions.

1. ちかてつは　あさと　ゆうがたと　どちらが　こんでいますか。
2. どうして　でんしゃの　ほうが　くるまより　はやいですか。
3. スミスさんは　なにを　ききながら、にほんごの　テキストを　よんでいますか。
4. スミスさんは　まいあさ　なんじに　うちを　でて、なんで　かいしゃに　いきますか。
5. ちかてつは　なんじごろが　いちばん　こんでいますか。

II　Put the appropriate particles or inflections in the parentheses.

1. しんかんせんは　くるま（　　）　はやいです。
2. どうやって　べんきょうしていますか。
　カセットテープを　きき（　　）　べんきょうしています。
3. ちかてつは　あさも　ゆうがた（　　）　こんでいますか。
　ゆうがたは　あさ（　　）　こんでいません。
4. こちらの　ほう（　　）　しずかですから、ここ（　　）　はなしを　しましょう。
5. かいしゃ（　　）　なか（　　）　だれが　いちばん　よく　はたらきますか。
6. えきの　ひとが　じょうきゃく（　　）　でんしゃの　なか（　　）　おしこんでいました。

III Complete the questions so that they fit the answers.

1. ちかてつと バスと （　　　） が べんりですか。
   ちかてつの ほうが べんりです。
2. ちかてつは （　　　） が いちばん こんでいますか。
   あさが いちばん こんでいます。
3. （　　　） が いちばん テニスが じょうずですか。
   リンダさんが いちばん じょうずです。
4. くだものの なかで （　　　） が いちばん すきですか。
   みかんが いちばん すきです。
5. のみものは コーヒーと こうちゃと （　　　） が いいですか。
   コーヒーを おねがいします。

IV Complete the sentences with the appropriate form of the verbs indicated.

1. スミスさんは はやしさんと （　　　） ながら、（　　　） います。
   （あるきます、はなします）
2. スミスさんは まいにち なんで （　　　） いますか。
   （つうきんします）
3. その レストランは （　　　） いますか。（すきます）
4. せなかを （　　　） ないでください。（おします）
5. きのうは ホテルで ともだちと しょくじを （　　　） ながら、はな
   しを （　　　）。（します、します）
6. この くるまを （　　　） も いいですか。（つかいます）
   わたしが （　　　） ますから、 （　　　） ないでください。
   （つかいます、つかいます）

V Answer the following questions.

1. あなたは スポーツの なかで なにが いちばん すきですか。
2. ごかぞくの なかで どなたが いちばん せが たかいですか。
3. あなたの まちの こうつうきかんの なかで なにが いちばん
   べんりですか。
4. すしと すきやきと どちらが すきですか。

LESSON 2 LOST AND FOUND

Mr. Chang realizes he left something on the train and tells a station employee about it.

チャン： すみません。

えきいん：はい、なんでしょうか。

チャン： わすれものを しました。

えきいん：どの 電車ですか。

チャン： 20分ぐらい 前の 電車で、うしろから 二ばんめの しゃりょうです。

えきいん：なにを わすれましたか。

チャン： くろくて 大きい かみの ふくろです。

えきいん：なかみは なんですか。くわしく せつめいしてください。

チャン： マフラーと セーターです。マフラーは ウールで、くろと しろの しまの もようです。セーターは あかくて、むねに うまの もようが あります。

えきいん：いま しゅうてんの 駅に でんわを かけて、といあわせますから、ちょっと まってください。

チャン： すみません。

After calling the terminal, the man comes back to Mr. Chang.

えきいん：ありました。ウールの マフラーと あかい セーターですね。東京駅の じむしつに とどいていますから、きょうじゅうに とりに 行ってください。

Chang:	Excuse me.
Station Employee:	Yes. May I help you?
Chang:	I forgot something (in the train).
Employee:	Which train (was it)?
Chang:	It was the train (which left) about twenty minutes ago, second car from the back.
Employee:	What did you forget?
Chang:	It's a big black paper bag.
Employee:	What're the contents? Please describe (them) in detail.
Chang:	(There's) a scarf and a sweater. The scarf is wool and has a pattern of black and white stripes. The sweater is red with a horse design on the chest.
Employee:	I'll call the terminal now and ask. Please wait a moment.
Chang:	Thank you.

18

Employee: (Your bag) is there. A wool scarf and a red sweater, right? They're at the clerks' office in Tokyo Station. (So) Please go pick them up today.

Vocabulary

えきいん	**ekiin**, station employee	もよう	**moyō**, pattern, design
でしょうか	**deshō ka**, (softer than **desu ka**)	むね	**mune**, chest
		うま	**uma**, horse
わすれもの	**wasuremono**, forgotten or lost article	しゅうてん	**shūten**, terminal, last stop
うしろ	**ushiro**, back	でんわを　かけて	**denwa o kakete**, telephone
～ばんめ	**-bamme**, counter for ordinal numbers	かける	**kakeru**, call
しゃりょう	**sharyō**, car, vehicle	といあわせます（といあわせる）	**toiawasemasu (toiawaseru)**, ask
わすれます（わすれる）	**wasuremasu (wasureru)**, forget	じむしつ	**jimu-shitsu**, clerks' office
かみ	**kami**, paper	とどいています	**todoite imasu**, have arrived
ふくろ	**fukuro**, bag		
なかみ	**nakami**, contents	とどく	**todoku**, arrive, reach
くわしく	**kuwashiku**, in detail	きょうじゅうに	**kyō-jū ni**, (within) today
くわしい	**kuwashii**, detailed	～じゅう/ちゅう　に	**-jū/-chū ni**, within, throughout
マフラー	**mafurā**, scarf		
ウール	**ūru**, wool	とりに　いきます	**tori ni ikimasu**, go to pick up
くろ	**kuro**, black(ness)		
しろ	**shiro**, white(ness)	とります（とる）	**torimasu (toru)**, pick up, get, take, pass
しま	**shima**, stripe		

GRAMMAR & LESSON OBJECTIVES

- **De**, connective form of **desu**

  20-pun gurai mae no densha de, ushiro kara 2-bamme no sharyō desu.
  Mafurā wa ūru de, kuro to shiro no shima no moyō desu.
  De is for **desu** the equivalent of the **-te** form of verbs. Each of these sentences has the same meaning as two independent sentences, each ending in **desu**.

- **-te/-de** form of adjectives as a connective

  Kurokute ōkii kami no fukuro desu.
  Sētā wa akakute, mune ni uma no moyō ga arimasu.
  The **-te** form of adjectives can be a connective, just as the **-te** form of verbs is used to combine two phrases, clauses or sentences. Another usage of the **-te** forms is to give a reason, as shown in lesson 14.

  Both **-i** and **-na** adjectives have various forms and functions. The form of **-i** adjectives found in dictionaries can be used as it is as a noun modifier or predicatively. For **-na** adjectives, bilingual dictionaries generally give the stem, so it is necessary to add **-na** when modifying nouns. A problem in English terminology arises because spaces between words are left in romanized Japanese (for easier reading), with the result that the **da** and **ni** of, for example, **shizuka da** and **shizuka ni** look like the plain form of **desu** and the particle **ni**. But this is not the case. It is better to think of **-na** adjectives in the same way as **-i** adjectives, words composed of a stem, which has independent uses as nouns, to which are added inflections. (There is no confusion in Japanese, since words are written without spaces between them, as seen in the supplement to the text.) For plain forms of the two kinds of adjectives and the copula **desu**, see lesson 8.

-i adj: ōkii → ōkikute; yasui → yasukute

ex. **Ano kōen wa hiroi desu. Shizuka desu.** → **Ano kōen wa hirokute shizuka desu.**
"That park is spacious and quiet."

-na adj: **kireina** → **kirei de; shizukana** → **shizuka de**

ex. **Chikatetsu wa benri desu. Hayakute yasui desu.** → **Chikatetsu wa benri de hayakute yasui desu.** "Subways are convenient, fast and cheap."

Adjectives: Stem and Inflections

		Connective form	Adverbial form	Stem
-i adj.	kuroi ōkii hayai	kurokute ōkikute hayakute	kuroku ōkiku hayaku	kuro ōki haya
-na adj.	shizukana benrina	shizuka de benri de	shizuka ni benri ni	shizuka benri

• . . . ni iku

Tori ni itte kudasai.

The **-masu** stem of a verb followed by **ni ikimasu/kimasu/kaerimasu** is a pattern for expressing the objective of "coming/going/returning." (For other verbs other patterns are necessary.)

ex. 1. **Kinō Kamakura ni oyogi ni ikimashita.** "(I) went to Kamakura yesterday to swim."
2. **Sukiyaki o tabe ni ikimasen ka.** "Wouldn't you like to go and have sukiyaki?"

NOTES

1. **Nan deshō ka.** (*lit.*) "What might it be (that you want)?"
This sounds softer than **Nan desu ka**, which may be heard in the appropriate situation.

2. **Wasuremono**
This belongs to a category of nouns formed by adding **mono**, "thing," to the **-masu** stem of a verb. Another example previously encountered was **nomimono** (in the first volume). A couple more everyday words not in this text but worth remembering are **tabemono**, "food"; **yomimono**, "reading material," especially light stuff; and **kowaremono** (**kowareru**, "break, be broken"), a "breakable thing."

3. **Dono densha desu ka.**
Note that the Japanese is the equivalent of "Which train is (it)?" whereas the English would normally be "Which train was it?" There were similar cases of differences in verb form or tense in the first volume and more will be encountered later on.

4. **Kuwashiku**, the adverbial form of **kuwashii**
Note the following.
-i adj: **hayai** → **hayaku; hiroi** → **hiroku; ii/yoi** → **yoku**
ex. **Yasuku utte imasu.** "(They) sell (them) cheap."
-na adj: **kireina** → **kirei ni; genkina** → **genki ni**
ex. **Shizuka ni terebi o mite imasu.** "(He's) quietly watching TV."
Being in charge of the platform, the station employee straightforwardly ascertains the contents, as well as the appearance, of the lost bag so as to be able to identify them, know whether anything is missing, and see that the bag is returned to the right person. A policeman or any person in charge of lost articles would do the same and, if appropriate, check for explosives. In a similar vein, after making his phone call, the employee reconfirms the contents of the bag, saying **Ūru no mafurā to akai sētā desu ne**, indicating the contents of the bag have also been checked at Tokyo Station.

5. **Arimashita.**
The translation of the dialogue is fairly literal. Since this word is heard when a person finds something he has been looking for, a free translation would be "(It's been) found!" **Basu ga kimashita**, "(Ah) here comes the bus," and **Omoidashimashita**, "(I've just) recalled (it)," are

expressions in a similar vein.

6. **Kyō-jū ni**

This **-jū ni** indicates the time within which something is expected to happen. **Jū** is a phonetic variation of **chū**. Other examples: **kotoshi-jū ni**, "(within) this year"; **raishū-chū ni**, "(within) next week," "sometime next week."

7. **Tōkyō eki no jimu-shitsu ni todoite imasu kara, . . .**

This literally means "(They) have reached the clerks' office in Tokyo Station and are still there," a usage of the **-te imasu** form explained in the first volume (p. 168).

PRACTICE

KEY SENTENCES

1. はやしさんは　にほんじんで、ABCの　ぶちょうです。
2. ここは　ひろくて　しずかな　こうえんです。
3. かんじを　きれいに　かいてください。
4. ひるごはんを　たべに　レストランに　いきました。

1. Mr. Hayashi is (a) Japanese and is a department head at ABC.
2. This is a quiet spacious park.
3. Please write the *kanji* neatly.
4. (I) went to a restaurant to eat lunch.

> **Vocabulary**

ぶちょう	**buchō**, department head, division chief
ぶ	**bu**, department, division
ひろい	**hiroi**, spacious, wide

EXERCISES

Make dialogues by changing the underlined parts as in the examples given.

A. *ex.* **Q**：どんな　かばんですか。
　　A：くろくて　おおきい　かばんです。

    1. ぐあい、あたまが　いたい、ねつが　あります
    2. こうえん、ひろい、しずかな　こうえんです
    3. たてもの、しろい、たかい　たてものです
    4. まち、れきしが　ふるい、ゆうめいな　まちです

B. *ex.* **Q**：どんな　こうえんですか。
　　A：きれいで　しずかな　こうえんです。

    1. ところ、にぎやか、とても　おもしろい　ところです
    2. レストラン、べんり、サービスが　よくて　はやいです
    3. もんだい、ふくざつ、むずかしい　もんだいです

4. ひと、ABCの　べんごし、とうきょうに　すんでいます
5. ひと、ちゅうがっこうの　せんせい、すうがくを　おしえています

C. *ex.* **Q**：やまださんは　どんな　ひとですか。
　　 A：<u>まじめで　よく　はたらきます。</u>

1. かみが　ながい、きれいな　ひとです
2. あたまが　いい、しんせつな　ひとです
3. おしゃべり、なまけものです
4. うそつき、がんこです

D. *ex.* **Q**：チャンさんは　<u>みちを　せつめいしましたか。</u>
　　 A：ええ、<u>くわしく　せつめいしました。</u>

1. はたらいています、いそがしい
2. もう　おきました、あさ　はやい
3. つきました、ゆうべ　おそい
4. はなしを　しています、たのしい

E. *ex.* **Q**：チャンさんは　<u>かんじを　かきますか。</u>
　　 A：ええ、<u>きれいに　かきます。</u>

1. うたを　うたいます、じょうず
2. わたなべさんに　おしえました、しんせつ
3. ともだちと　はなしを　しています、にぎやか
4. べんきょうしています、しずか

F. *ex.* **A**：どこに　いきますか。
　　 B：<u>ぎんざに　いきます。</u>
　　 A：なにを　しに　いきますか。
　　 B：<u>えいがを　みに　いきます。</u>

1. きょうと、ふるい　おてらを　みます
2. デパート、くつを　かいます
3. かとうさんの　へや、てがみを　とどけます
4. こうえん、しゃしんを　とります

G. *ex.* **Q**：なにを　しに　<u>いきますか。</u>
　　 A：<u>デパートに　シャツを　かいに　いきます。</u>

1. かえります、うち、ひるごはんを　たべます
2. いきます、にほん、あたらしい　ぎじゅつを　べんきょうします
3. いきます、きっさてん、コーヒーを　のみます
4. かえります、りょうしんの　うち、やすみます
5. きました、ここ、にほんごを　ならいます

Vocabulary

かばん	**kaban**, bag, briefcase, suitcase	うそつき	**usotsuki**, liar
ぐあい	**guai**, condition	がんこ（な）	**ganko(na)**, stubborn
サービス	**sābisu**, service	みちを　せつめいします	**michi o setsumei shimasu**, give directions (*lit.* explain the way)
もんだい	**mondai**, problem		
ふくざつ（な）	**fukuzatsu(na)**, complicated	おきます（おきる）	**okimasu (okiru)**, get up
ちゅうがっこう	**chūgakkō**, middle school	はやい	**hayai**, early
すうがく	**sūgaku**, mathematics	ゆうべ	**yūbe**, last night/evening
まじめ（な）	**majime(na)**, serious, diligent	うた	**uta**, song
かみが　ながい	**kami ga nagai**, long-haired	うたいます（うたう）	**utaimasu (utau)**, sing
かみ	**kami**, hair	シャツ	**shatsu**, shirt
ながい	**nagai**, long	ぎじゅつ	**gijutsu**, technique, technology
あたまが　いい	**atama ga ii**, bright	やすみます（やすむ）	**yasumimasu (yasumu)**, rest
おしゃべり（な）	**oshaberi(na)**, chatterbox	ならいます（ならう）	**naraimasu (narau)**, learn
なまけもの	**namakemono**, lazybones		

SHORT DIALOGUES

1. ホワイト：おかねを　ひろいました。
   けいかん：どこに　おちていましたか。
   ホワイト：スーパーの　まえの　おおどおりに　おちていました。
   けいかん：なんじごろ　ひろいましたか。
   ホワイト：15ふんぐらい　まえです。

   White:　　I found (this) money.
   Policeman: Where was (it)? (*lit.* "Where had (it) been dropped?")
   White:　　It was on the main street in front of the supermarket.
   Policeman: Around what time did you pick it up?
   White:　　About fifteen minutes ago.

2. すずき：　さいふを　おとしました。
   けいかん：どんな　さいふですか。
   すずき：　ちゃいろで　おおきい　かわの　さいふです。
   けいかん：なかに　なにが　はいっていますか。
   すずき：　げんきんが　3まんえんぐらいと　めいしです。

Suzuki: I lost my wallet.
Policeman: What kind of wallet is it?
Suzuki: It's a big, brown leather wallet.
Policeman: Is there something (contained) in it?
Suzuki: Cash, about ¥30,000, and business cards.

Vocabulary

ひろいます　**hiroimasu (hirou)**, find,
　（ひろう）　　pick up

おちています　**ochite imasu (ochiru)**,
　（おちる）　　drop, fall

おおどおり　**ōdōri**, main street

さいふ　**saifu**, wallet, purse

おとします　**otoshimasu (otosu)**, lose,
　（おとす）　　drop

ちゃいろ　**chairo**, brown

かわ　**kawa**, leather

はいっています　**haitte imasu (hairu)**, con-
　（はいる）　　tain, include

げんきん　**genkin**, cash

QUIZ

I　Read this lessons's opening dialogue and answer the following questions.

1. チャンさんは　どんな　ふくろを　わすれましたか。
2. うしろから　なんばんめの　しゃりょうに　わすれましたか。
3. あかい　セーターは　むねに　うまの　もようが　ありますか。
4. えきいんは　チャンさんの　せつめいを　きいて、なにを　しましたか。
5. チャンさんは　わすれものを　どこに　とりに　いきますか。

II　Put the appropriate particles in the parentheses.

1. チャンさんは　ウール（　　）　マフラー（　　）　あかい　セーター
　（　　）　わすれました。
2. まえ（　　）　3ばんめ（　　）　しゃりょうです。
3. くろ（　　）　しろ（　　）　しまの　シャツで、むね（　　）　ちい
　さい　かさの　もよう（　　）　あります。
4. じむしつ（　　）　とどいています（　　）、きょうじゅう（　　）　と
　り（　　）　きてください。

III　Complete the questions so that they fit the answers.

1. （　　）　さいふを　ひろいましたか。
　くろい　かわの　さいふです。
2. （　　）に　おちていましたか。
　こうえんに　おちていました。
3. （　　）　でんしゃに　のっていましたか。
　10ぷんぐらい　まえの　でんしゃです。
4. なかに　（　　）が　はいっていますか。
　ほんと　ペンが　2ほん　はいっています。

IV Complete the sentences with the appropriate form of the words in parentheses.

1. ブラウンさんは　（　　）　かんじを　かきます。（じょうず）
2. （　　）　せつめい　してください。（くわしい）
3. きょうは　（　　）　かいしゃに　いきます。（はやい）
4. あたまが　（　　）、ねつが　あります。（いたい）
5. こどもは　（　　）　ほんを　よんでいます。（しずか）
6. れきしが　（　　）、（　　）　まちです。（ふるい、ゆうめい）
7. かんじを　（　　）　かいてください。（おおきい）

V Connect the sentences using the appropriate verb or adjective form.

1. この　でんしゃに　のります。4つめの　えきで　おりてください。
2. あの　レストランは　やすいです。おいしいです。
3. この　きっさてんは　あたらしいです。きれいです。すいています。
4. それは　あおい　セーターです。はなの　もようが　あります。
5. わたなべさんは　あたまが　いいです。しんせつです。
6. チャンさんは　まじめです。よく　はたらきます。
7. じむしつに　でんわを　かけます。といあわせます。

VI Answer the following questions.

1. あなたの　おとうさんは　どんな　ひとですか。(use···**te/de**···**te/de**)
2. あなたの　まちは　どんな　ところですか。(use···**te/de**···**te/de**)
3. こうえんに　なにを　しに　いきますか。
4. あなたは　あした　どこに　なにを　しに　いきますか。

LESSON 3 THE HEALTH CLUB

Mr. Brown visits a health club.

ブラウン：　あのう、ちょっと　おねがいします。こちらの　クラブに　もうし
　　　　　　こみを　する　前に、　中を　見る　ことが　できますか。

クラブの人：はい。しつれいですが、どちらさまでしょうか。

ブラウン：　ブラウンです。

クラブの人：ああ、はやしさんの　ごしょうかいの　ブラウンさんですね。
　　　　　　ごあんないしましょう。

The clerk invites Mr. Brown in and shows him around.

ブラウン：　とても　ひろくて　きれいな　ところですね。

クラブの人：こちらの　テニスコートには　コーチも　いますから、コーチに
　　　　　　ならう　ことも　できます。こちらは　おんすいプールで、一年
　　　　　　中　およぐ　ことが　できます。

ブラウン：　こちらでは　みんな　いろいろな　マシーンを　つかっています
　　　　　　ね。

クラブの人：ええ。どれでも　おすきな　ものを　つかう　ことが　できます
　　　　　　が、はじめる　前に　トレーナーに　ごそうだんください。

ブラウン：　ええ、そう　します。

クラブの人：いかがでしたか。

ブラウン：　とても　気に　入りました。

クラブの人：では、こちらに　お名前と　ご住所を　おかきください。

Brown: Er, can you help me? May I look around inside before applying?
Clerk: Yes. Excuse me, but may I have your name?
Brown: It's Brown.
Clerk: Ah, the Mr. Brown introduced by Mr. Hayashi, isn't it? Let me show you around.

Brown: It's a very spacious and nice place, isn't it?
Clerk: Since there's (even) a coach at this tennis court, you can learn from the coach. Here (we) have a heated swimming pool. You can swim all year round.
Brown: Everyone here uses machines of various kinds, I see.
Clerk: Yes, you can use anything you like, but please consult the trainer before starting.
Brown: All right, I'll do (that).
Clerk: How do you like it?
Brown: It's very satisfactory.
Clerk: Well, then, would you write your name and address here, please?

26

あのう	**anō**, er	いちねんじゅう	**ichi-nen-jū**, all year round
もうしこみ	**mōshikomi**, application	およぐ	**oyogu**, swim
ことが できます（できる）	**koto ga dekimasu (dekiru)**, can	マシーン	**mashīn**, machine
どちらさま	**dochira-sama**, who	どれでも	**dore demo**, any (thing)
ああ	**ā**, Ah!	でも	**demo**, any (particle)
ごあんないする	**go-annai suru**, show around	もの	**mono**, thing, goods, wear
あんない	**annai**, guidance	トレーナー	**torēnā**, trainer
テニスコート	**tenisu kōto**, tennis court	ごそうだん	**go-sōdan**, consultation
コーチ	**kōchi**, coach	きに いりました	**ki ni irimashita**, was/is satisfactory
おんすいプール	**onsui pūru**, heated (swimming) pool	き	**ki**, feeling
おんすい	**onsui**, warm water		

GRAMMAR & LESSON OBJECTIVES

- Dictionary form of verbs

    The basic verb form introduced in this lesson is known as the *dictionary form* because it is the one under which verbs are listed in dictionaries. Without exception the final vowel is always *u*. (See the first volume, p. 54.)

    The three conjugations—Regular I, Regular II and Irregular (**shimasu** and **kimasu** only)—are introduced in the first volume (pp. 130–1). In the charts there and in this volume, it can be seen that there is a direct relation between vowel order (*a, i, u, e, o*) and the conjugation of Regular I verbs.

    Regular I: Five-vowel conjugation

	-nai stem	-masu stem	dictio-nary	conditional	volitional	-te	-ta
use	**tsukawa-**	**tsukai-**	**tsukau**	**tsukaeba**	**tsukaō**	**tsukatte**	**tsukatta**
swim	**oyoga-**	**oyogi-**	**oyogu**	**oyogeba**	**oyogō**	**oyoide**	**oyoida**
go	**ika-**	**iki-**	**iku**	**ikeba**	**ikō**	**itte**	**itta**

    The penultimate vowel of all Regular II verbs is either **i** or **e** and the dictionary form (if written in rōmaji) ends in **-iru** or **-eru** (It should be noted that verbs having these endings are not invariably Regular II. A small number are Regular I. Common examples are **kaeru**, "return"—**kaerimasu, kaeranai; hashiru**, "run"—**hashirimasu, hashiranai**; and **kiru**, "cut"—**kirimasu, kiranai**.)

    To tell whether a verb is Regular I or Regular II, look at the **-nai** stem. For Regular I verbs this stem has the final vowel a.

    Regular II: Single-vowel conjugation

	-nai stem	-masu stem	dictionary	conditional	volitional	-te	-ta
be	**i-**	**i-**	**iru**	**ireba**	**iyō**	**ite**	**ita**
begin	**hajime-**	**hajime-**	**hajimeru**	**hajimereba**	**hajimeyō**	**hajimete**	**hajimeta**
eat	**tabe-**	**tabe-**	**taberu**	**tabereba**	**tabeyō**	**tabete**	**tabeta**

Irregular

come	ko-	ki-	kuru	kureba	koyō	kite	kita
do	shi-	shi-	suru	sureba	shiyō	shite	shita

- **Plain forms of verbs**

   The dictionary form is also referred to as the *plain present form*. Other plain forms are the **-nai** plain negative and the **-ta** plain past forms. A fourth one, the plain past negative made with the verb/adjective inflection **-nakatta** (past form of **-nai**) is shown in the chart below. As noted in the first volume, a sentence ending in a plain form is less polite than one ending in the **-masu** form. Within a sentence plain forms do not affect the politeness level and, as in this lesson's dialogue, certain phrase and sentence patterns are commonly formed with plain forms.

	-masen form	plain negative
Past neg.	ikimasen deshita mimasen deshita	ikanakatta minakatta

- **. . .koto ga dekimasu**

   Naka o miru koto ga dekimasu ka.
   Ichinen-jū oyogu koto ga dekimasu.

   The pattern consisting of the dictionary form and **koto ga dekiru** indicates possibility or capability. An even more common way of expressing the same thing (using verb inflections) is given in lesson 19.

- **hajimeru mae ni**

   The verb coming before **mae ni** is always in the dictionary form.
   ex. **Nihon ni kuru mae ni kanji o naraimashita.** "(I) learned Sino-Japanese characters before coming to Japan."

NOTES

1. **Anō**
   Anō is an informal expression used at the beginning of a sentence and indicates hesitation or deference. Here it keeps the sentence from sounding brusque.

2. **Dochira-sama deshō ka.**
   Dochira-sama is a very polite alternative for **donata**. Literally, this sentence is "Who might (you) be?"

3. **Kochira no tenisu kōto niwa . . .**
   Kochira dewa . . .
   The use of **(ni)wa** and **(de)wa** serves to emphasize the topics of the sentences.

4. **Dore demo**, any(thing)
   This is formed with the interrogative **dore**, "any," "which (one)," plus the particle **demo**. Other terms of this type include **nan demo**, "anything"; **doko demo**, "anywhere"; **dare demo**, "anyone"; and **itsu demo**, "anytime."
   ex. **Itsu demo ii desu.** "Anytime will do."

5. **go-shōkai, go-annai, o-sukina mono, go-sōdan, o-namae, go-jūsho**
   These words are examples of the usage given in the first volume (pp. 69, 88) to show respect to the person spoken to or persons or things connected with him or her. There are a few cases where usage is determined not by the addressee but by the subject matter, e.g. **o-kane**, "money": **o-satō**, "sugar": **o-cha**, "tea." Whether **o-** or **go-** is added is simply a matter of usage, which is more common among women.

6. **Go-sōdan kudasai**

   Rather than **sōdan shite kudasai**, **o-/go-** with a noun and **kudasai** may be used.

   ex. **O-denwa kudasai**, "Please call (me)."

   Go-kinyū kudasai, "Please fill in (the form)."

   Still polite but slightly more businesslike is the pattern **o** with the **-masu** stem followed by **kudasai**.

   ex. **O-machi kudasai** (instead of **Matte kudasai**), "Please wait."

   O-tsukai kudasai (instead of **Tsukatte kudasai**). "Please use (it)."

PRACTICE

KEY SENTENCES

1. この　プールでは　いちねんじゅう　およぐ　ことが　できます。
2. まいあさ　かいしゃへ　いく　まえに、しんぶんを　よみます。

1. As for this pool, it can be swum in all year round.
2. (I) read the newspaper every morning before going to work.

EXERCISES

I　Verbs: Study the examples, convert into the dictionary form, and memorize.

A. Regular I

ex. いきます→いく　　　あそびます→あそぶ　　　いいます→いう
のみます→のむ　　　はなします→はなす　　　あります→ある
しにます→しぬ　　　たちます→たつ

1. あいます	6. はいります	11. なおします	16. つくります
2. おとします	7. いそぎます	12. もちます	17. すきます
3. うります	8. とびます	13. わかります	18. こみます
4. ききます	9. もらいます	14. ぬぎます	19. おくります
5. すいます	10. とどきます	15. あらいます	20. はたらきます

B. Regular II

ex. たべます→たべる　　　みます→みる

1. みせます	4. あげます	7. います	10. しめます
2. おきます	5. かんがえます	8. とめます	
3. おります	6. おちます	9. あびます	

C. Irregular

ex. きます→くる　　　します→する

1. けっこんします　　　3. あんないします
2. もってきます　　　4. せつめいします

II Make dialogues by changing the underlined parts as in the examples given.

A. *ex.* **Q** : この　プールで　いま　<u>およぐ</u>　ことが　できますか。
   Aa : はい、できます。
   An : いいえ、できません。

    1. この　へやを　つかいます
    2. きょうじゅうに　とどけます
    3. とうきょうえきに　とりに　いきます
    4. その　しゃしんを　もってきます

B. *ex.* **Q** : 〔あなたは〕にほんごを　<u>はなす</u>　ことが　できますか。
   A : ええ、できますが、あまり　じょうずでは　ありません。

    1. にほんの　うたを　うたいます
    2. かんじを　かきます
    3. くるまを　うんてんします
    4. にほんりょうりを　つくります

C. *ex.* **Q** : <u>ねる</u>　まえに　なにを　しましたか。
   A : <u>はを　みがき</u>ました。

    1. しょくじを　します、てを　あらいます
    2. えいがかんに　はいります、きっぷを　かいます
    3. ねます、さけを　すこし　のみます
    4. とうきょうに　きます、とうきょうの　ともだちに　でんわします

D. *ex.* **Q** : いつ　<u>でんわを　かけ</u>ますか。
   A : <u>うちに　かえる</u>　まえに　<u>でんわを　かけ</u>ます。

    1. シャワーを　あびます、でかけます
    2. コーヒーを　のみます、しごとを　はじめます
    3. しょくじを　します、おおさかに　つきます
    4. かえります、みちが　こみます

E. *ex.* **Q** : <u>もうしこみを　する</u>　まえに　<u>なかを　みる</u>　ことが　できますか。
   A : ええ、できますよ。

    1. はじめます、せんせいに　そうだんします
    2. かいしゃに　いきます、たいしかんで　あいます

3. しゃしんを　とります、かがみを　みます
4. レコードを　かいます、ちょっと　ききます

Vocabulary			
しぬ	**shinu**, die	うんてん	**unten**, driving
あそぶ	**asobu**, play	つくる	**tsukuru**, cook, prepare
たつ	**tatsu**, stand up	ねる	**neru**, sleep, go to bed
いそぐ	**isogu**, hurry	みがく	**migaku**, brush, polish
とぶ	**tobu**, fly	て	**te**, hand, arm
なおす	**naosu**, correct, improve	えいがかん	**eigakan**, movie theater
もつ	**motsu**, have, hold	～かん	**-kan**, building, hall
ぬぐ	**nugu**, take off	シャワーを　あ	**shawā o abiru**, take a
あらう	**arau**, wash	びる	shower
かんがえる	**kangaeru**, think, consider	シャワー	**shawā**, shower
あびる	**abiru**, bathe, pour	でかける	**dekakeru**, go out
うんてんする	**unten suru**, drive	かがみ	**kagami**, mirror

NB: From here on the verb form in the vocabulary lists is the dictionary form.

SHORT DIALOGUE

ホワイト：いけばなの　クラスを　みに　いっても　いいでしょうか。
なかむら：ええ。こんど　いっしょに　いきましょう。
ホワイト：いつ　クラスが　ありますか。
なかむら：1しゅうかんに　2かい、か、もくに　あります。

White:　　May I go to see the flower-arranging class?
Nakamura: Um. Let's go together next time.
White:　　When are the classes?
Nakamura: Twice a week. Tuesdays and Thursdays.

Vocabulary			
いけばな	**ikebana**, flower arrang-	こんど	**kondo**, next (time)
	ing	か	**ka**, Tuesday
クラス	**kurasu**, class	もく	**moku**, Thursday

QUIZ

I Read this lesson's opening dialogue and answer the following questions.

1. ブラウンさんは　はやしさんと　いっしょに　この　クラブに　いきましたか。
2. だれが　ブラウンさんを　あんないしましたか。
3. この　クラブでは　いちねんじゅう　プールで　およぐ　ことが　できますか。

4. ブラウンさんは この クラブの なかを みる まえに、もうしこみ を しましたか。

II Put the appropriate particles in the parentheses.

1. わたしは アメリカ (　　) にほんじんの せんせい (　　) にほんご (　　) ならいました。

2. どれ (　　) おすきなもの (　　) つかうこと. (　　) できます (　　)、はじめる まえ (　　) トレーナー (　　) ごそうだんく ださい。

3. この かみ (　　) おなまえ (　　) ごじゅうしょ (　　) おか きください。

4. 1かげつ (　　) 1かい おおさか (　　) いきます。

III Convert the following verbs into the dictionary form.

1. いきます	6. みます	11. きます
2. あいます	7. あります	12. たべます
3. あんないします	8. けします	13. つうきんします
4. おしえます	9. とめます	14. でんわを かけます
5. わすれます	10. まがります	15. もってきます

IV Complete the sentences with the appropriate form of the verbs indicated.

1. ここで スライドを (　　) ことが できますか。(みます)

2. ひるごはんを (　　) に (　　) も いいでしょうか。
(たべます、いきます)

3. (　　) まえに でんわを (　　) ください。(きます、かけます)

4. つぎの かどを (　　) ことが できますか。(まがります)

5. あした たなかさんに (　　) に (　　) ことが できますか。
(あいます、いきます)

6. ここに くるまを (　　) ことが できますか。(とめます)
いいえ、ここは ちゅうしゃきんしですから、くるまを (　　) でく ださい。(とめます)

V Answer the following questions.

1. あなたは およぐ ことが できますか。

2. あなたは かんじを よむ ことが できますか。

3. あなたは まいにち ねる まえに なにを しますか。

4. あなたは あさごはんを たべる まえに なにを しますか。

5. 1しゅうかんに なんかい にほんごの じゅぎょうが ありますか。

LESSON 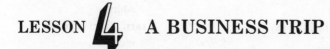 4 — A BUSINESS TRIP

Mr. Kimura and Mr. Brown chat about Brown's upcoming business trip to the Sapporo branch office.

きむら：　ブラウンさん、しゅっちょうですか。

ブラウン：ええ、あしたから　さっぽろ支店に　しゅっちょうです。
　　　　　きむらさんは　ほっかいどうに　行った　ことが　ありますか。

きむら：　ええ、がくせいの　ころ　いちど　ほっかいどうへ　りょこうに　行
　　　　　った　ことが　あります。車で　ほっかいどうを　まわりました。

ブラウン：さっぽろは　どんな　ところですか。

きむら：　さっぽろの　町は　にぎやかで、なかなか　おもしろいですよ。
　　　　　ブラウンさんは　はじめてですか。

ブラウン：ええ、しゃしんを　見た　ことは　ありますが、行った　ことは　あ
　　　　　りません。

きむら：　ひとりで　しゅっちょうですか。

ブラウン：かとうさんも　いっしょです。ふたりで　さっぽろしないの　とりひ
　　　　　きさきを　まわったり、銀行に　あいさつに　行ったり　します。

きむら：　かとうさんは　住んでいた　ことが　ありますから、さっぽろを　よ
　　　　　く　知っていますよ。

ブラウン：そうですか。あんしんしました。

Kimura:　Mr. Brown, is it a business trip you're going on?

Brown:　Yes. From tomorrow, to the Sapporo branch office. Have you ever been to Hokkaido?

Kimura:　Yes, at the time (I was) a (college) student, (we) once made a trip to Hokkaido. We toured Hokkaido by car.

Brown:　What kind of place is Sapporo?

Kimura:　The city of Sapporo is a really bustling (place) and quite interesting. Is this (your) first time?

Brown:　Um. I've seen pictures, but (I've) never gone there.

Kimura:　Are you making (this) trip alone?

Brown:　(No,) with Mr. Katō. The two of us will go around to (our) business contacts within Sapporo and pay our respects at the banks (and so on).

Kimura:　Mr. Katō has lived in Sapporo, so he knows (it) well.

Brown:　Is that right? I (can) relax!

Vocabulary

しゅっちょう	**shutchō**, business/official trip	なかなか	**nakanaka**, quite
		しない	**shinai**, within a city
してん	**shiten**, branch (office/store)	とりひきさき	**torihikisaki**, business contact

ほっかいどう	**Hokkaidō**, Hokkaido (prefecture)	あいさつ	**aisatsu**, civility, greeting, address
ことが　ある	**koto ga aru**, had the experience of	～たり～たりする	**tari...tari suru**, do X, Y etc.
ころ	**koro**, time	あんしんする	**anshin suru**, relax
まわる	**mawaru**, tour, go round	あんしん	**anshin**, peace of mind

GRAMMAR & LESSON OBJECTIVES

• -ta koto ga arimasu

Hokkaidō ni itta koto ga arimasu ka.

As can be seen in the dialogue, the **-ta** form of a verb plus **koto ga aru** expresses the fact that a person has experienced a particular thing.

ex. **Sapporo ni sunde ita koto ga arimasu.** "(He) has lived in Sapporo."

• -te and -ta forms from -masu form

Certain **-te** forms were given and used in the first volume. Now let's see how they can be made from the **-masu** form.

With Regular II and the two Irregular verbs it is only necessary to replace **-masu** with **-te** or **-ta**.

Regular II: **tabe(masu)** → **tabete** → **tabeta**; **mi(masu)** → **mite** → **mita**

Irregular: **ki(masu)** → **kite** → **kita**; **shi(masu)** → **shite** → **shita**

For Regular I verbs there are three types of euphonic change, depending on the syllable which immediately precedes **-masu**.

Regular I Type 1: **kaki(masu)** → **kaite** → **kaita**; **oyogi(masu)** → **oyoide** → **oyoida**

Type 2: **ii(masu)** → **itte** → **itta**; **mochi(masu)** → **motte** → **motta**; **kaeri(masu)** → **kaette** → **kaetta**

Type 3: **asobi(masu)** → **asonde** → **asonda**; **nomi(masu)** → **nonde** → **nonda**; **shini(masu)** → **shinde** → **shinda**

Note that no euphonic change occurs when the syllable is **shi**, e.g., **hanashi(masu)** → **hanashite** → **hanashita**, and for **ikimasu** the transformation is **iki(masu)** → **itte** → **itta**.

• ...-tari...-tari shimasu

Sapporo shinai no torihikisaki o mawattari, ginkō ni aisatsu ni ittari shimasu.

In the dialogue this pattern implies doing X, Y and other things, which is also the implication when only one verb is used. In other cases, the pattern means that two or more actions are done alternatively or repeatedly.

The **-tari** form is made by adding **ri** to the **-ta** form.

ex. 1. **Nichi-yōbi niwa hon o yondari, ongaku o kiitari shimasu.** "On Sundays I read books, listen to music (and so on)."

2. **Doa o aketari shimetari shinaide kudasai. Urusai desu.** "Please don't (keep on) opening and closing the door. It's (too) noisy."

NOTES

1. **Shutchō desu ka.**

   Desu can be used in place of **suru** because the situation is mutually understood. This is the same as **desu** in place of **arimasu** (first volume, p. 67). In fact, the question itself is asked merely for confirmation and could be freely interpreted as meaning, "I understand you're going on a business trip."

2. **Kuruma de Hokkaidō o mawarimashita.**

   o as used here is the same as **shingo o migi ni magatte** (first volume, p. 141). Some other verbs of motion taking the particle **o** when the action is through, along or from a certain place, are **tōru**, "pass along/through"; **aruku**, "walk"; **tobu**, "fly"; **deru**, "go out, leave."

ex. 1. **Watashi wa Ginza dōri o arukimashita.** "I walked along the (main) Ginza street."
2. **Hikōki ga sora o tonde imasu**. "The plane is flying through the air."

3. **Sapporo no machi wa nigiyaka de, nakanaka omoshiroi desu yo.**
Dictionaries equate **nakanaka** with "quite," "very," "considerably," "exceedingly," reflecting the good impression or high evaluation of whatever the speaker is commenting on.

4. **Shashin o mita koto wa arimasu ga, itta koto wa arimasen.**
Besides being a topic marker, the particle **wa** is used for contrast or to particularize or emphaisize the subject. Particles such as **ni**, **de** and **kara** can be combined with **wa**, but not **ga** and **o**. These are replaced by **wa**.
   ex. 1. **Minna kara henji o moraimashita ka.** "Did you get answers from everybody?"
   Iie, mada desu. Kimura-san to Tanaka-san kara wa moraimashita. "No, not yet. (I) got (them only) from Kimura and Tanaka."
   2. **Koko kara mae no seki dewa tabako o suwanaide kudasai.** "Please, no smoking in the seats ahead of these."
   3. **Maitoshi Kurisumasu kādo o kakimasu ka.** "Do (you) send (*lit.* write) Christmas cards every year?"
   Kurisumasu kādo wa kakimasen ga, nenga-jō wa maitoshi kakimasu. "(I) don't (always) send Christmas cards, but (I) send New Year's cards every year."

5. **Hokkaidō ni/e . . .**
Either **ni** or **e** can occur with such verbs as **iku**. On the interchangeability of these particles, see p. 53 of the first volume.

PRACTICE

KEY SENTENCES

1. わたなべさんは　ホンコンに　いった　ことが　あります。
2. にちようびは　ほんを　よんだり、おんがくを　きいたり　します。

1. Ms. Watanabe has been to Hong Kong.
2. Sundays, (I) read books, listen to music (and so on).

EXERCISES

I Verbs: Study the examples, convert into **-te** and **-ta** forms, and memorize.

A. Reg. I
   ex. かきます→　かく→　かいて→　かいた
   よみます→　よむ→　よんで→　よんだ
   あいます→　あう→　あって→　あった
   おわります→おわる→おわって→おわった

1. ならいます	6. のぼります	11. ぬぎます	16. はなします
2. およぎます	7. おきます	12. おとします	17. すわります
3. しにます	8. みがきます	13. はたらきます	18. なおします
4. あそびます	9. もちます	14. かいます	19. あるきます
5. たちます	10. とびます	15. いきます	20. やすみます

B. Reg. II and Irreg.

    ex. Reg. II   つけます→つける→つけて→つけた

                おきます→おきる→おきて→おきた

    Irreg.   きます→　くる→　きて→　きた

               します→　する→　して→　した

    1. きます（wear）   6. わすれます   11. れんしゅうします
    2. かんがえます   7. みせます   12. うっています
    3. おちます   8. でかけます   13. でます
    4. ねます   9. もってきます   14. はじめます
    5. あんしんします   10. すんでいます   15. おります

II Make dialogues by changing the underlined parts as in the examples given.

A. *ex.* **Q** : スミスさんは　まえに　<u>きゅうしゅうに　いった</u>　ことが　あります

    か。

    A : はい、いちど　<u>いった</u>　ことが　あります。

    1. はやしさんの　おくさんに　あいました
    2. ふじさんに　のぼりました
    3. しんかんせんに　のりました
    4. ヨーロッパを　まわりました

B. *ex.* **Q** : スミスさんは　<u>ユーフォー（UFO）を　みた</u>　ことが　ありますか。

    A : いいえ、ざんねんですが、<u>みた</u>　ことが　ありません。

    1. なんきょくへ　いきました
    2. じゅうどうを　ならいました
    3. ほうりつを　べんきょうしました
    4. だいとうりょうに　あいました

C. *ex.* **Q** : <u>さっぽろの　まちを　しっていますか。</u>

    A : <u>しゃしんを　みた</u>　ことは　ありますが、<u>いった</u>　ことは　ありま

    せん。

    1. ジョンソンさん、なまえを　ききました、あいました
    2. シェークスピアの　ハムレット、えいがを　みました、しばい
      を　みました
    3. ドリアン、しゃしんで　みました、たべました
    4. スフィンクス、はなしを　ききました、みました

D. *ex.* **Q**：しゅうまつに　なにを　しましたか。

    A：<u>かいものに　いったり</u>、<u>ともだちに　あったり</u>しました。

1. テニスを　する、さんぽを　する
2. ドライブに　いく、こどもと　あそぶ
3. てがみを　かく、ざっしを　よむ
4. ともだちと　はなす、レコードを　きく
5. うみで　およぐ、つりを　する

Vocabulary

のぼる	**noboru**, climb	なんきょく	**nankyoku**, South Pole
おく	**oku**, put, set up	じゅうどう	**jūdō**, judo
すわる	**suwaru**, sit, take a seat	ほうりつ	**hōritsu**, law
きる	**kiru**, wear, put on	だいとうりょう	**daitōryō**, president
れんしゅうする	**renshū suru**, practice	シェークスピア	**Shēkusupia**, Shakespeare
れんしゅう	**renshū**, practice		
きゅうしゅう	**Kyūshū** (place name)	ハムレット	**Hamuretto**, Hamlet
ふじさん	**Fuji-san**, Mount Fuji	しばい	**shibai**, play
～さん	**-san**, mount	ドリアン	**dorian**, durian
ユーフォー	**yūfō**, UFO (unidentified flying object)	スフィンクス	**sufinkusu**, the Sphinx
		つりを　する	**tsuri o suru**, fish
ざんねん	**zannen**, disappointing	つり	**tsuri**, fishing

SHORT DIALOGUES

1. A：きょうとに　いった　ことが　ありますか。
   B：はい、あります。
   A：いつ　いきましたか。
   B：きょねんの　8がつに　いきました。

   A: Have (you) ever been to Kyoto?
   B: Yes, I have.
   A: When did (you) go?
   B: (I) went last August.

2. たなか：よく　おおさかに　しゅっちょうしますね。
   かとう：ええ。1かげつに　5かいぐらい　とうきょうと　おおさかを　いったり　きたり　しています。

   Tanaka: You often make business trips to Osaka, don't you?
   Katō: Yes. I come and go (between) Tokyo and Osaka about five times a month.

QUIZ

I Read this lesson's opening dialogue and answer the following questions.

1. ブラウンさんは　だれと　ほっかいどうに　いきますか。

2. ブラウンさんは　ほっかいどうに　いった　ことが　ありますか。

3. きむらさんも　いっしょに　さっぽろしてんに　いきますか。

4. ブラウンさんは　さっぽろへ　いって　なにを　しますか。

II　Put the appropriate particles in the parentheses.

1. ヨーロッパ（　　）　りょこう（　　）　いった　ことが　あります。

2. くるま（　　）　ほっかいどう（　　）　まわりました。

3. すしを　たべた　こと（　　）　あります（　　）、つくった　こと
   （　　）　ありません。

4. スミスさんは　ひとり（　　）　こうえん（　　）　あるいています。

III　Convert the following verbs into the -ta form.

1. のぼります	6. おとします	11. まわります
2. あいます	7. よみます	12. せつめいします
3. たべます	8. わすれます	13. およぎます
4. ききます	9. みます	14. ならいます
5. います	10. あそびます	15. でかけます

IV　Complete the sentences with the appropriate form of the verbs indicated.

1. ふじさんに　（　　）　ことが　ありますか。（のぼります）

2. パーティーで　いちど　スミスさんの　おくさんに　（　　）　ことが
   あります。（あいます）

3. この　ラジオで　がいこくの　ニュースを　（　　）　ことが　できま
   すか。（ききます）

4. きのうの　ばん　ほんを　（　　）だり、てがみを　（　　）たり
   しました。（よみます、かきます）

5. しゅうまつに　えいがを　（　　）たり、ともだちに　（　　）たり
   します。（みます、あいます）

V　Answer the following questions.

1. あなたは　かぶきを　みた　ことが　ありますか。

2. あなたは　ちゅうごくに　いった　ことが　ありますか。

3. あなたは　しんかんせんに　のった　ことが　ありますか。

4. あなたは　にちようびに　なにを　しますか。(Use…**tari**…**tari**
   shimasu)

5. あなたは　きょねんの　なつやすみに　なにを　しましたか。
   (Use…**tari**…**tari shimasu**)

LESSON 5 A NEW WORD PROCESSOR

Mr. Hayashi gives Mr. Chang some advice about work procedures.

はやし：ワープロの カタログが たくさん ありますね。

チャン：ええ、きのう セールスの 人が くれました。
　　　　来月から うちの 課の ワープロの きしゅを かえます。

はやし：どの きしゅに しますか。

チャン：A社の 45Sが やすく なりましたが・・・。でも、まだ きめてい
　　　　ません。

はやし：システム部の おがわさんに そうだんしましたか。

チャン：いいえ、まだ 話していません。

はやし：ちょっと まずいですねえ。まず おがわさんに 話してください。

チャン：わかりました。

はやし：きっと システム部の いこうも わかりますよ。
　　　　話が まとまってから、みんなに 知らせてください。

チャン：はい、そう します。はやしさんは いつも かんけいしゃと そうだ
　　　　んしてから きめますか。

はやし：そうですねえ。しごとの すすめかたに かんしては たいてい そう
　　　　だんしてから きめますが、じんじに かんしては きめた 後で は
　　　　っぴょうします。

Hayashi:	(You) have a lot of word processor catalogues, I see.
Chang:	Yes, a salesman gave (them to me) yesterday. We're going to change the type of word processor in our section next month.
Hayashi:	Which type have (you) decided on?
Chang:	A Company's 45S has become less expensive. Still, we haven't decided yet.
Hayashi:	Have you consulted Mr. Ogawa in the Systems Department?
Chang:	No, I haven't spoken (with him) yet.
Hayashi:	(That makes things) a little awkward. Talk to Mr. Ogawa before (doing) anything else.
Chang:	I see.
Hayashi:	Surely (you'll also) know the Systems Department's views. After (your) consultations are concluded, please inform everyone.
Chang:	Right, (I'll do (that). Do you always decide after consulting the persons concerned?
Hayashi:	Well, concerning ways of proceeding with the work, I usually decide after consulting (people), but regarding personnel matters, I make announcements after deciding.

39

ワープロ	**wāpuro**, word processor	まとまる	**matomaru**, conclude
セールスの	**sērusu no hito**, salesper-	から	**kara**, after
ひと	son	しらせる	**shiraseru**, inform
セールス	**sērusu**, sales	いつも	**itsumo**, always
か	**ka**, section	かんけいしゃ	**kankei-sha**, person con-
きしゅ	**kishu**, type of machine		cerned
かえる	**kaeru**, change	かんけい	**kankei**, connected
～に する	**ni suru**, decide		with, related to
なる	**naru**, become	～しゃ	**-sha**, person (suffix)
きめる	**kimeru**, decide	すすめかた	**susume-kata**, way of pro-
システムぶ	**shisutemu-bu**, systems		ceeding
	department	すすめる	**susumeru**, proceed
システム	**shisutemu**, system	～かた	**-kata**, way, how to
～ぶ	**-bu**, department, divi-	～にかんして	**ni kanshite (wa)**, concern-
	sion	(は)	ing
まずい	**mazui**, awkward, un-	たいてい	**taitei**, usually, mostly
	savory	じんじ	**jinji**, personnel matters
まず	**mazu**, before anything	はっぴょうする	**happyō suru**, make an an-
	(else)		noucement
きっと	**kitto**, sure(ly)	はっぴょう	**happyō**, announcement
いこう	**ikō**, views		

GRAMMAR & LESSON OBJECTIVES

• -ku/ni narimasu, -ku/ni shimasu

A-sha no 45S ga yasuku narimashita.
Dono kishu ni shimasu ka.
When they come before **naru** (or other verbs), the **i** of **-i** adjectives is changed to **-ku**, as in **ōkiku narimasu**, "become big," and **akaku narimasu**, "get red."
With **-na** adjectives and nouns, **ni** is used.
ex. **shizukana → Shizuka ni narimasu.** "It'll get quiet."
   Arashi ni narimashita. "It got stormy."
   Pianisuto ni naritai desu. "(I) want to become a pianist."
This usage of **shimasu** expresses the speaker's intention or conscious decision.
ex. 1. **Rajio no oto o chiisaku shite kudasai.** "Please turn the radio down a little."
   2. **Doko de o-cha o nomimashō ka.** "Where shall we have tea?"
      Ano kissaten ni shimashō. "Let's make it that coffee shop."
   3. **Kono koto wa naimitsu ni shite kudasai.** "Please keep this matter confidential."

• -te kara and -ta ato de

Hanashi ga matomatte kara minna ni shirasete kudasai.
Taitei sōdan shite kara kimemasu.
The **-te** form plus **kara** means "after -ing" or "and then." It should not be confused with **kara** meaning "because."
ex. **Watashi no setsumei o kiite kara shitsumon shite kudasai.** "After listening to my explanation, please ask questions."
Ato de in **kimeta ato de** has approximately the same meaning but places more emphasis on the order in which things are done.
A common decision-making method in Japanese business and political circles is to consult the

people concerned before making a final decision. **Nemawashi** is the term given to this process of informally sounding people out and building a concensus.

● -te imasen

Mada kimete imasen.

Ogawa-san ni sōdan shimashita ka./Iie, mada hanashite imasen.

One meaning of **-te imasen** is to indicate that something has not occurred or been achieved; it conveys a feeling of unfinishedness. The answer above could not be **hanashimasen deshita**, as that would imply Chang does not intend to consult Ogawa. Compare this with the following examples.

ex. 1. **Kyō no shimbun o yomimashita ka.** "Did you read today's newspaper?"
   Iie, made yonde imasen. "No, not yet."
2. **Kodomo no toki, shimbun o yomimashita ka.** "Did you read newspapers when (you were) a child?"
   Iie, yomimasen deshita. "No, (I) didn't read (them)."

NOTES

1. **Sērusu no hito ga kuremashita.**
   As pointed out in the first volume (p. 109), **kureru** is used in this case because the receiver is the speaker and his group.

2. **Kankei-sha to sōdan shimasu.**
   Ogawa-san ni sōdan shimasu.
   The nuances of **to** and **ni** differ in that **to** suggests mutuality and interactiveness, while with the particle **ni** the feeling is more of one-sidedness.

3. **Shigoto no susume-kata**
   -kata added to the **-masu** stem of a verb is a common way to indicate "how" or "way (of doing)."
   ex. **kanji no yomi-kata**, "how to read kanji"
   hashi no tsukai-kata, "the way to use chopsticks"
   kōshū denwa no kakekata, "how to make a call from a public telephone"

4. **Boku**
   This word, which comes up in this lesson's short dialogues, is sometimes heard in familiar conversation instead of **watashi**, as is **kimi** in place of **anata**. Both are men's words and neither is appropriate when talking to older people.

PRACTICE

KEY SENTENCES————————————————————

1. ふゆものの　セールが　はじまって、コートや　セーターが　やすく　なりました。
2. デザートは　アイスクリームに　します。
3. てを　あらってから　サンドイッチを　たべましょう。
4. せつめいを　きいた　あとで、スライドを　みました。
5. もう　きめましたか。
   いいえ、まだ　きめていません。

1. The winter goods sale has started and coats and sweaters have become cheap.
2. We'll make ice cream (our) dessert.
3. Let's eat the sandwiches after washing our hands.
4. After listening to the explanation (we) watched the slides.

5. Did you decide?
   No, I haven't decided yet.

Vocabulary

ふゆもの	**fuyu-mono**, winter goods/ wear	セール	**sēru**, sale
ふゆ	**fuyu**, winter	はじまる	**hajimaru**, start
		コート	**kōto**, coat

EXERCISES

I Make dialogues by changing the underlined parts as in the examples given.

ex. **A**：どう　なりましたか。
   B：よく．なりました。/　げんきに　なりました。

   1. おおきい
   2. にぎやか
   3. つまらない
   4. くらい

   5. あかるい
   6. しずか
   7. ふくざつ
   8. べんり

   9. じょうず
   10. かんたん
   11. つよい
   12. きれい

II Practice the following pattern by changing the underlined parts as in the example given.

ex. わたしは　ピアニストに　なりたいです。

   1. ゆうめい、なりたい
   2. あたまが　いい、なりたい
   3. うちゅうひこうし、なりたかった
   4. びょうき、なりたくない
   5. びんぼう、なりたくなかった

III Make dialogues by changing the underlined parts as in the examples given.

A. ex. **Q**：ワープロは　どの　きしゅに　しますか。
   A：Aしゃの　45Sに　します。

   1. りょこう、どこ、ヨーロッパ
   2. ひっこし、いつ、らいげつ
   3. かいぎ、どの　へや、おおきい　へや
   4. デザート、なに、アイスクリーム

B. ex. **Q**：なにを　たべましょうか。
   A：てんぷらに　しましょう。

   1. どこで、おちゃを　のみます、あの　きっさてん

2. なんで、いきます、タクシー
3. なにを、つくります、とうふの　みそしる
4. どこで、スライドを　みます、2かいの　かいぎしつ
5. だれに、たのみます、ハンサムな　ひと

C. *ex.* **Q**：いつから　にほんごの　べんきょうを　はじめましたか。
   A：にほんに　きてから　はじめました。

1. ゴルフ、けっこんする
2. テニス、スポーツクラブに　はいる
3. この　しごと、だいがくを　でる
4. うんてん、18さいに　なる

D. *ex.* **Q**：いつも　そうだんしてから　きめますか。
   A：はい、たいてい　そうだんしてから　きめます。

1. カタログを　みる、かう
2. コーヒーを　のむ、しごとを　はじめる
3. よやくを　する、レストランに　いく
4. でんわを　かける、ともだちを　たずねる

E. *ex.* **Q**：いつ　シャワーを　あびますか。
   A：ジョギングを　した　あとで　シャワーを　あびます。

1. ビールを　のむ、しごとが　おわる
2. さんぽを　する、(お)ひるごはんを　たべる
3. みんなに　しらせる、はやしさんと　はなす
4. はっぴょうする、けいかくを　かえる

F. *ex.* **Q**：しょくじを　する　まえに　はを　みがきますか、しょくじを　し
   た　あとで　みがきますか。
   A：しょくじを　してから　みがきます。

1. ごはんを　たべます、くすりを　のみます
2. かんがえます、そうだんします
3. フランスに　いきます、フランスごの　べんきょうを　します
4. しなものが　とどきます、おかねを　はらいます

G. *ex.* **Q**：もう　この　ほんを　よみましたか。
   A：いいえ、まだ　よんでいません。

1. きっぷを　かう
2. でんわを　かける
3. にもつが　とどく
4. てがみを　だす

H. *ex.* スミス：　たなかさんは　かとうさんに　なにを　あげましたか。
わたなべ：はいざらを　あげました。
スミス：　あなたには？
わたなべ：わたしには　かびんを　くれました。

1. きょうとの　おかし、きょうとの　やきもの
2. あかい　ネクタイ、きぬの　スカーフ
3. えいがの　きっぷ、かぶきの　きっぷ
4. ウイスキー、はなたば

Vocabulary

どうなりました か	**Dō narimashita ka**, (*lit.*) How have (things) become? (See page 237, Note 1.)	たのむ	**tanomu**, request
		ハンサム（な）	**hansamu(na)**, handsome
		だいがく	**daigaku**, university, college
あめ	**ame**, rain	でる	**deru**, graduate, leave
あかるい	**akarui**, bright	かう	**kau**, buy
かんたん（な）	**kantan(na)**, simple	たずねる	**tazuneru**, visit
あらし	**arashi**, storm	けいかく	**keikaku**, plan, project
つよい	**tsuyoi**, strong	しなもの	**shinamono**, goods, article
ピアニスト	**pianisuto**, pianist	はらう	**harau**, pay
うちゅうひこう し	**uchū hikōshi**, astronaut	にもつ	**nimotsu**, baggage, cargo
		だす	**dasu**, mail
うちゅう	**uchū**, universe	あかい	**akai**, red
ひこうし	**hikōshi**, aviator	やきもの	**yakimono**, pottery
びょうき	**byōki**, sickness	きぬ	**kinu**, silk
びんぼう（な）	**bimbō(na)**, poor	スカーフ	**sukāfu**, scarf
ひっこし	**hikkoshi**, moving (house)	ウイスキー	**uisukī**, whisky
とうふ	**tōfu**, tofu	はなたば	**hanataba**, bouguet
みそしる	**miso shiru**, miso soup		
みそ	**miso**, bean paste		
しる	**shiru**, soup		

SHORT DIALOGUES

1. A：なんに　しますか。
B：ぼくは　コーヒーに　します。
C：そうですねえ。わたしは　ジュースに　します。
D：わたしは　アイスクリームです。

A: What'll you have?
B: I'll have coffee.
C: Let's see . . . I'll have juice.
D: Ice cream for me.

2. A：この　しょるいは　どう　しましょうか。

　　B：すぐ　ファックスで　おくりましょう。

　　A：べんりに　なりましたね。

A: What should we do with this document?
B: Let's send it immediately by fax.
A: It's become (very) convenient, hasn't it?

| **Vocabulary** |

| ぼく | **boku**, I (informal male speech) | すぐ | **sugu**, immediately |
| しょるい | **shorui**, document | ファックス | **fakkusu**, fax |

QUIZ

I　Read this lessons's opening dialogue and answer the following questions.

1. Aしゃの　ワープロの　45Sは　たかく　なりましたか、やすく　なりましたか。

2. チャンさんは　ワープロの　カタログを　もらう　まえに、おがわさんに　そうだんしましたか。

3. はやしさんは　しごとの　すすめかたに　かんしては　かんけいしゃと　そうだんしてから　きめますが、じんじに　かんしては　どうですか。

4. チャンさんは　だれに　ワープロの　カタログを　もらいましたか。

II　Put the appropriate particles in the parentheses.

1. ともだちが　わたし（　　）　しま（　　）　シャツ（　　）　くれました。

2. デザートは　アイスクリーム（　　）　しましょう。

3. はなし（　　）　まとまって（　　）、みんな（　　）　しらせてください。

4. ワープロ（　　）　かんしては　ひしょ（　　）　ほう（　　）　よく　しっています。

5. ひるごはん（　　）　たべた　あと（　　）、こうえん（　　）　さんぽ　しましょう。

6. わたしは　こども（　　）　ころ　ピアニスト（　　）　なりたかったです。

III   Complete the questions so that they fit the answers.

1. （　　）きしゅを　かいますか。
   45Sに　します。
2. （　　）でんわを　かけますか。
   うちに　かえってから　かけます。
3. （　　）に　そうだんしましたか。
   システムぶの　おがわさんに　そうだんしました。

IV   Complete the sentences with the appropriate form of the verbs indicated.

1. みそしるの　（　　）かたを　（　　）ください。（つくる、おしえる）
2. わすれものは　まだ　じむしつに　（　　）いません。（とどく）
3. まいにち　うちに　（　　）から、1じかんぐらい　にほんごを　べんきょうします。（かえる）
4. しごとが　（　　）あとで、ビールを　（　　）ませんか。
   （おわる、のむ）
5. こどもに　（　　）まえに、かないと　よく　そうだんします。
   （はなす）
6. ワープロの　きしゅを　（　　）ことが　できますか。（かえる）

V   Answer the following questions.

1. あなたは　にほんごが　じょうずに　なりましたか。
2. あなたは　もう　きょうの　しんぶんを　よみましたか。
3. あさ　しょくじを　する　まえに　はを　みがきますか、しょくじを　したあとで　はを　みがきますか。
4. あなたの　すきな　りょうりの　つくりかたを　かんたんに　せつめいしてください。（use…**te kara**,…**ta atode**,…**mae ni**）

LESSON 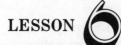 A PALE FACE

After meeting Mr. Chang in the elevator Mr. Katō advises him to take the rest of the day off.

かとう：かおいろが　よく　ありませんね。かぜですか。

チャン：ええ、おととい　いしゃに　行って　くすりを　もらってきましたが、
　　　　なかなか　よくなりません。けさは　ねつが　38度　ありました。

かとう：それじゃ、早く　うちに　かえって　休んだ　ほうが　いいですよ。

チャン：でも、この　プロジェクトが　はじまったばかりですから・・・。

かとう：むりを　しない　ほうが　いいですよ。来しゅうは　もっと　いそがし
　　　　く　なりますから、いまの　うちに　なおした　ほうが　いいですよ。

チャン：それでは　もうしわけありませんが、すずきくんか　きむらくんに　後
　　　　を　よく　たのんでから、かえります。

かとう：すずきくんには　さっき　べつの　用事を　たのんだばかりですから、
　　　　きむらくんの　ほうが　いいですよ。

チャン：わかりました。では、おさきに　しつれいします。

かとう：おだいじに。

Katō: (Your) complexion isn't good. Caught cold?
Chang: Eh, I went to the doctor the day before yesterday and got medicine, but it's not getting
        any better. My temperature this morning was 38 degrees.
Katō: In that case it's better to go home early and get some rest.
Chang: Actually, since this project has just started—
Katō: It's better not to overdo it. Next week'll be (even) busier. It'd be better if you got well
        right away.
Chang: Well then, I'm sorry but I'll leave after asking Suzuki or Kimura (to look after) the rest
        (of my work).
Katō: I just asked Suzuki a little while ago (to do) some other work. It'll have to be Kimura.
Chang: I see. Good-bye, then.
Katō: Take care of yourself.

Vocabulary			
かおいろ	**kaoiro**, complexion	もうしわけあり	**mōshiwake arimasen**,
かぜ	**kaze**, cold	ません	I'm sorry (*lit.* "There's
なかなか～ない	**nakanaka. . .nai**, not		no excuse.")
	any/at all	もうしわけ	**mōshiwake**, excuse,
それじゃ	**sore-ja**, in that case		apology
～た　ほうが	**-ta hō ga ii**, it's better	～くん	**-kun**, Mr., Master (infor-
いい	to . . .		mal male speech)

プロジェクト	**purojekuto**, project	か	**ka**, or (particle)
〜たばかり	**-ta bakari**, (have) just	あと	**ato**, rest
むりを　する	**muri o suru**, overdo (lit. be unnatural)	さっき	**sakki**, a short time ago
		べつの	**betsu no**, some other (thing)
〜ない　ほうが　いい	**-nai hō ga ii**, it's better not to	ようじ	**yōji**, work, business
もっと	**motto**, = -er, more	おさきに　しつれいします	**o-saki ni shitsurei shimasu**, goodbye
いまの　うちに	**ima no uchi ni**, right-away, before it's too late	さき	**saki**, ahead, before, beyond
それでは	**soredewa**, well then	おだいじに	**o-daiji ni**, Take care of yourself. (Said to sick people.)

GRAMMAR & LESSON OBJECTIVES

● **hō ga ii desu**

Uchi ni kaette yasunda hō ga ii desu yo.
Muri o shinai hō ga ii desu yo.
Ima no uchi ni naoshita hō ga ii desu yo.
Kimura-kun no hō ga ii desu yo.

As in these sentences, which are suggestions, before **hō ga ii desu**, the **-ta** form is more common, although recently the dictionary form has also come to be used. For negatives, whether verbs or adjectives, always use the plain **-nai** form. For either type of adjective, use the ordinary form, such as **ōkii hō ga ii desu** or **benrina hō ga ii desu**. After nouns add the particle **no**.

● **-ta bakari**

Kono purojekuto ga hajimatta bakari desu kara.
Suzuki-kun niwa sakki betsu no yōji o tanonda bakari . . .

The pattern **-ta bakari** indicates something has just happened.
ex. 1. **Watashi wa ima kita bakari desu.** "I just now arrived."
    2. **Sono nyūsu o shitta bakari desu.** "I just learned that news."

NOTES

1. **Yoku arimasen**
   This is the same as **yoku nai desu** (first volume, p. 97).
   ex. 1. **Ōkiku arimasen/nai desu.**
       2. **Takaku arimasen/nai desu.**
   Similarly with **-na** adjectives: **Shizuka dewa/ja arimasen** or **Benri dewa/ja arimasen** (introduced in the first volume) can be **Shizuka dewa/ja nai desu** or **Benri dewa/ja nai desu**. These alternative patterns are interchangeable in meaning.

2. **Isha ni itte kusuri o moratte kimashita.**
   This **-te kuru** pattern sometimes has its literal meaning: "go, do something, and return." (See p. 00 for a fuller discussion of this pattern.) The sentence can be translated, "I went to the doctor, got (some) medicine, and came back."
   ex. **Pan o katte kimasu.** "I'll buy bread (and come back)."

3. **Nakanaka yoku narimasen.**
   Nakanaka plus a negative implies that contrary to expectations something does not exist or has not happened or a favorable outcome is lacking despite a person's efforts or expectations.
   ex. 1. **Eigo ga nakanaka jōzu ni narimasen.** "(I) still haven't become good at English."

2. **Tanaka-san kara tegami ga nakanaka todokimasen.** "The letter (I've been waiting for) from Tanaka hasn't arrived."

4. **Suzuki-kun ka Kimura-kun ni . . .**
   -kun is less polite than **-san**. Typically heard when younger boys or men are being spoken to, it is never used between women or when addressing elders.

5. **O-saki ni shitsurei shimasu.**
   The sense of this is that by leaving before others, one is doing something he should excuse himself for. It is a very common expression, often shortened to either **o-saki ni** or **shitsurei shimasu**. (See the first volume, p. 61.) As noted on p. 15 of the first volume, **o-saki ni** may also be said when proceeding others through a door or into a car and so on.

PRACTICE

KEY SENTENCES

1. すぐ けいさつに でんわした ほうが いいです。
2. チャンさんは 4がつに ホンコンしてんから きたばかりです。
3. あの みせへ いって、たばこを かってきます。

1. You'd better telephone the police immediately.
2. Chang just came from the Hong Kong branch in April.
3. I'm going to that shop to buy tobacco.

Vocabulary

けいさつ   **keisatsu**, police

EXERCISES

I   Review: Study the examples again and convert the verbs into the **-nai** form.

A. Reg. I
   ex. いく →いかない   はなす→はなさない
        いそぐ→いそがない   まつ →またない
        のむ →のまない   ならう→ならわない
        しぬ →しなない   なおる→なおらない
        あそぶ→あそばない   ある →ない

1. およぐ	4. もらう	7. すむ	10. ひろう
2. つくる	5. おとす	8. かかる	11. けす
3. みがく	6. もつ	9. よぶ	12. つかう

B. Reg. II and Irreg.
   ex. しめる→しめない   くる→こない
        おりる→おりない   する→しない

1. はじめる	3. いる	5. もってくる	7. でんわする
2. できる	4. きめる	6. せつめいする	8. わすれる

II　Make dialogues by changing the underlined parts as in the examples given.

A. *ex.* **A**：なんで　いきましょうか。
　　　B：<u>ちかてつで</u>　<u>いった</u>　ほうが　いいですよ。

　　　　　1.　だれに　きく、かとうさんに
　　　　　2.　なんじごろ　でんわする、あさ　10じごろ
　　　　　3.　いつ　この　しょるいを　おくる、いま　すぐ
　　　　　4.　パーティーに　なんにん　ともだちを　よぶ、たくさん

B. *ex.* **Q**：どう　しましょうか。
　　　Aa：<u>はやしさんに　はなした</u>　ほうが　いいです。
　　　An：<u>はやしさんに　はなさない</u>　ほうが　いいです。

　　　　　1.　まどを　しめる　　　　　4.　バスで　いく
　　　　　2.　たなかさんに　いう　　　5.　はやしさんに　そうだんする
　　　　　3.　すぐ　でかける　　　　　6.　（お）さけを　もってくる

C. *ex.* **Q**：いつが　いいですか。
　　　A：<u>あしたの</u>　ほうが　いいです。

　　　　　1.　どれ、きれい　　　　　　4.　どこ、しずかな　ところ
　　　　　2.　なんじ、ごご　　　　　　5.　だれ、たなかくん
　　　　　3.　どちら、あかい

D. *ex.* **Q**：<u>いく　まえに　でんわした</u>　ほうが　いいですか。
　　　A：ええ、その　ほうが　いいでしょう。

　　　　　1.　ねる　まえに　くすりを　のむ
　　　　　2.　ふなびんで　おくる
　　　　　3.　ストーブを　けす
　　　　　4.　たなかさんに　しらせる

E. *ex.* **Q**：<u>いま　でんわしても</u>　いいですか。
　　　A：もう　おそいですから、<u>しない</u>　ほうが　いいですよ。

　　　　　1.　たばこを　すう、けんこうに　よくないです
　　　　　2.　ここに　くるまを　とめる、こうさてんに　ちかいです
　　　　　3.　すこし　あるく、まだ　びょうきが　なおっていません
　　　　　4.　もう　はっぴょうする、まだ　ぶちょうに　はなしていません

F. *ex.* **A**：リンダさんは　たぶん　<u>みちが　わかりません</u>よ。

    B：どうしてですか。

    A：<u>にほんへ　きたばかりです</u>から。

1. まだ　この　てがみを　よんでいません、いま　かいしゃに　きました
2. この　カメラの　つかいかたが　わかりません、きのう　かいました
3. まだ　あさごはんを　たべていません、いま　おきました
4. その　ニュースを　しりません、しゅっちょうから　かえりました

G. *ex.* **Q**：<u>だれが</u>　いいですか。

    A：<u>すずきくんか　きむらくんが</u>　いいです。

1. なに、ちゅうかりょうり、フランスりょうり
2. いつ、げつよう、かよう
3. どこ、ぎんざ、しんじゅく
4. いくら、1,500えん、2,000えん

H. *ex.* **Q**：どちらへ？

    A：<u>いしゃに　いって、くすりを　もらって</u>きます。

1. ほんやに　いく、しゅうかんしを　かう
2. あの　しょくどうへ　いく、しょくじを　する
3. うちへ　かえる、ひるごはんを　たべる
4. ぎんこうに　よる、おかねを　はらう
5. ゆうびんきょくへ　いく、てがみを　だす

Vocabulary

なおる	**naoru**, get well, be fixed	ぎんざ	**Ginza** (place name)
いま　すぐ	**ima sugu**, at once	しんじゅく	**Shinjuku** (place name)
ストーブ	**sutōbu**, (heating) stove	しゅうかんし	**shūkan-shi**, weekly magazine
けんこう	**kenkō**, health		
たぶん	**tabun**, probably, perhaps	よる	**yoru**, stop by
ちゅうか　りょ　うり	**Chūka ryōri**, Chinese cooking		

SHORT DIALOGUES

1. わたなべ：おかぜですか。

    チャン：　ええ。たいした　ことは　ありませんが、せきが　とまりません。

わたなべ：それは　いけませんね。

Watanabe: (Do you have) a cold?
Chang:　　Yes, It's nothing serious, but the coughing doesn't stop.
Watanabe: That's too bad. (*lit.* "It doesn't go [well], does it?")

2. すずき：もしもし、これから　びょういんに　よっていきますから、すこし
　　　　　　おそく　なります。
　すずき：どうか　しましたか。
　すずき：ころんで　あしに　けがを　しました。

Suzuki: Hello. I'm going to stop by the hospital so I'll be a little late.
Katō:　 What's the matter? (*lit.* "If it's [something unfortunate/out of the ordinary that's] happened. . .?")
Suzuki: (I) fell down and hurt my leg.

Vocabulary

たいした	**taishita**, serious, important	ころぶ	**korobu**, fall down
せき	**seki**, coughing, cough	あし	**ashi**, leg, foot
とまる	**tomaru**, stop	けがを　する	**kega o suru**, (be) hurt
これから	**korekara**, from now (on)	けが	**kega**, injury, wound
どうかする	**dō ka suru**, something is wrong		

QUIZ

I   Read this lessons's opening dialogue and answer the following questions.

1. チャンさんは　だれに　くすりを　もらいましたか。
2. チャンさんの　かぜは　すぐ　よく　なりましたか。
3. チャンさんの　かでは　あたらしい　プロジェクトが　はじまったばかりですか。
4. かとうさんは　すずきさんに　ようじを　たのんだ　あとで　チャンさんと　はなしましたか。

II   Put the appropriate particles in the parentheses.

1. いまの　うち（　　）　かえった　ほう（　　）　いいですよ。
2. かとうさんは　げつようび（　　）　かようび（　　）　とうきょうに　かえります。
3. ［わたしは］　さっき　すずきくん（　　）　べつ（　　）　ようじを　たのみました。
4. かいぎが　はじまったばかりです（　　）、へや（　　）　はいらないで　ください。
5. では、おさき（　　）　しつれいします。

52 LESSON 6

III Complete the sentences with the appropriate form of the verbs indicated.

1. けがを　していますから、いしゃを　（　　　）　ほうが　いいですよ。
（よぶ）

2. この　りんごは　ふるいですから、（　　　）　ほうが　いいですよ。
（たべる）

3. いま　（　　　）　ばかりですから、その　ニュースを　まだ　（　　　）い
ません。（くる、きく）

4. はやく　かぞくに　（　　　）　ほうが　いいですよ。　　（しらせる）

5. わたなべさんの　へやに　（　　　）、タイプを　（　　　）きます。
（いく、たのむ）

6. きょうは　みちが　（　　　）　いますから、くるまで　（　　　）　ほうが
いいですよ。（こむ、いく）

IV Circle the correct words in the parentheses.

1. わたしは（あまり、たいてい）でんしゃの　なかで　しんぶんを　よみ
ます。

2. タクシーを　まっていますが、（なかなか、ゆっくり）きません。

3. （はじめて、まず）はやしさんに　しらせて、（それでは、それから）み
んなに　しらせてください。

4. すずきくんは（さっき、もうすぐ）きたばかりです。

V Choose a sentence to make a suggestion appropriate to the situation described.

A. Your friend is embarrassed about having left his bag on the train.

1. でんしゃを　おりて、えきいんに　はなしたばかりです。

2. えきの　じむしつに　いって、えきいんに　はなした　ほうが　いい
です。

3. でんしゃに　のって、えきいんに　はなした　ことが　あります。

B. Your friend, despite having a fever, is drinking sake.

1. おさけを　たくさん　のんだ　ほうが　いいですよ。

2. はやく　ねた　ほうが　いいですよ。

3. すこし　おさけが　のみたいです。

LESSON 7 MR. JOHNSON'S ARRIVAL

Mr. Katō and Mr. Suzuki are talking about Mr. Johnson's arrival tomorrow.

かとう：あしたは　ジョンソンさんが　日本に　来る　日ですね。

すずき：ええ、そうです。

かとう：だれか　なりたくうこうまで　むかえに　行ってくれませんか。

すずき：わたしが　行きます。時間が　ありますから。

かとう：けさ　たのんだ　しごとは　きょうじゅうに　おわりますか。

すずき：はい、できます。

かとう：じゃ、おねがいします。ところで、ジョンソンさんを　知っています
　　　　か。

すずき：ロンドンの　じむしょに　いた　人ですね。

かとう：ええ。

すずき：しゃしんで　見た　ことが　あります。

かとう：なりたくうこうに　つく　時間は　14時50分です。ひこうきは　早く
　　　　つく　ことも　ありますから、早めに　ちゅうしょくを　すませて
　　　　出発してください。

すずき：はい。ジョンソンさんの　とまる　ホテルは　どこですか。

かとう：わたなべさんが　知っていますから、わたなべさんに　きいてくださ
　　　　い。

すずき：はい。

Katō:　　Tomorrow is the day Mr. Johnson comes to Japan, isn't it?
Suzuki:　Yes, that's right.
Katō:　　Won't someone be going to meet (him) at Narita Airport?
Suzuki:　I'll go. I have time.
Katō:　　Will the work (I) asked (you to do) this morning be finished today?
Suzuki:　Yes, I can (do it).
Katō:　　All right, please meet him. By the way, do you know Mr. Johnson?
Suzuki:　He's (one of the) people in the London Office, I believe.
Katō:　　Um hm.
Suzuki:　(I've) seen (his) picture.
Katō:　　Arrival time at Narita Airport is 14:50. Since planes sometimes arrive early, please finish lunch earlier and leave.
Suzuki:　Yes, sir. Where's the hotel Mr. Johnson's staying at?
Katō:　　Ms. Watanabe knows. Please ask her.
Suzuki:　I see.

だれか　　　　**dare ka**, someone, anyone　　　ちゅうしょく　　**chūshoku**, lunch

むかえにいく　　**mukae ni iku**, go to meet　　　すませる　　　　**sumaseru**, finish

　むかえる　　　　**mukaeru**, meet, greet　　　しゅっぱつする　**shuppatsu suru**, leave

ところで　　　　**tokorode**, by the way　　　　　しゅっぱつ　　　**shuppatsu**, departure

じむしょ　　　　**jimusho**, office　　　　　　　とまる　　　　　**tomaru**, stay, stop at

はやめに　　　　**hayame-ni**, early

GRAMMAR & LESSON OBJECTIVES

- Modifying nouns

A pattern corresponding to the relative clause in English is made by placing the modifiers before the noun. A verb appearing in the middle of the sentence is in a plain form, as noted earlier (p. 28).

present	aff.	**ashita kuru hitotachi**, "people (who are) coming tomorrow"
	neg.	**ashita konai hitotachi**, "people (who are) not coming tomorrow"
past	aff.	**kinō kita hitotachi**, "people (who) came yesterday"
	neg.	**kinō konakatta hitotachi**, "people (who) didn't come yesterday"

The following show how a sentence is converted into a modifying clause.

ex. 1. **Watashi wa hon o kaimashita.** → **Watashi ga/no katta hon,** "the book (that) I bought"

　　2. **Watashi wa kinō Ginza de hon o kaimashita.** → **Watashi ga kinō Ginza de katta hon,** "the book (which) I bought in the Ginza yesterday"

Note the changes in word order, the verb forms and the particles. Particle **wa** is replaced by **ga**, or when a clause is very short, it often becomes **no**.

ex. 1. **tenisu no jōzuna hito,** "a person (who is) good at tennis"

　　2. **ashi no nagai otoko,** "a man who has/having long legs." Alternatively, "a man with long legs" or "a long-legged man."

As well as with **-i** and **-na** adjectives and nouns plus **no**, nouns are modified with the plain past of **-i** adjectives. With a noun or **-na** adjective, plain forms of **desu** are used, as in the following examples. (For **desu**, the plain past is **datta** and the negative present is **dewa nai**, examples of which appear in later lessons.)

ex. 1. **takakatta hon,** "a book which used to be expensive"

　　2. **suki datta hito,** "a person (I) once liked"

　　3. **kyonen no natsu made byōin datta tatemono,** "the building which was a hospital until last summer"

Take careful note of five sentences in the dialogue in which this type of modification pattern occurs.

1. **Ashita wa Jonson-san ga Nihon ni kuru hi desu ne.**
2. **Kesa tanonda shigoto wa kyō-jū ni owarimasu ka.**
3. **Rondon no jimusho ni ita hito desu ne.**
4. **Narita Kūkō ni tsuku jikan wa 14-ji 50-pun desu.**
5. **Jonson-san no tomaru hoteru wa doko desu ka.**

NOTES

1. **Dare ka kūkō made mukae ni itte kuremasen ka.**

   -te kuremasen ka is a form of request but it would not be used when speaking to a superior. The meaning is "do (something) for (me/us)."

   ex. **Kite kuremasen ka.** "Won't you please come?"

Some other interrogatives of the same type as **dare ka** are **nani ka**, "something"; **itsu ka**, "sometime"; and **doko ka**, "somewhere."

ex. 1. **Dare ka mite imashita ka.** "Was anyone watching?"
   2. **Kyōto ni itsu ka ikitai desu.** "(I) want to go to Kyoto sometime."

2. **Hikōki wa hayaku tsuku koto mo arimasu.**
   In addition to the information given in lesson 4, you should observe that **koto** is a noun meaning "thing," "happening," "experience" and in the present case conveys the idea "it sometimes happens that . . ." "There are/have been cases of . . ."

ex. 1. **Ōsaka e wa taitei Shinkansen de ikimasu ga, hikōki de iku koto mo arimasu.** "(I) usually go to Osaka on the Shinkansen but sometimes (I) go by plane."
   2. **Do-yōbi wa shigoto wa yasumi desu ga, kaigi o suru koto mo arimasu.** "Saturday is a day off but sometimes meetings are held."
   3. **Nihon no chūgakkō dewa seito ni Eigo o oshiemasu ga, Furansu-go o oshieru gakkō mo arimasu.** "Japanese middle schools teach English to (their) students, but there are some schools which teach French."

PRACTICE

KEY SENTENCES

1. スミスさんは　ABCで　はたらいている　べんごしです。
2. きゅうしゅうは　あたたかい　ところですが、ふゆは　ゆきが　ふる　こと　も　あります。

1. Mr. Smith is a lawyer who works for ABC.
2. Kyushu is a warm region but in winter sometimes it snows.

Vocabulary			
あたたかい	**atatakai**, warm	ゆき	**yuki**, snow
ゆきが　ふる	**yuki ga furu**, it snows (lit. "snow falls")	ふる	**furu**, fall

EXERCISES

I Noun-modifying patterns: Memorize the following sentences.

A. 1. これは　おもしろい　ほんです。
   2. リンダさんは　かみが　ながい　ひとです。

B. 1. これは　きれいな　ざっしです。
   2. あれは　ちちが　すきな　えです。
   3. これは　こどものころ　わたしが　すきだった　おかしです。

C. 1. これは　ふなびんで　おくる　にもつです。
   2. あそこで　ほんを　よんでいる　ひとは　たなかさんです。
   3. これは　ははが　かいた　てがみです。

D. 1. <u>ぎんこうに　いく</u>　じかんが　ありません。
   2. <u>あなたが　とまった</u>　ホテルは　どこですか。
   3. <u>きってを　うっている</u>　ところを　しっていますか。
   4. <u>ロンドンから　きた</u>　ともだちに　あいました。

II Noun-modifying patterns: Study the following sentences, concentrating on the underlined patterns.

   1. かれは　<u>おもしろくない</u>　ひと　です。
   2. これは　<u>わたしが　ほしかった</u>　ゆびわです。
   3. この　なかで　<u>りょこうに　いかなかった</u>　ひとは　だれですか。
   4. たなかさんが　<u>かいしゃに　こなかった</u>　ひは　せんしゅうの　きん
      ようびです。

III Make dialogues by changing the underlined parts as in the examples given.

A. ex. **Q**：これは　なんですか。
     A：<u>えを　かく</u>　どうぐです。

      1. ゆでたまごを　きります
      2. トイレを　そうじします
      3. おもい　にもつを　はこびます
      4. ケーキを　やきます

B. ex. **Q**：すみません、<u>とうきょうへ　いく</u>　バスは　どれですか。
     A：あの　えきの　まえに　とまっている　バスです。

      1. 10じに　でます
      2. ぎんざを　とおります
      3. おおさかから　きました
      4. おおさかを　10じに　しゅっぱつしました

C. ex. **Q**：<u>しんぶんを　うっている</u>　ところを　しっていますか。
     A：さあ、ちょっと　わかりません。

      1. しずかです
      2. やすくて　おいしいです
      3. テニスが　できます
      4. たなかさんの　むすこさんが　つとめています
      5. こんでいません

D. *ex.* **Q** : まいにち　いそがしいですか。

　　A : ええ、<u>てがみを　かく</u>　じかんも　ありません。

1. しんぶんを　よみます
2. こどもと　あそびます
3. ともだちと　おしゃべりします
4. ふうふげんかを　します

E. *ex.* **Q** : <u>パーティーに　きた</u>　ひとは　だれですか。

　　A : きむらさんです。

1. きょねん　けっこんしました
2. なかむらさんが　すきでした
3. パーティーで　いっしょに　おどりたかったです
4. かいぎに　しゅっせきしませんでした
5. まだ　きていません
6. まだ　もうしこんでいません

F. *ex.* **A** : あの　ひとは　だれですか

　　B : どの　ひとですか。

　　A : <u>きの　したで　ほんを　よんでいる</u>　ひとです。

　　B : ああ、あの　<u>きの　したで　ほんを　よんでいる</u>　ひとですか。
　　　　　あれは　ホワイトさんです。

1. おおきい　こえで　わらっています
2. せきを　しています
3. うわぎを　きていません
4. いま　たちました
5. かみが　みじかいです
6. せが　たかいです

IV　Practice the following pattern by changing the underlined parts.

ex. <u>だれか</u>　<u>きました</u>か。

1. なに、いってください
2. どこ、いきたいですね
3. いつ、いきましょうか
4. だれ、よびましょうか

V   Make dialogues by changing the underlined parts as in the example given.

ex. **Q**：いつも　<u>ひこうきで　いきます</u>か。

　　A：ええ、たいてい　<u>ひこうきで　いきます</u>が、<u>しんかんせんで　いく</u>
　　　　ことも　あります。

1. うちで　しんぶんを　よみます、でんしゃの　なかで　よみます
2. じぶんで　ネクタイを　えらびます、かないが　えらびます
3. あさごはんを　たべます、ときどき　たべません
4. やくそくの　じかんんを　まもります、たまに　まもりません

Vocabulary

かれ	**kare**, he	ふうふ	**fūfu**, husband and wife
ほしい	**hoshii**, want, wish	けんか	**kenka**, quarrel, fight
ゆびわ	**yubiwa**, ring	おどる	**odoru**, dance
どうぐ	**dōgu**, implement, machine, appliance, tool	しゅっせきする しゅっせき	**shusseki suru**, attend **shusseki**, attendance
ゆでたまご	**yude tamago**, boiled egg	もうしこむ	**mōshikomu**, apply
きる	**kiru**, cut	こえ	**koe**, voice
トイレ	**toire**, toilet	わらう	**warau**, laugh, smile
はこぶ	**hakobu**, carry, transport	うわぎ	**uwagi**, jacket, coat
そうじする そうじ	**sōji suru**, clean **sōji**, cleaning	みじかい じぶんで	**mijikai**, short **jibun de**, by oneself
やく	**yaku**, bake, grill, roast	じぶん	**jibun**, oneself
とおる	**tōru**, go through/past	えらぶ	**erabu**, choose
おしゃべりする	**o-shaberi suru**, chat	やくそく	**yakusoku**, promise, appointment
ふうふげんか	**fūfu-genka**, marital disagreement	まもる たまに	**mamoru**, keep, obey **tama ni**, once in a while

SHORT DIALOGUES

1. かちょう：だれか　ちょっと　てを　かしてください。
　　すずき：　なんでしょうか。
　　かちょう：この　しりょうを　かたづけてくれませんか。
　　すずき：　はい、わかりました。

　　Section Chief: Won't someone lend me a hand for a moment?
　　Suzuki:　　　What is it (you want)?
　　Section Chief: Do me the favor of putting away these papers.
　　Suzuki:　　　Yes, certainly.

2. A：だれか　ここに　あった　しんぶんを　しりませんか。
　　B：あ、いま　わたしが　よんでいます。
　　A：じゃ、あとで　みせてください。

A: Doesn't anyone know where the newspaper that was here is?
B: Ah, I'm reading (it).
A: Well, please let me see it later (when you finish).

Vocabulary

かちょう	**kachō**, section chief	しりょう	**shiryō**, papers, document
てを かして	**te o kashite**, lend a hand	かたづける	**katazukeru**, put away, ti-
かす	**kasu**, lend		dy up

QUIZ

I Read this lesson's opening dialogue and answer the following questions.

1. だれが ジョンソンさんを くうこうまで むかえに いきますか。
2. ジョンソンさんは どこの じむしょに いた ひとですか。
3. かとうさんは ジョンソンさんの とまる ホテルを しっていますか。
4. すずきさんは ジョンソンさんに あった ことが ありますか。

II Put the appropriate particles in the parentheses.

1. これは わたし（　　） かいた えです。
2. えき（　　） つく じかんは なんじですか。
3. わたしは ジョンソンさん（　　） あった ことは ありませんが、
   しゃしん（　　） みた ことは あります。
4. はやく しごと（　　） すませて、うちに かえります。
5. くうこうまで くるま（　　） むかえ（　　） いきます。
6. たいてい ひとり（　　） りょこうしますが、ともだち（　　） い
   っしょに いく こと（　　） あります。

III Complete the sentences with the appropriate form of the verbs indicated.

1. スペインごが （　　） ひとは だれですか。(できます)
2. 〔あなたが〕 やまださんに （　　） ひは いつですか。(あいます)
3. きのう スライドを （　　） ひとは きょう みてください。
   (みませんでした)
4. えいごが （　　） ひとには にほんごで せつめいしましょう。
   (わかりません)
5. きのう （　　） ひとに この てがみを おくってください。
   (きませんでした)
6. きょう （　　） ものの なかで これが いちばん たかかったで
   す。(かいました)
7. ジョンソンさんが （　　） ホテルを しっていますか。
   (とまっています)
8. これは わたしの （　　） いろです。(すきです)
9. これは こどもの ころ わたしが （　　） おかしです。
   (すきでした)

10. あの （　　　） ひとは だれですか。（せが たかいです）

VI　Look at the picture and answer the questions.

1. いすに すわっている ひとは だれですか。
2. うわぎを きている ひとは だれですか。
3. セーターを きている ひとは だれですか。
4. かさを もっている ひとは だれですか。
5. たっている ひとは だれですか。

スミスさん　スミスさんの おくさん　たなかさん

V　Answer the following questions.

1. あなたが すんでいる ところは どこですか。
2. あなたの すきな りょうりは なんですか。
3. あなたが いきたい ところは どこですか。
4. いままで りょこうに いった ところの なかで どこが いちばん
　 すばらしかったですか。

LESSON 8 THE O-BON FESTIVAL

Mr. Chang, who's thinking about a trip to Sendai, asks Mr. Katō for advice.

チャン：8月の　10日ごろ　せんだいへ　あそびに　行きたいと　思いますが、
　　　　しんかんせんと　ひこうきと　どちらが　べんりですか。

かとう：しんかんせんの　ほうが　べんりだと　思いますよ。でも　しんかんせ
　　　　んの　していけんは　もう　ないと　思います。ひこうきの　きっぷも
　　　　たぶん　うりきれでしょう。

チャン：どうしてですか。

かとう：8月の　中ごろは　おぼんで、くにへ　かえる　人が　おおぜい　いま
　　　　す。10日ごろから、この　きせいラッシュが　はじまりますから、りょ
　　　　こうは　やめた　ほうが　いいですよ。

チャン：すずきくんも　10日に　せんだいの　家に　かえると　ききましたが・
　　　　・・。

かとう：ええ、かれは　1か月　前に　きっぷを　かったと　言っていました。

チャン：そうですか。じゃ、せんだいまで　車で　どのぐらい　かかりますか。

かとう：おぼんの　シーズンは　10時間　いじょう　かかると　思いますよ。
　　　　すずきくんは　きょ年は　車で　行きましたが、すごい　じゅうたいだ
　　　　ったと　言っていました。それに、おぼんの　後は　東京へ　かえる
　　　　車で　みちが　こむでしょう。Uターンラッシュですよ。

チャン：日本は　人が　おおいですからね。ラッシュの　ない　ところへ　行き
　　　　たいですねえ。

かとう：ラッシュの　ない　ところが　ありますよ。

チャン：どこですか。

かとう：どこだと　思いますか。おぼんの　ころの　東京ですよ。人も　車も
　　　　少ないし、つうきんラッシュも　ないし、いいですよ。

チャン：なるほど。

Chang:　Around August 10, I think I'd like to take a (pleasure) trip to Sendai. (Between) the
　　　　Shinkansen and a plane, which is more convenient?
Katō:　 I reckon the Shinkansen is more convenient. But then I'm afraid there aren't any more
　　　　Shinkansen reserved tickets. Plane tickets are probably sold out, too.
Chang:　Why is that?
Katō:　 The O-Bon Festival is around the middle of August. There are hordes of people return-
　　　　ing to their home towns. This homecoming rush begins around the 10. It'd be best to
　　　　give up your trip.
Chang:　I heard Suzuki's going back to his home in Sendai on the 10, too.
Katō:　 Um. He said he bought a ticket a month early.

Chang: Is that so? How long does it take to Sendai by car?

Katō: During the O-Bon period, I guess it'd take more than ten hours. Suzuki went by car last year and he said the congestion was terrible. And besides, after O-Bon the roads are most likely to be (very) crowded with cars returning to Tokyo. It's a "U-turn rush."

Chang: It's because Japan has a lot of people, wouldn't you say? I'd like to go someplace where there's no rushing around.

Katō: There is a place without a (big) rush.

Chang: Where's that?

Katō: Where do you think it is? It's Tokyo around O-Bon. With people and cars few and no commuter rush (hours), it's (quite) pleasant.

Chang: I see.

| Vocabulary |

せんだい	**Sendai** (city)	おおぜい	**ōzei**, hordes/lots of people
おもう	**omou**, think	きせい	**kisei**, homecoming
していけん	**shitei-ken**, reserved ticket	ラッシュ	**rasshu**, rush
		やめる	**yameru**, give up, stop
してい	**shitei**, appointment, designation, specification	シーズン	**shīzun**, period, time
		いじょう	**ijō**, more than
		じゅうたい	**jūtai**, congestion
けん	**ken**, ticket	それに	**soreni**, besides
もう〜ない	**mō . . . nai**, any/no more, any/no longer	ユーターン	**yūtān**, U-turn
		すくない	**sukunai**, a little, few
うりきれ	**urikire**, sold out	〜し	**shi**, and, moreover (particle)
なかごろ	**naka-goro**, around the middle	なるほど	**naruhodo**, I see, it's reasonable
おぼん	**O-Bon** (midsummer festival)		
くに	**kuni**, home town, birthplace, country		

GRAMMAR & LESSON OBJECTIVES

• to omou, to kiku, to iu

Sendai e asobi ni ikitai to omoimasu. (I think)

Shinkansen no hō ga benri da to omoimasu yo. (I reckon)

Shinkansen no shitei ken wa mō nai to omoimasu. (I'm afraid)

Suzuki-san mo 10-ka ni Sendai no ie e kaeru to kikimashita ga. (I heard)

Kare wa 1-kagetsu mae ni kippu o katta to itte imashita. (He said)

Suzuki-san wa kyonen wa kuruma de ikimashita ga, sugoi jūtai datta to itte imashita. (He said)

. . . **to iu** obviously signals quoted material and . . . **to kiku** may do so too. It should be noted that when a third person's statement is cited, the verb is **to itte imashita** or **to kiite imashita**, when the meaning of the latter is "asked." (**To iimashita** is not used; it is found in story-telling style, written or verbal. See appendix B.)

ex. **Hayashi-san wa . . . to itte imashita/kiite imashita.** "Hayashi said/asked. . ."

A verb tense form in quoted material has no relation to the tense form of the verb ending the sentence, so it may be the same or it may be different. It is quite common for negation to be expressed in the first, rather than the main, verb, and this sometimes contrasts with the pattern in English, as in **Sumisu-san wa ashita konai to omoimasu** if this is translated, "I don't think Smith is coming tomorrow."

When the subject is the speaker or the listener **to omou** is the preferred form. If the subject is a third person **to omotte iru** is used exclusively.

As in the examples above, verbs and adjectives coming at the end of quoted material are in plain forms, and with nouns and **-na** adjectives, patterns with **da** and **datta** are usual. (See appendix A.)

- **deshō**

  Hikōki no kippu mo tabun urikire deshō.

  O-bon no ato wa Tōkyō e kaeru kuruma de michi ga komu deshō.

  Deshō, seen in lessons 2 and 3 as a way to soften a direct question, may indicate conjecture or probability, what the speaker believes to be true. Words coming before **deshō** are in a plain form and in the case of **-na** adjectives, **deshō** comes directly after the stem.

  ex. 1. **Ano kōen wa shizuka desu.** → **Ano kōen wa shizuka deshō.** "That park is probably quiet."
  2. **Kare wa bengoshi desu** → **Kare wa bengoshi deshō.** "He's a lawyer, I suppose."
  3. **Chan-san wa mada Ogawa-san ni hanashite inai deshō.** "Chang probably hasn't told Ogawa yet."

  Since it implies tentativeness, **deshō** would sound awkward or irresponsible if it referred to the speaker's own action.

  ex. **Sumisu-san wa ashita Ōsaka ni iku deshō.**

  However, **Watashi mo ashita Ōsaka ni iku deshō** is awkward.

- Connective particle **shi**

  Hito mo kuruma mo sukunai shi, tsūkin rasshu mo nai shi, ii desu yo.

  The particle **shi** joins clauses, which are usually explanations, excuses or reasons, with the main clause. Before **shi**, either plain or **desu/-masu** verb forms (including their past and negative derivatives) can occur.

  ex. **Kirei desu shi, yasui desu shi, kaimashō.** "It's lovely, besides it's inexpensive, let's buy it."

NOTES

1. The **O-Bon** Festival

   For this festival on August 13–15 (there are a few local variations on the dates) many companies close down and millions of people desert the big cities. Originating in Buddhist beliefs fused with folk traditions, it celebrates the return of ancestral spirits to their birthplaces for a three-day visit and is, together with the New Year's holidays, a major event among the literally hundreds of annual festivals. Secularized to some extent in recent times, **O-Bon** is an occasion for family reunions, and the highlights are the **Bon Odori**, "Bon Dance," **O-haka-mairi**, "visits to (ancestral) graves," and the lighting of fires and lanterns to welcome and send-off the spirits of the dead.

2. **Shitei ken wa mō nai to omoimasu.**

   The usage of **mō**, "already"; **mō nai**, "not any more/longer"; and **mada**, "yet, still," need not be confusing. Study the following examples.

   ex. 1. Q: **Mada kippu wa arimasu ka.** "Do (you) still have tickets?"
   A*a*: **Hai mada arimasu.** "Yes, there are still (some available)."
   A*n*: **Iie, mō arimasen.** "No, there aren't any more."
   2. Q: **Kare wa mō dekakemashita ka.** "Has he gone out already?"
   A*a*: **Hai, mō dekakemashita.** "Yes, he's already gone out."
   A*n*: **Iie, mada dekakete imasen. Mada ie ni imasu.** "No, he hasn't left yet. He's still at home."

   As shown in the first volume (p. 95), **mō** can also mean simply "more," i.e., **Mō 1-mai kippu o kudasai**, "Give me one more ticket, please."

3. **Doko da to omoimasu ka.**

   Expressions similar to this one are:
   1. **Naze da to omoimasu ka.** "Why is it, do you think?"
   2. **Dare ga sō itta to omoimasu ka.** "(Can) you guess who said so?"

PRACTICE

KEY SENTENCES

1. あしたは　ストライキですから、でんしゃも　バスも　うごかないと　おもいます。
2. きむらさんは　さっぽろを　しっていると　いっていました。
3. あしたは　たぶん　あめでしょう。
4. おいしいし、やすいし、きれいだし、あの　レストランは　いいですよ。

1. There's a strike tomorrow, so I expect trains and buses won't be running.
2. Kimura said he knows Sapporo.
3. Tomorrow will probably be rain(y).
4. That restaurant is cheap and clean and (the food) is good, so its's OK.

Vocabulary	
ストライキ	**sutoraiki**, strike
うごく	**ugoku**, run, move, operate

EXERCISES

Make dialogues by changing the underlined parts as in the examples given.

A. *ex.* **Q**：あたらしい　プロジェクトを　どう　おもいますか。
    A：<u>たんへんだ</u>と　おもいます。

    1. むずかしいです　　　　4. たいくつです
    2. おもしろいです　　　　5. リサーチが　ひつようです
    3. つまらないです　　　　6. むずかしい　しごとです

B. *ex.* **Q**：<u>たなかさんは　きますか</u>。
    Aa：はい、<u>くる</u>と　おもいます。
    An：いいえ、<u>こない</u>と　おもいます。

    1. この　しごとは　あしたまでに　できます
    2. にもつは　きょうじゅうに　つきます
    3. しゅしょうは　この　ニュースを　もう　しっています
    4. たなかさんは　こどもが　あります

C. *ex.* **Q**：<u>たなかさんは　もう　かえりましたか</u>。
    Aa：ええ、もう　<u>かえった</u>と　おもいます。
    An：いいえ、まだ　<u>かえっていない</u>と　おもいます。

    1. しゅうかいは　もう　はじまりました

2. だいじんは この ニュースを もう ききました
3. たなかさんは おきゃくさんに もう あいました
4. けんきゅうしりょうは もう まとまりました

D. *ex.* **Q**: <u>すずきさん</u>は なんと いっていますか。
   A: <u>すずきさん</u>は <u>きのうは どこにも いかなかった</u>と いっています。

1. リンダ、さくらは とても きれいでした
2. ブラウン、あの ミュージカルは あまり おもしろくありませんでした
3. スミス、あした かいぎに でたくないです
4. やまだ、あまり スポーツを する じかんが ありません

E. *ex.* **Q**: あの ひとの <u>まえの しごと</u>を しっていますか。
   A: <u>がいこうかんだった</u>と ききましたが・・・。

1. じむしょが ある ところ、けいさつの となりです
2. おくに、あたたかい ところです
3. そつぎょうした だいがく、にほんの だいがくでは ありません
4. しけんの けっか、あまり よくありませんでした
5. わかい ころの しごと、かんごふさんでした

F. *ex.* **Q**: <u>あしたの てんき</u>は どうですか。
   A: たぶん <u>あめ</u>でしょうね。

1. あの みせ、たかいです
2. あの しばい、おもしろくないです
3. にちようびの こうえん、にぎやかです
4. これ、てきとうじゃ ないです
5. あしたの てんき、ゆきが ふります
6. たなかさん、くる ことが できません
7. チャンさんの かぜ、よく なりました

G. *ex.* **Q**: <u>あたらしい うち</u>は どうですか。
   A: <u>ひろいし きれいだし</u> すばらしいです。

1. ぎんざの まち、にぎやか、おもしろい、いい ところです
2. あたらしい カメラ、かるい、べんり、きに いっています

3. いまの　しごと、いそがしい、ざんぎょうが　おおい、たいへん
   です
4. いまの　アパート、せまい、やかましい、ひっこしたいと　おも
   っています

H. *ex.* **A**：たいへんですね。
   B：ええ。<u>おかねが　かかるし</u>　<u>じかんも　かかるし</u>。

1. ざんぎょうが　あります、よく　しゅっちょうも　します
2. おそくまで　はたらく　ことも　あります、あさ　はやく　でか
   ける　ことも　あります
3. しごとが　かわります、ひっこしも　します

Vocabulary

たいへん（な）	**taihen(na)**, hard, difficult	しけん	**shiken**, examination, test
たいくつ（な）	**taikutsu(na)**, boring	けっか	**kekka**, result
リサーチ	**risāchi**, research	わかい	**wakai**, young
ひつよう（な）	**hitsuyō(na)**, necessary	かんごふ（さん）	**kangofu(-san)**, nurse
しゅしょう	**shushō**, prime minister	てきとう（な）	**tekitō(na)**, suitable, ap-
しゅうかい	**shūkai**, gathering,		propriate
	assembly	かるい	**karui**, light
だいじん	**daijin**, minister (of state)	ざんぎょう	**zangyō**, overtime
けんきゅう	**kenkyū**, research, study	アパート	**apāto**, apartment, apart-
まとまる	**matomaru**, brought		ment house
	together, be in order	せまい	**semai**, small cramped,
さくら	**sakura**, cherry (blossom)		narrow
ミュージカル	**myūjikaru**, musical	やかましい	**yakamashii**, noisy
でる	**deru**, attend	ひっこす	**hikkosu**, move
がいこうかん	**gaikōkan**, diplomat	つかれる	**tsukareru**, be/get tired,
そつぎょうする	**sotsugyō suru**, graduate		tire,
そつぎょう	**sotsugyō**, graduation	かわる	**kawaru**, change

SHORT DIALOGUES

1. ブラウン：　　しんかんせんの　ざせきしていけんは　どこで　うっていま
   すか。

   つうこうにん：あそこの　みどりの　まどぐちで　うっています。

   ブラウン：　　きょうとまで　おとな　2まい　こども　1まい　おねがい
   します。

   えきいん：　　とっきゅうけんも　いりますか。

   ブラウン：　　ええ、おねがいします。

Brown:　　　Where are Shinkansen reserved seat tickets sold?
Passerby:　(They're) sold at the Green (Ticket) Window over there.

Brown:　　　　　　I'd like two adult tickets and one child's to Kyoto.
Station Employee: (Do you) want special express tickets too?
Brown:　　　　　　Yes, please.

2. A：10じ30ぷんはつの　しんおおさかいきの　しんかんせんは　なんばんせ
　　んから　でますか。

　　B：17ばんせんです。

A: What (number) track does the 10:30 Shinkansen going to Shin-Osaka depart from?
B: It's track number seventeen.

> **Vocabulary**

ざせき	**zaseki**, seat	とっきゅうけん	**tokkyū-ken**, special express ticket
つうこうにん	**tsūkōnin**, passerby		
みどりの　まど　ぐち	**Midori no Madoguchi**, Green (Ticket) Window (for reserved seat and express tickets)	とっきゅう	**tokkyū**, special/limited express
		いる	**iru**, need
		〜はつ	**-hatsu**, departure
みどり	**midori**, green	〜いき	**-iki**, going to, bound for
まどぐち	**madoguchi**, window, clerk	〜ばんせん	**-bansen** (counter for tracks)
おとな	**otona**, adult		

QUIZ

I　Read this lessons's opening dialogue and answer the following questions.

1. チャンさんは　8がつの　10かごろ　どこへ　あそびに　いきたいと
おもっていますか。

2. おぼんの　ころは　どうして　はやく　ひこうきや　しんかんせんの
きっぷが　うりきれに　なりますか。

3. すずきさんは　きょねん　くるまで　くにへ　かえりましたか、しんか
んせんで　かえりましたか。

4. おぼんの　ころの　とうきょうには　ラッシュが　ないと　だれが　い
っていますか。

5. あなたは　チャンさんが　8がつ10かに　せんだいへ　いくと　おもい
ますか、いかないと　おもいますか。

II　Put the appropriate particles in the parentheses.

1. スミスさんは　いまごろ　きょうとの　おてら（　　）　まわっている
（　　）　おもいます。

2. スミスさんは　その　しごと（　　）　おがわさん（　　）　たのんだ
（　　）　いっていました。

3. ねつが　ある（　　）、のども　いたい（　　）、かぜだ（　　）　おも
います。

4. かれも 10か（　　）　せんだい（　　）　うち（　　）　かえる
（　　）　ききました。

III　Complete the questions so that they fit the answers. (Use a question word.)

1. すずきくんと　きむらくんと　（　　）が　わかいですか。
きむらくんの　ほうが　わかいと　おもいます。
2. リンダさんは　（　　）　にほんに　くるでしょうか。
たぶん　らいねん　くるでしょう。
3. かれは　（　　）と　いっていましたか。
あしたは　つごうが　わるいと　いっていました。
4. この　えを　（　　）　おもいますか。
なかなか　すばらしいと　おもいます。
5. あなたは　（　　）　いきませんか。
あついし、ひとが　おおいし、いきたくないです。

IV　Complete the sentences with the appropriate form of the verbs indicated.

1. かれは　きのう　たいしかんへ　（　　）と　おもいます。（いきません
でした）
2. すずきさんは　あした　（　　）と　いっていました。（きません）
3. かとうさんは　（　　）と　わたなべさんが　いっていました。（げんき
でした）
4. かれは　ジョンソンさんに　あった　ことが　（　　）と　いってい
ました。（ありません）
5. きのうの　えいがは　（　　）と　いっていました。（おもしろくなかっ
たです）
6. あの　ひとは　ブラウンさんの　（　　）と　おもいます。（おくさんで
は　ありません）
7. リンダさんは　この　いろが　（　　）でしょう。（きに　いりません）
8. きょうは　さむいし、（　　）し、でかけたくないです。（あめです）
9. かいぎは　まだ　（　　）と　おもいます。（おわっていません）

V　Answer the following questions.

1. あしたは　いい　てんきでしょうか。
2. あなたは　いつから　にほんごを　ならっていますか。
3. にほんごの　べんきょうは　おもしろいと　おもいますか。
4. あなたは　なつやすみに　どこか　りょこうに　いきますか。

LESSON 9 PREP SCHOOL

On going to their house, Mr. Johnson meets Mr. Tanaka's daughter Keiko on her way out.

けい子：　　あら、ジョンソンさん。

ジョンソン：あ、けい子さん、お出かけですか。

けい子：　　ええ、これから　出かけなければ　なりません。

ジョンソン：今　すぐ　出なくては　いけませんか。

けい子：　　ごめんなさい。今日中に　よびこうの　もうしこみを　しなければ　なりませんから。

ジョンソン：よびこう？　けい子さんは　大学に　ごうかくしたと　ききましたが・・・。

けい子：　　ええ、第二しぼうの　大学には　ごうかくしましたが、第一しぼうの　こくりつ大学は　ふごうかくでした。来年　また　じゅけんします。

ジョンソン：そうですか。じゃ、行ってらっしゃい。

けい子：　　行ってまいります。

At the prep school.

けい子：　　　もうしこみの　しょるいは　これで　いいですか。これ、入学金と　3か月分の　じゅぎょうりょうです。
それから　サマーコースも　もうしこみたいと　思いますが、よく　かんがえてから　後で　ゆうびんで　もうしこんでは　いけませんか。

まどぐちの人：ええ、ゆうびんでも　いいです。しはらいも　わざわざ　ここまで　来なくても　いいですよ。銀行に　ふりこんでください。

けい子：　　　げんきんかきとめでも　いいですか。

まどぐちの人：はい、どちらでも　けっこうです。

Keiko:　　Oh, Mr. Johnson.
Johnson:　Ah, Keiko, are you going out?
Keiko:　　Yes, I have to (go out).
Johnson:　Do you have to leave right now?
Keiko:　　Sorry, (yes). I have to register at a prep school today.
Johnson:　Prep school? I heard you passed (your) college entrance exams.
Keiko:　　Yes, that's true. I passed (the exams) for the university of my second choice, but (the

70

ones) for the national university, my first choice, were a failure. I'll take the exams
again next year.
Johnson: Well, well. Bye-bye.
Keiko: Bye-bye.

Keiko: Are (my) application papers all right (like) this? This is the entrance fee and (here's)
three months' tuition. I think I'd like to register for the summer course too. After giving
it some thought, can't I register later by mail?
Clerk: Yes, mail is OK. As for payment, you don't have to go to the trouble of coming (all the
way) here. Please transfer (it) to our bank.
Keiko: Is sending it by registered-cash mail all right?
Clerk: Yes, either will be fine.

Vocabulary

あら	**ara**, Oh! (female speech)	にゅうがくきん	**nyūgaku kin**, entrance/matriculation fee
～なければ な らない	**-nakereba naranai**, must	にゅうがく	**nyūgaku**, matriculation
～なくては いけない	**-nakute wa ikenai**, must	さんかげつ ぶん	**san-kagetsu-bun**, 3-months' (worth)
ごめんなさい	**gomen-nasai**, I'm sorry, Excuse me	じゅぎょうりょ う	**jugyō-ryo**, tuition
よびこう	**yobikō**, preparatory school	じゅぎょう りょう	**jugyō**, instruction ryō, fee, charge
ごうかくする	**gōkaku suru**, pass, succeed	サマーコース	**samā kōsu**, summer course
ごうかく	**gōkaku**, success, eligibility	ゆうびん	**yūbin**, mail
だいに	**dai-ni**, second	でも いい	**demo ii**, is all right
だい～	**dai-** (prefix for ordinal number)	しはらい	**shiharai**, payment
		わざわざ～する	**wazawaza (suru)**, go to the trouble of
しぼう	**shibō**, choice, desire	わざわざ	**wazawaza**, especially
こくりつ	**kokuritsu**, national	～なくても いい	**-nakute mo ii**, don't have to
ふごうかく	**fu-gōkaku**, failure		
ふ～	**fu-** (negating prefix)	ふりこむ	**furikomu**, transfer
じゅけんする	**juken suru**, take an examination	げんきんかきと め	**genkin kakitome**, registered cash
じゅけん	**juken**, undergoing examination	かきとめ	**kakitome**, registered mail
いってらっしゃ い	**itterasshai**, bye-bye	どちらでも	**dochira demo**, either
いってまいりま す	**ittemairimasu**, so long	けっこう	**kekkō**, fine

GRAMMAR & LESSON OBJECTIVES

• Obligations, orders, prohibitions and permission
Kore kara dekakenakereba narimasen.
Kyō-jū ni mōshikomi o shinakereba narimasen.
-nakereba (made from the **-nai** form) **narimasen**, basically a pattern expressing obligation,

may be used, as here, in making excuses. As an order—"you must"—it sounds harsh and willful (not the kind of thing heard in polite society). On the other hand, the tone is fairly neutral if it reflects conditions beyond the speaker's or listener's control.

ex. **Kyō wa basu mo chikatetsu mo suto desu kara, kuruma de ikanakereba narimasen yo.** "Since both buses and subways are on strike today, you'll have to go by car."

Sentences ending with **-te wa ikemasen**, either affirmative or negative, have an imperative tone.

ex. **Ima denakute wa ikemasen.** "You must leave now."

Ima dete wa ikemasen. "You mustn't leave now."

Imasugu denakute wa ikemasen ka.

Ato de yūbin de mōshikonde wa ikemasen ka.

Both these patterns and **-nakereba narimasen ka** are freely used in asking questions. With almost the same meaning as **-te mo ii desu ka** (pattern after next), **-te wa ikemasen ka** can be a way of asking permission. Compare the translation of the sentence above with the following example.

ex. **Ato de yūbin de okutte mo ii desu ka.** "May I send it later by mail?"

Yūbin demo ii desu.

Genkin kakitome demo ii desu ka.

One meaning of **demo** being "even," the sense of **demo ii desu** is that it's all right even if X happens or a certain condition exists.

Koko made konakute mo ii desu.

By using this negative verb form, this pattern says it is OK not to do something.

NOTES

1. **o-dekake desu ka**

   This common expression is formed with **o** plus the **-masu** stem and **desu**. It is used in its literal sense here but may occur simply as a greeting not particularly requiring an answer.

2. **Itte rasshai, itte mairimasu**

   Tadaima, o-kaeri-nasai

   Itte rasshai is said to a person who will return to the place he or she is leaving, so it may be heard in offices and other places as well as homes. The person who leaves generally replies with **itte mairimasu/ittekimasu**. The expressions used when the person returns are **tadaima** and **o-kaeri-nasai**, as given in the short dialogues in this lesson and on p. 15 of the first volume.

3. **Yobikō**

   Students attend **yobikō**, "prep schools," to prepare for college entrance examinations. The ratio of applicants to openings, especially at the top schools, is quite high and aspirants may take entrance exams for two or more years before meeting with success. Good prep schools may also have more applicants than openings, which explains why Keiko wants to apply early for the summer course.

4. **Fu-gōkaku deshita.**

   Fu (不), a prefix which changes words into their opposite meanings, is similar to English "non-," "un-" or "in-." Another example is **fu-ben**, "inconvenient." (Although the common term is **benri**, the character (便, **ben**) by itself has the meaning "convenience," "facility."

5. **Kore de ii desu ka.**

   After a noun or pronoun, asking permission or confirmation is done with **de ii desu ka** and giving it with **de ii desu**.

   . . . de yoku nai desu cannot be used for refusals, the style of which is apt to vary with the situation.

   ex. **Superu wa kore de ii desu ka.** "Is this spelling right?"

   Hai, sore de ii desu. "Yes, that's right."

6. **Wazawaza koko made konakute mo ii desu yo.**

   An adverb meaning "go to the trouble of," **wazawaza** may express appreciation or reluctance.

ex. 1. **Wazawaza kite kudasatte, arigatō gozaimasu.** "Thank you for coming (all this way to see us)."
2. **Parēdo o mi ni ikimasen ka.** "Wouldn't you like to watch the parade?"
   Nichi-yōbi ni wazawaza Ginza made. "All the way to the Ginza? On Sunday?" (implying, "No thanks.")

7. **Dochira demo kekkō desu.**
   Compared with **dochira demo ii desu**, this is a little politer.
   In questions, **dochira demo/kore de ii desu ka** can be used, but **dochira demo/kore de kekko desu ka** cannot.

PRACTICE

KEY SENTENCES

1. きょうじゅうに　もうしこみを　しなければ　なりません。
2. ここに　また　こなくては　いけませんか。
3. いいえ、こなくても　いいです。
4. ゆうびんで　おくっては　いけませんか。
5. ええ、ゆうびんでも　いいです。

1. (I) must apply today.
2. Do I have to come here again?
3. No, you need not come here.
4. May I send it by mail?
5. Yes, mail is OK.

EXERCISES

I Verbs: Review the examples and convert the verbs into the plain negative form.

ex. Reg. I　はじまる→はじまらない
　　Reg. II　いる→　　いない
　　Irreg.　くる→　　こない
　　　　　　する→　　しない

1. まとまる	11. たずねる	21. おどる
2. かえる (change)	12. しゅっぱつする	22. わらう
3. たのむ	13. ふる	23. かたづける
4. しらせる	14. きる (cut)	24. えらぶ
5. はらう	15. むかえる	25. まもる
6. だす	16. やく	26. そつぎょうする
7. すすめる	17. そうじする	27. かわる
8. とまる	18. とおる	28. いる (need)
9. よぶ	19. やめる	29. かす
10. でる	20. かってくる	30. もらってくる

II Make dialogues by changing the underlined parts as in the examples given.

A. ex. Q：<u>いま</u>　<u>おかねを</u>　<u>はらわ</u>なければ　なりませんか。
　Aa：はい、おねがいします。
　An：いいえ、<u>いま</u>　<u>はらわ</u>なくても　いいです。

　　　1．わたしも　くる
　　　2．あしたまでに　する
　　　3．いま　もうしこむ
　　　4．パスポートを　みせる
　　　5．きょうじゅうに　しらせる

B. ex. Q：<u>なまえを</u>　<u>かか</u>なくても　いいですか。
　Aa：はい、<u>かか</u>なくても　いいです。
　An：すみませんが、<u>かいて</u>ください。

　　　1．スミスさんを　むかえに　いく
　　　2．みなさんに　せつめいする
　　　3．ひしょに　しらせる
　　　4．コピーを　たのむ

C. ex. Q：<u>この　へやを</u>　<u>つかって</u>は　いけませんか。
　Aa：どうぞ、<u>つかって</u>も　いいですよ。
　An：すみませんが、<u>つかわ</u>ないでください。

　　　1．ここで　たばこを　すう
　　　2．なまえを　はっぴょうする
　　　3．クーラーを　つける
　　　4．くるまで　くる
　　　5．にわで　しゃしんを　とる

D. ex. Q：<u>あした　かいぎに</u>　<u>でなくて</u>は　いけませんか。
　A：<u>でなくて</u>も　いいですよ。

　　　1．くすりを　のむ
　　　2．スミスさんにも　いう
　　　3．くつを　ぬぐ
　　　4．これを　おぼえる
　　　5．でんわを　かける

E. *ex.* **Q**：いま　はんこが　ありません。サインでも　いいですか。

　　　A：はい、サインでも　けっこうです。

　　　　1．ペン、えんぴつ
　　　　2．じかん、あと
　　　　3．ひま、にちようび
　　　　4．げんきん、カード

F. *ex.* **Q**：ここに　ごみを　すてても　いいですか。

　　　A：ここに　すてては　いけません。

　　　　1．ここに　くるまを　とめる
　　　　2．きょうしつで　コーヒーを　のむ
　　　　3．しばふに　はいる

Vocabulary

パスポート	**pasupōto**, passport	えんぴつ	**empitsu**, pencil
クーラー	**kūrā**, air conditioner	カード	**kādo**, (credit) card
おぼえる	**oboeru**, remember,	ごみ	**gomi**, rubbish
	memorize	すてる	**suteru**, throw out
はんこ	**hanko**, seal	きょうしつ	**kyōshitsu**, class room
サイン	**sain**, signature	しばふ	**shibafu**, lawn

SHORT DIALOGUES

1. おとこの　ひと：ここで　たばこを　すっても　いいですか。
　　かんごふ：　　　いいえ、すっては　いけません。この　びょういんでは
　　　　　　　　　きんえんです。

   Man:　May I smoke here?
   Nurse:　No, (you) may not (smoke). No smoking in this hospital.

2. A：もうしこみの　きげんは　いつですか。
　 B：3がつ　まつじつです。ゆうびんでも　いいですが、31にちまでに　こ
　　　ちらに　おねがいします。

   A: When is the application deadline?
   B: March, the last day. You can mail it, but please (do it) no later than the 31.

3. やまだ：　　ただいま。
　 わたなべ：おかえりなさい。なかやまさんは　いましたか。
　 やまだ：　　ええ、あって　しょるいを　わたしてきました。

Yamada: I'm back!
Watanabe: Oh, good. Was Ms. Nakayama (there)?
Yamada: Yes, I saw her and handed her the documents.

Vocabulary

きんえん	**kin'en**, no smoking	まつじつ	**matsujitsu**, last day
きげん	**kigen**, deadline	わたす	**watasu**, hand (over)

QUIZ

I Read this lesson's opening dialogue and answer the following questions.

1. けいこさんは　だいいちしぼうの　こくりつだいがくにも　ごうかくし
   ましたか。
2. けいこさんは　ごうかくした　だいがくに　はいりますか。
3. けいこさんは　サマーコースの　もうしこみに　また　よびこうまで
   いかなければ　なりませんか。
4. サマーコースの　しはらいは　げんきんかきとめでも　いいですか。
5. けいこさんは　サマーコースの　しはらいを　ぎんこうに　ふりこむで
   しょうか、げんきんかきとめで　おくるでしょうか。

II Put the appropriate particles in the parentheses.

1. とうふを　ちいさく　きりましたが、これ（　　）　いいですか。
2. うち（　　）　むすこは　ことし　だいがく（　　）　ごうかくしまし
   た。
3. ペン（　　）　かかなくては　いけませんか。
   えんぴつ（　　）　けっこうです。
4. よく　かんがえて（　　）、あとで　ゆうびん（　　）　おくります。
5. にゅうがくきんを　ぎんこう（　　）　ふりこみます。

III Complete the questions so that they fit the answers.

1. （　　）までに　もうしこまなくては　いけませんか。
   らいしゅうちゅうに　もうしこんでください。
2. （　　）　はらわなければ　なりませんか。
   5,000えんです。
3. （　　）　たいしかんへ　いかなければ　なりませんか。
   パスポートが　ひつようですから。
4. コーヒーと　こうちゃと　（　　）が　いいですか。
   どちらでも　けっこうです。
5. （　　）ぶんの　じゅぎょうりょうですか。
   6かげつぶんです。

VI Complete the sentences with the appropriate form of the verbs indicated.

1. あしたの　あさ　5じに　（　　）なければ　なりません。（おきる）
2. しょるいを　（　　）は　いけませんよ。（わすれる）
3. この　ほんを　きょうじゅうに　（　　）なければ　なりません。
　　（よむ）
4. おさけを　（　　）なくては　いけませんか。（やめる）
　　そうですね。　（　　）ほうが　いいでしょう。（やめる）
5. いつまでに　おかねを　（　　）なければ　なりませんか。（はらう）
　　らいしゅうちゅうに　（　　）ください。（はらう）
6. ここを　（　　）も　いいですか。（かたづける）
　　まだ　つかいますから、（　　）なくても　いいです。（かたづける）
7. ここは　ちゅうしゃきんしですから、くるまを　（　　）は　いけませ
　　ん。（とめる）

V Answer the following questions.

1. にほんに　いる　がいこくの　ひとは　みんな　にほんごを　べんきょ
　　うしなければ　なりませんか。
2. こうさてんに　くるまを　とめても　いいですか。
3. ひこうきの　なかで　たばこを　すっては　いけませんか。
4. あなたは　あした　なにを　しなければ　なりませんか。

たなかさん、おげんきですか。

わたしは　今　かぞくと　いっしょに　きゅうしゅうに　来ています。きのう、前から　行きたかった　あそ山に　行きました。すばらしい　ながめでした。

わたしたちが　とまっている　りょかんの　にわで　ゆうべ　ほたるを　見ました。前に　東京の　りょうていで　かごの　中の　ほたるを　見た　ことは　ありますが、しぜんの　ほたるは　はじめてです。のうやくの　しようを　やめてから、川が　きれいに　なって、ほたるが　ふえたと　りょかんの　しゅじんが　言っていました。

あさって、わたしたちは　ここを　出て、くまもと市内を　けんぶつした　後、ながさきへ　行きます。ながさきは　えど時代の　日本の　たった　一つの　ぼうえきこうで、その　ころは　日本の　中で　一番　こくさいてきな　町だったと　ざっしで　よんだ　ことが　あります。家内は　日本の　れきしに　きょうみが　ありますから、とても　たのしみに　しています。

みなみきゅうしゅうにも　行きたいと　思いますが、来しゅう　木よう日に　アメリカ本社から　社長が　来ますから、それまでに　東京に　かえらなければ　なりません。

おくさまにも　どうぞ　よろしく　おつたえください

7月30日

ジョン・ブラウン

July 30

Dear Mr. Tanaka,

How are you?

I've come to Kyushu with my family. We went to Mt. Aso yesterday where we've wanted to go from quite some time ago. The view was splendid.

Last evening in the garden of the inn we're staying at we saw fireflies and this was the first time (for me) to see fireflies in their natural (setting). I once saw fireflies in a cage at a Tokyo teahouse. After they stopped using agricultural chemicals, the rivers became cleaner and the fireflies proliferated, the innkeeper said.

The day after tomorrow we leave here and after sightseeing Kumamoto (City), go to Nagasaki. I once read, in a magazine, that in the Edo period Nagasaki was Japan's only trading port and at that time it was the most international-like city in Japan. My wife is interested in Japanese history. She's looking forward (to seeing Nagasaki) with great anticipation.

I'd like to go to southern Kyushu, too, but (our) president's coming from the U.S. head office Thursday of next week, so I have to get back to Tokyo by then.

Please give my best regards to your wife.

John Brown

Vocabulary

あそさん	**Aso-san**, Mt. Aso	えどじだい	**Edo jidai**, Edo period
ながめ	**nagame**, view	えど	**Edo** (former name for Tokyo)
りょかん	**ryokan**, inn		
ほたる	**hotaru**, firefly	じだい	**jidai**, period
りょうてい	**ryōtei**, teahouse	たった ひとつ	**tatta hitotsu**, one only
かご	**kago**, cage, basket	たった	**tatta**, only
しぜん	**shizen**, nature	ぼうえき	**bōeki**, trading
のうやく	**nōyaku**, agricultural chemical	～こう	**-kō**, port
しよう	**shiyō**, using, use, application	こくさいてき(な)	**kokusai-teki(na)**, international (like)
かわ	**kawa**, river, creek, stream	～てき	**-teki**, like, resembling (suffix)
ふえる	**fueru**, proliferate, increase	～に きょうみ が ある	**ni kyōmi ga aru**, be interested in
しゅじん	**shujin**, proprietor	きょうみ	**kyōmi**, interest
くまもと	**Kumamoto** (city and prefecture)	みなみ	**minami**, south
		ほんしゃ	**honsha**, head office, main company
けんぶつする けんぶつ	**kembutsu suru**, sight-see **kembutsu**, sight-seeing, visit	おくさま	**oku-sama**, (your) wife (polite)
ながさき	**Nagasaki** (city and prefecture)	つたえる	**tsutaeru**, convey, impart

NOTES

1. **Ryōtei**
   Ryōtei are restaurants so exclusive that they accept reservations only from regular customers or referrals by established patrons. They are typically buildings preserving a traditional, residential style of architecture, with gardens, and the waitresses dress in kimono. Decor and atmosphere, traditional and varying with the season, may include such touches as displaying fireflies to heighten the feeling of a summer evening.

2. **Edo jidai**
   Having ended over a century of civil unrest by being victorious at the Battle of Sekigahara in 1600, Ieyasu, the first of the Tokugawa shoguns, then established (in 1603) the military government that stabilized the country and maintained peace until the Meiji Restoration in 1868.

3. **Kokusaitekina**
   Adding the suffix **-teki** to nouns makes them **-na** adjectives. Other examples: **josei**, "woman, female," **josei-tekina**, "womanly, effeminate"; **dentō**, "tradition," **dentō-tekina**, "traditional."

4. **Dōzo yoroshiku o-tsutae kudasai.**
   This sentence, conventionally included at the end of personal letters, is politer than **Dōzo yoroshiku**.

QUIZ

I Put the appropriate words in the parentheses.

たなかさん、おげんきですか。

わたしは　いま　かぞく（　　）　いっしょに　きゅうしゅうに　きて
（　　）。

きのう、まえから　いきたかった　あそさんに　いきました。すばらしい
ながめ（　　）。

わたしたち（　　）　とまっている　りょかんの　にわ（　　）　ゆうべ
ほたるを　みました。まえに　とうきょうの　りょうていで　かご（　　）
なかの　ほたるを　みた　（　　）は　ありますが、しぜんの　ほたる
（　　）　はじめてです。のうやくの　しようを　やめて（　　）、かわが
きれい（　　）　なって、ほたるが　ふえた（　　）　りょかんの　しゅじ
んが　（　　　）いました。

あさって、わたしたちは　ここ（　　）　でて、くまもとしない（　　）
けんぶつした　（　　）、ながさきへ　いきます。ながさきは　えどじだい
（　　）にほんの　（　　）　ひとつの　ぼうえきこう（　　）、　その　こ
ろは　にほんの　なか（　　）　いちばん　こくさいてきな　まち
（　　）と　ざっし（　　）　よんだ　ことが　あります。かないは　にほんの
れきし（　　）　きょうみが（　　）から、とても　たのしみに　していま
す。

みなみきゅうしゅうにも　いきたい（　　）　おもいますが、らいしゅう
もくようび（　　）　アメリカほんしゃから　しゃちょうが　きますから、
（　　）とうきょうに　かえらなければ　（　　）。

おくさま（　　）も　どうぞ　（　　）　おつたえください。

II Write a letter in Japanese to a friend about a trip you have taken.

LESSON 11 JOB INTERVIEW

Mr. Hayashi looks over Ms. Nakamura's resume while interviewing her.

はやし： （りれきしょを 見ながら）なかむらさんは おととし 大学を そ
つぎょうしたんですか。

なかむら：はい。そつぎょうしてから しょう社に つとめていました。

はやし： なぜ やめたんですか。

なかむら：わたしの せんもんの 仕事が できませんでしたから、おもしろく
なかったんです。

はやし： どうして この 会社を えらんだんですか。

なかむら：こちらでは コンピューターを つかう 仕事が 多いと きいたか
らです。わたしは 大学で コンピューターサイエンスを べんきょ
うしていました。この 会社では わたしの 好きな 仕事が でき
ると 思ったんです。

はやし： 会社に 入ってから 1か月 けんしゅうしなければ ならない こ
とを 知っていますか。

なかむら：ええ、知っています。

はやし： それに 外国に しゅっちょうする ことも 多いですよ。

なかむら：はい、だいじょうぶです。

はやし： そうですか。では けっかは 後で れんらくします。

Hayashi: You graduated from college the year before last?
Nakamura: Yes. After graduating, I worked for a trading company.
Hayashi: Why did you quit?
Nakamura: (I) couldn't work at my specialty, so it wasn't satisfactory.
Hayashi: Why did you pick this company?
Nakamura: Because I heard that here there's a lot of work using computers. I studied computer
                  science in college. In this company I feel I'd be able to do the kind of work I like.
Hayashi: Are you aware that after joining the company there's a one-month training (pro-
                  gram)?
Nakamura: Yes, I know (that).
Hayashi: And overseas business trips are frequent.
Nakamura: That's (quite) all right.
Hayashi: Is it? Well, then, (we'll) contact you later regarding the outcome.

Vocabulary

りれきしょ	**rirekisho**, resume	サイエンス	**saiensu**, science
〜しょ	**sho**, (*lit.*) book, document, note	けんしゅうする けんしゅう	**kenshū suru**, study, train **kenshū**, (in-service) training (program)
おととし	**ototoshi**, year before last		
〜んです（か）	**n desu (ka)**, (*lit.*) Is it the case that	こと	**koto**, matter, fact
		だいじょうぶ （な）	**daijōbu(na)**, all right, safe
しょうしゃ	**shōsha**, trading company		
なぜ	**naze**, why	れんらくする	**renraku suru**, contact
せんもん	**semmon**, speciality	れんらく	**renraku**, contact, communication, connection
コンピューター	**kompyūtā**, computer		

GRAMMAR & LESSON OBJECTIVES

• n desu

To understand the usage of **. . . n desu**, it is best to look at the situation. Since Hayashi has Nakamura's resume in front of him, it is hardly necessary to ask when she finished college. Instead of **sotsugyō shimashita ka**, he evokes confirmation and supplemental information with this pattern. Although the sentence ending **n desu** occurs freely after the plain forms of adjectives, verbs and the copula **desu**, remember the patterns for nouns and **-na** adjectives are, for example, **kaigi na n desu** and **shizukana n desu**. (See appendix A.) In writing or more formal speech, **no desu** is the pattern used. (See p. 154.)

The difference between **-masu** and **n desu** is very subtle, and word-for-word translation of the latter can be difficult. All the following examples have an explanatory or confirmatory function.

ex. 1. (On seeing a coworker in the office with a big suitcase) **Doko ni iku n desu ka**. "Well, well, where are you off to?"

2. (On seeing snake meat in a grocery store show case) **Hebi o taberu n desu ka**. "Is that snake meat sold for food?"
   Ee. "Um."
   Honto ni taberu n desu ka. "You mean to say you actually eat it?"

3. **Kaihi o haratte kudasai.** "Would you mind paying the membership fee now, please?"
   Ashita demo ii desu ka. Ima o-kane ga nai n desu. "Wouldn't tomorrow be all right? I don't have the money (with me) now."

4. (To a roommate putting on pajamas early in the evening) **Mō neru n desu ka**. "You're going to bed already?"
   Ee. Ashita wa 4-ji ni okiru n desu. "Eh, 4:00 A.M. is the time I have to get up tomorrow.
   Compare this with the situation of simply asking a person what he intends to do: **Ashita nan-ji ni okimasu ka**. "What time are you getting up tomorrow?" **6-ji ni okimasu.** "I'll get up at 6 o'clock."

NOTES

1. **Daigaku o sotsugyō shita n desu ka.**
   Note that the particle is **o**, although what comes before **o** is not strictly speaking a direct object. (See p. 34.) Some other verbs in this category, which are alike in that a place or thing is being left, are **deru**, **shuppatsu suru** and **oriru**.

2. **1-kagetsu kenshū shinakereba naranai koto o shitte imasu ka.**
   In this case as well, plain forms come before the noun **koto**. Refer to lesson 7 regarding noun-modifying patterns.
   ex. **Kare ga kinō kono hon o motte kita koto wa himitsu desu.** "That he brought this book yesterday is a secret."

PRACTICE

KEY SENTENCES

1. あした　かいぎが　ありますから、いま　しりょうを　コピーしているんです。
2. ブラウンさんが　きゅうしゅうへ　りょこうした　ことを　しっていますか。

1. Since there's a meeting tomorrow, I'm copying the material now.
2. Do you know the Browns took a trip to Kyushu?

EXERCISES

I　Practice the following patterns.

  A. *ex.* いきます→　いくんです　　　　　いかないんです
             いったんです　　　　いかなかったんです

1. およぎます	6. あいます	11. すんでいます
2. よみます	7. いいます	12. あげます
3. あそびます	8. できます	13. みます
4. けします	9. あります	14. きます
5. まちます	10. います	15. そうだんします

  B. *ex.* やすいです→　やすいんです　　　　やすくないんです
              やすかったんです　　　やすくなかったんです

1. おいしいです	4. たかいです	7. あたまが　いいです
2. あぶないです	5. つめたいです	8. つごうが　わるいです
3. むずかしいです	6. つまらないです	9. やすみたいです

  C. *ex.* すきです→　すきなんです　　　　　すきでは　ないんです
             すきだったんです　　　　すきでは　なかったんです

1. じょうずです	5. かいぎです
2. ひまです	6. しごとです
3. べんりです	7. びょうきです
4. あんぜんです	8. けんしゅうです

II　Make dialogues by changing the underlined parts as in the examples given.

  A. *ex.* **Q**：あした　パーティーに　きませんか。
      A：ざんねんですが、いそがしいんです。

      1. かいぎが　あります
      2. じかんが　ありません
      3. びょういんに　いかなければ　なりません
      4. ともだちと　あう　やくそくを　しました

5. くにから　ははが　きています
6. あしたから　しゅっちょうです
7. かないが　びょうきです
8. からだの　ぐあいが　よくないです

B. *ex.* Q：なぜ　きのう　パーティーに　こなかったんですか。
A：<u>いそがしかった</u>んです。

1. かいぎが　ありました
2. しょうたいじょうを　もらいませんでした
3. きゅうに　つごうが　わるく　なりました
4. パーティーが　ある　ことを　しりませんでした

C. *ex.* Q：<u>けんしゅうしなければ　ならない</u>　ことを　しっていますか。
A：そうですか。しりませんでした。

1. なかむらさんが　こんやくしました
2. あした　こなくても　いいです
3. たなかさんが　たいきんを　おとしました
4. ジョーンズさんが　こちらに　きています
5. すずきさんの　おかあさまが　なくなりました

D. *ex.* A：かのじょは　よく　<u>ざんぎょう</u>しますね。
B：ええ、でも　<u>はやく　かえる</u>　ことも　おおいですよ。

1. テニスを　する、ゴルフを　やります
2. レストランで　たべる、うちで　たべます
3. かいしゃの　ひとと　のむ、ひとりで　のみます
4. べんきょうする、あそびに　いきます

E. *ex.* A：いつから　<u>ジョギング</u>を　はじめましたか。
B：<u>けっこんして</u>から　はじめました。
A：どうして　やめたんですか。
B：<u>けがを　した</u>からです。

1. ピアノ、しょうがっこうに　はいります、きょうみが　なくな
りました
2. えいかいわ、だいがくを　そつぎょうします、いそがしく　な
りました
3. やまのぼり、かいしゃに　はいります、こどもが　うまれまし
た

あぶない	**abunai**, dangerous	なくなる	**nakunaru**, pass away, be lost/missing, disappear
つめたい	**tsumetai**, cold, cool, chilled	かのじょ	**kanojo**, she
あんぜん（な）	**anzen(na)**, safe	やる	**yaru**, do, give (more collo-
からだの　ぐあい	**karada no guai**, health (*lit.* body condition)		quial than **suru**, **ageru**), play
からだ	**karada**, body, health	ピアノ	**piano**, piano
しょうたいじょう	**shōtai-jō**, invitation card/ letter	しょうがっこう	**shōgakkō**, elementary school
しょうたい	**shōtai**, invitation	えいかいわ	**eikaiwa**, spoken English (*lit.* English conversa-
～じょう	**-jō**, letter (suffix)		tion)
きゅうに	**kyū ni**, suddenly		
こんやくする	**kon'yaku suru**, become engaged	かいわ	**kaiwa**, conversation
		やまのぼり	**yamanobori**, mountain
こんやく	**kon'yaku**, engagement		climbing
たいきん	**taikin**, large sum of money	うまれる	**umareru**, be born
おかあさま	**okāsama**, (his/her) mother (polite)		

SHORT DIALOGUES

1. きゃく：　　　　　　とけいを　かいたいんですが　なんかいですか。
   デパートの　てんいん：とけいうりばは　6かいでございます。

   Customer:　　I'd like to buy a watch. What floor is it?
   Store Clerk: The watch counter is (on) the sixth floor.

2. スミス：　スポーツクラブに　はいったんですか。
   ブラウン：ええ、すいえいと　テニスを　はじめたんです。
   スミス：　スポーツを　することは　からだに　いいですね。

   Smith:　You've joined a health club, have you?
   Brown: Yes. I've taken up swimming and tennis.
   Smith:　Sports are good for the health, wouldn't you say?

で　ございます	**de gozaimasu**, is/are (polite for **desu**)	すいえい	**suiei**, swimming
		からだに　いい	**karada ni ii**, good for the health
スポーツクラブ	**supōtsu kurabu**, health club		

QUIZ

I Read this lessons's opening dialogue and answer the following questions.

1. はやしさんは　なにを　みながら、なかむらさんに　きいていますか。

2. なかむらさんが　しょうしゃで　していた　しごとは　かのじょの　せんもんでしたか。

3. なかむらさんは　しょうしゃで　していた　しごとは　おもしろかったと　いっていますか。

4. なかむらさんは　ABC では　すきな　しごとが　できると　おもっていますか。

II Put the appropriate particles in the parentheses.

1. なかむらさんは　しょうしゃ（　　）　つとめていました。

2. かれは　1965ねん（　　）　Aだいがく（　　）　そつぎょうしました。

3. かれが　かいしゃ（　　）　やめる　こと（　　）　しっていますか。

4. けっかは　あと（　　）　れんらくします。

5. どうして　この　かいしゃ（　　）　えらんだんですか。
   こちらでは　にほんごを　つかう　しごと（　　）　おおい（　　）
   きいた（　　）　です。

III Complete the questions so that they fit the answers.

1. （　　）　パーティーに　こなかったんですか。
   あたまが　いたかったんです。

2. （　　）　したんですか。
   てに　けがを　したんです。

3. この　コンピューターは　（　　）　つかうんですか。
   ちょっと　ふくざつですから、わたなべさんに　きいてください。

4. （　　）を　みているんですか。
   きょうとで　とった　しゃしんを　みているんです。

IV Complete the sentences with the appropriate form of the verbs indicated.

1. すずきさんは　いませんね。もう　うちに　（　　）んですか。
   ええ、30ぷんぐらい　まえに　かえりましたよ。（かえりました）

2. おがわさんに　（　　）んですか。
   ええ、おがわさんは　きのう　（　　）んです。（しらせませんでした、
   やすみでした）

3. どこに　（　　）んですか。でんわが　ありましたよ。
   どうも　すみません。ちょっと　コーヒーを　のみに　いっていました。
   （いっていました）

4. なにも　（　　）んですか。
   ええ、（　　）んです。（たべません、たべたくありません）

5. タクシーで　（　　）んですか。

ええ、じかんが あまり　（　　）んです。（でかけます、ありません）
6. すずきさんは　やすみですか。
　　ええ、（　　）んです。（びょうきです）
7. きのう　あなたが　（　　）　ことを　かれにも　（　　）ください。
　（いいました、はなします）
8. かんじを　（　　）　ことは　むずかしく　ないです。（おぼえます）

V　Choose a statement appropriate to the situation described.

A. You hear a friend has quit his job and you ask him about it.

1. いつ　かいしゃを　やめるんですか。
2. かいしゃを　やめては　いけませんか。
3. ほんとうに　かいしゃを　やめたんですか。

B. You see a friend doing something ridiculous.

1. なにを　しているんですか。
2. なにを　しなければ　なりませんか。
3. かれは　なんと　いっていますか。

C. You tell a friend that you didn't go to her party because of a headache.

1. とても　あたまが　いたいんです。
2. きゅうに　あたまが　いたく　なったんです。
3. あたまが　いたかったと　おもいます。

LESSON 12 HOTEL RESERVATIONS

Mr. Smith makes a reservation at an inn in Kyoto by phone.

よやくがかり：みやこりょかんでございます。

スミス：　　　もしもし、来月の　4日と　5日に　よやくを　おねがいしたい
　　　　　　　んですが、部屋は　あいていますか。

よやくがかり：はい、ございます。何名さまですか。

スミス：　　　ふたりです。いくらですか。

よやくがかり：1ぱく2しょくつきで、おひとり　18,000円でございます。ぜい
　　　　　　　金と　サービスりょうは　べつでございます。

スミス：　　　はい、じゃ、それで　おねがいします。

よやくがかり：お名前と　お電話ばんごうを　どうぞ。

スミス：　　　スミスと　言います。電話ばんごうは　東京03-405-3636です。
　　　　　　　そちらは　きょうとの　駅から　近いですか。

よやくがかり：駅から　車で　10分ぐらいです。

スミス：　　　駅に　ついた　時、電話を　しますから、そらちから　むかえに
　　　　　　　来てくれませんか。

よやくがかり：はい、かしこまりました。ごとうちゃくは　何時ごろですか。

スミス：　　　4時ごろです。

よやくがかり：はい、わかりました。8時より　おそく　なる　ばあいは、かな
　　　　　　　らず　ごれんらくください。

スミス：　　　はい。それで、りょう金は　いつ　はらいましょうか。

よやくがかり：おそれいりますが、内金として　18,000円　ごゆうそうくださ
　　　　　　　い。

スミス：　　　わかりました。

Reservation

Clerk: (This is the) Miyako Inn.

Smith: Hello, I'd like to make a reservation for the 4 and 5 of next month. Are rooms available (*lit.* "vacant").

Clerk: Yes, sir. (For) how many people?

Smith: Two. How much is it?

Clerk: Per day, with two meals per person, is ¥18,000. Tax and service charge are extra.

Smith: I see. Will you do me the favor, then (of making the reservation)?

Clerk: Your name and phone number, please.

Smith: My name is Smith. The telephone number is Tokyo 03-405-3636. Are you near Kyoto Station?

Clerk: It's about ten minutes by car from the station.
Smith: When (we) arrive at the station, if I call will you come to pick (us) up?
Clerk: Certainly, sir. Your arrival will be about what time?
Smith: Around four o'clock.
Clerk: I see. In case (it's) later than eight o'clock, be sure to call us.
Smith: All right. When should I pay the (room) charge?
Clerk: Excuse (my asking) but could you please send ¥18,000 by mail as a deposit?
Smith: Yes, of course.

Vocabulary

よやくがかり	**yoyaku-gakari**, reservation clerk	かしこまりました	**kashikomarimashita**, certainly
かかり/〜が かり	**kakari/-gakari**, person in charge	ごとうちゃく	**go-tōchaku**, arrival
あく	**aku**, be empty, be vacant, (be) open	ばあい	**baai**, (in) case, occasion, circumstance
ございます	**gozainasu**(polite, for **arimasu**)	かならず	**kanarazu**, be sure to, certainly
〜めい（さま）	**-mei(-sama)**, (counter for people; polite)	それで	**sorede**, and then
〜はく/ぱく	**-haku/-paku**, night (counter)	りょうきん	**ryōkin**, charge, fee
〜しょく	**-shoku**, meal (counter)	おそれいります	**osoreirimasu**, excuse me, be sorry (polite for **sumimasen**)
〜つき	**-tsuki**, included, attached	うちきん	**uchikin**, deposit, partial payment
ぜいきん	**zeikin**, tax	〜として	**to shite**, as, in the capacity of
サービスりょう	**sābisu-ryō**, service charge	ごゆうそう	**go-yūsō**, mail
べつ（な/の）	**betsu(na/no)**, extra, distinctive		
〜とき	**toki**, when		

GRAMMAR & LESSON OBJECTIVES

• Verb tense

In the second grammar section in the first volume (p. 54), it was pointed out that the two verb tense forms in Japanese are present and past, and with the present form expressing habitual or future action and the past being sometimes past and sometimes present perfect, there is a basis for correspondence with English verb tenses. In complex sentences, however, non-final verbs do not necessarily have the same relation to the main verbs as English verbs do. In translating, preservation of the Japanese tense may require some adjustment in the sentence. Look again at the translation of the dialogue sentence **Eki ni tsuita toki, denwa o shimasu kara, sochira kara mukae ni kite kuremasen ka**, translated as "Once we('ve) arrive(d) at the station, I'll call, so . . ." Think of the underlying meaning as being "Once arrival at the station has become an accomplished fact, a telephone call will be made, so . . ."
Compare the following sentences which differ from each other only in the verb forms in the first clause.

ex. 1. **Nihon ni kuru toki kūkō de kaimashita**. "While coming to Japan I bought (it) at the airport." (Implicitly means an airport outside of Japan.)
2. **Nihon ni kita toki kūkō de kaimashita**. "When I came (i.e., having come) to Japan (I) bought (it) at the airport." (Meaning an airport in Japan.)

• **Toki** and **baai**

Basically **toki** is "time" and **baai** is "case," but these nouns are interchangeable at certain times while at other times this is not the case. Keep in mind that (1) if something has actually occurred **baai** cannot be used. And (2) clues to the intended meaning lie in thinking of *time* and *circumstances* or *situation* in a contrastive way. Some examples:

1. **Kesa watashi ga okita toki,** "When I got up this morning, . . ."
2. **Denwa de renraku suru toki/baai,** "When contacts are made by phone, . . ."
3. **Muzukashii toki/baai,** "If it's difficult, . . ."
4. **Fubenna toki/baai,** "If it's inconvenient,"
5. **Shigoto ga yasumi no toki/baai,** "When (there's) time-off (from) work, . . ."
6. **Kodomo no toki,** "during childhood"
7. **Kodomo no baai,** "in the case of children"

NOTES

1. **yoyaku-gakari**
   Like many other words, **kakari** undergoes a phonetic change when compounded with other terms. Other examples: **hako** becomes **hom-bako**, "bookcase"; **hi** becomes **nichiyō-bi**; **hanashi**, becomes **otogi-banashi**, "fairy tale"; **kuchi**, "mouth," "door," becomes **iri-guchi**.

2. **shitai n desu ga**
   -tai n desu is more frequently heard than **-tai desu**.

3. **Nan-mei-sama desu ka.**
   Only such people as restaurant and hotel employees commonly use **nan-mei-sama** as a polite alternative for **nan-nin**, but **nan-mei**, which is more formal than **nan-nin**, is widely used.

4. **1-paku 2-shoku (ip-paku ni-shoku)**
   One night with supper and breakfast is the most conspicuous formula for **ryokan** charges. It is not common in western-style hotels, which are more apt to quote room charge only or room charge plus, optionally, breakfast. There is no general pattern for asking or not asking for a deposit or including or not including tax and service charge in the quoted room rate.

5. **O-namae to o-denwa-bangō o dōzo.**
   Sentences like this, ending with **dōzo** instead of **-te kudasai**, may be used when the situation is clear; they suggest the action to be taken. Similarly, **Kono denwa o dōzo** can mean "Please use this phone."

6. **Sumisu to iimasu.**
   The literal translation is "I'm called/I call myself Smith." **To mōshimasu** means the same but is more humble, hence politer. The pattern is like others introduced previously, **to omou**, **to kiku** and so on, as in **Kore wa Nihon-go de nan to iimasu ka.** "What is this called in Japanese."

7. **Kashikomarimashita**
   More formal than **wakarimashita**, this expression, "I understand and will do it," is a standard one often said by servants, clerks and others when receiving requests, orders or instructions. It is not appropriate in a classroom or among friends or family members.

8. **Uchikin to shite**
   To shite is used as follows:
   ex. 1. **Kanojo wa hisho to shite kono ka de hataraite imasu.** "She works in this section as a secretary."
   2. **Kitte-dai to shite 200-en haratte kudasai.** "Please pay ¥200 for the postage." (**dai**, "charge, price")

PRACTICE

KEY SENTENCES

1. スミスさんは　ほんを　よむ　とき、めがねを　かけます。
2. えきに　ついた　とき、でんわを　します。
3. おそく　なる　ばあいは　れんらくします。
4. わたしは　スミスと　いいます。

1. Smith wears glasses when he reads (books).
2. When I get to the station I'll phone.
3. If it's late I'll contact you.
4. My name is Smith.

Vocabulary

かける　　　　　　　**kakeru**, wear, put on

EXERCISES

I Make dialogues by changing the underlined parts as in the examples given.

A. *ex.* **Q**：よく　さんぽしますか。
　　　　A：ええ、ときどき　あさ　すずしい　とき、さんぽします。
　　　　　　1. この　くすりを　のむ、あたまが　いたい
　　　　　　2. ジョギングを　する、てんきが　よくて　さむくない
　　　　　　3. クーラーを　つかう、とても　あつい

B. *ex.* **Q**：ひまな　とき　なにを　しますか。
　　　　A：ひまな　ときですか。そうですねえ、レコードを　きいたりして
　　　　　　います ね。
　　　　　　1. こどもと　あそぶ
　　　　　　2. スポーツクラブに　およぎに　いく
　　　　　　3. ともだちに　でんわする
　　　　　　4. すきな　ほんを　よむ

C. *ex.* **Q**：こどもの　とき　どこに　すんでいましたか。
　　　　A：おおさかに　すんでいました。
　　　　　　1. かいぎ、どの　へやを　つかいますか、この　へやを
　　　　　　2. めんせつ、だれと　はなしましたか、ぶちょうと
　　　　　　3. がくせい、どこを　りょこうしましたか、ヨーロッパを
　　　　　　4. しけん、なにを　もっていきますか、えんぴつと　けしゴムを

II Practice the following pattern by changing the underlined parts.

　　ex. くにに　かえる　とき、おみやげを　かいます。

1. みちが　わかりません、けいかんに　ききます
2. みちが　こんでいます、タクシーより　でんしゃの　ほうが　はやいです
3. さいふを　ひろいました、こうばんに　とどけます
4. にほんに　きました、にほんごが　わかりませんでした

III　Make dialogues by changing the underlined parts as in the examples given.

A. *ex.* **A**：なんじごろ　<u>えき</u>に　つきますか。

　　B：さあ　ちょっと　わかりません。<u>えき</u>に　ついた　とき、でんわします。

　　A：そうしてください。むかえに　いきますから。

1. くうこう
2. とうきょうえき
3. ホテル
4. みなと

B. *ex.* **Q**：<u>はじめて　ひとに　あった</u>　とき、なんと　いいますか。

　　A：「<u>はじめまして</u>」と　いいます。

1. しょくじを　します、いただきます
2. しょくじが　おわりました、ごちそうさまでした
3. うちを　でます、いってまいります
4. うちに　かえりました、ただいま
5. ひとと　わかれます、さようなら

C. *ex.* **Q**：しゅうまつの　りょこうは　どう　しましょうか。

　　A：<u>あめの</u>　ばあいは　やめましょう。

1. でんしゃが　ストです
2. たなかさんの　つごうが　わるいです
3. てんきが　よくないです
4. たいふうです

D. *ex.* **Q**：<u>おそく　なる</u>　ばあいは　れんらくしてください。

　　A：はい、そうします。

1. おくれます
2. きません
3. おかねが　たりません

4. よていが かわりました
5. びょうきに なりました
6. ごうかくしました

E. *ex.* **Q**：<u>rose</u>は にほんごで なんと いいますか。
      A：<u>ばら</u>と いいます。

1. ball point pen、ボールペン
2. pants、ズボン
3. politician、せいじか
4. contract、けいやく
5. to celebrate、いわう

Vocabulary

すずしい	**suzushii**, cool	たりる	**tariru**, be enough
めんせつ	**mensetsu**, interview	よてい	**yotei**, plan, schedule
けしゴム	**keshigomu**, eraser	ばら	**bara**, rose
おみやげ	**o-miyage**, souvenir	ボールペン	**bōru pen**, ball-point pen
みなと	**minato**, port, harbor	ズボン	**zubon**, trousers
わかれる	**wakareru**, part, split up	せいじか	**seijika**, politician
スト	**suto**, strike	けいやく	**keiyaku**, contract
たいふう	**taifū**, typhoon	いわう	**iwau**, celebrate, con-
おくれる	**okureru**, be late		gratulate

SHORT DIALOGUES

1. きむら：あしたの スポーツたいかいの けんですが、あめが ふった と
      きは どう しますか。
  すずき：あさ 6じまでに やまない ばあいは ちゅうしです。
  きむら：よく わからない ときは どう しますか。
  すずき：その ばあいは ここに でんわを して たしかめてください。

Kimura: About tomorrow's athletic meeting, if it rains what happens?
Suzuki: If it doesn't stop by 6 in the morning, it'll be called off.
Kimura: If it's not clear (*lit.* "not understandable"), what should I do?
Suzuki: In that case, please make sure by phoning here.

2. わたなべ： にほんの せいかつに なれましたか。
  ジョンソン：ええ、すこしずつ。
  わたなべ： こまった ときは いつでも いってください。

Watanabe: Are (you) getting used to living in Japan?
Johnson: Well, little by little.
Watanabe: If (you're at all) inconvenienced, please tell me about it anytime.

たいかい	**taikai**, (big) meeting, conference, tournament	なれる	**nareru**, get used to
けん	**ken**, about, concerning (*lit.* subject)	すこしずつ	**sukoshi-zutsu**, little by little
		～ずつ	**-zutsu** (suffix)
やむ	**yamu**, stop	こまる	**komaru**, be inconvenienced/troubled/embarrassed
ちゅうし	**chūshi**, discontinuance, interruption		
たしかめる	**tashikameru**, make sure	いつでも	**itsu demo**, any-/sometime
せいかつ	**seikatsu**, living, life		

QUIZ

I   Read this lessons's opening dialogue and answer the following questions.

1. スミスさんは どこに でんわを しましたか。
2. りょかんの ひとは へやが あいていると いっていましたか。
3. みやこりょかんは えきから くるまで なんぷんぐらい かかりますか。
4. スミスさんは 1ぱく2しょくの りょうきんと なにを はらわなければ なりませんか。
5. みやこりょかんの ばあいは とまる まえに うちきんを はらわなければ なりませんか。

II   Put the appropriate particles in the parentheses.

1. りょうきんは おひとり 10,000えん （　　）ございます。
2. わたしは スミス（　　）いいます。
3. えき（　　）ついたとき、でんわを します（　　）、そちら（　　）むかえ（　　）きてくれませんか。
4. 6じ（　　）おそく なる ばあいは、かならず れんらくしてください。
5. 1ぱく2しょくつき（　　）ひとり 15,000えん かかりますが、いいですか。
6. かれは がいこうかん（　　）して、にほんに きています。
7. かいぎ（　　）とき、おちゃを もってきてください。

III   Complete the questions so that they fit the answers.

1. リンダさんは （　　） きたんですか。
   7じの ニュースを きいている とき きました。
2. これは にほんごで （　　）と いいますか。
   けしゴムと いいます。
3. （　　） りょかんに おそく なると いわなかったんですか。
   でんわを する じかんが なかったんです。

IV Complete the sentences with the appropriate form of the words indicated.

1. きょねん　きょうとに　（　　）　とき、きれいな　かみの　かさを
   かいました。（いきました）
2. うけつけの　ひとが　（　　）　ばあいは　1かいから　でんわを　し
   てください。（いません）
3. あさ　（　　）　とき、あめが　（　　）いました。（おきました、ふ
   ります）
4. あしたまでに　（　　）　ばあいは、れんらくを　（　　）ください。
   （できません、します）
5. さいふを　（　　）　ときは、こうばんに　（　　）なければ　いけま
   せん。（ひろいました、とどけます）
6. きのう　ちゅうしょくを　（　　）　とき、きゅうに　おなかが
   （　　）なりました。（たべていました、いたい）
7. わたなべさんに　はじめて　（　　）　とき、（　　）　ひとだと　お
   もいました。（あいました、きれい）
8. じかんが　（　　）　とき、サンドイッチを　たべます。（ありません）
9. （　　）　とき、イギリスを　（　　）　ことが　あります。（わかい、
   りょこうします）
10. （　　）　とき、ほんを　（　　）だり、こどもと　（　　）だりして
    います。（ひま、よみます、あそびます）

V Choose the most polite statement appropriate to the situation described.

A. You're at work and you answer the phone.

1. ABC でございます。
2. ABC と　いいます。
3. ABC が　ございます。

B. You tell a client you will show him around when it's convenient for him.

1. ごつごうの　いい　とき、ごあんないください。
2. じかんが　ある　とき、あんないしますよ。
3. ごつごうの　いい　とき、ごあんないしますよ。

C. You call Kato's house and ask if he is at home.

1. かとうさんに　ごれんらくください。
2. かとうさんは　いらっしゃいますか。
3. かとうさんと　いいますか。

LESSON 13 — A GIFT OF CHOCOLATE

Mr. Chang hands Mr. Johnson a small box with a card.

チャン： ジョンソンさん、これ、わたなべさんから ジョンソンさんへの
プレゼントですよ。きのう ジョンソンさんが いなかったので、
ぼくが あずかりました。カードも ありますよ。

ジョンソン：どうも ありがとう。わたなべさんからの おくりもの、うれしい
ですね。

チャン： なかみは チョコレートでしょう。

ジョンソン：開けたんですか。

チャン： カードは ラブレターかもしれませんよ。

ジョンソン：えっ、よんだんですか。

チャン： ははは・・・。じつは ぼくも 同じ ものを もらったんです。
すずきくんも もらっただろうと 思いますよ。

ジョンソン：えっ？ みんな もらったんですか。

チャン： ギリチョコですよ、ギリチョコ。

ジョンソン：ギリチョコって 何ですか。

チャン： ぎりの チョコレートです。日本の バレンタインデーの しゅう
かんです。しょくばでも よく 女性から 男性の じょうしや
どうりょうに チョコレートを プレゼントします。

ジョンソン：「いつも おせわに なっています。これからも よろしく。マイ
ケルへ まゆみより。」
やっぱり ギリチョコでした。

チャン： ざんねんでした。

ジョンソン：でも、ギリチョコを たくさん もらった 人は どう するんで
しょうか。

チャン： たぶん おくさんや ガールフレンドが 食べるんでしょう。

ジョンソン：じゃ、よろこぶ 人は 女性と かしやですね。

チャン： もらった 男性も たのしいですよ。

Chang: Mr. Johnson, here's a present for you from Ms. Watanabe. Since you weren't (here) yesterday, I took care of it. There's a card too.
Johnson: Thank you. A present from Ms. Watanabe, how delightful!
Chang: Chocolates inside, I suppose.
Johnson: You opened it?
Chang: Maybe the card is a love letter.
Johnson: Huh! You read it?

Chang:	Ha, ha! As a matter of fact I got the same thing. I think Suzuki got (one) too.		
Johnson:	Eh? Did everyone get one?		
Chang:	Um, It's *giri-choko*.		
Johnson:	*Giri-choko*? What do you mean?		
Chang:	Chocolate (given) out of a sense of obligation. It's a Japanese Valentine's Day custom. It's a gift from women to male superiors or coworkers.		
Johnson:	"Thank you for your helpfulness and kindness. Please continue to treat me with favor. To Michael from Mayumi." Just as you said, *giri-choko*.		
Chang:	Disappointing, isn't it?		
Johnson:	Um. What does a man who gets a lot of *giri-choko* do?		
Chang:	Probably his wife or girl friend (get to) eat it.		
Johnson:	Well then, the happy people are most likely the women and the confectioners.		
Chang:	The man who gets (it) is pleased too.		

Vocabulary

プレゼント	**purezento**, present	〜って	**-tte = to iu no wa** (informal)
ので	**node**, since, because		
あずかる	**azukaru**, take care of, keep	バレンタインデー	**Barentain dē**, Valentine's Day
おくりもの	**okurimono**, gift	しゅうかん	**shūkan**, custom, habit
うれしい	**ureshii**, delighted, happy	しょくば	**shokuba**, workplace
チョコレート	**chokorēto**, chocolate	じょせい	**josei**, woman, female
ラブレター	**rabu retā**, love letter	だんせい	**dansei**, male, man
かもしれません	**kamo shiremasen**, may be	じょうし	**jōshi**, superior
		どうりょう	**dōryō**, coworker
はは	**haha**, ha ha	おせわ	**o-sewa**, help, kindness, good offices
じつは	**jitsuwa**, as a matter of fact		
		やっぱり	**yappari**, (just) as you said
おなじ	**onaji**, same	ざんねん（な）	**zannen(na)**, disappointing
だろう	**darō**, (plain form of deshō)		
		ガールフレンド	**gāru furendo**, girl friend
ギリチョコ	**giri-choko**, *giri* chocolate	よろこぶ	**yorokobu**, be happy
ぎり	**giri**, (sense of) obligation	かしや	**kashi-ya**, confectioner, confectionery
〜って なんですか	**-tte nan desu ka**, What do you/does mean		

GRAMMAR & LESSON OBJECTIVES

- **kamo shiremasen, darō to omoimasu**, expressing uncertainty

  Kādo wa rabu retā kamo shiremasen.

  Suzuki-san mo moratta darō to omoimasu.

  These patterns follow **-i** adjectives, plain verb forms, nouns and the stem of **-na** adjectives.

  e.g. **benri deshō/darō to omoimasu/kamo shiremasen**. They also follow plain past and negative forms. (See appendix A.)

  Unlike the other two, **kamo shiremasen** can be used in referring to one's own actions.

  ex. **Watashi mo Ōsaka e iku kamo shiremasen.** "I may go to Osaka (myself)."

- **inakatta node**

Like **kara**, **node** indicates reason or cause but it sounds a bit softer. It follows **-i** adjectives and plain verb forms. For nouns and **-na** adjectives **na** is used, as in **benrina node**, **ame na node**. (See appendix A.)

NOTES

1. **Jonson-san e no purezento**
   Dōryō ni/e chokorēto o purezento shimasu.
   As seen in these examples, a distinction is made between cases of combining **e** or **ni** with **no**. When a noun is being modified, only **e no** occurs. Besides **ni**, the particles **wa**, **ga** and **o** never come before **no**. (See also the first volume, p. 55.)
   Other examples of particles combined with **no**:
   ex. 1. **Tōkyō de no kaigi**, "a meeting in Tokyo"
       2. **Ōsaka made no kippu**, "a ticket to Osaka"
       3. **Tanaka-san kara no moraimono**, "a present from Tanaka"

2. **Giri-choko**
   This term combines, rather humorously, a traditional social relationship and the shortened form of the word **chokorēto**. Having **giri**, "(a sense of) obligation," to one's seniors goes back many centuries. **Giri-choko** is, needless to say, a custom of modern times.

3. **Giri-choko tte nan desu ka.**
   The function of **tte** is to draw attention to the meaning. It is the informal equivalent of **to iu no wa**, which is found in lesson 28. Johnson's utterance could be translated more directly as, "What's *giri* chocolate?"

4. 「いつも おせわに なっています。これからも よろしく。マイケルへ
   まゆみより。」
   The half brackets in this passage signify the beginning (「) and end (」) of a direct quotation.

5. **Yappari**
   This word, the more formal form of which is **yahari**, sometimes expresses a feeling akin to deja vu and may be translated as "after all," "as I expected" or "as is usually the case."
   ex. **Yappari Tōkyō no rasshu awā wa sugoi desu ne.** "As might be expected, rush hours in Tokyo are awful."

6. **Zannen deshita.**
   Chang is teasing, of course, using a common expression said when there is cause for regret or one finds things not to one's liking.

PRACTICE

KEY SENTENCES

1. ゆきが たくさん ふっているから、ひこうきは とばないかもしれません。
2. すずきさんは リンダさんを しらないだろうと おもいます。
3. ひこうきが とばないので、りょこうに いく ことが できません。

1. It's snowing hard so planes probably aren't flying.
2. I don't think Suzuki knows Linda.
3. Since planes aren't flying, I can't go on (my) trip.

EXERCISES

I Make dialogues by changing the underlined parts as in the examples given.

A. *ex.* **A** : たなかさんは　こないかもしれませんよ。
　　　B : そうですか。
　　　A : おくさんが　びょうきだと　いっていましたから。

　　1.　じかんが　あります、きょうは　ひまです
　　2.　いません、でかけます
　　3.　りょこうに　いきました、こんしゅうは　やすみます
　　4.　かいぎに　しゅっせきしませんでした、しゅっちょうです

B. *ex.* **A** : しごとが　ぜんぶ　おわりました。
　　　B : あしたは　ひまかもしれませんね。

　　1.　あめが　やみました、はれです
　　2.　ちゅうもんが　たくさん　きました、いそがしいです
　　3.　あした　おきゃくさんが　すうにん　きます、かいぎを　する
　　　　じかんが　ありません

C. *ex.* **Q** : かいぎは　いつですか。
　　　A : あしたの　ごぜんちゅうだろうと　おもいます。

　　1.　たなかさん、どこ、かいぎしつ
　　2.　たんとうしゃ、だれ、すずきさん
　　3.　しけん、なんかから　なんかまで、35かから　40かまで
　　4.　とうちゃく、なんじ、よなかの　1じごろ
　　5.　あの　はでな　コート、だれの、スミスさんの

D. *ex.* **Q** : きっぷは　よやくした　ほうが　いいでしょうか。
　　　A : ええ、こんでいるから　よやくした　ほうが　いいだろうと　おも
　　　いますよ。

　　1.　この　ほうが　べんりです、みんなが　つかっています
　　2.　ニューヨークは　いま　さむいです、12がつです
　　3.　やまださんは　かいしゃを　やめます、やめたいと　いってい
　　　　ました
　　4.　たなかさんは　もう　かえりました、かばんが　ありません

E. *ex.* **Q**：<u>あの　ひとは　くる</u>でしょうか。

　　A*a*：ええ、たぶん　<u>くる</u>だろうと　おもいますよ。

　　A*n*：<u>こない</u>だろうと　おもいますよ。

　　　　1.　さくらは　さいています
　　　　2.　あの　みせで　アイスクリームを　うっています
　　　　3.　あの　ひとは　スペインごが　わかります
　　　　4.　スミスさんは　わたしを　しっています

F. *ex.* **Q**：どうして　<u>それを　つかって</u>いますか。

　　A：<u>べんりなので　つかって</u>います。

　　　　1.　まどを　あけました、あついです
　　　　2.　ビタミンを　のみました、からだが　だるいです
　　　　3.　すぐ　わかりました、かんたんでした
　　　　4.　みせは　しまっています、さいじつです
　　　　5.　やめました、じょうずに　なりません

G. *ex.* **Q**：どう　しましたか。

　　A：<u>たなかさんから　へんじが　こない</u>ので　こまっています。

　　　　1.　くるまが　うごきません
　　　　2.　いそがしい　ときに　おきゃくさんが　きます
　　　　3.　だいじな　ときに　スミスさんが　いません
　　　　4.　さいふを　わすれました
　　　　5.　しけんの　まえに　かぜを　ひきました

II　Practice the following dialogues.

　A. **Q**：これは　わたなべさん<u>から　もらった</u>　おくりものですか。

　　A：はい、わたなべさん<u>からの</u>　おくりものです。

　B. **Q**：これは　たなかさん<u>に　だす</u>　てがみですか。

　　A：はい、たなかさん<u>への</u>　てがみです。

　C. **Q**：これは　ジョンソンさん<u>に　あげる</u>　プレゼントですか。

　　A：はい、ジョンソンさん<u>への</u>　プレゼントです。

　D. **Q**：これは　ど<u>こで　おきた</u>　もんだいですか。

　　A：おおさかししゃ<u>での</u>　もんだいです。

　E. **Q**：これは　どの　かいしゃ<u>と　した</u>　けいやくですか。

　　A：ABC<u>との</u>　けいやくです。

ぜんぶ	**zembu**, all, every	さく	**saku**, bloom
はれ	**hare**, fair, clear	スペインご	**Supein-go**, Spanish
ちゅうもん	**chūmon**, order	ビタミン	**bitamin**, vitamin
すうにん	**sūnin**, many people	だるい	**darui**, logy, tired, dull
すう〜	**sū-**, a few, many, several (prefix)	しまる	**shimaru**, be closed
		さいじつ	**saijitsu**, legal holiday
きらい（な）	**kirai(na)**, dislike, unlike	どう	**dō**, what
たんとうしゃ	**tantō-sha**, person in charge	へんじ	**henji**, reply
		だいじ（な）	**daiji(na)**, critical, important
か	**-ka**, lesson (counter)		
よなか	**yonaka**, middle of the night, midnight	ひく	**hiku**, catch
		おきる	**okiru**, happen, occur
はで（な）	**hade(na)**, flashy, gorgeous		

SHORT DIALOGUES

1. たなかふじん：あのう、これ、つまらない　ものですが、きょうとの　おみやげです。

   かとうふじん：まあ、いつも　すみません。えんりょなく　いただきます。

   Tanaka: Er . . . this is a trifling thing (really, but it's) a souvenir from Kyoto.
   Katō: Ahh, (you're) always so thoughtful. (*lit.* I accept (it) without hesitation.)

2. A：みそしるって　なんですか。
   B：にほんじんが　よく　のむ　ポタージュです。

   A: What's *miso shiru*?
   B: It's a soup. Japanese often have (it with their meals).

ふじん	**fujin**, Mrs., lady, woman	えんりょ	**enryo**, reserve, restraint, diffidence
つまらない	**tsumaranai**, trifling, worthless		
		いただく	**itadaku**, accept, receive (politer than **morau**)
まあ	**mā**, ah, oh, my (female speech)		
		ポタージュ	**potāju**, soup, potage
えんりょなく	**enryo naku**, without hesitation/reserve		

QUIZ

I Read this lessons's opening dialogue and answer the following questions.

1. ジョンソンさんが　もらった　チョコレートは　だれからの　プレゼントですか。

2. チャンさんも　チョコレートと　カードを　もらいましたか。

3. チャンさんが　ジョンソンさんへの　プレゼントを　あずかった　ひは　なんの　ひですか。

4. ギリチョコを　たくさん　もらった　だんせいは　ひとりで　ぜんぶ　たべるだろうと　チャンさんは　いっていますか。

II　Put the appropriate words in the parentheses.

1. ガールフレンド（　　）の　プレゼントを　かいに　いきました。

2. とうきょう（　　）の　せいかつは　ほんとうに　たのしかったです。

3. ロンドン（　　）の　にもつが　とどきました。

4. いつも　おせわ（　　）　なっています。これ（　　）も　どうぞ　よろしく。マイケルへ　まゆみ（　　）。

5. よびこうっ（　　）　なんですか。

III　Complete the questions so that they fit the answers.

1. きのう　（　　）　こなかったんですか。
   いそがしかったので、しつれいしました。

2. （　　）　しましたか。
   べんごしが　こないので、こまっています。

3. あたらしい　ぶちょうは　（　　）　ひとでしょうか。
   あたまが　よくて　まじめな　ひとだろうと　おもいますよ。

4. みそしるって（　　）ですか。
   みその　スープですよ。

IV　Complete the sentences with the appropriate form of the words indicated.

1. かれが　（　　）ので、あんしんしました。（げんきです）

2. これは　（　　）だろうと　おもいます。（スミスさんの　ものでは　ありません）

3. たなかさんは　（　　）かもしれませんよ。（びょうきです）

4. かれは　（　　）ので、えいごが　（　　）だろうと　おもいますよ。（がいこうかんでした、じょうずです）

5. しゅじんは　たぶん　かさを　（　　）だろうと　おもいます。（もっていきませんでした）

6. この　ちかてつは　ぎんざを　（　　）だろうと　おもいます。（とおりません）

7. しんぶんは　いすの　うえに　（　　）かもしれません。（おきました）

8. すぐ　あたらしい　せいかつに　（　　）でしょう。（なれます）

9. でんしゃが　（　　）ので、バスで　きました。（うごきませんでした）

10. さくらは　まだ　（　　）だろうと　おもいます。（さいていません）

V Choose a statement appropriate to the situation described.

A. It's April and, although you are not in Tokyo, you are asked if the cherry trees are blooming there.

1. さくらは　もう　さいているだろうと　おもいます。
2. さくらは　きれいな　はなだと　おもいます。
3. さくらは　もう　さかないかもしれません。

B. You tell your section chief you have to go to the hospital to see your father.

1. ちちが　びょうきなので、びょういんへ　いくかもしれません。
2. おとうさんが　びょうきなので、びょういんへ　いっては　いけませんか。
3. ちちが　びょうきなので、びょういんへ　いかなければ　なりません。

C. You want to be know the meaning of the acronym UFO.

1. ユーフォーって　なんですか。
2. ユーフォーと　いいます。
3. ユーフォーは　なんと　いいますか。

LESSON 14 THE REFEREE'S ROLE

On entering the Sumo arena Mr. Smith and Mr. Tanaka first look around for Linda and Mr. Smith's wife.

スミス：わあ、すごい 人ですね。

たなか：すもうの しょ日は いつも まんいんです。人が たくさん いて、
リンダさんや おくさんが よく 見えませんね。

スミス：あ、あそこに いました。ほら、すもうを 見ながら やきとりを 食べているのが 見えますよ。

たなか：さあ、わたしたちも あそこへ 行って、ビールでも 飲みながら すわって 見ましょう。

スミス：ええ、でも この とりくみが おわるまで ここで いいです。うるさくて アナウンスが よく 聞こえませんが、どひょうの 上に いるのは？

たなか：ふじのみねと さくらりゅうです。

スミス：はでな きものを きて、どひょうの 上で 動きまわっているのは どういう 人ですか。

たなか：あれは ぎょうじです。

スミス：ああ、ジャッジですね。

たなか：ええ、でも それは たてまえです。くろい きものを きて、どひょうの まわりに すわっているのが しんぱんいいんで、ほんとうのジャッジです。あの 人たちは りきしの OB で、えらいんですよ。

スミス：じゃ、ぎょうじは ジャッジの けんげんが ないんですか。

たなか：ええ、じつは けっていけんは ないんです。

スミス：そうですか。ちょっと なっとくできませんね。

たなか：でも 発言けんは ありますよ。

スミス：それを 聞いて 安心しました。

Smith: Wow! An awful lot of people, aren't there?
Tanaka: It's always full on the first day of a *sumo* tournament. With so many people we aren't going to find Linda and your wife (easily).
Smith: Oh, they're over there. Look! (I see) they're watching the *sumo* and eating *yakitori*.
Tanaka: Well, let's go over there ourselves and while drinking (some) beer (or something), sit down and watch (the bouts).
Smith: Umm, it's just as well (to stay) here until this bout is over. It's noisy and (I) can't hear the announcements very well. (The ones) on the ring are . . .?
Tanaka: Fujinomine and Sakuraryū.

Smith: (And the one) wearing the gay kimono, moving around the ring, what's his role?

Tanaka: That's the *gyōji*.

Smith: Ah, he's the judge.

Tanaka: Yes, but that's only the half of it (*lit.* only the [obvious] system). The ones sitting around the ring wearing black kimono are the judges, the real judges. They're OBs among the wrestlers; they're quite important men.

Smith: Doesn't the referee have any judgemental authority?

Tanaka: To tell the truth, he doesn't have any decisive powers.

Smith: Is that so. That (makes it) a little hard to understand, doesn't it?

Tanaka: He has a right to (his) views, though.

Smith: That's a relief! (i.e., "Hearing that I feel relieved.")

Vocabulary

わあ **wā**, wow, oh

すもう **sumō** (wrestling)

しょにち **shonichi**, first/opening day

まんいん **man'in**, full (of people)
　まん〜 **man-**, full (prefix)

みえる **mieru**, can see, be visible

ほら **hora**, look!, there!

やきとり **yakitori**, grilled chicken

でも **demo**, let's say, for example

とりくみ **torikumi**, bout

アナウンス **anaunsu**, announcement

きこえる **kikoeru**, can hear, be audible

どひょう **dohyō**, (sumō) ring

うごきまわる **ugokimawaru**,* move around

どういう **dō iu**, what role, what kind of

ぎょうじ **gyōji**, referee

ジャッジ **jajji**, judge

たてまえ **tatemae**, system, principle, policy

〜の まわりに **no mawari ni**, around

しんぱん **shimpan**, judgement

いいん **iin**, committee member

ほんとう（の） **hontō (no)**, real

りきし **rikishi**, wrestler

OB **ōbī**, OB (old boy)

えらい **erai**, important, illustrious, eminent

けんげん **kengen**, judgmental authority

けっていけん **kettei-ken**, decisive say, authority

けってい **kettei**, decision, conclusion

〜けん **-ken**, power, authority, right

なっとく **nattoku**, understanding, consent

はつげんけん **hatsugen-ken**, right to views

はつげん **hatsugen**, view, observation, utterance

*Compound words like this (**ugoku** plus **mawaru**) are very common.

GRAMMAR & LESSON OBJECTIVES

- **-te** form indicating reason or condition

  Hito ga takusan ite, Rinda-san ya okusan ga yoku miemasen.

  Urusakute anaunsu ga yoku kikoemasen.

  Sore o kiite anshin shimashita.

  In these sentences the words and clauses ending with **-te** give the reason for making the concluding statement. Similarly, as seen in the exercises in this lesson, **-na** adjectives are used in this way too.

ex. **Kimura-san wa aruku no ga kirai de, yoku takushī ni norimasu.** "Kimura doesn't like walking so he often takes taxis."

Suwatte mimashō.

Hadena kimono o kite dohyō no ue de ugokimawatte iru no wa . . .?

In these cases the **-te** form specifies the condition or manner in which action or activity takes place. As here, the clause refers to the subject of the sentence, whether or not the subject is explicitly stated.

- **no** in noun clauses

Yakitori o tabete iru no ga miemasu yo.

Dohyō no ue de ugokimawatte iru no wa dō iu hito desu ka.

Kuroi kimono o kite, dohyō no mawari ni suwatte iru no ga shimpan iin de . . .

The pattern of clause followed by **no** plus a particle—**wa**, **ga** or **o**—identifies that segment of the sentence as the topic or subject or object of the sentence as a whole. It is called a noun clause and, as in these examples, frequently pinpoints a situation or person. Comparable to this is putting **no** after an adjective for a similar purpose.

ex. **ōkii no**, "a big one"; **kantanna no**, "a simple one"

- **mieru** and **kikoeru**

Rinda-san ya okusan ga miemasen ne.

Anaunsu ga yoku kikoemasen.

The real meanings of these two verbs is that something is within sight or something emits sound. Strictly translated, these sentences would be "Linda and your wife can't be seen" and "The announcements can't be heard well." The particle is **ga** (not **o**).

NOTES

1. **Sā, watashi tachi mo . . . suwatte mimashō.**
   Sā at the beginning of a sentence is an attention getter and suggests and invites action.

2. **Bīru demo nominagara . . .**
   Bīru o nomimasen ka often sounds brusque. With **demo** added, the sense is "drink (something), even (if it's only) beer."

3. **Kono torikumi ga owaru made koko de ii desu.**
   The sense of **de ii** is "will do, is satisfactory, is OK" and so on.
   ex. 1. **Tegami o taipu shimashita ga, kore de ii desu ka.** "I typed the letter. Is it all right?"
      2. **Sumimasen. Kōhī mo jūsu mo arimasen.** "Sorry. We have neither coffee nor juice."
         Mizu de ii desu. "Water's fine."
         cf: **Nani ka nomimasu ka. Kōhī. O-cha.** "What'll you have to drink? Coffee? Tea?"
         Mizu ga ii desu. "I'd prefer water."

4. **Kono torikumi ga owaru made . . .**
   When **made** ends a clause, the verb is in the plain present tense form. Remember that the mid-sentence and sentence-final verb forms are not interdependent (as they sometimes are in English).
   ex. **Kinō watashi-tachi wa kuraku naru made tenisu o shimashita.** "We played tennis yesterday until it got dark."

5. **Fujinomine, Sakuraryū**
   These names mean "Summit of (Mount) Fuji" and "Cherry Dragon." One genre of sumo wrestlers' names evokes things beautiful, noble, fierce, everlasting or variations on these themes. Other names are taken from rivers, seas or mountains in or near the wrestlers' birthplaces. Still others, wholly or in part, give the wrestler a bond with an admired predecessor.

6. **Dō iu hito desu ka.**
   Although both **dō iu** and **donna** are translated "what kind of," **dō iu** implies expectation of an answer going beyond simple appearances or obvious qualities.

7. **Gyōji wa jajji no kengen ga nai n desu ka.**
   Ee, jitsu wa kettei-ken wa nai n desu.
   This is an example of answering a negative question with **ee** signifying agreement ("Yes, that's right"), whereas the English would be "no." (See the first volume, p. 20.)

8. **Chotto nattoku dekimasen ne.**
   Thinking of the meaning of **nattoku** as "consent, agree." A freer translation would be "I'm not convinced," that is, "I can't agree with what you say," here implying "That's strange."

PRACTICE

KEY SENTENCES

1. その　はなしを　きいて、あんしんしました。
2. ビールでも　のみながら、すわって　みましょう。
3. ジョンソンさんを　なりたくうこうまで　むかえに　いったのは　すずきさんです。
4. あそこに　しろい　ビルが　みえます。
5. アナウンスが　よく　きこえません。

1. When I heard that, I felt relieved.
2. While (we're) having (our) beer, let's sit down and watch.
3. It was Suzuki who went all the way to Narita Airport to meet Johnson.
4. A white building is visible there.
5. (I) can't hear the announcements very well.

EXERCISES

I Make dialogues by changing the underlined parts as in the examples given.

A. *ex.* **Q**：どう　したんですか。
   A：あつくて　のむ　ことが　できないんです。

   1. おもい、ひとりで　もちます
   2. いそがしい、はやく　かえります
   3. ふべん、つかいます
   4. ふくざつ、せつめいする

B. *ex.* **A**：ニュースを　きいて　あんしんしました。
   B：なにか　あったんですか。

   1. しんぶんを　よみました、びっくりしました
   2. ははから　てがみを　もらいました、あんしんしました
   3. よなかに　でんわが　ありました、おどろきました
   4. しらせが　きません、こまっているんです

II Practice the following pattern by changing the underline part.

ex. すずきさんは あるいて かいしゃに いきました。

    1. すわる、すもうを みます
    2. いそぐ、しりょうを あつめます
    3. わらう、さようならを いいます
    4. でんわを する、おおさかししゃに といあわせます

III Make dialogues by changing the underlined parts as in the examples given.

A. ex. Q : まいにち べんきょうしていますか。
    A : ええ、まいにち べんきょうするのは たいへんです。

    1. よる おそくまで しごとを します、たいへん
    2. こどもと あそびます、たのしい
    3. しょくじを つくります、めんどう
    4. あさ 5じに おきます、むずかしい

B. ex. A : よく、えを かきますね。
    B : ええ、えを かくのが すきなんです。

    1. やまを あるきます
    2. じょうだんを いいます
    3. りょこうに いきます
    4. えいがを みます

C. ex. Q : なにを わすれたんですか。
    A : しゅくだいを もってくるのを わすれたんです。

    1. でんわします
    2. おかねを あずけます
    3. せっけんを かいます
    4. やくそくしました

D. ex. Q : きょう くるのは だれですか。
    A : ええと、きょう くるのは たなかさんです。

    1. みんなに れんらくします、だれ、わたなべさん
    2. パーティーに きません、だれ、スミスさん
    3. きのう いきました、どこ、としょかん
    4. ともだちに あいます、いつ、どようび

5.　あぶない、どこ、ニューヨーク
　　　6.　しんせつ、だれ、リンダさん

E. *ex.* **Q**：おたくから　<u>ふじさんが</u>　みえますか。
　　　A：てんきが　いい　ときは　よく　みえます。

　　　　1.　とおくの　やま
　　　　2.　うみ
　　　　3.　とうきょうタワー
　　　　4.　あたらしく　できた　たかい　ビル

F. *ex.* **Q**：なにが　きこえるんですか。
　　　A：<u>むしの　こえ</u>が　きこえるんです。
　　　Q：いつも　きこえるんですか。
　　　A：いえ、<u>よる　しずかな　ときに</u>　きこえるんです。

　　　　1.　でんしゃの　おと、あさ　はやく
　　　　2.　となりの　デレビの　おと、よる　おそく
　　　　3.　あかちゃんの　なきごえ、ひるま
　　　　4.　きんじょの　こどもの　こえ、ゆうがた

G. *ex.* **Q**：<u>ひるごはんを　たべない</u>んですか。
　　　Aa：ええ、<u>たべない</u>んです。
　　　An：いいえ、<u>たべます</u>。

　　　　1.　アシスタントは　けっていけんが　ありません
　　　　2.　じかんが　ありません
　　　　3.　わすれものを　とりに　いきませんでした
　　　　4.　あの　せんせいの　なまえを　しりません

H. *ex.* **Q**：きのう　いつまで　まっていたんですか。
　　　A：<u>かいぎが　おわるまで</u>　まっていました。

　　　　1.　くらく　なります
　　　　2.　へんじが　きます
　　　　3.　げんこうが　できます
　　　　4.　こたえが　でます

ふべん（な）	**fuben(na)**, inconvenient	ええと	**ēto**, let me see
びっくりする	**bikkuri suru**, be surprised	とおく	**tōku**, long distance
		タワー	**tawā**, tower
おどろく	**odoroku**, be surprised	むし	**mushi**, cricket,* insect
しらせ	**shirase**, news, information, notice	いえ	**ie＝iie**
		おと	**oto**, sound
あつめる	**atsumeru**, gather, collect, assemble	なきごえ	**naki-goe**, cry
		ひるま	**hiruma**, daytime
めんどう（な）	**mendō(na)**, troublesome, annoying, a nuisance	きんじょ	**kinjo**, neighborhood
		アシスタント	**ashisutanto**, assistant
じょうだんを いう	**jōdan o iu**, crack a joke	げんこう	**genkō**, manuscript
じょうだん	**jōdan**, joke	こたえが でる	**kotae ga deru**, get an answer
しゅくだい	**shukudai**, homework	こたえ	**kotae**, answer
あずける	**azukeru**, deposit, entrust		
せっけん	**sekken**, soap		

*Although bilingual dictionaries do not take note of it, it is clearly understood that **mushi no koe** is the "cry of a cricket."

SHORT DIALOGUES

1. すずき： もしもし、もしもし、きこえますか。
   やまかわ：もしもし、おでんわが とおいんですが、もう すこし おおき
   い こえで おねがいします。
   すずき： こちらは すずきですが、きこえますか。
   やまかわ：あ、きこえました。すずきさんですね。

   Suzuki: Hello, hello—can you here me?
   Yamakawa: Hello. I can't hear (you). Speak a little louder, please.
   Suzuki: This is Suzuki. Can you hear (now)?
   Yamakawa: Ah, I can hear now. It's Mr. Suzuki, isn't it?

2. A： しつれいですが、たなかさんじゃ ありませんか。
   B： はい、たなかですが・・・。

   A: Excuse me, but aren't you Mr. Tanaka?
   B: Yes, I'm Tanaka.

でんわが とおい **denwa ga tōi**, I can't hear (you) (*lit*. [Your voice over] the phone seems far away.)

QUIZ

I Read this lesson's opening dialogue and answer the following questions.

1. リンダさんと たなかさんの おくさんは すもうを みながら なに
   を していますか。
2. うるさくて アナウンスが よく きこえないと いったのは だれで
   すか。
3. しんぱんいいんは なにを きて、どこに すわっていますか。
4. ほんとうの ジャッジは ぎょうじですか、しんぱんいいんですか。

II Put the appropriate particles in the parentheses.

1. てんき（　　）いい とき、ふじさん（　　）みえます。
2. わたしは てがみ（　　）とどく（　　）を まっていました。
3. よる おそく くるま（　　）おと（　　）きこえました。
4. しろい うわぎ（　　）きている（　　）は スミスさんです。
5. おどろいたかもしれませんが、これは ほんとう（　　）はなしです。

III Complete the questions so that they fit the answers.

1. あの ひとは（　　）ひとですか。
   だいとうりょうの むすこで、ゆうめいな ピアニストです。
2. （　　）まで ここで まつんですか。
   かいぎが おわるまで まってください。
3. （　　）を みているんですか。
   ケーキを つくっているのを みているんです。
4. 3がつ 3かは（　　）ひですか。
   おんなの この おまつりの ひで、ともだちを よんで パーティー
   をしたり する ひです。

IV Complete the sentences with the appropriate form of the words indicated.

1. ニュースを（　　）、びっくりしました。（ききます）
2. しりょうを ぜんぶ（　　）のは たいへんです。（あつめます）
3. あそこで（　　）のが みえますか。
   いえ、（　　）、よく みえません。（つりを しています、とおいです）
4. てがみを（　　）のを わすれました。（だします）
5. じかんが（　　）、いく ことが できません。（ありません）
6. しょくじが（　　）まで、テレビでも みましょう。（できます）
7. はなしが（　　）、よく わかりません。（ふくざつです）

V Circle the correct words in the parentheses.

1. あついですね。ビール（や、でも、ほど）のみませんか。
   いいですね。

2. 6じまでに　（かならず、わざわざ、たいてい）　れんらくしてくださ
い。

3. ふごうかくだと　おもっていましたが、（かならず、やっぱり、たぶん）
ふごうかくでした。

4. あなたは　しらなかったんですか。
ええ、（ぜひ、それに、じつは）　しらなかったんです。

VI Answer the following questions.

1. あなたは　すもうを　みた　ことが　ありますか。
2. あなたの　へやから　なにが　みえますか。
3. よる　あなたの　へやに　いる　とき、くるまの　おとが　きこえます
か。
4. あなたは　やまに　のぼるのが　すきですか。
5. しょくじを　する　とき、にほんじんは　はじめに　なんと　いいます
か。

Mr. Brown takes care of Mr. Yamamoto's umbrella.

ブラウン：きのう　スポーツクラブに　行ったら　山本さんに　会いました。
わたなべ：おととい　ここに　来た　山本さんですか。
ブラウン：ええ。
わたなべ：山本さんが　かさを　わすれて　かえりましたが、どう　しましょうか。
ブラウン：私が　その　かさを　あずかりましょう。来週　スポーツクラブへ　行く　時、持って行きますから。山本さんに　会ったら　わたします。もし　会わなかったら、うけつけに　あずけます。
わたなべ：おねがいします。

At the health club.

うけつけ：おはようございます。
ブラウン：おはようございます。山本たろうさんと　いう　人は　もう　来ていますか。ここの　会員だと　思います。
うけつけ：会員の　山本さまですね。きょうは　山本さまは　ゆうがた　6時に　いらっしゃいます。
ブラウン：そうですか。山本さんの　かさを　あずかっているんですが、6時に　来るなら、今　ここに　あずけても　いいですか。
うけつけ：はい、どうぞ。
ブラウン：私は　ABCの　ブラウンと　言います。かれが　来たら　これを　わたしてください。
うけつけ：はい、たしかに。

Brown:　　　When I went to the health club yesterday, I ran into Mr. Yamamoto.
Watanabe:　The Mr. Yamamoto who came here the day before yesterday?
Brown:　　　Umm.
Watanabe:　He left and forgot his umbrella. What shall (I) do with it?
Brown:　　　I'll take care of the umbrella and when I go to the health club next week, I'll take it with me. If I see Mr. Yamamoto I'll give it to him. If I don't, I'll leave it at the reception desk.
Watanabe:　Oh, please.

Receptionist:　Good morning.
Brown:　　　　Good morning. Has a man by the name of Tarō Yamamoto come yet? He's a club member, I think.

Receptionist: Mr. Yamamoto is it? Mr. Yamamoto's coming today at six in the evening.
Brown: Is he? I've been keeping his umbrella. If he's coming at six, may (I) leave it here now?
Receptionist: Yes, of course.
Brown: My name is Brown. When he comes, please give it to him.
Receptionist: Yes, certainly.

Vocabulary

～たら	**-tara** = when, if (for completed action or supposition)	～さま	**-sama**, =**-san** (polite)
		～なら	**nara**, if
		たしかに	**tashika-ni**, certainly
もし	**moshi**, if		
かいいん	**kaiin**, club/society member		

GRAMMAR & LESSON OBJECTIVES

• -tara

Kinō supōtsu kurabu ni ittara Yamamoto-san ni aimashita.

A . . . **-tara** basically expresses completed action. **-tara** (**-kattara**, **dattara**) is combined with verbs, adjectives and nouns and means A has been done and B happened. Since B (**-mashita**) is unexpected, **-tara** is used here. In sentences like **Kinō Tanaka-san ga kita toki, kare ni hanashimashita**, "When Tanaka came yesterday, I told him (about it, as I had planned to)" **toki** (not a **-tara** pattern) occurs.

The difference between **-te** and **-tara** should be noted. If Brown had said **Kinō supōtsu kurabu ni itte Yamamoto-san ni aimashita**, ("I went to the health club yesterday and saw Yamamoto"), it would have meant that he had intended to see Yamamoto at the health club.

Yamamoto-san ni attara watashimasu. Moshi awanakattara uketsuke ni azukemasu.

If the time is the future (A . . . **-tara** B . . . **-masu/-mashō/-te kudasai**), this pattern expresses supposition, for nothing in the future is absolutely certain.

Verbs, adjectives and nouns are combined as follows:

	aff.	*neg.*
iku miru	ittara mitara	ikanakattara minakattara
takai	takakattara	takaku nakattara
shizukana	shizuka dattara	shizuka dewa/ja nakattara
ame	ame dattara	ame dewa/ja nakattara

• nara

6-ji ni kuru nara, ima koko ni azukete mo ii desu ka.

Although **nara** is also used when there is uncertainty, it may be subtly different from **-tara**. In this example, Brown has definitely decided to leave the umbrella assuming Yamamoto is coming to the club. At times either **-tara** or **nara** is used to mean the same thing. These two sentences, however, are different.

ex. 1. **Katō-san ga kitara kaerimasu.** "I'll leave after Katō comes."
    2. **Katō-san ga kuru nara kaerimasu.** "If Katō's coming, I'll leave (now)."

Nara can come after adjectives—**yasui nara, benri nara**—or nouns. **Ame nara kasa o motte ikimashō.** "If it's going to rain, (I'll) take (my) umbrella."

Additional cases will be introduced later. Also, **naraba**, with the same meaning as **nara**, may be encountered sometimes, but nowadays **nara** is far more frequent.

NOTES

1. **Yamamoto-sama**

   There is a gradation to be observed in terms of address.

   respect level   **Yamamoto-sama to iu kata**
   neutral   **Yamamoto-san to iu hito**
   humble level   **Yamamoto to iu/mōsu mono**

   Neutral terms are used among friends and equals. Note also that Brown uses the pattern he does, rather than simply Yamamoto-san, so as to confirm whether or not the receptionist knows him.

2. **Yamamoto-san no kasa o azukatte iru n desu ga, 6-ji ni kuru nara, ima koko ni azukete mo ii desu ka.**

   As can be seen, both **azukaru** (Regular I) and **azukeru** (Regular II) take the same object and the same particle in this sentence. Be careful not to confuse verbs like these.

   Compare: 1. **Buraun-san wa Watanabe-san kara kasa o azukarimashita.** (*lit.*) "Brown was entrusted with an umbrella by Watanabe."
   2. **Buraun-san wa uketsuke ni kasa o azukemashita.** "Brown had the receptionist take care of the umbrella."
   3. **Uketsuke no hito wa Buraun-san kara kasa o azukarimashita.** "The receptionist (was given) an umbrella to take care of by Brown."

PRACTICE

KEY SENTENCES

1. せんだいまで　くるまで　いったら、　10じかん　かかりました。
2. もし　あめが　ふったら、ハイキングは　やめます。
3. ひこうきで　いくなら、はやく　きっぷを　かった　ほうが　いいですよ。

1. We went to Sendai by car, it took ten hours.
2. If it rains, I'll give up (my) hiking (trip).
3. If you're going by plane, it's better to buy (your) tickets early.

EXERCISES

I Practice the following patterns by changing the underlined parts as in the examples given.

A. *ex.* ひるごはんを　たくさん　たべたら　ねむく　なりました。

    1. さけを　のみました、あたまが　いたく　なりました
    2. スポーツクラブに　いきました、むかしの　ともだちに　あいました
    3. さけを　のんで　うんてんしました、じこを　おこしました
    4. きのう　よしゅうを　しませんでした、きょう　ぜんぜん　わかりませんでした

B. *ex.* **Q**：かいぎは　いつ　はじめますか。
    A：10じに　なったら　すぐ　はじめます。

1. しゃちょうが きます
2. ぜんいんが そろいます
3. しょるいを ぜんぶ くばります
4. ちゅうしょくが すみます

C. ex. Q：ひまが あったら どう しますか。
A：もし ひまが あったら にほんじゅう りょこうしたいです。

1. おかねが あります
2. じかんが あります
3. くるまが あります

D. ex. Q：もし たくさん おかねが あったら どう しますか。
A：たくさん おかねが あったら おおきい うちを かいたいです。

1. りこんします
2. きふします
3. こいびとに ダイヤモンドを おくります
4. ちょきんします
5. せかいじゅう りょこうします

E. ex. Q：コーチが こないかもしれませんよ。どう しますか。
A：そうですねえ、もし かれが こなかったら いくのを やめます。

1. みちが わかりません
2. おかねが たりません
3. じかんが ありません
4. こどもが よろこびません

F. ex. A：あつかったら まどを あけてください。
B：はい、そうします。

1. さむいです、ヒーターを つけます
2. たかいです、かいません
3. いそがしくないです、あそびに きます
4. きぶんが よくないです、やすみます

II Make dialogues by changing the underlined parts as in the examples given.

A. *ex.* **A**：ひるごはんを　たべたいんですが。

　　　　B：ひるごはんを　たべるなら　あの　レストランが　いいですよ。

　　　1. スポーツクラブに　はいります、いい　クラブを　しょうかい
　　　　しましょう
　　　2. うみに　いきます、わたしの　くるまを　つかっても　いいで
　　　　すよ
　　　3. テープレコーダーを　かいます、ちいさい　ほうが　べんりで
　　　　すよ
　　　4. きゅうしゅうに　いきます、フェリーが　いいですよ

B. *ex.* **Q**：あめだったら　どうしますか。

　　　　A：あめなら　よていを　かえます。

　　　1. あめ、いきません
　　　2. たなかさんが　るす、また　あとで　でんわします
　　　3. ひま、ゴルフを　します
　　　4. だめ、もう　いちど　やります

C. *ex.* **Q**：あなたは　いきますか。

　　　　A：もし　あの　ひとが　いくなら　わたしは　いきません。

　　　1. でかけます　　　　　　4. はなします
　　　2. かえります　　　　　　5. てつだいます
　　　3. うたいます　　　　　　6. やめます

D. *ex.* **Q**：だれ（どなた）が　きましたか。

　　　　A：やまもとさんと　いう　ひとが　きました。

　　　1. たろう、こども
　　　2. はやしさま、かた
　　　3. グッドマンさん、おんなの　ひと

E. *ex.* **Q**：なんと　いう　ほんを　よみましたか。

　　　　A：「こころ」と　いう　ほんを　よみました。

　　　1. ところに　とまりました、かなざわ
　　　2. えいがを　みたいです、しちにんの　さむらい
　　　3. レコードを　かいました、つきの　ひかり

4. うたを　うたいます、ホワイトクリスマス

Vocabulary

ねむい	**nemui**, sleepy	おくる	**okuru**, give
むかし	**mukashi**, old	ちょきんする	**chokin suru**, save (money)
じこ	**jiko**, accident		
おこす	**okosu**, cause	ちょきん	**chokin**, savings, deposit
よしゅう	**yoshū**, preparation, rehearsal	せかいじゅう	**sekai-jū**, all over the world
ぜんいん	**zen'in**, all the staff, all members	せかい	**sekai**, world, society, realm
そろう	**sorou**, be present, assemble, be/become complete	じゅう	**-jū**, all over, throughout
		フェリー	**ferī**, ferry
くばる	**kubaru**, distribute	るす	**rusu**, be out/away
すむ	**sumu**, be finished	てつだう	**tetsudau**, help
りこんする	**rikon suru**, divorce, be divorced	かた	**kata**, person (polite)
		こころ	**kokoro**, heart, mind*
りこん	**rikon**, divorce	かなざわ	**Kanazawa** (place name)
きふする	**kifu suru**, donate, contribute	さむらい	**samurai****
		つきの　ひかり	**tsuki no hikari**, moonlight
きふ	**kifu**, donation, contribution	ひかり	**hikari**, light, rays
こいびと	**koibito**, sweetheart	ホワイトクリスマス	**Howaito Kurisumasu**, "White Christmas"
ダイヤモンド	**daiyamondo**, daimond		

*Title of one of Natsume Sōseki's novels.
***Shichi-nin no Samurai* is the title of one of Kurosawa Akira's films.

SHORT DIALOGUES

1. A：この　へんに　にもつを　あずける　ところは　ありませんか。
   B：あそこに　コインロッカーが　あります。もし　いっぱいなら、かいさ
   　　つぐちの　そばに　いちじあずかりじょが　あります。

   A: Isn't there a place to check baggage around here?
   B: There are pay lockers over there. If (they're) all full there's a temporary checkroom near the ticket gate.

2. ホワイト：かいぎは　なかなか　おわりませんね。
   わたなべ：7じに　なったら　おわるでしょう。
   ホワイト：そうですか。7じに　なるなら　おさきに　しつれいします。

   White:　　The meeting still isn't over, is it?
   Watanabe: It'll be over at seven, I suppose.
   White:　　Oh? Will it? If it's going on till 7 o'clock, I'm going till leave now.

Vocabulary

この　へん	**kono hen**, around here, this vicinity	いっぱい	**ippai**, full
		そば	**soba**, near, beside
へん	**hen**, neighborhood, vicinity	いちじ	**ichiji**, temporary, (at) one time
コインロッカー	**koin rokkā**, pay locker	あずかりじょ	**azukarijo**, checkroom

QUIZ

I Read this lesson's opening dialogue and answer the following questions.

1. ブラウンさんは　やまもとさんの　わすれた　かさを　だれから　あずかりましたか。

2. ブラウンさんは　どこで　やまもとさんに　その　かさを　わたしたいと　おもっていますか。

3. ブラウンさんは　スポーツクラブに　いった　とき、やまもとさんに　あう　ことが　できましたか。

4. やまもとさんは　この　スポーツクラブの　かいいんですか。

II Put the appropriate particles in the parentheses.

1. うけつけの　ひと（　　）　にもつ（　　）　あずけました。

2. かいいん（　　）　やまもとさまは　きょう　ゆうがた　6じ（　　）　いらっしゃいます。

3. やまもとさんが　かさ（　　）　わすれて　かえりました。
   じゃ、わたし（　　）　その　かさ（　　）　あずかりましょう。スポーツクラブ（　　）　やまもとさん（　　）　あったら、わたします。

4. 「7にんの　さむらい」　（　　）　いう　えいがを　みました。

III Complete the questions so that they fit the answers.

1. きのう　きた　ひとは　（　　）と　いう　ひとですか。
   ふじたさんと　いう　ひとです。

2. もし　やまもとさんが　こなかったら、　（　　）　しましょうか。
   てがみで　しらせてください。

3. （　　）　ひっこすんですか。
   うちが　できたら　ひっこします。

4. （　　）に　しょるいを　わたしましたか。
   たなかさんに　わたしました。

IV Complete the sentences with the appropriate form of the words indicated.

1. ワープロを　（　　）なら、いい　みせを　おしえましょう。（かいます）

2. ぜんいんが　（　　）たら、（　　）ください。（そろいます、はじめます）

3. さけを　（　　）だら、きぶんが　（　　）　なりました。（のみます、わるいです）

4. （　　）なら、えいがを　（　　）に　いきませんか。（ひまです、みます）

5. この　いすは　つかっていません。

（　　）なら、（　　）　ほうが　いいですよ。（つかいません、かたづけます）

6. （　　）たら、すこし　（　　）ください。（つかれます、やすみます）

7. （　　）たら、　（　　）ください。（いそがしくないです、てつだいます）

8. つくりかたが　（　　）なら、（　　）のを　やめます。（めんどうです、つくります）

9. あした　（　　）たら、でかけません。（あめです）

10. きょうとに　（　　）なら、この　ちずを　（　　）ましょう。（いきます、あげます）

11. にもつが　（　　）ので、（　　）ください。（おもいです、あずかります）

V　Answer the following questions.

1. おかねを　ひろったら、あなたは　どう　しますか。

2. 1かげつ　やすみが　あったら、なにを　しますか。

3. ともだちの　うちへ　いくとき、みちが　わからなかったら、あなたは　どう　しますか。

4. いままで　みた　えいがの　なかで、なんと　いう　えいがが　いちばん　おもしろかったですか。

LESSON 16 THE NEW SHOWROOM DESIGN

Mr. Yamakawa asks Mr. Hayashi on the phone if he likes the new design for the showroom.

山川: もしもし、はやし部長ですか。こちらは Mせっけいじむしょの 山川ですが、ごいらいの ショールームの せっけいが でき上がりました。さっき ファックスで ずめんを 送りましたが、いかがですか。

はやし: ええ、なかなか いいですねえ。

山川: 何か もんだいは ありませんか。あしたから こうじを はじめれば、来週 中に でき上がります。もし もんだいが なければ さっそく はじめたいと 思います。年末に なると ぎょうしゃも いそがしく なりますから、早ければ 早いほど いいと 思うんですが・・・。

はやし: そうですねえ。すみませんが、はじめる 前に もう 一度 会って そうだんしたいんですが。

山川: わかりました。そちらの ごつごうが よければ、これから うかがいます。

はやし: できれば そう してください。私は 8時ごろまで 会社に います。6時に なると おもての 入口は 閉まります。はんたいがわに まわると うら口が ありますから、そこから 入ってください。うら口は 10時まで 開いています。

山川: わかりました。

はやし: じゃ、よろしく おねがいします。

Yamakawa: Hello, is this Mr. Hayashi? This is Yamakawa (Office). (In accordance with) your request we have finished the showroom design. We sent the blueprint by fax (just) a little while ago. How is it?

Hayashi: It looks quite good to me.

Yamakawa: Are there any problems? If (we) start construction work tomorrow, it'll be finished next week. If there are no problems we'd like to start without delay. As it gets near the end of the year, businessmen get (quite) busy, so the earlier, the better, I think.

Hayashi: Yes, well, I'm afraid we'd prefer to meet (you) and have one more consultation before (you) start.

Yamakawa: I see. If you have time, I'll come (over) now.

Hayashi: If you can do that, please do. I'll be in the office until about eight o'clock. The front entrance is closed at six (*lit.* when it gets to be six). If you go around to the opposite side, there's the back entrance. Please come in that way. The back entrance is open until ten o'clock.

Yamakawa: Yes, of course.

Hayashi: I'll be expecting you then, (*lit.* "I request you to [act] properly.")

せっけい	**sekkei**, design, planning	〜（けれ）ば〜	**-(kere)ba . . . hodo**, if . . .
ごいらい	**go-irai**, (your) request,	ほど	-er/more/less, (then) . . .
	commission	うかがう	**ukagau**, visit, ask (polite)
ショールーム	**shōrūmu**, showroom	〜と	**to**, when (particle)
できあがる	**dekiagaru**, be finished/	おもて	**omote**, front, face, sur-
	ready/done		face
ずめん	**zumen**, blueprint, plan	はんたいがわ	**hantai-gawa**, opposite
なにか	**nanika**, some-/anything,		side
	some, any	はんたい	**hantai**, opposite,
こうじ	**kōji**, construction work		reverse
〜ば/〜ければ	**-ba/-kereba**, = if	〜がわ	**gawa**, side
さっそく	**sassoku**, without delay,	うらぐち	**uraguchi**, back entrance
	directly	うら	**ura**, back, reverse
ねんまつ	**nemmatsu**, end of the		(side)
	year	よろしく	**yoroshiku**, properly,
ぎょうしゃ	**gyōsha**, businessman,		well, at one's discretion
	supplier, trader		

GRAMMAR & LESSON OBJECTIVES

• -ba/-kereba

Ashita kara kōji o hajimereba raishū-chū ni dekiagarimasu.
Sochira no go-tsugō ga yokereba . . .
The **-ba/-kereba** form is called the conditional form and is made with verbs, the two types of adjectives and nouns as shown here.

	aff.	*neg.*
hajimeru (Reg. II) okuru (Reg. I) omou (Reg. I)	hajimereba okureba omoeba	hajimenakereba okuranakereba omowanakereba
hayai ii/yoi	hayakereba yokereba	hayaku nakereba yoku nakereba
benrina	(benri de areba) benri nara(ba)/dattara	benri de nakereba
ame	(ame de areba) ame nara(ba)/dattara	ame de nakereba

The expressions in parentheses and **naraba** are found in written Japanese and a formal way of speaking. **De areba** is derived from **de aru**, a literary counterpart of **desu**.
To see the conditional in relation to other forms, refer to the verb chart in appendix C.

• Hayakereba hayai hodo ii.

This pattern uses the conditional form of an **-i** adjective with the dictionary form of the same adjective plus **hodo** and leads to a conclusion.
ex. **Ōkikereba ōkii hodo ii desu.** "The larger the better."
For **-na** adjectives the pattern is: **Shizuka nara shizuka na hodo ii desu.** "The quieter the better."
Note also the negatives (practiced in the exercises in this lesson): **shizuka de nakereba**, "If it

isn't quiet"; **ame de nakereba**, "If it isn't raining/doesn't rain."
Essentially the same pattern consists of the conditional form of a verb and the dictionary form of the same verb with **hodo** coming after it.
ex. **Mireba miru hodo hoshiku narimasu.** "The more (I) look at (it), the more (I) want it."

• Particle **to**, when

6-ji ni naru to omote no iriguchi wa shimarimasu.
Hantai-gawa ni mawaru to uraguchi ga arimasu.
A clause ending with **to** followed by a main clause with a present form is a way of saying if or when A happens, B occurs as a natural or habitual result. The sense is often "whenever." Two points to remember are that **to** comes after the dictionary or plain negative form of a verb, and this pattern is not appropriate for expressing one's own requests, suggestions, intentions or the granting of permission. Specifically, it is not used in sentences ending in **-te kudasai**, **-mashō**, **masen ka** and so on.
ex. 1. **Taiyō ga shizumu to, kuraku narimasu.** "When the sun sets, it gets dark."
2. **Kono botan o osu to, kikai ga ugokimasu.** "If you push this button, the machine will (start) running."

To, **-tara**, **nara** and **-ba** are in some cases interchangeable, as when they are translated by "if." Beyond that, it is best to make case-by-case observations.

NOTE

Gyōsha
This word refers to traders, suppliers and manufacturers who provide goods and services to larger enterprises and government organizations. It can be compared with **torihiki-saki**, which implies a more equal relationship.

PRACTICE

KEY SENTENCES

1. じかんが あれば、きょうとししゃにも いきます。
2. ゆきが ふると、あの やまで スキーが できます。
3. さかなは あたらしければ あたらしいほど いいです。

1. If I have time, I'll go to the Kyoto branch too.
2. Whenever it snows, (you) can ski on that mountain.
3. As for fish, the fresher the better.

EXERCISES

I Verbs: Study the examples, convert into the conditional form, and memorize.

ex. いく → いけば　　　　たべる → たべれば　　　くる → くれば
はなす → はなせば　　みる → みれば　　　　する → すれば

1. あらう	5. つかう	9. おしえる	13. もってくる
2. たつ	6. あるく	10. おりる	14. あんないする
3. うる	7. できる	11. つとめる	15. もらってくる
4. たのむ	8. かける	12. しらせる	16. しんぱいする

II Adjectives: Study the examples, convert into the conditional form, and memorize.

ex. あつい→あつければ　　　はやくない→はやくなければ

1. すくない　　　　4. あたまが　いたい　　7. はなしたい
2. おもしろい　　　5. わるい　　　　　　　8. いきたくない
3. つごうが　いい　6. わるくない　　　　　9. かかない

III Make dialogues by changing the underlined parts as in the examples given.

A. ex. Q：よんだら　わかりますか。
　　　　A：ええ、よめば　わかりますが、よまなければ　わかりません。

1. ここに　いる　　　4. てつだう　　　　7. のむ
2. といあわせる　　　5. あした　くる　　8. つかう
3. りゅうがくする　　6. あう　　　　　　9. みる

B. ex. Q：やすかったら　かいますか。
　　　　A：ええ、やすければ　かいますが、やすくなければ　かいません。

1. あたらしい　　　4. おもしろい　　　7. ちかい
2. おいしい　　　　5. あかい　　　　　8. やわらかい
3. いい　　　　　　6. めずらしい　　　9. ほしい

IV Practice the following patterns by changing the underlined parts.

A. ex. はるに　なれば　はなが　さきます。

1. めがねを　かけます、よく　みえます
2. よく　ねむります、あたまが　はっきりします
3. ゆっくり　はなします、よく　わかります
4. しつもんが　ありません、これで　おわります
5. はっきり　いいません、わかりません
6. おかねと　じかんが　ありません、この　もんだいは　かいけ
　　つしません

B. ex. たかければ　かいません。

1. つごうが　わるい、でんわを　ください
2. いそがしい、ほかの　ひとに　たのみます
3. いそがしくない、いっしょに　えいがに　いきましょう
4. いきたくない、いかなくても　いいです

5. おかねが　たりない、かしましょう

6. ごめいわくでない、いっしょに　いきたいんですが

7. ごめんどうでない、おねがいします

V Make dialogues by changing the underlined parts as in the examples given.

A. ex. **A**：しごとは　はやければ　はやいほど　いいですね。

    B：ええ、わたしも　そう　おもいます。

1. にもつ、かるい　　　　4. ぜいきん、すくない

2. やちん、やすい　　　　5. やすみ、ながい

3. きゅうりょう、おおい　　6. やさい、あたらしい

B. ex. **Q**：そんなに　ほしいんですか。

    A：ええ、みれば　みるほど　ほしく　なります。

1. おもしろい、よむ　　　　4. うれしい、きく

2. すき、あう　　　　　　　5. たのしい、すむ

3. わからない、かんがえる

VI Practice the following patterns by changing the underlined parts.

A. ex. さけを　のむと　たのしく　なります。

1. （お）かねを　いれます、きっぷが　でます

2. つぎの　こうさてんを　まがります、びょういんが　あります

3. まっすぐ　いきます、ひだりがわに　ポストが　あります

4. たばこを　たくさん　すいます、がんに　なりますよ

5. コーヒーを　のみません、しごとが　できません

B. ex. **Q**：どう　すると　あくんですか。

    A：ボタンを　おすと　あきます。

1. ジュースが　ででくる、おかねを　いれる

2. みずが　でる、あしで　ペダルを　ふむ

3. でんきが　きえる、ドアを　しめる

4. まどが　あく、レバーを　ひく

C. ex. なにか　しつもんが　ありますか。

1. だれ、かいしゃの　ひとが　きましたか

2. いつ、ひまな　とき　いきたいです

3. どこ、しずかな　ところで　はなしましょう

4. いくつ、おいしい　ケーキを　かってきてください

5. なんさつ、おもしろい　ほんを　よういしてください

Vocabulary

しんぱいする	**shimpai suru**, be worried	でる	**deru**, come out
しんぱい	**shimpai**, worry	ポスト	**posuto**, mailbox
りゅうがくする	**ryūgaku suru**, study abroad	がん	**gan**, cancer
		ボタン	**botan**, button
りゅうがく	**ryūgaku**, studying overseas	でてくる	**dete kuru**, come out, appear
めずらしい	**mezurashii**, rare, unusual	ペダル	**pedaru**, pedal
やわらかい	**yawarakai**, soft, tender	ふむ	**fumu**, step on, trample
はる	**haru**, spring	きえる	**kieru**, go out, be extinguished, put out
ねむる	**nemuru**, sleep		
はっきりする	**hakkiri suru**, be/become clear, get better	レバー	**rebā**, lever
		ひく	**hiku**, pull
はっきり	**hakkiri**, clearly, exactly	いつか	**itsuka**, some/any time
		どこか	**dokoka**, some/any place
かいけつする	**kaiketsu suru**, solve, settle	いくつか	**ikutsu ka**, several, many, any number
かいけつ	**kaiketsu**, solution, decision	なんさつ　か	**nansatsu ka**, a few/many/several volumes
ごめいわく	**go-meiwaku**, trouble, inconvenience	〜さつ	**-satsu** (counter for books)
やちん	**yachin**, (house) rent	よういする	**yōi suru**, prepare, arrange, provide for
きゅうりょう	**kyūryō**, salary		
そんなに	**sonna ni**, that much/many	ようい	**yōi**, preparations, readiness
いれる	**ireru**, put in, insert		

SHORT DIALOGUE

A：たいへん。もう　10じはんですか。ひこうきの　じかんに　まにあわないか
　もしれません。

B：くるまで　くうこうまで　おくりましょう。いそげば　まにあうと　おもい
　ますよ。

A：それじゃ、おねがいします。

A: Oh, oh, it's 10:30 already. It looks like (I'll) be late for the plane.

B: I'll take (you) (*lit.* "send you off") to the airport by car. If (we) hurry, I think you'll be in time.

A: Oh, thank you.

たいへん　　　**taihen**, oh, oh!　　　　　おくる　　　　**okuru**, take, see/send off,
まにあう　　　**maniau**, be in/on time, be　　　　　　　　escort
　　　　　　　serviceable

QUIZ

I　Read this lessons's opening dialogue and answer the following questions.

1. だれが　だれに　ファックスで　ずめんを　おくりましたか。
2. はやしさんの　かいしゃに　なんじまでに　いけば　おもての　いりぐ
　ちから　はいる　ことが　できますか。
3. やまかわさんは　どうして　はやく　こうじを　はじめたいと　いって
　いますか。
4. ABC の　うらぐちは　なんじに　なると　しまりますか。

II　Put the appropriate word or word parts in the parentheses.

1. なに（　　）　つめたい　のみものは　ありませんか。
2. いつまで（　　）　はらわなくては　いけませんか。
　はやけれ（　　）　はやいほど　いいだろう（　　）　おもいます。
3. この　みせは　ひるから　よる　12じ（　　）　あいています。
4. ごいらい（　　）　せっけいが　できあがりましたので、ファックス
　（　　）　おくります。

III　Complete the questions so that they fit the answers.

1. さくらの　はなは　（　　）　さきますか。
　4がつに　なると　さきますよ。
2. （　　）か　しずかな　ところは　ないでしょうか。
　かいぎしつなら　しずかですよ。
3. やまださんが　かいた　えは　（　　）　でしたか。
　なかなか　よかったですよ。

IV　Convert the following verbs and adjectives into their **-ba/ -kereba** forms.

1. あう	4. ふる	7. かんがえる	10. ない
2. あく	5. みえる	8. けっこんする	11. めずらしい
3. しまる	6. よろこぶ	9. もってくる	12. いい

V　Complete the sentences with the appropriate form of the words indicated.

1. よく　（　　）ば、げんきに　（　　）でしょう。
　（やすみます、なります）
2. とうきょうタワーに　（　　）ば、うみが　（　　）でしょう。
　（のぼります、みえます）
3. つぎの　かどを　みぎに　（　　）と　はなやが　あります。
　（まがります）

4. おさけを　（　　）と、（　　）　なります。
　　（のみます、たのしいです）

5. ごつごうが　（　　）ば、ごご　（　　）たいと　おもいます。
　　（いいです、うかがいます）

6. （　　）ば、（　　）　なりますよ。
　　（れんしゅうします、じょうずです）

7. かとうさんに　（　　）ば、（　　）でしょう。
　　（ききません、わかりません）

8. （　　）ば、もっと　（　　）ましょう。
　　（ほしいです、もってきます）

9. （　　）ば、（　　）くれませんか。（できます、とどけます）

10. （　　）ば、（　　）ほど　わからなく　なります。
　　（かんがえます、かんがえます）

VI　Circle the correct words in the parentheses.

1. （すぐ、さっき、さっそく）　おきたばかりですから、まだ　しんぶんを
　　よんでいません。

2. なんじごろ　うかがいましょうか。
　　ごぜんちゅうは　いそがしいので、（できれば、なかなか、これから）
　　ごご　2じごろ　きてくれませんか。

3. じかんが　ないので、（さっき、たしかに、さっそく）　はじめてくれま
　　せんか。

Mr. Brown has to keep a diary as a part of his Japanese study.

12月31日（水）はれ　のち　くもり

　今日は　大みそかだ。となりの　おおのさんの　うちでは、朝から　かぞく全員で　そうじを　していた。みんなで　へいや　車や、そして　いぬまで　あらっていた。

　午後は　日本語で　ねんがじょうを　書いたが、じが　へただから　よみにくいだろう。ゆうがた、たなかさん　一家と　そばを　食べに　行った。

　よるは　ふだんは　あまり　見ない　テレビを　見たが、東京の　テレビの　チャンネルが　七つも　ある　ことを　はじめて　知った。チャンネルを　つぎつぎに　かえると、さわがしい　ショーや　さむらいの　時代げきや　ジョン・ウェインの　せいぶげきを　やっていた。えいせいちゅうけいで　パリや　ホンコンの　町を　見る　ことも　できた。3チャンネルでは　ベートーベンの　"第九"を　えんそうしていた。先日、なかむらさんが　「毎年、12月に　なると　日本かくちで　"第九"を　えんそうするんですよ。」と　言っていたが、おもしろい　国だ。

1月1日（木）はれ

　日本で　新年を　むかえた。町は　人も　車も　少なくて、たいへん　しずかだ。こうじょうも　会社も　休みなので、いつもは　よごれている　東京の　そらが、今日は　きれいで　きもちが　いい。近所の　店も　スーパーも　みんな

あけまして
おめでとう
ございます

一九九三年　元旦

休みだった。あの ラッシュアワーの サラリーマンや 学生は どこに 行っ
たのだろうか。

日本人の どうりょうや ともだちから ねんがじょうが とどいた。ぎょう
しゃからも 来た。いんさつの ものが 多いが、ふでで 書いた ものも あ
る。やはり うつくしい。もらった ねんがじょうは ほとんど 全部 くじつ
きである。

Wednesday, December 31st
Fair, later cloudy

Today is the (year's) final day. At the Ōno house next door, beginning in the morning, every member of the family did (some) cleaning up. Everybody washed (something)—the wall, the car, even the dog.

In the afternoon I wrote New Year's cards in Japanese, but they are probably difficult to read because of my poor handwriting. In the early evening we went to eat *soba* with the Tanakas.

(Later) in the evening, watching television, which I do not ordinarily see very often, I became aware for the first time that there are (as many as) seven TV channels in Tokyo. Switching channels one after another, I came across an uproarious show, a period *samurai* drama and a John Wayne western. By satellite relay (broadcast) I was able to see scenes in (places like) Paris and Hong Kong. On Channel 3 they were performing Beethoven's Ninth Symphony. The other day Nakamura told me, "Every year when December comes around Beethoven's Ninth Symphony is performed all over Japan." Interesting country!

Thursday, January 1
Fair

I salute the New Year in Japan! The city has few people or cars and is very quiet. Because factories and companies (are) on vacation Tokyo's usually dirty air is clean. (What a) good feeling. The neighborhood stores and the supermarket are all closed (too).

Where have those rush hour, white-collar workers and students gone, I wonder?

New Year's cards came from Japanese colleagues and friends. They came from business associates too. There were more printed ones but there were many written with a brush as well. Quite beautiful, as one would expect. Of the cards (I) received, almost all have lottery (numbers).

Vocabulary			
のち	**nochi**, later	ちゅうけい	**chūkei**, relay
くもり	**kumori**, cloudy	ベートーベン	**Bētōben**, Beethoven
おおみそか	**ō-misoka**, last day of year	だいく	**Dai-ku**, Ninth (Symphony)
へい	**hei**, wall, fence		
いぬ	**inu**, dog	えんそうする	**ensō suru**, perform
じ	**ji**, (hand)writing, character, letter	えんそう	**ensō**, performance, recital
へた（な）	**heta(na)**, poor, unskillful	まいとし	**maitoshi**, every year
～にくい	**-nikui**, difficult, awkward	せんじつ	**senjitsu**, the other day
いっか	**ikka**, family, household	かくち	**kakuchi**, all over, various districts
そば	**soba**, buckwheat noodles		
ふだん（は）	**fudan (wa)**, ordinarily	しんねん	**shinnen**, new year
チャンネル	**channeru**, channel	たいへん	**taihen**, very
も	**mo**, as many/much as	こうじょう	**kōjō**, factory
つぎつぎに	**tsugi-tsugi ni**, one after another, in turn	よごれる	**yogoreru**, be/become dirty

さわがしい	**sawagashii**, uproarious, noisy	そら	**sora**, sky
ショー	**shō**, show	きもち	**kimochi**, feeling
じだいげき	**jidai-geki**, period drama	ラッシュアワー	**rasshu awā**, rush hour
げき	**geki**, drama	サラリーマン	**sararīman**, white-collar (salaried) worker
せいぶげき	**seibu-geki**, western	（の）だろうか	**(no) darō ka**, I wonder
せいぶ	**seibu**, western part, the west	いんさつ	**insatsu**, printing
		ふで	**fude**, brush
えいせい ちゅ うけい	**eisei chūkei**, satellite relay (broadcast)	うつくしい	**utsukushii**, beautiful
		ほとんど	**hotondo**, almost
えいせい	**eisei**, satellite	くじ	**kuji**, lottery

GRAMMAR NOTES & LESSON OBJECTIVES

• Plain style

In this text, the plain forms of verbs have up to this point been used only in the middle of sentences. As sentence-final verbs, the plain forms are tied into, and are the main indicators of, the level of politeness. The plain style is used, for example, in a diary, a thesis or informal speech.

In informal speech there is a great variety of usage, related to the sex and age of the speakers and their relationships. Situation and topic may also be factors influencing the level of formality and politeness of forms and diction. The following chart summarizes these expressions, most of which have already been introduced.

desu/-masu style	plain style
1. Sumō o mita koto ga arimasu.	Sumō omita koto ga aru.
2. Kinō Ōsaka e ikimashita.	Kinō Ōsaka e itta.
3. Tanaka-san wa konai kamo shiremasen.	Tanaka-san wa konai kamo shirenai.
4. Ashita wa ame deshō.	Ashita wa ame darō.
5. Tōkyō wa omoshiroi machi desu.	Tōkyō wa omoshiroi machi da.
6. Kyō wa kimochi ga ii desu.	Kyō wa kimochi ga ii.

NOTES

1. **Ji ga heta da kara yominikui darō.**
   -nikui added to the **-masu** stem of a verb gives the meaning "difficult, hard," "awkward" and so on. In this context the translation can be "illegible." The opposite is **-yasui**, as in **yomiyasui**, "legible, easy to read." Both **-yasui** and **-nikui** are themselves inflected in just the same way as **-i** adjectives, e.g., **yominikuku nai**, "not hard to read."

2. **Tanaka-san ikka to soba o tabe ni itta.**
   Soba in many varieties is everyday fare in Japan. The buckwheat noodles prepared especially for New Year's Eve go by the name of **toshikoshi soba**, signifying the passing (**koshi**) of the year (**toshi**), thus by implication the imminent arrival of the New Year.

3. **Tōkyō no terebi no channeru ga nanatsu mo aru.**
   The particle **mo** here emphasizes the number of channels, Brown apparently not having realized how many there are. (Greater Tokyo also has several dozen cable channels and the number is on the increase.)
   ex. **Kaisha kara Narita Kūkō made kuruma de 2-jikan kakarimasu yo.** "By car, from the office to Narita Airport, it takes two hours."
   2-jikan mo kakaru n desu ka. "A full two hours?"

4. **Channeru o kaeru to . . . Jon Uein no seibu-geki o yatte ita.**
In addition to the **to . . . masu** pattern (p. 123) there is the **to . . . mashita** pattern meaning "A did X and happened to discover Y" or "X happened and then Y occurred."
ex. **Uketsuke no hito wa Yamamoto-san ga 6-ji ni kuru to, kasa o watashimashita.**
"When Yamamoto came at six, the receptionist handed him (his) umbrella."
In conversation, **yatte iru** is by far the most common way of saying something is being on TV, is being produced on stage and so on. If the time is the future, **yaru** is used.

5. **Ano rasshu awā no sararīman ya gakusei wa doko ni itta no darō ka.**
As noted in lesson 1 **ko, so, a** words are not limited to the tangible or what is immediately at hand. The expanded usage of **a** can denote "that which both you and I know about." In this sentence, **ano** underscores the unforgettableness of the rush hour subway experience.

6. **Moratta nengajō wa hotondo zembu kuji-tsuki de aru.**
Christmas cards are sent in Japan but in nowhere near the quantities of the more traditional New Year's cards (over 3 billion in one recent year). These regular size but specially printed postcards, bearing lottery numbers, go on sale at post offices in November and if mailed by the deadline (around December 20), are delivered on New Year's Day. The lottery is held on January 15—**Seijin no Hi**, "Coming-of-Age Day"—and the lucky winners receive things like bicycles or portable radios or consolation prizes of small panes of commemorative postage stamps.
The ending of this sentence, **de aru**, is the equivalent of **desu** and belongs to a bookish style of writing.

PRACTICE

KEY SENTENCES

1. きのうは いい てんきだったから、 ドライブに いった。
2. ジョンソンさんが はこを あけると、なかみは ギリチョコでした。

1. Yesterday was (such) fine weather I went for a drive.
2. When Johnson opened the box, the contents (turned out) to be *giri-choko*.

EXERCISES

I Practice the following patterns by changing verbs and adjectives as in the examples given.

A. *ex.* わたしは きょうとへ いきます。
→わたしは きょうとへ いく。
わたしは きょうとへ いかない。
わたしは きょうとへ いった。
わたしは きょうとへ いかなかった。

1. スミスさんと ダンスを します
2. たなかさんは 10じに きます
3. ジョンソンさんに あいます
4. ともだちと えいがを みます
5. ここに かぎが あります

B. *ex.* たなかさんは　いそがしいです。
　　→たなかさんは　いそがしい。
　　　たなかさんは　いそがしくない。
　　　たなかさんは　いそがしかった。
　　　たなかさんは　いそがしくなかった。

　　1. べんきょうは　たのしいです
　　2. くるまが　すくないです
　　3. あたまが　いいです
　　4. あの　レストランは　まずいです
　　5. つごうが　わるいです

C. *ex.* スミスさんは　げんきです。
　　→スミスさんは　げんきだ。
　　　スミスさんは　げんきでは　ない。
　　　スミスさんは　げんきだった。
　　　スミスさんは　げんきでは　なかった。

　　1. やまの　みずうみは　しずかです
　　2. スミスさんは　ワルツが　すきです
　　3. スミスさんは　りょうりが　じょうずです
　　4. デパートは　やすみです
　　5. やまもとさんは　パイロットです

D. *ex.* きのう　がっこうを　やすんだ。
　　→きのう　がっこうを　やすみました。

　　1. あした　ぜいむしょに　いかなければ　ならない
　　2. 6じに　うちに　かえる　ことが　できない
　　3. つきに　いった　ことが　ない
　　4. たいきんを　ひろった　ことが　ある
　　5. テニスを　したり　つりを　したり　した
　　6. たなかさんは　いくだろう
　　7. はやく　やすんだ　ほうが　いい
　　8. たなかさんは　スライドを　みていた
　　9. あしたは　ゆきかもしれない
　　10. まだ　ジョンソンさんに　あっていない

II Make dialogues by changing the underlined parts as in the examples given.

A. *ex.* **Q**：あの　ひとの　はなしかたは　どうですか。
     A：はやくて　ききにくいです。

1. この　しんぶん、　じが　ちいさい、よむ
2. あの　ひとの　せつめい、くどい、わかる
3. この　テープ、おとが　わるい、きく
4. なっとう、くさい、たべる
5. この　くすり、にがい、のむ

B. *ex.* **Q**：その　くつは　いかがですか。
     A：はきやすくて　きに　いっています。

1. この　アパート、すむ
2. その　ペン、かく
3. この　じしょ、ひく
4. その　スーツ、きる
5. あたらしい　ワープロ、つかう

III Practice the following pattern by changing the underlined parts.

ex. へやに　はいると　でんわが　なっていました。

1. まどを　あけました、すずしい　かぜが　はいってきました
2. そとに　でました、あめが　ふっていました
3. チャンネルを　かえました、ふるい　えいがを　やっていました
4. うちに　かえりました、ともだちが　まっていました
5. きんこを　あけました、なかは　からっぽでした

Vocabulary

ダンス	**dansu**, dance, dancing	はきやすい	**hakiyasui**, easy to put on
みずうみ	**mizuumi**, lake	はく	**haku**, put on, wear
ワルツ	**warutsu**, waltz		(shoes, pants, etc.)
パイロット	**pairotto**, pilot	～やすい	**-yasui**, easy to
ぜいむしょ	**zeimusho**, tax office	ひく	**hiku**, consult
しょ	**-sho**, office, bureau	スーツ	**sūtsu**, suit
くどい	**kudoi**, tedious, wordy, garrulous	なる	**naru**, ring
		かぜ	**kaze**, wind
なっとう	**nattō**, fermented soy-beans	そと	**soto**, outside, exterior, outer
くさい	**kusai**, smelly	きんこ	**kinko**, strong box, safe, vault
にがい	**nigai**, bitter		
		からっぽ	**karappo**, empty

1. おとこＡ：もう　あの　えいが　みた？
　　おとこＢ：ううん、まだ。きみは？
　　おとこＡ：うん、もう　みた。
　　おとこＢ：どうだった？
　　おとこＡ：あんまり　おもしろくなかった。

　　Man A:　Have you already seen that movie?
　　Man B:　Unh-unh, not yet. How about you?
　　Man A:　Um, I saw (it).
　　Man B:　How was it?
　　Man A:　Not very interesting.

2. おんな：もうすぐ　おしょうがつね。しごとは　いつまで？
　　おとこ：12がつ30にちまで。ねんまつは　いそがしくて　いやだ。
　　おんな：おしょうがつは　どっかに　いく？
　　おとこ：ううん、どこにも。しょうがつは　のんびりしたいね。

　　Woman:　New Year's will soon (be here), won't it? (*lit.* [Your] work [is] until when?)
　　Man:　　Until December 30. The end of the year is (so) busy. It's horrible!
　　Woman:　Are you going someplace for New Year's?
　　Man:　　No, nowhere. (I) want to take it easy.

Vocabulary

ううん	**ūn**, unh-unh, nope, no (informal)	おしょうがつ	**o-shōgatsu**, New Year's, January
きみ	**kimi**, you (informal male speech)	いや（な）	**iya(na)**, horrible, nasty, unwelcome
うん	**un**, um, un-huh, yeah (informal)	どっか	**dokka**, some-/anyplace (informal contraction of **doko ka**)
あんまり	**ammari**, not very (colloquial for **amari**)	のんびりする	**nombiri suru**, take it easy

QUIZ

I　Read this lessons's opening passage and answer the following questions.

　1. ブラウンさんは　おおみそかの　ゆうがた　だれと　なにを　たべに　いきましたか。
　2. 12がつには　にほんかくちで　ベートーベンの　"だいく"を　えんそうすると　ブラウンさんに　はなしたのは　だれですか。
　3. おしょうがつに　ブラウンさんの　きんじょの　みせは　あいていましたか。
　4. ブラウンさんは　だれから　ねんがじょうを　もらいましたか。
　5. ブラウンさんは　ふでで　かいた　ねんがじょうを　うつくしいと　おもっていますか。

II Read the following, supplying the appropriate words or word parts.

12がつ 31にち （すい）　　はれ　のち　くもり

　　きょうは　おおみそかだ。となりの　おおのさんの　うちでは　あさか
ら　かぞく　（　　）で　そうじを　して（　　）。みんなで　へいや
くるまや、そして　いぬ　（　　）　あらっていた。

　　ごごは　にほんごで　ねんがじょうを　（　　）が、じが　へただから、
よみ　（　　）だろう。ゆうがた　たなかさん　（　　）と　そばを
（　　）　いった。

1がつ　ついたち （もく）　　はれ

　　にほんで　しんねんを　むかえた。まちは　ひとも　くるまも　すくな
く　（　　）、たいへん　（　　）。こうじょうも　かいしゃも　やすみ
（　　）、いつもは　（　　）とうきょうの　そらが、きょうは　きれいで、
（　　）。きんじょの　みせも　スーパーも　みんな　やすみ　（　　）。
（　　）ラッシュアワーの　サラリーマンや　がくせいは　どこに　（　　）
のだろうか。

　　にほんじんの　どうりょうや　ともだち　（　　）　ねんがじょうが　と
どいた。いんさつの　ものが　（　　）が、（　　）で　かいた　ものも
ある。やはり　（　　）。もらった　ねんがじょうは　（　　）　ぜんぶ
くじつきである。

III Complete the questions so that they fit the answers.

1. （　　）に　でかける？
　　9じに　でる。
2. きのうの　えいが　（　　）だった？
　　あんまり　おもしろくなかった。
3. （　　）に　すみたい？
　　あんぜんな　ところが　いい。
4. かれは　（　　）くる？
　　あした　くるだろう。
5. （　　）と　いっしょに　いく？
　　ひとりで　いく。

IV Complete the sentences with the appropriate form of the words indicated.

1. この　にくは　（　　）、（　　）やすい。（やわらかい、たべる）
2. かれの　せつめいは　（　　）、（　　）にくい。（ふくざつ、わかる）
3. この　テープレコーダーは　（　　）、（　　）にくい。（ふるい、つかう）
4. まどを　（　　）と、すずしい　かぜが　（　　）きた。（あける、はい
　　る）
5. ことしは　（　　）、ねんがじょうを　ぜんぜん　（　　）ことが　で
　　きなかった。（いそがしい、かく）
6. へやが　（　　）、きもちが　いい。（きれい）

LESSON 18 BIRTHDAY FLOWERS

Mr. Johnson wants to find out whether giving flowers to a woman friend is an acceptable practice in Japan.

ジョンソン：すずきさん、ちょっと。

すずき：　何でしょう。

ジョンソン：日本の　しゅうかんを　知らないので　おしえてくださいません
　　　　　か。女の　友だちの　たんじょう日に　花を　あげようと　思うん
　　　　　ですが、おかしくないですか。とくべつの　女友だちでは　ないん
　　　　　ですが・・・。

すずき：　おかしくないですよ。だいじょうぶです。ジョンソンさん、たんじ
　　　　　ょう日いわいの　デートですか。いいですねえ。

ジョンソン：ううん、まあ。

At the florist.

ジョンソン：友だちに　花を　おくろうと　思うんですが、おねがいできます
　　　　　か。

花屋：　　はい。おとどけですね。できます。何日の　おとどけでしょうか。

ジョンソン：あした　とどけてください。

花屋：　　かしこまりました。

ジョンソン：この　ばらは　いくらですか。

花屋：　　1本　250円です。

ジョンソン：じゃ、これを　20本　おねがいします。たんじょう日の　プレゼン
　　　　　トに　する　つもりですから、この　カードを　つけて　とどけて
　　　　　くれませんか。

> 田中けい子さま
> 　　おたんじょう日　おめでとうございます。
> 　　　　　　　　　　マイケル

花屋：　　はい。おとどけ先は　都内ですか。

ジョンソン：いいえ、よこはまです。

花屋：　　送料が　500円　かかりますが、よろしいですか。

ジョンソン：ええ。

花屋： 　　では、こちらに　おきゃくさまの、そして　こちらに　おとどけ先
　　　　の　ご住所、お電話番号、お名前を　お書きください。

Johnson: Say, Mr. Suzuki.
Suzuki: Yes, what is it?
Johnson: Since I don't know Japanese customs, would you please tell me (something)? I'm thinking of giving flowers to a woman friend for (her) birthday. It wouldn't be strange, would it? She's not a special girl friend.
Suzuki: It's not strange. It's (quite) OK. (Are you going to have) a congratulatory birthday date, Mr. Johnson? (I'm jealous.)
Johnson: Umm well . . .

Johnson: I'm thinking of sending flowers to a friend. Can you take care of it?
Florist: Yes, of course. Delivered, you say? We can do that. What's the deliver day (you have in mind)?
Johnson: Please deliver (them) tomorrow.
Florist: Certainly.
Johnson: How much are these roses?
Florist: ¥250 each.
Johnson: All right. I'd like twenty of them. (They're) meant to be a birthday gift, so would you include this card and deliver (them)?

> Miss Tanaka Keiko,
> 　　　Congratulations on your birthday.
> 　　　　　　　　Michael

Florist: Yes, of course. Is the person their being delivered to in Tokyo Metropolitan Prefecture?
Johnson: No, Yokohama.
Florist: There'll be a ¥500 delivery charge. Is that all right?
Johnson: OK.
Florist: Please write your name, address and telephone number here and the recipient's name, address and telephone number here.

Vocabulary

～（よ）う	**-(y)ō** (volitional form)	おとどけさき	**o-todoke-saki**, con- signee, destination
おかしい	**okashii**, strange, funny		
とくべつの/な	**tokubetsu no/na**, special extraordinary	とない	**tonai**, within (Tokyo) Prefecture
いわい	**iwai**, congratulations, celebration	と	**to**, metropolitan pre- fecture
デート	**dēto**, date	そうりょう	**sōryō**, delivery charge, postage
つもり	**tsumori**, intention, pur- pose	よろしい	**yoroshii**, all right
つける	**tsukeru**, include (*lit.* at- tach)		

GRAMMAR & LESSON OBJECTIVES

• **-(y)ō**, volitional verb ending
Tomodachi ni hana o ageyō to omou n desu ga, . . .

Verbs ending in **-(y)ō** (plain form) and **-mashō** are in the volitional form and, in general, are translatable by "I'll," "we'll" or "let's." As in other cases the usage of plain forms indicates familiar speech.

ex. **Takushī de ikō ka.** "Shall we go by taxi?"

Chikai kara arukō yo. "Since (it's) close, let's walk."

As for the volitional form of Regular I verbs, note **arukō** in the example and keep in mind the correlation with the **a, i, u, e, o** vowel order.

	-masu form	dict. form	volitional form
Reg. I	okurimasu kakimasu aimasu	okuru kaku au	okurō kakō aō
Reg. II	agemasu todokemasu mimasu	ageru todokeru miru	ageyō todokeyō miyō
Irreg.	kimasu shimasu	kuru suru	koyō shiyō

- **tsumori**

Tanjōbi no purezento ni suru tsumori desu.

Tsumori is actually a noun and is much used in this pattern to show intent or purpose.

ex. 1. **Kyō Yoshida-san ga kimasu ga, awanai tsumori desu.** "Mr. Yoshida is coming today, but I don't plan to see him."

2. **Ashita Tōkyō ni kaerimasu ka.** "Will you go back to Tokyo tomorrow?"

Ee, sono tsumori desu. "Yes, I intend to."

- Polite expressions

The polite expressions in this lesson can be compared with others previously introduced.

Yoroshii desú ka is the same as **ii desu ka** but is more polite. **O-kaki kudasai** is the same meaning as **Kaite kudasai** but is more polite even though the tone is rather businesslike. (See pp. 28, 29.)

O-todoke desu ka. "Is it to be delivered?" In this case, too, prefacing the verb with the honorific **o-** is one way of expressing politeness or respect.

ex. 1. **Itsu o-kaeri desu ka.** "When are (you) coming back?"

2. **Hayashi-san wa taihen o-yorokobi deshita.** "Mrs. Hayashi was very pleased."

Oshiete kudasaimasen ka. "Would you please tell me?" **-te kudasaimasen ka** has the same meaning as **-te kuremasen ka** but is more polite.

PRACTICE

KEY SENTENCES

1. まいにち にほんごを べんきょうしようと おもいます。
2. あした はれたら、テニスを する つもりです。

1. I intend to study Japanese every day.
2. If it clears up tomorrow, (I) plan to play tennis.

Vocabulary

はれる **hareru**, clear up

EXERCISES

I Verbs: Study the examples, convert into the volitional form, and memorize.

ex. かく→かこう   たべる→たべよう   くる→こよう
　　いう→いおう   おきる→おきよう   する→しよう

1. かえる （return）	5. やすむ	9. みる
2. あずかる	6. おぼえる	10. かりる
3. およぐ	7. あずける	11. かってくる
4. えらぶ	8. みせる	12. りょうりする

II Make dialogues by changing the underlined parts as in the examples given.

A. *ex.* **Q**：だいがくに　いきますか。
　　　A：ええ、いこうと　おもいます。

    1. たばこを　やめる
    2. この　しゅうまつは　あそぶ
    3. しゃちょうに　そうだんする
    4. おかねを　かりる
    5. ともだちに　こどもを　あずける
    6. あさ　はやく　くる

B. *ex.* **Q**：かいしゃを　やめて　なにを　するんですか。
　　　A：ひとりで　しごとを　はじめる　つもりです。

    1. だいがくに　のこります、けいえいがくを　けんきゅうします
    2. ハワイに　いきます、およいだり　にっこうよくを　したり
    　します
    3. くにに　かえります、しょうらいの　ことを　かんがえます
    4. だいがくを　やめます、デザイナーに　なります

C. *ex.* **Q**：けっこん　しないんですか。
　　　A：ええ、けっこんしない　つもりです。

    1. もう　たばこを　すいません
    2. もう　アイスクリームを　たべません
    3. だれにも　みせません
    4. カメラを　もっていきません

D. *ex.* **Q**：すみませんが、しおを　とってくださいませんか。
　　　A：はい。

1. いすを　はこぶのを　てつだう
2. シャッターを　おす
3. さきに　いく
4. ここで　まっている
5. しずかに　する
6. クーラーを　よわく　する

Vocabulary

かりる	**kariru**, borrow, rent	にっこう	**nikkō**, sunshine
りょうりする	**ryōrisuru**, cook	しょうらい	**shōrai**, future
りょうり	**ryōri**, food	デザイナー	**dezainā**, designer
のこる	**nokoru**, remain, be left, linger	もっていく	**motte iku**, take
		しお	**shio**, salt
けいえいがく	**keiei-gaku**, business administration	シャッター	**shattā**, shutter
		よわい	**yowai**, weak, faint, delicate
にっこうよくを　する	**nikkōyoku o suru**, sunbathe		
にっこうよく	**nikkōyoku**, sunbathing, sunbath		

SHORT DIALOGUE

かちょう：かえりに　どう？　いっぱい　のもう。
おがわ：　きょうは　かないが　かぜを　ひいているので・・・。
かちょう：ちょっとなら　いいだろう。
おがわ：　いえ、やっぱり　だめなんです。
かちょう：そうか。じゃ、あきらめよう。

Section Chief: On the way home shall we have a drink?
Ogawa:　　　My wife has a cold today.
Section Chief: If it's just a short one, it'll be OK (I think).
Ogawa:　　　No, it's really out of the question.
Section Chief: Is it now? Oh well then, I give up.

Vocabulary

そうか	**sō ka = sō desu ka** (informal)	あきらめる	**akirameru**, give up, be resigned

QUIZ

I　Read this lessons's opening dialogue and answer the following questions.

1. ジョンソンさんは　おんなの　ともだちへの　プレゼントについて　どうして　すずきさんに　そうだんしましたか。

2. ジョンソンさんは　だれに　プレゼントを　おくろうと　おもっていますか。

3. ジョンソンさんが かった ばらは 20ぽんで いくらですか。

4. けいこさんは どこに すんでいるでしょうか。

II Convert the following verbs into their volitional form.

1. はなす　　　4. やめる　　　7. わかれる　　　10. まつ

2. とどける　　5. のぼる　　　8. はらう　　　　11. デイトする

3. あう　　　　6. あるく　　　9. はっぴょうする　12. もってくる

III Complete the sentences with the appropriate form of the verbs indicated.

1. なにを （　　） いるんですか。
   たなの うえの はこを （　　）と おもうんですが、てが （　　）
   んです。（します、とります、とどきません）

2. どんな テープレコーダーを （　　） つもりですか。
   ちいさくて、おとが いい テープレコーダーを （　　）と おもう
   んですが、どれが いいでしょうか。（かいます、かいます）

3. いまから ゆうびんきょくへ （　　）と おもうんですが、なにか
   ようじが ありませんか。
   すみませんが、この てがみを （　　）くださいませんか。（いってき
   ます、だします）

4. ほんとうに こいびとと （　　）んですか。
   ええ、もう （　　） つもりです。 （　　）ば、また けんかしま
   すから。（わかれました、あいません、あいます）

5. にほんごの べんきょうを （　　）と おもうんですが、てきとうな
   がっこうを （　　）くださいませんか。（はじめます、おしえます）

IV Choose a sentence appropriate to the situation described.

A. Congratulate a friend for passing his examination.

1. ごうかくを いわいます。

2. ごうかく おめでとうございます。

3. ふごうかくで、ざんねんでした。

B. You want to ask your section chief if it's all right to call him very late tomorrow evening.

1. あしたの ばん おそく おでんわくださいませんか。

2. あしたの ばん おそく かえってから でんわする。

3. あしたの ばん おそく でんわを しても よろしいですか。

C. On the phone you ask his wife what time an acquaintance of yours will get home.

1. ごしゅじんは なんじごろ かえりましたか。

2. ごしゅじんは なんじごろ おかえりでしょうか。

3. しゅじんは なんじごろ かえる つもりですか。

D. You answer a question by saying you really do intend to quit your job.

1. はい、ほんとうに　やめる　つもりです。
2. はい、たぶん　やめようと　おもいます。
3. はい、たぶん　やめるだろうと　おもいます。

V Answer the following questions.

1. あなたは　あした　なにを　しようと　おもっていますか。
2. にほんごの　べんきょうが　おわったら、にほんの　かいしゃで　はたらく　つもりですか。
3. あなたは　せかいじゅうを　りょこうしたいと　おもっていますか。
4. あなたの　らいしゅうの　よていを　はなしてください。

Mr. Chang and his neighbor Daisuke go for a walk together.

チャン：　あれは　何ですか。

だいすけ：都立の　図書館です。

チャン：　都立の　図書館は　東京都民しか　入れませんか。外国人も　りょうできますか。

だいすけ：ええ、もちろんです。だれでも　入れますよ。それに　チャンさんは　東京都民でしょう。あそこは　自分で　本を　手に　とって　見られますから、とても　りようしやすいですよ。

チャン：　それは　いいですね。ぼくは　カードを　見て　えらぶのは　にがてなんです。

だいすけ：でも　チャンさんは　かんじが　読めるでしょう。

チャン：　ええ、いみは　わかります。でも、ぼくは　自分で　本を　見ながら　えらべる　図書館が　好きなんです。

だいすけ：ちょっと　ふべんな　所に　あるけど　ひろいし　しずかだし、いいですよ。

チャン：　本を　かりたり　コピーしたり　する　ことも　できますか。

だいすけ：ええ、てつづきを　すれば　かりられます。ぼくも　今　2さつ　かりています。じしょとか　きちょうな　本とか、かりられない　ものも　あるけれど。

チャン：　新聞や　ざっしも　かりられますか。

だいすけ：かりられないけど、コピーを　たのめます。これから　いっしょに　行きませんか。2、3分で　行けますよ。

Chang:　　What's that?

Daisuke: It's a metropolitan library.

Chang:　　Can only residents of Tokyo Metropolis go into metropolitan libraries? Can a foreigner use (them) too?

Daisuke: Yes, of course. Anyone can go in. Besides, aren't you a resident of Tokyo? You yourself can get books and look at them, so it's very easy to use.

Chang:　　That's nice. Choosing books by looking through (the card catalogue) is difficult for me.

Daisuke: But I suppose you can read kanji, can't you?

Chang:　　Yes. I understand meanings. But I like libraries where I myself can look at the books and choose.

Daisuke: It's in a slightly inconvenient location, but it's roomy and quiet, so it's a pleasant (place).

Chang:　　Can you borrow books and make photocopies?

Daisuke: Yes. If you go through the formalities, you can borrow books. I have two borrowed

144

books now. Things like dictionaries and rare books can't be borrowed, however.

Chang: Can you borrow newspapers and magazines?

Daisuke: You can't borrow them but you can ask for photocopies. Shall we go (there) now? We can get there in a couple of minutes.

Vocabulary

だいすけ	**Daisuke** (male given name)	にがて	**nigate**, difficult, poor at
		よめる	**yomeru**, can read
とりつ	**toritsu**, metropolitan	いみ	**imi**, meaning
とみん	**tomin**, resident/citizen of Tokyo Metropolis	えらべる	**eraberu**, can choose
		けど	**kedo**, but, however
～しか～ない	**shika . . . nai**, only	てつづき	**tetsuzuki**, formality, procedure
はいれる	**haireru**, can go in		
がいこくじん	**gaikokujin**, foreigner	かりられる	**karirareru**, can borrow
りようする	**riyō suru**, make use of, take advantage of	～とか～とか	**toka . . . toka**, things like/such as . . . and
もちろん	**mochiron**, of course	きちょう（な）	**kichō(na)**, rare, valuable
だれでも	**dare demo**, anyone, everyone, someone	けれど	**keredo**, but, however
		たのめる	**tanomeru**, can ask
てに とる	**te ni toru**, get, take in one's hands	いける	**ikeru**, get to, reach, can go

GRAMMAR & LESSON OBJECTIVES

- Potential form of verbs

Gaikokujin mo riyō dekimasu ka.

Dare demo hairemasu.

Ano toshokan de hon ga kariraremasu.

2, 3-pun de ikemasu.

Potentiality can be expressed by the verb **dekiru** and the pattern **koto ga dekiru**. (See the first volume for the first and p. 28 for the latter.) In addition many verbs have a potential form made by conjugation. It will be noted that in terms of pronunciation, the final **u** of Regular I verb is replaced by **eru**, for example, **yomu → yomeru**, "can read," "be readable." And **erabu → eraberu**, "can choose," "can be chosen." (Although it is technically correct to call **yomeru** and **eraberu** dictionary forms, in the great majority of cases this form does not appear in bilingual dictionaries, since the verbs are made by regular transformations of other verbs.)

I Regular I

	-nai	-masu	conditional	-te	-ta
yomeru eraberu	yomenai erabenai	yomemasu erabemasu	yomereba erabereba	yomete erabete	yometa erabeta

Potential verbs conjugate the same as Regular II verbs but have no volitional form.

Other examples: **iku → ikeru, hanasu → hanaseru, kaeru → kaereru, okuru → okureru, kaku → kakeru, hairu → haireru**

The following sentences compare the meanings of the verb and its potential form:

ex. 1. **Chan-san wa toshokan ni hairirmasu.** "Chang enters the library."

2. **Chan-san wa toshokan ni hairemasu.** "Chang can enter the library."

For Regular II verbs add **-rareru** to the stem of **-nai** form as, for example, **minai → mirareru**, "can see," "can be seen" and **karinai → karirareru**, "can borrow," "can be borrowed." The Irregular **kuru** becomes **korareru**, "can come" and **suru** is replaced by **dekiru**.

II Regular II and Irregular

	-nai	-masu	conditional	-te	-ta
mirareru karirareru	mirarenai karirarenai	miraremasu kariraremasu	mirarereba karirarereba	mirarete karirarete	mirareta karirareta
korareru dekiru	korarenai dekinai	koraremasu dekimasu	korarereba dekireba	korarete dekite	korareta dekita

Other examples: **taberu** → **taberareru, todokeru** → **todokerareru, iru** → **irareru**

suru → **dekiru:** *ex.* **Gaikokujin mo riyō shimasu.** "Foreigners use (it) too."
Gaikokujin mo riyō dekimasu. "Foreigners can use (it) too."
The topic or subject of a potential verb can be either animate or inanimate. For example,
Kono naifu wa yoku kiremasu. "This knife cuts well."
ex. 1. **Sumisu-san wa kanji ga yomemasu.** "Smith can read Sino-Japanese characters."
    2. **Kono ji wa totemo chiisakute yomemasen** means "the letters are unreadable."
Potential verbs have customarily taken the particle **ga**, but recently **o** has also come into use.
ex. 1. **Chan-san wa kanji ga/o yomemasu.** "Chang can read Sino-Japanese characters."
    2. **Hon ga/o kariraremasu.** "You can borrow books."
    3. **Kopī ga/o tanomemasu.** "(You) can ask for copies."
When it comes to a choice between the potential form and **koto ga dekiru**, it can be said that the former, being slightly shorter, is often preferred. **Chan-san wa toshokan ni hairu koto ga dekimasu**, although grammatically correct, sounds a bit stilted. Still the forms are interchangeable and it is not necessary to be overly cautious concerning the differences between them.
ex. 1. **Sumisu-san wa shimbun ga yomemasu.** "Smith can read a (Japanese) newspaper."
    2. **Toshokan ni ikeba, jūnen mae no shimbun o yomu koto ga dekimasu.** "If (you) go to the library, (you) can read newspapers from ten years ago."

NOTES

1. **Tōkyō tomin shika hairemasen ka.**
   Shika with a negative means "only," "merely," emphasizing that besides X there's nothing else. This contrasts with the usage of **mo** to emphasize how many or much. (See p. 131.)
   ex. 1. **Saifu no naka ni 2000-en shika arimasen.** "I only have ¥2000 (in my purse)."
       2. **Kyōto ni shika ikimasen deshita.** "I visited Kyoto only."

2. **Demo Chan-san wa kanji ga yomeru deshō.**
   Deshō/deshō when used like this normally have a rising tone and imply, "I suppose . . . Aren't I right?"

3. **Jisho toka kichōna hon toka . . .**
   The particle **toka** is repeated as a colloquial way of mentioning or suggesting examples.

4. **kedo** and **keredo**
   Chotto fubenna tokoro ni aru kedo.
   Karirarenai mono mo aru keredo.
   Both these forms are colloquial shortenings of **keredomo**, "although," "but." In some contexts they are comparable to the particle **ga** and convey no particular meaning. (See the first volume, p. 89.)
   ex. **Moshi moshi, Jonson desu ga/kedo Keiko-san wa irasshaimasu ka.**

5. **2,3-pun de ikemasu yo.**
   One way to indicate the time or money required is with the pattern **de** plus potential form. In meaning, this sentence forms a pair with **2,3-pun shika kakarimasen**, rather than **2,3-pun kakarimasu.**
   ex. **Shīzun-ofu niwa 4000-en de kaemasu yo.** "In the off-season (it) can be bought for ¥4000."

PRACTICE

KEY SENTENCES

1. ブラウンさんは　にほんごが　はなせます。
2. てつづきを　すれば、だれでも　ほんが　かりられます。
3. わたなべさんは　やさいしか　たべません。
4. あなたも　いっしょに　いくでしょう。
   ええ、いきます。

1. Mr. Brown can speak Japanese.
2. If they go through the formalities, anybody can borrow books.
3. Watanabe eats only vegetables.
4. You are going with us, aren't you?
   Yes, I'm going.

EXERCISES

I Verbs: Study the examples, convert into the potential form, and memorize.

   ex. かく →かける　　　いる→　　いられる　　　くる→こられる
        かけない　　　　　　いられない　　　　　　こられない
    かう →かえる　　　おぼえる→おぼえられる　する→できる
       かえない　　　　　　おぼえられない　　　　できない

1. きく	5. はいる	9. つとめる
2. とぶ	6. すすめる	10. つうきんする
3. おす	7. おしえる	11. よんでくる
4. あらう	8. おきる	12. れんしゅうする

II Make dialogues by changing the underlined parts as in the examples given.

  A. *ex.* **Q**：この　かんじが　よめますか。
     A：はい、よめます。

      1. がいこくごで　うたを　うたう
      2. あした　あさ　7じに　でかける
      3. がいこくじんの　なまえを　すぐ　おぼえる
      4. にほんごで　あんないする

  B. *ex.* **Q**：えきまえに　くるまが　とめられますか。
     A：いいえ、とめられません。

      1. すぐ　しりょうを　あつめる
      2. あの　ひとの　はなしを　しんじる
      3. この　できごとを　わすれる

4. 100メートルを　10びょうで　はしる

C. *ex.* **Q**：ひらがなも　かんじも　かけますか。
　　　A：ひらがなは　かけますが、かんじは　かけません。

　　1. フランスご、ドイツご、はなす
　　2. じてんしゃ、オートバイ、のる
　　3. さかな、にく、たべる
　　4. たなかさん、やまもとさん、くる
　　5. テニス、ゴルフ、する

D. *ex.* **Q**：なんじごろ　かえれますか。
　　　A：8じまでに　かえれると　おもいます。

　　1. なんメートル　およぐ、200メートルも　およがない
　　2. だれが　なおす、たなかさんが　なおす
　　3. だれに　あずける、だれにも　あずけない
　　4. いつ　たなかさんに　あう、らいしゅうの　もくようびに　あう
　　5. どこで　かりる、としょかんで　かりる

E. *ex.* **Q**：なんでも　たべますか。
　　　A：やさいしか　たべません。

　　1. だれでも　りようできる、20さい　いじょうの　ひと
　　2. いま　おかねを　たくさん　もっている、500えん
　　3. おおぜい　きた、すこし
　　4. おこさんは　なんにん　いる、ひとり
　　5. ゆっくり　ねむれた、3じかん

F. *ex.* **Q**：なんでも　うっていますか。
　　　A：かぐとか　だいどころようひんとか、うっていない　ものも　あります。

　　1. できる、きかく、せんでん
　　2. てに　はいる、アフリカの　しんぶん、なんべいの　ざっし
　　3. そろっている、ふとん、もうふ
　　4. ある、てぶくろ、マフラー

G. *ex.* だいすけ：チャンさんは　かんじが　よめるでしょう？
　　　チャン：　ええ、よめます。

1. はじめてです
2. ABCの　しゃいんです
3. たべません
4. なっとうが　すきです
5. つごうが　いいです
6. こどもの　とき　おおきかったです

H. ex. **Q**: てつづきは　いつが　いいですか。
   A: いつでも　いいです。

1. りょうり、なに
2. ホテル、　どこ
3. やくそく、なんじ
4. むかえに　いく　ひと、だれ

I. ex. **Q**: これを　つかっても　いいですか。
   A: どうぞ、どれでも　すきな　ものを　つかってください。

1. ともだちを　つれてくる、だれ、すきな　ひとを
2. ここに　すわる、どこ、いい　ところに
3. あした　くる、いつ、ごつごうの　いい　じかんに
4. いろいろな　ものを　かう、なん、ひつような　ものを

Vocabulary

がいこくご	**gaikoku-go**, foreign language	てに　はいる	**te ni hairu**, be obtainable, come into one's hands
しんじる	**shinjiru**, believe	アフリカ	**Afurika**, Africa
できごと	**dekigoto**, happening, affair	なんべい	**Nambei**, South America
メートル	**mētoru**, meter	ふとん	**futon**, bedding, mattress, quilt
びょう	**-byō**, second (counter)	もうふ	**mōfu**, blanket
はしる	**hashiru**, run	てぶくろ	**tebukuro**, glove, mitten
じてんしゃ	**jitensha**, bicycle	しゃいん	**shain**, company employee
オートバイ	**ōtobai**, motorcycle	つれてくる	**tsurete kuru**, bring (a person)
ようひん	**yōhin**, utensil, supplies, article	つれる	**tsureru**, bring, take, be accompanied by
きかく	**kikaku**, planning, plan		
せんでん	**senden**, publicity, propaganda, advertising		

SHORT DIALOGUE

A: ちょっと　あついんですが、まどを　あけてくださいませんか。
B: この　ビルは　まどが　あかないんですよ。

A：えっ、じゃ、かじの　ときは　どう　するんですか。
B：ろうかの　つきあたりの　ひじょうぐちから　にげられますよ。

A: It's a little too hot. Would you mind opening the window?
B: The windows of this building can't be opened.
A: What? Well, what'll happen in case of fire?
B: We can escape through the emergency exit at the end of the hall.

Vocabulary			
かじ	**kaji**, fire	ひじょうぐち	**hijō-guchi**, emergency exit
ろうか	**rōka**, hall		
つきあたり	**tsukiatari**, end, foot (of passage, street)	にげる	**nigeru**, escape

QUIZ

I　Read this lessons's opening dialogue and answer the following questions.

1. とりつの　としょかんは　とうきょうとみんしか　りようできませんか。
2. チャンさんは　どんな　としょかんが　すきですか。
3. この　としょかんは　ひろくて　しずかですか。
4. ほんを　かりたい　ひとは　どう　すれば　かりられますか。

II　Put the appropriate words in the parentheses.

1. かいいんで　なければ、その　スポーツクラブを　りようできませんか。
   いいえ、だれ（　　）　りようできます。
2. ゆうべは　4じかん（　　）　ねむれませんでした。
3. ここ（　　）　ぎんざ（　　）　どのぐらい　かかりますか。
   15ふん（　　）　いけますよ。
4. くるま（　　）　きゅうしゅう（　　）　まわりましたか。
5. らいねんの　やすみも　ヨーロッパへ　いこうか。
   らいねんは　ちゅうごく（　　）　アフリカ（　　）、ほかの　ところへ
   いきたい。

III　Without changing the level of politeness, convert the following verbs into the potential form.

1. およぎます　　4. やくそくしません　7. うたう　　　10. きる（wear）
2. かきません　　5. いいません　　　　8. あわない　　11. もってくる
3. はなします　　6. ねます　　　　　　9. わすれない　12. やすまない

IV　Complete the questions so that they fit the answers.

1. （　　）　およげますか。
   100メートルぐらい　およげます。
2. つぎの　かいぎは　（　　）が　いいですか。
   いつでも　けっこうです。

3. （　　）に　いけば　かえますか。
　　デパートで　うっていますよ。
4. （　　）　いっしょに　いけないんですか。
　　むすめの　たんじょうびなので、かえらなければ　ならないんです。

V　Complete the sentences with the polite-level potential form of the verbs indicated.

1. ここは　ちゅうしゃきんしなので、くるまが　（　　）。（とめない）
2. スキーに　いって　けがを　したので、（　　）。（あるかない）
3. 1ねんに　なんにち　かいしゃを　（　　）か。（やすむ）
4. らいねん　（　　）か。（そつぎょうする）
5. いますぐ　（　　）か。（でかける）
6. ホワイトさんは　みそしるが　（　　）か。（つくる）
7. うけつけに　ある　でんわは　（　　）か。（つかう）
8. どこに　いけば　おいしい　すしが　（　　）か。（たべる）
9. しけんに　ごうかくしなければ、この　だいがくに　（　　）。（はいらない）
10. テレビで　にほんの　ふるい　えいがが　（　　）。（みる）

VI　Answer the following questions.

1. あなたは　フランスごが　はなせますか。
2. あなたは　かんじが　よめますか。よめる　ばあいは　いくつぐらい　よめますか。
3. あなたは　ゆうべ　よく　ねむれましたか。
4. あなたは　にほんの　うたが　うたえますか。
5. あなたは　にほんごで　てがみが　かけますか。

LESSON 20 CHERRY BLOSSOMS

桜前線と いう ことばを 聞いた ことが ありますか。

日本の 春を だいひょうする 花は 何と いっても 桜でしょう。人々は 春が 近づくと、桜の さく 日を よそくしたり、友だちと お花見に 行く 日を やくそくしたり します。

ところで、日本は 南から 北へ 長く のびている しま国です。きゅうし ゅう、しこく、ほんしゅう、ほっかいどうでは ずいぶん きおんの さが あ りますから、桜の さく 日も 少しずつ ことなっています。きゅうしゅうの 南部では、3月の 末ごろ さきますが、ほっかいどうでは 5月の はじめご ろ さきます。このように やく 40日も かかって、日本れっとうを 南から 北へ 花が さいていく ようすを 線で あらわした ものが 桜前線です。 桜前線の ほかに うめ前線や つつじ前線などの 花前線も あります。うめ は 桜より ずっと 早く きゅうしゅうを 出発しますが、ほっかいどうに

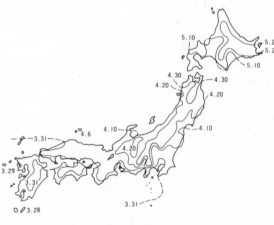

桜 前 線
（そめいよしのの 開花日）

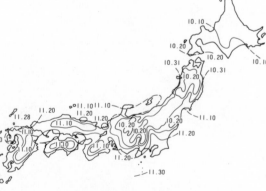

紅 葉 前 線
（いろはかえでの 紅葉日）

152

つくのは　だいたい　桜と　同じころです。ですから、5月の　上じゅんから
中じゅんに　かけて　ほっかいどうへ　りょこうすれば、一度に　春の　花が
見られるのです。これとは　はんたいに、秋に　なると、こうよう前線は　山の
木々を　あかや　きいろに　そめながら、北から　南へ　すすんでいきます。
　人々は　春には　お花見、秋には　もみじがりなどを　して、きせつを　たの
しみます。

Have you heard the term *sakura zensen*? The flower typifying spring in Japan is, undoubtedly, *sakura*, the "cherry" blossom. As spring approaches, people predict the day the cherry (trees) will blossom and agree with friends on a day to go blossom viewing.

Japan is an island country extending in a long (line) from south to north. Kyushu, Shikoku, Honshu, Hokkaido—there's quite a difference in temperatures, so the day the cherries blossom differs somewhat too. In the southern part of Kyushu the cherries bloom around the end of March, but in Hokkaido they bloom around the beginning of May. Thus, the cherry blossom "front," a line starting in the south of the Japanese archipelago and (moving) north, shows the state of the cherry trees' blossoming. This takes as long as forty days.

In addition to the cherry blossom front there are other flower fronts, such as the apricot blossom front and the azalea front. Apricots start in Kyushu a whole lot earlier than the cherry trees, but they reach Hokkaido at almost the same time (as the cherries). Therefore, if (you) travel to Hokkaido in early or mid May, (you) can see (various) spring flowers at the same time. On the other hand, when it gets to be autumn the autumn leaves front makes its way from north to south, dying the trees in the mountains crimson or yellow.

With flower viewing in the spring, maple (leaf) excursions in the autumn and so on, people enjoy each season (in turn).

Vocabulary

さくらぜんせん	**sakura zensen**, cherry blossom front	さいていく	**saite iku**, be (in the process of) blooming
ぜんせん	**zensen**, front	ようす	**yōsu**, state, circumstance, appearance
ことば	**kotoba**, word	せん	**sen**, line
だいひょうする	**daihyō suru**, typify, represent	あらわす	**arawasu**, show, express
だいひょう	**daihyō**, representation	～の　ほかに	**no hoka ni**, in addition to
なんといっても	**nan to itte mo**, undoubtedly	うめ	**ume**, apricot
ひとびと	**hito-bito**, people	つつじ	**tsutsuji**, azalea
ちかづく	**chikazuku**, approach	などの	**nado no**, such as
よそくする	**yosoku suru**, predict	など	**nado**, and so forth (particle)
よそく	**yosoku**, prediction, estimate	ずっと	**zutto**, a whole lot, all the time/way
おはなみ	**o-hanami**, (cherry) blossom viewing	だいたい	**daitai**, almost
ところで	**tokorode**, well, incidentally	ですから	**desukara**, therefore (same as **dakara**)
のびる	**nobiru**, extend, stretch, postpone	じょうじゅん	**jōjun**, first third of month
		ちゅうじゅん	**chūjun**, second third of month
しまぐに	**shima-guni**, island country	～から～にかけて	**kara ... ni kakete**, from ... to
しこく	**Shikoku** (place name)	こうよう	**kōyō**, autumn (*lit.* "red") leaves
ほんしゅう	**Honshū** (place name)		

ずいぶん	**zuibun**, quite	きぎ	**ki-gi**, trees
きおん	**kion**, (air) temperature	あか	**aka**, red
さ	**sa**, difference	きいろ	**kiiro**, yellow
ことなる	**kotonaru**, differ, be different	そめる	**someru**, dye
なんぶ	**nambu**, southern part	すすんでいく	**susunde iku**, be advancing
すえ	**sue**, end	もみじがり	**momiji-gari**, maple leaf excursion
はじめ	**hajime**, beginning, first		
このように	**kono yō ni**, thus, in this way	もみじ	**momiji**, maple
〜よう	**yō**, way, manner	かり/がり	**kari/-gari**, excursion, hunting
やく	**yaku**, about	きせつ	**kisetsu**, season
れっとう	**rettō**, archipelago		

Supplemental vocabulary

そめいよしの	**somei yoshino**, a species of cherry	こうようび	**kōyō-bi**, day the leaves turn
かいかび	**kaika-bi**, day of blooming	へいきん	**heikin**, average
いろはかえで	**iroha kaede**, a species of maple		

NOTES

1. **Sakura zensen, kōyō zensen**
   These **zensen** are analogous to warm and cold weather fronts, so perhaps it is not surprising that information on their progress comes from the **Kishō-chō**, the "Meteorological Agency." Among its weather-related functions are predicting the harvest time of fruits, but the **sakura** and **kōyō** are the most eagerly awaited predictions and reports. The harbinger for the many varieties of cherry blossoms is the species known as **somei yoshino** and for the maples it is **iroha kaede**.

2. **Nan to itte mo**
   More literally this means "No matter what anyone says . . ."

3. **Hana ga saite iku.** (*lit.*) "The flowers bloom progressively."
   Adding **iku** to this sentence serves to indicate the progressive nature of the action.

4. **Ichido ni haru no hana ga mirareru no desu.**
   no desu is quivalent to **n desu** but less colloquial. (See p. 82.)

5. 木々 **(kigi)**
   The kanji 々 indicates the repetition of the syllable(s) coming immediately before it, sometimes with a phonetic change. Nouns in Japanese are generally written and pronounced the same whether singular or plural (as noted in Characteristics of Japanese Grammar in the first volume), but this is one way of specifying plurality. Other examples: 花々 **hanabana**, "flowers"; 国々 **kuniguni**, "countries"; 島々 **shimajima**, "islands"; 山々 **yamayama**, "mountains."
   Words made plural with suffixes are comparatively few and must be learned as they are encountered. **Anata-gata**, for example, is one way of pluralizing "you." From familiar to formal, there are a number of words for "we," such as **boku-ra**, **wata(ku)shi-tachi** (the most common) and **watashi-domo**.

6. **Haru niwa o-hanami, aki niwa momiji-gari**
   When things are listed or enumerated, it is sometimes permissible to omit predicates and, in fact, this can create a dramatic effect.

QUIZ

Put the appropriate words in the parentheses.

　さくらぜんせん　（　　）　ことばを　きいた　（　　）が　ありますか。

　にほんの　はるを　だいひょうする　はなは　なんと　いっても　さくら　で
しょう。ひとびとは　はるが　ちかづく　（　　）、さくらの　さく　ひを　よそ
くし（　　）、ともだちと　おはなみに　いく　ひを　やくそくし（　　）　し
ます。

　（　　）、にほんは　みなみ（　　）　きた（　　）　ながく　のびている
しまぐにです。　きゅうしゅう、しこく、ほんしゅう、ほっかいどうでは
（　　）きおんの　さが　ありますから、さくらの　さく　ひも　すこし（　　）
ことなっています。きゅうしゅうの　なんぶでは、3がつの　すえごろ　さきま
すが、ほっかいどうでは　5がつの　はじめごろ　さきます。　（　　）　やく
40にちも　かかって、にほんれっとうを　みなみから　きたへ　はなが（　　）
いく　ようすを　せんで　あらわした　ものが　さくらぜんせんです。さくらぜ
んせん　（　　）　うめぜんせんや　つつじぜんせんなどの　はなぜんせんも
あります。うめは　さくらより　（　　）　はやく　きゅうしゅう（　　）　し
ゅっぱつしますが、ほっかいどう（　　）　つくのは　だいたい　さくら（　　）
おなじころです。　（　　）、5がつの　じょうじゅんから　ちゅうじゅんに
かけて　ほっかいどうへ　りょこうすれば、（　　）　はるの　はなが　みられ
る（　　）。これとは　（　　）、あきに　なる（　　）、こうようぜんせんは
やまの　きぎを　あかや　きいろに　そめながら、きたから　みなみへ　すすん
で（　　）。

　ひとびとは　はる（　　）は　おはなみ、あき（　　）は　もみじがりなどを
して、　（　　）を　たのしみます。

PART
II

Mr. Johnson is puzzled by young men in dark suits lined up in front of a building.

ジョンソン：ビルの 前に こんの せびろを 着た 人が たくさん ならん
でいますが、あれは 何を しているんですか。

加藤： ああ、今日は 9月5日ですね。今日から 学生の 会社ほうもん
が 始まります。

ジョンソン：みんな 若くて、大学生のような ふんいきですが、ふくそうは
サラリーマンのようですね。

加藤： あの 人たちは 来年の 春 そつぎょうする 大学生なんです
よ。しゅうしょくしたい 会社へ めんせつを 受けに 来たんで
すよ。

ジョンソン：今、いっぱんてきな けいこうとして、会社は どんな 人物を
もとめているのですか。

加藤： 10年ぐらい 前までは "こんじょうの ある 人" と 言ってい
ましたが、今は "こせいてきな 人" を もとめているそうです
よ。

ジョンソン：そうですか。でも ふくそうは せいふくのようで、ちっとも こ
せいてきじゃ ありませんね。ところで、学生の ほうは どんな
会社に 入りたがっているんですか。

加藤： きゅうりょうとか 会社の しょうらいせいとか、やりがいの あ
る 仕事とか、人に よって えらぶ きじゅんは いろいろだと
思いますよ。

ジョンソン：がいしけいの 会社の ひょうばんは どうですか。

加藤： がいしけいの 会社は 女性の 間で 人気が あるようです。

ジョンソン：なぜでしょう。われわれ 外人男性が ハンサムだからですか。あ
はは・・・。

加藤： あはは・・・。がいしけいの 会社では のうりょくが あれば
男性と びょうどうに 仕事の チャンスが あると 言っている
人も いますよ。

Johnson: Lots of people wearing dark blue suits are lined up in front of a building. What are
they doing?
Katō: Ah, today is September 5, isn't it? From today students begin company visits.
Johnson: They're all young and look like college students, but their style of dress is like white
color workers.

Katō: Those people will graduate from college next spring. They came to have interviews at
          a company where they want to get a job.
Johnson: As a general trend, what kind of people do companies look for now?
Katō: Until about ten years ago it was said (they wanted) people with fighting spirit, but
          now they look for people with originality, I hear.
Johnson: Is that so? But in clothes (looking) like uniforms there's no individuality at all. Inciden-
          tally, as for the students themselves what kind of companies do they want to join?
Katō: Salary, a company with a future, worthwhile work, things like that—depending on the
          person, I suppose there are various criteria for making a choice.
Johnson: How is the reputation of foreign firms?
Katō: It seems foreign firms are popular among women.
Johnson: Why, I wonder. Is it because we foreign men are so handsome? Ha, ha!
Katō: Ha, ha! There are people who say that in a foreign company, there's a chance (for
          women), if they have ability, to do work (on a level) equal with men.

Vocabulary

こん	**kon**, dark blue, navy	～そうです	**sō desu**, I hear, they say
せびろ	**sebiro**, (man's) suit	せいふく	**seifuku**, uniform
ならぶ	**narabu**, be lined up	ちっとも…ない	**chittomo . . . nai**, not at all
ほうもん	**hōmon**, visit		
だいがくせい	**daigakusei**, college student	～たがる	**-tagaru**, want to
		しょうらいせい	**shōrai-sei**, future, prospects
よう（な/です）	**yō (na/desu)**, like, seem		
ふんいき	**fun'iki**, (*lit.*) air, atmosphere, ambience	～せい	**-sei**, (*lit.*) attribute, nature, sex
ふくそう	**fukusō**, (style of) dress	やりがいのある	**yarigai no aru**, worthwhile
しゅうしょくする	**shūshoku suru**, get a job	～によって	**ni yotte**, depending on
うける	**ukeru**, have, receive, undergo, take	きじゅん	**kijun**, criterion, standard
		がいしけい	**gaishi-kei**, foreign capital affiliation
いっぱんてき（な）	**ippan-teki(na)**, general		
いっぱん（の）	**ippan (no)**, general, widespread	がいし	**gaishi**, foreign capital
		～けい	**-kei**, origin, lineage, system
けいこう	**keikō**, trend, tendency	ひょうばん	**hyōban**, reputation
じんぶつ	**jimbutsu**, person, character, figure	～の　あいだで	**no aida de**, among, between
もとめる	**motomeru**, look for, want, seek	にんき	**ninki**, popularity
		われわれ	**wareware**, we
こんじょう	**konjō**, fighting spirit, willpower, disposition	がいじん	**gaijin**, foreigner
		のうりょく	**nōryoku**, ability
こせいてき（な）	**kosei-teki(na)**, original, individual	びょうどう（に）	**byōdo (ni)**, equally
		チャンス	**chansu**, chance
こせい	**kosei**, individuality		

GRAMMAR & LESSON OBJECTIVES

• yō desu

Daigaku-sei no yō na fun'iki desu ga, fukusō wa sararīman no yō desu ne. More literally,
this would be, "They seem to have the air of college students about them, . . ."

Gaishi-kei no kaisha wa josei no aida de ninki ga aru yō desu.

yō desu comes after verbs, nouns and adjectives as follows.

After a verb: **Kare wa onaka ga suite iru yō desu.** "He seems to be hungry."

After a noun: **Ano biru wa byōin no yō desu.** "That building looks like a hospital."

After -i adj: **Chichi wa byōki desu ga, kyō wa sukoshi ii yō desu.** "My father is sick but he seems a little better today."

After -na adj: **Tōkyō dewa chikatetsu ga benrina yō desu.** "In Tokyo, subways would seem to be (the most) convenient."

This pattern may be used metaphorically.

ex. **Ano hito wa sūpāman no yō desu.** "That man is like Superman."

Within a sentence, **yō** is like a **-na** adjective.

ex. 1. **Yuki no yō ni shiroi desu.** "(It's) white like snow."

2. **Ningyō no yō na kodomo,** "a child like a doll"

• sō desu

"Kosei-tekina hito" o motomete iru sō desu.

Another way of conveying reported information is by adding **sō desu** after plain forms of adjectives, **desu** or a verb. The source of information can be identified by the expression **ni yoru to**, the verb **yoru** having the meaning "depend," "be based on." (See appendix A.)

ex. **Tenki yohō ni yoru to ashita wa ame da sō desu.** "According to the weather forecast, it'll rain tomorrow."

• -tagaru

Gakusei no hō wa donna kaisha ni hairi-tagatte iru n desu ka.

-tai basically expresses one's own or ask another's wishes or desires in a direct manner. As noted in the first volume (p. 175), as a predicate it cannot refer to the desires of a third person. For this purpose **-tagatte iru**, "to act as if one desires," can be used, but somewhat limitedly, i.e., as when the person under discussion is a child, a subordinate or an equal.

ex. **Kodomo-tachi wa soto ni de-tagatte imasu.** "The children want to go outside."

-tai can occur before expressions like **to iu**, **to omou** etc., and it is used freely to modify nouns, as in **shūshoku shitai kaisha.**

NOTES

1. **Kon no sebiro o kita hito**
   Phrases ending in the **-ta** form of a verb can be modifiers with the same meaning as the **-te iru** pattern, as in these examples.
   1. **megane o kaketa hito,** "the person wearing glasses"
   2. **kowareta terebi,** "a broken TV set"
   3. **magatta michi,** "a winding road"
   In some cases, the meanings differ.
   ex. 1. **Asa-gohan o tabete iru hito,** "The person eating breakfast."
   2. **Asa-gohan o tabeta hito,** "The person who ate breakfast." (See Lessons 25 and 27 in the first volume.)

2. **gakusei no kaisha hōmon**
   The school year runs from April to March and job recruitment begins in late summer or early autumn. Business and industrial circles agree on a date for the first interviews to take place, but the desire on the part of companies for good recruits and on the part of students to join the best companies is quite strong. In this competitive atmosphere, jumping the gun and meeting secretly occurs rather frequently.

3. **Ima wa "kosei-tekina hito" o motomete imasu.**
   Quotation marks have recently appeared in written Japanese to suggest the idea, "so called."

4. **Tokorode gakusei no hō wa . . .**
   One usage of **tokorode** is to change the topic of conversation.
   No hō wa gives the statement the sense of "from the students' viewpoint," the conversation having shifted from what the companies expect to what the students might be interested in.

5. **Hito ni yotte erabu kijun wa . . .**
   Here is another example of **ni yotte**:
   Ōsaka ni iku toki wa Shinkansen de ikimasu ka, hikōki de ikimasu ka. "When you go to Osaka, do you go on the Shinkansen or by plane?"
   Toki to baai ni yotte, Shinkansen mo hikōki mo tsukaimasu. "Depending on time and circumstances, I use either the Shinkansen or a plane."

PRACTICE

KEY SENTENCES

1. かいぎしつの　でんきが　ついています。かいぎは　まだ　おわっていない　ようです。
2. かとうさんは　あした　おおさかへ　いくそうです。

1. The conference room lights are still on. The meeting isn't over yet, it seems.
2. I hear Katō is going to Osaka tomorrow.

Vocabulary

つく　　　　　　　**tsuku**, be lit/ignited

EXERCISES

I Practice the following patterns by changing the underlined parts.

A. *ex.* あのひとは　どくしんのようです。

1. あしたは　あめだ
2. やましたさんは　しんにゅうしゃいんだ
3. チャンさんは　びょうきでは　ない
4. あの　えいがは　ひょうばんが　いい
5. あの　みせは　よくない
6. たなかさんは　さしみが　きらいだ

B. *ex.* **Q**：あの　かいしゃは　じょせいの　あいだで　にんきが　あるんですか。
   　A：ええ、にんきが　あるようですよ。

1. あの　ひとは　えいごが　ぜんぜん　わかりません
2. ぶちょうは　きのう　しゅっちょうから　かえりました
3. あの　こどもは　がっこうに　いきたくありません
4. あの　きょうじゅは　がくせいの　なまえを　しりませんでした
5. チャンさんは　ねつが　あります

II Make dialogues by changing the underlined parts as in the examples given.

A. *ex.* **Q**：〔あの　ひとたちは〕なにか　いりますか。
　　A：いいえ、なにも　いらないようです。

　　　1. となりの　へやに　だれか　いますか
　　　2. かれは　あした　どこか　いきますか
　　　3. だれか　きましたか
　　　4. かのじょは　なにか　かいましたか
　　　5. だれか　れんらくしましたか

B. *ex.* **Q**：どんな　ふくそうですか。
　　A：サラリーマンのような　ふくそうです。

　　　1. あじ、くすり
　　　2. かたち、ふね
　　　3. ひと、こども
　　　4. てんき、はる
　　　5. ふんいき、がくしゃ

III Practice the following pattern by changing the underlined parts.

ex. きょうは　はるのように　あたたかいですね。

　　　1. あの　やま、ふじさん、うつくしい
　　　2. ここ、ぎんざ、にぎやか
　　　3. あの　ひと、せんもんか、くわしい
　　　4. この　たてもの、げきじょう、おおきい

IV Make dialogues by changing the underlined parts as in the examples given.

A. *ex.* **Q**：たなかさんは　いつ　いきますか。
　　A：あした　いくそうです。

　　　1. どこへ、ロンドンへ
　　　2. だれと、かいしゃの　ひとと
　　　3. なんじに、11じはんに
　　　4. なんで、じぶんの　くるまで

B. *ex.* **Q**：ブラウンさんは　すしが　すきですか。
　　Aa：ええ、すきだそうです。
　　An：いいえ、すきでは　ないそうです。

1. テニスが　じょうずです
2. がっこうの　せんせいでした
3. つごうが　わるいです
4. きのう　いそがしかったです
5. やまださんを　しっています
6. こどもが　あります
7. あした　こられます
8. りょこうに　いきました

V　Practice the following patterns by changing the underlined parts.

A. *ex.* <u>かれの　はなし</u>に　よると　メキシコで　じしんが　あったそうです。

1. しんぶん
2. テレビ
3. ゴンザレスさんの　てがみ
4. メキシコししゃからの　レポート

B. *ex.* <u>こせいてきな　ひとを　もとめている</u>そうです。

1. なかむらさんは　アメリカに　りゅうがくしていました
2. にちようびも　はたらかなければ　なりません
3. あしたまでに　できないかもしれません
4. にほんごを　おしえようと　おもっています
5. あしが　いたくて　あるけません
6. あの　ひとは　だいとうりょうの　しんせきです
7. おっとにも　はなさない　つもりです

VI　Make dialogues by changing the underlined parts as in the examples given.

A. *ex.* **A**：わたしは　<u>かいしゃを　やめ</u>たいと　おもっています。
　　B：そういえば、やまださんも　<u>やめ</u>たがっていますよ。

1. にほんじゅうを　りょこうする
2. ゴルフを　ならう
3. えいぎょうぶで　はたらく
4. がいしけいの　かいしゃに　はいる

B. *ex.* **Q**：たなかさんは　どの　ひとですか。
　　A：あの　<u>こんの　せびろを　きた</u>ひとです。

1. サングラスを　かけています

2. しろい ぼうしを かぶっています
3. グリーンの ズボンを はいています
4. おおきい にもつを もっています
5. せが たかくて やせています

C. *ex.* **Q**：おわる じかんは おなじですか。
　　　　A：いいえ、<u>かいしゃ</u>に よって ちがうと おもいます。

1. しごと
2. ときと ばあい
3. くに

Vocabulary

どくしん	**dokushin**, single	じしん	**jishin**, earthquake
しんにゅうしゃいん	**shinnyū shain**, new company employee	レポート	**repōto**, report
		しんせき	**shinseki**, relative
しんにゅう〜	**shinnyū**, (*lit.*) newly entered	おっと	**otto**, (my, your, her) husband
さしみ	**sashimi**, raw fish	そういえば	**sō ieba**, speaking of . . .
きょうじゅ	**kyōju**, professor	えいぎょうぶ	**eigyō-bu**, sales/ marketing department
あじ	**aji**, taste, flavor		
かたち	**katachi**, shape, form, appearance	えいぎょう	**eigyō**, sales, marketing, business
ふね	**fune**, ship, boat	サングラス	**sangurasu**, sunglasses
がくしゃ	**gakusha**, scholar, savant	ぼうし	**bōshi**, hat, cap
せんもんか	**semmonka**, specialist, professional	かぶる	**kaburu**, wear, put on (headgear)
げきじょう	**gekijō**, theater, playhouse	グリーン	**gurīn**, green
		やせる	**yaseru**, be/become thin, lose weight
〜によると	**ni yoru to**, according to		
メキシコ	**Mekishiko**, Mexico		

SHORT DIALOGUE

A：このごろ がっこうに いきたがらない こどもが ふえているようです
　　ね。
B：そうだそうですね。こまった もんだいです。

A: The number of children who don't want to go to school seems to be on the increase these days.
B: That's what I hear too. It's a tough problem.

Vocabulary

このごろ	**konogoro**, these days, recently

QUIZ

I Read this lesson's opening dialogue and answer the following questions.

1. ジョンソンさんと　かとうさんが　はなしているのは　9がつ5かです
   が、この　ひは　どういう　ひですか。
2. サラリーマンのような　せびろを　きて、ビルの　まえに　ならんでい
   る　ひとは　どういう　ひとたちですか。
3. かいしゃの　ほうは　まえも　"こせいてきな　ひと"を　もとめてい
   ましたか。
4. がいしけいの　かいしゃは　じょせいの　あいだで　にんきが　あるよ
   うだと　だれが　いっていますか。

II Put the appropriate words in the parentheses.

1. この　せいじかは　わかい　ひと（　　）　あいだ（　　）　にんき
   （　　）あります。
2. まえの　しゃちょうは　がくしゃ（　　）　よう（　　）　ふんいきで
   した。
3. じょせいも　だんせいと　びょうどう（　　）、しごと（　　）　チャン
   スが　あります。
4. しんぶん（　　）　ぎんざ（　　）　かじが　あったそうです。
5. かいしゃ（　　）　がくせいを　えらぶ　きじゅんは　おなじでは　あ
   りません。

III Complete the questions so that they fit the answers.

1. そちらの　てんきは　（　　）ですか。
   はるのように　あたたかいです。
2. （　　）　かいしゃに　はいりたいんですか。
   がいしけいの　かいしゃに　はいりたいと　おもっています。
3. あの　くろい　ズボンを　はいた　ひとは　（　　）ですか。
   はやしさんです。
4. （　　）　がいしけいの　かいしゃに　しゅうしょく　したいんですか。
   がいこくに　いく　チャンスが　おおいと　おもったからです。

IV Complete the sentences with the appropriate pattern using the words in the parentheses.

1. かちょうは　（　　）ようです。（どくしんです）
2. ニュースに　よると　しゅしょうは　（　　）そうです。（びょうきです）
3. かちょうは　えいごが　（　　）ようです。（にがてです）
4. てがみに　よると　リーさんは　にほんごが　（　　）そうです。（にが
   てです）
5. この　かいしゃは　あまり　ひょうばんが　（　　）ようです。（よくな
   いです）

6. ブラウンさんの はなしに よると リーさんは こどもが （　）
そうです。（ありません）

7. かとうさんの むすこさんは きょねん だいがくの しけんを
（　）そうです。（うけました）

8. やまださんは えいぎょうぶで （　）たがっています。（はたらきま
す）

V Choose a statement appropriate to the situation described.

A. You tell your section chief Kimura called and said he'd be late.

1. きむらさんは おくれるそうです。
2. きむらさんは おくれたそうです。
3. きむらさんは おくれる つもりです。

B. You hear snoring and wonder who's taking a nap.

1. だれか ねたがっています。
2. だれか ねるそうです。
3. だれか ねているようです。

LESSON  A CANCELED RESERVATION

Mr. Smith has to change his plans.

スミス：　もしもし、東京の　スミスですが、先日の　予約を　とりけした
　　　　　いんですが。

予約がかり：何日の　ご予約でしょうか。

スミス：　あしたです。たいふうの　ために　ひこうきが　けっこうして、
　　　　　出発できないんです。

予約がかり：はあ。もうしわけありませんが、前日の　おとりけしの　ばあいは
　　　　　キャンセルチャージが　50パーセント　かかりますが・・・。

スミス：　50パーセントも！　私の　つごうでは　ないんですよ。たいふうで
　　　　　行けないんです。

予約がかり：はあ。まことに　もうしわけありません。ごじじょうは　よく　わ
　　　　　かりますが、そういう　きまりなので、よろしく　おねがいいたし
　　　　　ます。

スミス：　そうですか。

予約がかり：おきゃくさま、後日　こちらに　おとまりの　ご予定は　ありませ
　　　　　んか。

スミス：　先に　のばす　ばあいは　キャンセルチャージは　はらわなくても
　　　　　いいですか。

予約がかり：はい、けっこうでございます。来週なら　お部屋が　ございます。

スミス：　日本に　いたら　行くんですが、来週から　海外しゅっちょうで、
　　　　　むりなんです。今　決めなければ　いけませんか。つまとも　そう
　　　　　だんしたいので・・・。

予約がかり：いつでも　けっこうでございますが、今　シーズン中で　こんでい
　　　　　ますので、なるべく　早く　ごれんらくください。

スミス：　わかりました。それから　内金の　18,000円は　とどきましたか。
　　　　　4、5日前に　送りましたから、もう　とどいている　はずですが
　　　　　・・・。

予約がかり：はい、昨日　たしかに　うけとりました。内金は　おとまりの　時
　　　　　の　料金から　おひきします。では、お電話を　お待ちしていま
　　　　　す。

Smith:　　　Hello. This is Smith in Tokyo. I'd like to cancel the reservation (I made) the other day.

Reservation

Clerk:	What date is the reservation for?
Smith:	Tomorrow. Because of the typhoon planes aren't flying and I can't leave (here).
Clerk:	Well, I'm sorry, but in the case of a previous-day cancellation, a 50-percent cancellation charge is necessary.
Smith:	Fifty percent! It's not for personal reasons! I can't go because of the typhoon.
Clerk:	Yes, well, I really am sorry. I understand your situation well enough, but since there's a rule like that . . .
Smith:	Oh.
Clerk:	Do you have any plans to stay here at a later date, sir?
Smith:	If it's postponed (to the future), is it OK not to pay the cancellation charge?
Clerk:	Yes, that's all right. If it's next week, we have rooms.
Smith:	If I were going to be in Japan I'd go. But next week is an overseas business trip, so that's out of the question. Does it have to be decided now? I'd like to talk it over with my wife.
Clerk:	Anytime is fine. But (we're) in the (tourist) season now and we're full so please get in touch with us as soon as possible.
Smith:	I see. By the way did the ¥18,000 deposit reach (you)? I sent it four or five days ago, and it should have arrived (by now).
Clerk:	Yes, we got (it) yesterday (I'm) sure. The deposit will be deducted from the room charge when (you) stay (here). We'll be expecting your call.

Vocabulary

とりけす	**torikesu**, cancel		おとまり	**o-tomari**, (your) stay
～のために	**no tame ni**, because of		さき	**saki**, future
けっこうする	**kekkō suru**, not flying/ sailing, suspension of service		のばす	**nobasu**, postpone, extend
			かいがい	**kaigai**, abroad, foreign countries
はあ	**hā**, yes, I understand		むり（な）	**muri (na)**, out of the ques- tion, unreasonable
ぜんじつ	**zenjitsu**, previous day			
おとりけし	**o-torikeshi**, (your) cancellation		つま	**tsuma**, (my) wife
			なるべく	**narubeku**, as . . . as possi- ble
キャンセルチャ ージ	**kyanseru chāji**, cancella- tion charge		はず	**hazu**, have to, should
パーセント	**pāsento**, percent		さくじつ	**sakujitsu**, yesterday (less colloquial than **kinō**)
で	**de**, because of			
まことに	**makoto ni**, really		うけとる	**uketoru**, get
（ご）じじょう	**(go)jijō**, (your) situation		おひきする	**o-hiki suru**, deduct
きまり	**kimari**, rule, decision		ひく	**hiku**, deduct, discount, subtract
いたす	**itasu**, do (humble)			
ごじつ	**gojitsu**, later date, another day			

GRAMMAR & LESSON OBJECTIVES

- **no tame ni, de**, giving reasons

 Taifū no tame ni
 Taifū de
 Raishū kara kaigai shutchō de
 Ima shīzun-chū de

 Guidelines for the various patterns expressing reason or cause can be summarized as follows.

(For **kara**, **node** and **-te**, see the first volume [p. 73] and pp. 97 and 105, respectively.)
For requests or suggestions, that is, sentences ending in, for example, **-te kudasai**, **-masen ka** or **mashō**, or statements of the speaker's intention, neither the patterns with the connective **-te** form, noun plus **de** or noun plus **no tame ni** are ever used. The preferred patterns are formed with **node** or **na node**. And of the patterns introduced so far, it can be said that **kara**, as well as **node** and **na node**, can be used freely.
To express the meaning "(We) won't go for a drive because it's snowing," do not say **Yuki ga futte/yuki de doraibu ni ikimasen**. In this case use **Yuki ga furu node/yuki na node ...**
If the meaning is "(We) can't go for a drive because it's snowing," then **Yuki ga futte/yuki de doraibu ni ikemasen** is acceptable.

- **Hazu desu**

  4,5-nichi mae ni okurimashita kara mō todoite iru hazu desu.
  Like **tsumori**, **hazu** is a noun and, rather than supposition, is a way of saying something is deducible on a factual basis. It can come after verbs, adjectives, or other nouns plus **no**.
  ex. 1. **Kono nyūsu wa nan-kai mo terebi de itte ita kara, ōku no hito ga shitte iru hazu desu.** "Since this news has been on TV many times, a great many people must be aware of it."
  2. **Tegami wa senshū dashimashita kara, Suzuki-san wa yonda hazu desu.** "I sent the letter last week, so Suzuki must have (already) read it."
  3. **Tegami wa kinō dashimashita kara, Suzuki-san wa mada yonde inai hazu desu.** "I sent the letter yesterday, so Suzuki can't have read it yet."
  4. **Sono ie wa beddorūmu ga yottsu arimasu kara, jūbun hiroi hazu desu.** "Since that house has four bedrooms, it should be roomy enough."
  5. **Maitsuki no kaigi wa dai-2 moku-yōbi desu kara, tsugi wa 6-gatsu 12-nichi no hazu desu.** "The monthly meeting is on the second Thursday; the next one will be on June 12."
  (See appendix A.)

NOTES

1. **Nihon ni itara iku n desu ga ...**
   The implication of this sentence is, "I'm afraid I can't go." In other words, one function of the conditional form (**-tara**, **-ba**, **-nara**) is to say that the situation is the opposite of what has been supposed.

2. **Narubeku hayaku go-renraku kudasai.**
   Here is another example of **narubeku**.
   Narubeku takusan mottekite kudasai. "Please bring as many as possible."

3. **Uchikin wa o-tomari no toki no ryōkin kara o-hiki shimasu. Dewa o-denwa o o-machi shite imasu.**
   The pattern with the honorific **o** attached to the **-masu** stem and followed by **suru** downplays the importance of one's own, or one's group's actions. For certain verbs the same polite effect comes from use of an alternative word. As noted in the vocabulary list, the humble word for **suru** is **itasu**. **O-negai-shimasu** (verb **negau**) is an example of the one pattern; **o-negai-itashimasu** is an example of both formations.

PRACTICE

KEY SENTENCES

1. じしんの　ために　しんかんせんが　とまりました。
2. わたなべさんは　かぜで　かいしゃに　きませんでした。
3. スミスさんは　8じの　しんかんせんで　とうきょうを　でましたから、11じごろ　そちらに　つく　はずです。

1. The Shinkansen stopped (running) because of an earthquake.
2. Watanabe has a cold and didn't come to the office.
3. Smith left Tokyo on the eight o'clock Shinkansen so he should arrive there about eleven o'clock.

EXERCISES

I Make dialogues by changing the underlined parts as in the examples given.

A. *ex.* **Q**：どうか　したんですか。
  A：<u>たいふうの　ために</u>　<u>ひこうきが　でない</u>んです。

   1. じこ、でんしゃが　うごきません
   2. せんそう、くにの　かぞくと　れんらくが　できません
   3. おおゆき、でんしゃが　とまっています
   4. ストライキ、　じてんしゃで　いかなければ　なりません

B. *ex.* **A**：<u>やきゅうの　しあいが　できなく</u>　なりました。
  B：どうしてですか。
  A：<u>あめ</u>で　<u>できなく</u>　なりました。

   1. エレベーターが　つかえません、ていでん
   2. らいしゅう　いけません、こどもの　びょうき
   3. あの　くにに　にもつが　おくれません、かくめい
   4. でんわが　つかえません、かじ

II Practice the following pattern by changing the underlined parts.

ex. <u>まんいんで　はいれない</u>から　<u>べつの　ところを　さがしましょう</u>。

   1. ストで　でんしゃが　うごきません、あるいて　かえります
   2. かじで　けがを　しました、きゅうきゅうしゃを　よんでください
   3. あめの　ために　テニスが　できません、しつないプールで　およぎませんか
   4. きょうは　どようびで　12じまでです、らいしゅう　きてください

III Make dialogues by changing the underlined parts as in the examples given.

A. *ex.* **Q**：かいぎは　なんじに　<u>おわります</u>か。
  A：3じごろ　<u>おわる</u>　はずです。

   1. たなかさん、もどります
   2. あかちゃん、めが　さめます

3. リンダさん、つきます
4. おきゃくさん、きます

B. *ex.* **A**：ジョンソンさんは　<u>フランスごが　わかる</u>　はずです。
　　　B：どうしてですか。
　　　A：<u>5ねんも　フランスに　いました</u>から。

1. この　ほんを　よみません、かんじが　おおいです
2. おかねが　あります、また　あたらしい　じどうしゃを　かい
　ました
3. きょう　やすみました、ねつが　あると　いっていました
4. かいませんでした、すきでは　ないと　いっていました

C. *ex.* **Q**：さとうさんは　<u>えいごが　じょうず</u>でしょうか。
　　　A：ええ、<u>じょうずな</u>　はずです。<u>アメリカに　いました</u>から。

1. しあわせです、けっこんしたばかりです
2. ひまです、コーヒーを　のみながら　しんぶんを　よんでいま
　す
3. つごうが　わるいです、　おおさかに　いかなければ　なりま
　せん
4. いそがしいです、かいぎが　あります
5. まだ　がくせいです、おととし　だいがくに　はいりました
6. りょこうです、せんしゅうから　なつやすみです

D. *ex.* **Q**：<u>たなかさんに　あえます</u>か。
　　　A：<u>あした　くれば</u>　<u>たなかさんに　あえる</u>　はずです。

1. みっかで　つきます、こうくうびんで　だします
2. いいものが　かえます、30,000えん　だします
3. ひるごろまでに　つきます、9じの　しんかんせんに　のりま
　す
4. やせられます、たくさん　たべません

E. *ex.* **Q**：<u>この　ほんを　よみます</u>か。
　　　A：いいえ、<u>よみません</u>。<u>じかんが　あったら　よむ</u>んですが。

1. これが　わかります、もっと　あたまが　いいです
2. これが　わかります、てんさいです
3. コンピューターを　つかいます、つかいかたが　やさしいです

4. これを　たべます、もっと　やわらかいです
5. しょくじに　いきます、かいぎが　ありません

Vocabulary			
せんそう	**sensō**, war	しつない	**shitsunai**, indoor, interior
おおゆき	**ōyuki**, heavy snow(fall)	もどる	**modoru**, come/go/be back
やきゅう	**yakyū**, baseball	めが　さめる	**me ga sameru**, wake up
しあい	**shiai**, game, match, bout	め	**me**, eye
エレベーター	**erebētā**, elevator	さめる	**sameru**, wake up
ていでん	**teiden**, power failure	じどうしゃ	**jidōsha**, automobile
かくめい	**kakumei**, revolution	しあわせ（な）	**shiawase(na)**, happy
さがす	**sagasu**, look for	だす	**dasu**, pay, invest
きゅうきゅう	**kyūkyūsha**, ambulance	てんさい	**tensai**, genius
しゃ			

SHORT DIALOGUE

A：この　コップ、つかっても　いいですか。
B：ええ、どうぞ。いま　あらったばかりだから、きれいな　はずです。

A: Can I use this cup?
B: Yes, please (do so). That one should be clean as I've just washed it.

QUIZ

I Read this lesson's opening dialogue and answer the following questions.

1. スミスさんは　くるまで　りょこうする　つもりでしたか、ひこうきで
　でかける　つもりでしたか。
2. ひこうきは　ストライキの　ために　けっこうしましたか。
3. とまる　よていを　さきに　のばす　ばあいも　キャンセルチャージを
　はらわなければ　なりませんか。
4. どうして　スミスさんは　もう　うちきんが　とどいている　はずだと
　おもっていますか。

II Put the appropriate words in the parentheses.

1. きのうは　かぜ（　　）　かいしゃ（　　）　やすみました。
2. じしん（　　）　ために　でんしゃ（　　）　とまっています。
3. やきゅうの　しあいを　1しゅうかん　さき（　　）　のばしましょう。
4. 5（　　）　3を　ひくと　2（　　）　なります。

III Complete the questions so that they fit the answers.

1. （　　）　ひこうきが　とばないんですか。
　たいふうの　ために　けっこうしたそうです。

2. しゃちょうは　（　　　）　かえりますか。
   らいげつの　はじめに　かえる　はずです。

3. キャンセルチャージは　（　　　）　かかりますか。
   ぜんじつの　とりけしの　ばあいは　50パーセント　かかります。

4. けっこんしきは　（　　　）に　はじまりますか。
   10じごろ　はじまる　はずです。

IV Complete the sentences with the appropriate form of the words indicated.

1. かくめいで、ひこうきが　（　　　）　はずです。（とんでいません）

2. あの　ワープロは　（　　　）にくかったので、べつのに　（　　　）　はずです。（つかいます、かえました）

3. かちょうは　いちにちじゅう　（　　　）ので、きょうは　（　　　）　はずです。（かいぎです、いそがしいです）

4. きょう　てがみを　（　　　）ば、あした　（　　　）　はずです。（だします、つきます）

5. きのうは　おきゃくが　（　　　）から、たなかさんは　たいしかんに　（　　　）はずです。（ありました、いきませんでした）

6. じかんが　（　　　）たら、いくんですが、いそがしくて　（　　　）だろうと　おもいます。（あります、いけません）

V Circle the most appropriate words in the parentheses.

1. （きゅうに、きっと、たしかに）　つごうが　わるく　なったので、よやくを　とりけしてください。

2. よやくを　とりけす　ばあいは　（まことに、たしかに、かならず）ごれんらくください。

3. うちきんを　おくりましたが、とどいたでしょうか。
   はい、さくじつ　（きっと、たしかに、かならず）　うけとりました。

LESSON 23 A MESSAGE FROM CHANG

Mr. Chang arranges for concert tickets from a ticket agency.

スタジオＱ：チケット予約の　スタジオＱでございます。

チャン：　　あのう、チャンと　言いますが、中野さんを　おねがいします。

スタジオＱ：中野は　外出中です。

チャン：　　何時ごろ　帰るか　わかりますか。

スタジオＱ：1時すぎに　もどる　はずです。

チャン：　　じゃ、言づけを　おねがいします。
　　　　　　6月28日の　武道館の　コンサートの　きっぷ　3まいの　代金を
　　　　　　きのう　そちらの　銀行こうざに　ふりこんだと　伝えてください。
　　　　　　それから、もう　1まい　きっぷが　ほしいんですが、あるか　ど
　　　　　　うか　聞いてください。

スタジオＱ：はい、わかりました。

チャン：　　それから・・・とにかく　店に　もどったら、こちらに　電話する
　　　　　　ように　言ってくれませんか。

スタジオＱ：はい。そちらの　お電話番号を　どうぞ。

チャン：　　292-3365に　おねがいします。これは　直通電話です。

スタジオＱ：はい、292-3365ですね。中野が　もどりましたら、すぐ　お電話す
　　　　　　るように　伝えます。

Ms. Nakano hears about Chang's phone call.

スタジオＱ：さっき、チャンさんと　いう　おきゃくさんから　電話が　ありま
　　　　　　した。きっぷの　代金は　ふりこんだそうですが、もう　1まい
　　　　　　きっぷが　あるか　どうか　聞いていました。あなたからの　電話
　　　　　　を　待っていると　言っていました。これが　電話番号です。

Studio Q: Studio Q, ticket reservations.
Chang: Umm, my name is Chang. Ms. Nakano, please.
Studio Q: Nakano is out.
Chang: Do you know about what time (she'll) be back?
Studio Q: (She's) expected back after one o'clock.
Chang: I'd like (to leave) a message, then. Please tell her I transferred the money for three
            tickets to the concert at the Budōkan on June 28 to your bank account yesterday.
            Also, I want one more ticket. Please ask (her) whether there's another ticket
            (available).
Studio Q: Yes, of course.

Chang: Then—anyway, when she gets back please tell her to call me.
Studio Q: Certainly. Your telephone number, please?
Chang: (Call me at) 292-3365. This is a direct line (*lit*. phone).
Studio Q: That's 292-3365, right? When she returns I'll tell (her) to call you immediately.

Studio Q: A while ago there was a call from a customer named Chang. He said he transferred the money for the tickets and asked if there is one more ticket (available). He said he's expecting your call. This is his number.

Vocabulary			

スタジオ	**sutajio**, studio	だいきん	**daikin**, money, charge, fee
チケット	**chiketto**, ticket		
がいしゅつちゅう	**gaishutsu-chū**, is out	こうざ	**kōza**, account
		〜かどうか	**ka dō ka**, whether (or not)
がいしゅつ	**gaishutsu**, going out, outing	とにかく	**tonikaku**, anyway, in any case
〜すぎ（に）	**sugi (ni)**, after	ように	**yō ni** (for indirect statements)
ことづけ	**kotozuke**, message		
ぶどうかん	**Budōkan**, Hall of the Martial Arts (Tokyo)	ちょくつう	**chokutsū**, (*lit*.) direct communication, through service
コンサート	**konsāto**, concert		

GRAMMAR & LESSON OBJECTIVES

- **tsutaete/itte kudasai/kuremasen ka**

  Kippu 3-mai no daikin o . . . furikonda to tsutaete kudasai.
  Kochira ni denwa suru yō ni itte kuremasen ka.
  These patterns are appropriate when one wishes to leave a message. The effect of **yō ni** in the second sentence is to make the request indirect. When quoting directly or requesting verbatim repetition of one's own wording, **to** is used. Among other verbs occurring in this situation is **kiite** (when it means "ask"), as in **Mō 1-mai kippu ga hoshii n desu ga, aru ka dō ka kiite kudasai**.
  The patterns here are basically continuations of those introduced in lessons 8 and 21 for quoting material.
  Kippu no daikin wa furikonda sō desu ga, mō 1-mai kippu ga aru ka dō ka kiite imashita.
  Anata kara no denwa o matte iru to itte imashita.
  The two patterns—**sō desu (ga)** and **to itte imashita**—can be used to pass on messages. When an indirect quotation is in a question pattern, it is followed by **kiite iru**.
  ex. **Tanaka-san wa Sumisu-san ga ashita doko ni iku ka kiite imashita.** "Tanaka asked where Smith is going tomorrow."

- **da** (or other plain forms), **yō ni**, **ka dō ka** or **ka** for quotations

  Certain patterns are directly related to the type of sentence being cited.
  1. For quoted statements: **Chan-san wa kippu no daikin wa furikonda sō desu/to itte imashita.** "Chang said he transferred the money for the tickets." (See appendix A.)
  2. For quoted requests: *aff.* **Denwa suru yō ni itte kuremasen ka.** "Would (you) tell (her) to call (me)?" (dict. form + **yō ni**) *neg.* **Denwa shinai yō ni itte kudasai.** "Please tell (him) not to call (me)." (-**nai** form + **yō ni**)
  Since these patterns sound like orders, they wouldn't be heard in polite society. To indicate appropriate respect for the person referred to, honorific expressions should be used, such as -**te kudasaru yō ni** or -**te itadaku yō ni**. (See lesson 31.)
  ex. **Sumisu-san ni denwa shite kudasaru yō ni o-tsutae kudasai.** Would you please tell

Mr. Smith to call me." (The object of respect is Smith rather than the person answering the phone. This is clear in the Japanese sentence.)

3. For quoted yes/no questions: **Mō 1-mai kippu ga aru ka dō ka kiite kudasai.** "Please ask whether (or not) there's another ticket (available)." (The **ka** in **ka dō ka** and **nanji goru kaeru ka** is the same as **ka** at the end of a question sentence.) In the following examples, note how patterns are formed with plain verbs, the two types of adjectives and with nouns.

   ex. a. **Kippu no daikin ga todoita ka dō ka kiite kudasai.** "Please ask if the money for the tickets arrived."
   b. **Ōkii ka dō ka kiite kudasai.** "Please ask whether it's big or not."
   c. **Benri ka dō ka kiite kudasai.** "Ask whether it's convenient, please."
   d. **Nihon-jin ka dō ka kiite kudasai.** "Please ask if they're Japanese."

4. For quoted question-word questions: **Nanji goro kaeru ka wakarimasu ka.** "Do (you) know about what time (she'll) be back?"
   Additional examples:
   a. **Itsu okutta ka kiite kudasai.** "Please ask when (she) sent it?"
   b. **Nani ga suki ka kiite kudasai.** "Please ask what (they) like."

Here are some slightly more complex examples of making longer sentences by this process.

1. **Watashi wa kinō ryokan ni denwa o shite, taifū de ikenai to tsutaemashita.** "I called the inn yesterday and told (them) I couldn't go because of the typhoon."
2. **Kare ga doko kara kita ka dare mo shirimasen.** "No one knows where he comes from."
3. **Kare ni ima sain suru yō ni tanomimashō.** "Let's ask him to sign now."

NOTES

1. **Nakano wa gaishutsu-chū desu.**
   It is a common practice among business people when talking to outsiders to drop the **-san** from the names of members of one's own group, just as family members are apt to do.

2. **gaishutsu-chū**
   This **-chū** is similar to the **-jū** suffix in **kyō-jū ni** and **Nihon-jū** (see p. 21). It indicates "being busy with" or "in the process of," as in **shokuji-chū**, "having lunch (*lit.* "a meal")/out to lunch," and **kaigi-chū**, "in conference."

3. **Mō 1-mai kippu ga hoshii n desu ga.**
   The pattern is noun plus **ga** and **hoshii** and the usage is limited to **hoshii (n) desu**, "(I) want," and **hoshii (n) desu ka**, "Do (you) want?" Note the parallel between **hoshii** and **-tai** (p. 161). For referring to third persons there is the verb **hoshigaru (hoshigatte iru)**.

PRACTICE

KEY SENTENCES

1. さかやに　でんわして、ビールを　20ぽん　もってくるように　いってくだ
   さい。
2. 〔あなたが〕　あした　ゴルフに　いくか　どうか　かとうさんが　きいてい
   ました。
3. たなかさんが　なんじに　かえるか　しっていますか。

1. Please phone the liquor store and tell (them) to bring twenty bottles of beer.
2. Katō asked if you're going golfing tomorrow.
3. Do you know what time Tanaka's coming back?

I Make dialogues by changing the underlined parts as in the examples given.

    A. *ex.* **A** : ブラウンさんに　<u>また　あとで　でんわする</u>と　つたえてください。

        B : はい、しょうちしました。

        1.　あしたから　2しゅうかん　しゅっちょうします
        2.　そくたつが　とどきました
        3.　しらべたけれど　わかりませんでした
        4.　あした　しごとの　あとで　あいたいです
        5.　あしたより　あさっての　ほうが　いいです
        6.　もうしこんだけれど　だめでした
        7.　たなかさんは　いま　りょこうちゅうです
        8.　パーティーは　とても　たのしかったです

    B. *ex.* **A** : すずきくんを　おねがいします。

        B : いま　いませんが。

        A : じゃ、すずきくんに　<u>あとで　こちらに　でんわする</u>ように　いってください。

        B : はい、そう　つたえます。

        1.　パーティーに　おくさんと　いっしょに　きます
        2.　かいぎに　おくれません
        3.　はんこを　もってきます
        4.　へやを　かたづけます
        5.　じかんを　まちがえません

II Practice the following pattern by changing the underlined part.

    ex. きむらさんに　あしたの　あさ　8じに　くるように　<u>いいました</u>。

        1.　たのみました
        2.　つたえました
        3.　しらせました
        4.　いってください
        5.　いってくれませんか

III Make dialogues by changing the underlined parts as in the examples given.

    A. *ex.* **A** : なかのさんに　<u>もう　いちまい　きっぷが　ある</u>か　どうか　きいてください。

B： はい、ちょっと　おまちください。ただいま　きいてきます。

    1.　りょうしゅうしょが　いります
    2.　ほんとうに　いきません
    3.　でんごんが　ありました
    4.　なにも　きいていませんでした
    5.　あうのは　あしたです
    6.　あしたの　ばんは　ひまです
    7.　らいしゅうの　げつようびは　いそがしいです

B. *ex.* **Q**： たなかさんは　<u>いつ　かえりますか</u>。
    A： さあ、<u>いつ　かえるか</u>　ちょっと　わかりません。

    1.　どこへ　いきましたか
    2.　だれと　でかけましたか
    3.　なにを　しらべていますか
    4.　なんじに　かえりましたか
    5.　なんじの　ひこうきに　のりますか
    6.　なにが　すきですか
    7.　いつまで　いそがしいですか

IV Practice the following patterns by changing the underlined parts.

A. *ex.*　いつ　かえるか　<u>きいてください</u>。

    1.　きいてくれませんか
    2.　わかりますか
    3.　しっていますか
    4.　わかりません
    5.　しりません
    6.　まだ　きめていません

B. *ex.*　じかんが　あるか　どうか　<u>ききました</u>。

    1.　きいていました
    2.　きいてください
    3.　しっていますか
    4.　しりません
    5.　たなかさんに　きいたら　わかります
    6.　れんらくしてください

V   Make dialogues by changing the underlined parts as in the examples given.

A. *ex.* A：とうきょうでんきの　たなかですが、はやしさんを　おねがいします。

B：はやしは　いま　<u>かいぎちゅう</u>ですので、<u>あとで</u>　こちらから　れんらくするように　いいましょうか。

A：はい、では　おねがいします。

1.　でんわちゅう、でんわが　おわりましたら
2.　らいきゃくちゅう、あとで
3.　がいしゅつちゅう、もどりましたら
4.　しゅっちょうちゅう、かえりましたら

B. *ex.* Q：<u>もう　いちまい　きっぷ</u>が　ほしいんですが。

A：はい、どうぞ。

1.　もう　いっぱい　みず
2.　とうきょうの　ちず
3.　じこくひょう
4.　あんないしよ
5.　りょうしゅうしょ

Vocabulary

しょうちしました	**shōchi shimashita,** * I understand, certainly	でんごん	**dengon**, message
そくたつ	**sokutatsu**, special delivery	かいぎちゅう	**kaigi-chū**, in conference/a meeting
しらべる	**shiraberu**, check, investigate,	でんわちゅう	**denwa-chū**, on the phone
まちがえる	**machigaeru**, mistake	らいきゃくちゅう	**raikyaku-chū**, (busy) with a guest
ただいま	**tadaima**, right now, just now, in a minute	らいきゃく	**raikyaku**, guest
りょうしゅうしょ	**ryōshūsho**, receipt	じこくひょう	**jikoku-hyō**, timetable
		あんないしょ	**annai-sho**, guidebook, handbook

*The usage of this word is very similar to **kashikomarimashita**, but it is not quite as polite.

SHORT DIALOGUES

1.　A：やすくて　しゃれた　しょっきを　さがしているんですが・・・。

B：やすいか　どうか　わかりませんが、しゃれた　ものを　うっている　みせは　しっていますよ。

A: I'm looking for some inexpensive, well-designed tableware.
B: Whether it's cheap or not, I don't know, but I know a shop selling well-designed things.

2. すずき：これから　よこはまししゃに　いきますが、なにか　ごようは　あ
　　　　　りませんか。

　　かとう：やましたさんに　あって、みつもりしょが　できたか　どうか　き
　　　　　いてください。まだなら　はやく　つくるように　たのんでくださ
　　　　　い。

Suzuki:　I'm going to the Yokohama (branch) office now. Do you have any business (you want me to take care of)?
Katō:　Please see Yamashita, ask him if the estimate is ready, and if it isn't, please ask him to prepare it soon.

Vocabulary

しゃれた　　　　**shareta**, well designed,　　ごよう　　　　**go-yō**, (your) business
　　　　　　　(*lit.*) tasteful, chic　　みつもりしょ　　**mitsumori-sho**, (written)
しょっき　　　　**shokki**, tableware, dinner　　　　　　　estimate, quotation
　　　　　　　set, flatware

QUIZ

I　Read this lesson's opening dialogue and answer the following questions.

1. チャンさんは　きっぷを　キャンセルしようと　おもって　でんわを
　しましたか、もう　1まい　かおうと　おもって　でんわを　しました
　か。
2. スタジオQの　ひとは　なかのさんが　なんじごろ　かえるか　しって
　いましたか。
3. チャンさんは　なかのさんが　もどったら、なんばんに　でんわするよ
　うに　たのみましたか。
4. なかのさんが　みせに　もどると、スタジオQの　ひとは　どう　しま
　したか。
5. チャンさんは　コンサートの　きっぷを　ぜんぶで　なんまい　かう
　つもりですか。

II　Put the appropriate words in the parentheses.

1. とうきょうの　ちず（　　）　ほしいんですが、ありますか。
2. きょうは　そちらに　うかがえない（　　）　つたえでください。
3. なかのさんに　ごご　みせに　いる（　　）　どう（　　）　きいてく
　ださい。
4. いつ　ほっかいどうへ　いきますか。
　いつ　いく（　　）　まだ　きめていません。
5. すずきさんは　3じすぎ（　　）　　もどると　いっていました。
6. さっき　たなかさん（　　）　あなたに　でんわが　ありました。

III Circle the appropriate words in the parentheses.

1. ゴンザレスさんは　スペインごが　わかりますか。
   メキシコじんですから、（なかなか、もちろん、ほとんど）　わかる　は
   ずです。

2. いつまでに　レポートを　ださなくては　いけませんか。
   （なるべく、ほとんど、ずいぶん）　はやく　だしてください。

3. いつまでに　ずめんを　おくりましょうか。
   いそがなくても　いいですが、（さっき、ところで、とにかく）　できた
   ら、おくってください。

IV Complete the sentences with the appropriate form of the words indicated.

1. さいふを　どこで　（　　）か　おぼえていません。（おとしました）

2. かちょうが　（　　）か　どうか　わかりません。（きに　いります）

3. なかむらさんに　なにを　（　　）か　きいてください。（たべたいです）

4. くるまが　（　　）いるので、かれに　（　　）ように　いってくださ
   い。（よごれます、そうじします）

5. うちきんは　たしかに　（　　）と　つたえてください。（うけとりまし
   た）

6. きむらさんに　あさっては　しごとが　やすみで　（　　）と　つたえ
   てください。（ひまです）

V Choose a statement appropriate to the situation described.

A. You call a coworker's house and leave a message telling her to come to the office at
   eight tomorrow morning.

   1. あした　8じに　いくと　つたえてください。
   2. あした　8じに　きてください。
   3. あした　8じに　くるように　つたえてください。

B. You inform a caller that you don't know whether a coworker is coming back to the office today.

   1. かいしゃに　もどるか　どうか　わかりません。
   2. かいしゃに　もどるか　きいてください。
   3. かいしゃに　もどると　いっていました。

Mrs. Smith and Mrs. Tanaka look at pottery.

スミス夫人：あの　おさら、いいですね。ほしいけれど　高そうですね。

田中夫人：　ちょっと　待ってください。店の　人に　聞きますから。

田中夫人：　30万円ですって。有名な　人の　作品らしいです。

スミス夫人：そうですか。やっぱり　いい　物は　高いんですね。

田中夫人：　もう　1まいの　おさらは　もっと　高いそうです。

スミス夫人：1まい　1,500円ぐらいのは　ないんでしょうか。

田中夫人：　これは　1,700円ですが、こうしょうすれば　安く　なりそうです
　　　　　　　よ。

スミス夫人：安く　なるなら　買おうかしら。

Mrs. Smith buys some plates.

スミス夫人：すみません、これは　いくらですか。

店の人：　　1まい　1,700円です。いい　品ですよ。この　さらを　使うと
　　　　　　　りょうりが　おいしそうに　見えますよ。

スミス夫人：6まい　ほしいんですが、もう　少し　安く　してくださいません
　　　　　　　か。

店の人：　　そうですねえ。じゃあ、お安く　しましょう。1まい　1,600円に
　　　　　　　しましょう。

スミス夫人：どうも　ありがとう。　それから、この　はしおきも　おねがいします。

店の人：　　じゃ、全部で　12,600円に　なります。
ぜんぶ

Smith: That plate is nice, isn't it? I'd like (to have) it but it looks expensive.
Tanaka: Just a minute, I'll ask the shopkeeper.

Tanaka: He said it's ¥300,000. It seems to be the work of a famous person.
Smith: Is that right? After all, good things are expensive, aren't they?
Tanaka: He said the other plate (there) is more expensive.
Smith: Aren't there any plates for around ¥1,500, say?
Tanaka: This one is ¥1,700 yen, but if (we) negotiate it'll get cheaper, I guess.
Smith: If it's made cheaper, should I buy it, I wonder?

Smith: Excuse me. How much is this?
Shopkeeper: 1,700 yen for one. These are good wares. If (you) use these plates, food will look delicious.
Smith: I'd like six. Couldn't you make them a little cheaper?
Shopkeeper: Let me see. . . . All right, I'll make them cheaper. Let's say ¥1,600 each.
Smith: Thank you so much. And I'll take these chopstick rests too.
Shopkeeper: Fine, that comes to ¥12,600 all together.

Vocabulary

おさら	**o-sara**, plate, dish	～かしら	**kashira**, I wonder (informal female speech)
たかそうです	**takasō desu**, looks expensive	しな	**shina**, wares, article, goods
～そうです	**-sō desu** = looks		
～（です）って	**(desu) tte**, (he) said that	おいしそうに	**oishisō ni mieru**, looks delicious
さくひん	**sakuhin**, work, composition	みえる	
		に　する	**ni suru**, make/do (it), decide
らしい	**rashii**, seems to be		
もう	**mō**, the other, another	はしおき	**hashioki**, chopstick rest
こうしょうする	**kōshō suru**, bargain, negotiate	はし	**hashi**, chopstick
		ぜんぶで	**zembu de**, all together
こうしょう	**kōshō**, negotiation		

GRAMMAR & LESSON OBJECTIVES

- **sō desu**, "looks (as if), seems"

  Hoshii keredo taka sō desu ne.

  Yasuku nari sō desu.

  Note the forms taken by this **sō desu**. For adjectives, it is attached to the stem: **takasō**, for example, and **Benri sō desu**, "It seems to be convenient." For verbs, it is attached to the **-masu** stem.

  ex. **Ame ga furisō desu.** "It looks as if it's going to rain."

  With negative forms it patterns as follows.

  ex. 1. **Ame wa furanasa sō desu.** "It looks as if it's not going to rain."

  2. **Takakunasa sō desu.** "It doesn't look expensive."

  3. **Benri dewa nasa sō desu.** "It seems to be inconvenient." (*lit.* "not to be convenient")

  The adjective **ii/yoi** becomes **yosa sō desu**.

  Kono o-sara o tsukau to ryōri ga oishi sō ni miemasu yo.

  As used in this lesson, **sō** never follows a past form. When modifying nouns or verbs, the pattern becomes **sō na** or **sō ni**, as in **Kono o-sara o tsukau to ryōri ga oishi sō ni miemasu yo**.

ex. **yosa sō na sara**, "an apparently good dish." **takasō na sara**, "an expensive looking plate."

- **-ku/ni suru, -ku/ni naru**

  Kōshō sureba yasuku nari sō desu yo.
  Mō sukoshi yasuku shite kudasaimasen ka.
  O-yasuku shimashō.
  1-mai 1,600-en ni shimashō.
  1,600-en ni narimashita.

  -ku/ni suru expresses the speaker's intention, in this case what he has decided to do. From the listener's viewpoint, the pattern would be **. . . -ku/ni naru**, indicating the result—what has been decided. It is important to remember this distinction and also that after nouns and **-na** adjectives the pattern is **ni suru/naru**. Think of the meaning of **-ku/ni naru** as "be settled." At times, however, **-ku/ni naru**, which is softer than **-ku/ni suru**, is utilized to make it sound as if the speaker himself is not responsible for a decision.

NOTES

1. **Ano o-sara, ii desu ne.**
   Note the absence of a particle after **o-sara**. This actually draws attention to the subject and here is like saying, "Look at that plate."

2. **30,000-en desu tte.**
   tte, which follows the **desu/-masu** form, is the same in meaning as **da sō desu** and occurs mostly in female speech. **Datte** (in the short dialogues) has the same meaning, and is used by men as well.

3. **Yūmeina hito no sakuhin rashii desu.**
   As seen in the translation, "seems to be," **rashii** suggests some uncertainty on the part of the speaker. It comes after verbs and adjectives too. (See appendix A.)

4. **Mō 1-mai no o-sara wa motto takai sō desu.**
   From the **mō** here it can be assumed Mrs. Smith and Mrs. Tanaka are looking at two dishes on display.
   ex. **Onna no hito ga 3-nin Eigo de hanashite imasu. Futari wa Amerika-jin desu ga, mō hitori wa Igirisu-jin no yō desu**. "Three ladies are talking in English. Two are Americans but the other seems to be English."
   Some learners confuse **mō** and **motto**. Take note of these examples.
   1. **Mō sukoshi yasuku shite kudasai.** "Please make it a little bit cheaper."
   2. **Kōhī o mō ippai kudasai.** "Please give me one more/another cup of coffee."
   3. **Are wa motto takai desu.** "That's more expensive."

5. **1,500-en gurai no wa**
   The complete phrase is **1,500-en gurai no sara**, but **sara** is omitted because it is understood.

6. **Kaō kashira.**
   Kashira reflects the speaker's hesitation or indicisiveness. The corresponding term in male speech is **. . . ka na**.

7. **O-yasuku shimashō.**
   The meaning is no different from **yasuku shimashō** but this is politer. This is heard mostly from sales people.

PRACTICE

KEY SENTENCES

1. あの　かびんは　きれいですが、たかそうですね。

2. ねだんを　やすく　しましょう。　1,600えんに　しましょう。

3. ねだんが　やすく　なりました。　1,600えんに　なりました。

4. おおゆきで、しんかんせんが　うごいていないらしいです。

1. That vase is beautiful but it looks expensive.
2. I'll make the price cheaper. I'll make it ¥1,600.
3. The price has been reduced. It's become ¥1,600.
4. The Shinkansen (probably) isn't running because of the heavy snow.

Vocabulary

ねだん　　　　　　　**nedan**, price

EXERCISES

I　Practice the following patterns by changing the underlined parts.

A. *ex.* あの　りんごは　おいしそうです。

1. くつ、はきやすい
2. セーター、あたたかい
3. あたらしい　うち、ひろくて　きもちが　いい
4. ようふく、やすくない
5. みせの　ひと、ひま
6. けいかん、しんせつ
7. ひと、まじめ
8. どうぐ、べんりでは　ない

B. *ex.* てんきが　わるく　なりそうです。

1. はなが　さく
2. あめが　ふる
3. かびんが　おちる
4. ひが　きえる
5. あめは　ふらない
6. この　ふくの　ほうが　にあう
7. こどもが　よろこぶ

II　Make dialogues by changing the underlined parts as in the examples given.

A. *ex.* A：たかそうな　レストランですね。
　　　 B：たかそうに　みえますが、そんなに　たかくないですよ。

1. むずかしい、ほん
2. おもい、かばん

186 LESSON 24

3. やさしい、おとうさん
4. こわい、ひと
5. ひま、ポスト
6. らく、しごと

B. *ex.* **Q** : すずきさんは　なにを　していますか。
　　　A : <u>いそがしそうに</u>　<u>はたらいています</u>。

1. おいしい、おべんとうを　たべる
2. ひま、たばこを　すう
3. たのしい、はなす
4. さびしい、おんがくを　きく

C. *ex.* **Q** : もう　すこし　<u>やすく</u>　してくださいませんか。
　　　A : じゃ、<u>やすく</u>　しましょう。

1. はやい
2. すくない
3. あつい
4. しずか
5. きれい
6. かんたん

D. *ex.* **A** : <u>つぎの　かいぎは　いつに</u>　しますか。
　　　B : らいしゅうの　げつようびに　します。

　　　A : かとうさん、<u>つぎの　かいぎは　げつようびに</u>　なりました。

1. めんせつ、いつ、らいげつの　15にち
2. へやだい、いくら、60,000えん
3. しゅっぱつの　じかん、なんじ、あさ　8じ
4. しゃいんりょこう、どこ、ほっかいどう

E. *ex.* **Q** : だれが　<u>ドイツに　ふにんするん</u>ですか。
　　　A : たなかさんが　<u>ふにんする</u>らしいです。

1. ギターが　ひけます
2. しょるいを　わすれました
3. ロシアごが　わかりません
4. やくそくを　まもりませんでした

F. *ex.* **A**：スミスさんは　すもうに　くわしいらしいですよ。

　　　B：そうですか、ちっとも　しりませんでした。

1. あたらしい　じむしょ、やちんが　すごく　たかい
2. あの　レストラン、ゆうめい
3. かちょう、びょうき
4. あの　くるま、たなかさんの
5. やまださん、かいしゃを　やめる　つもり

Vocabulary

ようふく	**yōfuku**, (western) clothes	～だい	**-dai**, charge, fee
ひ	**hi**, fire	しゃいん　りょ	**shain ryokō**, company
ふく	**fuku**, clothes	こう	(employees' pleasure)
にあう	**niau**, suit, match (well)		trip
そんなに～ない	**sonna ni . . . nai**, not so	ふにんする	**funin suru**, be assigned,
やさしい	**yasashii**, gentle, kind		be sent, (*lit.*) proceed to
こわい	**kowai**, scary, fearful,		a post
	terrible	ギター	**gitā**, guitar
ポスト	**posuto**, position, post	ひく	**hiku**, play (musical instru-
らく（な）	**raku(na)**, easy, comfor-		ment)
	table	ロシアご	**Roshia-go**, Russian
（お）べんとう	**o-bentō**, (box) lunch	すごく	**sugoku**, very (colloquial),
さびしい	**sabishii**, lonely, cheerless		terrible
へやだい	**heya-dai**, room charge,		
	rent		

SHORT DIALOGUES

1. **A**：たなかさん　らいねん　ていねんだそうですよ。

　　B：ほんとうですか。しんじられません。おわかく　みえますね。

A: I hear Tanaka (will reach) retirement age next year.
B: Really? I can't believe it. He looks (so) young.

2. すずき：あしたから　あの　みせで　ふゆものの　バーゲンが　あるんだっ
　　　　　て？

　　さとう：うん、ずいぶん　やすく　するらしいよ。40パーセントびきだって。

Suzuki: Did you hear about the bargain sale on winter wear at that shop from tomorrow?
Satō:　Yeah, it seems they're going to be real cheap. Forty percent discount, I hear.

Vocabulary

ていねん	**teinen**, retirement age	～びき	**-biki (hiki)**, discount
バーゲン	**bāgen**, bargain (sale)		
～だって	**datte**, I hear (informal for		
	desu tte)		

QUIZ

I Read this lesson's opening dialogue and answer the following questions.

1. スミスさんが　ほしいけれど　たかそうだと　いった　さらは　いくら
   ですか。
2. スミスさんは　いくらぐらいの　さらが　ほしいと　いっていますか。
3. 1,700えんの　さらを　みて、こうしょうすれば　やすく　なりそうだと
   いっているのは　だれですか。
4. みせの　ひとは　1,700えんの　さらを　いくらに　しましたか。

II Put the appropriate words in the parentheses.

1. いくらですか。
   ぜんぶ（　　）　55,000えん（　　）　なります。
2. こちらは　いかがですか。
   ちょっと　ちいさいですね。おおきい（　　）は　ありませんか。
   それでは　こちらは　いかがですか。25,000えんです。
   すこし　たかいですね。
   それでは　23,000えん（・）　しましょう。
3. おもそう（　　）　かばんですね。
   おもそう（　　）　みえますが、そんなに　おもくないですよ。

III Circle the appropriate words in the parentheses.

1. いかがですか。
   すこし　おおきいですね。（もっと、もう）すこし　ちいさいのは　あり
   ませんか。
2. うるさいですね。
   ええ。（もっと、もう）　しずかな　ところで　はなしましょう。
3. あの　さらは　すばらしいですが、たかいんでしょう？
   ひだりの　さらは　50まんえんだそうです。（もっと、もう）　1まいの
   は　（もっと、もう）　たかいそうです。
4. コーヒーを　（もっと、もう）　1ぱい　いかがですか。
   いいえ、　（もっと、もう）　けっこうです。ありがとう。
5. こちらは　いかがですか。
   （もっと、もう）　やすいのは　ありませんか。

IV Complete the sentences with the appropriate form of the words indicated to convey the
meaning "seems (to be/that)."

1. スミスさんは　いつも　（　　）そうですね。
   ええ、しごとが　おおくて　（　　）らしいです。（いそがしい、たいへ
   んだ）
2. この　じしょと　あの　じしょと　どちらが　いいでしょうか。
   こちらの　ほうが　（　　）そうです。（いい）

3. じしんですね。

　あっ、たなから　ほんが　（　　）そうですよ。(おちる)

4. たなかさんは　（　　）、けがを　（　　）らしいです。(ころんだ、した)

5. すずきさんは　ふるい　にわに　きょうみが　（　　）らしいです。(ない)

6. あの　レストランは　（　　）、（　　）らしいです。(やすい、おいしい)

V Choose a sentence appropriate to the situation described.

A. Politely ask a neighbor to make less noise.

　1. しずかに　しましょう。

　2. うるさいです。やめてください。

　3. すみませんが、もう　すこし　しずかに　してくださいませんか。

B. You want to say, in a colloquial manner, that Nakamura can't come to the party.

　1. なかむらさんは　パーティーに　こられないんですって。

　2. なかむらさんは　パーティーに　こられないそうです。

　3. なかむらさんは　パーティーに　こられないと　いっていました。

LESSON **25** HOUSE FOR RENT

Ms. Nakamura goes house hunting.

中村： この へんで うちを さがしているんですが・・・。事務所が
　　　 いてんして、今の うちから とおく なってしまったんです。

ふどうさん屋：広さは、どのくらいの ものが よろしいでしょうか。

中村： 居間の ほかに 部屋が 一つ あれば いいんです。

ふどうさん屋：これなんか いかがですか。ダイニングキッチンと ほかに 部
　　　 屋が 二つ、一つは 和室です。

中村： 犬を かっても いいでしょうか。

ふどうさん屋：大家さんに 電話して、犬を かっても いいか どうか 聞い
　　　 てみましょう。よかったら これから 行ってみませんか。

中村： あの、家ちんは？

ふどうさん屋：1か月 11万円ですが、はじめの 月は 家ちんの ほかに し
　　　 き金、れい金として 6か月分 ひつようです。

中村： そうですか。では、見てから かりるか どうか きめたいと
　　　 思います。

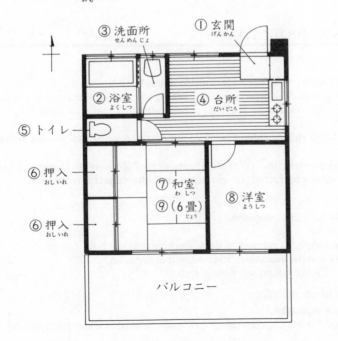

① genkan
② yokushitsu
③ senmen-jo
④ daidokoro
⑤ toire
⑥ oshiire
⑦ washitsu
⑧ yōshitsu
⑨ ~jo

191

Nakamura: I'm looking for a house in this neighborhood. Our office has been moved and it's ended up being (*lit.* "becoming") far from my present house.
Agent: About how much space would you like?
Nakamura: If there's one room, besides the living room, that'll be fine.
Agent: How about something like this? Besides the dining-room-kitchen there are two rooms and one is Japanese style.
Nakamura: Is it all right to have a dog?
Agent: I'll call the landlord and ask if it's OK to keep a dog. If you have time now (*lit.* If it's OK with you), wouldn't you like to go and look at it?
Nakamura: Well, what's the rent?
Agent: It's ¥110,000 a month. The first month, in addition to the rent, it's necessary (to pay) a deposit and appreciation money, six-month's worth (all together).
Nakamura: I see. I think I'll decide whether to rent it after looking at it.

Vocabulary

いてんする　**iten suru**, move
　いてん　**iten**, move, moving
〜てしまう　**-te shimau** (indicates completion, regret)
　しまう　**shimau**, finish, put an end to
ふどうさんや　**fudōsan-ya**, realty dealer
ひろさ　**hirosa**, space, (*lit.*) area
　〜さ　**-sa** (suffix, adj. to noun)
くらい　**kurai** = **gurai**
なんか　**nanka** (colloquial)=**nado**, like, such as, and so on

ダイニングキッチン　**dainingu kitchin**, dining-room-kitchen
わしつ　**washitsu**, Japanese-style room
かう　**kau**, keep, raise (not children)
おおやさん　**ōya-san**, landlord, owner
〜てみる　**-te miru**, (do and see result)
しききん　**shikikin**, deposit
れいきん　**reikin**, appreciation money
どうか　**dōka**, if, whether

GRAMMAR & LESSON OBJECTIVES

• -te shimau

Jimusho ga iten shite ima no uchi kara tōku natte shimatta n desu.

-te shimau expresses regret or dissatisfaction with a result, sometimes reluctance or resignation, and as indicated in the vocabulary list, this pattern signifies that something has been completely finished.

ex. 1. **Aiken no Burakkī ga shinde shimatta.** "(To my regret) my dog Blacky died. (**aiken**, "pet dog")
2. **Zembu tabete shimaimashita.** "(We) ate (them) all up." Both **-te/de shimau** and **-te/de shimatta** are often contracted, to **-chau/jau** and **-chatta/jatta**, respectively.

• -te miru

Inu o katte mo ii ka dō ka kiite mimashō.
Kore kara itte mimasen ka.

The meaning of this **-te** form plus **miru** is to do something and see how it goes.

ex. 1. **Kono doresu o kite mite kudasai.** "Please try this dress on."
2. **Tabete mimasu.** "I'll eat it (and see how it tastes)."

• -tara and -eba used idiomatically

Yokattara korekara itte mimashō.

Yokattara and **yokereba**, "If it's OK/convenient . . ." may be used in making suggestions or requests.

Ima no hoka ni heya ga hitotsu areba ii n desu.
Similarly with the pattern verb **-tara/-(re)ba ii**, which can be paraphrased as meaning "If you do it this way, the results should be satisfactory."
ex. **Dō ikeba/ittara ii desu ka.** "What's the (best) way to go?"
   Kono basu ni notte shūten de orireba/oritara ii desu. "If you take this bus and get off at the last stop (you'll be there)."
These are applications of the conditional verb forms introduced in lessons 15 and 16.

NOTES

1. **Hirosa**
   Hirosa is an example of an adjective being converted into a noun. This may be done with either type of adjective.
   -i adj: **nagasa**, "length"; **omosa**, "weight"; **ōkisa**, "size"
   -na adj: **benrisa**, "convenience"; **taisetsusa**, "importance"

2. **shikikin, reikin**
   In addition to a deposit, generally returnable, tenants are expected to give the landlord a certain amount of money, which varies from district to district, for the privilege of obtaining housing or office space. The **rei** of **reikin** means "thanks, gratitude."

PRACTICE

KEY SENTENCES

1. みちが こんでいて、よこはまから ここまで 3じかんも かかってしまいました。
2. この くつは いかがですか。はいてみてください。
3. あした なんじに きたら いいですか。
   10じに くれば いいです。

1. The roads were crowded and (we) ended up taking three hours from Yokohama to here.
2. How do you like these shoes? Try them on, please.
3. What would be a good time (for me) to come tomorrow?
   If (you come) at ten, it'll be OK.

EXERCISES

Make dialogues by changing the underlined parts as in the examples given.

A. *ex.* **A**：あまり じかんが ありません。
   B：そうですか、じゃ はやく <u>かたづけて</u>しまいましょう。

   1. きめる
   2. しごとを する
   3. なおす
   4. たべる
   5. とどける

B. *ex.* **Q**：もう　もらった　チョコレートを　ぜんぶ　たべてしまいましたか。
A：いいえ、まだ　たべていません。

1. しょくじを　する
2. てがみを　かく
3. コーヒーを　のむ
4. ぜんぶ　つかう

C. *ex.* **Q**：どう　したんですか。
A：ナイフで　てを　きってしまったんです。

1. コップを　わる
2. さいふを　おとす
3. しりょうが　なくなる
4. かっていた　いぬが　しぬ
5. ていでんで　コンピューターが　つかえなく　なる
6. すずきさんから　ラブレターを　もらう

D. *ex.* **Q**：どうして　でんわを　かけなかったんですか。
A：でんわばんごうを　わすれてしまったんです。

1. おくれました、くるまが　こしょうしました
2. ないています、しけんに　しっぱいしました
3. ひっこしました、じむしょが　とおく　なりました
4. おこっています、こどもが　となりの　ガラスを　わりました
5. がっこうを　やすみました、かぜを　ひきました

E. *ex.* **A**：できるか　どうか　やってみます。
B：どうぞ、ぜひ　やってみてください。

1. わかる、しらべる
2. にあう、きる
3. おもしろい、よむ
4. いい　みせ、いちど　いく

F. *ex.* **Q**：おいしそうな　おかしですね。たべてみても　いいですか。
A：はい、どうぞ。

1. はきやすい、くつ、はく
2. おもしろい、ほん、よむ

3. かんたん、ワープロ、つかう
4. いい、ステレオ、きく
5. べんり、じしょ、ひく

G. *ex.* **Q**：<u>きてみ</u>ましたか。
     A：ええ、<u>きてみ</u>ましたが、<u>にあいません</u>でした。

    1. しらべる、わかりません
    2. でんわを　かける、だれも　いません
    3. こうしょうする、やすく　なりません
    4. さがす、どこにも　ありません
    5. あう、きに　いりません

H. *ex.* **Q**：<u>なんじに　きた</u>ら　いいですか。
     A：<u>10じに　くれ</u>ば　いいですよ。

    1. だれに　きく、けいかんに
    2. どこで　かいぎを　する、あの　へやで
    3. なんで　いく、ちかてつで
    4. どこで　のりかえる、とうきょうで

I. *ex.* **Q**：<u>ふじさんの　たかさ</u>は　どのくらいですか。
     A：<u>3800メートル</u>くらいです。

    1. にもつ、おもい、　15キログラム
    2. しんかんせん、はやい、じそく　200キロ
    3. へや、ひろい、6じょう
    4. テーブル、おおきい、90センチ　かける　160センチ
    5. はし、ながい、2マイル

J. *ex.* **A**：<u>あたたかい</u>ですね。
     B：ええ、<u>はる</u>のような　<u>あたたかさ</u>ですね。

    1. くらい、ゆうがた
    2. あかるい、ひるま
    3. さむい、ふゆ
    4. にぎやか、まつり

ナイフ	**naifu**, knife	のりかえる	**norikaeru**, transfer
わる	**waru**, break	たかさ	**takasa**, height, altitude
こしょうする	**koshō suru**, break down, be out of order	じそく	**jisoku**, speed per hour
こしょう	**koshō**, breakdown, trouble	キロ（メートル）	**kiro(mētoru)**, kilo(meter)
なく	**naku**, cry	6じょう	**6-jō**, six-tatami-mat (area)
しっぱいする	**shippai suru**, fail	〜じょう	**-jō** (counter for **tatami**)
しっぱい	**shippai**, failure, mistake	90センチ かける 160セン チ	**90 senchi kakeru 160 senchi**, 90 by 160 centimeters
おこる	**okoru**, be/get angry	センチ	**senchi**, centimeter
となり	**tonari**, neighbor	かける	**kakeru**, multiply
ガラス	**garasu**, glass	はし	**hashi**, bridge
ステレオ	**sutereo**, stereo	マイル	**mairu**, mile

SHORT DIALOGUES

1. なかむら：あのこと、もう　しゃべってしまったんですか。
   すずき：　あ、いけなかったんですか。うっかり　しゃべってしまいました。

   Nakamura: Did you (go) chattering about that matter already?
   Suzuki:　　Oh, shouldn't I have? I talked about it without thinking.

2. **A**：とうきょうタワーへ　いきたいんですが、どう　いったら　いいですか。
   B：88ばんの　バスに　のって、しゅうてんで　おりてください。

   A: I'd like to go to Tokyo Tower. Which is the best way to go?
   B: Take the No. 88 bus and get off at the last stop.

3. こうはい：せんぱい、おもしろそうな　ざっしですね。
   せんぱい：うん、すごく　おもしろいよ。よかったら　あげるよ。
   こうはい：いいんですか。
   せんぱい：ああ、いいよ。もう　みちゃったから。

   Junior:　That seems to be an interesting magazine.
   Senior:　Unh, extremely interesting. I'll give it to you (if you want it).
   Junior:　Is it OK?
   Senior:　Ah, sure. I'm done looking (at it).

4. **A**：それだけ　べんきょうすれば、にほんごが　じょうずに　なりますよ。
   B：そうだと　いいんですが。

   A: If (you go on) studying so hard, (I'm sure your) Japanese will become quite good.
   B: (I) hope so. (*lit.* If so, that's [all to the] good.)

Vocabulary

しゃべる	**shaberu**, chatter, talk (colloquial)	せんぱい	**sempai**, senior, older person
うっかり	**ukkari**, without thinking, inadvertantly, carelessly	みちゃった	**michatta** (colloquial for **mite shimaimashita**)
こうはい	**kōhai**, junior, younger person (coworker or schoolmate)		

QUIZ

I   Read this lesson's opening dialogue and answer the following questions.

1. なかむらさんは　なぜ　うちを　さがしていますか。
2. なかむらさんは　いまの　ほかに　へやが　いくつ　あれば　いいと　いっていますか。
3. なかむらさんは　あたらしい　うちで、なにを　かいたがっていますか。
4. この　うちを　かりる　ひとが　はじめの　つきに　はらわなければ　ならない　おかねは　ぜんぶで　いくらに　なりますか。
5. なかむらさんは　この　うちを　かりるでしょうか。

II   Put the appropriate words in the parentheses.

1. いま（　　）　ほか（　　）　へやが　ふたつ　あります。
2. みて（　　）、かりる（　　）　どうか　きめたい（　　）　おもいます。
3. しききん、れいきん（　　）　6かげつぶんの　やちんを　はらってください。
4. この　へん（　　）　うち（　　）　さがしています。

III   Complete the questions so that they fit the answers.

1. にもつの　おもさは　（　　）くらいに　なりますか。
   やく　10キロです。
2. はじめに　（　　）かげつぶん　はらわなければ　なりませんか。
   ぜんぶで　7かげつぶんに　なります。
3. （　　）から　この　うちに　はいれますか。
   いま　すぐ　はいれます。
4. かりる　ばあいは　（　　）までに　へんじすれば　いいですか。
   らいしゅうちゅうに　おねがいします。

IV   Complete the sentences with the appropriate form of the verbs indicated.

1. じこの　ために　でんしゃが　（　　）しまいました。（とまる）
2. でんわを　かけるのを　（　　）しまいました。（わすれる）

3. れいぞうこの　なかの　たべものを　ぜんぶ　（　　）しまいました。
（たべる）

4. これで　ほんとうに　いいか　どうか　かちょうに　（　　）みてくだ
さい。（きく）

5. この　くつを　（　　）みてください。　（　　）たら、あげますよ。（は
く、きに　いる）

6. ぎんざに　いきたいんですが、どこで　（　　）たら　いいですか。
（のりかえる）

7. やちんは　いつまでに　（　　）ば　いいですか。（はらう）

V　Choose a sentence appropriate to the situation described.

A. Ask for directions to Tokyo Hospital.

1. すみませんが、とうきょうびょういんまで　いってくださいません
か。

2. こんにちは。とうきょうびょういんに　いこうと　おもいます。

3. すみませんが、とうきょうびょういんは　どう　いったら　いいです
か。

B. Ask a store clerk if it's all right to try on a jacket.

1. この　うわぎを　きてみても　いいですか。

2. よかったら、この　うわぎを　きてみませんか。

3. この　うわぎを　ください。

Mr. Suzuki and Ms. Watanabe get ready for a meeting.

鈴木：会議は　3時からですから、そろそろ　つくえや　いすを　ならべておいてください。

渡辺：どんな　かたちに　ならべましょうか。

鈴木：まず　スライドを　見てから、新しい　きかくの　せつめいを　しますから、コの字がたに　ならべてください。

渡辺：出席者は　18人ですね。

鈴木：はい。いすが　たりない　時は　となりの　部屋のを　使ったら　どうですか。しょるいは　人数分　コピーしてありますか。

渡辺：はい、20部　コピーしてあります。

鈴木：ところで、スライドの　じゅんびは　してありますか。

渡辺：はい、さっき　きかいを　ためして、セットしておきました。

鈴木：スライドを　見終わったころ　コーヒーを　出しますから、下の　コーヒーショップに　ちゅうもんしておいてくれませんか。

渡辺：3時半ごろ　持って来るように　言いましょうか。

鈴木：3時半は　早すぎます。4時ごろで　いいでしょう。

渡辺：はい、わかりました。

Suzuki:　　The meeting is from three, so please arrange the tables and chairs now (*lit.* soon).
Watanabe:　What shape should I arrange them in?
Suzuki:　　Since we'll look at slides first and explain the new plan, put them in the shape of [katakana] *ko* [コ].
Watanabe:　There'll be eighteen attendees, right?
Suzuki:　　Right. If there aren't enough chairs, how about using (those) in the next room? Are there copies of the materials for the (right) number of people?
Watanabe:　Yes, twenty sets have been made up.
Suzuki:　　Well, then, have preparations (for showing) the slides been made?
Watanabe:　Yes, I tested the equipment a little while ago, I've already set it up.
Suzuki:　　When (we) finish looking at the slides we'll serve coffee. Would you order it from the coffee shop downstairs?
Watanabe:　Shall I tell them to bring (it) around 3:30?
Suzuki:　　Three thirty is too early. Around four o'clock should be OK.
Watanabe:　All right.

そろそろ	**sorosoro**, (*lit.*) soon, little by little	きかい	**kikai**, equipment, (*lit.*) machine
ならべる	**naraberu**, arrange	ためす	**tamesu**, test, try out
～ておく	**-te oku**, (prepare in advance)	セットする	**setto suru**, set (up)
		みおわる	**miowaru**, finish looking at
～じがた	**-ji-gata**, shape of a character/letter	～おわる	**(-)owaru**, finish —ing
～がた	**-gata**, -shaped (suffix)	だす	**dasu**, serve
しゅっせきしゃ	**shusseki-sha**, attendee	コーヒーショップ	**kōhī shoppu**, coffee shop
にんずうぶん	**ninzū-bun**, (sets/portions) for number of people	ちゅうもんする	**chūmon suru**, order
にんずう	**ninzū**, number of people	ちゅうもん	**chūmon**, order
～ぶ	**-bu**, copy (counter)	はやすぎる	**hayasugiru**, too early
じゅんび	**jumbi**, preparations	～すぎる	**(-)sugiru** = too (*lit.* pass)

GRAMMAR & LESSON OBJECTIVES

• -te oku

Tsukue ya isu o narabete oite kudasai.
Sakki kikai o tameshite, setto shite okimashita.
Kōhī o dashimasu kara, shita no kōhī shoppu ni chūmon shite oite kuremasen ka.
The idea conveyed by **-te oku** is to do something so it will be ready for the future.

• -te aru

Shorui wa ninzū-bun kopī shite arimasu ka.
The use of **-te aru** indicates that something, having been done or prepared, is in a particular state or condition.

Watashi wa shorui o kopī shite okimashita. "I copied the documents (so they're ready)."
Shorui wa kopī shite arimasu. "The documents have been copied."
These two sentences refer to the same situation from different viewpoints. With **-te oku**, the person who does the action, whether expressed or implied, is important. With **-te aru**, the focus is on the action and the result. It should be noted that in either case the action is intentional. When it is a natural occurrence or intention is irrelevent, as with the verbs **furu**, **naru** and **shinu**, these patterns are never used.
Since the **-te aru** pattern focuses on situation or status, the particle is **ga** or **wa**. When the **-te aru** pattern is used, the thing or situation is the subject, so the particle is normatively **ga**, but since the subject may function as the topic, the topic marker **wa** may also occur, as in **Suraido no jumbi ga/wa shite arimasu. (Watanabe-san ga/wa) suraido no jumbi o shimashita/shite okimashita.** As in this sentence, the object marker **o** comes before **suru** used independently or **-te oku**.

NOTES

1. **Sorosoro**
   This word often comes into a conversation when one starts to do something. It can be thought of as meaning, "Now it's time to . . ."
   ex. **Sorosoro dekakemashō.** "We'd better start now."

2. **Isu ga tarinai toki wa, tonari no heya no o tsukattara dō desu ka.**
   The patterns with **-tara** combined with **ikaga desu ka**, **dō desu ka** or **ii desu yo** can be sug-

gestions or warnings.

ex. 1. **Kōban de kiitara dō desu ka.** "Why don't you ask at the police box?"
2. **Heya o sōji shitara dō desu ka.** "You'd better clean your room."
3. **Denwa de shirasetara ii desu yo.** "If (you) let (him) know by phone, it'll be all right."

3. **Suraido o mi-owatta koro . . .**
Owaru added to the **-masu** stem of a verb gives the meaning "finish —ing." The same type of compound word can be made with **hajimeru**, **naosu** and certain other verbs.
ex. **tabe-owaru**, "finish eating"; **yomi-hajimeru**, "start reading"; **kaki-naosu**, "rewrite"

4. **3-ji-han wa hayasugimasu.**
Sugiru, "exceed," "pass," "go too far," combines with the stems of adjectives and the -**masu** stem of verbs to mean "too" or "too much."
ex. **ōkii** → **ōki-sugiru**, "too big"; **takai** → **taka-sugiru**, "too high/expensive"; **shizukana** → **shizuka-sugiru**, "too quiet"; **tabemasu** → **tabe-sugiru**, "eat too much"

PRACTICE

KEY SENTENCES

1. 〔わたしは〕　でんわで　レストランの　せきを　よやくしておきました。
2. レストランの　せきが　よやくしてあります。
3. こうばんで　きいたら　どうですか。

1. I reserved restaurant seats by telephone.
2. Restaurant seats have been reserved (since I did it).
3. How about asking at the police box?

> **Vocabulary**

せき　　　　　**seki**, seat

EXERCISES

I   Make dialogues by changing the underlined parts as in the examples given.

A. *ex.* **Q**：かいぎの　まえに、<u>いすと　つくえを　ならべて</u>おきましょうか。
A：ええ、<u>ならべて</u>おいてください。

　　　1. かいぎ、しょるいを　つくる
　　　2. かいぎ、はいざらを　つくえの　うえに　おく
　　　3. パーティー、　ビールを　かう
　　　4. りょこう、てがみで　しらせる
　　　5. しゅっちょう、でんわを　かける
　　　6. おでかけ、タクシーを　よぶ

B. *ex.* **Q**：もう　<u>きっぷを　かいました</u>か。
A：はい、<u>かって</u>おきました。

1. ぶちょうに こられるか どうか きく
2. ヒーターを つける
3. たいせつな しょるいを あずける
4. へやを かたづける
5. かいぎの じゅんびを する

C. ex. **Q**：しょるいは もう じゅんびしてありますか。
　　　A：はい、じゅんびしておきました。
　　　Q：スライドは？
　　　A：スライドも じゅんびしてあります。

1. のみもの、かう、くだもの
2. やちん、はらう、ガスだい
3. けいやくしょ、つくる、せいきゅうしょ
4. ぎゅうにく、きる、ねぎや とうふ
5. パスポート、よういする、トラベラーズチェック

D. ex. **Q**：あなたの くるまは どこですか。
　　　A：この ビルの まえに とめてあります。

1. タイプライター、となりの へやに おく
2. あたった たからくじ、きんこの なかに しまう
3. にもつ、くるまの うしろに つむ
4. スミスさんの てがみ、つくえの うえに だす

E. ex. **A**：みちが わからない ときは どう したら いいでしょう。
　　　B：こうばんで きいたら どうですか。

1. でんわばんごうを しりたい、104に でんわする
2. ゆううつに なった、（お）さけを のむ
3. こまった、じょうしに そうだんする
4. さびしい、りょこうに でかける
5. （お）かねが たりない、おやに たのむ

II　Make compound verbs like the one in the example for the following sentences.

　　ex. スライドを みおわりました。

1. スライドを セットする、おわりました
2. いすを ならべる、はじめてください
3. うらぐちの ドアを しめる、わすれました

4. あめが　ふる、つづいています

5. てがみを　かく、なおします

III　Make dialogues by changing the underlined parts as in the examples given.

　A. *ex.* **Q**：<u>あじ</u>は　どうですか。

　　　A：ちょっと　<u>から</u>すぎますね。

　　　1. あじ、あまい

　　　2. ねだん、たかい

　　　3. いろ、あかい

　　　4. この　へや、せまい

　　　5. この　まち、にぎやか

　　　6. こどもたち、げんき

　B. *ex.* **Q**：どう　しましたか。

　　　A：<u>たべ</u>すぎて、<u>おなか</u>が　いたいんです。

　　　1. のむ、あたま

　　　2. あるく、あし

　　　3. たばこを　すう、のど

　　　4. はたらく、かたや　こし

　　　5. テレビを　みる、め

Vocabulary

たいせつ（な）	**taisetsu(na)**, important, valuable, serious	しまう	**shimau**, keep, put away, save
ガスだい	**gasu-dai**, gas bill	つむ	**tsumu**, load, pile up
ガス	**gasu**, gas	だす	**dasu**, put out
けいやくしょ	**keiyaku-sho**, (written) contract	ゆううつ（な）	**yūutsu(na)**, gloomy, depressed
せいきゅうしょ	**seikyū-sho**, bill	おや	**oya**, parent(s)
ねぎ	**negi**, onion, leek	つづく	**tsuzuku**, continue
トラベラーズ チェック	**toraberāzu chekku**, traveler's check	かきなおす	**kakinaosu**, rewrite, redraft
タイプライター	**taipuraitā**, typewriter	からい	**karai**, salty, hot
あたった　たか らくじ	**atatta takarakuji**, winning lottery (ticket)	あまい	**amai**, sweet, indulgent
あたる	**ataru**, win, hit the mark, strike	かた	**kata**, shoulder
たからくじ	**takarakuji**, lottery	こし	**koshi**, lower back, waist, hips

SHORT DIALOGUES

1. かちょう：ねんがはがきは　もう　かってありますか。

   やまだ：　はい。　1,000まい　かっておきましたが、たりますか。

   かちょう：あと　500まい　かっておいてください。

   Section Chief: Did you buy New Year's cards already?
   Yamada:　　　Yes, I bought one thousand. Is that enough?
   Section Chief: Please buy five hundred more.

2. リンダ：きのうの　しんぶんに　みそしるの　つくりかたが　かいてありま
   した。

   けいこ：へえ。いちど　つくってみたら　どうですか。

   Linda: I read how to make *miso* soup in yesterday's newspaper.
   Keiko: Oh, that sounds interesting. Why don't you try making (it) once?

3. わたなべ：コーヒーを　いれました。すこし　やすんだら　いかがですか。

   かとう：　ありがとう。じゃ、ひとやすみしよう。ああ、つかれた。

   Watanabe: (I) made coffee. How about resting awhile?
   Katō:　　　Thanks. I will take a short rest. Ah, am I tired!

Vocabulary

ねんがはがき　　**nenga hagaki**, New
　　　　　　　　　Year's card
いれる　　　　　**ireru**, make (coffee, tea,
　　　　　　　　　etc.)

ひとやすみ　　　**hitoyasumi**, (short) rest
つかれる　　　　**tsukareru**, tire, be/get
　　　　　　　　　tired

QUIZ

I　Read this lesson's opening dialogue and answer the following questions.

　1. すずきさんは　わたなべさんに　かいぎが　はじまる　まえに　つくえ
　　　や　いすを　ならべておくように　いいましたか。
　2. かいぎの　しゅっせきしゃは　なんにんですか。
　3. しょるいは　なんぶ　コピーしてありますか。
　4. わたなべさんは　かいぎで　スライドを　つかう　ことを　しっていま
　　　したか。
　5. かいぎは　4じごろ　おわりますか。

II　Put the appropriate words in the parentheses.

　1. コのじがた　（　　）　つくえ　（　　）　ならべてください。
　2. コーヒーが　ないんです。
　　　じゃ、みず　（　　）　けっこうです。
　3. とだな　（　　）　なかに　コップ　（　　）　しまいました。

4. いす（　　）　たりない　ときは、わたし（　　）を　つかってくださ
   い。
5. でんわを　して、さかや（　　）　ビール（　　）　ちゅうもんしてく
   ださい。

III　Complete the questions so that they fit the answers.

1. つくえは　（　　）　かたちに　ならべましょうか。
   コのじがたに　ならべてください。
2. スライドの　きかいは　（　　）ですか。
   もう　かいぎしつに　はこんであります。
3. この　へやは　（　　）ですか。
   せますぎて、だめです。
4. コーヒーは　（　　）ぶん　ちゅうもんしましょうか。
   6にんぶん　おねがいします。

IV　Complete the sentences with the appropriate form of the words indicated.

1. （　　）すぎて、　（　　）ません。（あまい、たべられる）
2. でんきを　（　　）わすれて、（　　）しまったんです。（けす、でかけ
   る）
3. でんわばんごうが　（　　）たら、わたなべさんに　（　　）たら　ど
   うですか。（わからない、きく）
4. たなかさんから　でんわが　（　　）たら、ようじを　（　　）おいて
   ください。（ある、きく）
5. （　　）　しょるいは　きんこに　（　　）あります。（たいせつ、しま
   う）
6. けいやくしょは　どこに　ありますか。
   かちょうの　つくえの　うえに　（　　）おきました。（おく）
7. その　けんは　ぶちょうに　はなしましたか。
   ええ、　もう　（　　）あります。（はなす）

V　Answer the following questions.

1. あなたの　にほんごの　ほんに　なまえが　かいてありますか。
2. うちや　へやを　かりたい　とき、どこで　そうだんしたら　いいです
   か。
3. あなたの　せの　たかさは　どのぐらいですか。
4. おさけを　のみすぎると　からだに　よくないですか。
5. あなたは　にほんごの　じゅぎょうの　まえに、かならず　つぎに　な
   らう　ところを　じぶんで　べんきょうしておきますか。

LESSON 27 A SAVE-THE-TREES CAMPAIGN

Mrs. Hayashi asks Linda to sign a petition.

林夫人：あのう、おねがいが あるんですが。

リンダ：何でしょう。まあ、しょめい運動ですか。

林夫人：ええ、北海道の 山に かんこうどうろを 作るので、げんせいりん の木を たくさん 切るそうです。何千本も 切るらしいんですよ。

リンダ：それは もったいないですねえ。

林夫人：ええ、それで その 計画を やめてほしいと 思って、しょめい運 動を 始めたんです。

リンダ：そうですか。ちきゅう上から みどりが へっていくのは こまります すね。しぜんほごと 開発の バランスは むずかしいですねえ。

林夫人：ええ、でも ルートを かえれば、たくさん 木を 切らなくても どうろは 作れるそうです。木を 切ってしまったら、後で こうか いしても おそすぎます。

リンダ：わたくしも そう 思います。

林夫人：かんけいしゃの 人たちに しぜんの うつくしさと 大切さを も っと じかくしてほしいんです。来週 グループの 人たちと じも とへ 行って、かんけいしゃに うったえてくる つもりです。

リンダ：そうですか。みどりの 少ない 都会の 人の ほうが ねっしんな ようですね。わたくしも 木を 切らないでほしいと 思います。あ した うちで パーティーを しますから、友だちに 話して、しょ めいしてもらいましょう。

林夫人：ええ、ぜひ おねがいします。

リンダ：でも、外国人の しょめいでも いいんですか。

林夫人：かえって いいと 思いますよ。外国人の 声には 耳を かたむけ るかもしれませんから。

Hayashi: Um, I'd like to ask you a favor.
Linda: What might it be? Ah, a signature campaign?
Hayashi: Yes. It seems that to build a sightseeing route in the Hokkaido mountains, they'll cut down a great many trees in a virgin forest. They'll cut thousands of trees, I hear.
Linda: That's a real waste.
Hayashi: Yes, that's why this signature campaign was started—to stop the project.
Linda: I see. It's distressing, isn't it, the (way) greenery is diminishing from the surface of the earth. Balancing preservation of nature and development is difficult, isn't it?
Hayashi: Yes, but it's said that if they change the route, the road can be built without cutting a lot of trees. Once they've cut the trees, it'll be too late to be sorry about it.

206

Linda: I agree.

Hayashi: We want the people concerned to be more conscious of the beauty and importance of nature. Next week, I'm planning to go with our group to (that) locality and make an appeal to the people concerned.

Linda: Oh, are you? City people with little greenery (around them) seem to be more enthusiastic, don't they? I wish (they) wouldn't cut the trees. I'm having a party at my house tomorrow, and I'll tell (my) friends and have them sign (the petition).

Hayashi: Please do, by all means.

Linda: Still, will even foreigners' signatures be all right?

Hayashi: If it comes to that, I think (they're) better. Perhaps they'll listen to foreigners' opinions.

Vocabulary

しょめい	**shomei**, signature	こうかい	**kōkai**, regret, repentance
うんどう	**undō**, campaign		
かんこう	**kankō**, sightseeing	～ても	**-te mo**, even if
どうろ	**dōro**, route, road, street, highway	わたくし	**watakushi**, I (polite, formal)
げんせいりん	**genseirin**, virgin forest	じかくする	**jikaku suru**, be consious of
もったいない	**mottainai**, waste(ful)		
それで	**sorede**, That's why, for that reason	じかく	**jikaku**, awareness, self-knowledge
～てほしい	**-te hoshii**, want to have done	じもと	**jimoto**, locality, local
		うったえる	**uttaeru**, make an appeal, complain
ちきゅうじょう	**chikyū-jō**, earth's surface (*lit.* upper part)	とかい	**tokai**, city, town
～じょう	**-jō**, upper (part)	ねっしん（な）	**nesshin(na)**, enthusiastic, zealous, attentive
へる	**heru**, diminish, decrease		
ほご	**hogo**, preservation, protection	しょめいする	**shomei suru**, sign
		かえって	**kaette**, on the contrary
かいはつ	**kaihatsu**, development	みみを　かたむける	**mimi o katamukeru**,
バランス	**baransu**, balancing, balance		listen, give ear to
		かたむける	**katamukeru**, lean, tilt, slant
ルート	**rūto**, route		
こうかいする	**kōkai suru**, be sorry, regret		

GRAMMAR & LESSON OBJECTIVES

• -te iku and -te kuru

Raishū . . . jimoto e itte kankei-sha ni uttaete kuru tsumori desu.

Let's take a look at the literal and figurative senses of **-te iku**, **te kuru** patterns, some of which were introduced in lesson 6. Basically **-te iku** means to do something and then go, and **-te kuru** means to do something and then come (back). The above example is, of course, literal. The figurative use generally suggests changes over time, analogous to **Haru ga kimasu**, "Spring is coming."

The following are further examples of literal usage, where three actions are actually implied: going, doing and coming (back).

ex. A. **B-san o-bentō o katte kite kudasai.** "Miss B, please go buy (me) a box lunch."

　　 B. **Hai, katte kimasu.** "Sure. (I'll) buy (it) and come (right) back."

Chikyūjō kara midori ga hette iku no wa komarimasu ne.
The usage here is figurative, as is the following.
Kaze o hikimashita ga yoku natte kimashita. "(I) caught cold but (I've) gotten better."

● **-te morau, -te ageru, -te kureru**

Tomodachi ni hanashite, shomei shite moraimashō.
These three verbs have all appeared before. (See lesson 5 and the first volume.) The point to note now is that their employment in these patterns parallels their usage as main verbs.

    ex. 1. **(Watashi wa) Yamada-san ni tetsudatte moraimashita.** "Ms. Yamada kindly helped me. (*lit.* "I received help(ing) from Ms. Yamada.)"
        2. **Yamada-san ga tetsudatte kuremashita.** "Ms. Yamada helped me." (*lit.* "Ms. Yamada gave (me a) helping (hand)."

The choice of the verb depends on who is giving and who is receiving, who is acting and who is "receiving" the action from the viewpoint of the speaker. However, it is better not to be too free with **-te ageru**, because it may sound as if "I am doing you a favor." It is appropriate when the milieu is family or close friends, but to a person with heavy baggage, it is preferable to say simply, **Nimotsu o mochimashō.** "I'll carry (your) baggage." Or, even politer, **O-nimotsu o o-mochi shimashō.**

● **-te hoshii**

Sono keikaku o yamete hoshii.
Kankei-sha no hito-tachi ni shizen no utsukushisa to taisetsusa o motto jikaku shite hoshii n desu.
These are examples of **hoshii** coming after verbs. (See p. 177 for nouns.) The complete pattern is formed with person **ni** plus **-te** form followed by **hoshii**.

    ex. **Suzuki-san ni kūkō e itte hoshii.** (I) want Suzuki to go to the airport."

The dialogue sentence **Watashi mo ki o kiranaide hoshii to omoimasu** shows one way a negative can be expressed by this pattern.

● **-te mo**

Ato de kōkai shite mo ososugimasu.
"Even if they regret (it) later, it'll be too late" is a good way to think of the meaning of this sentence.
These patterns are made with the **-te** form (verb or **-i** adjective) and **mo**, or a noun or **-na** adjective stem and **demo**.

    ex. 1. **Ashita ame ga futte mo gorufu ni ikimasu.** "If it rains tomorrow (I'm) going golfing anyway."
        2. **Yasukute mo kaimasen.** "Even if it's cheap, (I) won't buy (it)."
        3. **Ashita ame demo gorufu ni ikimasu.** "Rain tomorrow–(I'll) go golfing anyway."
        4. **Benri demo urusai kara, chikatetsu wa kirai desu.** "Although convenient, (I) dislike subways because they're noisy."

After negative forms:
Ki o kiranakute mo dōro wa tsukureru sō desu.

    ex. **Omoshiroku nakute mo zembu yonde kudasai.** "Please read all (of it) even if it's not interesting."

NOTES

1. **Mā, shomei undō desu ka.**
    Mā shows that the speaker has made a discovery and is a woman's way of speaking.

2. **Nan-zen-bon mo**
    This pattern, **nan** with a counter and **mo**, conveys the feeling that a number, while not specific, is significant. The **mo** adds emphasis.
    ex. **Ano hikōki jiko de nan-byaku-nin mo shinimashita.** "Hundreds of people died in that plane accident."

3. **Sorede sono keikaku o yamete hoshii to omotte, shomei undō o hajimeta n desu.**
   The role of **sorede** is to introduce a conclusion after mentioning background, process, reason and so on.

4. **chikyū-jō**
   -jō is added as a suffix with the meaning "on the surface of" to words like this one and **kai-jō**, "on the surface of the sea," and **riku-jō**, "on the surface of the land."

5. **Kaette ii to omoimasu.**
   When a person thinks his judgement is contrary to commonly accepted ideas, **kaette** can be used to show this. It may also occur when actions are contrary to expectations.
   ex. **Kusuri o nondara, kaette waruku narimashita.** "(I) took medicine but (I) got worse."

PRACTICE

KEY SENTENCES

1. この まちも たかい ビルが ふえていくでしょう。
2. ともだちに たのんで、やすくて きれいな ホテルを よやくしてもらいました。
3. ホワイトさんにも きてほしいので、しょうたいじょうを おくりましょう。
4. あした ゆきが ふっても、〔わたしは〕 ゴルフに いきます。

1. Tall buildings will multiply in this town too.
2. I had a friend make reservations at a clean, inexpensive hotel.
3. I want Ms. White to come too; let's send her an invitation.
4. Even if it snows tomorrow I'll go golfing.

EXERCISES

I   Make dialogues by changing the underlined parts as in the examples given.

   A. *ex.* **Q**：ちきゅうの みどりは しょうらい どう なりますか。
     A：もっと へっていくでしょう。

       1. とかいの じんこう、ふえる
       2. この まちの ようす、かわる
       3. ぶっか、たかく なる
       4. こどもの かず、すくなく なる

   B. *ex.* **Q**：なにを みているんですか。
     A：おおきい とりが とんでいくのを みているんです。

       1. ともだちが かえる
       2. おおきい ふねが でる
       3. かわいい いぬが はしる

II Practice the following pattern by changing the underlined part.

ex. <u>みちが　こんで</u>きました。

      1. だんだん　つかれる
      2. （お）かねが　なくなる
      3. あめが　ふる
      4. そらが　くらく　なる

III Make dialogues by changing the underlined parts as in the examples given.

A. *ex.* **Q**：かんけいしゃに　<u>たのめ</u>ますか。
      A：ええ、<u>たのんで</u>くる　つもりです。

      1. さっぽろで　いっぱく　できる、いっぱくする
      2. らいしゅうまでに　しらべられる、　しらべる
      3. ようすを　みてこられる、みる
      4. がいこくで　せんでんできる、せんでんする
      5. やすいものが　かえる、かう

B. *ex.* **Q**：だれに　<u>（お）かねを</u>　<u>かして</u>もらいましたか。
      A：<u>しんせつな　ともだち</u>に　<u>かして</u>もらいました。

      1. てつだう、こども
      2. しゃしんを　みせる、うちの　おばあさん
      3. うちを　さがす、ひしょの　わたなべさん
      4. しゃしんを　とる、　しらない　ひと

C. *ex.* **Q**：じぶんで　<u>つくった</u>んですか。
      A：いいえ、ともだちが　<u>つくって</u>くれたんです。

      1. ほんやくする
      2. しらべる
      3. てつづきを　する
      4. くすりを　とりに　いく

D. *ex.* **Q**：とうきょうの　<u>まちを　あんないして</u>ほしいんですが。
      A：はい、いいですよ。

      1. しけんの　ことを　せつめいする
      2. だんぼうを　つける
      3. はやしさんに　たのむ

4. けいこさんを　しょうかいする
　　5. いすを　2れつに　ならべる

E. *ex.* **Q**：<u>せんせいに　はなしても</u>　いいですか。
　　A：すみませんが、<u>はなさ</u>ないでほしいんです。

　　1. たばこを　すう
　　2. ともだちに　みせる
　　3. らいしゅう　やすむ
　　4. ろくおんする

F. *ex.* **Q**：<u>あめが　ふっても</u>　ゴルフに　いきますか。
　　A：<u>あめが　ふったら</u>　いきません。

　　1. でんしゃが　こんでいる、のる
　　2. ねぼうする、あさごはんを　たべる
　　3. たかい、かう
　　4. おそい、いく
　　5. ふべん、つかう

G. *ex.* **Q**：<u>こうばんで　きいたら　わかる</u>でしょうか。
　　A：さあ、<u>こうばんで　きいても　わから</u>ないでしょう。

　　1. スポーツを　したら　やせる
　　2. はしったら　まにあう
　　3. いま　いったら　あえる
　　4. ビタミンを　のんだら　よく　なる
　　5. あさ　はやく　いったら　すいている

H. *ex.* **Q**：<u>きを　きらなくても　どうろは　つくれ</u>ますか。
　　A：たぶん　むりでしょう。

　　1. じしょを　みない、ほんが　よめます
　　2. いしゃに　みて　もらわない、よく　なります
　　3. いそがない、まにあうでしょう
　　4. はっきり　いわない、きもちが　わかります

I. *ex.* **A**：<u>きを　なんぼんも　きる</u>らしいですよ。
　　B：そんなに　<u>きる</u>んですか。

　　1. さんかしゃが　なんびゃくにん、あった

2. いちまい　なんまんえん、する
3. こどもが　10にん、いる
4. ほんを　いちにち　さんさつ、よむ

ぶっか	**bukka**, (commodity) prices	～れつ	**retsu**, row, line
かず	**kazu**, number	ろくおんする	**rokuon suru**, record
とり	**tori**, bird	ろくおん	**rokuon**, recording
かわいい	**kawaii**, cute	ねぼうする	**nebō suru**, oversleep, sleep late
だんだん	**dandan**, gradually, step by step	ねぼう	**nebō**, oversleeping, late riser
しらない　ひと	**shiranai hito**, stranger	いしゃに　みて　もらう	**isha ni mite morau**, see a doctor
ほんやくする	**hon'yaku suru**, translate		
ほんやく	**hon'yaku**, translation	さんかしゃ	**sankasha**, participant, entrant
だんぼう	**dambō**, heating		
２れつ	**2-retsu**, 2 rows	する	**suru**, cost, be worth

SHORT DIALOGUE

ちち：　くらく　なってきた。　さあ、もう　かえろう。
むすこ：いやだ。もっと　あそびたい。

Father: It's getting dark. Let's go home now.
Son:　　No! (*lit*. "[That's a] disagreeable [idea]!") I want to play more.

もう　　　　　　　　**mō**, now

QUIZ

I　Read this lesson's opening dialogue and answer the following questions.

1. きを　たくさん　きって　かんこうどうろを　つくる　けいかくは　どこの　けいかくですか。
2. はやしさんは　その　けいかくを　やめてほしいと　おもって、どうしましたか。
3. きを　たくさん　きらなければ、どうろは　つくれませんか。
4. はやしさんは　ほっかいどうへ　いって　だれに　しぜんの　たいせつさを　うったえてこようと　おもっていますか。
5. リンダさんは　ともだちにも　しょめいを　してもらう　つもりですか。

II　Put the appropriate words in the parentheses.

1. じしんで　なんびゃくにん　（　　）　しんだそうです。

ずいぶん　おおぜい　しんだんですね。

2. あと（　　　）　こうかいして（　　　）　おそすぎます。
3. ちきゅうじょう（　　　）　だんだん　みどり（　　　）　へっていきます。
4. あした　あめ（　　　）　ドライブに　いきますか。
　　いいえ、あめだったら　うちに　いたいです。

III　Complete the questions so that they fit the answers.

1. （　　　）で　この　かさを　かしてもらったんですか。
　　スポーツクラブで　かしてもらったんです。
2. （　　　）が　はなを　おくってくれたんですか。
　　じもとの　ひとが　おくってくれました。
3. スミスさんの　ようすは　（　　　）ですか。
　　たんへん　いそがしそうです。
4. とかいの　ひとと　じもとの　ひとと　（　　　）が　ねっしんですか。
　　とかいの　ひとの　ほうが　ねっしんなようです。

IV　Complete the sentences with the appropriate form of the verbs indicated.

1. さむく　（　　　）きましたから、へやに　（　　　）ましょう。（なる、はいる）
2. リンダさんに　りょこうの　しゃしんを　（　　　）もらいました。（みせる）
3. ヒーターの　こしょうを　（　　　）ほしいんですが。（なおす）
4. ルートを　（　　　）ば、たくさん　きを　（　　　）ても、どうろは　つくれます。（かえる、きらない）
5. くすりを　のみましたか。
　　ええ。でも　くすりを　（　　　）でも、なかなか　びょうきが　（　　　）ません。（のむ、なおる）
6. にもつを　ここに　（　　　）ほしいんですが。（おかない）

V　Answer the following questions.

1. こどもの　ころ、おとうさんに　どこに　つれていってもらいましたか。
2. あなたの　すんでいる　まちの　じんこうは　ふえていくでしょうか、へっていくでしょうか。
3. やちんが　たかくても　べんりな　ところに　すみたいですか。

LESSON  SIGHTSEEING EDO VILLAGE

Mr. Smith is shown around Edo Village by a guide.

ガイド：ここには　江戸時代の　建物が　集められています。

スミス：江戸時代と　いうのは　何せいきごろですか。

ガイド：17せいきの　はじめから　19せいきの　中ごろまでです。

スミス：この　家は　ずいぶん　古そうですが、いつごろ　建てられたんですか。

ガイド：200年ぐらい　前に　作られました。

スミス：中に　入ってみても　いいですか。

ガイド：どうぞ。ここは　さむらいが　住んでいた　家です。

スミス：広くて　りっぱですね。

ガイド：あちらは　のう民の　家です。

スミス：さむらいの　家より　ずっと　小さいですね。

ガイド：ええ、大部分の　のう民は　びんぼうでした。作った　こめを　ほとんど　だいみょうに　とり上げられて、のう民は　めったに　こめの　ごはんが　食べられなかったと　言われています。

スミス：この　部屋は　何に　使われていたんですか。

ガイド：ここは　居間です。いろりの　まわりで、ごはんを　食べたり、話を　したり、仕事を　したり　していた　部屋です。

スミス：冬は　さむかったでしょうね。

ガイド：ええ、冬　ゆきに　ふられると、ほんとうに　たいへんだっただろうと　思います。

スミス：今のような　べんりな　時代に　生まれて　よかったですね。

TARO

Guide: Edo-period houses have been brought together here.
Smith: Edo period? About what century would that be?
Guide: From the beginning of the seventeenth century to the middle of the nineteenth century.
Smith: This house looks pretty old. About when was it built?
Guide: It was built about two hundred years ago.
Smith: Is it all right to go in and look around?
Guide: Please. This is a house samurai lived in.
Smith: It's large and imposing (isn't it)?
Guide: The one over there is a farmer's house.
Smith: It's much smaller than the samurai's.
Guide: Yes, most farmers were poor. Almost all the rice they produced was appropriated by the *daimyō*, and it's said that almost never were farmers able to eat rice with meals.
Smith: What was this room used for?
Guide: This is a living room. (Sitting) around the hearth, they had meals, talked, worked and so on.
Smith: Winters must have been cold.
Guide: Yes, where there were winter snows, it was really hard, I suppose.
Smith: Being born in an age of convenience like the present is (a) good (thing), wouldn't you say?

Vocabulary

ガイド	**gaido**, guide	こめ	**kome**, (uncooked) rice
あつめられる	**atsumerareru**, be brought together/collected/assembled	だいみょう	**daimyō**, daimyo (feudal lord)
せいき	**seiki**, century	とりあげられる	**toriagerareru**, be appropriated/confiscated/taken away
たてられる	**taterareru**, be built		
つくられる	**tsukurareru**, be built/made	めったに～ない	**metta ni . . . nai**, almost never, rarely
りっぱ（な）	**rippa(na)**, imposing, magnificent	いわれる	**iwareru**, be said
のうみん	**nōmin**, farmer	つかわれる	**tsukawareru**, be used
だいぶぶん	**daibubun**, most, greater part, majority	いろり	**irori**, hearth
		ゆきに　ふられる	**yuki ni furareru**, (*lit.*) be snowed on

GRAMMAR & LESSON OBJECTIVES

- **taterareru, tsukawareru**, "passive" verbs

    Verb forms like these are identified with the passives of English verbs, but it is well to remember from the beginning that **-reru**—added to the **-nai** stem of Regular I verbs—and **-rareru**–added to the **-nai** stem of Regular II verbs—have other uses as well.

Reg. I	tsukuru → tsukura-reru furu → fura-reru	tatenaosu → tatenaosa-reru
Reg. II	atsumeru → atsume-rareru toriageru → toriage-rareru	tateru → tate-rareru

The Irregular verbs are: **kuru → ko-rareru** and **suru → sa-reru**.

Two points to be noted are that these conjugations are like Regular II conjugations, and for Regular II verbs this form is the same as the potential form. (See p. 145.) The occurrence of active-passive verb pairs parallels English usage. When the object of the active verb is animate, it can become the subject or topic in the passive-verb sentence. A person who performs an action is identified by **ni** or, less frequently, **ni yotte** or **kara**.

ex. **Sensei wa watashi o shikatta.** "The teacher scolded me."

Watashi wa sensei ni shikarareta. "I was scolded by the teacher."

Active-verb sentences with inanimate objects can be thought of as falling into two categories: objective description and individual viewpoint. There are examples of both in the dialogue.

Objective description

Koko niwa Edo jidai no tatemono ga atsumerarete imasu.

Kono ie wa ... itsu goro taterareta n desu ka.

Kono heya wa nani ni tsukawarete ita n desu ka.

In explanations of historical events, social systems, world affairs and similar topics the subject of a passive sentence can be a thing or a concept. The agent, if specified, is normally identified by **ni yotte**.

ex. **Hamuretto wa Shēkusupia ni yotte kakaremashita.** *"Hamlet* was written by Shakespeare."

Individual viewpoint

(Nōmin wa) tsukutta kome o hotondo daimyō ni toriagerarete, ...

Active: **Daimyō wa nōmin kara kome o toriagete.** "Daimyō took the rice away from the farmers."

The recipient of the action in this type of sentence may be the speaker or a person or animal with whom he emphasizes. The object of the passive verb is the same as the object of the active verb, which contrasts with the other type of passive sentence and serves as a means of differentiating the two.

ex. 1. **Otōto ga/wa watashi no nikki o yonda.** "My brother read my diary." As passive: **(Watashi wa) otōto ni nikki o yomareta.** (The sentence **Watashi no nikki ga/wa otōto ni yomareta** is awkwardly constructed.)

2. **Minna ga/wa kanojo no e o homemashita.** "Everybody praised her drawing." As passive: **(Kanojo wa) minna ni e o homeraremashita.** (Awkwardly stated, **Kanojo no e ga/wa minna ni homeraremashita.**)

Fuyu yuki ni furareru to, hontō ni taihen datta darō to omoimasu.

A unique usage of the passive is seen with such verbs as **nigeru**, "run away," **furu, shinu** and so on. Literal renderings are often impossible, but the sense of such sentences is translatable.

ex. 1. **Tsuma ni nigerareta.** "My wife ran off (and abandoned me)."

2. **Sono kodomo wa oya ni shinarete hitori ni natta.** "That child's parents died, leaving him (all) alone."

In situations where a person is the recipient of another person's action, **kara** as well as **ni** may be used. Typical verbs of this sort are **shikaru, homeru, azukeru,** and **tanomu**.

ex. 1. **Watashi wa sensei ni/kara ...** "I was (scolded/praised/asked [to do something]) by the teacher."

2. **Keiko-san wa Jonson-san kara hana o okuraremashita.** (*lit.*) "Keiko was sent flowers by Johnson."

A recent usage, seen among the younger generation, has impersonal objects for the subject of so-called passive verbs.

ex. **Boku no rajio ga kowasarete shimatta.** "My radio ended up being broken."

In the following sentences the difference in construction reflects a difference in the speaker's attitude.

ex. 1. **1970-nen goro, Tōkyō ni takai biru ga takusan taterareta.** "Around 1970, many tall buildings were built in Tokyo."

2. **Uchi no mae ni takai biru o taterareta.** "A tall building was built in front of my house." (Cutting off the sunlight.)

NOTES

1. **Edo jidai to iu no wa**

   The function of **to iu no wa** is to define, so this clause means "The time known as the Edo period."

2. **Kono heya wa nani ni tsukawarete ita n desu ka.**

The particle **ni** shows the purpose of use or a requirement.

ex. 1. **Nihon-go no benkyō ni tēpu-rekōdā ga irimasu.** "(We) need a tape recorder for Japanese lessons."

2. **Mōshikomu no ni anata no sain ga hitsuyō desu.** "Your signature is necessary (when you) apply."

3. **Nōmin wa metta ni kome no gohan ga taberarenakatta.**

As noted previously, **-rareru** may be the potential form. Context will tell whether it is this, the so-called passive or the honorific usage which is explained in Lesson 37.

PRACTICE

KEY SENTENCES

1. まいねん　たくさんの　きが　きられて、ビルや　どうろが　つくられます。
2. 〔わたしは〕　おとうとに　あたらしい　カメラを　こわされました。
3. かれは　おとうさんに　しなれて　こまっています。

1. Every year many trees are cut down and buildings and roads built.
2. My new camera was broken by my younger brother.
3. His father died and he's at a loss (since then).

Vocabulary

こわす　　　　　　　**kowasu**, break

EXERCISES

I　Verbs: Study the examples, convert into the **-reru** or **-rareru** form, and memorize.

ex. つくる→つくられる　　　ほめる→ほめられる　　　くる→こられる
たのむ→たのまれる　　　かりる→かりられる　　　する→される

1. かく	5. しぬ	9. いる
2. よぶ	6. つかう	10. もってくる
3. まつ	7. たてる	11. ゆにゅうする
4. おす	8. みる	12. うったえる

II　Make dialogues by changing the underlined parts as in the examples given.

A. *ex.* **Q**：だれが　おしたんですか。

A：〔わたしは〕　うしろの　ひとに　おされたんです。

1. よんだ、ともだち
2. しかった、せんせい
3. おしりを　たたいた、ちち
4. たのんだ、となりの　うちの　ひと
5. けっこんを　もうしこんだ、ジョンソン

B. *ex.* **Q**： <u>どろぼう</u>に　<u>なにを</u>　<u>とられた</u>んですか。
　　　A： <u>しんじゅの　ゆびわを</u>　<u>とられました</u>。

　　1. おかあさん、みる、てがみを
　　2. こども、こわす、とけいを
　　3. けいかん、しらべる、かばんの　なかを
　　4. ともだち、のむ、ワインを
　　5. ねずみ、たべる、チーズを　はんぶん

III　Read the sentence and answer the questions.

たなかさんは　あさ　でんしゃの　なかで　すりに　さいふを　すられました。

ex. だれが　すられましたか。→たなかさんが　すられました。

　　1. なにを　すられましたか。
　　2. どこで　すられましたか。
　　3. だれに　すられましたか。
　　4. だれが　すられましたか。
　　5. いつ　すられましたか。
　　6. だれが　すりましたか。

IV　Practice the following pattern by changing the underlined part.

ex. <u>2しゅうかんも　あめに　ふられて</u>、こまっています。

　　1. まいばん　となりの　ひとが　くる
　　2. つまが　しぬ
　　3. ひしょが　やめる
　　4. かとうさんが　やすむ
　　5. あかんぼうが　なく

V　Transform the following sentences as in the example given.

ex. むぎから　ビールを　つくります。→ビールは　むぎから　つくられます。

　　1. こめから　（お）さけを　つくります。
　　2. ブラジルから　コーヒーを　ゆにゅうします。
　　3. この　てらを　200ねんまえに　たてました。
　　4. その　にもつを　ちゅうごくに　おくります。

VI   Answer the questions as in the example given.

   ex. **Q**：せきゆは　どこから　ゆにゅうされますか。
   　　A：イランから　ゆにゅうされます。

   1.　この　じどうしゃは　どこへ　ゆしゅつされますか。（アメリカ）
   2.　この　やさいは　どこで　つくられますか。（ほっかいどう）
   3.　キリストきょうは　いつ　にほんに　つたえられましたか。（16
   　　せいきの　なかごろ）
   4.　オリンピックは　なんねんに　とうきょうで　おこなわれました
   　　か。（1964ねん）

VII   Practice the following patterns by changing the underlined parts.

   A. *ex.*　<u>この　てらは　にほんで　いちばん　ふるいと</u>　いわれています。

   1.　この　まちは　せかいで　いちばん　きれいです
   2.　れきしは　くりかえします
   3.　この　ぎょうじは　300ねんまえから　おこなわれています
   4.　ちきゅうは　46おくねんまえに　できました

   B. *ex.*　<u>えどじだいと</u>　いうのは　<u>なんせいきごろ</u>ですか。

   1.　ながさき、どんな　ところ
   2.　かなざわ、どこに　ある　まち
   3.　コピーライター、どんな　しょくぎょう
   4.　おもしろい　ほん、どんな　ほん

| Vocabulary |

ほめる	**homeru**, praise	あかんぼう	**akambō**, baby
たてる	**tateru**, build	むぎ	**mugi**, barley, wheat, oats, rye
ゆにゅうする	**yunyū suru**, import		
ゆにゅう	**yunyū**, importation	ブラジル	**Burajiru**, Brazil
しかる	**shikaru**, scold	せきゆ	**sekiyu**, oil, petroleum, kerosene
おしりを　たた	**ō-shiri o tataku**, spank		
く		イラン	**Iran**, Iran
おしり	**o-shiri**, bottom, buttocks	ゆしゅつする	**yushutsu suru**, export
		ゆしゅつ	**yushutsu**, exportation
たたく	**tataku**, strike, beat, slap, knock	キリストきょう	**Kirisuto-kyō**, Christianity
どろぼう	**dorobō**, thief	～きょう	**-kyō**, faith
とる	**toru**, rob/steal	つたえる	**tsutaeru**, introduce
しんじゅ	**shinju**, pearl	オリンピック	**Orimpikku**, Olympics
ねずみ	**nezumi**, rat, mouse	おこなう	**okonau**, hold, carry out

チーズ	**chīzu**, cheese	くりかえす	**kurikaesu**, repeat
はんぶん	**hambun**, half	ぎょうじ	**gyōji**, event
すり	**suri**, pickpocket	コピーライター	**kopīraitā**, copywriter
する	**suru**, pick a pocket	しょくぎょう	**shokugyō**, occupation

SHORT DIALOGUES

1. きゃく：　　しょうめいしょようの　しゃしんを　おねがいします。
　　しゃしんや：なんに　つかいますか。
　　きゃく：　　パスポートを　つくるのに　ひつようなんです。
　　しゃしんや：じゃ、たて　よこ　5センチですね。

　　Customer:　　　I'd like a photograph for (an identification) certificate.
　　Photographer: What's it to be used for?
　　Customer:　　　It's necessary for (having) my passport (made).
　　Photographer: Well, then, height and width will be 5 cm (each).

2. **A**：なんの　しごとを　しているんですか。
　　B：たいしかんから　たのまれた　しごとです。

　　A: What work are you doing?
　　B: The work requested by the embassy.

Vocabulary

しょうめいしょ	**shōmei-sho**, certificate	たて	**tate**, height, vertical
〜よう	**-yō**, for, (*lit.*) use, service		(direction)
しゃしんや	**shashin-ya**, photographer, photo studio	よこ	**yoko**, width, horizontal

QUIZ

I　Read this lesson's opening dialogue and answer the following questions.

　　1. えどむらと　いうのは　なにが　あつめられている　ところですか。
　　2. えどむらの　さむらいの　いえは　なんねんぐらい　まえに　たてられた　いえですか。
　　3. さむらいの　いえは　のうみんの　いえより　ちいさいですか。
　　4. だれが　のうみんから　こめを　とりあげましたか。
　　5. いまのような　べんりな　じだいに　うまれて　よかったと　スミスさんは　いっていますが、あなたも　そう　おもいますか。

II　Put the appropriate particles in the parentheses.

　　1. この　コップを　かびん（　　）　つかっても　いいですか。
　　2. この　てらは　にほん（　　）　いちばん　ふるい（　　）　いわれて　います。

3. けいこさんは　きょう　せんせい（　　）　じ（　　）　ほめられて
   うれしそうです。
4. ［わたしは］　とけい（　　）　こども（　　）　こわされてしまいまし
   た。
5. リーさんは　こうつうじこ（　　）　あって、びょういん（　　）　は
   こばれました。

III Complete the questions so that they fit the answers.

1. （　　）　かちょうに　しかられたんですか。
   かいぎの　じかんに　おくれてしまったんです。
2. （　　）で　カメラを　とられたんですか。
   こうえんで　やすんでいる　とき　とられたんです。
3. この　あおい　ビルは　（　　）　ごろ　たてられたんですか。
   1964ねんに　たてられました。
4. はやしさんと　いうのは　（　　）　ひとですか。
   ABCの　ぶちょうですが、まえは　すうがくの　きょうじゅだったそう
   です。

IV Convert the following verbs into their **-reru** or **-rareru** form.

1. きく　　　　　　　4. なく　　　　　　　7. つれてくる
2. しょうかいする　　5. こわす　　　　　　8. しらべる
3. たのむ　　　　　　6. あずける　　　　　9. おこなう

V Change the verbs into the **-reru** or **-rareru** form and make any necessary changes in the
  sentence patterns.

1. やまださんは　きむらさんに　けっこんを　（　　）　ました。（もうしこ
   む）
2. みちを　あるいている　とき、しゃしんを　（　　）　ました。（とる）
3. あの　ひとは　まじめな　ひとだと　みんなから　（　　）　います。（お
   もう）
4. ぶちょうは　ひしょに　（　　）、こまっています。（やめる）
5. くうこうで　なんども　かばんの　なかを　（　　）　ました。（しらべる）
6. こどもの　ころ　おばあさんの　うちに　（　　）　ました。（あずける）

VI Answer the following questions.

1. どろぼうに　おかねを　とられた　ことが　ありますか。
2. あなたは　ともだちから　よく　そうだん　されますか。
3. あなたの　くにでは　なにごが　はなされていますか。
4. あなたの　がっこうや　かいしゃでは　コンピューターが　つかわれて
   いますか。

LESSON  A COMPLICATED CONTRACT

Mr. Katō gets an inquiry by phone from the Yokohama office.

横浜支社：先週 もらった Ｎ社との けいやく書に あやまりが あると
思うんですが。

加藤：そうですか。そんな はずは ないと 思いますが。あれは うちの
鈴木に 作らせた ものです。さっそく 本人に 調べさせましょ
う。

p.3

Mr. Katō tells Mr. Suzuki to look into the matter.

加藤：鈴木くん、ちょっと 来てください。

鈴木：はい、何でしょうか。

加藤：先週 送った けいやく書の 件で、横浜支社から 問い合わせが
あったんだけど、たしかめてくれませんか。

鈴木：はい、わかりました。

Mr. Katō gives the Yokohama office an answer.

加藤：もしもし 先ほどの けいやく書の 件ですが、鈴木に 調べさせま
したが、まちがいは ないと 言っています。ただ、作った 時の
じじょうが ふくざつなので、わかりにくいかもしれませんね。

横浜支社：じゃ、だれか 説明に 来てくれませんか。

加藤：そうですね。じゃ、これから 鈴木を 行かせますが、いかがでしょ
うか。

横浜支社：ぜひ おねがいします。

Yokohama
Office: (I) think there's a mistake in the N Company contract (we) received last week.

Katō: Oh, I wouldn't think there'd be (any mistake). (More *lit*. "It can't be so.") We had
Suzuki here prepare it. I'll have (Suzuki) himself check it immediately.

Katō: Suzuki, come (here) a minute.

Suzuki: Yes, What is it?

Katō: There's been an inquiry from the Yokohama office about the contract (we) sent last
week, would you mind making sure?

Suzuki: No, of course not.

Katō: Hello. Regarding the contract you mentioned a little while ago, I had Suzuki check
it. He says there's no mistake. It's only that the conditions at the time the contract

222

was made were complicated, so perhaps it's difficult to understand.

Yokohama: Well, could someone come and explain it?
Katō: Hmm. I'll have Suzuki go, then. How'd that be?
Yokohama: We'd appreciate it very much.

| **Vocabulary** |

あやまり **ayamari**, mistake

そんな **sonna**, such, like that

つくらせる **tsukuraseru**, have (so-meone)prepare

ほんにん **honnin**, the person himself, said person

しらべさせる **shirabesaseru**, have (so-meone) check

といあわせ **toiawase**, inquiry

さきほど **sakihodo**, a little while ago (less colloquial than **sakki**)

まちがい **machigai**, mistake

ただ **tada**, only, but

いかせる **ikaseru**, have (someone) go

GRAMMAR & LESSON OBJECTIVES

- **tsukuraseru** and **shirabesaseru**, causative verbs

  Sassoku honnin ni shirabesasemashō.
  Suzuki o ikasemasu.
  This verb form, made by adding **-seru** or **-saseru** to the **-nai** stem, can mean "make/have" or "let" a person do something. Conjugation is like Regular II verbs.

Reg. I	**tsukuru → tsukura-seru, iku → ika-seru, shiru → shiraseru**
Reg. II	**shiraberu → shirabe-saseru, denwa o kakeru → denwa o kake-saseru**
Irreg.	**kuru → ko-saseru, suru → sa-seru**

As seen in the dialogue, the agent is sometimes marked by the particle **ni** and sometimes by **o**. Two factors determine which it is. One is that the particle **o** cannot occur twice in succession with verbs which normally take objects. The particle **ni** must be used even if the object and **o** are omitted.

ex. **Kore wa kodomo no hon desu. (Kore o) uchi no musume ni yomasemashō.** "This is a children's book. (I'll) let (our) daughter read it."

In the second instance, with verbs which do not take objects (**iku**, **kuru**, **hairu**, for example) either **ni** or **o** may occur. If the sentence suggests a commanding attitude, **o** is used. If the sentence implies giving permission, **ni** is used.

ex. **Hayashi-san wa kodomo o/ni gaikoku ni hitori de ikasemashita.** "Hayashi made/let (his) child go to foreign countries by himself."

- **-seru** and **-saseru**, additional usages

  This verb ending, as well as being the causative, has several more applications, which are introduced in the short dialogues. Study the examples below.
  Yasumasete kudasai. "Please let me take (the day) off."
  The **-te** form of the causative with **kudasai** is often used to ask permission.
  ex. 1. **Watashi ni ikasete kudasai.** "Please let me go."
      2. **Koko de hatarakasete kudasai.** "Please allow (me) to work here."
  Yasumasete itadakimasu. "(I'll) take a rest (and feel much obliged)."
  The **-te** form of the causative plus **itadaku** is a conventionally polite phrase meaning "I'll do such and such because you allow me to." Acknowledgement of permission can be made as follows:
  ex. 1. **Kono hon o motte kaette ii desu yo. Yondara kaeshite kudasai.** "It's all right to take this book (home). Please return it after you've read it."

Arigatō gozaimasu. Sō sasete itadakimasu. "Thank you very much. I'll do that."

2. **Kono heya o tsukawasete itadakimasu.** "I'll use this room (since you allow me to do so)."

3. **O-saki ni kaerasete itadakimasu.** "(I'll) leave ahead (of you, and I'm grateful for your letting me)."

-saserareru, causative and "passive" combined

Konshū wa minna nichi-yōbi ni shukkin saserareta kara ne. "All of you had to be at the office this Sunday, didn't you?"

As in this and the following sentences, the causative may be combined with **-reru/-rareru**.

ex. 1. **Shorui ni sain saseraremashita.** "(I) was forced to sign the document."

2. **Seito-tachi wa nikki o kakaseraremasu/kakasaremasu.** "Pupils are made to keep a diary."

Note: The pronunciation of Regular I verbs may be shortened to **-sareru**, as in **ikasareru**, **kawasareru**, **matasareru**, etc.

NOTES

1. **Sakihodo no keiyakusho no ken desu ga.**
   The implication of **sakihodo no** is "previously referred to."

2. **Keiyakusho no ken de . . .**
   The pattern noun plus **ken de** means "regarding," "with respect to."
   ex. **Kyanseru-chāji no ken de kikitai koto ga arimasu.** "There are some questions about the cancellation charge."

3. **Suzuki wa machigai wa nai to itte imasu, tada . . .**
   Tada is used here to introduce additional information to complete an explanation, or at least provide fuller information.

PRACTICE

KEY SENTENCES

1. かとうさんは　すずきさんに　けいやくしょを　つくらせました。
2. かとうさんは　すずきさんを　よこはまししゃへ　いかせました。

1. Katō had Suzuki make a contract.
2. Katō had Suzuki go to the Yokohama (branch) office.

EXERCISES

I　Verbs: Study the examples, convert into the causative form, and memorize.

ex. かく→かかせる　　　しらべる→しらべさせる　　くる→こさせる
　　およぐ→およがせる　　きる→きさせる　　　　　する→させる

1. けす	5. つくる	9. いる
2. まつ	6. つかう	10. もってくる
3. よぶ	7. かける	11. しゅっきんする
4. やすむ	8. たしかめる	12. そうたいする

II Make dialogues by changing the underlined parts as in the examples given.

A. *ex.* **Q**：ぶちょうは　すずきさんに　なにを　させていますか。
　　　　A：<u>しょるいを　つくらせて</u>います。

　　　1．けいやくしょ、しらべます
　　　2．よやく、たしかめます
　　　3．ないよう、せつめいします
　　　4．しりょう、あつめます

B. (Doctor to mother of sick child.)
　　ex. いしゃ：こどもを　<u>ゆっくり　やすませて</u>ください。
　　　　はは：　はい、わかりました。

　　　1．こどもを　ともだちと　あそばせません
　　　2．こどもを　そとに　いかせません
　　　3．こどもに　くすりを　のませます
　　　4．こどもに　つめたい　ものを　たべさせません

C. *ex.* **A**：わたしは　いそがしくて　<u>いけない</u>んですが。
　　　　B：じゃ、<u>やまださんに　いか</u>せましょう。

　　　1．そうじする、やまださんに
　　　2．てつだう、ひしょに
　　　3．おちゃを　いれる、すずきくんに
　　　4．しゅっせきする、うちの　かないを

D. *ex.* **A**：すみませんが、<u>あした　やすませて</u>ください。
　　　　Ba：はい、いいですよ。
　　　　Bn：それは　ちょっと　こまるんですが・・・。

　　　1．ちょうきょりでんわを　かける
　　　2．この　へやを　つかう
　　　3．さきに　かえる
　　　4．きょう　そうたいする
　　　5．あなたの　しゃしんを　とる

E. *ex.* **A**：<u>こんしゅうは　たいへん</u>でしたよ。
　　　　B：どうしたんですか。
　　　　A：<u>にちようびも　しゅっきん</u>させられたんです。

1. きのうの　レッスン、なんかいも　れんしゅうした
2. せんげつ、３かいも　しゅっちょうした
3. けさ、なんども　しょるいを　しらべた
4. きのう、５じすぎに　ほんしゃまで　みつもりしょを　とどけた

F. *ex.* **Q** : ごきげんが　わるいですね。どう　したんですか。
　　　　A : <u>ともだちに　１じかんも　またされたんですよ。</u>

1. ぶちょう、しごとを　おそくまで　てつだう
2. ともだち、たくさん　さけを　のむ
3. かない、おもい　にもつを　もつ
4. かちょう、なりたくうこうまで　いく

G. *ex.* **A** : <u>ゆっくり　やすんでください。</u>
　　　　B : では、<u>やすませていただきます。</u>

1. この　でんわを　つかう
2. さきに　かえる
3. この　いすに　かける
4. この　へやで　まつ

Vocabulary

しゅっきんする	**shukkin suru**, be at the office, report for work	ちょうきょりでんわ	**chōkyori denwa**, long-distance call
しゅっきん	**shukkin**, attendance, presence	ちょうきょり	**chōkyori**, long distance
		レッスン	**ressun**, lesson
そうたいする	**sōtai suru**, leave (office, school) early	なんかいも	**nan-kai mo**, many times
		なんども	**nan-do mo**, many times
そうたい	**sōtai**, leaving early	ごきげん	**go-kigen**, (your) mood, humor
ないよう	**naiyō**, contents, details		
ゆっくり	**yukkuri**, slowly, by easy stage		

SHORT DIALOGUES

1. すずき：どうも　からだの　ちょうしが　よく　ないので、あしたは　やすませてください。

　　かとう：こんしゅうは　にちようびも　しゅっきんさせられたからね。ゆっくり　やすんだら　いいよ。

　　すずき：じゃ、いそがしい　ときに　すみませんが、やすませていただきます。

Suzuki: I'm not feeling well. Would you mind letting me take off tomorrow.
Katō: You had to come in on Sunday this week. Better (take time to) get rested up.
Suzuki: Well, at a busy time I'm sorry (to be doing this), but I will take off (with your kind permission).

2. なかの：もしもし、すずきさん、いらっしゃいますか。

かとう：いま　でかけています。のちほど　でんわさせましょうか。

なかの：はい、おねがいします。

Nakano: Is Mr. Suzuki there?
Katō: No, he's out. Shall I have him call you later?
Nakano: Yes, thank you.

Vocabulary

どうも	**dōmo**, somehow	のちほど	**nochi-hodo**, later (more
ちょうし	**chōshi**, condition		formal than **ato de**)
～ていただく	**-te itadaku** (See grammar, p. 235.)		

QUIZ

I Read this lesson's opening dialogue and answer the following questions.

1. Ｎしゃとの　けいやくしょは　だれが　だれに　つくらせた　ものですか。

2. かとうさんは　けいやくしょに　あやまりが　あるか　どうか　じぶんで　しらべましたか。

3. その　けいやくしょは　なぜ　わかりにくいのですか。

4. この　あと　すずきさんは　どこに　いって、なにを　しますか。

II Put the appropriate particles in the parentheses.

1. にもつは　おもいですが、ひとり（　　）　もてますか。
   いいえ。でも　こども（　　）　もたせますから、ごしんぱいは　いりません。

2. よる　おそくまで　テレビを　みたがる　こども（　　）　ベッドに　いかせるのは　たいへんです。

3. かんこうどうろの　けいかく（　　）　けん（　　）　ごそうだんが　あるんですが。

4. ぶちょうに　よこはまししゃに　しょるい（　　）　とどけるよう（　　）　いわれたので、さっそく　なかむらさん（　　）　とどけさせました。

III Convert the following verbs into the causative form.

1. さがす	4. のむ	7. やめる
2. かく	5. てつだう	8. もってくる

3. たべる 　　　　　 6. とどける 　　　　　 9. しごとを　する

IV Change the verbs into the causative form and complete the sentences.

1. ひしょに　コピーを　（　　）ましょう。（する）
2. こどもを　あぶない　ところへ　（　　）ください。（いかない）
3. すこし　この　へやで　おまちください。
   　はい。では　（　　）いただきます。（まつ）
4. こどもを　さきに　（　　）ました。（かえる）
5. まちがいが　あるか　どうか　（　　）ます。（しらべる）
6. あたらしい　ショールームの　みつもりしょですが、いかがですか。
   　そうですねえ。もう　すこし　（　　）ください。（かんがえる）
7. すずきくんに　けいやくしょを　（　　）ください。（もってくる）

V Choose a sentence appropriate to the situation described.

A. You catch cold and ask your teacher for permission to be absent tomorrow.

1. かぜを　ひいたので、あした　やすませてください。
2. かぜで　あした　やすむんですって。
3. かぜを　ひいたら　やすんでもらいたいんです。

B. You say that it was inconvenient for you to go to the embassy, so you asked Suzuki to go.

1. わたしは　いそがしかったですが、すずきくんに　いかされました。
2. わたしは　つごうが　わるかったので、すずきくんに　いってもらいました。
3. すずきくんが　いそがしかったので、わたしが　いきました。

　1964年に　東京で　オリンピックが　開かれ、その　年に　東海道新幹線が
開通しました。それまでは　東京から　大阪まで　とっきゅうでも　7時間以
上　かかりましたが、新幹線が　できてから、東京、大阪間を3時間ほどで
行けるように　なりました。
　新幹線の　開通に　ともなって、サラリーマンの　出張の　ようすも　だい
ぶ　かわりました。以前は　東京から　かんさいほうめんに　出張する　時は
しゅくはくするのが　ふつうでしたが、今は　日帰りで　出張する　ことが　で
きるように　なりました。
　サラリーマンの　中には、てんきんを　めいじられ、じじょうに　よって　家
族と　はなれて　生活している　人が　かなり　います。週末や　休日に　な
ると、新幹線を　利用して、ふにんさきから　うちへ　帰る　たんしん　ふにん
の　人が　大ぜい　のっています。ひさしぶりに　家族に　会えるのを　たのし
みに　しているようです。
　新幹線は　その　後　きゅうしゅうほうめん、とうほくほうめん、そして　に
いがたほうめんにも　のび、かくちの　はってんに　大いに　やくだっていま
す。

The Olympic games were held in Tokyo in 1964, and in that year the Tokaidō Shinkansen
went into operation. Until then, (the trip) from Tokyo to Osaka had taken more than seven
hours by special express. After the Shinkansen was finished it became possible to go between
Tokyo and Osaka in about three hours.
　With the opening of the Shinkansen the situation (regarding) white collar workers' business
trips changed greatly. Previously, when (they) made business trips from Tokyo to the Kansai
district, putting up at a hotel was the usual (thing). Now, making a one-day business trip has
become possible.
　Among white color workers, there are a considerable (number) of people who are ordered (to
make) transfers and, because of the circumstances, live apart from (their) families. When
weekends and holidays come around, a lot of transferees use the Shinkansen to travel from
(their) places of assignment and return home. It seems (they really) look forward to being able to
see their families after a long time.
　(Some years) later, the Shinkansen was extended to Kyushu, Tōhoku and then Niigata and
has been of considerable use in the development of each region.

ひらく	**hiraku**, hold	てんきん	**tenkin**, transfer
とうかいどう	**Tōkaidō** (district name)	めいじる	**meijiru**, order
かいつうする	**kaitsū suru**, go into operation, be opened to traffic	はなれて	**hanarete**, apart, separately from
かいつう	**kaitsū**, opening to traffic	かなり	**kanari**, considerably, fairly
とうきょう　お　おさかかん	**Tōkyō-Ōsaka-kan**, between Tokyo and Osaka	きゅうじつ	**kyūjitsu**, holiday
		ふにんさき	**funin-saki**, place of appointment
～かん	**-kan**, between, among	～さき	**-saki**, (*lit.*) destination
ほど	**hodo**, about	たんしん	**tanshin**, alone, unaccompanied
～に　ともなって	**ni tomonatte**, with, accompanying	ひさしぶりに	**hisashiburi ni**, after/for a long time
だいぶ	**daibu**, greatly, considerably	その　ご	**sono go**, later, afterwards
		とうほく	**Tōhoku** (district name)
いぜん（は）	**izen (wa)**, previously	にいがた	**Niigata** (prefecture, city)
かんさい	**Kansai** (district name)	はってん	**hatten**, development, growth, expansion
ほうめん	**hōmen**, district, direction		
しゅくはくする	**shukuhaku suru**, put up at, stay (overnight)	おおいに	**ōi ni**, considerably, greatly
しゅくはく	**shukuhaku**, lodging	やくだつ	**yakudatsu**, be of use, serve a purpose
ふつう	**futsū**, usual		
ひがえり	**higaeri**, one-day, go and return the same day		

GRAMMAR & LESSON OBJECTIVES

- **-masu** stem as clause ending

  1964-nen ni Tōkyō de Orimpikku ga hirakare, sono toshi ni . . .
  Shinkansen wa sono go Kyūshū hōmen, Tōhoku hōmen, sōshite Niigata hōmen nimo nobi, kakuchi no hatten . . .
  The **-masu** stem at the end of a phrase has the same function as the **-te** form, but it's customary place of occurrence is in a formal written style.

- **yō ni naru**, "become possible" or indication of a change

  Tōkyō-Ōsaka-kan o 3-jikan hodo de ikeru yō ni narimashita.
  Ima wa higaeri de shutchō suru koto ga dekiru yō ni narimashita.
  Potential verbs in their dictionary form followed by **yō ni narimashita** indicate "it has become possible to . . ." (**Wakaru** and **dekiru** themselves express potentiality, so in this usage the pattern is **wakaru/dekiru yō ni naru**.)
  ex. 1. **Sumisu-san wa kanji ga yomeru yō ni narimashita.** "Smith has become able to read Sino-Japanese characters."
  2. **Sumisu-san wa unagi ga taberareru yō ni narimashita.** "Smith has become able to eat eels."
  3. **Mainichi Nihon-go no nyūsu o kiite ita node, Nihon-go ga wakaru yō ni narimashita.** "Since I've been listening to the news in Japanese every day, I've come to (be able to) understand Japanese."

  Coming after the plain non-past (dictionary) form of verbs **yō ni naru** indicates a change in habits, manners or conditions.

ex. **Kodomo no toki wa yasai ga kirai deshita ga, kono goro wa yoku taberu yō ni narimashita.** "When (I) was a child I disliked vegetables, but these days (I) eat (them) a lot."

NOTES

1. **Shinkansen no kaitsū ni tomonatte, ...**
   Ni tomonatte, meaning "with," "accompanying," "accordingly," is a rather formal expression. It comes from the verb **tomonau**, "accompany, go with, attend on."

2. **Funin-saki**
   Saki can refer to things, people or places as perceived from the speaker's or subject's viewpoint. Other examples are: **ryokō-saki**, "place traveled to"; **okuri-saki**, "place to which something is sent/mailed"; and **torihiki-saki**, "party to a contract."

3. **Tanshin funin**
   As noted in the vocabulary list, **tanshin** means "alone." The two components incorporated in **funin** are **fu**, "proceed," and **nin**, "duty" or "office." In recent years, many men transferred to distant places, especially middle-aged ones, have elected, usually for family reasons such as children's education, aged parents or a working wife, to live like bachelors until the situation changes.

PRACTICE

KEY SENTENCE

しんかんせんが できてから、とうきょうから おおさかまで 3じかんで いけるように なりました。

After the Shinkansen was finished, it became possible to go between Tokyo and Osaka in about three hours.

EXERCISES

Make dialogues by changing the underlined parts as in the examples given.

A. *ex.* **Q**：(お) さけが のめますか。
   A：まえは ぜんぜん のめませんでしたが、だんだん のめるように なりました。

   1. でんわで うまく はなせる
   2. こうしょうが じょうずに できる
   3. にほんごの しんぶんが よめる
   4. ひとりで まちを あるける
   5. にほんごが わかる

B. *ex.* **A**：いぜんは おんなの ひとだけでしたが、いまは おとこの ひとも だいどころに はいるように なりました。
   B：そうですか。しゅうかんが かわってきたんですね。

   1. にほんじん、がいこくじん、さんかする

2. さかな、にく、たべる
3. にちようび、どようび、やすむ
4. ひるま、よる、スーパーが　あいている
5. こくない、かいがい、いく

C. *ex.* **Q**：どうやって　<u>かえりますか</u>。
A：<u>しんかんせんを　りようして　かえります</u>。

1. べんきょうする、テープを　きく
2. かいしゃに　くる、ちかてつに　のる
3. いみを　しらべる、じしょを　ひく
4. たべる、やく
5. といあわせる、でんわを　かける

Vocabulary

うまく	**umaku**, easily, (*lit.*) well, skillfully	よる	**yoru**, night, nighttime
さんかする	**sanka suru**, participate, enter (a contest)	こくない	**kokunai**, inside the country, domestic, (*lit.*) interior
さんか	**sanka**, particpation		

SHORT DIALOGUE

ホワイト：こどもさんの　あしの　ぐあいは　いかがですか。
おがわ：　ありがとうございます。おかげさまで　もう　かなり　あるけるよう
　　　　　に　なりました。

White:　How's your child's leg?
Ogawa: Thank you for asking. He's gotten able to walk fairly well now.

Vocabulary

おかげさまで　　**okagesama de**, Thank you for asking, (*lit.* Thanks to you)

QUIZ

I　Put the appropriate words in the parentheses.

　　　1964ねんに　とうきょう（　　）　オリンピックが　（　　）、その　とし
　（　　）　とうかいどうしんかんせんが　かいつうしました。（　　）までは
とうきょうから　おおさかまで　とっきゅう（　　）　7じかん（　　）
かかりましたが、しんかんせんが　できて（　　）、とうきょう、おおさか
かんを　3じかん（　　）で　いける（　　）なりました。
　　　しんかんせんの　かいつうに　（　　）、サラリーマンの　しゅっちょう

の ようすも （　　） かわりました。（　　）は とうきょうから か
んさい ほうめんに しゅっちょうする （　　）は しゅくはくする
（　　）が ふつうでした（　　）、いまは （　　）で しゅっちょうする
（　　）が できるように なりました。
　　サラリーマンの なかには、てんきんを めいじられ、じじょうに
（　　） かぞくと （　　） せいかつしている ひとが （　　）い
ます。しゅうまつや きゅうじつに （　　）と、しんかんせんを りよう
して、ふにんさき（　　） うちへ かえる たんしんふにんの ひとが
（　　） のっています。（　　）に かぞくに あえるのを たのしみ
（　　） している ようです。
　　しんかんせんは （　　） きゅうしゅうほうめん、とうほくほうめん、
（　　） にいがたほうめんにも （　　）、かくちの はってん（　　）
おおいに やくだっています。

II　Complete the following sentences with the appropriate form of the verbs indicated.

1. このごろ にほんごが かなり うまく （　　）ように なりました。
（はなせます）
2. テープを （　　）、にほんごを べんきょうしています。（ききます）
3. あしの けがが なおって、（　　）ように なりました。（あるけます）
4. しんかんせんに （　　）、きょうとに いこうと おもいます。（のり
ます）
5. いぜんは どようびも （　　）いましたが、いまは （　　）ないよ
うに なりました。（しゅっきんします，しゅっきんします）
6. 4がつから ほっかいどうに （　　）ように めいじられました。（ふ
にんする）

LESSON 31 ANNIVERSARY PARTY

Mr. Katō checks on the preparations for ABC's anniversary party.

加藤：20日の　そうりつ10周年きねんパーティーについて　かくにんを　したいと　思います。まず　しょうたいじょうの　件ですが、もう　全部　送ってくれましたか。

鈴木：はい。渡辺さんに　出してもらいました。げんざい　出席の　返事が210名　とどいています。

加藤：それから、しょうたいした　おきゃくさまに　さしあげる　きねん品はどう　なっていますか。

鈴木：来週　早々　とどく　はずです。

加藤：社長の　あいさつの　げんこうは　できているでしょうね。

鈴木：はい。林部長に　まず　日本語で　書いていただいて、それを　ジョンソンさんに　ほんやくしてもらいました。最後に　社長が　目を　通してくださいました。これが　その　げんこうです。

加藤：会場の　てはいは　もんだいありませんか。

鈴木：出席の　人数が　決まったら、ホテルの　人と　もう　一度　会って、最終の　うち合わせを　します。

加藤：料理の　メニューは　決まりましたか。

鈴木：たんとうの　人を　よんで、林部長が　決めてくださいました。これがメニューです。

加藤：わかりました。

Katō:　About (our) tenth anniversary party on the 20, I'd like to confirm (certain things). First, about the invitation cards—have you sent all of them?

Suzuki:　Yes, I had Watanabe send (them). As of now, responses (indicating) attendance have arrived from 210 people.

Katō:　And what about the mementos for the invited guests?

Suzuki:　They should arrive early next week.

Katō:　The manuscript for the president's address is ready, isn't it?

Suzuki:　Yes. I first asked Mr. Hayashi to write (it) in Japanese and (then I) had Mr. Johnson translate it. Finally, the president looked (it) over. This is the manuscript.

Katō:　There aren't any problems with the arrangements for the reception hall?

Suzuki:　Once the number of guests is fixed, I'll meet with the hotel people again and make the final arrangements.

Katō:　Has the menu been decided?

Suzuki:　Mr. Hayashi called in the person in charge and made the decision. This is the menu.

Katō:　Fine.

そうりつきねん	**sōritsu kinen pātī**, (*lit.*	そうそう	**sōsō**, early, immediately
パーティー	establishment) anniver-	〜ていただく	**-te itadaku** (See gram-
	sary party		mar.)
そうりつ	**sōritsu**, establishment	さいごに	**saigo ni**, finally
きねん	**kinen**, commemoration	めを　とおす	**me o tōsu**, look over
10しゅうねん	**ju-sshū nen**, tenth (year)	とおす	**tōsu**, pass
〜しゅう	**-shū**, (*lit.*) circuit, lap	〜てくださる	**-te kudasaru** (See gram-
かくにんを　す	**kakunin o suru**, confirm		mar.)
る		かいじょう	**kaijō**, reception hall, (*lit.*)
かくにん	**kakunin**, confirmation		meeting place
〜てくれる	**-te kureru** (See gram-	てはい	**tehai**, arrangement,
	mar.)		preparations
げんざい	**genzei**, (as of) now,	さいしゅう	**saishū**, final
	presently	うちあわせを	**uchiawase o suru**, make
さしあげる	**sashiageru**, give (polite)	する	arrangements
きねんひん	**kinenhin**, memento,	うちあわせ	**uchiawase**, (*lit.*)
	souvenir		previous arrangement

GRAMMAR & LESSON OBJECTIVES

• itadaku, sashiageru, kudasaru

These three verbs are the polite counterparts of three learned earlier: **morau**, **ageru** (or **yaru**) and **kureru**. (See lesson 15 in the first volume and lessons 5 and 27 in this volume.) As has been seen, they occur in patterns for giving and receiving both objects and services.

Things:	Neutral	**morau**	**ageru/yaru**	**kureru**
	Polite	**itadaku**	**sashiageru**	**kudasaru**
Services:	Neutral	**-te morau**	**-te ageru/yaru**	**-te kureru**
	Polite	**-te itadaku**	**-te sashiageru**	**-te kudasaru**

Remember the following points concerning usage.

1. Although **yaru** was once the standard word for "give," its usage is now limited to the situation of giving or doing something for intimates, like one's own children, or pets.
2. The use of **-te ageru** is limited; **(Watashi wa) . . . -te agemasu** occurs only in familiar conversation. However, **-te agete kudasai** can be used more freely to ask a person to do something for a third person.
3. **-te itadaku** and **-te kudasaru** are commonly used, but **-te sashiageru** sounds patronizing and so cannot be used freely.

Study the sentences below thinking of the relationship of the people involved as shown in the diagrams.

Shachō	
Hayashi Buchō	Invited guests
Katō Kachō	
Suzuki Johnson Watanabe	
Within the group	Outside the group

Katō says: **Suzuki-kun, shōtaijō wa zembu okutte kuremashita ka.**

shōtai shita o-kyaku-sama ni sashiageru kinenhin

Suzuki says: **Watanabe-san ni dashite moraimashita.**

Hayashi buchō ni kaite itadaite . . .

Jonson-san ni hon'yaku shite moraimashita.

Shachō ga me o tōshite kudasaimashita.

Another comparison to make is between the opening dialogue and the short dialogues in this lesson. The main difference between the way men and women talk in familiar conversation is seen in the sentence endings. Generally speaking, **no yo**, **wa yo** and **wa** when said with a rising tone at the end of a sentence are characteristic of women's speech.

• **kimaru** and **kimeru**

Shusseki no ninzū ga kimattara . . .

Ryōri no menyū wa kimarimashita ka.

Hayashi buchō ga kimete kudasaimashita.

Whether the verb is **kimaru**, "be decided," or **kimeru**, "decide," makes a difference in the particles used. Since the particle **wa** is a topic marker and the topic is not necesarily the same as the grammatical subject of the sentence, nothing particular need be said about it.

1. **Kimaru** takes the subject marker **ga**, as in **Ryōri no menyū ga kimaru.**
2. **Kimeru** takes the particle **o**, as in **Buchō ga ryōri no menyū o kimeru.**

Just as **ni naru** is preferred to **ni suru** (lesson 29), **kimarimashita**, "It has been decided," is soft and is often used by a person making a decision. On the other hand, both negative forms **kimete imasen**, "(I) haven't decided (yet)," and **kimatte imasen**, "It hasn't been decided (yet)," are freely used.

An analogy has been made between pairs of verbs like these and the transitive and intransitive verbs of English. It is better, however, to regard the Japanese forms as so-called transitive and so-called intransitive. A similarity exists in that the direct object of verbs like **kimeru** becomes the subject of verbs like **kimaru**, but many "intransitive" verbs have applications distinctive from English verbs. In other words, there is some resemblance in patterns but usage differs to a great extent and in many instances literal translation is awkward. A number of verb pairs already presented are given here for comparative review.

1. **aku: Kaze de doa ga aita.** The door was opened by the wind."
   akeru: Watashi wa doa o aketa. "I opened the door."
2. **todoku: Kinō kakitome kozutsumi ga todokimashita.** "A registered parcel was delivered yesterday."
   todokeru: Kono jūsho ni bara o todokete kudasai. "Please send roses to this address."
3. **narabu: Biru no mae ni otoko no hito ga takusan narande imasu.** "Many men are lined up in front of the building."
   naraberu: Watanabe-san wa isu o narabemashita. "Watanabe lined up the chairs."
4. **hajimaru: Purojekuto ga hajimarimashita.** "The project has been started."
   hajimeru: Ashita kara kōji o hajimemasu. "We'll start construction (work) tomorrow."
5. **hairu: Gakusei wa donna kaisha ni hairitagatte imasu ka.** "What companies do students want to be employed by?"
   ireru: Posuto ni kono tegami o irete kudasai. "Please put this letter in the mail box."
6. **susumu: Takushī ga susumimasen deshita.** "The taxi did not move on." (*lit.* "proceed")
   susumeru: Shigoto o susumemashō. "Let's get on with the work."
7. **ochiru: Tōkyō dewa momiji no ha wa 12-gatsu no owari goro ochimasu.** "In Tokyo maple leaves fall around the end of December."
   otosu: Hashi no ue kara mono o otosanaide kudasai. "Please do not drop things from the bridge."
8. **kieru: Denki ga kiemashita. Teiden kamo shiremasen.** "The lights went out. There seems to have been a power failure."
   kesu: Denki o keshite, kagi o kakete kudasai. "Please turn off the lights and lock up."

• Comparison of **-te iru** and **-te aru**.

While **-te iru** and **-te aru** differ little in concrete meaning, the latter does imply that an individual's action has resulted in the state or condition described. In the following examples, **-te iru**, "is —ing," ("a" sentences) was introduced in lesson 25 of the first volume, **-te iru** ("b" sentences) in lesson 27 of the first volume (with a person as subject, which differs from these examples and those in Lesson 2), and **-te aru** in lesson 26.

ex. 1. a. **Mado o akete imasu.** "(Somebody) is opening the window."
    b. **Mado ga aite imasu.** "The window is open."
    c. **Mado ga akete arimasu.** "The window is open." (Someone having opened it.)
  2. a. **Watanabe-san wa isu o narabete imasu.** "Watanabe is arranging chairs."
    b. **Isu ga narande imasu.** "The chairs have been arranged."
    c. **Isu ga narabete arimasu.** "The chairs have been arranged." (Someone having arranged them.)
  3. a. **Haha ga kēki o tsukutte imasu.** "Mother is making a cake."
    b. **Kēki ga dekite imasu.** "The cake is ready."
    c. **Kēki ga tsukutte arimasu.** "The cake is ready." (Someone having baked it.)

NOTES

1. **O-kyaku-sama ni sashiageru kinenhin wa dō natte imasu ka.**
Dō natte imasu ka literally means "How has it become?" and is used to ask how things are going or a current condition. (See p. 44.)
ex. **Ashita no yotei wa dō natte imasu ka.** "What's your schedule tomorrow."

2. **Shachō ga me o tōshite kudasaimashita.**
Remember that the **-masu** form of **kudasaru** is **kudasaimasu** (not **kudasarimasu.**†) There are similar examples in lesson 33.

PRACTICE

KEY SENTENCES

1. ぶちょうが　パーティーの　メニューを　きめてくださいました。
2. ぶちょうに　パーティーの　メニューを　きめていただきました。
3. すずきくんが　てつだってくれました。
4. かれに　せつめいしてあげてください。

1. The division chief (did us the favor of) deciding the party menu.
2. The division chief decided the party menu. (Has the nuance, "since we asked him to.")
3. Mr. Suzuki helped (me).
4. Please explain (it) to him.

Vocabulary

～てあげる   **-te ageru**, do something for someone

EXERCISES

I. Make dialogues by changing the underlined parts as in the examples given.

  A. *ex.* **Q** :〔あなたは〕　たなかさんに　なにを　いただきましたか。
    A :〔わたしは　たなかさんに〕　かびんを　いただきました。

      1. せんせい、えはがき
      2. となりの　おおのさん、めずらしい　おかし
      3. しゃちょう、しゃちょうが　かいた　え

4. しゃちょうの　おくさん、ぼんさいの　ほん

B. *ex.* **Q**：<u>かびんを　くださったのは</u>　どなたですか。
A：<u>たなかさん</u>です。

1. えはがき、せんせい
2. この　めずらしい　おかし、かいしゃの　かた
3. え、ぶちょう
4. ぼんさいの　ほん、しゃちょうの　おくさん

C. *ex.* **Q**：<u>おれいに</u>　なにを　さしあげる　つもりですか。
A：<u>くだもの</u>を　さしあげようと　おもいます。

1. きねん、しゃしん
2. おみまい、くだもの
3. おみやげ、スイスせいの　チョコレート
4. おいわい、はな

D. *ex.* **Q**：<u>ともだちに</u>　<u>ほんを</u>　おくってもらったんですか。
A：いいえ、<u>せんせいに</u>　おくっていただきました。

1. ともだち、この　ほんを　かす、せんせい
2. なかむらさん、あんないする、はやしぶちょう
3. みせの　ひと、かぐを　とどける、かいしゃの　かた
4. すずきさん、あなたの　レポートを　よむ、かちょう

E. *ex.* **Q**：<u>すずきさんが</u>　<u>げんこうを</u>　かいてくれたんですか。
A：いいえ、<u>ぶちょうが</u>　かいてくださいました。

1. でんわを　かける、かちょう
2. その　じょうほうを　しらせる、とりひきさきの　かた
3. じぎょうけいかくしょに　めを　とおす、ぶちょう
4. その　ことばの　いみを　おしえる、えいかいわの　せんせい
5. やくしょに　こうしょうする、　しゃちょう

F. *ex.* **Q**：<u>ぶちょうが</u>　きめてくださいましたか。
A：はい、<u>ぶちょうに</u>　きめていただきました。

1. ぶちょう、くわしく　せつめいしました
2. してんちょう、でんわばんごうを　おしえました

3. せんせい、きょうかしょを もってきました
4. かちょう、とりひきさきに つれていきました
5. たなかさん、えきまで くるまで おくりました

G. ex. **Q** : だれか てがみを だしに いってくれない？
   A : ぼくが いってあげる。

1. いすを ならべるのを てつだう
2. てがみが きたか どうか みてくる
3. その にもつを はこぶ
4. この へやを かたづける

II. Make pairs of sentences like those in the example.

ex. ぶちょうが けいかくを きめました。→けいかくが きまりました。

1. きょうじゅ、しりょう、あつめる、しりょう、あつまる
2. かんりにん、ドア、あける、ドア、あく
3. しゃちょう、かいぎの ひ、かえる、かいぎの ひ、かわる
4. さかや、ビール、とどける、ビール、とどく
5. おてつだいさん、おもての いりぐち、しめる、おもての い
   りぐち、しまる
6. しゃちょう、きゅうりょう、あげる、きゅうりょう、あがる
7. たなかさん、でんわ、かけてくる、でんわ、かかってくる
8. ぎょうしゃ、こうじ、はじめる、こうじ、はじまる
9. なかむらさん、さいふ、おとす、さいふ、おちる
10. はは、ストーブ、けす、ストーブ、きえる
11. となりの ひと、うち、たてる、うち、たつ
12. エンジニア、コンピューター、なおす、コンピューター、なお
    る
13. うんてんしゅ、くるま、とめる、くるま、とまる

III. Make dialogues by changing the underlined parts as in the example given.

ex. **A** : まどが あいていますね。
   B : ええ、おきゃくさんが くるので あけてあります。

1. いすが たくさん ならぶ、ならべる
2. かいぎしつの でんきが つく、つける
3. こんな ところに しょるいが でる、だす
4. れいぞうこに ビールが たくさん はいる、いれる

えはがき	**e-hagaki**, picture post-card	やくしょ	**yakusho**, public/government office
ぼんさい	**bonsai** (dwarf tree)	してんちょう	**shitenchō**, branch manager
おれいに	**o-rei ni**, as a token of gratitude	きょうかしょ	**kyōkasho**, textbook
れい	**rei**, gratitude, courtesy, reward	あつまる	**atsumaru**, be collected
（お）みまい	**o-mimai**, gift (to a sick person), expression of sympathy	おてつだいさん	**o-tetsudai-san**, maid
		あげる	**ageru**, raise
		あがる	**agaru**, be raised, rise
まんねんひつ	**mannenhitsu**, fountain pen	でんわが かかってくる	**denwa ga kakatte kuru**, receive a phone call
レポート	**repōto**, report	でんわが かかる	**denwa ga kakaru**, get a phone call, (*lit.* be called by phone)
じょうほう	**jōhō**, information		
じぎょう	**jigyō**, business, enterprise, operations	たつ	**tatsu**, be built
		エンジニア	**enjinia**, engineer
けいかくしょ	**keikaku-sho**, plan (written)	れいぞうこ	**reizōko**, refrigerator

SHORT DIALOGUES

1. スミス： すずきさんに この てがみの ないようを せつめいしてあげてください。
   わたなべ：はい、わかりました。

   Smith:　　Please explain the contents of this letter to Suzuki.
   Watanabe: Yes, of course.

2. はは　　　　　：ちょっと おつかいに いってくれない？
   うえの むすめ：これから しゅくだいを はじめるのよ。あとでね。
   したの むすめ：じゃ、わたしが いってあげるわ。

   Mother:　　　　　　Will you do (*lit.* go on) an errand (for me)?
   Older Daughter:　　I'm going to do my homework now. Later, OK?
   Younger Daughter: I'll do it (for you).

おつかい	**o-tsukai**, errand, mission	したの	**shita no**, younger, lower
うえの	**ue no**, older, upper		

QUIZ

I. Read this lesson's opening dialogue and answer the following questions.

1. すずきさんは じぶんで しょうたいじょうを だしましたか。

2. しゃちょうの　あいさつの　げんこうは　まず　だれが　かいて、それ
　　を　だれが　ほんやくしましたか。
3. しょうたいされた　おきゃくさまは　200めいより　おおいですか。
4. しゅっせきの　にんずうが　きまったら、すずきさんは　なにを　する
　　つもりですか。

II. Put the appropriate particles in the parentheses.

1. わたしは　かとうさん（　　）　めずらしい　ほん（　　）　いただき
　　ました。
2. おみまいに　くだもの（　　）　さしあげよう（　　）　おもいます。
3. はなしたい　ことが　ありますから、みんな（　　）　あつめてくださ
　　い。
4. この　かいぎには　にほんの　かくち（　　）　おおぜいの　ひと
　　（　　）　あつまりました。
5. この　へやは　カード（　　）　いれると　かぎ（　　）　あきます。

III. Complete the questions so that they fit the answers.

1. きふを　して　くださったのは　（　　）ですか。
　　はやしぶちょうです。
2 （　　）　ホテルの　ひとと　さいしゅうの　うちあわせを　しますか。
　　しゅっせきの　にんずうが　きまったら、すぐ　します。
3. （　　）に　その　ほんを　かしていただいたんですか。
　　かちょうに　かしていただきました。
4. かいじょうの　てはいは　（　　）　なっていますか。
　　もう　てはいは　してあります。

IV. Complete the sentences with the appropriate form of the verbs indicated.

1. しゅうまつに　しゃちょうが　おたくに　（　　）くださいました。（し
　　ょうたいします）
2. わたなべさんが　へやを　（　　）のを　（　　）くれました。（かたづ
　　けます、てつだいます）
3. きむらさんに　くるまの　こしょうを　（　　）もらいました。（なおし
　　ます）
4. れいぞうこに　ビールが　（　　）あります。（いれます）
5. わたなべさんが　かいぎしつに　いすを　（　　）いますから、（　　）
　　あげてください。（はこびます、てつだいます）
6. リンダさんから　てがみが　（　　）います。（とどきます）

V. Choose a sentence appropriate to the situation described.

A. A coworker asks you what he should give his section chief for his birthday.

1. はなを　あげようと　おもいます。
2. はなを　あげても　いいです。

3. はなを　さしあげたら　どうですか。

B. In answer to a question, you say that while you were in Kyoto your professor took you to see an old temple.

1. きょうじゅに　ふるい　おてらへ　つれていっていただきました。
2. きょうじゅが　ふるい　おてらへ　つれていかれました。
3. きょうじゅが　ふるい　おてらへ　つれていってあげました。

LESSON 32 A BROKEN TV SET

Mrs. Suzuki asks about having their TV looked at.

鈴木夫人：　もしもし、あのう、こちら　鈴木と　言いますが、きのうから　うちの　テレビが　よく　うつらなくて　困っています。ちょっと　見に　来てもらえませんか。

サービスセンター：場所は　どの　へんでしょうか。

鈴木夫人：　六本木の　こうさてんを　渋谷に　むかって　200メートルぐらい　行くと　右がわに　大きい　スーパーマーケットが　あります。その　スーパーの　先を　右に　まがると　すぐ　左がわに　6階建ての　白い　建物が　あります。

サービスセンター：ああ、あの　ふねみたいな　かたちの　マンションですね。

鈴木夫人：　そこの　403号室です。今から　来れますか。

サービスセンター：午前中は　ちょっと　むずかしいですね。もう　一つ　しゅうりの　やくそくが　ありますから。

鈴木夫人：　むりですか。3時から　出かけたいんですが。

サービスセンター：そうですか。じゃ、昼に　センターに　もどらないで、ちょくせつ　うかがうように　します。

鈴木夫人：　だいたい　何時ごろに　なりますか。

サービスセンター：1時すぎに　なると　思います。

鈴木夫人：　じゃ、外出せずに　待っていますから、できるだけ　早く　おねがいします。

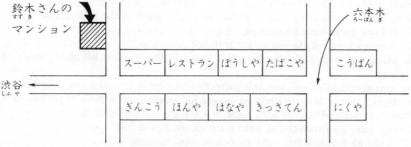

Mr. Suzuki: Hello, my name is Suzuki. (Our) TV (picture) hasn't been good since yesterday and it's annoying. Couldn't you come and look at it?

Service
Center: Your place is where?

Suzuki: About 200 meters from the Roppongi intersection going towards Shibuya there's a big supermarket on the right side. If (you) turn right just beyond the supermarket, there's a six-story white building immediately on the left side.
Center: Ah, is it the apartment house shaped to resemble a ship?
Suzuki: Um hm, that (place), number 403. Can you come now?
Center: It's difficult this morning. I already have an appointment (to do some) repairs.
Suzuki: Impossible, is it? I'd like to go out at 3:00.
Center: I see. Well, then, (I) won't come back to the center at noon; I'll go directly to your place.
Suzuki: Around what time will it be?
Center: After one o'clock, I suppose.
Suzuki: I won't go out then; I'll be waiting (for you). Make it as early as possible please.

Vocabulary

うつる	**utsuru**, (*lit.*) be reflected (appear as an image)	マンション	**manshon**, apartment building (usu. ferrocon-crete)
センター	**sentā**, center		
ばしょ	**basho**, place, seat, scene	しゅうり	**shūri**, repair, fix up
ろっぽんぎ	**Roppongi** (place name)	ちょくせつ	**chokusetsu**, directly, straightforwardly
しぶや	**Shibuya** (place name)		
むかう	**mukau**, go, face, confront	ように　する	**yō ni suru**, try to
スーパーマーケット	**supāmāketto**, super-market	～ずに	**-zu ni**, without —ing
6かいだて	**6-kai-date**, six story	できるだけ	**dekiru dake**, as . . . as possible, to the best of one's ability
～だて	**-date**, story, counter		
みたい（な）	**-mitai(na)**, resembling, like, a sort of	～だけ	**dake**, all there is, no more than

GRAMMAR & LESSON OBJECTIVES

- **-nakute, -naide, -zu ni**, negative connectives

Terebi ga yoku utsuranakute komatte imasu.
Jā, hiru ni sentā ni modoranaide, chokusetsu ukagau yō ni shimasu.
Gaishutsu sezu ni matte imasu.
All three of these connectives used to link phrases or subordinate clauses in a sentence follow the **-nai** stem of verbs. The **-te** form of **nai**, **-nakute**, is also combined with **-i** adjectives. **-nakute** indicates the reason for the state of affairs given in the main clause.

ex. 1. **O-kane ga nakute kaemasen.** "I don't have any money; I can't buy it."
  2. **Ame ga furanakute yokatta.** "It didn't rain—good!"
  3. **Michi ga wakaranakute komatte imasu.** "I'm worried because I don't know the way."

When **-nakute** supplies a reason, this pattern cannot express requests or suggestions, and the main clause never ends in **-te kudasai**, **masen ka**, **-mashō** or any form or pattern evincing the speaker's intention. Patterns with **node** or **kara** are suitable in such cases.

  Wrong: **Yuki ga furanakute, sukī o shimasen.**† (will not)
  OK: **Yuki ga furanakute, sukī ga dekimasen.** (cannot)
  OK: **Yuki ga furanai node/kara, sukī o shimasen.** (will not)

In the dialogue sentences above, **-naide** and **-zu ni** mean essentially the same thing: "without doing" or "not do . . . but . . ."

ex. 1. **Kinō wa hiru-gohan o tabenaide/-zu ni asa kara ban made hatarakimashita.** "Yesterday (I) worked from morning until evening without eating lunch."
  2. **Kare wa nani mo shinaide/sezu ni ichi-nichi-jū terebi o mite imasu.** "He (spends)

all day doing nothing but watching TV." (Note: **sezu ni** in the case of **suru**, not **shizu-ni**.†)

- **yō ni suru,** "try"

Chokusetsu ukagau yō ni shimasu.

The dictionary form followed by **yō ni suru** means "try," as seen in the dialogue, or "intend." Although a common expresion, bilingual dictionaries often omit this meaning of **yō ni suru.**

ex. 1. **Mainichi denwa de shiraseru yō ni shimasu.** "I intend to report by phone every day."

2. **Maiasa 6-ji mae ni okiru yō ni shite imasu.** "(I) try to get up before six every morning."

3. **Basu no naka ni kasa o wasurenai yō ni shite kudasai.** "Please don't (*lit.* "try not to") leave (your) umbrellas in the bus."

NOTES

1. **Mi ni kite moraemasen ka.**
   This is a request. Note that it is the potential form, **morae-**, not **morai-**. The pattern **-te itadakemasen ka** is politer. (See also pp. 235.)

2. **Ā, ano fune-mitaina katachi no manshon desu ne.**
   Mitaina, which has the same meaning as **no yō na** but is more colloquial, can mean "seemingly" as well as "resembling, looking like." **Mitai** occurs as a predicate with either meaning.
   ex. **Kare wa gaikoku-jin mitai (desu).** "He seems to be a foreigner." (Actually, it is not clear whether the speaker is sure about the fact or is making an assumption.)

3. **Ima kara koremasu ka.**
   Strictly speaking, the potential form of **kuru** is **korareru** but **koreru** has become acceptable usage. Similar simplified forms:

orthodox	**taberareru**	**mirareru**	**kirareru**	**orirareru**
popular	**tabereru**	**mireru**	**kireru**	**orireru**

4. **Dekiru-dake hayaku onegaishimasu.**
   Another word for **dekiru-dake,** "as . . . as possible," is **narubeku,** as in exercise I F (*ex.* question), p. 000.

5. **Nan-ji goro ni narimasu ka.**
   This is another case of using **naru** to make the question sound softer than the more direct **Nan-ji goro kimasu ka** would.

PRACTICE

KEY SENTENCES

1. がいしゅつ しないで/せずに まっています。
2. こくさいでんわの かけかたが わからなくて こまっています。
3. にほんごで あいさつするように しています。
4. えどじだいの いえみたいな レストランです。

1. (I) won't go out; I'll be waiting (for you).
2. Not knowing how to make international calls, I'm at a loss.
3. (I) try to greet people in Japanese.
4. (It's) a restaurant which looks like an Edo-period house.

EXERCISES

I. Make dialogues by changing the underlined parts as in the examples given.

A. *ex.* **Q**：スミスさんは　もう　でかけましたか。
   A：ええ、ひるごはんを　たべないで　でかけてしまいました。

   1. でんわを　かけません
   2. てがみを　よみません
   3. いつ　かえるか　いいません
   4. ぜんぜん　はなしを　しません

B. *ex.* **Q**：いつも　でんわを　してから　いきますか。
   A：いいえ、でんわを　しないで　いく　ことも　あります。

   1. よやくを　してから　いきます
   2. まちがいが　ないか　どうか　たしかめてから　おくります
   3. しんぶんに　めを　とおしてから　でかけます
   4. うちへ　でんわを　してから　かえります
   5. しゅくだいを　してから　ねます

C. *ex.* **Q**：じしょを　ひかなかったんですか。
   A：ええ、じしょを　ひかないで、にほんごの　しんぶんを　よみました。

   1. てつだってもらいませんでした、ひとりで　しました
   2. のりかえませんでした、とうきょうまで　いく　ことが　できました
   3. えいごを　つかいませんでした、にほんごで　はなしました
   4. だれにも　ききませんでした、ここに　くる　ことが　できました

D. *ex.* **Q**：ちょっと　おくれるかも　しれませんが、まっていてくださいませんか。
   A：はい、では　がいしゅつせずに　まっています。

   1. かいぎを　はじめません
   2. どこへも　でかけません
   3. しょくじに　いきません
   4. なにも　きめません

E. *ex.* **Q**：どうか　しましたか。
　　　A：<u>この　かんじが　よめなくて</u>　こまっています。

　　　　1.　でんわが　かけられません
　　　　2.　（お）かねが　ありません
　　　　3.　この　きかいの　つかいかたが　わかりません
　　　　4.　ひとりで　できません
　　　　5.　ハンドバッグが　みつかりません

F. *ex.* **A**：なるべく　はやく　<u>して</u>ほしいんですが・・・。
　　　B：ええ、できるだけ　はやく　<u>する</u>ように　します。

　　　　1.　とどける
　　　　2.　なおす
　　　　3.　かえす
　　　　4.　しらべる
　　　　5.　じゅんびする

G. *ex.* **Q**：いつも　なんじごろ　<u>おきる</u>んですか。
　　　A：<u>6じごろ　おきる</u>ように　しています。

　　　　1.　ねる、　12じまえに
　　　　2.　ばんごはんを　たべる、8じまえに
　　　　3.　べんきょうを　はじめる、ゆうしょくの　あと　すぐに
　　　　4.　うちを　でる、ラッシュアワーの　まえに

H. *ex.* **A**：<u>できるだけ　しおを　とらない</u>ように　してください。
　　　B：はい、<u>どりょくします</u>。

　　　　1.　まいにち　ちゃんと　くすりを　のみます、どりょくします
　　　　2.　よく　たしかめます、そうします
　　　　3.　ならった　ことを　できるだけ　わすれません、どりょくします
　　　　4.　かいぎに　ぜったいに　おくれません、わかりました

I. *ex.* **Q**：<u>テレビが　こわれたので、みに　きて</u>もらえませんか。
　　　A：はい、わかりました。

　　　　1.　とけいが　うごかない、しゅうりする
　　　　2.　へやが　きたない、かたづける
　　　　3.　いま　いそがしい、あとに　する

4. しごとが のこっている、さきに いく

II. Practice the following pattern by changing the underlined parts.

ex. ふねみたいです。→ふねみたいな かたちです。

1. こども、ひと
2. きょうと、ところ
3. はる、ひ
4. （お）しろ、いえ

Vocabulary

ハンドバッグ	**handobaggu**, handbag	ちゃんと	**chanto**, regularly, correctly, perfectly
みつかる	**mitsukaru**, be found		
かえす	**kaesu**, give back, repay	ぜったい（に）	**zettai (ni)**, absolutely, unconditionally
ゆうしょく	**yūshoku**, supper		
とる	**toru**, eat	こわれる	**kowareru**, be broken
どりょくする	**doryoku suru**, make an effort, do one's best	きたない	**kitanai**, dirty
どりょく	**doryoku**, effort	（お）しろ	**o-shiro**, castle

SHORT DIALOGUES

1. さとう：こんどの しゅうまつ、つりに いかない？
   すずき：こんしゅうは じかんが なくて いけないよ。

   Satō   Won't you (like to) go fishing this coming weekend?
   Suzuki: This week I don't have time so I can't go.

2. かちょう：さとうくんの いえに どろぼうが はいったそうだね。
   わたなべ：ええ。かぎを しめないで でかけたらしいですよ。

   Section Chief: A robber broke into Satō's house, I hear.
   Watanabe: Yes, it seems they went out without locking up.

Vocabulary

かぎを しめる **kagi o shimeru**, lock

QUIZ

I. Read this lesson's opening dialogue and answer the following questions.

1. すずきさんは どこから サービスセンターに でんわを かけていますか。
2. すずきさんは なぜ こまっていますか。

3. すずきさんの　すんでいる　マンションは　なんかいだてで、どんな
かたちですか。
4. サービスセンターの　ひとは　ひるに　センターに　もどらずに　ちょ
くせつ　すずきさんの　うちに　いこうと　おもっていますか。

II. Put the appropriate particles in the parentheses.

1. とうきょうえき（　　）　むかって　300メートルぐらい　いく（　　）
ひだりがわ（　　）　あります。
2. たばこやの　さき（　　）　みぎ（　　）　まがってください。
3. かど（　　）　10かいだて（　　）　ちゃいろの　マンション（　　）
あります。
4. これからは　ねぼう　しないよう（　　）　します。

III. Complete the questions so that they fit the answers.

1. ばしょは　（　　）　へんでしょうか。
きんざ　4ちょうめの　こうさてんの　ちかくです。
2. （　　）　したんですか。
コンピューターが　うごかなくて　こまっています。
3. じかんは　だいたい　（　　）　ごろに　なりますか。
3じすぎに　うかがえると　おもいます。
4. （　　）　こられないんですか。
もう　ひとつ　べつの　やくそくが　あるので、いかれないんです。

IV. Complete the sentences with the appropriate form of the verbs indicated.

1. なんかげつも　あめが　（　　）、のうみんは　こまっています。
（ふりません）
2. よる　でんきを　（　　）で、（　　）しまいました。（けしません、ね
ます）
3. よく　（　　）ずに、けいやくしょに　サインを　（　　）しまいまし
た。（たしかめます、します）
4. くつが　きたないので、（　　）もらえませんか。（みがきます）
5. だいじな　しょるいが　（　　）、こまっています。（みつかりません）
6. ゆうべは　シャワーを　（　　）で、ねました。（あびません）

V. Answer the following questions.

1. あなたは　あさ　なにも　たべずに　でかけますか。
2. あなたは　じしょを　ひかないで、にほんごの　しんぶんが　よめます
か。
3. あなたは　げんきんを　もたずに　かいものに　いく　ことが　ありま
すか。
4. あなたは　しょくじに　きを　つけていますか。きを　つけている　こ
とを　えらんでください。

a. できるだけ　しおを　とらないように　しています。
b. にくを　たべないように　しています。
c. あまり　たくさん　たべないように　しています。
d. あまい　ものを　たくさん　たべないように　しています。
e. やさいを　たくさん　たべるように　しています。

LESSON 33 A THANK YOU PHONE CALL

Mrs. Katō follows up a social visit.

加藤夫人： もしもし、スミスさんでいらっしゃいますか。

スミス夫人：はい、スミスでございます。

加藤夫人： 加藤でございますが、昨日は　お招きいただきまして、ありがとう
ございました。

スミス夫人：こちらこそ、みなさまに　来ていただいて、とても　楽しかったで
す。お送りする　つもりでしたが、あいにく　車の　調子が　悪く
て、しつれいいたしました。おつかれに　なりませんでしたか。

加藤夫人： いいえ。主人も　子どもたちも　とても　よろこんでいました。ほ
んとうに　ありがとうございました。

スミス夫人：こちらこそ　かきを　たくさん　いただきまして、ありがとうござ
いました。おにわで　りっぱなのが　できるんですねえ。

加藤夫人： ２、３日たつと、もっと　あまく　なりますから、それから　めし
上がってください。では、どうぞ　みなさまに　よろしく　おっし
ゃってください。

スミス夫人：はい。どうも　ごていねいに　お電話を　ありがとうございまし
た。

Mrs. Katō:	Hello, is this Mrs. Smith?
Mrs. Smith:	Yes, this is Mrs. Smith.
Katō:	This is Mrs. Katō. Thank you so much for inviting us yesterday.
Smith:	We should be the ones (to thank you. We're) very glad everybody could come. (We) intended to take you home, but unfortunately the car wasn't running well. I'm sorry. Weren't you all tired out?
Katō:	No, Both (my) husband and the children were very pleased. (We) really do want to thank you.
Smith:	(No, really,) thank you. (And we) got such a lot of persimmons—thank you. Such splendid persimmons and grown in your (own) garden!
Katō:	After a few days (pass), they'll be tastier so please eat (them then). Please give our best regards to everyone.
Smith:	Certainly. Thank you for calling. It's so considerate of you.

Vocabulary			
～でいらっしゃる	**-de irassharu**, be (respect lang.)	たつ	**tatsu**, pass
まねく	**maneku**, invite	めしあがる	**meshiagaru**, eat (or drink; respect lang.)

こそ	**koso**, (*lit.*) indeed	おっしゃる	**ossharu**, say (respect
お〜する	**o** + **-masu** stem **suru**		lang.)
	(humble)	（ご）ていねい	**(go-)teinei ni**, con-
あいにく	**ainiku**, unfortunately	に	siderate, (*lit.*) politely,
お〜になる	**o** + **-masu** stem **ni naru**		respectfully, conscien-
	(respect lang.)		tiously;
かき	**kaki**, persimmon	ていねい（な）	**teinei(na)**, polite

GRAMMAR & LESSON OBJECTIVES

- **o** + **-masu** stem **ni naru**, **o** + **-masu** stem **suru** and other polite expressions

O-tsukare ni narimasen deshita ka. (to show respect)

O-okuri suru tsumori deshita ga. . . . (to show humility)

The appropriate usage of **keigo** ("terms of respect") depends on the relationships between people, primarily between the speaker and his or her listener, secondarily when a third person is referred to. Let's look at two determinants and the related patterns and vocabulary. The first determinant is order of hierarchy. While the speaker chooses respect language when speaking to or about seniors or elders, social status, power or patronage are also factors which may come into play. The second determinant, as shown in the diagram, is ingroup-outgroup relationships.

outgroup
↑
speaker's group

strangers

When speaking or referring to a person in the outgroup, the speaker chooses terms of respect and he uses humble expressions to talk about himself and his group. **Keigo** is limited primarily to current relationships. It is not the usual thing where strangers are concerned, nor when people are famous or historical personages known only by name.

Especially in business circles, the ingroup-outgroup dichotomy is important; in ingroup relations hierarchy is important.

Certain words and patterns clearly identify expressions of respect and humility.

1. Expressions of respect

As in the first example above, ordinary verbs become respect language when put in the pattern **o** + **-masu** stem + **ni naru**.

ex. **O-denwa o o-kake ni narimasu ka.** "Will (you) phone?"

Two other points are relevant. For **miru**, the pattern is **go-ran ni naru** and for **iru** and **kuru** it is **o-ide ni naru**. And certain verbs have **keigo** equivalents. A few of the most common are: **taberu → meshiageru; suru → nasaru; iu → ossharu; kureru → kudasaru;** and **irassharu** for **iru**, **iku** and **kuru**. These are Regular I verbs conjugated as in the chart.

	-nai	-masu	conditional	-te	-ta
meshiagaru	meshiaga-ranai	meshiaga-rimasu	meshia-gareba	meshiagatte	meshiagatta
nasaru	nasaranai	nasaimasu	nasareba	nasatte	nasatta ·

Note that the **-masu** forms of the other respect verbs given here are like **nasaru**'s and certain others previously encountered, i.e., **osshaimasu, irasshaimasu, gozaimasu, kudasaimasu.**

2. Expressions of humility .

As in the second example on page 000, ordinary verbs become humble when put in the pattern of **o** + **-masu** stem + **suru/itasu**. This is the same type expression as **go-annai shimashō** (in leson 3), which might also be **go-annai itashimashō** (politer).

ex. **O-mise shimashō.** "(We'll) show (you)."
A few alternative humble words for common verbs are: **suru** → **itasu**; **iru** → **oru**; **iu** → **mōsu**; **morau, taberu** → **itadaku**; **iku, kuru** → **mairu/ukagau.**
The usage of **mairu** is unrestricted but **ukagau** is limited to cases where one goes to a place connected with the object of respect.
ex. 1. **Ashita o-taku ni ukagaimasu/mairimasu.** "(I'll) go to (your) house tomorrow."
    2. **Ashita Kyōto ni mairimasu.** "(I'm) going to Kyoto tomorrow."

● **de irasshaimasu, de gozaimasu**

Moshi moshi Sumisu-san de irasshaimasu ka.
Hai, Sumisu de gozaimasu.
These two patterns make what is said sound polite.
ex. 1. **Pātī wa 6-ji kara de gozaimasu.** (instead of **desu**) "The party is from six o'clock."
    2. **Achira ni uketsuke ga gozaimasu.** (instead of **arimasu**) "There's a reception (desk) over there."
Another expression of this type is **-te itadaku** as in **Mina-sama ni kite itadaite totemo tanoshikatta desu.** (Lesson 31)
The difference between **o** + **-masu** stem **itadaku** and **o** + **-masu** stem **suru** is that with the former an action is performed for the speaker and with the latter the speaker performs an action for another person. Nouns that combine with **suru**, such as **go-annai, o-denwa** and **go-sōdan**, frequently occur in these patterns.

NOTE

Kochira koso . . . arigatō gozaimashita
Koso coming after a word places stress on that word. As suggested by the translation, the sense of **kochira koso** is that the obligation is really on this side, i.e., on me/us.

PRACTICE

KEY SENTENCES

1. おつかれに　なりましたか。
2. みなさまを　くるまで　おおくりしましょう。
3. おまねきいただきまして、ありがとうございます。

1. Weren't you all tired out?
2. I'll send you all (home) by car.
3. Thank you very much for inviting (me/us).

EXERCISES

I. Practice the following dialogue as a telephone conversation.

（あなた）：もしもし、かとうさんでいらっしゃいますか。
かとう：　はい、かとうでございます。
（あなた）：（あなたの　なまえ）でございますが、ごしゅじん/おくさまは
　　　　　　いらっしゃいますか。
かとう：　きょうは　ようじが　ございまして、でかけております。
（あなた）：そうですか。では、また　のちほど　おでんわいたします。

II. Make dialogues by changing the underlined parts as in the examples given.

A. *ex.* **Q**：おつかれに　なりましたか。
A：はい、<u>つかれ</u>ました。

1. かく
2. よむ
3. つかう

4. はなす
5. きめる
6. えらぶ

B. *ex.* **A**：どうぞ　<u>なかに　おはいり</u>ください。
B：はい、ありがとうございます。

1. ゆっくり　やすむ
2. (お)すきなだけ　とる
3. よろしく　つたえる

4. そこに　かける
5. いつでも　たずねる

C. *ex.* **Q**：<u>くるまで　おおくり</u>しましょうか。
A：おねがいします。

1. にもつを　もつ
2. かわりに　きく
3. かさを　かす
4. しょるいを　とどける
5. みほんを　みせる

6. しばらく　まつ
7. とうきょうを　あんないする
8. みちを　せつめいする
9. みなさんに　しょうかいする

III. Practice the following patterns by changing the underlined parts as in the examples given.

A. *ex.* **Q**：ごしゅじんは　<u>います</u>か。→ごしゅじんは　<u>いらっしゃいます</u>か。
A：はい、<u>います</u>。　　　→はい、<u>おります</u>。

1. **Q**：いつ　とうきょうに　<u>きました</u>か
A：せんげつ　<u>きました</u>

2. **Q**：どうぞ　ケーキを　<u>たべてください</u>
A：はい、<u>たべます</u>

3. **Q**：<u>だれが</u>　<u>せつめいします</u>か
A：わたしが　<u>します</u>

4. **A**：あした　わたしの　うちに　<u>きてください</u>
B：はい、<u>いきます</u>

5. **Q**：おくさんの　なまえは　なんと　<u>いいます</u>か
A：ゆきこと　<u>いいます</u>

6. **Q**：どこへ　いきますか
   A：ぎんざへ　いきます

7. **Q**：だれが　くれましたか
   A：スミスさんに　もらいました

B. *ex.* さくじつは　おまねきいただきまして　ありがとうございました。

1. いい　ところを　おおしえいただく
2. きちょうな　ほんを　おかしいただく
3. けっこうな　ものを　おおくりいただく
4. くるまで　おくってくださる
5. しりょうを　とどけてくださる

Vocabulary

～ておる	**-te oru** (humble for **-te iru**)	みほん	**mihon**, sample
すきなだけ	**sukina dake**, as much as you like	しばらく	**shibaraku**, awhile, a moment, for the time being
かわりに	**kawari ni**, in place of	おる	**oru**, be (humble)
Responses			
まいる	**mairu**, go, come (humble)	なさる	**nasaru**, do (polite)

SHORT DIALOGUES

1. はやし：やあ、しばらくですね。いつ　にほんへ　おいでに　なりましたか。
   キム：　みっか　まえに　まいりました。

   Hayashi: Well, well, it's been awhile (since I saw you last), hasn't it? When did you come to Japan?
   Kim:　　 I got (here) three days ago.

2. **A**：なんじごろ　いらっしゃいますか。
   B：ごご　2 じごろ　うかがいたいのですが。
   A：ええ、けっこうです。おまちしております。

   A: Around what time are you coming?
   B: I'd like to come around two o'clock.
   A: Fine, I'll be waiting for you.

QUIZ

I. Read this lesson's opening dialogue and answer the following questions.

1. だれが　だれの　うちに　まねかれましたか。
2. スミスさんは　みんなを　くるまで　おくっていきましたか。

3. スミスさんが もらった かきは どこで できた ものですか。

4. おみやげの かきは いつごろに なると おいしく なると かとう
   さんは いっていますか。

5. 「みなさんに よろしく。」と「みなさまに よろしく おっしゃってく
   ださい。」と どちらが ていねいな いいかたですか。

II. Put the appropriate particles or inflections in the parentheses.

1. もしもし たなかさんでいらっしゃいますか。
   はい、たなか（　　）ございます。

2. このごろ からだ（　　）　ちょうし（　　）　よく ありません。

3. しゅじんも こどもたち（　　）　かき（　　）　とても すきです。

4. 1ねんぐらい べんきょうすれ（　　）、にほんご（　　）はなせるよう
   （　　）　なるでしょう。

III. Complete the questions so that they fit the answers.

1. デザートは （　　）を めしあがりますか。
   アイスクリームを いただきます。

2. おしょくじは （　　）に なさいますか。
   8じに おねがいします。

3. あしたは （　　）に いらっしゃいますか。
   いちにちじゅう うちに おります。

4. （　　）が ロンドンに いらっしゃるんですか。
   ぶちょうが いらっしゃるそうです。

IV. Complete the sentences with the appropriate form of the verbs indicated.

1. せんせいは らいねん だいがくを お（　　）に なります。（やめる）

2. どうぞ たくさん （　　）ください。（めしあがる）

3. おにもつを お（　　）しましょう。（もつ）

4. おすきな ものを お（　　）ください。（えらぶ）

5. なんじごろ お（　　）に なりましたか。（つく）
   お（　　）に なったでしょう。（つかれる）

6. せんせいは これを どう お（　　）に なりますか。（かんがえる）

7. きのう （　　）　かたから おでんわが ありました。（いらっしゃる）

8. わたくしが みなさまに ごせつめい（　　）ます。（いたす）

V. Choose a sentence appropriate to the situation described.

A. You wish to express polite thanks for a present sent to you the previous day.

1. さくじつは けっこうな ものを おおくりいただきまして ありが
   とうございました。

2. きのうは いいものを おくってくれて ありがとう。

3. さくじつは いい ものを もらいました。ありがとうございます。

B. You reply to a coworker's **Sakujitsu wa arigatō gozaimashita**.

1. そちらこそ　ほんとうに　ありがとうございました。
2. こちらも　ほんとうに　ありがとう。
3. こちらこそ　ほんとうに　ありがとうございました。

C. You want to ask in a polite way if it's convenient to visit Tanaka's company about 3:00 in the afternoon.

1. ごご　3じごろ　そちらに　うかがいたいと　おもいますが、ごつごうは　いかがでしょうか。
2. ごご　3じごろ　そちらに　いきたいと　おもいますが、つごうは　どうですか。
3. ごご　3じごろ　そちらに　いらっしゃりたいと　おもいますが、よろしいでしょうか。

Ms. Nakamura is irritated because Mr. Johnson hasn't come yet and she's afraid they'll be late for the concert.

中村：　ジョンソンさん、おそいですね。待ち合わせの　時間は　6時10分
　　　　でしょう？

チャン：　ええ。もう　6時半です。約束の　時間を　20分も　すぎているの
　　　　に、来ませんね。もう　会場に　行かないと、間に合いませんよ。

中村：　そうですね。ほんとうに　どう　したんでしょう。先に　行きまし
　　　　ょうか。けい子さんを　待たせると　悪いですから。

チャン：　そうですね。いっしょに　行かなくても　ジョンソンさんは　場所
　　　　を　よく　知っていますし、きっぷも　わたしてありますから、だ
　　　　いじょうぶでしょう。

Johnson apologizes.

ジョンソン：どうも　おそくなって　もうしわけありません。出かけようと　し
　　　　た　時、電話が　かかってきて・・・。それに　来る　とちゅう
　　　　デモに　あって　タクシーが　なかなか　進まなくて　困りまし
　　　　た。

チャン：　いったい　どう　したんだろうって、心配していたんですよ。

ジョンソン：ご心配かけてもうしわけありません。

中村：　さあ、急ぎましょう。

Nakamura: Mr. Johnson's quite late, isn't he? The time for meeting was 6:10, wasn't it?
Chang: Yes. It's already 6:30. Even though it's twenty minutes after the time agreed on, he (still) hasn't come. If we don't go to the concert hall now, we won't be in time.
Nakamura: That's right. What happened (to him), I wonder? Shall we go on ahead? It's impolite to keep Keiko waiting.
Chang: Isn't that (the truth). Even if we don't go together, it's OK because Mr. Johnson knows the place well and (I) already gave him a ticket.

Johnson: I'm terribly late. I do apologize. Just when I was about to go out, there was a phone call. Then on the way we ran into a demonstration and the taxi couldn't move at all. It was quite frustrating.
Chang: (We) wondered what on earth might have happened and we were worried.
Johnson: I'm awfully sorry to make you worry.
Nakamura: Well, then, let's hurry.

258

まちあわせ	**machiawase**, meeting (by appointment), waiting	とちゅう	**tochū**, on the way
のに	**noni**, even though (particle)	デモ	**demo**, demonstration
		いったい	**ittai**, what on earth!
～（よ）うと した とき	**-(y)ō to shita toki**, just when . . . happened	しんぱい（を）かける	**shimpai (o) kakeru**, make (someone) worry

GRAMMAR & LESSON OBJECTIVES

- Particle **noni**

    Yakusoku no jikan o 20-pun mo sugite iru noni kimasen ne.
    Noni links two contradictions or apparent contradictions. It comes after plain forms, nouns or **-na** adjectives, as in **ame na noni, shizukana noni**. (See appendix A.) In very polite speech, it follows **desu/-masu** endings.
    ex. **6-nenkan mo gakkō de Eigo o benkyō shita noni, hanasemasen.** "(I) studied English at school for six years but (I) can't speak (it)."
    This particle is appropriate when something has already occurred or obviously exists. It can be compared with **-te mo.**
    ex. 1. **Nankai mo denwa shita noni, kare ni renraku dekimasen deshita.** "Even though (I) phoned many times, I couldn't reach him."
       2. **Kaisha ni denwa shite mo, kyō wa kare wa kaisha ni imasen yo.** "(You can) phone the company, but he won't be at work today."

- **-(y)ō to shita toki**

    This pattern consists of the volitional form and **to shita toki**. Another example:
    Gaikoku-jin ni Eigo de hanasō to shita toki, kare ga Nihon-go de hanashi-ha-jimemashita. "Just as (I) was about to speak to a foreigner in English, he began speaking Japanese."

NOTES

1. **Hontō ni dō shita n deshō.**
    Honto ni may be used for its literal meaning, "really," but often it is only for emphasis.

2. **Keiko-san o mataseru to warui desu kara.**
    Warui implies a feeling of regret or deference about what has happened or is going to happen. It is like saying "It's impolite to . . ." or "I feel bad about . . ."
    ex. **Watashi no jitensha o konshu-chū tsukatte ii desu yo.** "I don't mind if you use my bicycle all this week."
    Arigatō. Warui desu nē. "Thank you. I feel bad (about depriving you of it)."

3. **Dekakeyō to shita toki denwa ga kakatte kite, . . .**
    Johnson is giving reasons for being late, so he leaves the sentence unfinished, rather than ending it with **okuremashita**. The addition of **kuru** after **kakaru** specifies the direction of the call.

4. **Kuru tochū demo ni atte . . .**
    The dictionary form plus **tochū** is a common way of saying "on the way."

5. **Go-shimpai kakete mōshiwake arimasen.**
    Two other expressions similar to this are: **O-tesū kakete mōshiwake arimasen** and **Go-mendō kakete moshiwake arimasen**, both of which are apologies meaning "(I'm/We're) awfully sorry to have caused (you) trouble/inconvenience."

PRACTICE

KEY SENTENCES

1. やくそくの　じかんを　20ぷんも　すぎているのに　ジョンソンさんは　きません。
2. でかけようと　した　とき、でんわが　かかってきました。

1. Even though it's twenty minutes past (*lit.* "have passed") the time agreed on, Johnson still hasn't come.
2. Just as (I) was about to go out, there was a phone call.

EXERCISES

I. Make dialogues by changing the underlined parts as in the examples given.

    A. *ex.* **A**：<u>30ぷんも　すぎている</u>のに　まだ　きませんね。
         B：ほんとうに　どう　したんでしょう。

        1. はやく　くると　いいました
        2. ぜったいに　おくれないと　いいました
        3. みちが　すいています
        4. ていねいに　ちずを　かいてあげました
        5. うちが　ちかいです

    B. *ex.* **Q**：<u>あめな</u>のに　ゴルフに　いくんですか。
        A：しかたが　ありません。しごとですから。

        1. かぜです
        2. おこさんが　びょうきです
        3. へたです
        4. きらいです

II. Practice the following pattern by changing the underlined part.

    ex. <u>くすりを　のんだ</u>のに　ねつが　さがりません。
        1. たしかめました、まだ　ミスが　ありました
        2. この　うちは　せまいです、やちんが　たかいです
        3. この　テレビは　たかかったです、すぐ　こしょうしました
        4. はるです、まだ　さむいです
        5. にちようびです、はたらかなければ　なりません
        6. じょうずです、にほんごを　つかいません
        7. たいせつな　ものでした、なくしてしまいました

III. Make dialogues by changing the underlined parts as in the examples given.

A. *ex.* **Q**：<u>ぶちょうから　でんわが</u>　ありましたか。

     A：ええ、<u>でかけようと　した　とき</u>　<u>ありました</u>。

       1. かちょうから　しごとを　たのまれましたか、かえる
       2. すずきさんは　きましたか、でんわを　する
       3. ゆうべ　じしんが　ありましたね、ねる
       4. さっき　ていでんで　エレベーターが　とまりましたね、そと
         に　でる

B. *ex.* **Q**：どこで　じこに　あいましたか。

     A：<u>ここに　くる</u>　とちゅう、　じこに　あいました。

       1. かいしゃに　きます
       2. うちに　かえります
       3. えきに　いきます
       4. かいものに　いきます

C. *ex.* **A**：どう　したんだろうって、しんぱいしていたんですよ。

     B：<u>ごしんぱい　かけて</u>　もうしわけありません。

       1. おそくなる
       2. まちあわせの　じかんに　おくれる
       3. ねぼうして　おくれてしまう
       4. おまたせする
       5. やくそくを　わすれてしまう

Vocabulary

しかたが　あり ません	**shikata ga arimasen**, It can't be helped, (*lit.*) There's no way of do- ing . . .	ミス	**misu**, mistake
		なくす	**nakusu**, lose
		じこに　あう	**jiko ni au**, meet with an accident
さがる	**sagaru**, go down, fall		

SHORT DIALOGUES

1. スミスふじん：　あしたから　1しゅうかん　りょこうで　るすに　するん
　　　　　　　　です が、とりを　あずかっていただけないでしょうか。
　となりの　ひと：ええ、どうぞ。おあずかりしましょう。
　スミスふじん：　ごめんどうを　おかけして、もうしわけありません。

Mrs. Smith: From tomorrow (we'll) be on a trip for a week. Since we'll be away, could you please take care of our bird?

Neighbor: Yes, I'll take care of (it).

Mrs. Smith: I'm afraid it'll be troublesome (for you), but . . .

2. なかむら：としょかんで あの ほん、みつかりましたか。

チャン： いいえ。わざわざ いったのに、みつかりませんでした。

Nakamura: Did you find that book in the library?

Chang: No. I went especially to do that but I didn't find it.

Vocabulary

（ご）めんどう を かける	**(go-)mendō o kakeru,** cause (a person) trouble	かける	**kakeru,** (*lit.*) impose
めんどう	**mendō,** trouble, difficulty		

QUIZ

I. Read this lesson's opening dialogue and answer the following questions.

1. なかむらさんたちと ジョンソンさんは なんじに まちあわせる やくそくを しましたか。
2. その ひ、ジョンソンさんの きっぷは だれが もっていましたか。
3. ジョンソンさんは ひとりで かいじょうに いけるだろうと チャンさんは おもっていますか。
4. けいこさんも なかむらさんたちと いっしょに ジョンソンさんを まっていますか。

II. Put the appropriate words in the parentheses.

1. けいこさん （　　） またせる （　　） わるいですから、さき （　　） いきましょう。
2. いっしょに いかなくて （　　）、ひとり （　　） いけます。
3. ねよう （　　） した とき、でんわ （　　） かかってきました。
4. たいしかん （　　） いく とちゅう デモ （　　） あって、おくれ てしまいました。
5. やくそく （　　） じかんを 40ぷんも すぎています。
6. どうしたんだろうっ （　　）、しんぱいしていました。

III. Circle the appropriate words in the parentheses.

1. にちようびは （めったに、あいにく、あまり） あめで はなみに いけませんでした。
2. （いったい、ぜったいに、たった） どこで さいふを おとしたんだろう。
3. いそいでいますから、しりょうを （かならず、できるだけ、ほとんど）

はやく　そろえてください。

4. かわの　みずが　よごれていて、（なるべく、いったい、めったに）　ほ
たるが　みられません。

5. よていの　じかんを　すぎているのに、かいぎは　（ほとんど、なかな
か、めったに）　おわりません。

IV. Complete the sentences with the appropriate form of the verbs indicated.

1. ちずを　かいて　（　　）のに、（　　）しまいました。（もらいました、
なくしました）

2. みずが　（　　）のに、うみで　（　　）います。（つめたいです、およ
ぎます）

3. にほんごが　（　　）のに、にほんごを　はなしません。（わかります）

4. うたが　（　　）のに、おおきい　こえで　（　　）います。（へたです、
うたいます）

5. あの　ひとは　（　　）のに、パーティーに　きました。（しょうたいさ
れていません）

6. ひるごはんを　（　　）と　した　とき、じしんが　ありました。（たべ
ます）

7. うちに　（　　）と　した　とき、かちょうに　よばれました。（かえり
ます）

V. Choose a sentence appropriate to the situation described.

A. You apologize for keeping a client waiting.

1. おそい　じかんで　すみません。
2. おまたせして　もうしわけありません。
3. ごめんどうかけて　もうしわけありません。

B. You want to say you are sure Suzuki will keep his promise.

1. けっこうですよ。
2. いいですよ。
3. だいじょうぶですよ。

LESSON 35 A TRANSFER, A RESIGNATION

Mr. Hayashi introduces Mr. Sato, recently transferred to the head office, to Mr. Johnson.

林：　　　　　ジョンソンさん、こちらは　今度　東京本社に　きんむする　ことに　なった　佐藤さんです。

佐藤：　　　　佐藤です。4月から　こちらの　えいぎょう部で　働く　ことに　なりました。

ジョンソン：京都に　出張に　行った　時、ちょっと　お目に　かかりましたね。

佐藤：　　　　ええ、おぼえています。どうぞ　よろしく　おねがいします。

ジョンソン：こちらこそ、どうぞ　よろしく。

Ms. Yamada plans to leave the company to do more congenial work.

鈴木：　　　　山田さんが　会社を　やめるんだって？

渡辺：　　　　ええ、前から　やめたがっていましたから。3月で　やめる　ことに　したそうです。

鈴木：　　　　それで、これから　どう　する　つもりだろう。

渡辺：　　　　つとめを　やめて、好きな　デザイン関係の　仕事を　自分で　始めるそうです。

Hayashi: Mr. Johnson, this is Mr. Satō. It's been decided he'll work at the Tokyo head office from now on.
Satō: I'm Satō. From April, I'll be working in the sales department here.
Johnson: When I went to Kyoto on business we met, didn't we?
Satō: Yes, I remember that. I'm glad I'll be working with you.
Johnson: The pleasure's all mine.

Suzuki: Did you hear—Yamada's leaving the company?
Watanabe: Um. She's been wanting to quit for some time. I heard she's decided to leave in March.
Suzuki: What's she planning to do, I wonder?
Watanabe: She said she's going to stop going to an office and start doing the design-related work she likes on her own.

きんむする	**kimmu suru**, work, serve	ことに する	**koto ni suru**, decide
きんむ	**kimmu**, service, duty	つとめ	**tsutome**, go to an office,
ことに なる	**koto ni naru**, be decided		work for a company,
おめに かかる	**o-me ni kakaru**, meet	デザイン	**dezain**, design
	(humble)		

Vocabulary

GRAMMAR & LESSON OBJECTIVES

• **koto ni naru/suru**

Kochira wa kondo Tōkyō ni kimmu suru koto ni natta Satō-san desu.
4-gatsu kara kochira no eigyō-bu de hataraku koto ni narimashita.
(Yamada-san wa) 3-gatsu de (kaisha o) yameru koto ni shita sō desu.

These patterns, the dictionary form with **koto ni naru/suru**, are the same in meaning as **ni naru** and **ni suru**. They are preceded by a clause summarizing the situation that has been decided on or changed. The negative pattern is **nai** form **koto ni naru/suru**.

ex. 1. **Ōsaka e ikanai koto ni narimashita.** "It's been decided that I won't go to Osaka."
2. **Ōsaka e ikanai koto ni shimashita.** "(I) decided not to go to Osaka."

NOTES

1. **Ē, oboete imasu.**

Attention must be given to which forms of **oboeru** express which meanings. The **-te iru** form is appropriate in this case because the meaning is "Something became fixed in my mind (once) and I (still) remember it." For the meaning "I'll memorize/learn," **oboemasu** can be used. To say "I remember (now)" or "I recall/have (just) recalled (it now)," a different verb is necessary, namely, **omoidashimashita**.

2. **Kaisha o yameru.**
Tsutome o yameru.

The particle **o** is used with **yameru**, also with **yasumu**, as in **kaisha o yasumu**.

PRACTICE

KEY SENTENCES

1. らいねん ほんしゃが いてんする ことに なりました。
2. わたしは たばこを やめる ことに しました。

1. It's been decided to move the head office next year.
2. I've decided to stop smoking.

EXERCISES

Make dialogues by changing the underlined parts as in the examples given.

A. *ex.* **Q**：かいぎの けっかは どう なりましたか。

    A：<u>かいしゃが いてんする</u> ことに なりました。

        1. ぜんいんの きゅうりょうが あがります
        2. ホンコンに してんを つくります

3. せいと　ぜんいんが　そつぎょうします
4. オフィスで　たばこを　すっては　いけません
5. きねんひんを　さしあげません

B. ex. **Q**：こちらは　どなたですか。
　　 A：こんど　えいぎょうぶで　はたらく　ことに　なった　さとうさんです。

1. しごとを　てつだってくれます
2. シドニーに　はけんされます
3. しちょうに　りっこうほします
4. せんでんぶで　デザインの　しごとを　します
5. こんど　うちの　かいしゃに　きてもらいます

C. ex. すずき：なつやすみが　2しゅうかん　とれる　ことに　なりましたが、
　　　　　　　チャンさんは　なにを　する　つもりですか。
　　 チャン：くにに　かえる　ことに　しました。

1. うちで　ゆっくり　やすみます
2. にほんごの　しゅうちゅうこうざを　うけます
3. ヒマラヤの　ちかくに　りょこうします
4. やすまないで　はたらきます
5. おんせんに　いきます

D. ex. **Q**：やっぱり　かいしゃを　やめるんですか。
　　 A：いろいろ　かんがえましたが、やめない　ことに　しました。

1. にわの　きを　きります
2. べっきょします
3. おみあいを　します
4. かいしゃの　ちかくに　ひっこします
5. しゃちょうに　ちょくせつ　はなします

E. ex. **Q**：にもつの　けんさを　されるんですか。
　　 A：すみません。そういう　ことに　なっていまして・・・。

1. たばこを　すっては　いけません
2. くつを　ぬいで　はいります
3. はんこじゃ　なくては　いけません
4. ここに　しょめいします

F. *ex.* **Q**：なかむらさんは　<u>やすみを　とらない</u>んだって？

A：そうらしいですよ。

1. ミスを　した　ことが　ありません
2. ぜんぜん　およげません
3. あたらしい　くるまを　かいました
4. らいしゅう　しゅっちょうします
5. アメリカに　りゅうがくした　ことが　あります

Vocabulary

せいと	**seito**, pupil	こうざ	**kōza**, course, lecture
オフィス	**ofisu**, office	ヒマラヤ	**Himaraya**, Himalayas
シドニー	**shidonī**, Sydney	べっきょする	**bekkyo suru**, live separately
はけんする	**haken suru**, send (a person)	べっきょ	**bekkyo**, separation
はけん	**haken**, dispatch	（お）みあいを	**o-miai o suru**, have a marriage interview
しちょう	**shichō**, mayor	する	
りっこうほする	**rikkōho suru**, be a candidate	みあい	**miai**, (*lit.*) meeting and looking over
りっこうほ	**rikkōho**, candidacy	けんさを　する	**kensa o suru**, inspect, examine, test
しゅうちゅう こうざ	**shūchu kōza**, intensive course	けんさ	**kensa**, inspection, examination, test
しゅうちゅう	**shūchū**, concentration		

SHORT DIALOGUES

1. やまだ：あのう、こんど　けっこんする　ことに　なりました。

   かとう：ほう、それは　おめでとう。おみあいですか、それとも　れんあい？

   やまだ：じつは　うちの　かの　さとうさんと　けっこんする　ことに　しました。

   Yamada: Er. I'm going to get married.
   Katō: Oh, congratulations! Is it an arranged (marriage) or a love (marriage)?
   Yamada: Actually, I'm marrying Mr. Satō in our section.

2. **A**：せんしゅう　みっかも　やすんでしまった。

   B：まじめに　はたらかないと　くびに　なるよ。

   A: I took three days off last week.
   B: If (you) don't settle down you'll get fired.

Vocabulary

ほう	**hō**, oh	れんあい（けっこん）	**ren'ai (kekkon)**, love (marriage)
おめでとう	**o-medetō**, congratulations	くびに　なる	**kubi ni naru**, get/be fired
それとも	**soretomo**, or	くび	**kubi**, neck

QUIZ

I. Read this lesson's opening dialogue and answer the following questions.

1. ジョンソンさんと さとうさんは いぜん あった ことが あります
   か。
2. さとうさんは いつから とうきょうほんしゃで はたらく ことに
   なりましたか。
3. やまださんは かいしゃを やめて なにを はじめる ことに しま
   したか。
4. やまださんが かいしゃを やめる ことを わたなべさんは まえか
   ら しっていましたか。
5. ジョンソンさんは どこから とうきょうに てんきんしてきたか あ
   なたは おぼえていますか。

II. Put the appropriate particles in the parentheses.

1. ねつ（　　）　40ども あるので、かいしゃ（　　）　やすむ ことに
   しました。
2. はやしさんは ぼうえきかんけい（　　）　（お）しごと（　　）　な
   さって いたそうです。
3. せんじつ パーティー（　　）　とうきょうでんきの しゃちょうに
   おめ（　　）　かかりました。
4. ともだち（　　）　てつだってもらわないで、じぶん（　　）にほんご
   の てがみを かいてみます。

III. Complete the questions so that they fit the answers.

1. なつやすみに　（　　）を する よていですか。
   ほっかいどうを りょこうする ことに しました。
2. （　　）が てつだいに きてくれるんですか。
   ちかくに すんでいる いとこが きてくれる ことに なりました。
3. かいぎの けっかは　（　　）　なりましたか。
   あの プロジェクトは やめる ことに なりました。

IV. Complete the sentences with the appropriate form of the verbs indicated.

1. おいわいに とけいを　（　　）　ことに します。（さしあげます）
2. えきまえの みちは くるまが　（　　）　ことに なりました。（とお
   れません）
3. つぎの かいぎは ロンドンで　（　　）　ことに なりました。（ひら
   かれます）
4. すずきさんを ロンドンに べんきょうに　（　　）　ことに しまし
   た。（いかせます）
5. ジョンソンさんが げんこうを　（　　）　ことに なりました。（ほん
   やくしてくれます）

6. しんにゅうしゃいんは　けんしゅうを　（　　）　ことに　なっていま
す。（うけます）

V. Choose a sentence appropriate to the situation described.

A. You want to ask someone if he or she remembers when Johnson's birthday is.

1. ジョンソンさんの　たんじょうびを　おぼえていますか。
2. ジョンソンさんの　たんじょうびを　おぼえますか。
3. ジョンソンさんの　たんじょうびを　おぼえましたか。

B. You acknowledge being introduced to a friend's section chief.

1. どうぞ　よろしく　おつたえください。
2. どうぞ　よろしく　おねがいいたします。
3. どうぞ　よろしくと　おっしゃっていました。

LESSON 36 SUZUKI CAUGHT LOAFING

Mr. Katō, faced with some urgent business, wants to know what Mr. Suzuki's been up to.

加藤：鈴木くん、大事な 書るいを 広げたまま どこに 行ってたんだ。きみ
　　　の いない 間に、大阪支社から 三度も 電話が あったよ。

鈴木：すみません。

加藤：もう 一度 書るいに 目を 通して、メモに 書いてある とおりに
　　　必要な 資料を そろえといてくれないか。

鈴木：いつまでに すれば よろしいんでしょうか。

加藤：あしたの 会議で 使うから、今日中に たのむよ。

鈴木：はい、わかりました。

Mr. Satō hears that Suzuki's been loafing.

佐藤：鈴木くん、ちょっと 話が あるんだけど。今日は ずいぶん いそがし
　　　そうだね。

鈴木：課長から 今日中に 資料を そろえろって 言われてるので、やってし
　　　まわなければ ならないんだ。

佐藤：それじゃ、じゃましない ほうが いいね。

鈴木：仕事を さぼるなって、さっき 言われたし。仕事が 終わったら、きみ
　　　の ところに 行くよ。

佐藤：じゃ、待ってるよ。

Katō:　Suzuki, (some) papers were left lying on your desk. Where have you been? There were three telephone calls from the Osaka office while you weren't around.

Suzuki:　Sorry.

Katō:　Look the papers over again and get the necessary documents ready, as was written up in the memorandum.

Suzuki:　When does (it) have to be finished?

Katō:　I want it (done) today since it's to be used at the meeting tomorrow.

Suzuki:　I'll do it (right away).

Satō:　I have something to talk to you about but you seem to be quite busy today.

Suzuki:　I was told by the section chief to get the documents ready sometime today and I have to finish doing it.

Satō:　I shouldn't be bothering you, then.

Suzuki:　I was just told not to loaf on the job. I'll come to you when I finish (my) work.

ひろげる	hirogeru, (lie) open, spread, unfold	〜って	tte (colloquial for to)
（〜た）まま	(-ta) mama, as it is/was	いわれてる	iwareteru (contraction of iwarete iru)
いってた	itteta (contraction of itte ita)	じゃまする	jama suru, bother, interfere
あいだに	aida ni, while	じゃま	jama, hindrance, barrier, inconvenience
メモ	memo, memorandum		
とおりに	tōri ni, as, like, (lit.) way	しごとを さぼる	shigoto o saboru, loaf on the job
そろえといて	soroetoite (contraction of soroete oite)	さぼる	saboru, loaf, play hooky
そろえる	soroeru, get ready		
〜てくれないか	-te kurenai ka (instead of -te kuremasen ka)	な	na = don't
		まってる	matteru (contraction of matte iru)
そろえろ	soroero (imperative of soroeru)		

GRAMMAR & LESSON OBJECTIVES

• itteta n da and kurenai ka

Doko ni itteta n da instead of **itte ita n desu ka.**

Hitsuyōna shorui o soroetoite kurenai ka instead of **soroete oite kuremasen ka.**

The use of plain or contracted forms and less polite imperatives is characteristic of informal speech. Young boys are apt to come out with such speech, as well as fathers talking to their offspring, and teachers or others in positions of authority talking to those under them. **Saboru na** also characterizes this way of speaking.

Some verb forms put to use as plain imperatives are formed as follows.

Reg. I: **iku → ike; nomu → nome; kaeru → kaere; iu → ie**

Reg. II: **soroeru → soroero; taberu → tabero; iru → iro; miru → miro**

Irreg: **kuru → koi, suru → shiro**

Note that **kureru** does not become **kurero.†** "Give!" is **Kure.**

Another common pattern—**-masu** stem **nasai** (imperative form of **nasaru**)—is favored by superiors speaking to those under them and is given in this lesson's short dialogues.

• Dictionary form followed by na

Saboru na instead of **sabotte wa ikemasen.**

Other examples of negative imperatives equivalent to "Don't!" are: **Kuru na,** "Don't come!" **Suru na,** "Don't do (it)!" **Nomu na,** "Don't drink (it)!"

• soroetoite, iwareteru, matteru

When speaking, the **e** of **-te** or the **i** of **iru** are frequently elided from the **-te iru** and **-te ita** patterns. **Soroete oite** becomes **soroetoite, iwarete iru** becomes **iwareteru, matte iru** becomes **matteru** and so on. Another example: **nonde oite → nondoite.**

NOTES

1. **Daijina shorui o hirogeta mama**

   Ta form of a verb followed by **mama** indicates there has been no change since something was done or occurred. Adjectives and demonstratives also come before **mama.**

   ex. 1. **Kirazu ni ōkii mama tabete kudasai.** "Eat it whole, without cutting it up."

   2. **Sono mama o-machi kudasai.** "Please wait (right there)."

2. **Kimi no inai aida ni**

Aida is a noun meaning "space" or "interval (of time)." It does not occur after the **-ta** form of verbs.

ex. 1. **Matte iru aida ni kono shiryō o yonde oite kudasai.** "Please (finish) reading this material while (you're) waiting."
2. **Rusu no aida ni dare ka kimashita ka.** "Did anybody come while I was out?"

3. **Memo ni kaite aru tōri (ni) . . .**

The particle **ni** is sometimes dropped. **Tōri** after nouns becomes **dōri**.

ex. 1. **Kono tōri (ni) tsukutte kudasai.** "Please make it like this."
2. **Kare no iu tōri (ni) shimashita.** "I did it just as he told me to."
3. **Iwareta tōri (ni) shimashita.** "I did (it) the way I was told to."
4. **Yakusoku-dōri (ni) 3-ji ni kite kudasai.** "Please come at three, the appointed time."

4. **Itsu made ni sureba yoroshii n deshō ka.**

Either **ii n deshō ka** or **ii n desu ka** might have been used here, but the speaker chose the more polite **yoroshii n deshō ka**.

5. **Suzuki-kun, chotto . . .**

Although **chotto** in this context defies translation and so seems meaningless, it makes the sentence softer, less demanding.

6. **Kimi no tokoro ni iku yo.**

This would never be **kimi ni iku.†** It is always the equivalent of "your place," "the place where you are." Similarly with objects in many cases, for example:
1. **Mado no tokoro ni itte kudasai.** "Go to the window, please."
2. **Doa no tokoro de matte imasu.** "I'll be waiting at the door."

PRACTICE

KEY SENTENCES

1. まどを しめろと いったのに、かれは あけたまま へやを でていった。
2. けいかんに ここに くるまを とめるなって いわれた。
3. いった とおりに ひつような しょるいを そろえといてくれ。
4. きみの いない あいだに、3ども でんわが あったよ。

1. I told him to close the window, but he went out of the room leaving it open.
2. I was told by a policeman not to park the car here.
3. Prepare the necessary papers as I told you to.
4. While you weren't around, there were three telephone calls.

Vocabulary

～てくれ   **-te kure** (equivalent to **-te kudasai**)

EXERCISES

I Verbs: Study the examples, convert into affirmative and negative imperative forms, and memorize.

ex. Reg. I   Reg. II

かく → かけ、かくな   たべる→たべろ、たべるな

はなす→はなせ、はなすな   みる→ みろ、みるな

いう→　いえ、いうな　　　　　　Irreg.
まつ→　まて、まつな　　　　　　くる→こい、くるな
　　　　　　　　　　　　　　　　　　する→しろ、するな

1. よむ　　　　　　　6. かす　　　　　　　11. しゅうりする
2. かたづける　　　　7. あそぶ　　　　　　12. とってくる
3. もってくる　　　　8. みせる　　　　　　13. およぐ
4. そうだんする　　　9. あける　　　　　　14. かう
5. まがる　　　　　　10. とめる　　　　　　15. はしる

II. Make dialogues by changing the underlined parts as in the examples given.

A. *ex.* ぶちょう　ちょっと　これを　しらべて　くれないか。
　　　すずき：はい、わかりました。

　　　　　1. しりょうを　せいりする
　　　　　2. おきゃくさんの　あいてを　する
　　　　　3. けいやくしょを　もう　いちど　みる
　　　　　4. この　しんぶんきじを　きりとる
　　　　　5. でんぴょうを　せいりする

B. *ex.* さとう：かちょうに　なんて　いわれたんだ？
　　　すずき：しりょうを　そろえろって　いわれたんだ。

　　　　　1. すぐ　かえる　　　　　6. きを　つける
　　　　　2. ゆっくり　はなす　　　7. しりょうを　もってくる
　　　　　3. ししゃに　いく　　　　8. コピーを　する
　　　　　4. さけを　のむ　　　　　9. はやく　けっこんする
　　　　　5. さっさと　かたづける

C. *ex.* **Q :**　　あそこに　なんて　かいてありますか。
　　A :　　みぎに　まがるなと　かいてあります。

　　　　　1. こうさてんの　ちかくに　くるまを　とめる
　　　　　2. ここを　わたる
　　　　　3. ここで　たばこを　すう
　　　　　4. スピードを　だす
　　　　　5. さけを　のんで　うんてんする
　　　　　6. ここに　ごみを　すてる
　　　　　7. ここで　こどもを　あそばせる

III. Practice the following patterns by changing the underlined parts.

A. *ex.* <u>じしんだ</u>！　<u>ひを　けせ</u>！

    1. じしんだ、ガスを　とめる
    2. かじだ、ひゃくじゅうきゅう（119）ばんに　でんわする
    3. かじだ、きゅうきゅうしゃを　よぶ
    4. どろぼうだ、ひゃくとお（110）ばんする
    5. あぶない、にげる
    6. かじだ、あわてない
    7. じしんだ、そとに　でない

B. *ex.* しゃしんを　<u>みています</u>。→しゃしんを　<u>みてます</u>。
    きのう　しりょうを　<u>よんでおきました</u>。→きのう　しりょうを　<u>よ</u>
<u>んどきました</u>。

    1. あめが　ふっています
    2. あそこで　ほんを　よんでいる　ひとは　だれですか
    3. けさは　おそくまで　ねていました
    4. コピーを　しておきました
    5. しょるいを　そろえておいてください
    6. しょくじの　まえに　くすりを　のんでおきました

IV. Make dialogues by changing the underlined parts as in examples given.

A. *ex.* **Q**：なにを　してるんですか。
    A：<u>ともだちを　まって</u>るんです。

    1. こしょうを　なおす
    2. エンジンの　ちょうしを　しらべる
    3. ぼうねんかいの　そうだんを　する
    4. めがねを　さがす

B. *ex.* **A**：<u>らいしゅうまでに　よん</u>どいてください。
    B：はい、わかりました。

    1. わたしが　かえってくるまでに　きめる
    2. そのままに　する
    3. あしたまでに　かう
    4. クーラーを　つける
    5. きんようびまでに　けいさんする

V. Practice the following patterns by changing the underlined parts.

ex. さとうさんは <u>まどを　あけたまま</u>　がいしゅつするそうです。

   1. テレビを　つけました、ねてしまいます
   2. みせの　まえに　くるまを　とめました、どこかへ　いって
      しまいました
   3. あそびに　いきました、かえってきません
   4. けいさんきを　かりていきました、かえしに　きません

VI. Make dialogues by changing the underlined parts as in the examples given.

A. *ex.* **Q**：<u>まどは　どう　しましょうか。</u>
     A：<u>あけたままで</u>　いいです。

   1. ヒーター、つけました
   2. ファイル、だしました
   3. コーヒーカップ、その
   4. ケーキ、きらずに　おおきい
   5. スープ、つめたい

B. *ex.* **Q**：どう　<u>かいたら</u>　いいですか。
     A：<u>いう</u>　とおりに　<u>かいて</u>ください。

   1. やります、いわれました
   2. します、おもっています
   3. じゅんびします、かいてあります
   4. せつめいします、みました
   5. しらせます、ききました

VII. Practice the following patterns by changing the underlined parts.

A. *ex.* <u>じかん</u>　どおりに　<u>きてください。</u>

   1. やくそく、3じに　きました
   2. よてい、じっこうします
   3. けいかく、おこなわれます
   4. せいきゅうしょ、おはらいします

B. *ex.* <u>こどもが　ねている</u>　あいだに　<u>かいものに　いってきます。</u>

   1. でかけています、どろぼうに　はいられました
   2. ここで　おまちに　なっています、できます

3. トラックで はこびます、くさってしまいました
4. りょこうしています、はなが かれてしまいました
5. るすです、だれか きたようです
6. きゅうかです、この ほんを よみたいです

Vocabulary

とってくる	**totte kuru**, go and get	あわてる	**awateru**, be flustered, confused, panic
せいりする	**seiri suru**, put in order, (re)adjust	ぼうねんかい	**bōnen-kai**, year-end party, (*lit.*) forget-the-year party
せいり	**seiri**, (re)arrangement, regulation	その まま	**sono mama**, as it is/was
あいてを する	**aite o suru**, deal with, wait on	けいさんする	**keisan suru**, calculate, compute
あいて	**aite**, partner, other party, opponent	けいさん	**keisan**, calculation, accounts
きじ	**kiji**, article	けいさんき	**keisanki**, calculator, computer
きりとる	**kiritoru**, cut out, tear off, amputate	ファイル	**fairu**, file
でんぴょう	**dempyō**, bill, (sales) check, voucher	じっこうする	**jikkō suru**, carry out, execute
さっさと	**sassato**, quickly	じっこう	**jikkō**, practice, action, implementation
わたる	**wataru**, cross	トラック	**torakku**, truck
スピードを だす	**supīdo o dasu**, (put on) speed	くさる	**kusaru**, rot, go bad, corrupt
スピード	**supīdo**, speed		
119ばん	**119 ban** (emergency number for fire, ambulance)	かれる	**kareru**, wither, die
110ばんする	**hyakutō ban suru**, dial 110 (emergency number for police)	きゅうか	**kyūka**, vacation, time off

---

SHORT DIALOGUES

1. はは： はやく しなさい。がっこうに おくれますよ。
   こども：こくごの きょうかしょが なくなっちゃった。
   はは： そこの ソファーの うえに あるでしょ。はやく いきなさい。

   Mother: Hurry up! You'll be late for school.
   Child: Japanese textbook's disappeared.
   Mother: It's on that sofa. Now, get going!

2. おんな： たすけて！ どろぼう！
   おとこ：あ、あいつだ。つかまえろ！ まて！

Woman: Help! thief!
Man: Oh-oh, such a guy. Catch him! (Hey you) Wait!

Vocabulary			
こくご	**kokugo**, Japanese, national language, mother tongue	いきなさい	**iki nasai**, go!
		たすける	**tasukeru**, help, save
		あいつ	**aitsu**, that guy, he (colloquial male speech)
～ちゃった	**-chatta**, (contraction of **-te shimatta**)		
		つかまえる	**tsukamaeru**, catch, grab, arrest
ソファー	**sofā**, sofa		

QUIZ

I. Read this lesson's opening dialogue and answer the following questions.

1. おおさかししゃから でんわが あった とき、すずきさんは しょるいを ひろげたまま どこかに いっていましたか。

2. すずきさんは かとうさんに しりょうを そろえておくように いわれましたか、おおさかししゃに でんわするように いわれましたか。

3. さとうさんと すずきさんは ていねいな ことばで はなしていますか。

4. さとうさんは すずきさんの ところへ しごとの はなしを しに きたと おもいますか、それとも おしゃべりを しに きたと おもいますか。

II. Put the appropriate particles in the parentheses.

1. その しごと（　）　おわったら、ぶちょう（　）　ところに いってくれないか。

2. メモ（　）　かいてある とおり（　）　でんわで つたえてください。

3. すずきさんは しごと（　）　さぼって、おちゃを のみ（　）　いった。

4. まちがい（　）　ない（　）　どうか もう いちど しょるい（　）　めを とおしてください。

5. ちょっと でかけてくるから、たなかさん（　）　でんわ（　）　あったら、きいておいてください。

6. きょうじゅう（　）　ひつよう（　）　しりょう（　）　そろえなければ ならない。

III. Complete the questions so that they fit the answers.

1. （　）までに すれば よろしいんでしょうか。
   らいしゅうちゅうに たのむよ。

2. （　）　かたちに しましょうか。

この　ずめん　どおりに　つくってください。

3. （　　）で　まちあわせる？
　　えきの　まえで　まってるよ。

4. （　　）　したら　いいんだろう。
　　まず　でんわで　たしかめろよ。

5. あそこに　（　　）と　かいてありますか。
　　ごみを　すてるなって　かいてあるんですよ。

IV. Complete the sentences with the appropriate form of the words in the parentheses.

1. さとうさんは　まどを　（　　）まま　でかけてしまった。（あけました）

2. せんせいから　（　　）　とおりに　しりょうを　しらべた。（いわれました）

3. きみが　（　　）　あいだに　でがみが　とどいた。（やすんでいます）

4. くるまに　（　　）まま　えいがが　みられます。（のります）

5. しばらく　（　　）　あいだに　ずいぶん　（　　）　なった。（あいません、おおきいです）

6. きみが　（　　）　とおりに　やりなさい。（おもいます）

V. Complete the sentences with a plain imperative form of the verbs indicated.

1. りょうしゅうしょを　（　　）。（もってきます）

2. だいじな　しょるいだから、（　　）。（なくしません）

3. やくそくを　（　　）。（まもります）

4. しょるいを　（　　）。（もってきてください）

VI. Choose a sentence appropriate to the situation described.

A. Tell a close friend not to be late (as man to man).

1. やくそくしたから　おくれないでくださいませんか。

2. やくそくの　じかんに　おくれるなよ。

3. やくそくの　じかんに　おくれるよ。

B. Ask a close friend to contact you when he arrives at the station.

1. えきに　ついたら、れんらくしてくれないか。

2. えきに　ついたら、れんらくしていただけませんか。

3. えきに　ついたら、れんらくしてあげてくれないか。

LESSON *37* WEIGHT CONTROL

Mr. Hayashi and Mr. Smith chat during their coffee break.

林: スミスさん、ずっと ジョギングを 続けておられますか。

スミス: 毎朝 続けるのは、なかなか むずかしいですね。夜は おそくまで 仕事が ありますし、日曜日の 朝は ゴルフに いきますし・・・。

林: つまも やせる ために ジョギングを 始めたんですけど、ぜんぜん こうかが 上がりません。

スミス: 私も このごろ かなり ふとってきましたから 食べすぎないように 注意しています。

林: つまは あまい ものが 好きで よく 食べますから、ちっとも やせません。

スミス: 先日、おくさんが 作られた ケーキを いただきましたが、とても おいしかったですよ。

林: スミスさんの おくさんの 日本料理も すばらしいですね。

スミス: このごろは ふとらないように、もっぱら 日本料理を 食べています。林さんは けんこうの ために、何か 運動を 始められたと うかがいましたが。

林: たいした ことでは ないんです。毎朝 15分くらい なわとびや たいそうを するように しています。

スミス: 今でも 山に のぼられるんですか。

林: ええ、たまに のぼります。運動を 始めてから、よく ねむれるように なりました。

Hayashi: Mr. Smith, have you kept up your jogging all this time?

Smith: To keep on (doing it) every morning is quite difficult. There are (days when) I have work to do until late at night and on Sunday mornings, I go golfing so . . .

Hayashi: My wife started jogging to lose weight, but it doesn't have any effect at all.

Smith: I'm getting fat these days too, so I take care not to overeat.

Hayashi: My wife likes sweet things and eats a lot. She doesn't lose weight at all.

Smith: The other day we had some cake your wife made. It was very good.

Hayashi: Mrs. Smith's Japanese cooking is also splendid.

Smith: Nowadays, so as not to gain weight, I eat nothing but Japanese cooking. I heard you started (taking) some exercise for (your) health.

Hayashi: Oh, it's nothing special. Mornings I try to do fifteen minutes of skipping rope or calisthenics.

Smith: Do you climb mountains, even now?

Hayashi: Yes, occasionally (I go climbing). Since starting (my) exercises I've begun to sleep very well.

つづける	**tsuzukeru**, keep up, continue, go on	ちゅういする	**chūi suru**, take care, pay attention
～ておられる	**-te orareru** (respect lang.)	ちゅうい	**chūi**, care, attention, warning
～（の）ために	**(no) tame ni**, (in order) to, for		
こうか	**kōka**, effect, efficiency	もっぱら	**moppara**, nothing but, solely
あがる	**agaru**, (*lit.*) be derived/attained	うかがう	**ukagau**, hear (humble)
ふとる	**futoru**, get fat, gain weight	なわとび	**nawatobi**, jumping rope
		たいそう	**taisō**, calisthenics, gymnastics
～ないように	**nai yō ni**, (so as) not to ...	たまに	**tama ni**, occasionally

GRAMMAR & LESSON OBJECTIVES

- **-reru/-rareru** as respect language

  Zutto jogingu o tsuzukete oraremasu ka.
  Nanika undō o hajimerareta to ukagaimashita.
  Ima demo yama ni noborareru n desu ka.

  These forms are given in lesson 28 as so-called passive verbs. In addition to the other polite expressions introduced thus far, the conventionally polite communication patterns in this lesson are more commonly used by men and are heard often in the world of commerce and industry.

  Remember that **orareru** is used for **iru** in this style of speech.

- **tame ni**, stating purpose

  Tsuma mo yaseru tame ni jogingu o hajimeta n desu kedo ...
  Kenkō no tame ni

  Tame is a noun found in such patterns as dictionary form + **tame ni** and noun + **no tame ni** and has meanings like "to, in order to," "for (the purpose of)" and so on.

  ex. 1. **Katsu tame ni gambarimashō.** "Let's do our best to win."
  2. **Kaigi no tame ni jumbi shite oite kudasai.** "Please prepare (things) for the meeting."

- **(-nai) yō ni**

  Tabesuginai yō ni chūi shite imasu.
  Konogoro wa futoranai yō ni, Nihon ryōri o tabete imasu.
  Maiasa 15-fun gurai nawatobi ya taisō o suru yō ni shite imasu.

  Nai yō ni means "not to" and the affirmative **yō ni** means "in order to."

  ex. **Yoku kikoeru yō ni ōkii koe de hanashimasu.** "(I'll) speak loudly so you can hear (me) easily."

  Compare this with the other usages of **yō ni** in previous lessons.

  1. Adverbial use in **no yō desu**, "seems": **Sararī-man no yō ni miemasu ga, minna daigakusei desu.** (pp. 160 and 161)
  2. **Yō ni** in requests or orders: **Denwa suru yō ni itte kuremasen ka.** And **Denwa shinai yō ni itte kudasai.** (pp. 176 and 177)
  3. A verb plus **yō ni naru** to express change: **Tōkyō-Ōsaka-kan o 3-jikan hodo de ikeru yō ni narimashita.** (p. 230)
  4. **Yō ni suru** to mean "try": **Chokusetsu ukagau yō ni shimasu.** (p. 245)

NOTE

Taishita koto dewa nai n desu.
This is a stock expression heard in a variety of contexts.

ex. **O-nīsan wa go-byōki datta sō desu ne.** "I hear your brother was sick."
Ē, demo taishita koto dewa nakatta n desu. "Umm, but it's nothing serious."

PRACTICE

KEY SENTENCES

1. ぶちょうは あした アメリカから かえられます。
2. フランスごを おぼえるために フランスじんの ともだちと いっしょに すんでいます。
3. やくそくの じかんに おくれないように、すこし はやく いえを でました。

1. The department chief is coming back from the United States tomorrow.
2. To learn French I'm living with a French friend.
3. (We) left the house a little early so as not to be late for (our) appointment.

EXERCISES

I. Make dialogues by changing the underlined parts as in the examples given.

A. *ex.* **Q**: いい えを かわれたと うかがいましたが・・・。
   A: ええ、でも たいした ものでは ないんです。

    1. すばらしい さくひんを かいた
    2. いい ろんぶんを はっぴょうした
    3. りっぱな うちを たてた
    4. レストランを はじめた

B. *ex.* **Q**: きょうじゅは もう かえられましたか。
   A: ええ、もう おかえりに なりました。

    1. しゃちょう、よむ
    2. しゅしょう、この きじに めを とおす
    3. せんせい、でかける
    4. しゃちょう、りょこうさきに つく
    5. かちょう、なおる

C. *ex.* **Q**: どこで カメラを かわれましたか。
   A: デパートで かいました。

    1. どこで のりかえる、ぎんざ
    2. いつ テニスを する、せんしゅうの にちようび
    3. なにを うけとる、おもい こづつみ
    4. だれに てがみを だす、ししゃの ひと

D. *ex.* **Q**：なんの　ために　べんきょうしているんですか。
　　　A：<u>べんごしに　なる</u>　ために　べんきょうしています。

　　　1. ちょきんしている、うちを　たてます
　　　2. （お）かねを　ためている、こどもを　いしゃに　します
　　　3. にほんに　きた、せんたんぎじゅつを　まなびます
　　　4. すいえいを　している、やせます

E. *ex.* **Q**：どうして　そんなに　いっしょうけんめい　はたらくんですか。
　　　A：<u>こどもの　きょういくの</u>　ために　はたらいているんです。

　　　1. より　ゆたかな　せいかつ
　　　2. ろうご
　　　3. かぞく

F. *ex.* **Q**：<u>かいぎの</u>　ための　じゅんびですか。
　　　A：いいえ、<u>パーティー</u>　のためです。

　　　1. りょこう、ちょきん、こどもの　けっこん
　　　2. わかい　ひと、しせつ、（お）としより
　　　3. きょうそう、スポーツ、けんこう

G. *ex.* **A**：<u>わすれない</u>ように　ちゅういしてください。
　　　B：はい、きを　つけます。

　　　1. おくれません
　　　2. かぜを　ひきません
　　　3. まちがえません
　　　4. たべすぎません
　　　5. すべりません

II. Practice the following pattern by changing the underlined parts.

　ex. <u>おくれない</u>ように　<u>はやく　うちを　でました</u>。

　　　1. つかれません、はやく　ねた
　　　2. おこられません、いそいで　かたづけた
　　　3. わすれません、ノートに　かいた
　　　4. はやく　びょうきが　なおります、いしゃに　みてもらった
　　　5. よく　きこえます、おおきい　こえで　はなした
　　　6. よみやすいです、かきなおした

ろんぶん　　　**rombun**, paper, thesis
りょこうさき　**ryokō-saki**, destination
こづつみ　　　**kozutsumi**, small parcel
ためる　　　　**tameru**, save, gather, accumulate
せんたんぎじゅ**sentan gijutsu**, high
　つ　　　　　　tech(nology)
　せんたん　　　**sentan**, (*lit.*) point, tip
まなぶ　　　　**manabu**, learn, study
いっしょうけん**isshō-kemmei**, eagerly,
　めい　　　　　as hard as one can
きょういく　　**kyōiku**, education

より　　　　　　**yori**, more
ゆたか（な）　**yutaka(na)**, affluent, rich, abundant
ろうご　　　　**rōgo**, old age
しせつ　　　　**shisetsu**, facilities, institution
（お）としより　**(o-)toshiyori**, old person
きょうそう　　**kyōsō**, competition, contest, race
すべる　　　　**suberu**, slip, slide, skate
ノート　　　　**nōto**, note

SHORT DIALOGUES

1. わかい　おっと：いつか　じぶんの　みせが　もちたいなあ。
　わかい　つま：　それじゃ、しょうらいの　ために　ふたりで　はたらいて
　　　　　　　　　おかねを　ためましょう。

Young Husband: I want to have my own shop someday.
Young Wife:　　Well, let's work together and save money for the future.

2. きむら：ひざしが　つよいね。
　すずき：うん。めを　わるくしないように　サングラスを　かけた　ほうが
　　　　　いいよ。

Kimura: The sunlight is strong, isn't it!
Suzuki: Yeah. It's better to wear sunglasses so your eyes don't go bad.

～なあ　　　　**nā** (particle; indicates emphasis; informal)
ひざし　　　　**hizashi**, sunlight

QUIZ

I. Read this lesson's opening dialogue and answer the following questions.

1. スミスさんは　まいあさ　ジョギングを　つづけるのは　むずかしいと
　おもっていますか。
2. はやしさんの　おくさんは　やせる　ために　ジョギングを　はじめた
　のに　どうして　やせませんか。
3. スミスさんは　なぜ　にほんりょうりを　たべていますか。
4. はやしさんは　いぜんも　やまに　のぼっていましたか。

II. Put the appropriate particles in the parentheses.

1. まいにち　あさ　はやく　（　　）　　よる　おそく　（　　）　　しごとを
   しなければ　ならないので、つかれます。
2. まいねん　なつ（　　）　　なると　やま（　　）　　のぼります。
3. けんこう　（　　）　　ために　スポーツを　はじめました。
4. ぶちょうの　おくさまが　なくなられた　（　　）　　うかがいました。
5. まいあさ　ジョギング（　　）　　つづける　（　　）は　むずかしいです。
6. わすれないよう　（　　）　ノート　（　　）　　かいておきました。

III. Circle the most appropriate words in the parentheses.

1. せんしゅうから　　（ずっと、もっと、ずいぶん）　　あめが　ふりつづい
   ています。
2. よく　えいがを　みられますか。
   いいえ。　（めったに、たまに、ほとんど）　　みる　ことも　あります
   が。
3. やすみの　ひは　（いったい、もう、もっぱら）　　かぞくの　ために
   じかんを　つかっています。
4. あまい　ものを　（なるべく、あいにく、なかなか）　　たべないように
   してください。

IV. Complete the sentences with the appropriate form of the verbs indicated.

1. けいえいがくを　　（　　）　　ために、だいがくに　はいりました。（まな
   びます）
2. （　　）ように　よく　ちゅういして　しょっきを　はこんでください。
   （こわしません）
3. うしろの　ほうに　（　　）いる　ひとが　よく　（　　）ように　お
   おきい　じを　かいた。（すわります、みえます）
4. いしゃに　（　　）　ために　べんきょうしている。（なります）
5. まちがいが　（　　）　ように、なんども　たしかめた。（ありません）

V. Complete the sentences with the **-reru** or **-rareru** form of the verbs indicated.

1. おくさんが　（　　）　ケーキは　とても　おいしいです。（つくりまし
   た）
2. かちょうは　どこへ　（　　）　か。（いきました）
3. あしたは　なんじに　かいしゃに　（　　）　か。（きます）
4. おにもつは　うけつけに　（　　）　か、それとも　（　　）　か。（あずけ
   ます、もっていきます）
5. ぶちょうが　ごじぶんで　（　　）　そうです。（せつめいします）

LESSON 38 ROCK CONCERT

Mr. Johnson, Ms. Nakamura and Mr. Chang arrive at the concert hall, where Keiko is waiting.

ジョンソン：待たせちゃって、ごめん。

けい子：　あたしも　たった　今　来た　ところよ。

中村：　　コンサートは　もう　始まっていますか。

けい子：　ちょうど　始まる　ところです。

チャン：　プログラム　買ってきますから、ちょっと　待っててください。

As they enter the auditorium.

ジョンソン：わあ、すごい　人だなあ。けい子さん、ここ・階段が　あるから　気を　つけて。

チャン：　わあ、ひさしぶりだなあ、こんな　すごい　コンサート。

中村：　　よく　きっぷが　とれましたね。

けい子：　ほんとうに　チャンさんの　おかげだわ。

As the performance begins.

ジョンソン：けい子さんの　好きな　歌手は　どれ？

けい子：　ほら、シンセサイザーの　前で　歌ってる　あの　人よ。よく　聞いて。

ジョンソン：歌は　うまいね。でも、まるで　女みたいな　かっこうを　してて　いやだなあ。

中村：　　シンセサイザーって　不思議な　音が　しますね。

けい子：　あら、あそこに　いるの　大介くんじゃない？

チャン：　そうだ、大介くんだ。となりに　いるのは　ガールフレンドの　まり子さんに　ちがいない。

けい子：　ねえ、コンサートが　終わったら、みんなで　どっかに　行かない？

ジョンソン：うん、大介くんたちも　さそって、みんなで　ディスコに　行こうよ。

みんな：　さんせい。

Johnson:	Sorry to have kept you waiting.		
Keiko:	I just got here too.		
Nakamura:	Has the concert already started?		
Keiko:	It's just about to (start).		
Chang:	I'll go buy a program. Wait a minute.		

Johnson: Wow, what a lot of people! Keiko, there are steps here. Be careful.
Chang: Oh, it's been a long time (since I've been) to a fantastic concert like this!
Nakamura: And we could get a ticket—how about that!
Keiko: Thanks to Chang, really.

Johnson: Who's your favorite singer, Keiko?
Keiko: There! That one singing in front of the synthesizer. Listen!
Johnson: He sings well but he's dressed like a woman.
Nakamura: The synthesizer makes an uncanny sound, doesn't it?
Keiko: Hey, isn't that Daisuke over there?
Chang: So it is. The one who's next (to him) must be his girl friend, Mariko.
Keiko: Say, after the concert's over, why don't we all go someplace?
Johnson: Unh, let's ask Daisuke (and his friend) and go to a disco.
All: We'll go along (with that).

Vocabulary

ごめん	**gomen**, sorry (informal)	かっこうを　し	**kakkō o shiteru**, be dres-
あたし	**atashi**, I (informal	てる	ed
	women's speech)	かっこう	**kakkō**, appearance,
（〜た）ところ	**(-ta) tokoro**, just (happen-		dress
	ed, about to happen)	してて	**shitete = shite ite**
ちょうど	**chōdo**, just	ふしぎ（な）	**fushigi(na)**, uncanny,
プログラム	**puroguramu**, program		strange, weird
わあ	**wā** (indicates surprise)	おとが　する	**oto ga suru**, make a
かいだん	**kaidan**, steps, stairs		sound,
おかげ	**o-kage**, (*lit.*)	〜に ちがいない	**ni chigainai**, must (be)
	indebtedness,	ねえ	**nē**, say!
	support, backing	さそう	**sasou**, ask, invite
かしゅ	**kashu**, singer	ディスコ	**disuko**, disco
シンセサイザー	**shinsesaizā**, synthesizer	さんせい	**sansei**, (*lit.*) agreement,
うまい	**umai**, well, skillful,		approval, endorsement
	delicious		
まるで〜みたい	**marude . . . mitai**, (be/		
	look) like		

GRAMMAR & LESSON OBJECTIVES

● Speech levels

Introduced in this lesson is conversation that is friendly but less polite than in earlier lessons. It will be noted that while Johnson and Keiko converse in an informal manner, Keiko and Chang's speech is less informal when they address Nakamura, who is older and sticks to a standard level with **desu/-masu** verbs.

Puroguramu (o) katte kimasu.

Koko (ni) kaidan ga aru kara ki o tsukete (kudasai).

Asoko ni iru no (wa) Daisuke-kun ja nai.

There were certain examples of omissions in the first volume. In this dialogue the particles and other words dropped are typical of informal conversation.

Hisashiburi da nā, konna sugoi konsāto.

Inverted word order is not at all unusual in this style of speech. Of course, the normal word order would be **Konna sugoi konsāto (wa) hisashiburi da nā. Nā** is for emphasis.

Matasechatte gomen.

Uta wa umai ne.

Minna de disuko ni ikō yo.

The plain expressions in these sentences were once heard exclusively from men but are now used by young women as well. You will also remember plain forms as sentence endings are found in certain writing styles, as in lesson 17.

Atashi mo tatta ima kita tokoro yo.

Hontō ni Chan-san no o-kage da wa.

The sentence endings (noun plus) **yo** and **(da) wa**, said in a rising tone, are characteristic of women's speech.

Men never use **atashi**.

- **Tokoro** as a time expression

  Atashi mo tatta ima kita tokoro yo.
  Chōdo hajimaru tokoro desu.

  As indicated on p. 189 in the first volume, the basic meaning of **tokoro** is related to space, but it also occurs in time expressions. When the **-ta** form precedes **tokoro**, it means that something has just happened. With the dictionary form, the meaning is "be about to." Similarly, **-te iru tokoro** means "be doing just now."

  ex. **Shimbun o yomimashita ka.** "Have you read the newspaper?"
  Ima yonde iru tokoro desu. "I'm reading it (just now)."

- **Suru**

  As you have seen, **suru** is a versatile verb which occurs with many types of words and in many contexts. The following summarizes examples in this lesson and related usages.

  1. **Shinsesaizā tte fushigina oto ga shimasu ne.** Similar to this are: **aji ga suru**, "it tastes," and **nioi ga suru**, "it smells."
  2. **Suru** is used with certain articles of clothing and accessories such as rings, bracelets, neckties, etc. **Nekutai o suru**, "put on a tie." **Tokei o suru**, "put on a watch." Similarly with a person's appearance: **Marude onna mitaina kakkō o shite ite . . .** which literally is "He has a girlish appearance." **Rinda-san wa aoi me o shite imasu.** "Linda has blue eyes."
  3. Occupation, in the pattern **o shite iru: Kare wa Ōsaka de bengoshi o shite imasu.** "He's a lawyer in Osaka."

NOTES

1. **Ara, asoko ni iru no Daisuke-kun ja nai.**
   Ara, heard in female speech, indicates discovery. **Ja nai** in a rising tone is informal for **dewa arimasen ka**.

2. **Tonari ni iru no wa gārufurendo no Mariko-san ni chigainai.**
   (ni) chigainai means "It isn't different from that," hence, "must be" or "I'm sure that." It is informal and also comes after verbs and adjectives. (See appendix A.)

3. **Nē, konsāto ga owattara, minna de dokka e ikanai.**
   Nē is an attention-getting word and occurs only in informal situations. **Ikanai** is, needless to say, informal for **ikimasen ka**, as noted in the first volume (p. 131).

4. **Sansei**
   Although the English translation makes use of a verb, **sansei** by itself signifies acceptance of a suggestion or proposal. In this situation, it would never be **sansei suru**, which may occur in other contexts. It is not limited to informal speech and may be used to indicate approval by a committee or other body.

PRACTICE

KEY SENTENCES

1. すずきくんは？
   たった いま でかけた ところだよ。
2. じょうずね、ジョンソンさんの にほんご。
3. わたしに その しゃしん、みせて。

1. Where's Suzuki?
   He just left.
2. Good, (your/Johnson's) Japanese!
3. Show me the pictures.

EXERCISES

I. Make dialogues by changing the underlined parts as in the examples given.

> *ex.* A おんなの がくせいA：あら、ひさしぶりね、げんき？
> おんなの がくせいB：うん、げんきよ。<u>いっしょに （お）ひるご</u>
> <u>はん たべない</u>？
> おんなの がくせいA：あら、いいわね。どこに いく？
> おんなの がくせいB：<u>おいしい カレーの みせ しってるわ</u>。
> おんなの がくせいA：じゃ、そこに しましょ。

> *ex.* B おとこの がくせいA：やあ、ひさしぶりだなあ、げんきか？
> おとこの がくせいB：うん、げんきだよ。<u>いっしょに ひるごはん</u>
> <u>たべないか</u>？
> おとこの がくせいA：ああ、いいね、どこに いく？
> おとこの がくせいB：<u>おいしい カレーの みせ しってるよ</u>。
> おとこの がくせいA：じゃ、そこに しよう。

> 1. ちょっと おちゃ（を） のむ、かっこいい （お）みせが あ
>   る
> 2. これから えいが（を） みる、ぎんざで おもしろいの（を）
>   やってる

II. Practice the following pattern by changing it as in the example given.

> *ex.* きを つけてください。→きを つけて。

> 1. すぐ タクシーを よんでください
> 2. だれか たすけてください
> 3. おいしいか どうか たべてみてください

4.　へやの　かたづけを　しといてください

5.　はやく　のんじゃってください

III.　Make dialogues by changing the underlined parts as in examples given.

A. *ex.* **Q**：かいぎは　もう　はじまりましたか。

　　A：たった　いま　はじまった　ところです。

　　1.　ミーティング

　　2.　かいかいしき

　　3.　たなかさんを　はげますかい

　　4.　（お）そうしき

B. *ex.* **Q**：もう　てがみを　おかきに　なりましたか。

　　A：ええ、いま　かいた　ところです。

　　1.　くすり、のみました

　　2.　じこの　ニュース、ききました

　　3.　かいひ、はらいました

　　4.　かりた　しりょう、かえしました

C. *ex.* **Q**：もう、なまえを　かきましたか。

　　A₁：いま　かいている　ところですが・・・。

　　A₂：わたしは　かき　おわった　ところです。

　　1.　ぶんぽうの　せつめいを　よむ

　　2.　じしょで　しらべる

　　3.　せっけいずを　みる

　　4.　つくえの　うえを　せいりする

D. *ex.* はは：　　　　はやく　かたづけてしまいなさい。

おとこの　こ：いま　かたづける　ところだよ。

　　1.　しゅくだいを　する

　　2.　おふろに　はいる

　　3.　たべる

　　4.　あしたの　じゅんびを　する

IV.　Practice the following sentences.

ex. **A**：そとで　へんな　おとが　しますよ。

　　B：そうですか。

1. この　スープは　へんな　あじが　する
2. この　はなは　とても　いい　においが　する
3. どこかで　ひとの　こえが　した
4. ねつが　あるような　きが　する
5. いい　ことが　ありそうな　よかんが　する

V. Practice the following pattern by changing the underlined part.

ex. **A**：いい　とけい　（を）　してますね。
 B：べんごしを　している　あにからの　プレゼントなんです。

1. すてきな　ネクタイ
2. きれいな　ゆびわ
3. しゃれた　サングラス
4. あたたかそうな　てぶくろ

VI. Make dialogues by changing the underlined parts as in the example given.

ex. **A**：いい　ひとですね、あの　ひとは。
 B：そう　おもいますよ、わたしも。

1. あの　ニュースは、ひどいです
2. あの　はなしは、すばらしいです
3. あんな　じけんは、いやです
4. そんな　すばらしい　ひとに、あってみたいです

VII. Practice the following sentences.

ex. もう　よんでしまいました。→もう　よんじゃいました。

1. あの　えいがは　もう　みてしまいました
2. はやく　たべてしまいましょう
3. おきゃくさんが　くる　まえに　ワインを　のんでしまった
   んですか
4. みんな　はなしてしまったら　どうですか

VIII. Practice the following patterns by changing the underlined parts.

ex. **Q**：もう　この　ほんを　よんじゃったの？
 A：うん、もう　よんじゃった。

1. ひるごはんを　たべる
2. ビールを　のむ
3. こどもは　ねる

4. やまださんは　でかける

IX. Make dialogues by changing the underlined part of the example.

> *ex.* おとこの　がくせい：<u>あそこに　いるのは　かみが　ながいから　まり</u>
> <u>こさんに　ちがいない。</u>
> おんなの　がくせい：きっと　そうね。

1. これは　かんじだけで　かいて　あるから　ちゅうごくの　ざっし
   です
2. これは　さっき　たなかさんが　つかっていたから　たなかさんの
   です
3. この　きかいは　しんせいひんだから　べんりです
4. ゆきが　ふったから　やまは　さむいです
5. みたいと　いっていたから　まりこさんも　きます
6. かれは　きっと　せいこうします
7. かれは　みちに　まよっています
8. かのじょは　しけんに　しっぱいしました

Vocabulary

カレー	**karē**, curry	へん（な）	**hen(na)**, strange, weird
やあ	**yā**, hi	においが　する	**nioi ga suru**, smell
かっこ（う）い　い	**kakko ii**, great, cool, super	におい	**nioi**, smell, odor
のんじゃって	**nonjatte** (contraction of **nonde shimatte**)	きが　する	**ki ga suru**, feel, think
		よかんが　する	**yokan ga suru**, have a hunch
ミーティング	**mītingu**, meeting	よかん	**yokan**, hunch, premonition
かいかいしき	**kaikai-shiki**, opening ceremony	すてき（な）	**suteki(na)**, fine, stunning, wonderful
かいかい	**kaikai-**, opening		
はげます　かい	**hagemasu-kai**, (*lit.*) encouragement party	ひどい	**hidoi**, terrible, harsh, severe
はげます　かい	**hagemasu**, encourage **-kai**, party, meeting	しんせいひん　しん〜	**shin-seihin**, new product **shin-**, new
（お）そうしき	**(o)-sōshiki**, funeral	せいひん	**seihin**, product
かいひ	**kaihi**, dues, membership fee	せいこうする　せいこう	**seikō suru**, succeed **seikō**, success
ぶんぽう	**bumpō**, grammar	みちに　まよう	**michi ni mayou**, lose one's way
せっけいず	**sekkeizu**, blueprint, plan	まよう	**mayou**, be lost, be puzzled
（お）ふろに　はいる	**(o-)furo ni hairu**, take a bath		
（お）ふろ	**(o-)furo**, bath		

SHORT DIALOGUES

1. **A**：ゆうべの　じしん、すごかったですね。

   B：そうだそうですね。ちょうど　そとを　あるいている　ところで、わたしは　きが　つきませんでした。

   A: Last night's earthquake was terrible, wasn't it!
   B: That's what I heard. I was walking outside just then and I didn't notice.

2. **A**：むすこさんの　おしごとは？

   B：いしゃを　しています。

   A: Your son's work?
   B: He's a doctor.

> **Vocabulary**

きが　つく　　**ki ga tsuku**, notice, realize, regain consciousness

QUIZ

I. Read this lesson's opening dialogue and answer the following questions.

   1. なかむらさんたちが　ついた　とき、コンサートは　もう　はじまって　いましたか。
   2. コンサートには　ひとが　おおぜい　きていましたか。
   3. おんなみたいな　かっこうを　して　うたっている　かしゅは　うたが　じょうずだと　ジョンソンさんは　いっていますか。
   4. だいすけくんと　まりこさんも　なかむらさんたちと　いっしょに　コンサートに　いきましたか。
   5. コンサートが　おわったら　どこに　いこうと　ジョンソンさんは　はなしていますか。

II. Put the appropriate particles in the parentheses.

   1. へんな　かっこう（　　）　している　ひとが　かいしゃの　まえに　たっています。
   2. ごうかく　おめでとうございます。
      ありがとうございます。ほんとう（　　）　せんせい（　　）おかげです。
   3. おぼんで　こんでいる　ときに、よく　しんかんせんの　きっぷ（　　）とれましたね。
   4. シンセサイザーって　ふしぎな　おと（　　）　します。
   5. あそこに　たっている（　　）は　けいこさんじゃない？

III. Complete the questions so that they fit the answers.

1. （　　　）を　してるんですか。
   めがねを　さがしてるんです。
2. （　　　）　かえってきたんですか。
   たった　いま　かえってきた　ところです。
3. （　　　）を　さそおうか。
   チャンさんと　ジョンソンさんを　さそおう。
4. （　　　）　あじが　する？
   くすりみたいな　あじが　する。

IV. Complete the sentence with the appropriate form of the verbs indicated.

1. しりょうは　もう　（　　　）おわりましたか。（よみます）
   いいえ、いま　（　　　）　ところですから、もう　すこし　（　　　）く
   ださい。（よんでいます、まちます）
2. どうも　（　　　）　もうしわけありません。（おそくなります）
   たった　いま　でんしゃが　（　　　）　ところです。つぎので　いきま
   しょう。（でました）
3. かちょう、げんこうが　できましたが、（　　　）いただけませんか。（め
   を　とおします）
   いま　（　　　）　ところだから、つくえの　うえに　（　　　）おいてく
   れないか。（でかけます、おきます）
4. いい　においが　しますね。
   いま　りょうりを　（　　　）　ところです。あなたも　（　　　）くださ
   い。（つくっています、てつだいます）

V. Convert the following sentences to a more polite level.

A：あそこに　いるのは　きむらさんじゃない？
B：そうだね。きむらさんだ。いっしょに　いるのは　やまださんに　ちが
   いない。
A：ふたりを　さそって、どっかに　いかない？
B：でも、じゃましない　ほうが　いいよ。ふたりは　けっこんするらしい
   から。

Mrs. Tanaka and Mr. Brown discuss the unusual fate of floating-world pictures.

田中夫人：きのう　上野の　美術館へ　行って　浮世絵の　さとがえりてんを
　　　　　見てきました。

ブラウン：アメリカや　ヨーロッパの　美術館から　いい　ものが　たくさん
　　　　　運ばれてきたようですね。

田中夫人：ええ、浮世絵は　日本より　外国の　ほうに　有名な　ものが　ある
　　　　　そうです。明治時代の　日本人が　どんどん　売ってしまったらしい
　　　　　です。

ブラウン：その　ころの　日本人には　外国の　ものは　みんな　よく　見え
　　　　　て、日本の　ものは　つまらなく　見えたんでしょうか。

田中夫人：そうですね。江戸時代の　さこくの　反動かもしれません。でも、外
　　　　　国人の　目には　浮世絵は　しんせんな　おどろきだったようです。
　　　　　それで　たくさんの　浮世絵が　日本から　出ていった　わけです。

ブラウン：日本の　すばらしい　でんとう美術が　外国へ　行ってしまって　日
　　　　　本人は　ざんねんに　思っていませんか。

田中夫人：そう　思っている　人は　多いかもしれませんが、私は　そうは　思
　　　　　いません。きのう　てんらん会を　見て　感心しました。みんな　と
　　　　　ても　よく　ほぞんされているんです。

ブラウン：浮世絵の　美しさを　みとめて、関係者が　大事に　してきたんでし
　　　　　ょうね。

田中夫人：そうですね。あの　ころは　日本は　今ほど、お金も　ぎじゅつも
　　　　　ありませんでしたから、よい　じょうたいで　ほぞんできたか　どう
　　　　　か　わかりませんしね。

ブラウン：美しい　ものは　すべて　大切に　ほぞんしてほしいですね。

田中夫人：ええ、後世の　人の　ためにもね。

ブラウン：でんとう美術は　みんなの　文化いさんと　いう　わけですね。

Tanaka:　Yesterday I went to the art museum in Ueno and saw an exhibition of ukiyo-e from abroad.

Brown:　It seems many good things were brought (back) from museums in the United States and Europe.

Tanaka:　Yes. They say there are more famous ukiyo-e in foreign countries than (in) Japan. It seems Meiji-period Japanese sold them off one after another.

Brown:　Could we say all foreign goods looked good to the Japanese at that time, and Japanese things seemed to be worthless?

Tanaka: Well, it might have been a reaction to the national isolation during the Edo period. Anyway, in foreigners' eyes ukiyo-e were apparently a new wonder. That's why a lot of ukiyo-e left Japan.

Brown: Don't Japanese feel regretful about this splendid traditional art going to foreign countries?

Tanaka: People who do feel that way are probably quite numerous, but I don't feel so. Seeing the exhibition yesterday, I was impressed. Everything had been very well taken care of.

Brown: Probably the people concerned, appreciating the beauty of ukiyo-e, valued (them) highly.

Tanaka: I think so too. Japan in those days did not have the wealth or technology of today, and I doubt whether they could have preserved (ukiyo-e) in good condition.

Brown: I'd like (to see) all beautiful things well taken care of.

Tanaka: Umm, (it'd be) for future generations too, wouldn't it.

Brown: Traditional art is the cultural heritage of all human beings, so to speak.

Vocabulary

びじゅつかん **bijutsukan**, art museum

うきよえ **ukiyo-e**, floating-world pictures

さとがえりてん **satogaeri-ten**, exhibition of returned works

さとがえり **satogaeri**, (*lit.*) return to (one's native) village

めいじじだい **Meiji-jidai**, Meiji period (1868–1912)

どんどん **dondon**, one after the other, steadily, rapidly

よく みえる **yoku mieru**, look good

つまらなく みえる **tsumaranaku mieru**, seem (to be) worthless

さこく **sakoku**, national isolation

はんどう **handō**, reaction

しんせん（な） **shinsen(na)**, new, fresh

おどろき **odoroki**, wonder, surprise, fright

わけです **wake desu**, (*lit.*) It is for this reason

わけ **wake**, reason, cause

でんとう **dentō**, tradition

びじゅつ **bijutsu**, art

ざんねんに おもう **zannen ni omou**, feel regret

てんらんかい **tenrankai**, exhibition

かんしんする **kanshin suru**, be impressed

ほぞんする **hozon suru**, take care of, preserve

ほぞん **hozon**, preservation, maintenance

みとめる **mitomeru**, appreciate, recognize

だいじに する **daiji ni suru**, value highly, take good care of

じょうたい **jōtai**, condition, state of affairs

すべて **subete**, all

こうせいの ひと **kōsei no hito**, future generation

こうせい **kōsei**, coming/later age

いさん **isan**, heritage, property, legacy

GRAMMAR & LESSON OBJECTIVES

• (to iu) wake desu

Sorede takusan no ukiyo-e ga Nihon kara dete itta wake desu.

Wake, a noun meaning "reason" which occurs in patterns like this, conveys the idea of a natural result. Like certain other nouns it follows verbs and adjectives.

ex. 1. A: **Ashita uchi no pātī ni konai to kikimashita ga, dōshite desu ka.** "You're not coming to our party tomorrow, I hear. Why is that?"

B. **Shutchō nan desu.** "Business trip."

C. **Aa, so iu wake desu ka.** "So that's why."

2. **Tonari ga o-tera desu kara, koko wa shizukana wake desu.** "Next door is a temple, so naturally it's quiet here."

Dentō bijutsu wa minna no bunka isan to iu wake desu ne.

To iu wake desu can be used for summing up, the sense being "in brief" or "so to speak."

NOTES

1. **Ukiyo-e no satogaeri-ten**
   Ukiyo-e, mostly woodblock prints, was a very popular genre of art from the seventeenth century through the nineteenth. From the late seventeenth century, **ukiyo**, "floating world" was a term applied to the milieu of entertainment districts, the licensed quarters and the kabuki theater, the setting for the best-known ukiyo-e. **Satogaeri** (**sato**, "home town"; plus **-masu** stem of **kaeru**, "return") actually refers to a bride's first visit to her parents' home and is here combined with **ten** to figuratively mean an exhibition of Japanese things on loan or repurchased from foreign collections.

2. **Sakoku**
   From 1639 until the end of the Edo period in 1868 the Tokugawa shoguns enforced a policy of not having intercourse with other countries. The only port permitted to engage in foreign trade was the island of Dejima in Nagasaki harbor, where there were at various times Dutch and Chinese traders. **Sakoku** is written with two Sino-Japanese characters meaning "closed country."

3. **Sonokoro no Nihonjin niwa ...**
   Niwa after a noun that refers to people means "for" or "to."
   ex. 1. **Kono hon wa kodomo niwa muzukashi sugimasu.** "This book is too difficult for children."
   2. **Tanaka-san niwa omoshiroi kamo shiremasen ga, watashi niwa taikutsu desu.** "(It) may be interesting to Tanaka, but to me it's boring."

4. **shinsenna odoroki datta yō desu.**
   The **-masu** stem of the majority of verbs functions as a noun. Some examples which are also separate dictionary entries are: **yorokobi**, "happiness"; **kanashimi**, "sadness"; **warai**, "smile, laughter"; **iki**, "going"; **tabesugi**, "overeating"; **nomisugi**, "intemperance."

5. **Watashi wa sō wa omoimasen.**
   The **wa** put into the simple negative **sō omoimasen** expression is for the sake of contrast, the sense being, "Whatever others may think, I think differently." **Sō omoimasen** is not usual.

PRACTICE

KEY SENTENCES

1. かのじょは あまいものが すきで よく たべますから、ふとる わけで す。

2. かとうさんは しゅっちょうちゅうで、すずきさんは びょうきで かいし ゃを やすんでいます。さとうさんも ごごは やくそくが あると いっ ていました。うちの かからは だれも ミーティングに しゅっせきでき ないと いう わけです。

1. She likes sweet things and eats a lot; naturally she gains weight.
2. Katō is on a business trip and Suzuki is off because he's sick. Satō says he has an afternoon appointment. That's why nobody in our section can attend the meeting.

EXERCISES

I. Practice the following patterns by changing the underlined parts.

A. *ex.* まいにち　おそくまで　はたらく<u>から</u>　<u>つかれる</u>　わけです。

   1. まいにち　テープを　きいている、じょうずに　なる
   2. からいものを　たべた、のどが　かわく
   3. きちんと　せいりしない、だいじな　ものが　なくなる
   4. みていなかった、わからない
   5. すずきさんは　いなかった、しらない
   6. むりを　する、かぜが　なおらない

B. *ex.* アメリカに　すんでいた<u>から</u>　<u>えいごが　じょうずな</u>　わけです。

   1. うみの　ちかくで　うまれた、すいえいが　じょうずです
   2. いちばん　あたらしい　きしゅだ、この　でんわは　べんりです
   3. ひろくて　べんりだ、やちんが　たかいです
   4. あの　かんとくの　さくひんだ、この　えいがは　おもしろいです

C. *ex.* **A**：なんで　わたなべさんは　しらないんでしょう。
     B：<u>やすんでいたから</u>　<u>しらない</u>　わけですよ。

   1. おくれてきました
   2. でかけてしまって　いませんでした
   3. しゅっちょうしていました
   4. でんわに　でていて　この　はなしを　きいていませんでした

D. *ex.* **A**：あの　ひとは　なぜ　<u>いか</u>ないんでしょう。
     B：<u>じかんと　（お）かねが　ない</u>から　<u>いき</u>たくても　<u>いけ</u>ないと
      いう　わけですよ。

   1. たべる、いの　しゅじゅつを　したばかりだ
   2. いけんを　いう、じぶんの　せんもんでは　ない
   3. ぶちょうに　なる、のうりょくと　じんぼうが　ない
   4. ふとる、ふきそくな　せいかつを　している

II. Make dialogues by changing the underlined parts as in the examples given.

A. *ex.* **Q**：どう　おもわれましたか。
     A：とても　<u>ざんねんに</u>　おもいました。

   1. ふしぎ

2. かなしい
3. うれしい
4. さびしい

B. ex. **Q**：いんしょうは　どうでしたか。
    A：<u>わかく　みえる</u>　ひとですね。

1. えらい
2. りっぱ
3. やさしそう
4. おとなしそう

Vocabulary

のどが　かわく	**nodo ga kawaku**, be/get thirsty	いけん	**iken**, opinion, suggestion
かわく	**kawaku**, become dry	じんぼうが　な い	**jimbō ga nai**, unpopular
きちんと	**kichin-to**, neatly, accurately	じんぼう	**jimbō**, popularity, reputation
かんとく	**kantoku**, director, supervisor	ふきそく（な）	**fukisoku(na)**, irregular
なんで	**nande**, why	かなしい	**kanashii**, sad, pathetic, unhappy
でんわに　でる	**denwa ni deru**, answer the phone	いんしょう	**inshō**, impression
い	**i**, stomach	おとなしそう	**otonashisō**, look gentle
しゅじゅつ	**shujutsu**, operation	おとなしい	**otonashii**, quiet, gentle, good-tempered, tame

---

SHORT DIALOGUES

1. さとう：スミスさんの　にほんごは　すごいですね。
　　チャン：まいにち　でんしゃの　なかでも　テープを　きいて　べんきょう
　　　　　　しているそうですよ。
　　さとう：それじゃ、じょうずに　なる　わけですね。

Satō:　Smith's Japanese is great, isn't it!
Chang: I hear he studies on the train every day by listening to tapes.
Satō:　Well, that explains why he gets better.

2. **A**：れんきゅうの　ドライブの　よていは　きまった？
　　B：その　こと　なんだけど、れんきゅうは　どこも　こんでいるし、てん
　　　　　きが　よくないらしいし、それに・・・。
　　A：ようするに　やめたいって　わけか。
　　B：まあ、そういう　わけ。

A: Have you made a plan to go driving over the holidays?
B: Oh, that, well, everywhere is crowded over the holidays, and the weather isn't expected
   to be good, and . . .
A: In other words, you don't want to go.
B: Well, yes, that's true.

Vocabulary

れんきゅう   **renkyū,** (consecutive)   ようするに   **yō suru ni,** in other
           holidays   words, in short

QUIZ

I. Read this lesson's opening dialogue and answer the following questions.

1. たなかさんが うえのの びじゅつかんで みた うきよえは どこか
   ら はこばれてきた ものですか。

2. めいじじだいに うきよえを つまらない ものだと おもったのは
   がいこくじんですか、にほんじんですか。

3. たなかさんは うきよえが がいこくに いってしまった ことを ざ
   んねんに おもっていますか。

4. たなかさんは なぜ めいじじだいの にほんでは うきよえを よい
   じょうたいで ほぞんできなかったかもしれないと おもっているので
   すか。

5. たなかさんも ブラウンさんも でんとうびじゅつは みんなが たい
   せつに しなければ ならないと おもっていますか。

II. Put the appropriate particles in the parentheses.

1. とうきょう（   ） きょうとの ほうに ふるい たてものが たく
   さん あります。

2. わかい ひと（   ）は かぶきは つまらなく みえるらしいです。

3. ふるい ものの よさ（   ） みとめて、だいじ（   ） しなけれ
   ば ならない。

4. アメリカ（   ） にほんに はこばれてきた えは よい じょうた
   い（   ） ほぞんされています。

III. Circle the most appropriate word in the parentheses.

1. かれの おくさんの びょうきは かなり わるいらしいです。
   （そこで、それで、それでは） よく やすむんですね。

2. おっとは チョコレートが だいすきなんです。
   （ちょうど、かなり、まるで） こどもみたいです。

3. これから たなかさんの うちに よります。（ここから、そこから、あ
   そこから） でんわで おたくに れんらくしますから、（これまで、そ
   れまで、あれまで） まっていてください。

IV. Complete the sentences with the appropriate form of the words indicated.

    1. ぜんぜん　れんしゅうしないから、うまく　（　　）　わけです。(なり
　　ません)

    2. くつが　ちいさすぎるから、（　　）　わけです。(つかれます)

    3. あなたに　（　　）、とても　（　　）　おもっています。(あえません、
　　ざんねんです)

    4. あの　ひとは　70すぎだそうですが、とても　（　　）　みえます。(わ
　　かいです)

    5. となりが　おてらだから、ここは　（　　）　わけです。(しずかです)

    6. あの　ひとの　せんもんでは　ないから、（　　）　わけです。(わかり
　　ません)

V. Choose a sentence appropriate to the situation described.

  A. You invite a friend, who's just come to see you, to join you for dinner.

    1. しょくじに　でた　ところだから、ちょっと　まっていて？

    2. しょくじを　すませた　ところだから、いっしょに　でかけない？

    3. しょくじに　でるところだから、いっしょに　たべに　いかない？

  B. You wish to disagree with an otherwise unanimous opinion at a meeting.

    1. みなさんは　さんせいのようですが、わたくしは　そうは　おもいま
　　せん。

    2. みなさんが　さんせいするなら、わたくしは　さんせいしません。

    3. みなさんは　さんせいしましたが、わたくしは　さんせいしませんで
　　した。

  C. You ask a friend to go on vacation with you.

    1. だれか　いきませんか。

    2. いつ　いく　つもり？

    3. どこかに　いかない？

　江戸時代には　まだ　とういつ的な　学校 教育せいどは　かくりつしていなかった。しかし、各藩では　藩の　学校を　作って、ぶじゅつばかりでなく、いろいろな　学問を　しょうれいした。17世紀後半には　全国で　240校あまりの　藩校が　あったと　言われる。

　この　藩校では　主に　ぶしかいきゅうの　子どもたちに　じゅ学や　国学などを　教えた。いっぽう、町人の　子どもたちは　寺子屋に　通って　べんきょうしていた。それまでは　主に　学校の　やくわりを　じいんなどが　していた。そして、その　場所を　寺子屋と　よんだのが、その　名の　おこりである。江戸時代の　中ごろに　なると、町人が　だんだん　経済力を　持ちはじめ、じいんばかりでなく、ふつうの　家を　使って、「読み　書き　そろばん」など　実用的な　ことを　教えるように　なったが、これも　やはり　寺子屋とよばれた。18世紀の　中ごろには　江戸の　町だけでも　800くらいの　寺子屋が　あったと　言われている。

　江戸時代の　有名な　学者の　本居宣長（1730〜1801）には　でしが　大ぜいいた。げんざい　わかっている　480人の　でしの　うち、町人は　166人、のう民は　144人、しんかん　67人、ぶし　58人、医者　27人などと　なっている。女性も　22人　いた。

　このように　すぐれた　学者を　中心とする　私じゅくが　はったつして、医学や　ちり学など　しぜん科学の　教育も　行われていたのである。

In the Edo period a unified educational system had not yet to be established. However, in each fief they created fief schools and promoted (the understanding of) not only military science but various (other) studies. It is said that in the latter half of the seventeenth century there were over 240 fief schools in the country as a whole.

At these fief schools they taught Confucianism, the Japanese classics and so on, mainly to the children of the samurai class. On the other hand, the children of townspeople attended private schools (to study). Prior to that, mainly temples had played the role of schools. Those places were called "temple schools" and this is the origin of the name *terakoya*. In the middle of the Edo period, townspeople began to have economic strength, and practical things like reading, writing and the abacus came to be taught, not particularly at temple schools but making use of ordinary houses. These, too, were also called *terakoya*. It is said that in the mid eighteenth century in Edo alone there were around eight hundred *terakoya*.

One famous scholar of the Edo period, Motoori Norinaga (1730–1801), had many students. Among the 480 students, as known (to us) now, were 166 townspeople, 144 farmers, 67 Shintō priests, 58 samurai, 27 doctors and others. There were 22 women.

In this way—(i.e.) centered on eminent scholars—private schools developed, (with) medicine, geography, natural sciences and so on being offered.

とういつてき（な）	**tōitsu-teki(na)**, unified	かよう	**kayou**, attend, go to and from, commute
とういつ	**tōitsu**, unification, uniformity	やくわり	**yakuwari**, role, part
がっこうきょういくせいど	**gakkō kyōiku seido**, (*lit.*) school education system	じいん	**jiin**, temple
		な	**na**, name
せいど	**seido**, system	おこり	**okori**, origin
かくりつする	**kakuritsu suru**, establish, settle	けいざいりょく	**keizai-ryoku**, economic strength
かくりつ	**kakuritsu**, establishment, settlement	～りょく	**-ryoku**, strength, power
しかし	**shikashi**, however	そろばん	**soroban**, abacus
かく	**kaku-**, each (prefix)	じつようてき（な）	**jitsuyō-teki(na)**, practical
はん	**han**, fief, domain	やはり	**yahari**, also
ぶじゅつ	**bujutsu**, military science	～には～いる	**niwa . . . iru**, (someone) has (students, children, etc.)
～ばかりでなく	**bakari de naku**, not only		
がくもん	**gakumon**, studies, learning	でし	**deshi**, student, follower, disciple
しょうれいする	**shōrei suru**, promote, encourage	～のうち	**no uchi**, among
		しんかん	**shinkan**, Shintō priest
しょうれい	**shōrei**, promotion, stimulation	～と　なる	**to naru**, (*lit.*) come/amount to
こうはん	**kōhan**, latter half	すぐれた	**sugureta**, eminent, outstanding, superior
ぜんこく	**zenkoku**, the whole country		
		ちゅうしんとする	**chūshin to suru**, be centered on
ぜん～	**zen-**, whole, all (prefix)		
～こう	**-kō** (counter for schools)	ちゅうしん	**chūshin**, center, core
あまり	**amari**, over	しじゅく	**shijuku**, private school/college
はんこう	**hankō** (obsolete), fief school		
		はったつする	**hattatsu suru**, develop, progress
おもに	**omo-ni**, mainly		
ぶし	**bushi**, warrior	はったつ	**hattatsu**, development, growth, advancement
かいきゅう	**kaikyū**, class, caste		
じゅがく	**jugaku**, Confucianism	いがく	**igaku**, medicine
こくがく	**kokugaku**, Japanese classics	ちりがく	**chirigaku**, geography
		しぜんかがく	**shizen kagaku**, natural science
いっぽう	**ippō**, (on the) other hand, (on) one hand/side		
		かがく	**kagaku**, science
ちょうにん	**chōnin**, townspeople		
てらこや	**terakoya**, temple/private school		

NOTES

The prose in this lesson, which is literary/reportorial in style, contains a number of expressions you are likely to come across in your reading.

1. **Motoori Norinaga (1730–1801) niwa deshi ga ōzei ita.**
   The pattern person(s) **niwa** person(s) **ga iru** means the former has the latter and carries the implication of an emphatic relationship.
   ex. 1. **Kaisha o yamesaserareta shi okane mo ushinatta. Demo watashi niwa kazoku ya tomodachi ga iru.** "I was fired by (my) company and lost money, yet I have family and friends (who believe in and support me)."
   2. **Kare niwa mikata mo iru ga teki mo ōi/ōzei iru.** "He has many friends but his enemies are numerous too."

2. **Chōnin wa 166-nin . . . isha 27-nin nado to natte iru.**
   To natte iru has the same meaning as **de aru** but when what is being said is based on a record, document or regulation, **to natte iru** is preferred. It sounds more formal and indirect.
   ex. 1. **Koko wa tachi iri kinshi to natte imasu.** "This place is posted."
   2. **Kaigi no kikan wa raishū no getsu-yō kara moku-yō made to natte iru.** "The period (set aside) for the conference is next week, from Monday till Thursday."

QUIZ

Put the appropriate words in the parentheses.

えどじだいには　（　　）　とういつてきな　がっこうきょういくせいどは
かくりつしていなかった。（　　）、かくはんでは　はんの　がっこうを　つくっ
て、ぶじゅつ（　　）、いろいろな　がくもんを　しょうれいした。17せいき
こうはんには　ぜんこく（　　）240こうあまりの　はんこうが　あった（　　）
いわれる。
　この　はんこうでは　おもに　ぶしかいきゅうの　こどもたちに　じゅがく
（　　）　こくがくなどを　おしえた。（　　）、ちょうにんの　こどもたちは
てらこや（　　）　かよって　べんきょうしていた。それまでは　（　　）　が
っこうの　やくわりを　じいんなど（　　）　していた。そして、（　　）　ば
しょを　てらこやと　よんだのが、その　なの　おこりである。えどじだいの
なかごろに　（　　）、ちょうにんが　（　　）　けいざいりょくを　もちはじ
め、じいんばかりでなく、（　　）の　いえを　つかって、「よみ　かき　そろば
ん」など　じつようてき（　　）　ことを、おしえる（　　）が、これも（　　）
てらこやと　よばれた。18せいきの　なかごろ（　　）は　えどのまち（　　）
800くらいの　てらこやが　あったと　いわれている。
　えどじだいの　ゆうめい（　　）　がくしゃ（　　）　もとおりのりなが（1730
～1801）には　でし（　　）　おおぜい　いた。（　　）　わかっている　480に
んの　でし（　　）、ちょうにんは　166にん、のうみんは　144にん、しんかん
67にん、ぶし　58にん、いしゃ　27にんなどと　（　　）。じょせいも　22にん
いた。
　（　　）　すぐれた　がくしゃ（　　）　ちゅうしんとする　しじゅく（　　）
はったつして、いがくや　ちりがく（　　）　しぜんかがくの　きょういくも
（　　）のである。

NEW KANJI

The numbers in parentheses indicate the number of strokes.

Counters, Day of the Week, Date

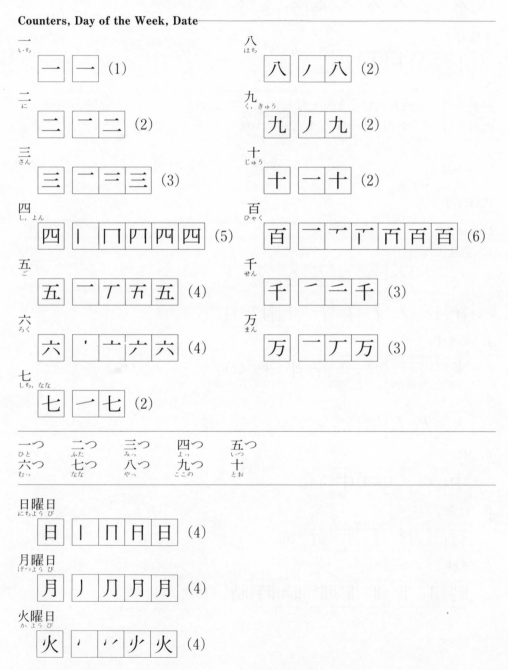

水曜日
すいようび

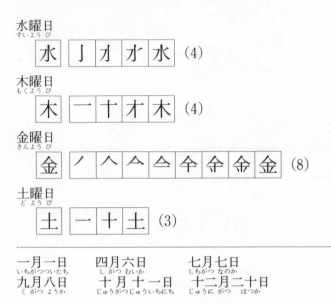

水 ｜ ｊ ォ 水 水 (4)

木曜日
もくようび

木 一 十 才 木 (4)

金曜日
きんようび

金 ノ 〈 亼 仐 全 仐 金 金 (8)

土曜日
どようび

土 一 十 土 (3)

一月一日　　四月六日　　七月七日
いちがつついたち　し がつ むいか　　しちがつ なのか
九月八日　　十月十一日　　十二月二十日
く がつ ようか　　じゅうがつじゅういちにち　じゅうに がつ　はつか

PART I

Lesson 1

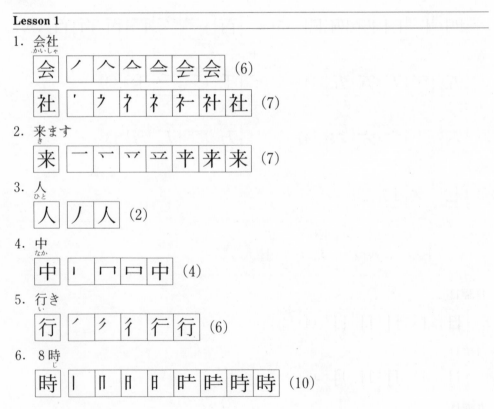

1. 会社
   かいしゃ

   会 ノ 〈 亼 仝 会 会 (6)

   社 ˋ ⺙ ⻊ ⻌ ⻍ 社 社 (7)

2. 来ます
   き

   来 一 ⼀ ⼀ 平 平 来 来 (7)

3. 人
   ひと

   人 ノ 人 (2)

4. 中
   なか

   中 ｜ ⼌ ⼐ 中 (4)

5. 行き
   い

   行 ˊ ⼃ ⼈ 行 行 (6)

6. 8時
   じ

   時 ｜ ⼆ ⽇ ⽇ 昨 昨 時 時 (10)

7. 日本語
にほんご

| 日 | 丨 | 冂 | 日 | 日 | (4) |

| 本 | 一 | 十 | 才 | 木 | 本 | (5) |

| 語 | 丶 | 二 | 三 | 言 | 言 | 言 | 訂 | 語 | 語 | 語 | (14) |

Lesson 2

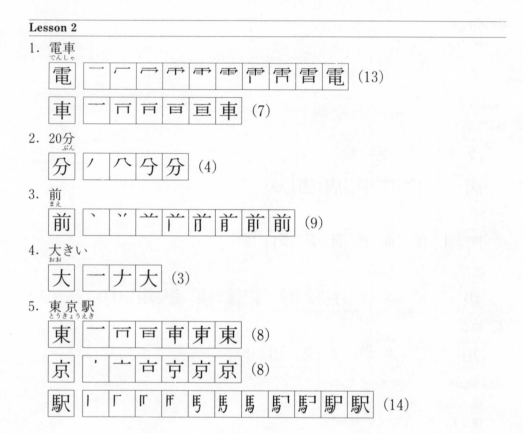

1. 電車
でんしゃ

| 電 | 一 | 厂 | 宀 | 雨 | 雨 | 雨 | 雨 | 雷 | 電 | (13) |

| 車 | 一 | 冂 | 亘 | 亘 | 亘 | 車 | (7) |

2. 20分
ぶん

| 分 | 丿 | 八 | 分 | 分 | (4) |

3. 前
まえ

| 前 | 丶 | 丷 | 丷 | 产 | 肖 | 前 | 前 | 前 | (9) |

4. 大きい
おお

| 大 | 一 | ナ | 大 | (3) |

5. 東京駅
とうきょうえき

| 東 | 一 | 冂 | 亘 | 申 | 東 | 東 | (8) |

| 京 | 丶 | 亠 | 亩 | 亨 | 京 | 京 | (8) |

| 駅 | 丨 | 厂 | 厂 | 厈 | 馬 | 馬 | 馬 | 駅 | 駅 | 駅 | 駅 | (14) |

Lesson 3

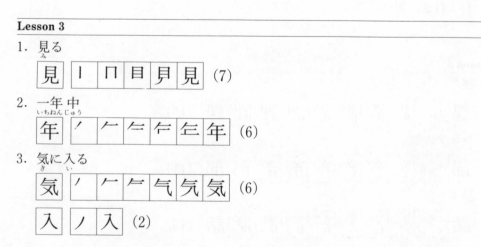

1. 見る
み

| 見 | 丨 | 冂 | 目 | 見 | 見 | (7) |

2. 一年中
いちねんじゅう

| 年 | 丿 | 𠂉 | 匕 | 午 | 年 | 年 | (6) |

3. 気に入る
き   い

| 気 | 丿 | 𠂉 | 匕 | 気 | 気 | 気 | (6) |

| 入 | 丿 | 入 | (2) |

4. 名前
<ruby>名<rt>な</rt></ruby><ruby>前<rt>まえ</rt></ruby>

| 名 | ノ | ク | タ | タ | 名 | 名 | (6) |

5. 住所
<ruby>住<rt>じゅう</rt></ruby><ruby>所<rt>しょ</rt></ruby>

| 住 | ノ | イ | 亻 | 仹 | 住 | 住 | (7) |

| 所 | 一 | 亍 | 彐 | 戸 | 戸 | 所 | 所 | 所 | (8) |

Readings :

中：中，一年中
<ruby>中<rt>なか</rt></ruby> <ruby>一年中<rt>いちねんじゅう</rt></ruby>

Lesson 4

1. 支店
<ruby>支<rt>し</rt></ruby><ruby>店<rt>てん</rt></ruby>

| 支 | 十 | 亍 | 支 | (4) |

| 店 | 一 | 广 | 广 | 庐 | 店 | 店 | (8) |

2. 町
<ruby>町<rt>まち</rt></ruby>

| 町 | 丨 | 冂 | 皿 | 田 | 田 | 町 | 町 | (7) |

3. 銀行
<ruby>銀<rt>ぎん</rt></ruby><ruby>行<rt>こう</rt></ruby>

| 銀 | ノ | 𠆢 | 𠆢 | 牟 | 牟 | 金 | 金 | 釖 | 鈩 | 鈩 | 鈩 | 銀 | (14) |

4. 知る
<ruby>知<rt>し</rt></ruby>る

| 知 | ノ | 𠂉 | 𠂉 | 矢 | 矢 | 知 | 知 | (8) |

Readings :

車：電車，車
<ruby>電車<rt>でんしゃ</rt></ruby> <ruby>車<rt>くるま</rt></ruby>
住：住所，住んでいた
<ruby>住所<rt>じゅうしょ</rt></ruby> <ruby>住<rt>す</rt></ruby>んでいた
行：行き，銀行
<ruby>行<rt>い</rt></ruby>き <ruby>銀行<rt>ぎんこう</rt></ruby>

Lesson 5

1. 課
<ruby>課<rt>か</rt></ruby>

| 課 | 言 | 言 | 訂 | 評 | 評 | 評 | 課 | 課 | 課 | (15) |

2. システム部
システム<ruby>部<rt>ぶ</rt></ruby>

| 部 | 亠 | 立 | 立 | 立 | 音 | 音 | 咅 | 部 | 部 | (11) |

3. 話す
<ruby>話<rt>はな</rt></ruby>す

| 話 | 二 | 言 | 言 | 言 | 訂 | 訐 | 訐 | 話 | 話 | (13) |

4. 後(あと)

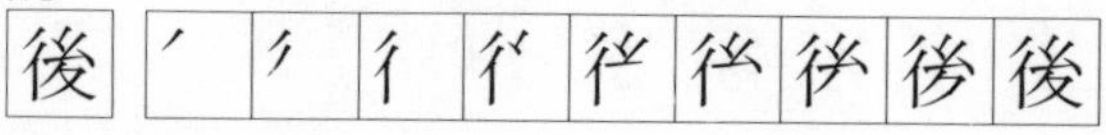
(9)

Readings :

来：来(き)ます，来月(らいげつ)

話：話(はな)す，話(はなし)

Lesson 6

1. 38度(ど)

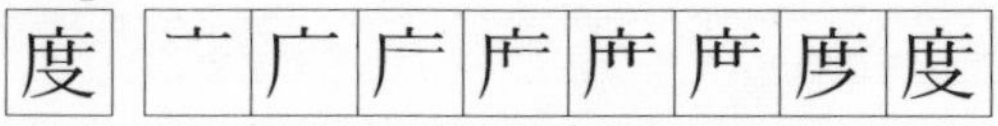
(9)

2. 早(はや)く

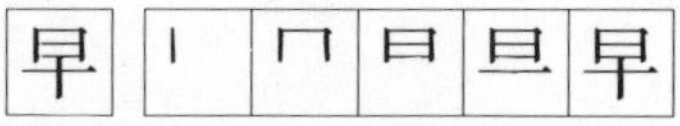
(6)

3. 休(やす)む

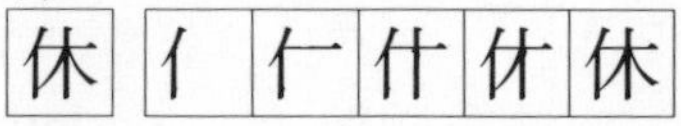
(6)

4. 用事(ようじ)

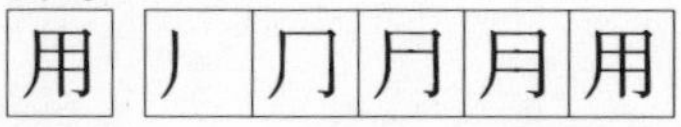
(5)

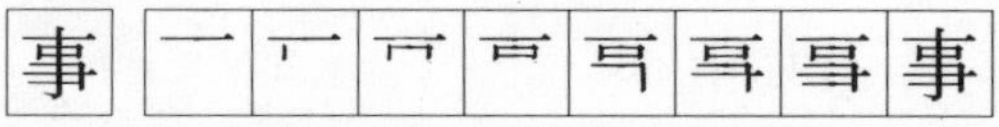
(8)

Lesson 7

1. 時間(じかん)

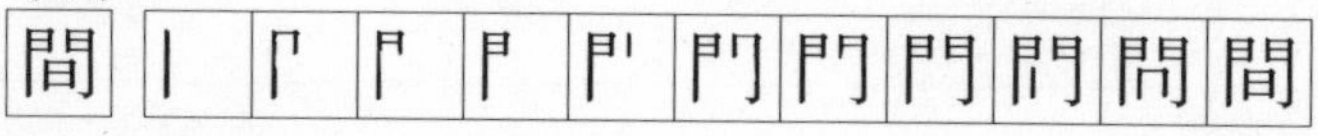
(12)

2. 出発(しゅっぱつ)

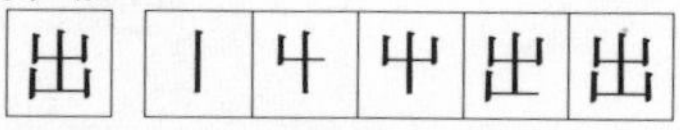
(5)

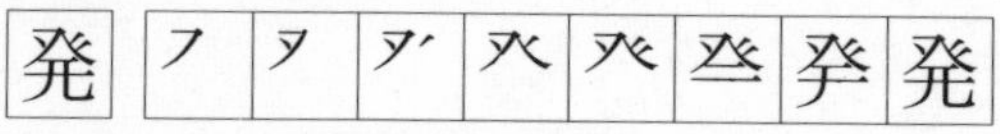
(9)

Readings :

日：日本語(にほんご)，日(ひ)

来：来(き)ます，来月(らいげつ)，来(く)る

Lesson 8

1. 思(おも)う

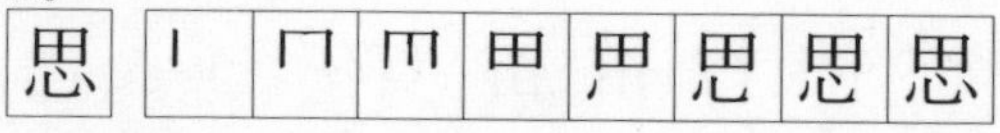
(9)

2. 家
_{いえ}

家 ` ´ ´ ⺤ ⺀ 宁 宇 安 家 家 家 (10)

3. 言う
_い

言 ⼀ ⼆ ⺫ ⺲ 言 言 言 (7)

4. 少ない
_{すく}

少 ⼃ ⼩ 小 少 (4)

Lesson 9

1. けい子
_こ

子 ⺆ 了 子 (3)

2. 今
_{いま}

今 ⼃ ⼈ ⼈ 今 (4)

3. 大学
_{だいがく}

学 ` ` ⺍ ⺍ ⺌ 学 (8)

Readings :

出：出発，出かける　　　　今：今，今日中
_{しゅっぱつ}_で　　　　　　　　_{いま}_{きょうじゅう}
大：大きい，大学　　　　　入：気に入る，入学金
_{おお}_{だいがく}　　　　　　_き_い_{にゅうがくきん}
分：20分，3か月分　　　　来：来ます，来月，来る，来ない
_{ぶん}_{げつぶん}　　　　　　　_き_{らいげつ}_く_こ

Kanji for recognition : 第一
_{だいいち}

Lesson 10

1. あそ山
_{さん}

山 ｜ ⼭ 山 (3)

2. 川
_{かわ}

川 ⼃ ⼅ 川 (3)

3. 市内
_{しない}

市 ⼇ 广 市 市 (5)

内 ｜ ⼌ 内 内 (4)

4. 一番
_{いちばん}

番 ⼃ ⼇ ⼌ ⼂ 平 采 采 番 番 番 (12)

5. 社長

しゃちょう

長　｜　广　巨　丘　丟　長　(8)

Readings :

家：家，家内

　　いえ　　かない

Kanji for recognition：時代

　　　　　　　　　　　じだい

Lesson 11

1. 仕事

しごと

仕　イ　仁　什　仕　(5)

2. 多い

おお

多　ノ　ク　タ　タ　多　多　(6)

3. 好きな

す

好　㇄　女　女　好　好　好　(6)

4. 外国

がいこく

外　ノ　ク　タ　列　外　(5)

国　｜　冂　冂　冚　用　国　国　国　(8)

Readings :

事：用事，仕事

　　ようじ　しごと

入：気に入る，入学金，入る

　　き　い　にゅうがくきん　はい

Lesson 12

1. 部屋

へや

屋　㇇　㇕　尸　尸　尸　居　居　屋　屋　(9)

2. 何名

なんめい

何　イ　广　何　何　(7)

3. 円

えん

円　｜　冂　冂　円　(4)

4. 近い

ちか

近　㇐　厂　斤　斤　沂　近　近　(7)

Readings :

名：名前，何名　　　　話：話します，話，電話
時：時間，時　　　　　内：市内，内金
部：システム部，部屋

Lesson 13

1. 開ける

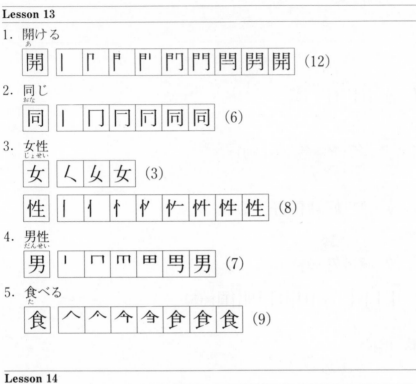

2. 同じ

3. 女性

4. 男性

5. 食べる

Lesson 14

1. 飲む

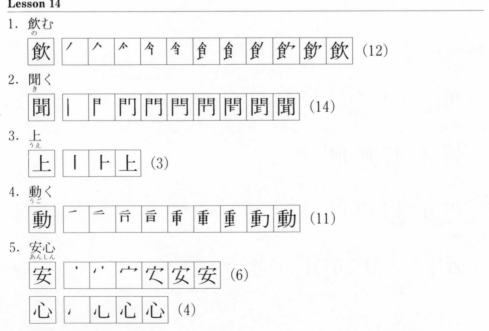

2. 聞く

3. 上

4. 動く

5. 安心

Readings :

言：言います，発言
　　い　　　　はつげん
発：出発，発言
　　しゅっぱつ　はつげん

Lesson 15

1. 私
　わたし

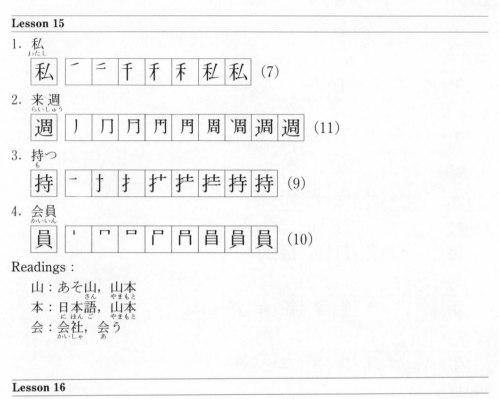

　私　｜ ˊ　｜ ˉ　｜ 千　｜ 禾　｜ 禾　｜ 私　｜ 私　(7)

2. 来週
　らいしゅう

　週　｜ ﾉ　｜ 刀　｜ 月　｜ 冎　｜ 円　｜ 周　｜ 冽　｜ 週　｜ 週　(11)

3. 持つ
　も

　持　｜ ｰ　｜ 十　｜ 扌　｜ 扩　｜ 护　｜ 拝　｜ 持　｜ 持　(9)

4. 会員
　かいいん

　員　｜ ｀　｜ 冂　｜ 口　｜ 尸　｜ 冎　｜ 昌　｜ 員　｜ 員　(10)

Readings :

山：あそ山，山本
　　　　　さん　やまもと
本：日本語，山本
　　にほんご　やまもと
会：会社，会う
　　かいしゃ　あ

Lesson 16

1. 送る
　おく

　送　｜ ﾉ　｜ ﾝ　｜ 兰　｜ 关　｜ 关　｜ 关　｜ 送　｜ 送　(9)

2. 年末
　ねんまつ

　末　｜ ﾆ　｜ 干　｜ 才　｜ 末　(5)

3. 入口
　いりぐち

　口　｜ ｜　｜ 冂　｜ 口　(3)

4. 閉まる
　し

　閉　｜ ｜　｜ ﾄ　｜ 門　｜ 門　｜ 門　｜ 閉　｜ 閉　(11)

Readings :

上：上，でき上がる
　　うえ　　　あ
中：中，一年中，来週中
　　なか　いちねんじゅう　らいしゅうちゅう
何：何名，何か
　　なんめい　なに

Lesson 17

1. 朝

あさ

| 朝 | ナ | 古 | 卓 | 朝 | 朝 | (12) |

2. 全員

ぜんいん

| 全 | 人 | 宀 | 仐 | 全 | 全 | (6) |

3. 午後

ご ご

| 午 | ノ | ヒ | 二 | 午 | (4) |

4. 書く

か

| 書 | 一 | 一 | 三 | 聿 | 聿 | 書 | 書 | (10) |

5. 先日

せんじつ

| 先 | ノ | ヒ | 屮 | 生 | 牛 | 先 | (6) |

6. 毎年

まい

| 毎 | ノ | 一 | 仁 | 勾 | 毎 | 毎 | (6) |

7. 新年

しんねん

| 新 | 亠 | 立 | 辛 | 辛 | 亲 | 斩 | 新 | 新 | (13) |

8. 学生

がくせい

| 生 | ノ | 一 | 牛 | 牛 | 生 | (5) |

Readings :

国：外国，国

　　がいこく　くに

店：支店，店

　　してん　みせ

日：日本語，日，先日

　　にほんご　ひ　せんじつ

後：後，午後

　　あと　ご

年：一年中，毎年

　　いちねんじゅう　まいとし

近：近い，近所

　　ちか　　きんじょ

所：住所，近所

　　じゅうしょ　きんじょ

Lesson 18

1. 友

とも

| 友 | 一 | ナ | 方 | 友 | (4) |

2. 花

はな

| 花 | 一 | 艹 | 艹 | 艹 | 花 | 花 | (7) |

3. 都内

と ない

| 都 | 十 | 土 | 耂 | 耂 | 者 | 者 | 者⻏ | 都⻏ | 都 | (11) |

4. 送料
   料　｀ゝ　ゞゝ　半　半　米　米-　料　(10)

5. 番号
   号　｜　口　口　号　号　(5)

6. 田中
   田　｜　冂　川　田　田　(5)

Readings :

女 : 女性, 女
　　 じょせい　おんな
送 : 送る, 送料
　　 おく　　そうりょう
先 : 先日, おとどけ先
　　 せんじつ　　　　さき

Lesson 19

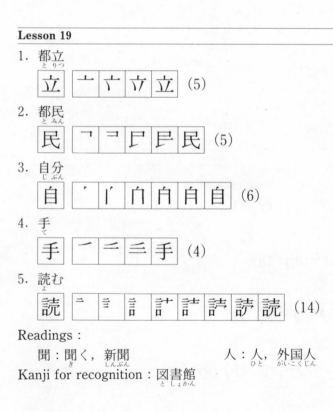

1. 都立
   立　亠　六　立　立　(5)

2. 都民
   民　フ　コ　尸　尸　民　(5)

3. 自分
   自　′　′　冂　自　自　自　(6)

4. 手
   手　一　二　三　手　(4)

5. 読む
   読　゠　言　言　計　詰　詰　詰　読　(14)

Readings :

聞 : 聞く, 新聞　　　　　人 : 人, 外国人
　　 き　　しんぶん　　　　　　ひと　がいこくじん
Kanji for recognition : 図書館
　　　　　　　　　　　　　 としょかん

Lesson 20

1. 桜 前線
   さくらぜんせん
   線　′　幺　糸　糸　糺　糺　紵　紵　線　線　(15)

2. 春
   はる
   春　一　三　丰　夫　春　(9)

3. 南

南 ｜ 一 亠 宀 冇 肎 南 南 (9)

4. 北
北 ｜ 一 ｜ 十 才 北 (5)

5. 秋
秋 ｀ 二 千 千 禾 秒 秒 秋 (9)

6. 木々
々 ｜ ノ 夕 々 (3)

Readings :

長：社長，長い   南：南，南部
上：上，上がる，上じゅん   末：年末，末ごろ
少：少ない，少し   木：木よう日，木々

Kanji for recognition：桜

PART II

Lesson 21

1. 着る
着 ｀ 丷 ﾒ 羊 羊 着 着 (12)

2. 始まる
始 ｜ 女 女 妁 妁 始 (8)

3. 若い
若 ｜ 一 十 艹 ﾌ 芧 芋 若 (8)

4. 受ける
受 ｜ 一 ⺍ 爫 爫 严 受 受 (8)

5. 人物
物 ｜ ノ ｜ 牛 牛 牜 牞 物 物 (8)

Readings :

人：人，人物，人気

Kanji for recognition：加藤

1. 予約
予  (4)

約 (9)

2. 予定
定 (8)

3. 海外
海 (9)

4. 決める
決 (7)

5. 昨日
昨 (9)

6. 待つ
待 (9)

Readings :
前：名前，前日

Lesson 23

1. 帰る
帰 (10)

2. 伝える
伝 (6)

3. 直通
直 (8)

通 (10)

Readings :
言：言う，発言，言づけ

Kanji for recognition：中野，武道館

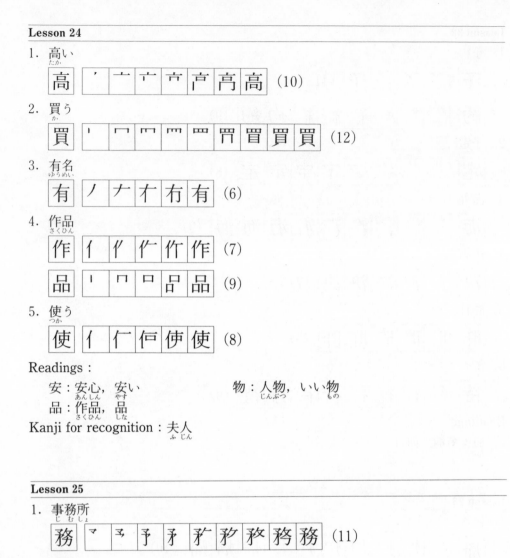

1. 高い
たか

高　　ハ　亠　宀　亠　声　高　高　(10)

2. 買う
か

買　　レ　ロ　ワ　四　四　罒　買　買　買　(12)

3. 有名
ゆうめい

有　　ノ　ナ　オ　冇　有　(6)

4. 作品
さくひん

作　　イ　イ　仁　竹　作　(7)

品　　ト　ロ　口　品　品　(9)

5. 使う
つか

使　　イ　仁　仨　伊　使　(8)

Readings :

　安：安心，安い　　　　　　物：人物，いい物
　　　あんしん　やす　　　　　　　　じんぶつ　　もの
　品：作品，品
　　　さくひん　しな
Kanji for recognition : 夫人
　　　　　　　　　　　　ふじん

---

1. 事務所
じ むしょ

務　　マ　ヲ　予　矛　矜　矜　矜　務　務　(11)

2. 広さ
ひろ

広　　亠　广　広　広　広　(5)

3. 和室
わ しつ

和　　ノ　二　千　禾　禾　和　(8)

室　　ヽ　ヽ　宀　宀　灾　灾　宏　宰　室　(9)

4. 犬
いぬ

犬　　一　ナ　大　犬　(4)

Readings :

　家：家，家内，大家
　　　いえ　かない　おおや
Kanji for recognition : 居間，中村
　　　　　　　　　　　　いま　なかむら

Lesson 26

1. 会議
   <ruby>会議<rt>かい ぎ</rt></ruby>
   議 ｜ 言 ｜ 言 ｜ 言 ｜ 誄 ｜ 議 ｜ 議 ｜ 議 ｜ 議 ｜ 議 (20)

2. コの字がた
   <ruby>字<rt>じ</rt></ruby>
   字 ｜ ｀ ｜ ｀｀ ｜ 宀 ｜ 宁 ｜ 字 ｜ 字 (6)

3. 出席者
   <ruby>出 席 者<rt>しゅっ せき しゃ</rt></ruby>
   席 ｜ ｀ ｜ 广 ｜ 广 ｜ 庐 ｜ 庐 ｜ 席 ｜ 席 (10)
   者 ｜ 一 ｜ 十 ｜ 土 ｜ 耂 ｜ 者 ｜ 者 ｜ 者 (8)

4. 人数
   <ruby>人数<rt>にんずう</rt></ruby>
   数 ｜ ゛ ｜ ゛ ｜ 米 ｜ 米 ｜ 类 ｜ 娄 ｜ 娄 ｜ 数 ｜ 数 ｜ 数 (13)

5. 終わる
   <ruby>終<rt>お</rt></ruby>わる
   終 ｜ ｀ ｜ 幺 ｜ 糸 ｜ 糸 ｜ 紒 ｜ 紻 ｜ 終 ｜ 終 (11)

6. 下
   <ruby>下<rt>した</rt></ruby>
   下 ｜ 一 ｜ 丁 ｜ 下 (3)

7. 半
   <ruby>半<rt>はん</rt></ruby>
   半 ｜ ゛ ｜ ゛ ｜ 兰 ｜ 半 (5)

Readings :

新：新聞，新しい
<ruby>新聞<rt>しんぶん</rt></ruby> <ruby>新<rt>あたら</rt></ruby>しい
Kanji for recognition：鈴木，渡辺
<ruby>鈴木<rt>すずき</rt></ruby> <ruby>渡辺<rt>わたなべ</rt></ruby>

Lesson 27

1. 運動
   <ruby>運動<rt>うんどう</rt></ruby>
   運 ｜ 冖 ｜ 冖 ｜ 冒 ｜ 冒 ｜ 軍 ｜ 軍 ｜ 渾 ｜ 運 (12)

2. 北海道
   <ruby>北海道<rt>ほっかいどう</rt></ruby>
   道 ｜ ゛ ｜ ゛ ｜ 首 ｜ 道 (12)

3. 切る
   <ruby>切<rt>き</rt></ruby>る
   切 ｜ 一 ｜ 七 ｜ 切 ｜ 切 (4)

4. 計画
   <ruby>計画<rt>けいかく</rt></ruby>
   計 ｜ 言 ｜ 計 ｜ 計 (9)

画 | 一 | 冂 | 币 | 帀 | 画 | 画 (8)

5. 声
<ruby>声<rt>こえ</rt></ruby>
声 | 士 | 吉 | 吉 | 吉 | 声 (7)

6. 耳
<ruby>耳<rt>みみ</rt></ruby>
耳 | 一 | 丁 | 丆 | 耳 | 耳 (6)

Readings:

北：北，北海道　　　　　動：動く，運動
<ruby>北<rt>きた</rt></ruby>　<ruby>北海道<rt>ほっかいどう</rt></ruby>　　　<ruby>動<rt>うご</rt></ruby>く　<ruby>運動<rt>うんどう</rt></ruby>

開：開ける，開発　　　　作：作品，作る
<ruby>開<rt>あ</rt></ruby>ける　<ruby>開発<rt>かいはつ</rt></ruby>　　　<ruby>作品<rt>さくひん</rt></ruby>　<ruby>作<rt>つく</rt></ruby>る

大：大きい，大学，大切　切：切る，大切
<ruby>大<rt>おお</rt></ruby>きい　<ruby>大学<rt>だいがく</rt></ruby>　<ruby>大切<rt>たいせつ</rt></ruby>　<ruby>切<rt>き</rt></ruby>る　<ruby>大切<rt>たいせつ</rt></ruby>

Kanji for recognition：林
<ruby>林<rt>はやし</rt></ruby>

Lesson 28

1. 建てる
<ruby>建<rt>た</rt></ruby>てる
建 | ⁊ | ⌐ | 聿 | 建 | 建 (9)

2. 集める
<ruby>集<rt>あつ</rt></ruby>める
集 | 亻 | 宀 | 什 | 隹 | 隹 | 隼 | 集 (12)

3. 古い
<ruby>古<rt>ふる</rt></ruby>い
古 | 一 | 十 | 古 (5)

4. 小さい
<ruby>小<rt>ちい</rt></ruby>さい
小 | 亅 | 小 | 小 (3)

5. 冬
<ruby>冬<rt>ふゆ</rt></ruby>
冬 | 夂 | 夂 | 冬 | 冬 (5)

Readings:

建：建てる，建物
<ruby>建<rt>た</rt></ruby>てる　<ruby>建物<rt>たてもの</rt></ruby>

生：学生，生まれる
<ruby>学生<rt>がくせい</rt></ruby>　<ruby>生<rt>う</rt></ruby>まれる

Kanji for recognition：江戸
<ruby>江戸<rt>えど</rt></ruby>

Lesson 29

1. 調べる
<ruby>調<rt>しら</rt></ruby>べる
調 | 言 | 訂 | 訂 | 訮 | 調 (15)

2. 件
けん
件 イ イ 仁 件 (6)

3. 問い合わせ
と あ
問 丨 冖 冂 冂 門 門 問 (11)
合 ノ 人 合 合 (6)

4. 説明
せつめい
説 言 訁 評 訝 説 (14)
明 冂 日 明 明 (8)

Readings :
　書：書く，けいやく書
　　　か　　　　しょ
Kanji for recognition：横浜
　　　　　　　　　　　よこはま

Lesson 30

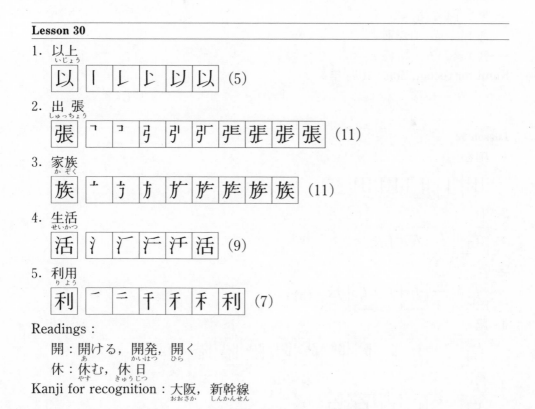

1. 以上
いじょう
以 丨 レ 以 以 以 (5)

2. 出張
しゅっちょう
張 フ フ 弓 引 引 張 張 張 張 (11)

3. 家族
かぞく
族 亠 宁 方 扩 扩 扩 旅 族 (11)

4. 生活
せいかつ
活 氵 氵 汗 汗 活 (9)

5. 利用
りよう
利 一 二 千 禾 禾 利 (7)

Readings :
　開：開ける，開発，開く
　　　あ　　　かいはつ　ひら
　休：休む，休日
　　　やす　　きゅうじつ
Kanji for recognition：大阪，新幹線
　　　　　　　　　　　おおさか　しんかんせん

1. 返事
へんじ

返 ｜一 厂 反 反 返｜ (7)

2. 最後
さいご

最 ｜日 旦 昌 冒 骨 最 最｜ (12)

3. 目
め

目 ｜｜ 冂 月 月 目｜ (5)

4. 会場
かいじょう

場 ｜土 圫 坦 垾 場 場｜ (12)

5. 料理
りょうり

理 ｜т 王 玾 理 理｜ (11)

Readings :

　早 : 早い，早々
　　　はや　　そうそう
　通 : 直通，目を通す
　　　ちょくつう　め　とお
　終 : 終わる，最終
　　　お　　　さいしゅう

Kanji for recognition : 10周年
　　　　　　　　　しゅうねん

---

1. 困る
こま

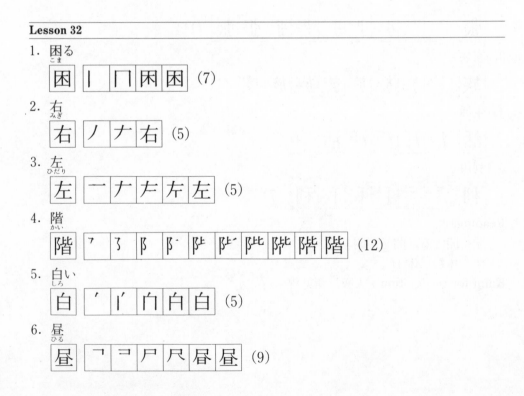

困 ｜｜ 冂 困 困｜ (7)

2. 右
みぎ

右 ｜ノ ナ 右｜ (5)

3. 左
ひだり

左 ｜一 ナ ナ 左 左｜ (5)

4. 階
かい

階 ｜ ⁊ ⻖ 阝 阼 阼 陛 陛 階 階｜ (12)

5. 白い
しろ

白 ｜ ´ ⺊ 白 白 白｜ (5)

6. 昼
ひる

昼 ｜ ⁊ ⁊ 尸 尺 昼 昼｜ (9)

Readings :

場：会場，場所
<ruby>か<rt></rt></ruby>

Kanji for recognition：渋谷<ruby>しぶや<rt></rt></ruby>

Lesson 33

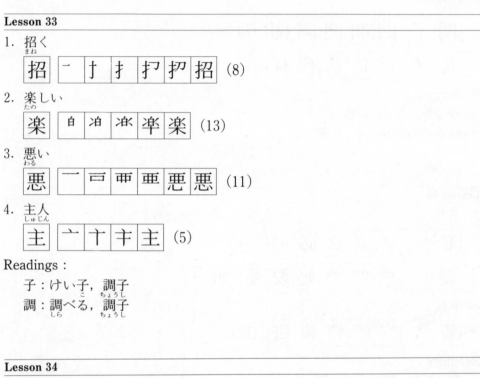

1. 招く
まね

招 ｜ 一 ｜ 十 ｜ 扌 ｜ 护 ｜ 护 ｜ 招 (8)

2. 楽しい
たの

楽 ｜ 白 ｜ 冶 ｜ 冹 ｜ 単 ｜ 楽 (13)

3. 悪い
わる

悪 ｜ 一 ｜ 戸 ｜ 亜 ｜ 亜 ｜ 悪 ｜ 悪 (11)

4. 主人
しゅじん

主 ｜ 亠 ｜ 十 ｜ 丰 ｜ 主 (5)

Readings :

子：けい子，調子
<ruby>こ<rt></rt></ruby>　<ruby>ちょうし<rt></rt></ruby>

調：調べる，調子
<ruby>しら<rt></rt></ruby>　<ruby>ちょうし<rt></rt></ruby>

Lesson 34

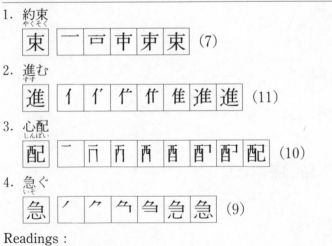

1. 約束
やくそく

束 ｜ 一 ｜ 戸 ｜ 申 ｜ 束 ｜ 束 (7)

2. 進む
すす

進 ｜ 亻 ｜ 亻 ｜ 俨 ｜ 什 ｜ 隹 ｜ 淮 ｜ 進 (11)

3. 心配
しんぱい

配 ｜ 一 ｜ 亓 ｜ 万 ｜ 西 ｜ 酉 ｜ 酉 ｜ 酉 ｜ 配 (10)

4. 急ぐ
いそ

急 ｜ ノ ｜ ケ ｜ 刍 ｜ 刍 ｜ 急 ｜ 急 (9)

Readings :

間：時間，間に合う
<ruby>じかん<rt></rt></ruby>　<ruby>ま<rt></rt></ruby> <ruby>あ<rt></rt></ruby>

Lesson 35

1. 働く
   _{はたら}
   働 亻 仁 佢 佴 値 衝 働 (13)

2. 関係
   _{かんけい}
   関 門 門 門 閂 閈 関 (14)

   係 亻 仁 仔 佟 佟 係 (9)

Readings :

今：今，今日，今度
_{いま} _{きょう} _{こんど}
Kanji for recognition：佐藤
_{さとう}

Lesson 36

1. 必要
   _{ひつよう}
   必 丶 丿 必 必 必 (5)

   要 一 冂 西 西 更 要 要 (9)

2. 資料
   _{しりょう}
   資 冫 汀 次 浒 沓 資 (13)

Readings :

間：時間，間に合う，間
_{じかん} _ま _あ _{あいだ}

Lesson 37

1. 続ける
   _{つづ}
   続 糸 続 続 続 (13)

2. 曜
   _{よう}
   曜 日 旷 旷 矅 瞱 曜 (18)

3. 注意
   _{ちゅうい}
   注 氵 氵 汁 注 (8)

   意 亠 立 音 意 (13)

4. 夜
   _{よる}
   夜 亠 亠 夜 夜 夜 (8)

Lesson 38

1. 階段
段 ［ ˊ ｜ ｝ ｝ ｝ 段 段 (9)

2. 歌手
歌 一 ｧ 可 哥 歌 歌 (14)

3. 不思議
不 一 ｧ 不 不 (4)

4. 音
音 ｧ 立 音 音 (9)

Readings :
手：手，歌手
歌：歌手，歌う
思：思う，不思議
Kanji for recognition：大介

Lesson 39

1. 売る
売 ｧ 声 売 (7)

2. 反動
反 一 厂 反 反 (4)

3. 感心
感 丿 厂 厂 后 咸 咸 感 (13)

4. 美しい
美 ｧ ｧ 羊 羊 羊 美 (9)

5. 後世
世 一 十 廿 廿 世 (5)

6. 文化
文 ｧ ナ 文 (4)
化 亻 亻 化 (4)

Readings :

運：運動，運ぶ
後：後，午後，後世
Kanji for recognition：浮世絵，上野，明治，美術館

Lesson 40

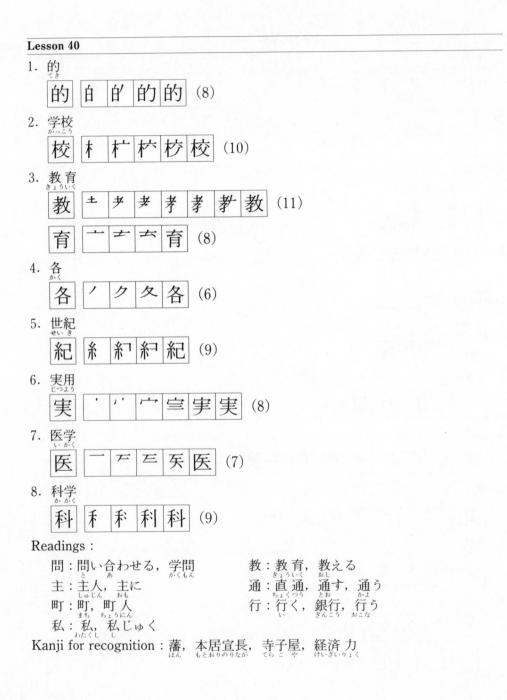

1. 的
   的 自 自 的 的 (8)

2. 学校
   校 木 朾 栌 栌 校 (10)

3. 教育
   教 土 尹 尹 孝 孝 孝 教 (11)
   育 亠 云 云 育 (8)

4. 各
   各 ノ ク 久 各 (6)

5. 世紀
   紀 糸 紅 紅 紀 (9)

6. 実用
   実 丶 丷 宀 宙 実 実 (8)

7. 医学
   医 一 匚 匡 医 医 (7)

8. 科学
   科 禾 禾 科 科 (9)

Readings :

問：問い合わせる，学問　　教：教育，教える
主：主人，主に　　　　　通：直通，通す，通う
町：町，町人　　　　　　行：行く，銀行，行う
私：私，私じゅく
Kanji for recognition：藩，本居宣長，寺子屋，経済力

APPENDIX A: Connective Patterns

The plain adjective and verb forms given in the charts below are used in a number of patterns. Exceptions, which occur only in the case of a **-na** adjective or a noun followed by **da**, are shown in parentheses.

Verbs

	Present		Past	
	aff.	neg.	aff.	neg.
Reg. I	tsukau	tsukawanai	tsukatta	tsukawanakatta
Reg. II	iru	inai	ita	inakatta
Irr.	kuru	konai	kita	konakatta
	suru	shinai	shita	shinakatta

Adjectives, Noun + **desu**

	Present		Past	
	aff.	neg.	aff.	neg.
-i adj.	akai	akaku nai	akakatta	akaku nakatta
-na adj.	(shizuka da)	shizuka dewa/ja nai	shizuka datta	shizuka dewa/ja nakatta
N + **desu**	(N da)	N dewa/ja nai	N datta	N dewa/ja nakatta

1. **To omou/iu/kiku** (lesson 8), **sō desu** ("I hear, They say," lesson 21), **to tsutaeru** (lesson 23)
   These follow the forms in the charts, no exceptions.

2. Nouns (lesson 7), **toki, baai** (lesson 12), **tsumori** (lesson 18), **yō desu** (lesson 21), **hazu** (lesson 22), **wake** (lesson 39)
   -na adjectives and nouns plus **da** are the exceptions.
   -na adj: **shizukana toki/hazu/kōen**
   　　　　　　shizukana yō desu
   Noun: **kodomo no toki/hazu/hon**
   　　　　kodomo no yō desu

3. **Deshō** (lesson 8), **darō** (lesson 13), **kamo shiremasen** (lesson 13), **rashii** (lesson 24), **ni chigainai** (lesson 38)
   -na adjectives and nouns plus **da** are the exceptions. The stem of **-na** adjective and noun come directly before these words.
   -na adj: **shizuka deshō/kamo shirenai/rashii**
   Noun: **kodomo deshō/kamo shirenai/rashii**

4. **No/n desu** (lesson 11), **node** (lesson 13), **noni** (lesson 32)
   -na adjectives and nouns plus **da** are the exceptions.
   -na adj: **shizukana no/n desu**
   　　　　　　shizuka na node/noni
   　　　　　N + **desu**: **kodomo na no/n desu**
   　　　　　　　　　　　kodomo na node/noni

APPENDIX B: The Centipede's Errand

むしの　くにの　とのさまが　おもい　びょうきに　なりました。

「くるしい。くるしい。早く　いしゃを　よんでくれ。」と　言いました。

そこで、むしたちは　あつまって、そうだんしました。

「だれか　足の　はやい　むしは　いませんか。」

「だれが　いいでしょうか。」

「そうだ。百足が　いいと　思いますよ。百足は　足が　100本も　あるから、きっと　はやいでしょう。」と　ひとりが　言いました。

「むかでさん。むかでさん。いしゃを　むかえに　行って、つれてきてくれませんか。早く　してください。」と　百足に　たのみました。

「わかりました。100本の　足で　はしって　いきます。」と　百足は　こたえました。

みんなは　しばらく　まっていましたが、いしゃは　来ません。百足も　かえってきません。

「おかしいねえ。どうしたか　見に　行ってきます。」と　言って、ある　むしが　げんかんまで　行くと、そこに　百足が　いました。

「いしゃは　どこだ。　早く　早く。」と　言うと、

「いま　わらじを　はいている　ところです。これから　いしゃを　むかえに　行ってきます。」と　言いながら、百足は　99足めの　わらじを　はいていました。

Mushi no kuni no tono-sama ga omoi byōki ni narimashita.
"Kurushii, kurushii, hayaku isha o yonde kure," to iimashita.
Sokode, mushi-tachi wa atsumatte, sōdan shimashita.
"Dare ka ashi no hayai mushi wa imasen ka."
"Dare ga ii deshō ka."
"Sō da. Mukade ga ii to omoimasu yo. Mukade wa ashi ga 100-pon mo aru kara, kitto hayai deshō," to hitori ga iimashita.

"Mukade-san, Mukade-san, isha o mukae ni itte, tsurete kite kuremasen ka. Hayaku shite kudasai," to mukade ni tanomimashita.
"Wakarimashita. 100-pon no ashi de hashitte ikimasu," to mukade wa kotaemashita.

Minna wa shibaraku matte imashita ga, isha wa kimasen. Mukade mo kaette kimasen.
"Okashii nē. Dō shita ka mi ni itte kimasu," to itte, aru mushi ga genkan made iku to, soko ni mukade ga imashita.
"Isha wa doko da. Hayaku, hayaku," to iu to, "Ima waraji o haite iru tokoro desu. Kore kara isha o mukae ni itte kimasu," to iinagara, mukade wa 99-soku-me no waraji o haite imashita.

The King of the Kingdom of Insects became seriously ill.

"(Oh), the pain, (oh, the pain), quick! Call the doctor," (he) said.

"(Among us) insects, isn't there someone who's swift of foot?"

"Who'd be good, do you suppose?"

"That's it! The centipede would be good, I think. Since the centipede has (as many as) a hundred legs. Surely he's fast," one (insect) said.

(They asked the centipede, saying, "Mr. Centipede, Mr. Centipede, won't you please (call the doctor and) bring him (here)? Do it quickly, please."

"Of course. I'll go running on (my) hundred legs," the centipede answered.

Everyone waited for some time but the doctor didn't come. Nor did the centipede return.

Saying, "Strange, isn't it. I'll go and see why," one insect went to the entrance hall, and (when he did) there was the centipede.

When (the insect) said, "Where's the doctor? Quick! Quick!" the centipede, while saying "(I'm) now putting on my straw sandals. Then I'll go get the doctor," put on the ninety-ninth sandal.

Vocabulary

とのさま	**tono-sama**, lord
くるしい	**kurushii**, painful, suffocating, difficult, awkward
いしゃをよぶ	**isha o yobu**, send for the doctor
～でくれ	**-de kure** (see lesson 36)
くれ	**kure** (plain imperative of **kureru**)
そこで	**sokode**, thereupon
あしの　はやい	**ashi no hayai**, swift of foot
そうだ	**sō da**, That's it!
むかで	**mukade**, centipede
はしっていく	**hashitte iku**, go running
こたえる	**kotaeru**, answer
ある	**aru**, one, a certain
わらじ	**waraji**, straw sandals
はいている　と ころです	**haite iru tokoro desu**, (just) now putting on (see Lesson 38)
99そくめ	**99-soku-me**, the ninety-ninth
そく	**-soku**, (*lit.*) pair (shoes, socks, etc; counter)
め	**-me**, (suffix added to numbers and counters to make ordinal numbers)

(The title of this story is a direct translation of the Japanese **Mukade no O-tsukai**, the word **(o-) tsukai** meaning "errand," "mission.")

APPENDIX C: Verb Chart

Form	Reg. I Verbs			
-nai	**kikanai**	**morawanai**	**erabanai**	**osanai**
-masu	**kikimasu**	**moraimasu**	**erabimasu**	**oshimasu**
dict.	**kiku**	**morau**	**erabu**	**osu**
conditional	**kikeba**	**moraeba**	**erabeba**	**oseba**
volitional	**kikō**	**moraō**	**erabō**	**osō**
-te	**kiite**	**moratte**	**erande**	**oshite**
-ta	**kiita**	**moratta**	**eranda**	**oshita**

Form	Reg. II Verbs		Irreg. Verbs	
-nai	**wasurenai**	**orinai**	**konai**	**shinai**
-masu	**wasuremasu**	**orimasu**	**kimasu**	**shimasu**
dict.	**wasureru**	**oriru**	**kuru**	**suru**
conditioal	**wasurereba**	**orireba**	**kureba**	**sureba**
volitional	**wasureyō**	**oriyō**	**koyō**	**shiyō**
-te	**wasurete**	**orite**	**kite**	**shite**
-ta	**wasureta**	**orita**	**kita**	**shita**

330

GLOSSARY

ā, Ah! 27
abiru, bathe, pour, 31
abunai, dangerous, 85
abura, oil, grease, 15
agaru, *(lit.)* be derived/attained, 280
agaru, be raised, rise, 240
ageru, raise, 240
aida ni, while, 271
ainiku, unfortunately, 252
aisatsu, civility, greeting, address, 34
aite, partner, other party, opponent; *aite o suru*, deal with, wait on, 276
aitsu, that guy, he, 277
aji, taste, flavor, 165
aka(i), red, crimson, scarlet, 44, 154
akambō, baby, 219
akarui, bright, 44
akirameru, give up, be resigned, 141
aku, be vacant, be empty, (be) open, 89
amai, sweet, indulgent, 203
-amari, over, 302
ame, rain, 44
ammari, not very, 135
anaunsu, announcement, 105
annai, guidance, 27; *annai-sho*, guidebook, handbook, 180
anō, er, 27
anshin, peace of mind; *anshin suru*, relax, 34
anzen(na), safe, 85
apāto, apartment, apartment house, 67
ara, Oh!, 71
arashi, storm, 44
arau, wash, 31
arawasu, show, express, 153
aru, one, a certain, 328
ashi, foot, leg, 52
ashisutanto, assistant, 110
asobu, play, 31
ataru, win, hit the mark, strike, 203
atashi, I, 286
atatakai, warm, 56
ato, rest, remainder, more, 48
atsumaru, be collected, get together, 240
atsumeru, gather, collect, assemble, 110, 215
awateru, be flustered, confused, panic, 276
ayamari, mistake, 223
azukarijo, checkroom, 119
azukaru, take care of, keep, 97
azukeru, deposit, entrust, 110

baai, *(in) case, occasion, circumstance*, 89

bāgen, bargain sale, 188
bakari de naku, not only, 302
-bamme (counter for ordinal number), 19
-bansen (counter for tracks), 68
bara, rose, 93
baransu, balancing, balance, 207
basho, place, seat, scene, 244
bekkyo, separation; *bekkyo suru*, live separately, 267
bentō, (box) lunch, 188
betsu(na)/no, some other (thing); extra, distinctive, 48, 89
bijutsu, art; *bijutsukan*, art museum, 295
-biki (hiki), discount, 188
bikkuri suru, be surprised, 110
bimbō(na), poor, 44
bitamin, vitamin, 101
bōeki, trade, 79
boku, I, 45
bōnen-kai, year-end (forget-the-year) party, 276
bonsai, dwarf tree, 240
bōru pen, ball-point pen, 93
bōshi, hat, cap, 165
botan, button, 126
bu, department, division, 40; *buchō*, department head, division chief, 21
-bu, copy (counter), 200
bujutsu, military arts, 302
bukka, (commodity) prices, 212
bumpō, grammar, 291
bushi, warrior, 302
-byō, second (counter), 149
byōdō ni, equally, 160
byōki, sickness, 44

chairo, brown, 24
channeru, channel, 130
chansu, chance, 160
chanto, regularly, correctly, perfectly, 248
chikazuku, approach, 153
chiketto, ticket, 176
chikyū, earth, globe; *chikyū-jō*, earth's surface, 15, 207
chirigaku, geography, 302
chittomo . . . (ja) nai, not at all, 160
chīzu, cheese, 220
chōdo, just, 286
chokin, savings, deposit; *chokin suru*, save (money), 118
chokorēto, chocolate, 97
chokusetsu, directly, straitforwardly, 244

chokutsū, direct communication, through service, 176

chōkyori denwa, long-distance call; *chōkyori*, long distance, 226

chōnin, townspeople, 302

chōshi, condition, 227

chūgakkō, middle school, 23

chūi, care, attention, warning; *chūi suru*, take care, pay attention, 280

-*chū*/-*jū*, all over, throughout, 19, 180

-*chū*/-*jū ni*, within, 19

chūjun, second third of month, 153

chū-ka-ryōri, Chinese cooking, 51

chūkei, relay, 130

chūmon, order; *chūmon suru*, order, 101, 200

chūshi, discontinuance, interruption; *chūshi (suru)*, be, called off, call off, 94

chūshin, center, core; *chūshin to suru*, be centered on, 302

chūshoku, lunch, 55

dai- (prefix for ordinal number), 71

-*dai*, charge, fee, 188

daibu, greatly, considerably, 230

daibubun, most, greater part, majority, 215

daigaku, university, college, 44; *daigakusei*, college student, 160

daihyō, representation; *daihyō suru*, typify, represent, 153

daiji(na), critical, important; *daiji ni suru*, value highly, take good care of, 101, 295

daijin, minister (of state), 67

daijōbu(na), all right, safe, 82

daikin, money, charge, fee, 176

daimyō, daimyo (feudal lord), 215

dainingu kitchin, dining room-kitchen, 192

daitai, almost around, generally, 153

daitōryō, president, 37

daiyamondo, diamond, 118

dake, all there is, no more than, 244

dambō, heating, 212

dandan, gradually, step by step, 212

dansei, male, man, 97

dansu, dance, dancing, 134

dare demo, anyone, everyone, someone, 145

dare ka, someone, anyone, 55

darui, logy, tired, dull, 101

dasu, mail; pay, invest; serve; put out, 44, 173, 200, 203

-*date*, story, storied, 244

de, because, 169

dekakeru, go out, 31

dekiagaru, be finished, ready, done, 122

dekigoto, happening, affair, 149

demo, any, 27

demo, demonstration, 259

demo, let's say, for example, 105

demo, though, 12

dempyō, bill, (sales) check, voucher, 276

dengon, message, 180

dentō, tradition, 295

denwa-chū, on the phone, 180

denwa ga kakaru/kakatte kuru, get a phone call; *denwa o kakeru*, telephone, 19, 240

denwa ga tōi, I can't hear (you), 110

denwa ni deru, answer the phone, 298

deru, graduate, leave; attend; come out; *dete kuru*, come out, appear, 44, 67, 126

deshi, student, follower, disciple, 302

deshō, may, can possibly be, 97

desukara, therefore (same as *dakara*), 153

dēto, date, 138

dezain, design; *dezainā*, designer, 141, 265

disuko, disco, 286

dō, what, 101

dochira, which; *dochira-sama*, who, 27; *dochira demo*, either, 14, 71

dōgu, implement, machine, appliance, tool, 59

dohyō, (sumō) ring, 105

dō iu, what role, what kind of, 105

dōka, if, whether, 192

dōka suru, something is wrong, 52

dokoka, some-/anyplace; *dokka = dokoka*, 126, 135

dokushin, single, 165

dōmo, somehow, 227

dondon, one after the other, steadily, rapidly, 295

dore demo, any(thing), 27

dorian, durian, 37

dorobō, thief, 219

dōro, route, road, street, highway, 207

dōryō, coworker, 97

doryoku, effort; *doryoku suru*, make an effort, do one's best, 248

dotchi = dochira, 15

Edo jidai, Edo period, 79

e-hagaki, picture postcard, 240

eigakan, movie theater, 31

eigyō, sales, marketing, business; *eigyō-bu*, sales/marketing department, 165

eikaiwa, spoken English, 85

eisei chūkei, satellite relay (broadcast); *eisei*, satellite, 131

ekiin, station employee, 19

empitsu, pencil, 75

enjinia, engineer, 240

enryo, reserve, restraint, diffidence; *enryo naku*, without, hesitation/reserve, 101

ensō, performance, recital; *ensō suru*, perform, 130

erabu, choose, 59, 145

erai, important, illustrious, eminent, 105

erebētā, elevator, 173

ēto, let me see, 110

fairu, file, 276

fakushimiri/fakkusu, facsimile/fax, 15, 45

ferī, ferry, 118

fu-, negating prefix, 71
fuben(na), inconvenient, 110
fudan(wa), ordinarily, 130
fude, brush, 131
fudōsan-ya, realty dealer, 192
fueru, proliferate, icrease, 79
fūfu-genka, marital disagreement; *fūfu*, husband and wife, 59
fu-gōkoku, failure, 71
fujin, Mrs., lady, woman, 101
fukisoku(na), irregular, 298
fuku, clothes, 188
fukuro, bag, 19
fukusō, (style of) dress, 160
fukuzatsu(na), complicated, 23
fumu, step on, trample, 126
fune, ship, boat, 165
fun'iki, air, atmosphere, ambience, 160
funin-saki, place of appointment; *funin suru*, proceed to a post, 188, 230
furikomu, transfer, 71
furo, bath; *furo ni hairu*, take a bath, 291
furu, fall, 56
fushigi(na), uncanny, strange, weird, 286
futon, bedding, mattress, quilt, 149
futoru, get fat, gain weight, 280
futsū, usual, 230
fuyu, winter, 42

gaido, guide, 215
gaikōkan, diplomat, 67
gaikoku-go, foreign language, 149
gaikokujin/gaijin, foreigner, 145, 160
gaishi, foreign capital; *gaishi-kei*, foreign capital affiliation, 160
gaishutsu, going out, outing; *gaishutsu suru*, go/be out; *gaishutsu-chū*, is out, 176
gakumon, studies, learning, 302
gakusha, scholar, savant, 165
gan, cancer, 126
ganko(na), stubborn, 23
garasu, glass, 196
gāru furendo, girl friend, 97
gasu, gas; *gasu-dai*, gas bill, 203
-gata, -shaped, 200
gawa, side, 122
geki, drama; *gekijō*, theater, playhouse, 131, 165
genkin, cash, 24; *genkin kakitome*, registered cash, 71
genkō, manuscript, 110
genseirin, virgin forest, 207
genzai, (as of) now, presently, 235
gijutsu, technology, technique, skill, 23
girichoko, *giri* chocolate; *giri*, (sense of obligation), 97
gitā, guitar, 188
go-chisō, treat, banquet, entertainment; *go-chisō shimasu*, treat; *go-chisō ni narimasu*, be treated/entertained, 16
gojitsu, later date, another day, 169

gōkaku, success, eligibility; *gōkaku suru*, pass, succeed, 71
gomen-nasai, I'm sorry, Excuse me, 71, 286
gomi, rubbish, 75
gozaimasu (polite = *arimasu*), 89
guai, condition, 23
gurīn, green, 165
gyōji, event, 220
gyōji, referee, 105
gyōsha, businessman, supplier, trader, 122

hā, yes, 169
hade(na), flashy, gorgeous, 101
hagemasu, encourage; *hagemasu-kai*, encouragement party, 291
haha, ha ha, 97
haitte iru, contian, include, 24
hajimaru, start, 42
hajime (no), beginning, first, 154
hajimete, for the first time, 12
haken, dispatch; *haken sareru*, be sent, 267
hakkiri, clearly, exactly; *hakkiri suru*, be/become clear, get better, 126
hakobu, carry, 59, 141
-haku/-paku, night (counter), 89
haku, put on, wear (shoes, pants, etc.), 134
hambun, half, 220
han, fief, domain; *hankō*, fief school, 302
hanami, flower viewing, 153
hanarete, apart, separately from, 230
hanasu, talk, speak, tell, 16
hanataba, bouquet, 44
handō, reaction, 295
handobaggu, handbag, 248
hanko, seal, 75
hansamu(na), handsome, 44
hantai, opposite, reverse; *hantai-gawa*, opposite side, 122
happyō, announcement; *happyō suru*, make an announcement, 40
harau, pay, 44
hare, fair, clear, 101
hareru, clear up, 139
haru, spring, 126
hashi, bridge, 196
hashi, chopstick; *hashioki*, chopstick rest, 184
hashiru, run, 149
hataraku, work, 15
-hatsu, departure, 68
hatsugen, view, observation, utterance; *hatsugen-ken*, right to, views, 105
hattatsu, development, growth, advancement; *hattatsu suru*, develop, progress, 302
hatten, development, growth, expansion, 230
hayai, fast, early; *hayame-ni*, early, earlier than usual; 12, 23, 55
hayasugiru, too early, 200
hazu(da), have to, should, 169
hē, oh, 12
hei, wall, fence, 130

heikin, average, 154
hen, neighborhood, vicinity, 119
henji, reply, 101
hen(na), strange, weird, 291
heru, diminish, decrease, 207
heta(na), poor, unskillful, 130
heya-dai, room charge, rent, 188
hi, fire, 188
hidoi, terrible, harsh, severe, 291
higaeri, one-day, go and return the same day, 230
hijō-guchi, emergency exit, 150
hikari, light, ray, 118
hikkosu, move, *hikkoshi*, moving; 44, 67
hikōshi, aviator, 44
hiku, catch; pull; consult, 101, 126, 134
hiku, deduct, discount, subtract, 169
hiku, play, 188
hiraku, hold, 229
hirogeru, (lie) open, spread, unfold, 271
hiroi, spacious, wide; *hirosa*, area, 21, 192
hirou, find, pick up, 24
hiruma, daytime, 110
hisashiburi ni, after/for a long time, 230
hito-bito, people, 153
hitoyasumi, (short) rest, 204
hitsuyō(na), necessary, 67
hizashi, sunlight, 283
hō, oh, 267
hō, side, direction, 12
hodo, about, 230
hodo . . . nai, not so . . . as, 12
hogo, preservation, protection, 207
hōmen, district, direction, 230
homeru, praise, 219
hōmon, visit, 160
honnin, the person himself, said person, 223
honsha, head office, main company, 79
hontō (no), real, 105
hon'yaku, translation; *hon'yaku suru*, translate, 212
hora, look!, there!, 105
hōritsu, law, 37
hoshii, want, desire, 59, 207
hotaru, firefly, 79
hotondo, almost, almost all, 131
hozon, preservation, maintenance; *hozon suru*, take care of, preserve, 295
hyōban, reputation, 160

i, stomach, 298
ichiban, most, number one, 12
ichiji, temporary, (at) one time, 119
igaku, medicine, 302
iin, committee member, 105
ijō, more than, 63
ikebana, flower arranging, 31
iken, opinion, suggestion, 298
-iki, going to, bound for, 68
ikka, family, household, 130

ikō, views, 40
ikutsu, several, many, any number, 126
ima no uchi ni, rightaway, before it is too late; *ima sugu*, at once, 48, 51
imi, meaning, 145
insatsu (no), printing, printed, 131
inshō, impression, 298
inu, dog, 130
ippai, full, 119
ippan (no), general, widespread; *ippan-teki(na)*, general, 160
ippō, (on the) other hand, (on) one hand/side, 302
irai, request, commission, 122
ireru, put in, insert; make (coffe, tea, etc.), 126, 204
iroha kaede, a species of maple, 154
irori, hearth, 215
iru, attain, 27
iru, need, 68
isan, heritage, property, legacy, 295
isha, doctor, 328
isogu, hurry, 31
isshō-kemmei, eagerly, as hard as one can, 283
itadaku, accept, receive (politer than morau), 101, 227, 235
itasu, do (humble for suru), 169
iten, move, moving; *iten suru*, move, 192
itsu demo, any-/sometime, 94
itsu ka, some/any time, 126
itsumo, always, 40
ittai, what on earth, 259
itte mairimasu, bye-bye, 71
itte rasshai, bye-bye, 71
iwai, congratulation, celebration, 138
iwau, celebrate, congratulate, 93
iya, horrible, disagreeable, nasty, unwelcome, 135
izen (wa), previously, 230

jajji, judge, 105
jama, hinderance, barrier, inconvenience; *jama suru*, bother, interfere, 271
ji, (hand)writing, character, letter, 130
jibun, oneself; *jibun de*, by oneself, 59
jidai, period; *jidai-geki*, period drama, 79, 131
jidōsha, automobile, 173
-ji-gata, shape of character, 200
jigyō, business, enterprise, operations, 240
jiin, temple, 302
jijō, situation, 169
jikaku, awareness, self-knowledge; *jikaku suru*, be consicous of, 207
jikkō, practice, action, implementation; *jikkō suru*, carry out, execute, 276
jiko, accident, 118, 261
jikoku-hyō, timetable, 180
jimbō, popularity, reputation, 298
jimbutsu, person, charactter, figure, 160
jimoto (no), locality, local, 207

jimu-shitsu, clerks' office, 19
jimusho, office, 55
jinji, personnel matters, 40
jinkō, population, 15
jishin, earthquake, 165
jisoku, speed per hour, 196
jitensha, bicycle, 149
jitsuwa, as a matter of fact, 97
jitsuyō-teki(na), practical, 302
jō, upper (part), 207
-jō, letter, 85
-jō, (counter for tatami), 196
jōdan, joke, 110
jōhō, information, 240
jōjun, first third of month, 153
jōkyaku, passenger, 12
josei, woman, female, 97
jōshi, superior, 97
jōtai, condition, state of affairs, 295
-jū, throughout, 19, 27, 118
jūdō, judo, 37
jugaku, Confucianism, 302
jugyō, instruction; *jugyō-ryo*, tuition, 71
juken, undergoing examination; *juken suru*, take an examination, 71
jumbi, preparations (preliminary) arrangements, 200
jūtai, congestion, 63

ka, section, 40
ka, or, 48
ka, Tuesday, 31
-ka, lesson (counter), 101
kaban, bag, briefcase, suitcase, 23
kabin, vase, 44
kaburu, wear, put on (headgear), 165
kachō, section chief, 60
kādo, (credit) card, 75
ka dō ka, whether (or not), 176
kaeru, change, 40
kaesu, give back, repay, 248
kaette, on the contrary, 207
kagaku, science, 302
kagami, mirror, 31
kagi o shimeru, lock, 248
kago, cage, basket, 79
-kai, party, meeting; *kaihi*, dues, membership fee; 291
kaiin, club/socity member, 114, 291
kaidan, steps, stairs, 286
kaigai, abroad, foreign countries, 169
kaigi-chū, in conference/a meeting, 180
kaihatsu, development, 207
kaijō, meeting place, 235
kaika-bi, day of blooming, 154
kaikai, opening; *kaikai-shiki*, opening ceremony, 291
kaiketsu, solution, decision; *kaiketsu suru*, solve, settle, 126
kaikyū, class, caste, 302

kaitsū, opening to traffic; *kaitsū suru*, go into operation, be opened to traffic, 230
kaiwa, conversation, 85
kaji, fire, 150
kakari/-gakari, person in charge, 89
kakeru, call; wear, put on; multiply; impose, 19, 91, 196, 262
kaki, persimmon, 252
kakinaosu, rewrite, redraft, 203, 282
kakitome, registered mail, 71
kakkō, appearance, dress; *kakko ii*, great, cool, super, 286, 291
kakkō o shite iru, be dressed, 286
kaku, each, 302
kakuchi, all over, various districts, 130
kakumei, revolution, 173
kakunin, confirmation; *kakunin o suru*, confirm, 235
kakuritsu, establishment, settlement; *kakuritsu suru*, establish, settle, 302
kami, hair, 23
kami, paper, 19
kamo shiremasen, may be, 97
-kan, building, 31
-kan, between, among, 230
kanarazu, be sure to, certainly, 89
kanari, considerably, fairly, 230
kanashii, sad, pathetic, unhappy, 298
kangaeru, think, consider, 31
kangofu(-san), nurse, 67
kankei, connected with, related; *kankei-sha*, person concerned, 40
kankō, sightseeing, 207
kanojo, she, 85
kanshin suru, be impressed, 295
kantan(na), simple, 44
kantoku, director, supervisor, 298
kaoiro, complexion, 47
kara, after, 40
karada, body, health, 85, 86
kara . . . ni kakete, from . . . to, 153
karai, salty, hot, 203
karappo, empty, 134
kare, he, 59
karē, curry, 291
kareru, wither, die, 276
kari/-gari, excursion, hunting, 154
kariru, borrow, rent, 141, 145
karui, light, 67
kasetto tēpu, cassette tape, 12
kashikomarimashita, certainly, 89
kashira, I wonder (informal female speech), 184
kashi-ya, confectioner, confectionary, 97
kashu, singer, 286
kasu, lend, 60
kata, shoulder, 203
kata, person, 118
-kata, way, how to, 40
katachi, shape, form, appearance, 165
katamukeru, lean, tilt, slant, 207

katazukeru, put away, tidy up, 60
kau, buy, 44
kau, keep, raise (not children), 192
kawa, leather, 24
kawa, river, creek, stream, 79
kawaii, cute, 212
kawaku, become dry, 298
kawari ni, in place of, 255
kawaru, change, 67
kayou, attend, go to and from, commute, 302
kaze, cold, 47
kaze, wind, 134
kazu, number, 212
kedo, but, however, 145
kega, injury, wound; *kega o suru*, (be) hurt, 52
-kei, origin, lineage, system, 160
keiei administration, management; *keiei-gaku*, business administration, 141
keikaku, plan, project, 44; *keikaku-sho*, plan (in writing), 240
keikō, trend, tendency, 160
keisan, calculation, accounts; *keisan suru*, calculate, compute, 276
keisanki, calculator, computer, 276
keisatsu, police, 49
keiyaku, contract; *keiyaku-sho*, contract (written), 93, 203
keizai-ryoku, economic strength, 302
kekka, result, 67
kekkō, fine, 71
kekkō suru, not flying/sailing, suspension of service, 169
kembutsu, sight-seeing, visit; *kembutsu suru*, sight-see, 79
ken, ticket, 63
ken, about, concerning, 94
-ken, power, authority, right, 105
kengen, judgmental authority, 105
kenka, quarrel, fight, 59
kenkō, health, 51
kenkyū, research, study, 67
kensa, inspection, examination, test, 267
kenshū, (in-service) training, *kenshū suru*, study, train, 82
keredo, but, however, 145
kesa, this morning, 12
keshigomu, eraser, 93
kettei, decision, conclusion; *kettei-ken*, decisive say/authority, 107
ki, feeing, 27; *ki ni irimashita*, was/is satisfactory, 27; *ki ga suru*, feel think, 291; *ki ga tsuku*, notice, realize, 292
kichin-to, neatly, accurately, 298
kichō(na), rare, valuabl, 145
kieru, go out, be extinguished, put out, 126
kifu, donation, contribution; *kifu suru*, donate, contribute, 118
kigen, deadline, 76
kigen, mood, humor, 226

ki-gi, trees, 154
kiiro, yellow, 154
kiji, article, 276
kijun, criterion, standard, 160
kikai, equipment, *(lit.)* machine, 200
kikaku, planning, plan, 149
kikan, system, 12
kikoeru, can hear, be audible, 105
kimari, rule, decision, 169
kimeru, decide, 40
kimi, you, 135
kimmu, service, duty; *kimmu suru*, work, serve, 265
kimochi, feeling; *kimochi ga ii*, comfortable, 131
kinen, commemoration; *kinenhin*, memento, souvenir, 235
kin'en, no smoking, 76
kinjo, neighborhood, 110
kinko, strong box, safe, vault, 134
kinu, silk, 44
kion, (air) temperature, 154
kirai, dislike, unlike, 101
kiritoru, cut out/off, tear off, amputate, 276
kiro(mētoru), kilo(meter), 196
kiru, cut, 59
kiru, wear, put on, 37
kisei, homecoming, 63
kisetsu, season, 154
kishu, type of machine, 40
kita, north, 15
kitanai, dirty, 248
kitto, sure(ly), 40
-kō, port, 79
-kō, (counter for schools), 302
kōchi, coach, 27
koe, voice, 59
kōhai, junior, younger, 197
kōhan, latter half, 302
kōhī shoppu, coffee shop, 200
koibito, sweetheart, 118
koin rokkā, pay locker, 119
kōji, construction work, 122
kōjō, factory, 130
kōka, effect, efficiency, 280
kōkai, regret, repentance; *kōkai suru*, be sorry, regret, 207
kokoro, heart, mind, 118
kokugaku, Japanese classics, 302
kokugo, Japanese, national language, mother tongue, 277
kokunai, inside the country, domestic, *(lit.)*, interior, 232
kokuritsu, national, 71
kokusaiteki(na), international (like), 79
komaru, be inconvenienced, troubled, embarrassed, 94
kome, (uncooked) rice, 215
kompyūtā, computer, 82
kon, dark blue, navy, 160

kondo, next (time), 31

konjō, fighting spirit, willpower, disposition, 160

konogoro, these days, recently, 165

kono hen, around here, this vicinity, 119

kono yō ni, thus, in this way, 154

konsāto, concert, 176

kon'yaku, engagement; *kon'yaku suru*, become engaged, 85

kopīraitā, copywriter, 220

korekara, from now (on), 52

koro, time, 34

korobu, fall down, 52

kōsei, coming/later age, 295

kosei, individuality; *kosei-teki(na)*, original, individual, 160

koshi, lower back, waist, hips, 203

kōshō, negotiation; *kōshō suru*, bargain, negotiate, 184

koshō, breakdown, trouble; *koshō suru*, break down, be out of order, 196

koso, indeed, 252

kotae, answer; *kotae ga deru*, get an answer; *kotaeru*, answer, 110, 328

koto, matter, fact, 82

koto ni suru, decide; *koto ni naru*, be decided, 265

koto ga aru, had the experience of, 34

koto ga dekiru, can, 27

kōto, coat, 42

kotoba, word, 153

kotonaru, differ, be different, 154

kotozuke, message, 176

kōtsū, transportation, 12

kowai, scary, fearful, terrible, 188

kowareru, be broken, 248

kowasu, break, 217

kōyō, autumn (*lit.* red) leaves; *kōyō-bi*, day the leaves turn, 153, 154

kōza, account, 176

kōza, course, lecture, 267

kozutsumi, small parcel, 283

kubaru, distribute, 118

kubi, neck; *kubi ni naru*, get/be fired, 267

kudoi, tedious, wordy, garrulous, 134

kuji, lottery, 131

kumori, cloudy, 130

-kun, Mr.,Master, 47

kuni, home town, birthplace, country, 63

kūrā, air conditioner, 75

kurabu, club, 26

-kurai = -gurai, 192

kurasu, class, 31

kurikaesu, repeat, 220

kuro, black(ness), 19

kurushii, painful, suffocating, difficult, 328

kusai, smelly, 134

kusaru, rot, go bad, corrupt, 276

kuwashii, detailed, precise; *kuwashiku*, in detail, 19

kyanseru chāji, cancellation charge, 169

kyō, faith, 219

kyoīku, education, 283, 302

kyōju, professor, 165

kyōkasho, textbook, 240

kyōmi, interest; *kyōmi ga aru*, be interested in, 79

kyōshitsu, class room, 75

kyōsō, competition, contest, race, 283

kyū ni, suddenly, 85

kyūjitsu, holiday, 230

kyūka, vacation, time off, 276

kyūkyūsha, ambulance, 173

kyūryō, salary, 126

mā, ah, oh, my; well, 101

machiawase, meeting (by appointment), waiting, 259

machigaeru, mistake, 180

machigai, mistake, 223

mado-guchi, window, clerk, 68

mafurā, scarf, 19

mairu, go, come, 255

mairu, mile, 196

maitoshi, every year, 130

majime(na), serious, diligent, 23

makoto ni, really, 169

mama, as it is/was, 271

mamoru, keep, obey, 59

manabu, learn, study, 283

man-, full; *man'in*, full of people, 105

maneku, invite, 251

maniau, be in/on time, 127

mannenhitsu, fountain pen, 240

manshon, apartment building, 244

marude . . . mitai, (be/look) like, 286

mashīn, machine, 27

matomaru, brought together, be in order; conclude, 40, 67

matsujitsu, last day, 76

mawari ni, around, 105

mawaru, tour, go round, 34

mayou, be lost, be puzzled, 291

mazu, before anything (else), 40

mazui, awkward, unsavory, 40

me, eye; *me ga sameru*, wake up; *me o tōsu*, look over, 173

Meiji jidai, Meiji period, 295

meijiru, order, 229

-mei(-sama) (counter for people), 89

meiwaku, trouble, inconvenience, 126

memo, memorandum, 271

mendō(na), troublesome, annoying, (a) nuisance; *mendō o kakeru*, cause (a person) trouble, 110, 262

mensetsu, interview, 93

meshiagaru, eat (or drink), 251

mētoru, meter, 149

metta ni . . . nai, almost never, rarely, 215

mezurashii, rare, unusual, 126

miai, meeting and looking over, 267

michi, road, street; *michi ni mayou*, lose one's way, 12, 23, 291

midori, green, 68

mieru, can see, be visible, 105

migaku, brush, polish, 31

mihon, sample, 255

mijikai, short, 59

mimi, ear; *mimi o katamukeru*, listen, give ear to, 207

mimai, gift (to a sick person), expression of sympathy, 240

minami, south, 79

minato, port, harbor, 93

miowaru, finish looking at, 200

miso shiru, miso soup, 44

misu, mistake, 261

-mitai(na), resembling, like, a sort of, 244

mītingu, meeting, 291

mitomeru, appreciate, recognize, 295

mitsukaru, be found, find, 248

mitsumori, estimate, quotation; *mitsumori-sho*, estimate (written), 181

mizuumi, lake, 134

mo, as many/much as, 130

mō, now, 212

mō, the other, another, 184

mochiron, of course, 145

modoru, come/go/be back, 173

mōfu, blanket, 149

moku, Thursday, 31

momiji, maple; *momiji-gari*, maple leaf excursion, 154

mo . . . mo . . . , both . . . and, 12

mō . . . nai, any/no more, any/no longer, 63

mondai, problem, 23,

mono, goods, wear, thing, 27, 42

moppara, nothing but, solely, 280

moshi, if, 114

mōshikomu, apply; *mōshikomi*, application, 59

moshiwake arimasen, There's no excuse; *moshiwake*, excuse, apology, 47

motomeru, look for, want, seek, 160

motsu, have, hold, 31

mottainai, waste(ful), 207

motto = -er, more, less, 48

moyō, pattern, design, 19

mugi, barley, wheat, oats, rye, 219

mukaeru, meet, greet, 55

mukashi(no), old, 118

mukau, go, face, confront, 244

mune, chest, 19

muri na, out of the question, unreasonable; muri o suru, be unnatural, 48, 169

mushi, cricket, insect, 110

myūjikaru, musical, 67

na, name, 302

na = don't, 271

nado, and so forth; *nado no*, such as, 153

nagai, long, 23

nagame, view, 79

naifu, knife, 196

naiyō, contents, details, 226

naka-goro, around the middle, 63

nakami, contents, 19

nakanaka, quite, 33; *nakanaka . . . nai*, not any/at all, 47

naki-goe, cry, 110

naku, cry, 196

nakunaru, pass away, be lost/missing, disappear, 85

nakusu, lose, 261

namakemono, lasybones, 23

nambu, southern part, 154

nan to itte mo, undoubtedly,153

nande, why, 298

nan-do/kai mo, many times, 226

nanika, some-/any(thing), 122

nanka, like, such as, and so on, 192

nansatsu, a few/any/several volumes, 126

naoru, get better, be fixed, 51

naosu, correct, get well, improve, 31

nara, if, 114

naraberu, arrange, 200

narabu, be lined up, 150

narau, learn, 23

nareru, get used to, 94

naru, become, 40

naru, ring, 134

narubeku, as . . . as possible, 169

naruhodo, I see, 63

nattō, fermented soybeans, 134

nattoku, understanding, consent, 105

nawatobi, jumping rope, 280

naze, why, 82

nē, say!, 286

nebō, oversleeping, late riser; *nebō suru*, oversleep, sleep late, 212

nedan, price, 186

negi, onion (also leek), 203

nemmatsu, end of the year, 122

nemui, sleepy, 118

nemuru, sleep, 126

nenga hagaki, New Year's card, 204

neru, sleep, go to bed, 31

nesshin(na), enthusiastic, zealous, attentive, 207

nezumi, rat, mouse, 219

ni chigainai, must (be), 286

niau, suit, match (well), 188

nigai, bitter, 134

nigate, difficult, poor at, 145

nigeru, escape, 150

(ni) kanshite wa, concerning, 40

nikkōyoku, sunbathing, sunbath; *nikkōyoku o suru*, sunbathe, 141

-nikui, difficult, awkward, 130

ni kyōmi ga aru, be interested in, 79

nimotsu, baggage, cargo, 44

ninki, popularity, 160

ninzū, number of people; *ninzū -bun,* (portion/
  sets) for, number of people, 200

nioi, smell, odor; *nioi ga suru,* smell, 291

ni suru, decide, make/do (it), 40, 184

ni tomonatte, with, accompanying, 230

ni yoru to, according to; *ni yotte,* depending on,
  160, 165

no aida de, among, between, 160

nobasu, extend, stretch, postpone, 169

nobiru, extend, 153

noboru, climb, 37

nochi(hodo), later, 130, 227

node, since, because, 97

nodo ga kawaku, be/get thirsty, 298

no hō ga, = -er/more/less, 12

no hoka ni, in addition to, 153

nokoru, be left, remain, linger, 141

nombiri suru, take it easy, 135

nōmin, farmer, 215

no naka de, of all, among, 12

no ni, even though, 259

nōryoku, ability, 160

norikaeru, transfer, 196

nōto, note, 283

no uchi, among, 302

nōyaku, agricultural chemical, 79

nugu, take off, 31

nyūgaku, matriculation; *nyūgaku kin,* matrucula-
  tion fee, 71

ōbī, OB (old boy), 105

oboeru, remember, memorize, 75

ochiru, drop, fall, 24

o-daiji ni, Take care of yourself, 48

ōdōri, main street, 24

odoroku, be surprised; *odoroki,* wonder, surprise, fright, 110, 295

odoru, dance, 59

ofisu, office, 267

ōi, many, much; *ōi ni,* considerably, greatly, 15,
  230

okagesama de, Thank you for asking, 232, 286

okāsama, (your) mother, 85

okashii, strange, funny, 138

okiru, get up; happen, occur, 23, 101

okonau, hold, carry out, 219, 276

okori, origin, 302

okoru, be/get angry, 196

okosu, cause, 118

oku, put, set up, 37

okureru, be late, 93

okuri-mono, gift, 97

okuru, give, 118

okuru, take, see/send off, escort, 126

oku-sama, (your) wife, 79

omedetō, congratulations, 267

o-me ni kakaru, meet (humble for *au*), 265

ō-misoka, last day of year, 130

o-miyage, souvenir, 93

omoi, heavy, serious, 15

omo-ni, mainly, 302

omote, front, face, surface, 122

omou, think, 63

onaji, same, 97

onsui, warm water, 27; *onsui pūru,* heated
  (swimming) pool, 27

o-sewa, help, kindness, good offices, 97

oshaberi, chatterobox, 23; *oshaberi suru,* chat,
  59

oshikomu, squeeze, 12

osoreirimasu, Excuse me, be sorry, 89

ossharu, say, 252

o-tetsudai-san, maid, 240

o-todoke-saki, consignee, destination, 138

oto, sound, 110; *oto ga suru,* make a sound, hear
  a sound, 110, 286

ōtobai, motorcycle, 149

otonashii, gentle, quiet, good-tempered, tame,
  298

otona, adult, 68

otosu, lose, drop, 24

ototoshi, year before last, 82

o-tsukai, errand, mission, 240

otto, husband, 165

oya, parent, 203

ōya-san, landlord, owner, 192

oyogu, swim, 27

ōyuki, heavy snow(fall), 173

ōzei, hordes of people, 63

pairotto, pilot, 134

pāsento, percent, 169

pasupōto, passport, 75

pedaru, pedal, 126

piano, piano, 85; *pianisuto,* pianist, 44, 85

pīku, peak, 12

posuto, position, post, 126, 188

potāju, potage, soup, 101

purezento, present, 97

puroguramu, program, 286

purojekuto, project, 48

pūru, pool, 26

rabu retā, love letter, 97

raikyaku, guest; *raikyaku-chū,* (busy) with a
  guest, 180

raku(na), easy, comfortable, 188

rashii, seems to be, 184

rasshu, rush; *rasshuawā,* rush hour, 63, 131

rebā, lever, 126

rei, gratitude, courtesty, reward; *reikin,* appreciation money, 192, 240

reizōko, refrigerator, 240

ren'ai (kekkon), love (marriage), 267

renkyū, consecutive holidays, 299

renraku, contact, communication, connection;
  renraku suru, contact, 82

renshū, practice; *renshū suru,* practice, 37

repōto, report, 165, 240

ressun, lesson, 226
retsu, row, line (counter), 212
rettō, archipelago, 154
rikishi, sumō wrestler, 105
rikkōho, candidacy; *rikkōho suru*, be a candidate, 267
rikon, divorce; *rikon suru*, divorce, be divorced, 118
ripōto, report, 241
rippa(na), imposing, magnificent, 215
rirekisho, resume, 82
risāchi, research, 67
riyō, use; *riyō suru*, use, 145
rōgo, old age, 283
rōka, hall, 150
rokuon, recording; *rokuon suru*, record, 212
rombun, paper, thesis, 283
rusu, be out/away, 118
rūto, route, 207
ryō, fee, charge, 71
ryōhō, both, 16
ryokan, inn, 79
ryōkin, charge, fee, 89
ryokō-saki, destination, 283
-ryoku, strength, power, 302
ryōrisuru, cook, 141
ryōshūsho, receipt, 180
ryōtei, teahouse, 79
ryūgaku, studying overseas; *ryūgaku suru*, study overseas, 126

sa, difference, 154
sabishii, lonely, cheerless, 188
sābisu, service, 23
sābisu-ryō, service charge, 89
saboru, loaf, play hooky; *shigoto o saboru*, loaf on the job, 271
sagaru, go down, fall, 261
sagasu, look for, 173
saiensu, science, 82
saifu, wallet, purse, 24
saigo ni, finally, 235
saijitsu, legal holiday, 101
sain, signature, 75
saishū (no), final, 235
saite iku, be (in the process of) blooming, 153
saki, before, ahead, beyond, future, 48
-saki, destination, 169, 230
sakihodo, a little while ago, 23
sakki, a short time ago, 48, 223
sakoku, national isolation, 295
saku, bloom, 101, 153
sakuhin, work, production, 184
sakujitsu, yesterday, 169
sakura, cherry blossom, 67, 153
-sama = san, 114
samākōsu, summer course, 71
sameru, wake up, 173
samurai, samurai, 118
-san, mount, 79

sangurasu, sunglasses, 165
sanka, participation; *sanka suru*, participate, enter (a contest); *sankasha*, participant, entrant, 212, 232
sansei, agreement, approval, endorsement; *sansei (suru)*, go along with, agree, approve, 286
sara, plate, dish, 184
sararīman, white-collar worker, 131
sashiageru, give, 235
sashimi, raw, 165
sasou, ask, invite, 286
sassato, quickly, 276
sassoku, without delay, directly, 122
satogaeri, return to (one's native) village; *satogaeri-ten*, exhibition of returned works, 295
-satsu, (counter for books), 126
sawagashii, uproarious, noisy, 131
se, height, back; *se ga takai*, tall, 15
sebiro, (man's) suit, 150
sei, attribute, nature, sex, 160
seibu, western part, the west; *seibu-geki*, western, 131
seido, system, 302
seifuku, uniform, 160
seihin, product, 291
seijika, politician, 93
seikatsu, living, life, 94
seiki, century, 215
seikō, success; *seikō suru*, succeed, 291
seikyū-sho, bill, 203
seiri, (re)arrangement, regulation; *seiri suru*, put in order, (re)adjust, 276
seito, pupil, 267
sekai, world, society, realm, 118
seki, coughing, cough, 52
seki, seat, 201
sekiyu, oil, petroleum, 219
sekkei, design, planning, 122
sekkeizu, blueprint, plan, 291
sekken, soap, 110
semai, small cramped, narrow, 67
semmon, speciality; *semmonka*, speacialist, professional, 82, 165
sempai, senior, older person, 197
sen, line, 153
senaka, back, 12
senchi, centimeter, 196
senden, publicity, propaganda, advertising, 149
senjitsu, the other day, 130
sensō, war, 173
sentā, center, 244
sentan gijutsu, high tech(nology); *sentan*, point, tip, 283
sērusu, sales, 40; *sērusu no hito*, salesperson, 40
sēru, sale, 42
setto suru, set up, set, 200
-sha, person, 40

shaberu, chatter, talk, 197
shachō, president, 15
shain, company employee, 149, 188
shareta, tasteful, chic, 181
sharyō, car, vehicle, 19
shashin-ya, photographer, photo studio, 220
shatsu, shirt, 23
shattā, shutter, 141
shawā, shower; *shawā o abiru*, take a shower, 31
shi, and, moreover, 63
shiai, game, match bout, 173
shiawase(na), happy, 173
shibafu, lawn, 75
shibai, play, 37
shibaraku, awhile, a moment, for the time being, 255
shibō, choice, desire, 71
shichō, mayor, 267
shiharai, payment, 71
shijuku, private school/college, 302
shikaru, scold, 219
shikashi, however, 302
shikata, way of doing, 261
shiken, examination, test, 67
shikikin, deposit, 192
shima, stripe, 19
shima-guni, island country; *shima*, island, 153
shimaru, be closed, 101
shimau, finish, put an end to; keep, put away, save, 192, 203
shimpai, worry; *shimpai suru*, worry, be worried; *shimpai (o) kakeru*, make (someone) worry, 126, 259
shimpan, judgement, 105
shin-, new, 291
shina, wares, article, goods, 184
shinai, within a city, 33
shinamono, goods, article, 44
shinjiru, believe, 149
shinju, pearl, 219
shinkan, shintō priest, 302
shinnen, new year, 130
shinnyū shain, new company employee; *shin-nyū*, newly entered, 165
shin-seihin, new product, 291
shinseki, relative, 165
shinsen(na), new, fresh, 295
shinsesaizā, synthesizer, 286
shinu, die, 31
shio, salt, 141
shippai, failure, mistake; *shippai suru*, fail, 196
shiraberu, check, investigate, 180, 223
shiranai hito, stranger, 212
shirase, news, information, notice, 110
shiraseru, inform, 40
shiri, bottom, buttocks, 219
shiro, white(ness), 19
shiro, castle, 248
shiryō, papers, document, material, 60

shisetsu, facilities, institution, 283
shisutemu, system, 40; *shisutemu-bu*, systems department, 40
shita no, younger, 240
shitei, designation, specification; *shitei-ken*, reserved ticket, 63
shiten, branch (office/store), 33; *shitenchō*, branch manager, 240
shitsunai, indoor, interior, 173
shiyō, using, use, application, 79
shizen, nature; *shizen kagaku*, natural science, 79, 302
shīzun, period, time, 63
shō, show, 131
-sho, book, document, note, 82, 180
shōchi shimashita, I understand, certainly, 180
shōgakkō, elementary school, 85
shōgatsu, New Year's, January, 135
shōkai, introduction; *shōkai suru*, introduce, 27
shokki, tableware, dinner set, flatware, 181
-shoku, meal (counter), 89
shokuba, work place, 97
shokugyō, occupation, 220
shomei, signature, 207
shomei suru, sign, 207
shōmei-sho, certificate, 220
shonichi, first/opening day, 105
shōrai, future; *shōraisei*, future, prospects, 141, 160
shōrei, promotion, stimulation; *shōrei suru*, promote, encourage, 302
shorui, document, paper, 45
shōrūmu, showroom, 122
shōsha, trading company, 82
shōtai, ivitation; *shōtai suru*, invite; *shōtai-jō*, invitation card/letter, 85
-shū, circuit, lap (counter), 235
shūchū, concentration; *shūchu kōza*, intensive course, 267
shujin, proprietor, 79
shujutsu, operation, 298
shūkai, gathering, assembly, 67
shūkan, custom, habit, 97
shūkan-shi, weekly magazine, 51
shukkin, attendance, presence; *shukkin suru*, be at the office, report for work, 226
shukudai, homework, 110
shukuhaku, lodging; *shukuhaku suru*, put up at, stay (overnight), 230
shuppatsu, departure; *shuppatsu suru*, leave, 55
shūri, repair, 244
shushō, prime minister, 67
shūshoku suru, get a job, 160
shusseki, attendance; *shusseki suru*, attend; *shusseki-sha*, attendee, 59, 200
shutchō, business/official trip, 33
shūten, terminal, last stop, 19,
soba, buckwheat noodles, 130
soba, near, beside, 119
sōda, That's it!, 328

sō desu, I hear, they say, 160
-sō desu, = looks (like), seem, 184
sōdan, consultation, 27: *sōdan suru*, consult, 40
sofā, sofa, 277
sō ieba, speaking of . . . , 165
sōji, cleaning; *sōji suru*, clean, 59
sō ka = *sō desu ka*, 141
sokode, thereupon, 328
-soku, pair (shoes, socks, etc.; counter), 328
sokutatsu, special delivery, 180
somei yoshino, a species of cherry, 154
someru, dye, 154
sonna, such, like that, 223
sonna ni, that much/many; *sonna ni . . . nai*, not so, 126, 188
sono-go, later, afterwards, 230
sono mama, as it is, 276
sora, sky, 131
sorede, and then; That's why, for that reason, 89, 207
sore-dewa, well then, 48
sore-ja, in that case, 47
soreni, besides, 63
soretomo, or, 267
sōritsu, establishment, 235
soroban, abacus, 302
soroeru, get ready, 271
sorosoro, soon, little by little, 200
sorou, assemble, be present, be/become complete, 118
sōryō, delivery charge, postage, 138
sōshiki, funeral, 291
sōsō, early, immediately, 235
sōtai, leaving early; *sōtai suru*, leave (office, school) early, 226
soto, outside, exterior, outer, 134
sotsugyō, graduation; *sotsugyō suru*, graduate, 67
sū-, a few, many, several, 101
suberu, slip, slide, skate, 283
subete, all, 295
sue, end, 154
sūgaku, mathematics, 23
sugi (ni), after, 176
-sugiru = too; pass, 200
sugoi, terrible, wonderful; *sugoku*, very terrible, 12, 188
sugu, immediately, 45
sugureta, eminent, outstanding, superior, 302
suiei, swimming, 85
sukāfu, scarf, 44
sukina dake, as much as one likes, 255
sukoshi-zutsu, little by little, 94
suku, be/become empty/uncrowded, 12
sukunai, a little, few, 63
sumaseru, finish, 55
sumō, (wrestling), 105
sumu, be finished, 118
sū-nin, several people, 101
supāmāketto, supermarket, 244

supīdo, speed; *supīdo o dasu*, put on speed, 276
supōtsu, sports, 14
supōtsu kurabu, health club, 85
suri, pickpocket, 220
suru, pick a pocket, 220
suru, cost, be worth, 212
susumeru, proceed, make one's way, advance, *susume-kata*, way of proceeding, 40
susumu, advance make one's way, 154
sutajio, studio, 176
suteki(na), fine, stunning, wonderful, 291
sutereo, stereo, 196
suteru, throw out, 75
suto/sutoraiki, strike, 65, 93
sutōbu, stove (heating), 51
sūtsu, suit, 134
suwaru, sit, take a seat, 37
suzushii, cool, 93

tabun, probably, perhaps, 51
tada, only, but, 223
tadaima, right now, just now, in a minute, 180
-tagaru, want, 160
taifū, typhoon, 93
taihen, very; oh, oh!, *taihen(na)*, hard, difficult, 67, 127, 130
taikai, (big) meeting, conference, tournament, 94
taikin, large sum of money, 85
taikutsu(na), boring, 67
taipuraitā, typewriter, 203
taisetsu(na), important, valuable, serious, 203
taishita, serious, important, 52
taisō, calisthenics, gymnastics, 280
taitei, usually, mostly, 40
takarakuji, lottery, 203
takasa, height, altitude, 196
takasō desu, looks expensive, 184
tama ni, once in a while, 59, 280
tame ni, (in order) to, for, 169, 280
tameru, save, gather, accumulate, 283
tamesu, test, try out, 200
tanomu, request, 44, 145
tanshin, alone, unaccompanied, 230
tantō-sha, person in charge, 101
tariru, be enough, 93
tashikameru, make sure, 94
tashika-ni, certainly, 114
tasukeru, help, save, 277
tataku, strike, beat, slap, knock, 219
tate, height, vertical (direction), 220
tatemae, system, principle, policy, 105
tatemono, building, 23
tateru, build, 215, 219
tatsu, be built, 240
tatsu, pass, 251
tatsu, stand up, 31
tatta hitotsu, one only; *tatta*, only, 79
tawā, tower, 110
tazuneru, visit, 44

te, hand, arm, 31; *te o kasu*, lend a hand, 60; *te ni toru*, get, taken in one's hands, 145; *te ni hairu*, be obtainable, come into one's hands, 149

tebukuro, glove, mitten, 149

tehai, arrangement, preparations, 235

teiden, power failure, 173

teinei(na), polite, 252

teinen, retirement age, 188

-teki, like, resembling, 79

tekitō(na), suitable, appropriate, 67

tempura, tempura, 15

tenisu kōto, tennis court, 27

tenkin, transfer, 229

tenrankai, exhibition, 295

tensai, genius, 173

terakoya, temple/private school, 302

tetsudau, help, 118

tetsuzuki, formality, procedure, 145

to, when, 122

tobu, fly, 31

tōchaku, arrival, 89

tochū (de), on the way, 259

todoke-saki, consignee, destination, 138

todoku, arrive, reach, 19,

tōfu, tofu, 44

toiawase, inquiry, 19

toiawaseru, inform, 19, 223

toire, toilet, 59

tōitsu, unification, uniformity; *tōitsu-teki(na)*, unified, 302

toka . . . toka, things like/such, 145

tokai, city, town, 207

toki, when, 89

tokkyū, special express; *tokkyū-ken*, special express ticket, 68

tokorode, by the way; well, incidentally, 55, 153

tōku, long distance, 110

tokubetsu no/na, special extraordinary, 138

tomaru, stop, be stopped; stay, stop at; *tomari*, stay, 52, 55, 169

tomin, resident/citizen of Tokyo Prefecture, 145

tonai, within (Tokyo) Prefecture, 138

tonari, neighbor, 196

to naru, come/amount to

tonikaku, anyway, in any case, 176

tonosama, 328

toraberāzu chekku, traveler's check, 203

torakku, truck, 276

torēnā, trainer, 27

tori, bird, 212

tōri ni, way, 271

toriagerareru, be appropriated, confiscated, taken away, 215

torihikisaki, business contact, 33

torikesu, cancel; *torikeshi*, cancellation, 169,

torikumi, bout, 105

toritsu, metropolitan, 145

toru, pick up, get, take, pass, rob, steal, 19, 219

toru, eat, 248

tōru, go through/past, 59

toshi, age, year; *toshi ga ue*, older, senior; *toshiyori*, old person, 12, 283

tōsu, pass, 235

to shite, as, in the capacity of, 89

totte kuru, go and get, 276

tsugi-tsugi ni, one after another, in order, 130

tsukamaeru, catch, grab, arrest, 277

tsukareru, be/get tired, tire, 67, 204

tsukeru, attach, include, 138

-tsuki, included, attached, 89

tsuki, moon, month, 15, 118

tsukiatari, end, foot (of passage, street), 150

tsūkin, commuting; *tsūkin suru*, commute, 12

tsūkō-nin, passer-by, 68

tsuku, be lit/ignited, 162

tsukuru, cook, prepare, make, 31, 215, 223

tsuma, (my) wife, 169

tsumaranai, trifling, worthless, insignificant, 101, 295

tsumetai, cold, cool, chilled, 85

tsumori, intention, purpose, 138

tsumu, load, pile up, 203

tsureru, bring, take, be accompanied by; *tsurete kuru*, bring, (person), 149

tsuri, fishing; *tsuri o suru*, fish, 37

tsutaeru, convey, impart, tell; make known, transmit, introduce, 79, 219

tsutome, go to an office, work for a company, duty, service, 265

tsutsuji, azalea, 153

tsuyoi, strong, 44

tsuzukeru, keep up, continue, go on, 280

tsuzuku, continue, 203

uchiawase, previous arrangement; *uchiawase o suru*, make arrangements, 235

uchikin, deposit, partial payment, 89

uchū, universe; *uchū hikōshi*, astronaut, 44

ue, upper, above; older, 15, 240

ugokimawaru, move around, 105

ugoku, move, run, operate, 65

uisukī, whisky, 44

ukagau, visit, ask; hear, 122, 280

ukeru, have, receive, undergo, take, 160

uketoru, get, 169

ukiyo-e, floating-world pictures, 295

ukkari, without thinking, inadvertantly, carelessly, 197

uma, horse, 19

umai, well, skillful, delicious; *umaku*, easily, *(lit)* well, skillfully, 232, 286

umareru, be born, 85

ume, apricot, 153

un, um, un-huh, yeah, 135

ūn, unh-unh, nope, no, 135

undō, campaign, 207

unten, driving; *unten suru*, drive, 31

ura, back, reverse (side); *uraguchi*, back entrance, 122

ureshii, delighted, happy, 97

urikire, sold out, 63

ūru, wool, 19

ushiro, back, 19

usotsuki, liar, 23

uta, song, 23; *utau*, sing, 23

utsukushii, beautiful, 131

utsuru, be reflected, appear as an image, 244

uttaeru, make an appeal, complain, 207

uwagi, jacket, 59

wā, wow, oh, 105, 286

wakai, young, 67

wakareru, part, split up, 93

wake, reason, cause, 295

wāpuro, word processor, 40

waraji, straw sandals, 328

warau, laugh, 59

wareware, we, 160

waru, break, 196

warutsu, waltz, 134

washitsu, Japanese-style room, 192

wasureru, forget, 19

wasuremono, forgotten or lost article, 19

watakushi, I, 207

wataru, cross, 276

watasu, hand (over), 76

wazawaza, especially; *wazawaza . . . suru*, go to the trouble of, 71

yā, hi, 291

yachin, (house) rent, 126

yahari, also, 302

yakamashii, noisy, 67

yakimono, pottery, 44

yakitori, grilled chicken, 105

yaku, about, 154

yaku, bake, grill, fry, 59

yakudatsu, be of use, serve a purpose, 230

yakusho, public/govenment office, 240

yakusoku, promise, appointment, 59

yakuwari, role, part, 302

yakyū, baseball, 173

yamanobori, mountain climbing, 85

yameru, give up, stop, 63

yamu, stop, 94

yappari, (just) as you said, 97

yarigai, worthwhile, 160

yaru, do, give, play, 85

yasashii, gentle, kind, 188

yaseru, lose weight, be/become thin, 165

-yasui, easy to, 134

yasumu, rest, 23

yawarakai, soft, tender, 126

yō, way, manner, 154, 160

yō, business, use, service, 181, 220

yobikō, preparatory school, 71

yobu, call, send for, 328

yōfuku, (western) clothes, 188

yogoreru, be/become dirty, 130

yōhin, utensil, supplies, article, 149

yoī, preparations, readiness; *yoī suru*, prepare, arrange, provide for, 126

yōji, work, business, 48

yokan, hunch, premonition; *yokan ga suru*, have a hunch, 291

yoko, width, horizontal, 220

yonaka, middle of the night, midnight, 101

yori, more, 283

yori, than, 12

yorokobu, be happy, 97

yoroshii, all right; *yoroshiku*, properly, well, at one's discretion, 122, 138

yoru, night, nighttime, 232

yoru, stop by, 51

yoshū, preparation, rehearsal, 118

yosoku, prediciton, estimate; *yosoku suru*, predict, 153

yōsu, state, circumstance, appearance, 153

yōsuru ni, in other words, in short, 299

yotei, plan, schedule, 93

yoyaku-gakari, reservation clerk, 89

yowai, weak, faint, delicate, 141

yūbe, last night/evening, 23

yūbin, mail, 71

yubiwa, ring, 59

yude tamago, boiled egg, 59

yūfō, UFO, 37

yuki, snow; *yuki ga furu*, snow falls, 56, 215

yukkuri, by easy stages, slowly, 226

yunyū, importation; *yunyū suru*, import, 219

yūshoku, supper, 248

yushutsu, exportation; *yushutsu suru*, export, 219

yūsō (suru), mail, 89

yutaka(na), affluent, rich, abundant, 283

yūtān, U-turn, 63

yūutsu(na), gloomy, depressed, 203

zangyō, overtime, 67

zannen(na), disappointing, 37; *zannen ni omou*, feel regret, 97, 295

zaseki, seat, 68,

zeikin, tax; *zeimusho*, tax office, 89, 134

zembu, all, every; *zembu de*, all together, 101, 184

zen-, whole, all, 302

zen'in, all the staff, all members, 118

zenjitsu, previous day, 169

zenkoku, the whole country, 302

zensen, front, 153

zettai (ni), absolutely, unconditionally, 248

zubon, trousers, 93

zuibun, quite, 154

zumen, blueprint, plan, 122

-zutsu (suffix), 94

zutto, a whole lot, all the time/way, 153

INDEX

SUPPLEMENT TO THE TEXT

ROMANIZED TEXT

1 RUSH HOUR

Opening Dialogue

Chang: Kesa hajimete densha de kaisha ni kimashita. Totemo konde imashita. Eki no hito ga jōkyaku no senaka o oshite, naka ni oshikonde imashita. Sugokatta desu yo.

Sumisu: Demo densha no hō ga kuruma yori hayai desu yo. Michi mo konde imasu kara.

Chang: Sumisu-san wa nan de tsūkin shite imasu ka.

Sumisu: Watashi wa iki mo kaeri mo chikatetsu desu. Tōkyō no kōtsu kikan no naka de chikatetsu ga ichiban benri desu yo.

Chang: Chikatetsu wa asa mo yūgata mo konde imasu ka.

Sumisu: Ee, demo yūgata wa asa hodo konde imasen. Asa no 8-ji han goro ga pīku desu kara, watashi wa maiasa 7-ji ni uchi o demasu.

Chang: Sono jikan wa suite imasu ka.

Sumisu: Ee, 7-ji goro wa 8-ji goro yori suite imasu yo. Watashi wa maiasa chikatetsu no naka de Nihongo o benkyō shite imasu. Kasetto tēpu o kikinagara, tekisuto o yonde imasu.

Chang: Hē, sō desu ka.

Key Sentences

1. Tōkyō wa Ōsaka yori ōkii desu.
2. Tōkyō to Ōsaka to dochira ga ōkii desu ka. Tōkyō no hō ga ōkii desu.
3. 3-gatsu wa 1-gatsu hodo samukunai desu.
4. [Watashi wa] supōtsu no naka de tenisu ga ichiban suki desu.
5. Sumisu-san wa kōhi o nominagara, terebi o mite imasu.

EXERCISES

Make dialogues by changing the underlined parts as indicated in the examples given.

A. *ex.* Q: Chikyū wa tsuki yori ōkii desu ka.
   A: Ee, tsuki yori ōkii desu.
   1. Tōkyō no jinkō, Rondon no jinkō, ōi desu   2. mizu, abura, omoi desu   3. Hayashi-san, Katō-san, toshi ga ue desu   4. Furansu no Pari, Nihon no Sapporo, kita ni arimasu

B. *ex.* Q: Tori-niku to gyū-niku to dochira/dotchi ga yasui desu ka.
   A: Tori-niku no hō ga yasui desu.
   1. fakushimiri, tegami, benri desu   2. Hayashi-san, Katō-san, Eigo ga jōzu desu   3. asa, yūgata, konde imasu   4. Katō-san, Suzuki-san, takusan o-sake o nomimasu

C. *ex.* Q: Nomimono wa kōhī to kōcha to dochira/dotchi ga ii desu ka.
   A: Kōhī no hō ga ii desu.
   1. ryōri, tempura, shabu-shabu   2. jikan, gozen, gogo   3. dezāto, aisukurīmu, kudamono   4. pātī, kin-yōbi, do-yōbi

D. *ex.* Q: Supōtsu no naka de nani ga ichiban suki desu ka.
   A: Tenisu ga ichiban suki desu.

1. shisha, doko, ōkii desu, Nyūyōku   2. go-kyōdai, donata, se ga takai desu, otōto   3. ichi-nichi, itsu, konde imasu, asa 8-ji goro   4. kaisha, dare, yoku hatarakimasu, shachō

E. *ex.* A: Ryōri ga jōzu desu ne.
   B: Iie, [watashi wa] Rinda-san hodo jōzu dewa arimasen.
   1. tenisu, Hayashi-san   2. sukī, Sumisu-san   3. Nihon-go, Buraun-san

F. *ex.* A: Ōsaka wa ōkii desu ne.
   B: Ee, demo Tōkyō hodo ōkiku nai desu.
   1. Shinkansen, takai desu, hikōki   2. Tōkyō, atsui desu, Honkon   3. denwa, benri desu, fakushimiri

G: ex. Q: Katō-san wa nani o shite imasu ka.
   A: Rajio o kikinagara shimbun o yonde imasu.
   1. kōhī o nomimasu, shigoto o shimasu   2. tabako o suimasu, tegami o kakimasu   3. hanashi o shimasu, basu o machimasu   4. iyahōn de ongaku o kikimasu, benkyō shimasu

Short Dialogues

1. A: Chotto hanashi ga arimasu. Shokuji o shinagara, hanashimasen ka.
   B: Sō shimashō.
   A: Kyō wa watashi ga go-chisō shimasu.
   B: Sō desu ka. Ja, go-chisō ni narimasu.

2. A: Kōhī to kōcha to dochira ga suki desu ka.
   B: Ryōhō suki desu.

Quiz

   I   Read this lesson's opening dialogue and answer the following questions.
   1. Chikatetsu wa asa to yūgata to dochira ga konde imasu ka. 2. Dōshite densha no hō ga kuruma yori hayai desu ka. 3. Sumisu-san wa nani o kikinagara, Nihon-go no tekisuto o yonde imasu ka. 4. Sumisu-san wa maiasa nan-ji ni uchi o dete, nan de kaisha ni ikimasu ka. 5. Chikatetsu wa nan-ji goro ga ichiban konde imasu ka.

   II   Put the appropriate particles or inflections in the parentheses.
   1. Shinkansen wa kuruma (   ) hayai desu. 2. Dō yatte benkyō shite imasu ka./Kasetto tēpu o kiki (   ) benkyō shite imasu. 3. Chikatetsu wa asa mo yūgata (   ) konde imasu ka./Yūgata wa asa (   ) konde imasen. 4. Kochira no hō (   ) shizuka desu kara, koko (   ) hanashi o shimashō. 5. Kaisha (   ) naka (   ) dare ga ichiban yoku hatarakimasu ka. 6. Eki no hito ga jōkyaku (   ) densha no naka (   ) oshikonde imashita.

   III   Complete the questions so that they fit the answers.
   1. Chikatetsu to basu to (   ) ga benri desu ka./Chikatetsu no hō ga benri desu. 2. Chikatetsu wa (   ) ga ichiban konde imasu ka./Asa ga ichiban konde imasu. 3. (   ) ga ichiban tenisu ga jōzu desu ka./Rinda-san ga ichiban jōzu desu. 4. Kudamono no naka de (   ) ga ichiban suki desu ka./Mikan ga ichiban suki desu. 5. Nomimono wa kōhī to kōcha to (   ) ga ii desu ka./Kōhī o onegaishimasu.

   IV   Complete the sentences with the appropriate form of the verbs indicated.
   1. Sumisu-san wa Hayashi-san to (   ) nagara, (   ) imasu. (arukimasu, hanashimasu) 2. Sumisu-san wa mainichi nan de (   ) imasu ka. (tsūkin shimasu) 3. Sono resutoran wa (   ) imasu ka. (sukimasu) 4. Senaka o (   ) naide kudasai. (oshimasu) 5. Kinō wa hoteru de tomodachi to shokuji o (   ) nagara, hanashi o (   ). (shimasu, shimasu) 6. Kono kuruma o (   ) mo ii desu ka. (tsukaimasu)/Watashi ga (   ) masu kara, (   ) naide kudasai.(tsukaimasu, tsukaimasu)

   V   Answer the following questions.
   1. Anata wa supōtsu no naka de nani ga ichiban suki desu ka. 2. Go-kazoku no naka de donata ga ichiban se ga takai desu ka. 3. Anata no machi no kōtsū kikan no naka de nani ga ichiban benri desu ka. 4. Sushi to sukiyaki to dochira ga suki desu ka.

2 LOST AND FOUND

Opening Dialogue

Chan: Sumimasen.
Ekiin: Hai, nan deshō ka.
Chan: Wasuremono o shimashita.
Ekiin: Dono densha desu ka.
Chan: 20-pun gurai mae no densha de, ushiro kara 2-bamme no sharyō desu.
Ekiin: Nani o wasuremashita ka.
Chan: Kurokute ōkii kami no fukuro desu.
Ekiin: Nakami wa nan desu ka. Kuwashiku setsumei shite kudasai.
Chan: Mafurā to sētā desu. Mafurā wa ūru de, kuro to shiro no shima no moyō desu. Sētā wa akakute, mune ni uma no moyō ga arimasu.
Ekiin: Ima shūten no eki ni denwa o kakete, toiawasemasu kara, chotto matte kudasai.
Chan: Sumimasen.

Ekiin: Arimashita. Ūru no mafurā to akai sētā desu ne. Tōkyō eki no jimu-shitsu ni todoite imasu kara, kyō-jū ni tori ni itte kudasai.

Key Sentences

1. Hayashi-san wa Nihon-jin de ABC no buchō desu.
2. Koko wa hirokute shizukana kōen desu.
3. Kanji o kirei ni kaite kudasai.
4. Hiru-gohan o tabe ni resutoran ni ikimashita.

EXERCISES

Make dialogues by changing the underlined parts as in the examples given.

A. *ex.* Q: Donna kaban desu ka.
  A: Kurokute ōkii kaban desu.
    1. guai, atama ga itai, netsu ga arimasu 2. kōen, hiroi, shizukana kōen desu 3. tatemono, shiroi, takai tatemono desu 4. machi, rekishi ga furui, yumeina machi desu

B. *ex.* Q: Donna kōen desu ka.
  A: Kirei de shizukana kōen desu.
    1. tokoro, nigiyaka, totemo omoshiroi tokoro desu 2. resutoran, benri, sābisu ga yokute hayai desu 3. mondai, fukuzatsu, muzukashii mondai desu 4. hito, ABC no bengoshi, Tōkyō ni sunde imasu 5. hito, chūgakkō no sensei, sūgaku o oshiete imasu

C. *ex.* Q: Yamada-san wa donna hito desu ka.
  A: Majime de yoku hatarakimasu.
    1. kami ga nagai, kireina hito desu 2. atama ga ii, shinsetsuna hito desu 3. oshaberi, namakemono desu 4. usotsuki, ganko desu

D. *ex.* Q: Chan-san wa michi o setsumei shimashita ka.
  A: Ee, kuwashiku setsumei shimashita.
    1. hataraite imasu, isogashii 2. mō okimashita, asa hayai 3. tsukimashita, yūbe osoi 4. hanashi o shite imasu, tanoshii

E. *ex.* Q: Chan-san wa kanji o kakimasu ka.
  A: Ee, kirei ni kakimasu.
    1. uta o utaimasu, jōzu 2. Watanabe-san ni oshiemashita, shinsetsu 3. tomodachi to hanashi o shite imasu, nigiyaka 4. benkyō shite imasu, shizuka

F. *ex.* A: Doko ni ikimasu ka.
  B: Ginza ni ikimasu.
  A: Nani o shi ni ikimasu ka.
  B: Eiga o mi ni ikimasu.
    1. Kyōto, furui o-tera o mimasu 2. depāto, kutsu o kaimasu 3. Katō-san no heya,

tegami o todokemasu 4. kōen, shashin o torimasu

G. *ex.* Q: Nani o shi ni ikimasu ka.
   A: Depāto ni shatsu o kai ni ikimasu.
   1. kaerimasu, uchi, hiru-gohan o tabemasu 2. ikimasu, Nihon, atarashii gijutsu o benkyō shimasu 3. ikimasu, kissaten, kōhī o nominasu 4. kaerimasu, ryōshin no uchi, yasumimasu 5. kimashita, koko, Nihon-go o naraimasu

Short Dialogues

1. Howaito: O-kane o hiroimashita.
   Keikan: Doko ni ochite imashita ka.
   Howaito: Sūpā no mae no ōdōri ni ochite imashita.
   Keikan: Nan-ji goro hiroimashita ka.
   Howaito: 15-fun gurai mae desu.

2. Suzuki: Saifu o otoshimashita.
   Keikan: Donna saifu desu ka.
   Suzuki: Chairo de ōkii kawa no saifu desu.
   Keikan: Naka ni nani ga haitte imasu ka.
   Suzuki: Genkin ga 30,000-en gurai to meishi desu.

Quiz

I Read this lesson's opening dialogue and answer the following questions.
   1. Chan-san wa donna fukuro o wasuremashita ka. 2. Ushiro kara nan-bamme no sharyō ni wasuremashita ka. 3. Akai sētā wa mune ni uma no moyō ga arimasu ka. 4. Ekiin wa Chan-san no setsumei o kiite, nani o shimashita ka. 5. Chan-san wa wasuremono o doko ni tori ni ikimasu ka.

II Put the appropriate particles in the parentheses.
   1. Chan-san wa ūru (　) mafurā (　) akai sētā (　) wasuremashita. 2. Mae (　) 3-bamme (　) sharyō desu. 3. Kuro (　) shiro (　) shima no shatsu de, mune (　) chiisai kasa no moyō (　) arimasu. 4. Jimu-shitsu (　) todoite imasu (　), kyō-jū (　) tori (　) kite kudasai.

III Complete the questions so that they fit the answers.
   1. (　) saifu o hiroimashita ka./Kuroi kawa no saifu desu. 2. (　) ni ochite imashita ka./Kōen ni ochite imashita. 3. (　) densha ni notte imashita ka./10-pun gurai mae no densha desu. 4. Naka ni (　) ga haitte imasu ka./Hon to pen ga 2-hon haitte imasu.

IV Complete the sentences with the appropriate form of the word in parentheses.
   1. Buraun-san wa (　) kanji o kakimasu. (jōzu) 2. (　) setsumei shite kudasai. (kuwashii) 3. Kyō wa (　) kaisha ni ikimasu. (hayai) 4. Atama ga (　), netsu ga arimasu. (itai) 5. Kodomo wa (　) hon o yonde imasu. (shizuka) 6. Rekishi ga (　), (　) machi desu. (furui, yūmei) 7. Kanji o (　) kaite kudasai. (ōkii)

V Connect the following sentences using the appropriate verb or adjective form.
   1. Kono densha ni norimasu. 4-tsu-me no eki de orite kudasai. 2. Ano resutoran wa yasui desu. Oishii desu. 3. Kono kissaten wa atarashii desu. Kirei desu. Suite imasu. 4. Sore wa aoi sētā desu. Hana no moyō ga arimasu. 5. Watanabe-san wa atama ga ii desu. Shinsetsu desu. 6. Chan-san wa majime desu. Yoku hatarakimasu. 7. Jimu-shitsu ni denwa o kakemasu. Toiawasemasu.

VI Answer the following questions.
   1. Anata no otō-san wa donna hito desu ka. (use the pattern . . . **te/de** . . . **te/de**) 2. Anata no machi wa donna tokoro desu ka. (use the pattern . . . **te/de** . . . **te/de**) 3. Kōen ni nani o shi ni ikimasu ka. 4. Anata wa ashita doko ni nani o shi ni ikimasu ka.

3 THE HEALTH CLUB

Opening Dialogue

Buraun: Anō, chotto onegaishimasu. Kochira no kurabu ni mōshikomi o suru mae ni, naka o miru koto ga dekimasu ka.

Kurabu
no hito: Hai. Shitsurei desu ga, dochira-sama deshō ka.

Buraun: Buraun desu.

Kurabu: Aa, Hayashi-san no go-shōkai no Buraun-san desu ne. Go-annai shimashō.

Buraun: Totemo hirokute kireina tokoro desu ne.

Kurabu: Kochira no tenisu-kōto niwa kōchi mo imasu kara, kōchi ni narau koto mo dekimasu. Kochira wa onsui pūru de, ichinen-jū oyogu koto ga dekimasu.

Buraun: Kochira dewa minna iroirona mashīn o tsukatte imasu ne.

Kurabu: Ee. Dore demo o-sukina mono o tsukau koto ga dekimasu ga, hajimeru mae ni torēnā ni go-sōdan kudasai.

Buraun: Ee, sō shimasu.

Kurabu: Ikaga deshita ka.

Buraun: Totemo ki ni irimashita.

Kurabu: Dewa, kochira ni o-namae to go-jūsho o okaki kudasai.

Key Sentences

1. Kono pūru dewa ichinen-jū oyogu koto ga dekimasu.
2. Maiasa kaisha e iku mae ni shimbun o yomimasu.

EXERCISES

I Verbs: Study the examples, convert into the dictionary form, and memorize.
   A. Regular I: *ex.* ikimasu → iku; nomimasu → nomu; shinimasu → shinu; asobimasu → asobu; hanashimasu → hanasu; tachimasu → tatsu; iimasu → iu; arimasu → aru
      1. aimasu 2. otoshimasu 3. urimasu 4. kikimasu 5. suimasu 6. hairimasu 7. isogimasu 8. tobimasu 9. moraimasu 10. todokimasu 11. naoshimasu 12. mochimasu 13. wakarimasu 14. nugimasu 15. araimasu 16. tsukurimasu 17. sukimasu 18. komimasu 19. okurimasu 20. hatarakimasu
   B. Regular II: *ex.* tabemasu → taberu; mimasu → miru
      1. misemasu 2. okimasu 3. orimasu 4. agemasu 5. kangaemasu 6. ochimasu 7. imasu 8. tomemasu 9. abimasu 10. shimemasu
   C. Irregular: *ex.* kimasu → kuru; shimasu → suru
      1. kekkon shimasu 2. mottekimasu 3. annai shimasu 4. setsumei shimasu

II Make dialogues by changing the underlined parts as in the examples given.
   A. *ex.* Q: Kono pūru de ima oyogu koto ga dekimasu ka.
      A*a*: Hai, dekimasu.
      A*n*: Iie, dekimasen.
         1. kono heya o tsukaimasu 2. kyō-jū ni todokemasu 3. Tōkyō eki ni tori ni ikimasu 4. Sono shashin o mottekimasu
   B. *ex.* Q: [Anata wa] Nihon-go o hanasu koto ga dekimasu ka.
      A: Ee, dekimasu ga, amari jōzu dewa arimasen.
         1. Nihon no uta o utaimasu 2. kanji o kakimasu 3. kuruma o unten shimasu 4. Nihon ryōri o tsukurimasu
   C. *ex.* Q: Neru mae ni nani o shimashita ka.
      A: Ha o migakimashita.
         1. shokuji o shimasu, te o araimasu 2. eigakan ni hairimasu, kippu o kaimasu 3. nemasu, sake o sukoshi nomimasu 4. Tōkyō ni kimasu, Tōkyō no tomodachi ni denwa shimasu
   D. *ex.* Q: Itsu denwa o kakemasu ka.
      A: Uchi ni kaeru mae ni denwa o kakemasu.

1. shawā o abimasu, dekakemasu 2. kōhī o nomimasu, shigoto o hajimemasu 3. shokuji o shimasu, Ōsaka ni tsukimasu 4. kaerimasu, michi ga komimasu

E. *ex.* Q: <u>Mōshikomi o suru</u> mae ni <u>naka o miru</u> koto ga dekimasu ka.
    A: Ee, dekimasu yo.
        1. hajimemasu, sensei ni sōdan shimasu 2. kaisha ni ikimasu, taishikan de aimasu
        3. shashin o torimasu, kagami o mimasu 4. rekōdo o kaimasu, chotto kikimasu

Short Dialogue

Howaito: Ikebana no kurasu o mi ni itte mo ii deshō ka.
Nakamura: Ee. Kondo issho ni ikimashō.
Howaito: Itsu kurasu ga arimasu ka.
Nakamura: 1-shū-kan ni 2-kai, ka, moku ni arimasu.

Quiz

I   Read this lesson's opening dialogue and answer the following questions.
     1. Buraun-san wa Hayashi-san to issho ni kono kurabu ni ikimashita ka. 2. Dare ga Buraun-san o annai shimashita ka. 3. Kono kurabu dewa ichinenjū pūru de oyogu koto ga dekimasu ka. 4. Buraun-san wa kono kurabu no naka o miru mae ni mōshikomi o shimashita ka.

II   Put the appropriate particles in the parentheses.
     1. Watashi wa America ( ) Nihon-jin no sensei ( ) Nihon-go ( ) naraimashita. 2. Dore ( ) o-sukina mono ( ) tsukau koto ( ) dekimasu ( ), hajimeru mae ( ) torēnā ( ) go-sōdan kudasai. 3. Kono kami ( ) o-namae ( ) go-jūsho ( ) o-kaki kudasai. 4. 1-kagetsu ( ) 1-kai Ōsaka ( ) ikimasu.

III Convert the following verbs into the dictionary form.
     1. ikimasu 2. aimasu 3. annai shimasu 4. oshiemasu 5. wasuremasu 6. mimasu 7. arimasu 8. keshimasu 9. tomemasu 10. magarimasu 11. kimasu 12. tabemasu 13. tsūkin shimasu 14. denwa o kakemasu 15. mottekimasu

IV Complete the sentences with the appropriate form of the verbs indicated.
     1. Koko de suraido o ( ) koto ga dekimasu ka. (mimasu) 2. Hiru-gohan o ( ) ni ( ) mo ii deshō ka. (tabemasu, ikimasu) 3. ( ) mae ni denwa o ( ) kudasai (kimasu, kakemasu) 4. Tsugi no kado o ( ) koto ga dekimasu ka. (magarimasu) 5. Ashita Tanaka-san ni ( ) ni ( ) koto ga dekimasu ka. (aimasu, ikimasu) 6. Koko ni kuruma o ( ) koto ga dekimasu ka. (tomemasu)/Iie, koko wa chūsha kinshi desu kara, kuruma o ( ) de kudasai. (tomemasu)

V   Answer the following questions.
     1. Anata wa oyogu koto ga dekimasu ka. 2. Anata wa kanji o yomu koto ga dekimasu ka. 3. Anata wa mainichi neru mae ni nani o shimasu ka. 4. Anata wa asa-gohan o taberu mae ni nani o shimasu ka. 5. 1-shū-kan ni nan-kai Nihon-go no jugyō ga arimasu ka.

4 A BUSINESS TRIP

Opening Dialogue

Kimura: Buraun-san, shutchō desu ka.
Buraun: Ee, ashita kara Sapporo shiten ni shutchō desu. Kimura-san wa Hokkaidō ni itta koto ga arimasu ka.
Kimura: Ee, gakusei no koro ichi-do Hokkaidō e ryokō ni itta koto ga arimasu. Kuruma de Hokkaidō o mawarimashita.
Buraun: Sapporo wa donna tokoro desu ka.
Kimura: Sapporo no machi wa nigiyaka de, nakanaka omoshiroi desu yo. Buraun-san wa hajimete desu ka.
Buraun: Ee, shashin o mita koto wa arimasu ga, itta koto wa arimasen.
Kimura: Hitori de shutchō desu ka.
Buraun: Katō-san mo issho desu. Futari de Sapporo shinai no torihikisaki o mawattari, ginkō ni aisatsu ni ittari shimasu.

Kimura: Katō-san wa sunde ita koto ga arimasu kara, Sapporo o yoku shitte imasu yo.
Buraun: Sō desu ka. Anshin shimashita.

Key Sentences

1. Watanabe-san wa Honkon ni itta koto ga arimasu.
2. Nichi-yōbi wa hon o yondari, ongaku o kiitari shimasu.

EXERCISES

I   Verbs: Study the examples, convert into **-te** and **-ta** forms, and memorize.
   A. Regular I

kakimasu	kaku	kaite	kaita	aimasu	au	atte	atta
yomimasu	yomu	yonde	yonda	owarimasu	owaru	owatte	owatta

1. naraimasu 2. oyogimasu 3. shinimasu 4. asobimasu 5. tachimasu 6. noborimasu 7. okimasu 8. migakimasu 9. mochimasu 10. tobimasu 11. nugimasu 12. otoshimasu 13. hatarakimasu 14. kaimasu 15. ikimasu 16. hanashimasu 17. suwarimasu 18. naoshimasu 19. arukimasu 20. yasumimasu

   B. Regular II and Irregular

tsukemasu	tsukeru	tsukete	tsuketa	okimasu	okiru	okite	okita
kimasu	kuru	kite	kita	shimasu	suru	shite	shita

1. kimasu (wear) 2. kangaemasu 3. ochimasu 4. nemasu 5. anshin shimasu 6. wasuremasu 7. misemasu 8. dekakemasu 9. mottekimasu 10. sunde imasu 11. renshū shimasu 12. utte imasu 13. demasu 14. hajimemasu 15. orimasen

II   Make dialogues by changing the underlined parts as in the examples given.
   A. ex. Q: Sumisu-san wa mae ni <u>Kyūshū ni itta</u> koto ga arimasu ka.
      A: Hai, ichido <u>itta</u> koto ga arimasu.
      1. Hayashi-san no okusan ni aimashita. 2. Fuji-san ni noborimashita 3. Shinkansen ni norimashita 4. Yōroppa o mawarimashita
   B. ex. Q: Sumisu-san wa <u>yūfō o mita</u> koto ga arimasu ka.
      A: Iie, zannen desu ga, <u>mita</u> koto ga arimasen.
      1. Nankyoku e ikimashita 2. jūdō o naraimashita 3. hōritsu o benkyō shimashita 4. daitōryō ni aimashita
   C. ex. Q: <u>Sapporo no machi</u> o shitte imasu ka.
      A: <u>Shashin o mita</u> koto wa arimasu ga, <u>itta</u> koto wa arimasen.
      1. Jonson-san, namae o kikimashita, aimashita 2. Shēkusupia no Hamuretto, eiga o mimashita, shibai o mimashita 3. dorian, shashin de mimashita, tabemashita 4. sufinkusu, hanashi o kikimashita, mimashita
   D. ex. Q: Shūmatsu ni nani o shimashita ka.
      A: <u>Kaimono ni ittari</u>, <u>tomodachi ni attari</u> shimashita.
      1. tenisu o suru, sampo o suru 2. doraibu ni iku, kodomo to asobu 3. tegami o kaku, zasshi o yomu 4. tomodachi to hanasu, rekōdo o kiku 5. umi de oyogu, tsuri o suru

Short Dialogues

1. A: Kyōto ni itta koto ga arimasu ka.
   B: Hai, arimasu.
   A: Itsu ikimashita ka.
   B: Kyonen no 8-gatsu ni ikimashita.

2. Tanaka: Yoku Ōsaka ni shutchō shimasu ne.
   Katō: Ee. 1-kagetsu ni 5-kai gurai Tōkyō to Ōsaka o ittari kitari shite imasu.

I   Read this lesson's opening dialogue and answer the following questions.
    1. Buraun-san wa dare to Hokkaidō ni ikimasu ka. 2. Buraun-san wa Hokkaidō ni itta koto ga arimasu ka. 3. Kimura-san mo issho ni Sapporo shiten ni ikimasu ka. 4. Buraun-san wa Sapporo e itte, nani o shimasu ka.

II Put the appropriate particles in the parentheses.
    1. Yōroppa (   ) ryokō (   ) itta koto ga arimasu. 2. Kuruma (   ) Hokkaidō (   ) mawarimashita. 3. Sushi o tabeta koto (   ) arimasu (   ), tsukutta koto (   ) arimasen. 4. Sumisu-san wa hitori (   ) kōen (   ) aruite imasu.

III Convert the following verbs into the **-ta** form.
    1. noborimasu 2. aimasu 3. tabemasu 4. kikimasu 5. imasu 6. otoshimasu 7. yomimasu 8. wasuremasu 9. mimasu 10. asobimasu 11. mawarimasu 12. setsumei shimasu 13. oyogimasu 14. naraimasu 15. dekakemasu

IV Complete the sentences with the appropriate form of the verbs indicated.
    1. Fuji-san ni (   ) koto ga arimasu ka. (noborimasu) 2. Pātī de ichido Sumisu-san no okusan ni (   ) koto ga arimasu. (aimasu) 3. Kono rajio de gaikoku no nyūsu o (   ) koto ga dekimasu ka. (kikimasu) 4. Kinō no ban hon o (   ) dari, tegami o (   ) tari shimashita. (yomimasu, kakimasu) 5. Shūmatsu ni eiga o (   ) tari, tomodachi ni (   ) tari shimasu. (mimasu, aimasu)

V   Answer the following questions.
    1. Anata wa kabuki o mita koto ga arimasu ka. 2. Anata wa Chūgoku ni itta koto ga arimasu ka. 3. Anata wa Shinkansen ni notta koto ga arimasu ka. 4. Anata wa Nichi-yōbi ni nani o shimasu ka. (use . . . tari . . . tari shimasu.) 5. Anata wa kyonen no natsu-yasumi ni nani o shimashita ka.

5 A NEW WORD PROCESSOR

Opening Dialogue

Hayashi: Wāpuro no katarogu ga takusan arimasu ne.
Chan: Ee, kinō sērusu no hito ga kuremashita. Raigetsu kara uchi no ka no wāpuro no kishu o kaemasu.
Hayashi: Dono kishu ni shimasu ka.
Chan: A-sha no 45S ga yasuku narimashita ga . . . Demo, mada kimete imasen.
Hayashi: Shisutemu-bu no Ogawa-san ni sōdan shimashita ka?
Chan: Iie, mada hanashite imasen.
Hayashi: Chotto mazui desu ne. Mazu Ogawa-san ni hanashite kudasai.
Chan: Wakarimashita.
Hayashi: Kitto shisutemu-bu no ikō mo wakarimasu yo. Hanashi ga matomatte kara, minna ni shirasete kudasai.
Chan: Hai, sō shimasu. Hayashi-san wa itsumo kankei-sha to sōdan shite kara kimemasu ka.
Hayashi: Sō desu ne. Shigoto no susume-kata ni kanshite wa taitei sōdan shite kara kimemasu ga, jinji ni kanshite wa, kimeta ato de happyō shimasu.

Key Sentences

1. Fuyu mono no sēru ga hajimatte, kōto ya sētā ga yasuku narimashita.
2. Dezāto wa aisukurīmu ni shimasu.
3. Te o aratte kara sandoitchi o tabemashō.
4. Setsumei o kiita ato de, suraido o mimashita.
5. Mō kimemashita ka.
   Iie, mada kimete imasen.

EXERCISES

I Make dialogues by changing the underlined parts as in the example given.
   ex. Q: Dō narimashita ka.
       A: Yoku narimashita./Genki ni narimashita.
          1. ōkii 2. nigiyaka 3. tsumaranai 4. kurai 5. akarui 6. shizuka 7. fukuzatsu 8. benri 9. jōzu 10. kantan 11. tsuyoi 12. kirei

II Practice the following pattern by changing the underlined parts.
   ex. Watashi wa pianisuto ni naritai desu.
       1. yumei, naritai 2. atama ga ii, naritai 3. uchū hikōshi, naritakatta 4. byōki, naritaku nai 5. bimbō, naritaku nakatta

III Make dialogues by changing the underlined parts as in the examples given.
   A. *ex.* Q: Wāpuro wa dono kishu ni shimasu ka.
          A: A-sha no 45S ni shimasu.
             1. ryokō, doko, Yōroppa 2. hikkoshi, itsu, raigetsu 3. kaigi, dono heya, ōkii heya 4. dezāto, nani, aisukurīmu
   B. *ex.* Q: Nani o tabemashō ka.
          A: Tempura ni shimashō.
             1. doko de, o-cha o nomimasu, ano kissaten 2. nan de, ikimasu, takushī 3. nani o, tsukurimasu, tōfu no miso shiru 4. doko de, suraido o mimasu, 2-kai no kaigi-shitsu 5. dare ni, tanomimasu, hansamuna hito
   C. *ex.* Q: Itsu kara Nihon-go no benkyō o hajimemashita ka.
          A: Nihon ni kite kara hajimemashita.
             1. gorufu, kekkon suru 2. tenisu, supōtsu kurabu ni hairu 3. kono shigoto, daigaku o deru 5. unten, 18-sai ni naru
   D. *ex.* Q: Itsumo sōdan shite kara kimemasu ka.
          A: Hai, taitei sōdan shite kara kimemasu.
             1. katarogu o miru, kau 2. kōhī o nomu, shigoto o hajimeru 3. yoyaku o suru, resutoran ni iku 4. denwa o kakeru, tomodachi o tazuneru
   E. *ex.* Q: Itsu shawā o abimasu ka.
          A: Jogingu o shita ato de shawā o abimasu.
             1. bīru o nomu, shigoto ga owaru 2. sampo o suru, (o)hiru-gohan o taberu 3. minna ni shiraseru, Hayashi-san to hanasu 4. happyō suru, keikaku o kaeru
   F. *ex.* Q: Shokuji o suru mae ni ha o migakimasu ka, shokuji o shita ato de migakimasu ka.
          A: Shokuji o shite kara migakimasu.
             1. gohan o tabemasu, kusuri o nomimasu 2. kangaemasu, sōdan shimasu 3. Furansu ni ikimasu, Furansu-go no benkyō o shimasu 4. shinamono ga todokimasu, o-kane o haraimasu
   G. *ex.* Q: Mō kono hon o yomimashita ka.
          A: Iie, mada yonde imasen.
             1. kippu o kau 2. denwa o kakeru 3. nimotsu ga todoku 4. tegami o dasu
   H. *ex.* Sumisu: Tanaka-san wa Katō-san ni nani o agemashita ka.
          Watanabe: Haizara o agemashita.
          Sumisu: Anata niwa.
          Watanabe: Watashi niwa kabin o kuremashita.
             1. Kyōto no okashi, Kyōto no yakimono 2. akai nekutai, kinu no sukāfu 3. eiga no kippu, kabuki no kippu 4. uisukī, hanataba

Short Dialogues

1. A: Nan ni shimasu ka.
   B: Boku wa kōhī ni shimasu.
   C: Sō desu ne. Watashi wa jūsu ni shimasu.
   D: Watashi wa aisukurīmu desu.

2. A: Kono shorui wa dō shimashō ka.
   B: Sugu fakkusu de okurimashō.
   A: Benri ni narimashita ne.

I Read this lesson's opening dialogue and answer the following questions.
1. A-sha no wāpuro no 45S wa takaku narimashita ka, yasuku narimashita ka. 2. Chan-san wa wāpuro no katarogu o morau mae ni, Ogawa-san ni sōdan shimashita ka. 3. Hayashi-san wa shigoto no susume-kata ni kanshite wa kankei-sha to sōdan shite kara kimemasu ga, jin-ji ni kanshite wa dō desu ka. 4. Chan-san wa dare ni wāpuro no katarogu o moraimashita ka.

II Put the appropriate particles in the parentheses.
1. Tomodachi ga watashi ( ) shima ( ) shatsu ( ) kuremashita. 2. Dezāto wa aisukurīmu ( ) shimashō. 3. Hanashi ( ) matomatte ( ), minna ( ) shirasete kudasai. 4. Wāpuro ( ) kanshite wa hisho ( ) hō ( ) yoku shitte imasu. 5. Hiru-gohan ( ) tabeta ato ( ), kōen ( ) sampo shimashō. 6. Watashi wa kodomo ( ) koro pianisuto ( ) naritakatta desu.

III Complete the questions so that they fit the answers.
1. ( ) kishu o kaimasu ka./45S ni shimasu. 2. ( ) denwa o kakemasu ka./Uchi ni kaette kara kakemasu. 3. ( ) ni sōdan shimashita ka./Shisutemu-bu no Ogawa-san ni sōdan shimashita.

IV Complete the sentences with the appropriate form of the verbs indicated.
1. Miso shiru no ( ) kata o ( ) kudasai. (tsukuru, oshieru) 2. Wasuremono wa mada jimu-shitsu ni ( ) imasen. (todoku) 3. Mainichi uchi ni ( ) kara, 1-jikan gurai Nihon-go o benkyō shimasu. (kaeru) 4. Shigoto ga ( ) ato de, bīru o ( ) masen ka. (owaru, nomu) 5. Kodomo ni ( ) mae ni, kanai to yoku sōdan shimasu. (hanasu) 6. Wāpuro no kishu o ( ) koto ga dekimasu ka. (kaeru)

V Answer the following questions.
1. Anata wa Nihon-go ga jōzu ni narimashita ka. 2. Anata wa mō kyō no shimbun o yomimashita ka. 3. Asa shokuji o suru mae ni ha o migakimasu ka, shokuji o shita ato de ha o migakimasu ka. 4. Anata no sukina ryōri no tsukurikata o kantan ni setsumei shite kudasai. (Make use of patterns with **te kara, ato de, mae ni**.)

6 A PALE FACE

Opening Dialogue

Katō: Kaoiro ga yoku arimasen ne. Kaze desu ka.
Chan: Ee, ototoi isha ni itte kusuri o moratte kimashita ga, nakanaka yoku narimasen. Kesa wa netsu ga 38-do arimashita.
Katō: Soreja, hayaku uchi ni kaette yasunda hō ga ii desu yo.
Chan: Demo, kono projekuto ga hajimatta bakari desu kara.
Katō: Muri o shinai hō ga ii desu yo. Raishū wa motto isogashiku narimasu kara, ima no uchi ni naoshita hō ga ii desu yo.
Chan: Soredewa mōshiwake arimasen ga, Suzuki-kun ka Kimura-kun ni ato o yoku tanonde kara kaerimasu.
Katō: Sō desu ne. Suzuki-kun niwa sakki betsu no yōji o tanonda bakari desu kara, Kimura-kun no hō ga ii desu yo.
Chan: Wakarimashita. Dewa, o-saki ni shitsurei shimasu.
Katō: O-daijini.

Key Sentences

1. Sugu keisatsu ni denwa shita hō ga ii desu.
2. Chan-san wa 4-gatsu ni Hon Kon shiten kara kita bakari desu.
3. Ano mise e itte, tabako o katte kimasu.

I Review: Study the examples again and convert the verbs into the **-nai** form.
A. Regular I: iku → ikanai; isogu → isoganai; nomu → nomanai; shinu → shinanai; asobu → asobanai; hanasu → hanasanai; matsu → matanai; narau → narawanai; naoru → naoranai; aru → nai
1. oyogu 2. tsukuru 3. migaku 4. morau 5. otosu 6. motsu 7. sumu 8. kakaru 9. yobu 10. hirou 11. kesu 12. tsukau
B. Regular II and Irregular: shimeru → shimenai; oriru → orinai; kuru → konai; suru → shinai
1. hajimeru 2. dekiru 3. iru 4. kimeru 5. mottekuru 6. setsumei suru 7. denwa suru 8. wasureru

II Make dialogues by changing the underlined parts as in the examples given.
A. *ex.* Q: <u>Nan de</u> ikimashō ka.
    A: <u>Chikatetsu de itta</u> hō ga ii desu yo.
    1. dare ni kiku, Katō-san ni 2. nan-ji goro denwa suru, asa 10-ji goro 3. itsu kono shorui o okuru, ima sugu 4. pātī ni nan-nin tomodachi o yobu, takusan
B. *ex.* Q: Dō shimashō ka.
    A*a*: <u>Hayashi-san ni hanashita</u> hō ga ii desu.
    A*n*: <u>Hayashi-san ni hanasanai</u> hō ga ii desu.
    1. mado o shimeru 2. Tanaka-san ni iu 3. sugu dekakeru 4. basu de iku 5. Hayashi-san ni sōdan suru 6. (o)sake o mottekuru
C. *ex.* Q: <u>Itsu</u> ga ii desu ka.
    A: <u>Ashita no</u> hō ga ii desu.
    1. dore, kirei 2. nan-ji, gogo 3. dochira, akai 4. doko, shizukana tokoro 5. dare, Tanaka-kun
D. *ex.* Q: Iku mae ni <u>denwa shita</u> hō ga ii desu ka.
    A: Ee, sono hō ga ii deshō.
    1. neru mae ni kusuri o nomu 2. funabin de okuru 3. sutōbu o kesu 4. Tanaka-san ni shiraseru
E. *ex.* Q: Ima <u>denwa shite</u> mo ii desu ka.
    A: <u>Mō osoi desu</u> kara, <u>shinai</u> hō ga ii desu yo.
    1. tabako o suu, kenkō ni yoku nai desu 2. koko ni kuruma o tomeru, kōsaten ni chikai desu 3. sukoshi aruku, mada byōki ga naotte imasen 4. mō happyō suru, mada buchō ni hanashite imasen
F. *ex.* A: Rinda-san wa tabun <u>michi ga wakarimasen</u> yo.
    B: Dōshite desu ka.
    A: <u>Nihon e kita</u> bakari desu kara.
    1. mada kono tegami o yonde imasen, ima kaisha ni kimashita 2. kono kamera no tsukai-kata ga wakarimasen, kinō kaimashita 3. mada asa-gohan o tabete imasen, ima okimashita 4. sono nyūsu o shirimasen, shutchō kara kaerimashita
G. *ex.* Q: <u>Dare</u> ga ii desu ka.
    A: <u>Suzuki-kun ka Kimura-kun</u> ga ii desu.
    1. nani, Chūka ryōri, Furansu ryōri 2. itsu, getsu-yō, ka-yō 3. doko, Ginza, Shinjuku 4. ikura, ¥1,500, ¥2,000
H. *ex.* Q: Dochira e
    A: <u>Isha ni itte kusuri o moratte</u> kimasu.
    1. hon-ya ni iku, shūkanshi o kau 2. ano shokudō e iku, shokuji o suru 3. uchi e kaeru, hiru-gohan o taberu 4. ginkō ni yoru, o-kane o harau 5. yūbinkyoku e iku, tegami o dasu

Short Dialogues

1. Watanabe: O-kaze desu ka.
   Chan: Ee. Taishita koto wa arimasen ga, seki ga tomarimasen.
   Watanabe: Sore wa ikemasen ne.

2. Suzuki: Moshi-moshi, kore kara byōin ni yotte ikimasu kara, sukoshi osoku narimasu.
   Katō:　Dōka shimashita ka.
   Suzuki: Koronde ashi ni kega o shimashita.

Quiz

I Read this lesson's opening dialogue and answer the following questions.
1. Chan-san wa dare ni kusuri o moraimashita ka. 2. Chan-san no kaze wa sugu yoku narimashita ka. 3. Chan-san no ka dewa atarashii purojekuto ga hajimatta bakari desu ka. 4. Katō-san wa Suzuki-san ni yōji o tanonda ato de Chan-san to hanashimashita ka.

II Put the appropriate particles in the parentheses.
1. Ima no uchi (　) kaetta hō (　) ii desu yo. 2. Katō-san wa getsu-yōbi (　) ka-yōbi (　) Tōkyō ni kaerimasu. 3. (Watashi wa) sakki Suzuki-kun (　) betsu (　) yōji o tanomimashita. 4. Kaigi ga hajimatta bakari desu (　), heya (　) hairanaide kudasai. 5. Dewa, o-saki (　) shitsurei shimasu.

III Complete the sentences with the appropriate form of the verbs indicated.
1. Kega o shite imasu kara, isha o (　) hō ga ii desu. (yobu) 2. Kono ringo wa furui desu kara, (　) hō ga ii desu yo. (taberu) 3. Ima (　) bakari desu kara, sono nyūsu o mada (　) imasen. (kuru, kiku) 4. Hayaku kazoku ni (　) hō ga ii desu yo. (shiraseru) 5. Watanabe-san no heya ni (　), taipu o (　) kimasu. (iku, tanomu) 6. Kyō wa michi ga (　) imasu kara, kuruma de (　) hō ga ii desu yo. (komu, iku)

IV Circle the correct words in the parentheses.
1. Watashi wa (amari, taitei) densha no naka de shimbun o yomimasu. 2. Takushī o matte imasu ga, (nakanaka, yukkuri) kimasen. 3. (Hajimete, mazu) Hayashi-san ni shirasete, (sore-dewa, sorekara) minna ni shirasete kudasai. 4. Suzuki-kun wa (sakki, mō sugu) kita bakari desu.

V Choose a sentence appropriate to the situation described.
　A. Your friend is embarrassed about having left his bag on the train.
　　1. Densha o orite, eki-in ni hanashita bakari desu. 2. Eki no jimu-shitsu ni itte, eki-in ni hanashita hō ga ii desu. 3. Densha ni notte, eki-in ni hanashita koto ga arimasu.
　B. Your friend, despite having a fever, is drinking sake.
　　1. O-sake o takusan nonda hō ga ii desu yo. 2. Hayaku neta hō ga ii desu yo. 3. Sukoshi o-sake ga nomitai desu.

7 MR. JOHNSON'S ARRIVAL

Opening Dialogue

Katō:　Ashita wa Jonson-san ga Nihon ni kuru hi desu ne.
Suzuki: Ee, sō desu.
Katō:　Dare ka Narita Kūkō made mukae ni itte kuremasen ka.
Suzuki: Watashi ga ikimasu. Jikan ga arimasu kara.
Katō:　Kesa tanonda shigoto wa kyō-jū ni owarimasu ka.
Suzuki: Hai, dekimasu.
Katō:　Ja, onegaishimasu. Tokorode, Jonson-san o shitte imasu ka.
Suzuki: Rondon no jimusho ni ita hito desu ne.
Katō:　Ee.
Suzuki: Shashin de mita koto ga arimasu.
Katō:　Narita Kūkō ni tsuku jikan wa 14-ji 50-pun desu. Hikōki wa hayaku tsuku koto mo arimasu kara, hayame ni chūshoku o sumasete shuppatsu shite kudasai.
Suzuki: Hai. Jonson-san no tomaru hoteru wa doko desu ka.
Katō:　Watanabe-san ga shitte imasu kara, Watanabe-san ni kiite kudasai.
Suzuki: Hai.

Key Sentences

1. Sumisu-san wa ABC de hataraite iru bengoshi desu.
2. Kyūshū wa atatakai tokoro desu ga, fuyu wa yuki ga furu koto mo arimasu.

EXERCISES

I Noun-modifying patterns: Memorize the following sentences.
  A. 1. Kore wa omoshiroi hon desu. 2. Rinda-san wa kami ga nagai hito desu.
  B. 1. Kore wa kireina zasshi desu. 2. Are wa chichi ga sukina e desu. 3. Kore wa kodomo no koro watashi ga suki datta okashi desu.
  C. 1. Kore wa funabin de okuru nimotsu desu. 2. Asoko de hon o yonde iru hito wa Tanaka-san desu. 3. Kore wa haha ga kaita tegami desu.
  D. 1. Ginkō ni iku jikan ga arimasen. 2. Anata ga tomatta hoteru wa doko desu ka. 3. Kitte o utte iru tokoro o shitte imasu ka. 4. Rondon kara kita tomodachi ni aimashita.

II Noun-modifying patterns: Study the following sentences, concentrating on the underlined patterns.
  1. Kare wa omoshiroku nai hito desu. 2. Kore wa watashi ga hoshikatta yubiwa desu. 3. Kono naka de ryokō ni ikanakatta hito wa dare desu ka. 4. Tanaka-san ga kaisha ni konakatta hi wa senshū no kin-yōbi desu.

III Make dialogues by changing the underlined parts as in the examples given.
  A. *ex.* Q: Kore wa nan desu ka.
      A: E o kaku dōgu desu.
        1. yude tamago o kirimasu 2. toire o sōji shimasu 3. omoi nimotsu o hakobimasu 4. kēki o yakimasu
  B. *ex.* Q: Sumimasen, Tōkyō e iku basu wa dore desu ka.
      A: Ano eki no mae ni tomatte iru basu desu.
        1. 10-ji ni demasu 2. Ginza o tōrimasu 3. Ōsaka kara kimashita 4. Ōsaka o 10-ji ni shuppatsu shimashita
  C. *ex.* Q: Shimbun o utte iru tokoro o shitte imasu ka.
      A: Sā, chotto wakarimasen.
        1. shizuka desu 2. yasukute oishii desu 3. tenisu ga dekimasu 4. Tanaka-san no musuko-san ga tsutomete imasu 5. konde imasen
  D. *ex.* Q: Mainichi isogashii desu ka.
      A: Ee, tegami o kaku jikan mo arimasen.
        1. shimbun o yomimasu 2. kodomo to asobimasu 3. tomodachi to o-shaberi shimasu 4. fūfu-genka o shimasu
  E. *ex.* Q: Pātī ni kita hito wa dare desu ka.
      A: Kimura-san desu.
        1. kyonen kekkon shimashita 2. Nakamura-san ga suki deshita 3. Pātī de issho ni odoritakatta desu 4. kaigi ni shusseki shimasen deshita 5. mada kite imasen 6. mada mōshikonde imasen
  F. *ex.* A: Ano hito wa dare desu ka.
      B: Dono hito desu ka.
      A: Ki no shita de hon o yonde iru hito desu.
      B: Aa, ano ki no shita de hon o yonde iru hito desu ka. Are wa Howaito-san desu.
        1. ōkii koe de waratte imasu 2. seki o shite imasu 3. uwagi o kite imasen 4. ima tachimashita 5. kami ga mijikai desu 6. se ga takai desu

IV Practice the following pattern by changing the underlined parts.
  ex. Dare ka kimashita ka.
    1. nani, itte kudasai 2. doko, ikitai desu ne 3. itsu, ikimashō ka 4. dare, yobimashō ka

V Make dialogues by changing the underlined parts as in the example given.
  ex. Q: Itsumo hikōki de ikimasu ka.
      A: Ee, taitei hikōki de ikimasu ga, Shinkansen de iku koto mo arimasu.
        1. uchi de shimbun o yomimasu, densha no naka de yomimasu 2. jibun de nekutai o erabimasu, kanai ga erabimasu 3. asa-gohan o tabemasu, tokidoki tabemasen 4. yakusoku no jikan o mamorimasu, tama ni mamorimasen

Short Dialogues

1. Kachō: Dare ka chotto te o kashite kudasai.
   Suzuki: Nan deshō ka.
   Kachō: Kono shiryō o katazukete kuremasen ka.
   Suzuki: Hai, wakarimashita.

2. A: Dare ka koko ni atta shimbun o shirimasen ka.
   B: A, ima watashi ga yonde imasu.
   A: Ja, ato de misete kudasai.

Quiz

I Read this lesson's opening dialogue and answer the following questions.
   1. Dare ga Jonson-san o kūkō made mukae ni ikimasu ka. 2. Jonson-san wa doko no jimusho ni ita hito desu ka. 3. Katō-san wa Jonson-san no tomaru hoteru o shitte imasu ka. 4. Suzuki-san wa Jonson-san ni atta koto ga arimasu ka.

II Put the appropriate particles in the paretheses.
   1. Kore wa watashi (   ) kaita e desu. 2. Eki (   ) tsuku jikan wa nan-ji desu ka. 3. Watashi wa Jonson-san (   ) atta koto wa arimasen ga, shashin (   ) mita koto wa arimasu. 4. Hayaku shigoto (   ) sumasete, uchi ni kaerimasu. 5. Kūkō made kuruma (   ) mukae (   ) ikimasu. 6. Taitei hitori (   ) ryokō shimasu ga, tomodachi (   ) issho ni iku koto (   ) arimasu.

III Complete the sentences with the appropriate form of the verbs indicated.
   1. Supein-go ga (   ) hito wa dare desu ka. (dekimasu) 2. (Anata ga) Yamada-san ni (   ) hi wa itsu desu ka. (aimasu) 3. Kinō suraido o (   ) hito wa kyō mite kudasai. (mimasen deshita) 4. Eigo ga (   ) hito niwa Nihon-go de setsumei shimashō. (wakarimasen) 5. Kinō (   ) hito ni kono tegami o okutte kudasai. (kimasen deshita) 6. Kyō (   ) mono no naka de kore ga ichiban takakatta desu. (kaimashita) 7. Jonson-san ga (   ) hoteru o shitte imasu ka. (tomatte imasu) 8. Kore wa watashi no (   ) iro desu. (suki desu) 9. Kore wa kodomo no koro watashi ga (   ) o-kashi desu. (suki deshita) 10. Ano (   ) hito wa dare desu ka. (se ga takai desu)

IV Look at the picture on page 00 of the main text and answer the questions.
   1. Isu ni suwatte iru hito wa dare desu ka. 2. Uwagi o kite iru hito wa dare desu ka. 3. Sētā o kite iru hito wa dare desu ka. 4. Kasa o motte iru hito wa dare desu ka. 5. Tatte iru hito wa dare desu ka.

V Answer the following questions.
   1. Anata ga sunde iru tokoro wa doko desu ka. 2. Anata no suki na ryōri wa nan desu ka. 3. Anata ga ikitai tokoro wa doko desu ka. 4. Ima made ryokō ni itta tokoro no naka de doko ga ichiban subarashikatta desu ka.

8 THE O-BON FESTIVAL

Opening Dialogue

Chan: 8-gatsu no 10-ka goro Sendai e asobi ni ikitai to omoimasu ga, Shinkansen to hikōki to dochira ga benri desu ka.

Katō: Shinkansen no hō ga benri da to omoimasu yo. Demo, Shinkansen no shitei-ken wa mō nai to omoimasu. Hikōki no kippu mo tabun urikire deshō.

Chan: Dōshite desu ka.

Katō: 8-gatsu no naka goro wa O-Bon de, kuni e kaeru hito ga ōzei imasu. 10-ka goro kara, kono kisei rasshu ga hajimarimasu kara, ryokō wa yameta hō ga ii desu yo.

Chan: Suzuki-san mo 10-ka ni Sendai no uchi ni kaeru to kikimashia ga . . .

Katō: Ee, kare wa 1-kagetsu mae ni kippu o katta to itte imashita.

Chan: Sō desu ka. Ja, Sendai made kuruma de donogurai kakarimasu ka.

Katō: O-bon no shīzun wa 10-jikan ijō kakaru to omoimasu yo. Suzuki-san wa kyonen wa kuruma de ikimashita ga, sugoi jūtai datta to itte imashita . . . Soreni, O-Bon no ato wa Tōkyō e kaeru kuruma de michi ga komu deshō. Yū-tān rasshu desu yo.

Chan: Nihon wa hito ga ōi desu kara ne. Rasshu no nai tokoro e ikitai desu ne.

Katō: Rasshu no nai tokoro ga arimasu yo.

Chan: Doko desu ka.

Katō: Doko da to omoimasu ka. O-Bon no koro no Tōkyō desu yo. Hito mo kuruma mo sukunai shi, tsūkin rasshu mo nai shi, ii desu yo.

Chan: Naruhodo.

Key Sentences

1. Ashita wa sutoraiki desu kara, densha mo basu mo ugokanai to omoimasu.
2. Kimura-san wa Sapporo o shitte iru to itte imashita.
3. Ashita wa tabun ame deshō.
4. Oishii shi, yasui shi, kirei da shi, ano resutoran wa ii desu yo.

EXERCISES

I Make dialogues by changing the underlined parts as in the examples given.

A. *ex.* Q: Atarashii purojekuto o dō omoimasu ka.
   A: Taihen da to omoimasu.
   1. muzukashii desu 2. omoshiroi desu 3. tsumaranai desu 4. taikutsu desu 5. risāchi ga hitsuyō desu 6. muzukashii shigoto desu

B. *ex.* Q: Tanaka-san wa kimasu ka.
   A*a*: Hai, kuru to omoimasu.
   A*n*: Iie, konai to omoimasu.
   1. Kono shigoto wa ashita made ni dekimasu 2. nimotsu wa kyō-jū ni tsukimasu 3. shushō wa kono nyūsu o mō shitte imasu 4. Tanaka-san wa kodomo ga arimasu

C. *ex.* Q: Tanaka-san wa mo kaerimashita ka.
   A*a*: Ee, mō kaetta to omoimasu.
   A*n*: Iie, mada kaette inai to omoimasu.
   1. shūkai wa mō hajimarimashita 2. daijin wa kono nyūsu o mō kikimashita 3. Tanaka-san wa o-kyaku-san ni mō aimashita 4. kenkyū shiryō wa mō matomarimashita

D. *ex.* Q: Suzuki-san wa nan to itte imasu ka.
   A: Suzuki-san wa kinō wa doko nimo ikanakatta to itte imasu.
   1. Rinda, sakura wa totemo kirei deshita 2. Buraun, ano myūjikaru wa amari omoshiroku arimasen deshita 3. Sumisu, ashita kaigi ni detakunai desu 4. Yamada, amari supōtsu o suru jikan ga arimasen

E. *ex.* Q: Ano hito no mae no shigoto o shitte imasu ka.
   A: Gaikōkan datta to kikimashita ga. . .
   1. jimusho ga aru tokoro, keisatsu no tonari desu 2. o-kuni, atatakai tokoro desu 3. sotsugyō shita daigaku, Nihon no daigaku dewa arimasen 4. shiken no kekka, amari yoku arimasen deshita 5. wakai koro no shigoto, kangofu-san deshita

F.*ex.* Q: Ashita no tenki wa dō desu ka.
   A: Tabun ame deshō ne.
   1. ano mise, takai desu 2. ano shibai, omoshiroku nai desu 3. nichi-yōbi no kōen, nigiyaka desu 4. kore, tekitō ja nai desu 5. ashita no tenki, yuki ga furimasu 6. Tanaka-san, kuru koto ga dekimasen 7. Chan-san no kaze, yoku narimashita

G. *ex.* Q: Atarashii uchi wa dō desu ka.
   A: Hiroi shi kirei da shi subarashii desu.
   1. Ginza no machi, nigiyaka, omoshiroi, ii tokoro desu 2. atarashii kamera, karui, benri, ki ni itte imasu 3. ima no shigoto, isogashii, zangyō ga ōi, taihen desu 4. ima no apāto, semai, yakamashii, hikkoshitai to omotte imasu

H. *ex.* A: Taihen desu ne.
   B: Ee, o-kane ga kakaru shi, jikan mo kakaru shi.
   1. zangyō ga arimasu, yoku shutchō mo shimasu 2. osoku made hataraku koto mo arimasu, asa hayaku dekakeru koto mo arimasu 3. shigoto ga kawarimasu, hikkoshi mo shimasu

Short Dialogues

1. Buraun: Shinkansen no zaseki shitei-ken wa doko de utte imasu ka.
   Tsūkōnin: Asoko no midori no madoguchi de utte imasu.

   Buraun: Kyōto made otona 2-mai, kodomo 1-mai onegaishimasu.
   Ekiin: Tokkyū-ken mo irimasu ka.
   Buraun: Ee, onegai shimasu.

2. A: 10-ji 30-pun hatsu no Shin-Ōsaka-iki no Shinkansen wa nan-ban sen kara demasu ka.
   B: 17-ban sen desu.

Quiz

I Read this lesson's opening dialogue and answer the following questions.
1. Chan-san wa 8-gatsu no 10-ka goro doko e asobi ni ikitai to omotte imasu ka. 2. O-Bon no koro wa dōshite hayaku hikōki ya Shinkansen no kippu ga urikire ni narimasu ka. 3. Suzuki-san wa kyonen kuruma de kuni e kaerimashita ka, Shinkansen de kaerimashita ka. 4. O-Bon no koro no Tōkyō niwa rasshu ga nai to dare ga itte imasu ka. 5. Anata wa Chan-san ga 8-gatsu 10-ka ni Sendai e iku to omoimasu ka, ikanai to omoimasu ka.

II Put the appropriate particles in the parentheses.
1. Sumisu-san wa ima goro Kyōto no o-tera (   ) mawatte iru (   ) omoimasu. 2. Sumisu-san wa sono shigoto (   ) Ogawa-san (   ) tanonda (   ) itte imashita. 3. Netsu ga aru (   ), nodo mo itai (   ), kaze da (   ) omoimasu. 4. Kare mo 10-ka (   ) Sendai (   ) uchi (   ) kaeru (   ) kikimashita.

III Complete the questions so that they fit the answers.
1. Suzuki-kun to Kimura-kun to (   ) ga wakai desu ka./Kimura-kun no hō ga wakai to omoimasu. 2. Rinda-san wa (   ) Nihon ni kuru deshō ka./Tabun rainen kuru deshō. 3. Kare wa (   ) to itte imashita ka./Ashita wa tsugō ga warui to itte imashita. 4. Kono e o (   ) omoimasu ka./Nakanaka subarashii to omoimasu. 5. Anata wa (   ) ikimasen ka./ Atsui shi, hito ga ōi shi, ikitaku nai desu.

IV Complete the sentences with the appropriate form of the verbs indicated.
1. Kare wa kinō taishikan e (   ) to omoimasu. (ikimasen deshita) 2. Suzuki-san wa ashita (   ) to itte imashita. (kimasen) 3. Katō-san wa (   ) to Watanabe-san ga itte imashita. (genki deshita) 4. Kare wa Jonson-san ni atta koto ga (   ) to itte imashita. (arimasen) 5. Kinō no eiga wa (   ) to itte imashita (omoshiroku nakatta desu) 6. Ano hito wa Buraun-san no (   ) to omoimasu. (okusan dewa arimasen) 7. Rinda-san wa kono iro ga (   ) deshō. (ki ni irimasen) 8. Kyō wa samui shi, (   ) shi, dekaketaku nai desu (ame desu) 9. Kaigi wa mada (   ) to omoimasu. (owatte imasen)

V Answer the following questions.
1. Ashita wa ii tenki deshō ka. 2. Anata wa itsu kara Nihon-go o naratte imasu ka. 3. Nihon-go no benkyō wa omoshiroi to omoimasu ka. 4. Anata wa natsu-yasumi ni dokoka ryokō ni ikimasu ka.

9 PREP SCHOOL

Opening Dialogue

Keiko: Ara, Jonson-san.
Jonson: A, Keiko-san. O-dekake desu ka.
Keiko: Ee, korekara dekakenakereba narimasen.
Jonson: Ima sugu denakute wa ikemasen ka.
Keiko: Gomennasai. Kyō-jū ni yobikō no mōshikomi o shinakereba narimasen kara.
Jonson: Yobikō. Keiko-san wa daigaku ni gōkaku shita to kikimashita ga.
Keiko: Ee, dai-ni shibō no daigaku niwa gōkaku shimashita ga, dai-ichi shibō no kokuritsu daigaku wa fu-gōkaku deshita. Rainen mata juken shimasu.
Jonson: Sō desu ka. Ja, itterasshai.
Keiko: Ittemairimasu.

Keiko: Mōshikomi no shorui wa kore de ii desu ka. Kore, nyūgaku kin to 3-kagetsu-bun no jugyō-ryō desu. Sorekara samā kōsu mo mōshikomitai to omoimasu ga, yoku kangaete kara ato de yūbin de mōshikonde wa ikemasen ka.

Madoguchi
no hito: Ee, Yūbin demo ii desu. Shiharai mo wazawaza koko made konakute mo ii desu yo. Ginkō ni furikonde kudasai.

Keiko: Genkin kakitome demo ii desu ka.

Madoguchi: Hai, dochira demo kekkō desu.

Key Sentences

1. Kyō-jū ni mōshikomi o shinakereba narimasen.
2. Koko ni mata konakute wa ikemasen ka.
3. Iie, konakute mo ii desu.
4. Yūbin de okutte wa ikemasen ka.
5. Ee, yūbin demo ii desu.

EXERCISES

I Verbs: Review the examples and convert the verbs into the plain negative form.

  ex. Reg. I: hajimaru → hajimaranai; Reg. II: iru → inai; Irreg: kuru → konai; suru → shinai
  1. matomaru 2. kaeru (change) 3. tanomu 4. shiraseru 5. harau 6. dasu 7. susumeru 8. tomaru 9. yobu 10. deru 11. tazuneru 12. shuppatsu suru 13. furu 14. kiru (cut) 15. mukaeru 16. yaku 17. sōji suru 18. tōru 19. yameru 20. katte kuru 21. odoru 22. warau 23. katazukeru 24. erabu 25. mamoru 26. sotsugyō suru 27. kawaru 28. iru (need) 29. kasu 30. moratte kuru

II Make dialogues by changing the underlined parts as in the examples given.

  A. *ex.* Q: Ima o-kane o harawanakereba narimasen ka.
    A*a*: Hai, onegaishimasu.
    A*n*: Iie, ima harawanakute mo ii desu.
    1. watashi mo kuru 2. ashita made ni suru 3. ima mōshikomu 4. pasupōto o miseru 5. kyō-jū ni shiraseru

  B. *ex.* Q: Namae o kakanakute mo ii desu ka.
    A*a*: Hai, kakanakute mo ii desu.
    A*n*: Sumimasen ga, kaite kudasai.
    1. Sumisu-san o mukae ni iku 2. minasan ni setsumei suru 3. hisho ni shiraseru 4. kopī o tanomu

  C. *ex.* Q: Kono heya o tsukatte wa ikemasen ka.
    A*a*: Dōzo, tsukatte mo ii desu yo.
    A*n*: Sumimasen ga, tsukawanaide kudasai.
    1. koko de tabako o suu 2. namae o happyō suru 3. kūrā o tsukeru 4. kuruma de kuru 5. niwa de shashin o toru

  D. *ex.* Q: Ashita kaigi ni denakute wa ikemasen ka.
    A: Denakute mo ii desu yo.
    1. kusuri o nomu 2. Sumisu-san nimo iu 3. kutsu o nugu 4. kore o oboeru 5. denwa o kakeru

  E. *ex.* Q: Ima hanko ga arimasen. Sain demo ii desu ka.
    A: Hai, sain demo kekkō desu.
    1. pen, empitsu 2. jikan, ato 3. hima, nichi-yōbi 4. genkin, kādo

  F. *ex.* Q: Koko ni gomi o sutete mo ii desu ka.
    A: Koko ni sutete wa ikemasen.
    1. koko ni kuruma o tomeru 2. kyōshitsu de kōhī o nomu 3. shibafu ni hairu

Short Dialogues

1. Otoko no hito: Koko de tabako o sutte mo ii desu ka.
   Kangofu: Iie, sutte wa ikemasen. Kono byōin dewa kin'en desu.

2. A: Mōshikomi no kigen wa itsu desu ka.
   B: 3-gatsu matsujitsu desu. Yūbin demo ii desu ga, 31-nichi made ni kochira ni o-negaishimasu.

3. Yamada: Tadaima.
   Watanabe: Okaeri nasai. Nakayama-san wa imashita ka.
   Yamada: Ee, atte shorui o watashite kimashita.

Quiz

I   Read this lesson's opening dialogue and answer the following questions.
    1. Keiko-san wa dai-ichi shibō no kokuritsu daigaku nimo gōkaku shimashita ka. 2. Keiko-san wa gōkaku shita daigaku ni hairimasu ka. 3. Keiko-san wa samā kōsu no mōshikomi ni mata yobikō made ikanakereba narimasen ka. 4. Samā kōsu no shiharai wa genkin kakitome demo ii desu ka. 5. Keiko-san wa samā kōsu no shiharai o ginkō ni furikomu deshō ka, genkin kakitome de okuru deshō ka.

II Put the appropriate particles in the parentheses.
    1. Tōfu o chiisaku kirimashita ga, kore (   ) ii desu ka. 2. Uchi (   ) musuko wa kotoshi daigaku (   ) gōkaku shimashita. 3. Pen (   ) kakanakute wa ikemasen ka./Empitsu (   ) kekkō desu. 4. Yoku kangaete (   ), ato de yūbin (   ) okurimasu. 5. Nyūgaku-kin o ginkō (   ) furikomimasu.

III Complete the questions so that they fit the answers.
    1. (   ) made ni mōshikomanakute wa ikemasen ka./Raishu-chū ni mōshikonde kudasai. 2. (   ) harawanakereba narimasen ka./¥5,000 desu. 3. (   ) taishikan e ikanakereba narimasen ka./Pasupōto ga hitsuyō desu kara. 4. Kōhī to kōcha to (   ) ga ii desu ka./Dochira demo kekkō desu. 5. (   ) bun no jugyōryō desu ka./6-kagetsu bun desu.

IV Complete the sentences with the appropriate form of the verbs indicated.
    1. Ashita no asa 5-ji ni (   ) nakereba narimasen. (okiru) 2. Shorui o (   ) wa ikemasen yo. (wasureru) 3. Kono hon o kyō-jū ni (   ) nakereba narimasen. (yomu) 4. O-sake o (   ) nakute wa ikemasen ka. (yameru)/Sō desu ne. (   ) hō ga ii deshō. (yameru) 5. Itsu made ni okane o (   ) nakereba narimasen ka. (harau)/Raishū-chū ni (   ) kudasai. (harau) 6. Koko o (   ) mo ii desu ka. (katazukeru)/Mada tsukaimasu kara, (   ) nakute mo ii desu. (katazukeru) 7. Koko wa chūsha kinshi desu kara, kuruma o (   ) wa ikemasen. (tomeru)

V   Answer the following questions.
    1. Nihon ni iru gaikoku no hito wa minna Nihon-go o benkyō shinakereba narimasen ka. 2. Kōsaten ni kuruma o tomete mo ii desu ka. 3. Hikōki no naka de tabako o sutte wa ikemasen ka. 4. Anata wa ashita nani o shinakereba narimasen ka.

10 LETTER FROM KYUSHU

Tanaka-san, o-genki desu ka.

Watashi wa ima kazoku to issho ni Kyūshū ni kite imasu. Kinō mae kara ikitakatta Aso-san ni ikimashita. Subarashii nagame deshita.

Watashi-tachi ga tomatte iru ryokan no niwa de, yūbe hotaru o mimashita. Mae ni Tōkyō no ryōtei de kago no naka no hotaru o mita koto wa arimasu ga, shizen no hotaru wa hajimete desu. Nōyaku no shiyō o yamete kara, kawa ga kirei ni natte, hotaru ga fueta to ryokan no shujin ga itte imashita.

Asatte watashi-tachi wa koko o dete, Kumamoto shinai o kembutsu shita ato, Nagasaki e ikimasu. Nagasaki wa Edo jidai no Nihon no tatta hitotsu no bōeki-kō de, sono koro wa Nihon no naka de ichiban kokusai-tekina machi datta to zasshi de yonda koto ga arimasu. Kanai wa Nihon no rekishi ni kyōmi ga arimasu kara, totemo tanoshimi ni shite imasu.

Minami Kyūshū nimo ikitai to omoimasu ga, raishū moku-yōbi ni Amerika honsha kara shachō ga kimasu kara, sore made ni Tōkyō ni kaeranakereba narimasen.

Oku-sama nimo dōzo yoroshiku o-tsutae kudasai.

7-gatsu 30-nichi

Jon Buraun

Put the appropriate words in the parentheses.

   Tanaka-san, o-genki desu ka.
   Watashi wa ima kazoku (   ) issho ni Kyūshū ni kite (   ). Kinō mae kara ikitakatta Aso-san ni ikimashita. Subarashii nagame (   ).
   Watashi-tachi (   ) tomatte iru ryokan no niwa (   ), yūbe hotaru o mimashita. Mae ni Tōkyō no ryōtei de kago (   ) naka no hotaru o mita (   ) wa arimasu ga, shizen no hotaru (   ) hajimete desu. Nōyaku no shiyō o yamete (   ), kawa ga kirei (   ) natte, hotaru ga fueta (   ), ryokan no shujin ga (   ) imashita.
   Asatte watashi-tachi wa koko (   ) dete, Kumamoto shinai (   ) kembutsu shita (   ), Nagasaki e ikimasu. Nagasaki wa Edo jidai (   ) Nihon no (   ) hitotsu no bōeki-kō (   ), sono koro wa Nihon no naka (   ) ichiban kokusai-tekina machi (   ) to zasshi (   ) yonda koto ga arimasu. Kanai wa Nihon no rekishi (   ) kyōmi ga (   ) kara, totemo tanoshimi ni shite imasu.
   Minami Kyūshū nimo ikitai (   ) omoimasu ga, raishū moku-yōbi (   ) Amerika honsha kara shachō ga kimasu kara, (   ) Tōkyō ni kaeranakereba (   ).
   Oku-sama (   ) mo dōzo (   ) otsutae kudasai.

11 JOB INTERVIEW

Opening Dialogue

Hayashi: [Rirekisho o minagara] Nakamura-san wa ototoshi daigaku o sotsugyō shita n desu ka.
Nakamura: Hai. Sotsugyō shite kara shōsha ni tsutomete imashita.
Hayashi: Naze yameta n desu ka.
Nakamura: Watashi no semmon no shigoto ga dekimasen deshita kara, omoshiroku nakatta n desu.
Hayashi: Dōshite kono kaisha o eranda n desu ka.
Nakamura: Kochira dewa kompūtā o tsukau shigoto ga ōi to kiita kara desu. Watashi wa daigaku de kompūtā saiensu o benkyō shite imashita. Kono kaisha dewa watashi no sukina shigoto ga dekiru to omotta n desu.
Hayashi: Kaisha ni haitte kara 1-kagetsu kenshū shinakereba naranai koto o shitte imasu ka.
Nakamura: Ee, shitte imasu.
Hayashi: Soreni gaikoku ni shutchō suru koto mo ōi desu yo.
Nakamura: Hai, daijōbu desu.
Hayashi: Sō desu ka. Dewa, kekka wa ato de renraku shimasu.

Key Sentences

1. Ashita kaigi ga arimasu kara, ima shiryō o kopī shite iru n desu.
2. Buraun-san ga Kyūshū e ryokō shita koto o shitte imasu ka.

EXERCISES

I Practice the following patterns.
   A. *ex.* ikimasu → iku n desu → ikanai n desu
                    → itta n desu → ikanakatta n desu
      1. oyogimasu 2. yomimasu 3. asobimasu 4. keshimasu 5. machimasu 6. aimasu 7. iimasu 8. dekimasu 9. arimasu 10. imasu 11. sunde imasu 12. agemasu 13. mimasu 14. kimasu 15. sōdan shimasu

   B. *ex.* yasui desu → yasui n desu → yasuku nai n desu
                       → yasukatta n desu → yasukunakatta n desu
      1. oishii desu 2. abunai desu 3. muzukashii desu 4. takai desu 5. tsumetai desu 6. tsumaranai desu 7. atama ga ii desu 8. tsugō ga warui desu 9. yasumitai desu

C. *ex.* suki desu → sukina n desu → suki dewa nai n desu
→ suki datta n desu → suki dewa nakatta n desu
1. jōzu desu 2. hima desu 3. benri desu 4. anzen desu 5. kaigi desu 6. shigoto desu 7. byōki desu 8. kenshū desu

II Make dialogues by changing the underlined parts as in the examples given.
A. *ex.* Q: Ashita pātī ni ikimasen ka.
A: Zannen desu ga, isogashii n desu.
1. kaigi ga arimasu 2. jikan ga arimasen 3. byōin ni ikanakereba narimasen 4. tomodachi to au yakusoku o shimashita 5. kuni kara haha ga kite imasu 6. ashita kara shutchō desu 7. kanai ga byōki desu 8. karada no guai ga yoku nai desu

B. *ex.* Q: Naze kinō pātī ni konakatta n desu ka.
A: Isogashikatta n desu.
1. kaigi ga arimashita 2. shōtai-jō o moraimasen deshita 3. kyū ni tsugō ga waruku narimashita 4. Pātī ga aru koto o shirimasen deshita

C. *ex.* Q: Kenshū shinakereba naranai koto o shitte imasu ka.
A: Sō desu ka. Shirimasen deshita.
1. Nakamura-san ga kon'yaku shimashita 2. ashita konakutemo ii desu 3. Tanaka-san ga taikin o otoshimashita 4. Jōnzu-san ga kochira ni kite imasu 5. Suzuki-san no okāsama ga nakunarimashita

D. *ex.* Q: Kanojo wa yoku zangyō shimasu ne.
A: Ee, demo hayaku kaeru koto mo ōi desu yo.
1. tenisu o suru, gorufu o yarimasu 2. resutoran de taberu, uchi de tabemasu 3. kaisha no hito to nomu, hitori de nomimasu 4. benkyō suru, asobi ni ikimasu

E. *ex.* A: Itsu kara jogingu o hajimemashita ka.
B: Kekkon shite kara hajimemashita.
A: Dōshite yameta n desu ka.
B: Kega o shita kara desu.
1. piano, shōgakkō ni hairimasu, kyōmi ga nakunarimashita 2. eikaiwa, daigaku o sotsugyō shimasu, isogashiku narimashita 3. yamanobori, kaisha ni hairimasu, kodomo ga umaremashita

Short Dialogues

1. Kyaku: Tokei o kaitai n desu ga, nan-kai desu ka.
Depāto no ten'in: Tokei uriba wa 6-kai de gozaimasu.

2. Sumisu: Supōtsu kurabu ni haitta n desu ka.
Buraun: Ee, suiei to tenisu o hajimeta n desu.
Sumisu: Supōtsu o suru koto wa karada ni ii desu ne.

Quiz

I Read this lesson's opening dialogue and answer the following questions.
1. Hayashi-san wa nani o minagara, Nakamura-san ni kiite imasu ka. 2. Nakamura-san ga shōsha de shite ita shigoto wa kanojo no semmon deshita ka. 3. Nakamura-san wa shōsha de shite ita shigoto wa omoshirokatta to itte imasu ka. 4. Nakamura-san wa ABC dewa sukina shigoto ga dekiru to omotte imasu ka.

II Put the appropriate particles in the parentheses.
1. Nakamura-san wa shōsha (   ) tsutomete imashita. 2. Kare wa 1965-nen (   ) A daigaku (   ) sotsugyō shimashita. 3. Kare ga kaisha (   ) yameru koto (   ) shitte imasu ka. 4. Kekka wa ato (   ) renraku shimasu. 5. Dōshite kono kaisha (   ) eranda n desu ka./Kochira dewa Nihon-go o tsukau shigoto (   ) ōi (   ) kiita (   ) desu.

III Complete the questions so that they fit the answers.
1. (   ) pātī ni konakatta n desu ka./Atama ga itakatta n desu. 2. (   ) shita n desu ka./Te ni kega o shita n desu. 3. Kono kompyūta wa (   ) tsukau n desu ka./Chotto fukuzatsu desu kara, Watanabe-san ni kiite kudasai. 4. (   ) o mite iru n desu ka./Kyōto de totta shashin o mite iru n desu.

IV Complete the sentences with the appropriate form of the words indicated.
1. Suzuki-san wa imasen ne. Mō uchi ni (   ) n desu ka./Ee, 30-pun gurai mae ni kaerimashita yo. (kaerimashita) 2. Ogawa-san ni (   ) n desu ka./Ee, Ogawa-san wa kinō (   ) n desu. (shirasemasen deshita, yasumi deshita) 3. Doko ni (   ) n desu ka. Denwa ga arimashita yo./Dōmo sumimasen. Chotto kōhī o nomi ni itte imashita. (itte imashita) 4. Nani mo (   ) n desu ka./Ee, (   ) n desu. (tabemasen, tabetaku arimasen) 5. Takushī de (   ) n desu ka. /Ee, jikan ga amari (   ) n desu. (dekakemasu, arimasen) 6. Suzuki-san wa yasumi desu ka./Ee, (   ) n desu. (byōki desu) 7. Kinō anata ga (   ) koto o kare nimo (   ) kudasai. (iimashita, hanashimasu) 8. Kanji o (   ) koto wa muzukashikunai desu. (oboemasu)

V Choose a statement appropriate to the situations described.
A. You hear a friend has quit his job and you ask him about it.
1. Itsu kaisha o yameru n desu ka. 2. Kaisha o yamete wa ikemasen ka. 3. Hontō ni kaisha o yameta n desu ka.
B. You see a friend doing something ridiculous.
1. Nani o shite iru n desu ka. 2. Nani o shinakereba narimasen ka. 3. Kare wa nan to itte imasu ka.
C. You tell a friend that you didn't go to the party because of a headache.
1. Totemo atama ga itai n desu. 2. Kyū ni atama ga itaku natta n desu. 3. Atama ga itakatta to omoimasu.

12 HOTEL RESERVATIONS

Opening Dialogue

Yoyaku-gakari: Miyako Ryokan de gozaimasu.
Sumisu: Moshi moshi, raigetsu no yokka to itsuka ni yoyaku o onegaishitai n desu ga, heya wa aite imasu ka.
Yoyaku-gakari: Hai, gozaimasu. Nan-mei-sama desu ka.
Sumisu: Futari desu. Ikura desu ka.
Yoyaku-gakari: 1-paku 2-shoku-tsuki de, o-hitori ¥18,000 de gozaimasu. Zeikin to sābisu-ryō wa betsu de gozaimasu.
Sumisu: Hai, ja, sore de onegaishimasu.
Yoyaku-gakari: O-namae to o-denwa-bangō o dōzo.
Sumisu: Sumisu to iimasu. Denwa-bangō wa Tōkyō 03-405-3636 desu. Sochira wa Kyōto no eki kara chikai desu ka.
Yoyaku-gakari: Eki kara kuruma de 10-pun gurai desu.
Sumisu: Eki ni tsuita toki, denwa o shimasu kara, sochira kara mukae ni kite kuremasen ka.
Yoyaku-gakari: Hai, kashikomarimashita. Go-tōchaku wa nanji goro desu ka.
Sumisu: 4-ji goro desu.
Yoyaku-gakari: Hai, wakarimashita. 8-ji yori osoku naru baai wa, kanarazu go-renraku kudasai.
Sumisu: Hai. Sorede, ryōkin wa itsu haraimashō ka.
Yoyaku-gakari: Osore-irimasu ga, uchikin to shite ¥18,000 go-yūsō kudasai.
Sumisu: Wakarimashita.

Key Sentences

1. Sumisu-san wa hon o yomu toki, megane o kakemasu.
2. Eki ni tsuita toki, denwa o shimasu.
3. Osoku naru baai wa renraku shimasu.
4. Watashi wa Sumisu to iimasu.

EXERCISES

I Make dialogues by changing the underlined parts as in the examples given.

A. *ex.* Q: Yoku sampo shimasu ka.

A: Ee, tokidoki asa suzushii toki, sampo shimasu.

1. kono kusuri o nomu, atama ga itai 2. jogingu o suru, tenki ga yokute samuku nai 3. kūrā o tsukau, totemo atsui

B. *ex.* Q: Himana toki nani o shimasu ka.

A: Himana toki desu ka. So desu nē, rekōdo o kiitari shite imasu ne.

1. kodomo to asobu 2. supōtsu kurabu ni oyogi ni iku 3. tomodachi ni denwa suru 4. sukina hon o yomu

C. *ex.* Q: Kodomo no toki doko ni sunde imashita ka.

A: Ōsaka ni sunde imashita.

1. kaigi, dono heya o tsukaimasuka, kono heya o 2. mensetsu, dare to hanashimashitaka, buchō to 3. gakusei, doko o ryokō shimashitaka, Yōroppa o 4. shiken, nani o motte ikimasuka, empitsu to keshigomu o

II Practice the following pattern by changing the underlined parts.

A. *ex.* Kuni ni kaeru toki, omiyage o kaimasu.

1. michi ga wakarimasen, keikan ni kikimasu 2. michi ga konde imasu, takushī yori densha no hō ga hayai desu. 3. saifu o hiroimashita, kōban ni todokemasu 4. Nihon ni kimashita, Nihon-go ga wakarimasen deshita

III Make dialogues by changing the underlined parts as in the examples given.

A. *ex.* A: Nan-ji goro eki ni tsukimasu ka.

B: Sā, chotto wakarimasen. Eki ni tsuita toki denwa shimasu.

A: Sō shite kudasai. Mukae ni ikimasu kara.

1. kūkō 2. Tōkyō eki 3. hoteru 4. minato

B. *ex.* Q: Hajimete hito ni atta toki, nan to iimasu ka.

A: "Hajimemashite" to iimasu.

1. shokuji o shimasu, itadakimasu 2. shokuji ga owarimashita, gochisosama deshita 3. uchi o demasu, itte mairimasu 4. uchi ni kaerimashita, tadaima 5. hito to wakaremasu, sayōnara

C. *ex.* Q: Shūmatsu no ryokō wa dō shimashō ka.

A: Ame no baai wa yamemashō.

1. densha ga suto desu 2. Tanaka-san no tsugō ga warui desu 3. tenki ga yoku nai desu 4. taifū desu

D. *ex.* Q: Osoku naru baai wa renraku shite kudasai.

A: Hai, sō shimasu.

1. okuremasu 2. kimasen 3. o-kane ga tarimasen 4. yotei ga kawarimashita 5. byōki ni narimashita 6. gōgaku shimashita

E. *ex.* Q: *Rose* wa Nihon-go de nan to iimasu ka.

A: Bara to iimasu.

1. ball point pen, bōru pen 2. *pants*, zubon 3. *politician*, seijika 4. *contract*, keiyaku 5. *to celebrate*, iwau

Short Dialogues

1. Kimura: Ashita no supōtsu taikai no ken desu ga, ame ga futta toki wa dō shimasu ka.
Suzuki: Asa 6-ji made ni yamanai baai wa chūshi desu.
Kimura: Yoku wakaranai toki wa dō shimasu ka.
Suzuki: Sono baai wa koko ni denwa o shite tashikamete kudasai.

2. Watanabe: Nihon-no seikatsu ni naremashita ka.
Jonson: Ee, sukoshi-zutsu.
Watanabe: Komatta toki wa itsu demo itte kudasai.

Quiz

I Read this lesson's opening dialogue and answer the following questions.

1. Sumisu-san wa doko ni denwa o shimashita ka. 2. Ryokan no hito wa heya ga aite iru to

itte imashita ka. 3. Miyako ryokan wa eki kara kuruma de nan-pun gurai kakarimasu ka. 4. Sumisu-san wa 1-paku 2-shoku no ryōkin to nani o harawanakereba narimasen ka. 5. Miyako ryokan no baai wa tomaru mae ni uchikin o harawanakereba narimasen ka.

II Put the appropriate particles in the parentheses.
1. Ryōkin wa o-hitori ¥10,000 (　　) gozaimasu. 2. Watashi wa Sumisu (　　) iimasu. 3. Eki (　　) tsuita toki, denwa o shimasu (　　), sochira (　　) mukae (　　) kite kuremasen ka. 4. 6-ji (　　) osoku naru baai wa, kanarazu renraku shite kudasai. 5. 1-paku 2-shoku tsuki (　　) hitori ¥15,000 kakarimasu ga, ii desu ka. 6. Kare wa gaikōkan (　　) shite, Nihon ni kite imasu. 7. Kaigi (　　) toki, o-cha o mottekite kudasai.

III Complete the questions so that they fit the answers.
1. Rinda-san wa (　　) kita n desu ka./7-ji no nyūsu o kiite iru toki kimashita. 2. Kore wa Nihon-go de (　　) to iimasu ka./Keshigomu to iimasu. 3. (　　) ryokan ni osoku naru to iwanakatta n desu ka./Denwa o suru jikan ga nakatta n desu.

IV Complete the sentences with the appropriate form of the words indicated.
1. Kyonen Kyōto ni (　　) toki, kirei na kami no kasa o kaimashita. (ikimashita) 2. Uketsuke no hito ga (　　) baai wa 1-kai kara denwa o shite kudasai. (imasen) 3. Asa (　　) toki, ame ga (　　) imashita. (okimashita, furimasu) 4. Ashita made ni (　　) baai wa, renraku o (　　) kudasai (dekimasen, shimasu) 5. Saifu o (　　) toki wa kōban ni (　　) nakereba ikemasen. (hiroimashita, todokemasu) 6. Kinō chūshoku o (　　) toki, kyū ni onaka ga (　　) narimashita. (tabete imashita, itai) 7. Watanabe-san ni hajimete (　　) toki, (　　) hito da to omoimashita. (aimashita, kirei) 8. Jikan ga (　　) toki, sandoitchi o tabemasu. (arimasen) 9. (　　) toki, Igirisu o (　　) koto ga arimasu. (wakai, ryokō shimasu) 10. (　　) toki, hon o (　　) dari, kodomo to (　　) dari shite imasu. (hima, yomimasu, asobimasu)

V Choose the most polite statement appropriate to the situation described.
A. You're at work and you answer the phone.
1. ABC de gozaimasu. 2. ABC to iimasu. 3. ABC ga gozaimasu.
B. You tell a client you will show him around when it's convenient for him.
1. Go-tsugō no ii toki, go-annai kudasai. 2. Jikan ga aru toki, annai shimasu yo. 3. Go-tsugō no ii toki, go-annai shimasu yo.
C. You call Kato's house and ask if he is at home.
1. Katō-san ni go-renraku kudasai. 2. Katō-san wa irasshaimasu ka. 3. Katō-san to iimasu ka.

13 A GIFT OF CHOCOLATE

Opening Dialogue

Chan: Jonson-san, kore, Watanabe-san kara Jonson-san e no purezento desu yo. Kinō Jonson-san ga inakatta node, boku ga azukarimashita. Kādo mo arimasu yo.

Jonson: Dōmo arigatō. Watanabe-san kara no okurimono, ureshii desu ne.

Chan: Nakami wa chokorēto deshō.

Jonson: Aketa n desu ka.

Chan: Kādo wa rabu retā kamo shiremasen yo.

Jonson: E, yonda n desu ka.

Chan: Haha. Jitsuwa boku mo onaji mono o moratta n desu. Suzuki-kun mo moratta darō to omoimasu yo.

Jonson: E. Minna moratta n desu ka.

Chan: Giri-choko desu yo, giri-choko.

Jonson: Giri-choko tte nan desu ka.

Chan: Giri no chokorēto desu. Nihon no Barentain dē no shūkan desu. Shokuba demo yoku josei kara dansei ya jōshi ya dōryō ni chokorēto o purezento shimasu.

Jonson: "Itsumo o-sewa ni natte imasu. Korekara mo yoroshiku. Maikeru e. Mayumi yori." Yappari giri-choko deshita.

Chan: Zannen deshita.

Jonson: Demo, giri-choko o takusan moratta hito wa dō suru n deshō ka.
Chan: Tabun okusan ya gāru furendo ga taberu n deshō.
Jonson: Ja, yorokobu hito wa josei to kashi-ya desu ne.
Chan: Moratta dansei mo tanoshii desu yo.

Key Sentences

1. Yuki ga takusan futte iru kara hikōki wa tobanai kamo shiremasen.
2. Suzuki-san wa Rinda-san o shiranai darō to omoimasu.
3. Hikōki ga tobanai node, ryokō ni iku koto ga dekimasen.

EXERCISES

I Make dialogues by changing the underlined parts as in the examples given.

A. *ex.* A: Tanaka-san wa konai kamo shiremasen yo.
　　　B: Sō desu ka.
　　　A: Okusan ga byōki da to itte imashita kara.
　　　　1. jikan ga arimasu, kyō wa hima desu 2. imasen, dekakemasu 3. ryokō ni ikimashita, konshū wa yasumimasu 4. kaigi ni shusseki shimasen deshita, shut-chō desu.

B. *ex.* A: Shigoto ga zembu owarimashita.
　　　B: Ashita wa hima kamo shiremasen ne.
　　　　1. ame ga yamimashita, hare desu 2. chūmon ga takusan kimashita, isogashii desu 3. ashita o-kyaku-san ga sūnin kimasu, kaigi o suru jikan ga arimasen

C. *ex.* Q: Kaigi wa itsu desu ka.
　　　A: Ashita no gozen-chū darō to omoimasu.
　　　　1. Tanaka-san, doko, kaigi-shitsu. 2. tantōsha, dare, Suzuki-san 3. shiken, nan-ka kara nan-ka made, 35-ka kara 40-ka made 4. tōchaku, nan-ji, yonaka no 1-ji goro 5. ano hadena kōto, dare no, Sumisu-san no

D. *ex.* Q: Kippu wa yoyaku shita hō ga ii deshō ka.
　　　A: Ee, konde iru kara yoyaku shita hō ga ii darō to omoimasu yo.
　　　　1. kono hō ga benri desu, minna ga tsukatte imasu 2. Nyūyōku wa ima samui desu, 12-gatsu desu 3. Yamada-san wa kaisha o yamemasu, yametai to itte imashita 4. Tanaka-san wa mō kaerimashita, kaban ga arimasen.

E. *ex.* Q: Ano hito wa kuru deshō ka.
　　　A*a*: Ee, tabun kuru darō to omoimasu yo.
　　　A*n*: Konai darō to omoimasu yo.
　　　　1. sakura wa saite imasu 2. ano mise de aisukurīmu o utte imasu 3. ano hito wa Supein-go ga wakarimasu 4. Sumisu-san wa watashi o shitte imasu

F. *ex.* Q: Dōshite sore o tsukatte imasu ka.
　　　A: Benri na node tsukatte imasu.
　　　　1. mado o akemashita ka, atsui desu. 2. bitamin o nomimashita ka, karada ga darui desu. 3. sugu wakarimashita ka, kantan deshita 4. mise wa shimatte imasu ka, saijitsu desu 5. yamemashita ka, jōzu ni narimasen

G. *ex.* Q: Dō shimashita ka.
　　　A: Tanaka-san kara henji ga konai node komatte imasu.
　　　　1. kuruma ga ugokimasen 2. isogashii toki ni o-kyaku-san ga kimasu 3. daijina toki ni Sumisu-san ga imasen 4. saifu o wasuremashita 5. shiken no mae ni kaze o hikimashita

II Practice the following dialogues.

A. Q: Kore wa Watanabe-san kara moratta okurimono desu ka.
　　A: Hai, Watanabe-san kara no okurimono desu.

B. Q: Kore wa Tanaka-san ni dasu tegami desu ka.
　　A: Hai, Tanaka-san e no tegami desu.

C. Q: Kore wa Jonson-san ni ageru purezento desu ka.
　　A: Hai, Jonson-san e no purezento desu.

D. Q: Kore wa doko de okita mondai desu ka.
　　A: Ōsaka shisha de no mondai desu.

E. Q: Kore wa dono kaisha to shita keiyaku desu ka.
   A: ABC to no keiyaku desu.

Short Dialogues

1. Tanaka-fujin: Anō, kore, tsumaranai mono desu ga, Kyōto no o-miyage
                desu.
   Kato-fujin: Mā, itsumo sumimasen. Enryo naku itadakimasu.

2. A: Miso shiru tte nan desu ka.
   B: Nihon-jin ga yoku nomu potāju desu.

Quiz

I   Read this lesson's opening dialogue and answer the following questions.
    1. Jonson-san ga moratta chokorēto wa dare kara no purezento desu ka. 2. Chan-san mo
    chokorēto to kādo o moraimashita ka. 3. Chan-san ga Jonson-san e no purezento o azukatta
    hi wa nan no hi desu ka. 4. Giri-choko o takusan moratta dansei wa hitori de zenbu taberu
    darō to Chan-san wa itte imasu ka.

II Put the appropriate words in the parentheses.
    1. Gāru-furendo (   ) no purezento o kai ni ikimashita. 2. Tokyō (   ) no seikatsu wa
    hontō ni tanoshikatta desu. 3. Rondon (   ) no nimotsu ga todokimashita. 4. Itsumo o-
    sewa (   ) natte imasu. Kore (   ) mo dōzo yoroshiku. Maikeru e Mayumi (   ). 5.
    Yobikō t(   ) nan desu ka.

III Complete the questions so that they fit the answers.
    1. Kinō (   ) konakatta n desu ka./Isogashikatta node, shitsurei shimashita. 2. (   )
    shimashita ka./Bengoshi ga konai node, komatte imasu. 3. Atarashii buchō wa (   ) hito
    deshō ka./Atama ga yokute majimena hito darō to omoimasu yo. 4. Miso shiru tte, (   )
    desu ka./Miso no sūpu desu yo.

IV Complete the sentences with the appropriate form of the words indicated.
    1. Kare ga (   ) node, anshin shimashita. (genki desu) 2. Kore wa (   ) darō to
    omoimasu. (Sumisu-san no mono dewa arimasen) 3. Tanaka-san wa (   ) kamo
    shiremasen yo. (byōki desu) 4. Kare wa (   ) node, Eigo ga (   ) darō to omoimasu yo.
    (gaikōkan deshita, jōzu desu) 5. Shujin wa tabun kasa o (   ) darō to omoimasu. (motte
    ikimasen deshita) 6. Kono chikatetsu wa Ginza o (   ) darō to omoimasu. (tōrimasen) 7.
    Shimbun wa isu no ue ni (   ) kamo shiremasen. (okimashita) 8. Sugu atarashii seikatsu
    ni (   ) deshō. (naremasu) 9. Densha ga (   ) node, basu' de kimashita. (ugokimasen
    deshita) 10. Sakura wa mada (   ) darō to omoimasu. (saite imasen)

V   Choose a statement appropriate to the situation described.
    A. It's April and, although you are not in Tokyo, you are asked if the cherry trees are
       blooming there.
       1. Sakura wa mō saite iru darō to omoimasu. 2. Sakura wa kireina hana da to
       omoimasu. 3. Sakura wa mō sakanai kamo shiremasen.
    B. You tell your section chief you have to go to the hospital to see your father.
       1. Chichi ga byōki na node, byōin e iku kamo shiremasen. 2. Otō-san ga byōki na node,
       byōin e itte wa ikemasen ka. 3. Chichi ga byōki na node, byōin e ikanakereba
       narimasen.
    C. You want to know the meaning of the acronym *UFO*.
       1. Yūfō tte nan desu ka. 2. Yūfō to iimasu. 3. Yūfō wa nan to iimasu ka.

14 THE REFEREE'S ROLE

Opening Dialogue

Sumisu: Wā, sugoi hito desu ne.
Tanaka: Sumō no shonichi wa itsumo man'in desu. Hito ga takusan ite, Rinda-san ya okusan ga
        yoku miemasen ne.

Sumisu: A, asoko ni imashita. Hora, sumō o minagara yakitori o tabete iru no ga miemasu yo.

Tanaka: Sā, watashi-tachi mo asoko e itte, bīru demo nominagara suwatte mimashō.

Sumisu: Ee, demo kono torikumi ga owaru made koko de ii desu. Urusakute anaunsu ga yoku kikoemasen ga, dohyō no ue ni iru no wa.

Tanaka: Fujinomine to Sakuraryū desu.

Sumisu: Hadena kimono o kite, dohyō no ue de ugokimawatte iru no wa dō iu hito desu ka.

Tanaka: Are wa gyōji desu.

Sumisu: Aa, jajji desu ne.

Tanaka: Ee, demo sore wa tatemae desu. Kuroi kimono o kite, dohyō no mawari ni suwatte iru no ga shimpan iin de, hontō no jajji desu. Ano hito-tachi wa rikishi no OB de, erai n desu yo.

Sumisu: Ja, gyōji wa jajji no kengen ga nai n desu ka.

Tanaka: Ee, jitsuwa kettei-ken wa nai n desu.

Sumisu: Sō desu ka. Chotto nattoku dekimasen ne.

Tanaka: Demo hatsugen-ken wa arimasu yo.

Sumisu: Sore o kiite anshin shimashita.

Key Sentences

1. Sono hanashi o kiite, anshin shimashita.
2. Bīru demo nominagara, suwatte mimashō.
3. Jonson-san o Narita Kūkō made mukae ni itta no wa Suzuki-san desu.
4. Asoko ni shiroi biru ga miemasu.
5. Anaunsu ga yoku kikoemasen.

EXERCISES

I   Make dialogues by changing the underlined parts as in the examples given.

    A. *ex.* Q: Dō shita n desu ka.

           A: Atsukute nomu koto ga dekinai n desu.

               1. omoi, hitori de mochimasu 2. isogashii, hayaku kaerimasu 3. fuben, tsukaimasu 4. fukuzatsu, setsumei suru

    B. *ex.* A: Nyūsu o kiite anshin shimashita.

           B: Nani ka atta n desu ka.

               1. shimbun o yomimashita, bikkuri shimashita 2. haha kara tegami o moraimashita, anshin shimashita 3. yonaka ni denwa ga arimashita, odorokimashita 4. shirase ga kimasen, komatte iru n desu

II Practice the following pattern by changing the underlined part.

    ex. Suzuki-san wa aruite kaisha ni ikimashita.

           1. suwaru, sumō o mimasu 2. isogu, shiryō o atsumemasu 3. warau, sayōnara o iimasu 4. denwa o suru, Ōsaka shisha ni toiawasemasu

III Make dialogues by changing the underlined parts as in the examples given.

    A. *ex.* Q: Mainichi benkyō shite imasu ka.

           A: Ee, mainichi benkyō suru no wa taihen desu.

               1. yoru osoku made shigoto o shimasu, taihen 2. kodomo to asobimasu, tanoshii 3. shokuji o tsukurimasu, mendō 4. asa 5-ji ni okimasu, muzukashii

    B. *ex.* Q: Yoku, e o kakimasu ne.

           A: Ee, e o kaku no ga sukina n desu.

               1. yama o arukimasu 2. jōdan o iimasu 3. ryokō ni ikimasu 4. eiga o mimasu

    C. *ex.* Q: Nani o wasureta n desu ka.

           A: Shukudai o mottekuru no o wasureta n desu.

               1. denwa shimasu 2. okane o azukemasu 3. sekken o kaimasu 4. yakusoku shimashita

    D. *ex.* Q: Kyō kuru no wa dare desu ka.

           A: Ēto, kyō kuru no wa Tanaka-san desu.

               1. minna ni renraku shimasu, dare, Watanabe-san 2. Pātī ni kimasen, dare, Sumisu-san 3. kinō ikimashita, doko, toshokan 4. tomodachi ni aimasu, itsu, do-yōbi 5. abunai, doko, Nyūyōku 6. shinsetsu, dare, Rinda-san

E. *ex.* Q: O-taku kara Fuji-san ga miemasu ka.
　　A: Tenki ga ii toki wa yoku miemasu.
　　　　1. tōku no yama 2. umi 3. Tōkyō tawā 4. atarashiku dekita takai biru

F. *ex.* Q: Nani ga kikoeru n desu ka.
　　A: Mushi no koe ga kikoeru n desu.
　　Q: Itsumo kikoeru n desu ka.
　　A: Ie, yoru shizukana toki ni kikoeru n desu.
　　　　1. densha no oto, asa hayaku 2. tonari no terebi no oto, yoru osoku 3. akachan no naki-goe, hiruma 4. kinjo no kodomo no koe, yūgata

G. *ex.* Q: Hiru-gohan o tabenai n desu ka.
　　A*a*: Ee, tabenai n desu.
　　A*n*: Iie, tabemasu.
　　　　1. ashisutanto wa kettei-ken ga arimasen 2. jikan ga arimasen 3. wasuremono o tori ni ikimasen deshita 4. ano sensei no namae o shirimasen

H. *ex.* Q: Kinō itsu made matte ita n desu ka.
　　A: Kaigi ga owaru made matte imashita.
　　　　1. kuraku narimasu 2. henji ga kimasu 3. genkō ga dekimasu 4. kotae ga demasu

Short Dialogues

1. Suzuki:　　　Moshi moshi, moshi moshi, kikoemasu ka.
　Yamakawa: Moshi moshi, o-denwa ga tōi n desu ga, mō sukoshi ōkii koe de onegaishimasu.
　Suzuki:　　　Kochira wa Suzuki desu ga, kikoemasu ka.
　Yamakawa: A, kikoemashita. Suzuki-san desu ne.

2. A: Shitsurei desu ga, Tanaka-san ja arimasen ka.
　B: Hai, Tanaka-desu ga.

Quiz

I　Read this lesson's opening dialogue and answer the following questions.
　　1. Rinda-san to Tanaka-san no okusan wa sumō o minagara nani o shite imasu ka. 2. Urusakute anaunsu ga yoku kikoenai to itta no wa dare desu ka. 3. Shimpan iin wa nani o kite, doko ni suwatte imasu ka. 4. Hontō no jajji wa gyōji desu ka, shimpan iin desu ka.

II　Put the appropriate particles in the parentheses.
　　1. Tenki ( ) ii toki, Fuji-san ( ) miemasu. 2. Watashi wa tegami ( ) todoku ( ) o matte imashita. 3. Yoru osoku kuruma ( ) oto ( ) kikoemashita. 4. Shiroi uwagi ( ) kite iru ( ) wa Sumisu-san desu. 5. Odoroita kamo shiremasen ga, kore wa hontō ( ) hanashi desu.

III　Complete the questions so that they fit the answers.
　　1. Ano hito wa ( ) hito desu ka./Daitōryō no musuko de, yūmei na pianisuto desu. 2. ( ) made koko de matsu n desu ka./Kaigi ga owaru made matte kudasai. 3. ( ) o mite iru n desu ka./Kēki o tsukutte iru no o mite iru n desu. 4. 3-gatsu 3-ka wa ( ) hi desu ka./Onna no ko no o-matsuri no hi de, tomodachi o yonde pātī o shitari suru hi desu.

IV　Complete the sentences with the appropriate form of the words indicated.
　　1. Nyūsu o ( ), bikkuri shimasu. (kikimasu) 2. Shiryō o zembu ( ) no wa taihen desu. (atsumemasu) 3. Asoko de ( ) no ga miemasu ka./Ie, ( ), yoku miemasen. (tsuri o shite imasu, tōi desu) 4. Tegami o ( ) no o wasuremashita. (dashimasu) 5. Jikan ga ( ), iku koto ga dekimasen. (arimasen) 6. Shokuji ga ( ) made, terebi demo mimashō. (dekimasu) 7. Hanashi ga ( ), yoku wakarimasen. (fukuzatsu desu)

V　Circle the correct words in the parentheses.
　　1. Atsui desu ne. Bīru (ya, demo, hodo) nomimasen ka./Ii desu ne. 2. 6-ji made ni (kanarazu, wazawaza, taitei) renraku shite kudasai. 3. Fugōkaku da to omotte imashita ga, (kanarazu, yappari, tabun) fugōkaku deshita. 4. Anata wa shiranakatta n desu ka./Ee, (zehi, soreni, jitsuwa) shiranakatta n desu.

VI　Answer the following questions.
　　1. Anata wa sumō o mita koto ga arimasu ka. 2. Anata no heya kara nani ga miemasu ka. 3. Yoru anata no heya ni iru toki, kuruma no oto ga kikoemasu ka. 5. Anata wa yama ni noboru no ga suki desu ka. 5. Shokuji o suru toki, Nihon-jin wa hajime ni nan to iimasu ka.

15 A FORGOTTEN UMBRELLA

Opening Dialogue

Buraun: Kinō supōtsu kurabu ni ittara, Yamamoto-san ni aimashita.
Watanabe: Ototoi koko ni kita Yamamoto-san desu ka.
Buraun: Ee.
Watanabe: Yamamoto-san ga kasa o wasurete kaerimashita ga, dō shimashō ka.
Buraun: Watashi ga sono kasa o azukarimashō. Raishū supōtsu kurabu ni iku toki, motte ikimasu kara. Yamamoto-san ni attara watashimasu. Moshi awanakattara, uketsuke ni azukemasu.
Watanabe: Onegaishimasu.

Uketsuke: Ohayō gozaimasu.
Buraun: Ohayō gozaimasu. Yamamoto Tarō-san to iu hito wa mō kite imasu ka. Koko no kaiin da to omoimasu.
Uketsuke: Kaiin no Yamamoto-sama desu ne. Kyō wa Yamamoto-sama wa yūgata 6-ji ni irasshaimasu.
Buraun: Sō desu ka. Yamamoto-san no kasa o azukatte iru n desu ga, 6-ji ni kuru nara, ima koko ni azukete mo ii desu ka.
Uketsuke: Hai, dōzo.
Buraun: Watashi wa ABC no Buraun to iimasu. Kare ga kitara, kore o watashite kudasai.
Uketsuke: Hai, tashika-ni.

Key Sentences

1. Sendai made kuruma de ittara, 10-jikan kakarimashita.
2. Moshi ame ga futtara, haikingu wa yamemasu.
3. Hikōki de iku nara, hayaku kippu o katta hō ga ii desu yo.

EXERCISES

I Practice the following patterns by changing the underlined parts as in the examples given.
   A. *ex.* Hiru-gohan o takusan tabetara nemuku narimashita.
      1. sake o nomimashita, atama ga itaku narimashita 2. supōtsu kurabu ni ikimashita, mukashi no tomodachi ni aimashita 3. sake o nonde unten shimashita, jiko o okoshimashita 4. kinō yoshū o shimasen deshita, kyō zenzen wakarimasen deshita

   B. *ex.* Q: Kaigi wa itsu hajimemasu ka.
            A: 10-ji ni nattara sugu hajimemasu.
               1. shachō ga kimasu 2. zen'in ga soroimasu 3. shorui o zembu kubarimasu 4. chūshoku ga sumimasu

   C. *ex.* Q: Hima ga attara dō shimasu ka.
            A: Moshi hima ga attara Nihon-jū ryokō shitai desu.
               1. o-kane ga arimasu 2. jikan ga arimasu 3. kuruma ga arimasu

   D. *ex.* Q: Moshi takusan o-kane ga attara dō shimasu ka.
            A: Takusan o-kane ga attara ōkii uchi o kaitai desu.
               1. rikon shimasu 2. kifu shimasu 3. koibito ni daiyamondo o okurimasu 4. chokin shimasu 5. sekai-jū ryokō shimasu

   E. *ex.* Q: Kōchi ga konai kamo shiremasen yo. Dō shimasu ka.
            A: Sō desu ne, moshi kare ga konakattara iku no o yamemasu.
               1. Michi ga wakarimasen 2. o-kane ga tarimasen 3. jikan ga arimasen 4. kodomo ga yorokobimasen

   F. *ex.* Q: Atsukattara mado o akete kudasai.
            A: Hai sō shimasu.
               1. samui desu, hītā o tsukemasu 2. takai desu, kaimasen 3. isogashiku nai desu, asobi ni kimasu 4. kibun ga yoku nai desu, yasumimasu

II Make dialogues by changing the underlined parts as in the examples given.
   A. *ex.* A: Hiru-gohan o tabetai n desu ga.
      B: Hiru-gohan o taberu nara ano resutoran ga ii desu yo.
      1. supōtsu kurabu ni hairimasu, ii kurabu o shōkai shimashō 2. umi ni ikimasu, watashi no kuruma o tsukatte mo ii desu yo 3. tēpurekōdā o kaimasu, chiisai hō ga benri desu yo 4. Kyūshū ni ikimasu, ferī ga ii desu yo

   B. *ex.* Q: Ame dattara dō shimasu ka.
      A: Ame nara yotei o kaemasu.
      1. ame, ikimasen 2. Tanaka-san ga rusu, mata ato de denwa shimasu 3. hima, gorufu o shimasu 4. dame, mō ichido yarimasu

   C. *ex.* Q: Anata wa ikimasu ka.
      A: Moshi ano hito ga iku nara watashi wa ikimasen.
      1. dekakemasu 2. kaerimasu 3. utaimasu 4. hanashimasu 5. tetsudaimasu 6. yamemasu

   D. *ex.* Q: Dare (donata) ga kimashita ka.
      A: Yamamoto-san to iu hito ga kimashita.
      1. Tarō, kodomo 2. Hayashi-sama, kata 3. Guddoman-san, onna no hito

   E. *ex.* Q: Nan to iu hon o yomimashita ka.
      A: "Kokoro" to iu hon o yomimashita.
      1. tokoro ni tomarimashita, Kanazawa 2. eiga o mitai desu, 7-nin no Samurai 3. rekōdo o kaimashita, Tsuki no Hikari 4. uta o utaimasu, Howaito Kurisumasu

Short Dialogues————————————————————————————————————
1. A: Kono hen ni nimotsu o azukeru tokoro wa arimasen ka.
   B: Asoko ni koin rokkā ga arimasu. Moshi ippai nara, kaisatsuguchi no soba ni ichiji azukari-jo ga arimasu.

2. Howaito: Kaigi wa nakanaka owarimasen ne.
   Watanabe: 7-ji ni nattara owaru deshō
   Howaito: Sō desu ka. 7-ji ni naru nara osaki ni shitsurei shimasu.

Quiz
 I Read this lesson's opening dialogue and answer the following questions.
   1. Buraun-san wa Yamamoto-san no wasureta kasa o dare kara azukarimashita ka. 2. Buraun-san wa doko de Yamamoto-san ni sono kasa o watashitai to omotte imasu ka. 3. Buraun-san wa supōtsu kurabu ni itta toki, Yamamoto-san ni au koto ga dekimashita ka. 4. Yamamoto-san wa kono supōtsu kurabu no kaiin desu ka.

 II Put the appropriate particles in the parentheses.
   1. Uketsuke no hito (   ) nimotsu (   ) azukemashita. 2. Kaiin (   ) Yamamoto-sama wa kyō yūgata 6-ji (   ) irasshaimasu. 3. Yamamoto-san ga kasa (   ) wasurete kaerimashita./Ja, watashi (   ) sono kasa (   ) azukarimashō. Supōtsu kurabu (   ) Yamamoto-san (   ) attara, watashimasu. 4. *7-nin no Samurai* (   ) iu eiga o mimashita.

III Complete the questions so that they fit the answers.
   1. Kinō kita hito wa (   ) to iu hito desu ka./Fujita-san to iu hito desu. 2. Moshi Yamamoto-san ga konakattara, (   ) shimashō ka./Tegami de shirasete kudasai. 3. (   ) hikkosu n desu ka./Uchi ga dekitara, hikkoshimasu. 4. (   ) ni shorui o watashimashita ka./Tanaka-san ni watashimashita.

IV Complete the sentences with the appropriate form of the words indicated.
   1. Wāpuro o (   ) nara, ii mise o oshiemashō. (kaimasu) 2. Zen'in ga (   ) tara, (   ) kudasai. (soroimasu, hajimemasu) 3. Sake o (   ) dara, kibun ga (   ) narimashita. (nomimasu, warui desu) 4. (   ) nara, eiga o (   ) ni ikimasen ka. (hima desu, mimasu) 5. Kono isu wa tsukatte imasen./(   ) nara, (   ) hō ga ii desu yo. (tsukaimasen, katazukemasu) 6. (   ) tara, sukoshi (   ) kudasai. (tsukaremasu, yasumimasu) 7. (   ) tara, (   ) kudasai. (isogashiku nai desu, tetsudaimasu) 8. Tsukurikata ga (   ) nara, (   ) no o yamemasu. (mendō desu, tsukurimasu) 9. Ashita (   ) tara, dekakemasen. (ame desu) 10. Kyōto ni (   ) nara, kono chizu o (   ) mashō. (ikimasu, agemasu) 11.

nimotsu ga (   ) node, (   ) kudasai. (omoi desu, azukarimasu)

V   Answer the following questions.
1. O-kane o hirottara, anata wa dō shimasu ka. 2. 1-kagetsu yasumi ga attara, nani o shimasu ka. 3. Tomodachi no uchi e iku toki, michi ga wakaranakattara, anata wa dō shimasu ka. 4. Ima made mita eiga no naka de, nan to iu eiga ga ichiban omoshirokatta desu ka.

16 THE NEW SHOWROOM DESIGN

Opening Dialogue

Yamakawa: Moshi moshi, Hayashi-buchō desu ka. Kochira wa M sekkei jimusho no Yamakawa desu ga, go-irai no shōrūmu no sekkei ga dekiagarimashita. Sakki fakkusu de zumen o okurimashita ga, ikaga desu ka?
Hayashi: Ee, nakanaka ii desu ne.
Yamakawa: Nanika mondai wa arimasen ka. Ashita kara kōji o hajimereba, raishū-chū ni dekiagarimasu. Moshi mondai ga nakereba, sassoku hajimetai to omoimasu. Nemmatsu ni naru to gyōsha mo isogashiku narimasu kara, hayakereba hayai hodo ii to omou n desu ga.
Hayashi: Sō desu nē. Sumimasen ga, hajimeru mae ni mō ichido atte sōdan shitai n desu ga.
Yamakawa: Wakarimashita. Sochira no go-tsugō ga yokereba, korekara ukagaimasu.
Hayashi: Dekireba sō shite kudasai. Watashi wa 8-ji goro made kaisha ni imasu. 6-ji ni naru to omote no iriguchi wa shimarimasu. Hantai-gawa ni mawaru to uraguchi ga arimasu kara, soko kara haitte kudasai. Uraguchi wa 10-ji made aite imasu.
Yamakawa: Wakarimashita.
Hayashi: Ja, yoroshiku onegaishimasu.

Key Sentences

1. Jikan ga areba, Kyōto shisha nimo ikimasu.
2. Yuki ga furu to, ano yama de sukī ga dekimasu.
3. Sakana wa atarashikereba atarashii hodo ii desu.

EXERCISES

I   Verbs: Study the examples, convert into the conditional forms, and memorize.
    ex. iku → ikeba, hanasu → hanaseba, taberu → tabereba, miru → mireba, kuru → kureba, suru → sureba
    1. arau 2. tatsu 3. uru 4. tanomu 5. tsukau 6. aruku 7. dekiru 8. kakeru 9. oshieru 10. oriru 11. tsutomeru 12. shiraseru 13. motte kuru 14. annai suru 15. moratte kuru 16. shimpai suru

II Adjectives: Study the examples, convert into the conditional forms, and memorize.
    ex. atsui → atsukereba, hayaku nai → hayakunakereba
    1. sukunai 2. omoshiroi 3. tsugō ga ii 4. atama ga itai 5. warui 6. waruku nai 7. hanashitai 8. ikitaku nai 9. kakanai

III Make dialogues by changing the underlined parts as in the examples given.
    A. *ex.* Q: Yondara wakarimasu ka.
           A: Ee, yomeba wakarimasu ga, yomanakereba wakarimasen.
           1. koko ni iru 2. toiawaseru 3. ryūgaku suru 4. tetsudau 5. ashita kuru 6. au 7. nomu 8. tsukau 9. miru
    B. *ex.* Q: Yasukattara kaimasu ka.
           A: Ee, yasukereba kaimasu ga, yasukunakereba kaimasen.
           1. atarashii 2. oishii 3. ii 4. omoshiroi 5. akai 6. mezurashii 7. chikai 8. yawarakai 9. hoshii

IV Practice the following patterns by changing the underlined parts.
    A. *ex.* Haru ni nareba, hana ga sakimasu.
           1. megane o kakemasu, yoku miemasu 2. yoku nemurimasu, atama ga hakkiri

shimasu 3. yukkuri hanashimasu, yoku wakarimasu 4. shitsumon ga arimasen, korede owarimasu 5. hakkiri iimasen, wakarimasen 6. o-kane to jikan ga arimasen, kono mondai wa kaiketsu shimasen

B. *ex.* Takakereba, kaimasen.
1. tsugō ga warui, denwa o kudasai 2. isogashii, hoka no hito ni tanomimasu 3. isogashiku nai, issho ni eiga ni ikimashō 4. ikitaku nai, ikanakute mo ii desu 5. o-kane ga tarinai, kashimashō 6. go-meiwaku de nai, issho ni ikitai n desu ga 7. go-mendō de nai, onegaishimasu

V Make dialogues by changing the underlined parts as in the examples given.
A. *ex.* A: Shigoto wa hayakereba hayai hodo ii desu ne.
B: Ee, watashi mo sō omoimasu.
1. nimotsu, karui 2. yachin, yasui 3. kyūryō, ōi 4. zeikin, sukunai 5. yasumi, nagai 6. yasai, atarashii

B. *ex.* Q: Sonna ni hoshii n desu ka.
A: Ee, mireba miru hodo hoshiku narimasu.
1. omoshiroi, yomu 2. suki, au 3. wakaranai, kangaeru 4. ureshii, kiku 5. tanoshii, sumu

VI Practice the following patterns by changing the underlined parts.
A. *ex.* Sake o nomu to, tanoshiku narimasu.
1. (o)-kane o iremasu, kippu ga demasu 2. tsugi no kōsaten o magarimasu, byōin ga arimasu 3. massugu ikimasu, hidari-gawa ni posuto ga arimasu 4. tabako o takusan suimasu, gan ni narimasu yo 5. kōhī o nomimasen, shigoto ga dekimasen

B. *ex.* Q: Dō suru to aku n desu ka.
A: Botan o osu to akimasu.
1. jūsu ga dete kuru, o-kane o ireru 2. mizu ga deru, ashi de pedaru o fumu 3. denki ga kieru, doa o shimeru 4. mado ga aku, rebā o hiku

C. *ex.* Nani ka shitsumon ga arimasu ka.
1. dare, kaisha no hito ga kimashita ka 2. itsu, himana toki ikitai desu 3. doko, shizukana tokoro de hanashimashō 4. ikutsu, oishii kēki o katte kite kudasai 5. nansatsu, omoshiroi hon o yōi shite kudasai

Short Dialogue

A: Taihen. Mō 10-ji han desu ka. Hikōki no jikan ni maniawanai kamo shiremasen.
B: Kuruma de kūkō made okurimashō. Isogeba maniau to omoimasu yo.
A: Soreja, onegaishimasu.

Quiz

I Read this lesson's opening dialogue and answer the following questions.
1. Dare ga dare ni fakkusu de zumen o okurimashita ka. 2. Hayashi-san no kaisha ni nan-ji made ni ikeba, omote no iriguchi kara hairu koto ga dekimasu ka. 3. Yamakawa-san wa dōshite hayaku kōji o hajimetai to itte imasu ka. 4. ABC no uraguchi wa nan-ji ni naru to shimarimasu ka.

II Put the appropriate words or word parts in the parentheses.
1. Nani (   ) tsumetai nomimono wa arimasen ka. 2. Itsu made (   ) harawanakute wa ikemasen ka./Hayakere (   ) hayai hodo ii darō (   ) omoimasu. 3. Kono mise wa hiru kara yoru 12-ji (   ) aite imasu. 4. Go-irai (   ) sekkei ga dekiagarimashita node, fakkusu (   ) okurimasu.

III Complete the questions so that they fit the answers.
1. Sakura no hana wa (   ) sakimasu ka./4-gatsu ni naru to sakimasu yo. 2. (   ) ka shizukana tokoro wa nai deshō ka./Kaigi-shitsu nara shizuka desu yo. 3. Yamada-san ga kaita e wa (   ) deshita ka./Nakanaka yokatta desu yo.

IV Convert the following verbs and adjectives into their **-ba/-kereba** form.
1. au 2. aku 3. shimaru 4. furu 5. mieru 6. yorokobu 7. kangaeru 8. kekkon suru 9. mottekuru 10. nai 11. mezurashii 12. ii

V Complete the sentences with the appropriate form of the words indicated.
1. Yoku ( ) ba, genki ni ( ) deshō. (yasumimasu, narimasu) 2. Tōkyō tawā ni ( )
ba, umi ga ( ) deshō. (noborimasu, miemasu) 3. Tsugi no kado o migi ni ( ) to, hanaya ga arimasu (magarimasu) 4. O-sake o ( ) to, ( ) narimasu. (nomimasu,
tanoshiidesu) 5. Go-tsugō ga ( ) ba, gogo ( ) tai to omoimasu. (ii desu, ukagaimasu)
6. ( ) ba, ( ) narimasu yo. (renshū shimasu, jōzu desu) 7. Katō-san ni ( ) ba,
( ) deshō. (kikimasen, wakarimasen) 8. ( ) ba, motto ( ) mashō. (hoshii desu, mottekimasu) 9. ( ) ba, ( ) kuremasen ka. (dekimasu, todokemasu) 10. ( ) ba, ( )
hodo wakaranaku narimasu. (kangaemasu, kangaemasu)

VI Circle the correct words in the parentheses.
1. (Sugu, sakki, sassoku) okita bakari desu kara, mada shimbun o yonde imasen. 2. Nan-ji
goro ukagaimashō ka./Gozen-chū wa isogashii node, (dekireba, nakanaka, korekara) gogo
2-ji goro kite kuremasen ka. 3. Jikan ga nai node, (sakki, tashika ni, sassoku) hajimete
kuremasen ka.

17 BROWN'S DIARY

12-gatsu 31-nichi (sui) hare nochi kumori
Kyō wa ō-misoka da. Tonari no Ōno-san no uchi dewa, asa kara kazoku zen'in de sōji o shite
ita. Minna de hei ya kuruma ya, soshite inu made aratte ita.
Gogo wa Nihongo de nengajō o kaita ga, ji ga heta da kara yominikui darō. Yūgata, Tanaka-
san ikka to soba o tabe ni itta.
Yoru wa fudan wa amari minai terebi o mita ga, Tōkyō no terebi no channeru ga nanatsu mo
aru koto o hajimete shitta. Channeru o tsugitsugi ni kaeru to, sawagashii shō ya samurai no
jidai-geki ya Jon Uein no seibu geki o yatte ita. Eisei chūkei de Pari ya Honkon no machi o miru
koto mo dekita. 3-channeru dewa Bētōben no Dai-ku o ensō shite ita. Senjitsu, Nakamura-san ga
"Maitoshi, 12-gatsu ni naru to Nihon kakuchi de Dai-ku o ensō suru n desu yo," to itte ita ga,
omoshiroi kuni da.

1-gatsu tsuitachi (moku) hare
Nihon de shinnen o mukaeta. Machi wa hito mo kuruma mo sukunakute, taihen shizuka da.
Kōjō mo kaisha mo yasumi na node, itsumo wa yogorete iru Tōkyō no sora ga, kyō wa kirei de
kimochi ga ii. Kinjo no mise mo sūpā mo minna yasumi datta. Ano rasshu awā no sararīman ya
gakusei wa doko ni itta no darō ka.
Nihon-jin no dōryō ya tomodachi kara nengajō ga todoita. Gyōsha kara mo kita. Insatsu no
mono ga ōi ga, fude de kaita mono mo aru. Yahari utsukushii. Moratta nengajō wa hotondo zembu kuji-tsuki de aru.

Key Sentences
1. Kinō wa ii tenki datta kara, doraibu ni itta.
2. Jonson-san ga hako o akeru to, nakami wa giri-choko deshita.

EXERCISES
I Practice the following patterns by changing the verbs and adjectives as in the examples
given.
A. *ex.* Watashi wa Kyōto e ikimasu. → Watashi wa Kyōto e iku. → Watashi wa Kyōto e
ikanai. → Watashi wa Kyōto e itta. → Watashi wa Kyōto e ikanakatta.
1. Sumisu-san to dansu o shimasu 2. Tanaka-san wa 10-ji ni kimasu 3. Jonson-san ni
aimasu 4. tomodachi to eiga o mimasu 5. koko ni kagi ga arimasu

B. *ex.* Tanaka-san wa isogashii desu. → Tanaka-san wa isogashii. → Tanaka-san wa
isogashiku nai. → Tanaka-san wa isogashikatta. → Tanaka-san wa isogashiku
nakatta.
1. benkyō wa tanoshii desu 2. kuruma ga sukunai desu 3. atama ga ii desu 4. ano
resutoran wa mazui desu 5. tsugō ga warui desu

C. *ex.* Sumisu-san wa genki desu. → Sumisu-san wa genki da. → Sumisu-san wa genki dewa nai. → Sumisu-san wa genki datta. → Sumisu-san wa genki dewa nakatta.
1. yama no mizuumi wa shizuka desu 2. Sumisu-san wa warutsu ga suki desu 3. Sumisu-san wa ryōri ga jōzu desu 4. depāto wa yasumi desu 5. Yamamoto-san wa pairotto desu

D. *ex.* Kinō gakkō o yasunda. → Kinō gakkō o yasumimashita.
1. ashita zeimusho ni ikanakereba naranai 2. 6-ji ni uchi ni kaeru koto ga dekinai 3. tsuki ni itta koto ga nai 4. taikin o hirotta koto ga aru 5. tenisu o shitari tsuri o shitari shita 6. Tanaka-san wa iku darō 7. hayaku yasunda hō ga ii 8. Tanaka-san wa suraido o mite ita 9. ashita wa yuki kamo shirenai 10. mada Jonson-san ni atte inai

II Make dialogues by changing the underlined parts as in examples given.
A. *ex.* Q: <u>Ano hito no hanashikata</u> wa dō desu ka.
A: <u>Hayakute kikinikui</u> desu.
1. kono shimbun, ji ga chiisai, yomu 2. ano hito no setsumei, kudoi, wakaru 3. kono tēpu, oto ga warui, kiku 4. nattō, kusai, taberu 5. kono kusuri, nigai, nomu

B. *ex.* Q: <u>Sono kutsu</u> wa ikaga desu ka.
A: <u>Hakiyasukute</u> ki ni itte imasu.
1. kono apāto, sumu 2. sono pen, kaku 3. kono jisho, hiku 4. sono sūtsu, kiru 5. atarashii wāpuro, tsukau

III Practice the following patterns by changing the underlined parts.
ex. <u>Heya ni hairu</u> to <u>denwa ga natte imashita</u>.
1. mado o akemashita, suzushii kaze ga haitte kimashita 2. soto ni demashita, ame ga futte imashita 3. channeru o kaemashita, furui eiga o yatte imashita 4. uchi ni kaerimashita, tomodachi ga matte imashita 5. kinko o akemashita, naka wa karappo deshita

Short Dialogues

1. Otoko A: Mō ano eiga mita.
   Otoko B: Ūn, mada. Kimi wa.
   Otoko A: Un, mō mita.
   Otoko B: Dō datta.
   Otoko A: Ammari omoshiroku nakatta.

2. Onna: Mō sugu O-shōgatsu ne. Shigoto wa itsu made.
   Otoko: 12-gatsu 30-nichi made. Nemmatsu wa isogashikute iya da.
   Onna: O-shōgatsu wa dokka ni iku.
   Otoko: Ūn, doko nimo. Shōgatsu wa nombiri shitai ne.

Quiz

I Read this lesson's opening passage and answer the following questions.
1. Buraun-san wa ō-misoka no yūgata dare to nani o tabe ni ikimashita ka. 2. 12-gatsu niwa Nihon kakuchi de Bētōben no Dai 9 o ensō suru to Buraun-san ni hanashita no wa dare desu ka. 3. O-shōgatsu ni Buraun-san no kinjo no mise wa aite imashita ka. 4. Buraun-san wa dare kara nengajō o moraimashita ka. 5. Buraun-san wa fude de kaita nengajō o utsukushii to omotte imasu ka.

II Read the following, supplying the appropriate words or word parts.
12-gatsu 31-nichi (sui) hare nochi kumori
Kyō wa ōmisoka da. Tonari no Ōno-san no uchi dewa asa kara kazoku (   ) de sōji o shite (   ). Minna de hei ya kuruma ya soshite inu (   ) aratte ita.
Gogo wa Nihon-go de nengajō o (   ) ga, ji ga heta da kara yomi (   ) darō. Yūgata Tanaka-san (   ) to soba o (   ) itta.

1-gatsu tsuitachi (moku) hare
Nihon de shinnen o mukaeta. Machi wa hito mo kuruma mo sukunaku (   ), taihen (   ). Kōjō mo kaisha mo yasumi (   ), itsumo wa (   ) Tōkyō no sora ga, kyō wa kirei de, (   ). Kinjo no mise mo sūpā mo minna yasumi (   ). (   ) rasshu awā no sararīman ya gakusei wa doko ni (   ) no darō ka.

Nihon-jin no dōryō ya tomodachi ( ) nengajō ga todoita. Insatsu no mono ga ( ) ga, ( ) de kaita mono mo aru. Yahari ( ). Moratta nengajō wa ( ) zembu kuji-tsuki de aru.

III Complete the questions so that they fit the answers.

1. ( ) ni dekakeru./9-ji ni deru. 2. Kinō no eiga ( ) datta./Ammari omoshiroku nakat-ta. 3. ( ) ni sumitai./Anzenna tokoro ga ii. 4. Kare wa ( ) kuru./Ashita kuru. 5. ( ) to issho ni iku./Hitori de iku.

IV Complete the sentences with the appropriate form of the words indicated.

1. Kono niku wa ( ), ( ) yasui. (yawarakai, taberu) 2. Kare no setsumei wa ( ), ( ) nikui. (fukuzatsu, wakaru) 3. Kono tēpurekōda wa ( ), ( ) nikui. (furui, tsukau) 4. Mado o ( ) to, suzushii kaze ga ( ) kita. (akeru, hairu) 5. Kotoshi wa ( ), nengajō o zenzen ( ) koto ga dekinakatta. (isogashii, kaku) 6. Heya ga ( ), kimochi ga ii. (kirei)

18 BIRTHDAY FLOWERS

Opening Dialogue

Jonson: Suzuki-san, chotto.

Suzuki: Nan deshō.

Jonson: Nihon no shūkan o shiranai node oshiete kudasaimasen ka. Onna no tomodachi no tan-jōbi ni hana o ageyō to omou n desu ga okashiku nai desu ka. Tokubetsu no onna tomodachi dewa nai n desu ga.

Suzuki: Okashiku nai desu yo. Daijōbu desu. Jonson-san, tanjōbi iwai no dēto desu ka. Ii desu nē.

Jonson: Ūn, mā.

Jonson: Tomodachi ni hana o okurō to omou n desu ga, onegai dekimasu ka.

Hanaya: Hai, o-todoke desu ne. Dekimasu. Nan-nichi no o-todoke deshō ka.

Jonson: Ashita todokete kudasai.

Hanaya: Kashikomarimashita.

Jonson: Kono bara wa ikura desu ka.

Hanaya: 1-pon ¥250 desu.

Jonson: Ja, kore o 20-pon onegaishimasu. Tanjōbi no purezento ni suru tsumori desu kara, kono kādo o tsukete, todokete kuremasen ka.

Hanaya: Hai. O-todoke-saki wa tonai desu ka.

Jonson: Iie, Yokohama desu.

Hanaya: Sōryō ga ¥500 kakarimasu ga, yoroshii desu ka.

Jonson: Ee.

Hanaya: Dewa kochira ni o-kyaku-sama no, soshite kochira ni o-todoke-saki no go-jūsho, o-denwa-bangō, o-namae o o-kaki kudasai.

> Tanaka Keiko sama
>
> O-tanjōbi omedetō gozaimasu.
>
> Maikeru

Key Sentences

1. Mainichi Nihon-go o benkyō shiyō to omoimasu.
2. Ashita haretara, tenisu o suru tsumori desu.

EXERCISES

I Verbs: Study the examples, convert into the volitional form, and memorize.

ex. kaku → kakō, iu → iō, taberu → tabeyō, okiru → okiyō, kuru → koyō, suru → shiyō

1. kaeru (*return*) 2. azukaru 3. oyogu 4. erabu 5. yasumu 6. oboeru 7. azukeru 8. miseru 9. miru 10. kariru 11. katte kuru 12. ryōri suru

II Make dialogues by changing the underlined parts as in the examples given.
A. *ex*. Q: <u>Daigaku ni ikimasu</u> ka.
   A: Ee, <u>ikō</u> to omoimasu.
   1. tabako o yameru 2. kono shūmatsu wa asobu 3. shachō ni sōdan suru 4. o-kane o kariru 5. tomodachi ni kodomo o azukeru 6. asa hayaku kuru

B. *ex*. Q: <u>Kaisha o yamete</u> nani o suru n desu ka.
   A: <u>Hitori de shigoto o hajimeru</u> tsumori desu.
   1. daigaku ni nokorimasu, keiei-gaku o kenkyū shimasu 2. Hawai ni ikimasu, oyoidari nikkōyoku o shitari shimasu 3. kuni ni kaerimasu, shōrai no koto o kangaemasu 4. daigaku o yamemasu, dezainā ni narimasu

C. *ex*. Q: <u>Kekkon shinai</u> n desu ka.
   A: Ee, <u>kekkon shinai</u> tsumori desu.
   1. mō tabako o suimasen 2. mō aisukurīmu o tabemasen 3. dare nimo misemasen 4. kamera o motte ikimasen

D. *ex*. Q: Sumimasen ga, <u>shio o totte</u> kudasaimasen ka.
   A: Hai.
   1. isu o hakobu no o tetsudau 2. shattā o osu 3. saki ni iku 4. koko de matte iru 5. shizuka ni suru 6. kūrā o yowaku suru

Short Dialogue

Kachō: Kaeri ni dō. Ippai nomō.
Ogawa: Kyō wa kanai ga kaze o hiite iru node . . .
Kachō: Chotto nara ii darō.
Ogawa: Ie, yappari dame na n desu.
Kachō: Sō ka. Ja, akirameyō.

Quiz

I Read this lesson's opening dialogue and answer the following questions.
1. Jonson-san wa onna no tomodachi e no purezento ni tsuite, dōshite Suzuki-san ni sodan shimashita ka. 2. Jonson-san wa dare ni purezento o okurō to omotte imasu ka. 3. Jonson-san ga katta bara wa 20-pon de ikura desu ka. 4. Keiko-san wa doko ni sunde iru deshō ka.

II Convert the following verbs into their volitional form.
1. hanasu 2. todokeru 3. au 4. yameru 5. noboru 6. aruku 7. wakareru 8. harau 9. happyō suru 10. matsu 11. dēto suru 12. mottekuru

III Complete the sentence with the appropriate form of the verbs indicated.
1. Nani o ( ) iru n desu ka. /Tana no ue no hako o ( ) to omou n desu ga, te ga ( ) n desu. (shimasu, torimasu, todokimasen) 2. Donna tēpurekōdā o ( ) tsumori desu ka. / Chiisakute, oto ga ii tēpurekōdā o ( ) to omou n desu ga, dore ga ii deshō ka. (kaimasu, kaimasu) 3. Ima kara yūbinkyoku e ( ) to omou n desu ga, nani ka yōji ga arimasen ka.)/ Sumimasen ga, kono tegami o ( ) kudasaimasen ka. (itte kimasu, dashimasu) 4. Hontō ni koibito to ( ) n desu ka. Ee, mō ( ) tsumori desu. ( ) ba, mata kenka shimasu kara. (wakaremashita, aimasen, aimasu) 5. Nihon-go no benkyō o ( ) to omou n desu ga, tekitō na gakkō o ( ) kudasaimasen ka. (hajimemasu, oshiemasu)

IV Choose a sentence appropriate to the situation described.
A. Congratulate a friend for passing his examination.
   1. Gōkaku o iwaimasu. 2. Gōkaku omedetō gozaimasu. 3. Fugōkaku de zannen deshita.
B. You want to ask your section chief if it's all right to call him very late tomorrow evening.
   1. Ashita no ban osoku o-denwa kudasaimasen ka. 2. Ashita no ban osoku kaette kara denwa suru. 3. Ashita no ban osoku denwa o shite mo yoroshii desu ka.
C. On the phone you ask his wife what time an acquaintance of yours will get home.
   1. Go-shujin wa nan-ji goro kaerimashita ka. 2. Go-shujin wa nan-ji goro o-kaeri deshō ka. 3. Shujin wa nan-ji goro kaeru tsumori desu ka.

D. You answer a question by saying you really do intend to quit your job.
1 Hai, hontō ni yameru tsumori desu. 2. Hai, tabun yameyō to omoimasu. 3. Hai, tabun yameru darō to omoimasu.

V Answer the following questions.
1. Anata wa ashita nani o shiyō to omotte imasu ka. 2. Nihon-go no benkyō ga owattara, Nihon no kaisha de hataraku tsumori desu ka. 3. Anata wa sekai-jū o ryokō shitai to omotte imasu ka. 4. Anata no raishū no yotei o hanashite kudasai.

19 THE PUBLIC LIBRARY

Opening Dialogue

Chan: Are wa nan desu ka.
Daisuke: Toritsu no toshokan desu.
Chan: Toritsu no toshokan wa Tōkyō tomin shika hairemasen ka. Gaikokujin mo riyō dekimasu ka.
Daisuke: Ee, mochiron desu. Dare demo hairemasu yo. Soreni Chan-san wa Tōkyō tomin deshō. Asoko wa jibun de hon o te ni totte miraremasu kara, totemo riyō shiyasui desu yo.
Chan: Sore wa ii desu ne. Boku wa kādo o mite erabu no wa nigate na n desu.
Daisuke: Demo, Chan-san wa kanji ga yomeru deshō.
Chan: Ee, imi wa wakarimasu. Demo, boku wa jibun de hon o minagara eraberu toshokan ga suki nan desu.
Daisuke: Chotto fubenna tokoro ni aru kedo, hiroi shi shizuka da shi ii desu yo.
Chan: Hon o karitari kopī shitari suru koto mo dekimasu ka?
Daisuke: Ee, tetsuzuki o sureba kariraremasu. Boku mo ima 2-satsu karite imasu. Jisho toka kichōna hon toka, karirarenai mono mo aru keredo.
Chan: Shimbun ya zasshi mo kariraremasu ka?
Daisuke: Karirarenai kedo kopī o tanomemasu. Korekara issho ni ikimasen ka. 2, 3-pun de ikemasu yo.

Key Sentences

1. Buraun-san wa Nihon-go ga hanasemasu.
2. Tetsuzuki o sureba, dare demo hon ga kariraremasu.
3. Watanabe-san wa yasai shika tabemasen.
4. Anata mo issho ni iku deshō.
   Ee, ikimasu.

EXERCISES

I Verbs: Study the examples, convert into the potential forms, and memorize.
   ex. kaku → kakeru, → kakenai; iru → irareru, →irarenai; kuru → korareru, korarenai; kau → kaeru, → kaenai; oboeru → oboerareru, → oboerarenai; suru → dekiru, dekinai
   1. kiku 2. tobu 3. osu 4. arau 5. hairu 6. susumeru 7. oshieru 8. okiru 9. tsutomeru 10. tsūkin suru 11. yonde kuru 12. renshū suru

II Make dialogues by changing the underlined parts as in examples given.
   A. *ex.* Q: Kono kanji ga yomemasu ka.
      A: Hai, yomemasu.
         1. gaikoku-go de uta o utau 2. ashita asa 7-ji ni dekakeru 3. gaikoku-jin no namae o sugu oboeru 4. Nihon-go de annai suru
   B. *ex.* Q: Eki mae ni kuruma ga tomeraremasu ka.
      A: Iie, tomeraremasen.
         1. sugu shiryō o atsumeru 2. ano hito no hanashi o shinjiru 3. kono dekigoto o wasureru 4. 100-mētoru o 10-byō de hashiru
   C. *ex.* Q: Hiragana mo kanji mo kakemasu ka.
      A: Hiragana wa kakemasu ga, kanji wa kakemasen.

1. Furansu-go, Doitsu-go, hanasu 2. jitensha, ōtobai, noru 3. sakana, niku, taberu
4. Tanaka-san, Yamamoto-san, kuru 5. tenisu, gorufu, suru

D. *ex.* Q: <u>Nan-ji goro kaeremasu</u> ka.
A: <u>8-ji made ni kaereru</u> to omoimasu.
1. nan-mētoru oyogu, 200-mētoru mo oyoganai 2. dare ga naosu, Tanaka-san ga
naosu 3. dare ni azukeru, dare nimo azukenai 4. itsu Tanaka-san ni au, raishū no
moku-yōbi ni au 5. doko de kariru, toshokan de kariru.

E. *ex.* Q: <u>Nan demo tabemasu</u> ka.
A: <u>Yasai shika tabemasen.</u>
1. dare demo riyō dekiru, 20-sai ijō no hito 2. ima o-kane o takusan motte iru,
¥500 3. ō-zei kita, sukoshi 4. o-ko-san wa nan-nin iru, hitori 5. yukkuri nemureta,
3-jikan

F. *ex.* Q: Nan demo <u>utte imasu</u> ka.
A: <u>Kagu toka daidokoro yōhin toka, utte inai</u> mono mo arimasu.
1. dekiru, kikaku, senden 2. te ni hairu, Afurika no shimbun, Nambei no zasshi 3.
sorotte iru, futon, mōfu 4. aru, tebukuro, mafurā

G. *ex.* Daisuke: Chan-san wa <u>kanji ga yomeru</u> deshō.
Chan: Ee, <u>yomemasu.</u>
1. hajimete desu 2. ABC no shain desu 3. tabemasen 4. nattō ga suki desu 5.
tsugō ga ii desu 6. kodomo no toki okikatta desu

H. *ex.* Q: <u>Tetsuzuki</u> wa <u>itsu</u> ga ii desu ka.
A: <u>Itsu</u> demo ii desu.
1. ryōri, nani 2. hoteru, doko 3. yakusoku, nan-ji, 4. mukae ni iku hito, dare

I. *ex.* Q: <u>Kore</u> o tsukatte mo ii desu ka.
A: Dōzo, <u>dore</u> demo <u>suki na mono</u> o tsukatte kudasai.
1. tomodachi o tsurete kuru, dare, suki na hito o 2. koko ni suwaru, doko, ii
tokoro ni 3. ashita kuru, itsu, go-tsugō no ii jikan ni 4. iroiro na mono o kau, nan,
hitsuyōna mono o

Short Dialogue

A: Chotto atsui n desu ga, mado o akete kudasaimasen ka.
B: Kono biru wa mado ga akanai n desu yo.
A: E, ja, kaji no toki wa dō suru n desu ka.
B: Rōka no tsukiatari no hijōguchi kara nigeraremasu yo.

Quiz

I Read this lesson's opening dialogue and answer the following questions.
1. Toritsu no toshokan wa Tōkyō tomin shika riyō dekimasen ka. 2. Chan-san wa donna
toshokan ga suki desu ka. 3. Kono toshokan wa hirokute shizuka desu ka. 4. Hon o karitai
hito wa dō sureba kariraremasu ka.

II Put the appropriate words in the parentheses.
1. Kaiin de nakereba, sono supōtsu kurabu o riyō dekimasen ka./Iie, dare (   ) riyō
dekimasu. 2. Yūbe wa 4-jikan (   ) nemuremasen deshita. 3. Koko (   ) Ginza (   )
dono gurai kakarimasu ka./15-fun (   ) ikemasu yo. 4. Kuruma (   ) Kyūshū (   )
mawarimashita ka. 5. Rainen no yasumi mo Yōroppa e ikō ka./Rainen wa Chūgoku (   ),
Afurika (   ), hoka no tokoro e ikitai.

III Without changing the level of politeness convert the following verbs into the potential
form.
1. oyogimasu 2. kakimasen 3. hanashimasu 4. yakusoku shimasen 5. iimasen 6. nemasu 7.
utau 8. awanai 9. wasurenai 10. kiru (wear) 11. mottekuru 12. yasumanai

IV Complete the questions so that they fit the answers.
1. (   ) oyogemasu ka./100-mētoru gurai oyogemasu. 2. Tsugi no kaigi wa (   ) ga ii
desu ka./Itsu demo kekkō desu. 3. (   ) ni ikeba kaemasu ka./Depāto de utte imasu yo. 4.
(   ) issho ni ikenai n desu ka./Musume no tanjōbi na node, kaeranakereba naranai n
desu.

V   Complete the sentences with the polite-level potential form of the verbs indicated.
    1. Koko wa chūsha kinshi na node, kuruma ga (   ). (tomenai) 2. Sukī ni itte kega o shita node, (   ). (arukanai) 3. 1-nen ni nan-nichi kaisha o (   ) ka. (yasumu) 4. Rainen (   ) ka. (sotsugyō suru) 5. Ima sugu (   ) ka. (dekakeru) 6. Howaito-san wa miso shiru ga (   ) ka? (tsukuru) 7. Uketsuke ni aru denwa wa (   ) ka. (tsukau) 8. Doko ni ikeba oishii sushi ga (   ) ka. (taberu) 9. Shiken ni gōkaku shinakere ba, kono daigaku ni (   ). (hairanai) 10. Terebi de Nihon no furui eiga ga (   ). (miru)

VI   Answer the following questions.
    1. Anata wa Furansu-go ga hanasemasu ka. 2. Anata wa kanji ga yomemasu ka. Yomeru baai wa ikutsu gurai yomemasu ka. 3. Anata wa yūbe yoku nemuremashita ka. 4. Anata wa Nihon no uta ga utaemasu ka. 5. Anata wa Nihongo de tegami ga kakemasu ka.

20 CHERRY BLOSSOMS

Sakura zensen to iu kotoba o kiita koto ga arimasu ka.

Nihon no haru o daihyō suru hana wa, nan to itte mo sakura deshō. Hito-bito wa haru ga chikazuku to, sakura no saku hi o yosoku shitari, tomodachi to o-hanami ni iku hi o yakusoku shitari shimasu.

Tokorode, Nihon wa minami kara kita e nagaku nobite iru shima-guni desu. Kyūshū, Shikoku, Honshū, Hokkaidō dewa, zuibun kion no sa ga arimasu kara, sakura no saku hi mo sukoshi-zutsu kotonatte imasu. Kyūshū no nambu dewa, 3-gatsu no sue goro sakimasu ga, Hokkaidō dewa, 5-gatsu no hajime goro sakimasu. Kono yō ni yaku 40-nichi mo kakatte, Nihon rettō o minami kara kita e hana ga saite iku yōsu o sen de arawashita mono ga sakura zensen desu. Sakura zensen no hoka ni ume zensen ya tsutsuji zensen nado no hana zensen mo arimasu. Ume wa sakura yori zutto hayaku Kyūshū o shuppatsu shimasu ga, Hokkaidō ni tsuku no wa daitai sakura to onaji koro desu. Desukara, 5-gatsu no jōjun kara chūjun ni kakete Hokkaidō e ryokō sureba, ichido ni haru no hana ga mirareru no desu. Kore to wa hantai ni, aki ni naru to, kōyō zensen wa yama no ki-gi o aka ya kiiro ni somenagara, kita kara minami e susunde ikimasu.

Hito-bito wa haru niwa o-hanami, aki niwa momiji-gari nado o shite, kisetsu o tanoshimimasu.

Quiz

Put the appropriate words in the parentheses.

Sakura zensen (   ) kotoba o kiita (   ) ga arimasu ka.

Nihon no haru o daihyō suru hana wa, nan to itte mo sakura deshō. Hito-bito wa haru ga chikazuku (   ), sakura no saku hi o yosoku shi (   ), tomodachi to o-hanami ni iku hi o yakusoku shi (   ) shimasu.

(   ), Nihon wa minami (   ) kita (   ) nagaku nobite iru shima-guni desu. Kyūshū, Shikoku, Honshū, Hokkaidō dewa, (   ) kion no sa ga arimasu kara, sakura no saku hi mo sukoshi (   ) kotonatte imasu. Kyūshū no nambu dewa, 3-gatsu no sue goro sakimasu ga, Hokkaidō dewa, 5-gatsu no hajime goro sakimasu. (   ) yaku 40-nichi mo kakatte, Nihon rettō o minami kara kita e hana ga (   ) iku yōsu o sen de arawashita mono ga sakura zensen desu. Sakura zensen (   ) ume zensen ya tsutsuji zensen nado no hana zensen mo arimasu. Ume wa sakura yori (   ) hayaku Kyūshū (   ) shuppatsu shimasu ga, Hokkaidō (   ) tsuku no wa daitai sakura (   ) onaji koro desu. (   ), 5-gatsu no jōjun kara chūjun ni kakete Hokkaidō e ryokō sureba, (   ) haru no hana ga mirareru (   ). Kore to wa (   ), aki ni naru (   ), kōyō zensen wa yama no ki-gi o aka ya kiiro ni some nagara, kita kara minami e susunde (   ).

Hito-bito wa haru (   ) wa o-hanami, aki (   ) wa momiji-gari nado o shite, (   ) o tanoshimimasu.

QUIZ ANSWERS

Lesson 1

I 1. Asa no hō ga (yūgata yori) konde imasu. 2. Michi ga konde imasu kara (densha no hō ga hayai desu). 3. Kasetto tēpu o kikinagara tekisuto o yonde imasu. 4. 7-ji ni uchi o dete, chikatetsu de kaisha ni ikimasu. 5. Asa no 8-ji han goro ga ichiban konde imasu.
II 1. yori 2. nagara 3. mo, hodo 4. ga, de 5. no, de 6. o, ni
III 1. dochira/dotchi 2. itsu 3. Dare 4. nani 5. dochira/dotchi
IV 1. aruki-, hanashite 2. tsūkin shite 3. suite 4. osa- 5. shi-, shimashita 6. tsukatte, tsukai-, tsukawa-

Lesson 2

I 1. Kurokute ōkii kami no fukuro o wasuremashita. 2. Ushiro kara 2-bamme no sharyō ni wasuremashita. 3. Hai, arimasu. 4. Shūten no eki ni denwa o kakete toiawasemashita. 5. Tōkyō eki (no jimusho) ni tori ni ikimasu.
II 1. no, to, o 2. kara, no 3. to, no, ni, ga 4. ni, kara, ni, ni
III 1. Donna 2. Doko 3. Dono 4. nani
IV 1. jōzu ni 2. Kuwashiku 3. hayaku 4. itakute 5. shizuka ni 6. furukute, yūmeina 7. ōkiku
V 1. Kono densha ni notte, 4-tsu-me no eki de orite kudasai. 2. Ano resutoran wa yasukute oishii desu. 3. Kono kissaten wa atarashikute kirei de suite imasu. 4. Sore wa aoi sētā de hana no moyō ga arimasu. 5. Watanabe-san wa atama ga yokute shinsetsu desu. 6. Chan-san wa majime de yoku hatarakimasu. 7. Jimu-shitsu ni denwa o kakete toiawasemasu.

Lesson 3

I 1. Iie, Hayashi-san to issho ni ikimasen deshita. 2. Kurabu no hito ga annai shimashita. 3. Hai, ichinen-jū oyogu koto ga dekimasu. 4. Iie, mōshikomi o suru mae ni naka o mimashita.
II 1. de, ni, o 2. demo, o, ga, ga, ni, ni 3. ni, to, o 4. ni, ni/e
III 1. iku 2. au 3. annai suru 4. oshieru 5. wasureru 6. miru 7. aru 8. kesu 9. tomeru 10. magaru 11. kuru 12. taberu 13. tsūkin suru 14. denwa o kakeru 15. mottekuru
IV 1. miru 2. tabe-, itte 3. Kuru, kakete 4. magaru 5. ai-, iku 6. tomeru, tomenai-

Lesson 4

I 1. Katō-san to ikimasu. 2. Iie, itta koto ga arimasen. 3. Iie, Kimura-san wa ikimasen. 4. Torihiki-saki o mawattari, ginkō ni aisatsu ni ittari shimasu.
II 1. ni/e, ni 2. de, o 3. wa, ga, wa 4. de, o
III 1. nobotta 2. atta 3. tabeta 4. kiita 5. ita 6. otoshita 7. yonda 8. wasureta 9. mita 10. asonda 11. mawatta 12. setsumei shita 13. oyoida 14. naratta 15. dekaketa
IV 1. nobotta 2. atta 3. kiku 4. yon-, kai- 5. mi-, at-

Lesson 5

I 1. Yasuku narimashita. 2. Iie, sōdan shimasen deshita. 3. Kimeta ato de happyō shimasu. 4. Sērusu no hito ni moraimashita.

II 1. ni, no, o 2. ni 3. ga, kara, ni 4. ni, no, ga 5. o, de, o 6. no, ni
III 1. Dono 2. Itsu 3. Dare
IV 1. tsukuri-, oshiete 2. todoite 3. kaette 4. owatta, nomi- 5. hanasu 6. kaeru

Lesson 6

I 1. Isha ni moraimashita. 2. Iie, nakanaka yoku narimasen deshita. 3. Hai, hajimatta bakari desu. 4. Hai, Katō-san wa Suzuki-san ni yōji o tanonda ato de Chan-san to hanashimashita imasu.
II 1. ni, ga 2. ka, ni 3. ni, no 4. kara, ni 5. ni
III 1. yonda 2. tabenai 3. kita, kiite 4. shiraseta 5. itte, tanonde 6. konde, ikanai
IV 1. taitei 2. nakanaka 3. mazu, sorekara 4. sakki
V A. 2 B. 2

Lesson 7

I 1. Suzuki-san ga ikimasu. 2. Rondon no jimusho ni ita hito desu. 3. Iie, shirimasen. 4. Iie, atta koto ga/wa arimasen.
II 1. ga/no 2. ni 3. ni, de/o 4. o 5. de, ni 6. de, to, mo
III 1. dekiru 2. au 3. minakatta 4. wakaranai 5. konakatta 6. katta 7. tomatte iru 8. sukina 9. suki datta 10. se ga takai
IV 1. Sumisu-san no okusan desu. 2. Sumisu-san desu. 3. Tanaka-san desu. 4. Sumisu-san desu 5. Sumisu-san to Tanaka-san desu.

Lesson 8

I 1. Sendai e ikitai to omotte imasu. 2. Kuni e kaeru hito ga ōzei imasu kara. 3. Kuruma de kaerimashita. 4. Katō-san ga itte imasu. 5. Ikanai to omoimasu/Wakarimasen.
II 1. o, to 2. o, ni, to 3. shi, shi, to 4. ni, no, ni/e, to
III 1. dochira/dotchi 2. itsu 3. nan 4. dō 5. dōshite
IV 1. ikanakatta 2. konai 3. genki datta 4. nai 5. omoshiroku nakatta 6. okusan dewa nai 7. ki ni iranai 8. ame da 9. owatte inai

Lesson 9

I 1. Iie, gōkaku shimasen deshita 2. Iie, harimasen. 3. Iie, ikanakute mo ii desu. 4. Hai, genkin kakitome demo ii desu. 5. Genkin kakitome de okuru deshō/Wakarimasen.
II 1. de 2. no, ni 3. de, demo 4. kara, de 5. ni
III 1. Itsu 2. Ikura 3. Dōshite 4. dochira/dotchi 5. Nankagetsu
IV 1. oki- 2. wasurete 3. yoma- 4. yame-, yameta 5. harawa-, haratte 6. katazukete, katazuke- 7. tomete

Lesson 10

First paragraph: to, imasu, deshita
Second paragraph: ga, de, no, koto, wa, kara, ni, to, itte
Third paragraph: o, o, ato, no, tatta, de, de, datta, de, ni, arimasu
Fourth paragraph: to, ni, sore made ni, narimasen
Fifth paragraph: ni, yoroshiku

Lesson 11

I 1. Nakamura-san no rirekisho o minagara kiite imasu. 2. Iie, kanojo no semmon dewa arimasen deshita. 3. Iie, omoshiroku nakatta to itte imasu. 4. Hai, dekiru to omotte imasu.
II 1. ni 2. ni, o 3. o, o 4. de 5. o, ga, to, kara
III 1. Dōshite 2. Dō 3. dōyatte 4. Nani

IV 1. Kaetta 2. shirasenakatta, yasumi datta 3. itte ita 4. tabenai, tabetakunai 5. dekakeru, nai
6. byōki na 7. itta, hanashite 8. oboeru
V A. 3 B. 1 C. 2

Lesson 12

I 1. (Kyōto no) Miyako Ryokan ni denwa o shimashita. 2. Hai, aite iru to itte imashita. 3. 10-pun gurai kakarimasu. 4. Zeikin to sābisu ryō o harawanakereba narimasen. 5. Hai, harawanakereba narimasen.
II 1. de 2. to 3. ni, kara, kara, ni 4. yori 5. de 6. to 7. no
III 1. itsu 2. nan 3. Dōshite
IV 1. itta 2. inai 3. okita, futte 4. dekinai, shite 5. hirotta, todoke- 6. tabete ita, itaku 7. atta, kireina 8. nai 9. Wakai, ryokō shita 10. Himana, yon-, ason-
V A. 1 B. 3 C. 2

Lesson 13

I 1. Watanabe-san kara no purezento desu. 2. Hai, moraimashita. 3. Barentain dē desu. 4. Iie. Tabun okusan ya gāru furendo ga taberu darō to itte imasu.
II 1. e 2. de 3. kara 4. ni, kara, yori 5. te
III 1. dōshite 2. Dō 3. donna 4. nan
IV 1. genkina 2. Sumisu-san no mono dewa nai 3. byōki 4. gaikōkan datta, jōzu 5. motte ikanakatta 6. tōranai 7. oita 8. nareru 9. ugokanakatta 10. saite inai
V A. 1 B. 3 C. 1

Lesson 14

I 1. Sumō o minagara yakitori o tabete imasu. 2. Sumisu-san desu. 3. Kuroi kimono o kite, dohyō no mawari ni suwatte imasu. 4. Shimpan iin desu.
II 1. ga, ga 2. ga, no 3. no, ga 4. o, no 5. no
III 1. dō iu 2. Itsu 3. Nani 4. dō iu
IV 1. kiite 2. atsumeru 3. tsuri o shite iru, tōkute 4. dasu 5. nakute 6. dekiru 7. fukuzatsu de
V 1. demo 2. kanarazu 3. yappari 4. jitsuwa

Lesson 15

I 1. Watanabe-san kara azukarimashita. 2. Supōtsu kurabu de watashitai to omotte imasu. 3. Iie, au koto ga dekimasen deshita. 4. Hai, sō desu.
II 1. ni, o 2. no, ni 3. o, ga, o, de, ni 4. to
III 1. nan 2. dō 3. Itsu 4. Dare
IV 1. kau 2. sorot-, hajimete 3. non-, waruku 4. Hima, mi 5. Tsukawanai, katazuketa 6. Tsukare-, yasunde 7. Isogashikunakat-, tetsudatte 8. mendō, tsukuru 9. ame dat- 10. iku, age- 11. omoi, azukatte

Lesson 16

I 1. Yamakawa-san ga Hayashi-san ni okurimashita. 2. 6-ji made ni ikeba hairu koto ga dekimasu. 3. Nemmatsu ni naru to gyōsha ga isogashiku narimasu kara. 4. 10-ji ni naru to shimarimasu.
II 1. ka 2. ni, -ba, to 3. made 4. no, de
III 1. itsu 2. Doko 3. dō
IV 1. aeba 2. akeba 3. shimareba 4. fureba 5. miereba 6. yorokobeba 7. kangaereba 8. kekkon sureba 9. mottekureba 10. nakereba 11. mezurashikereba 12. yokereba
V 1. yasume-, naru 2. nobore-, mieru 3. magaru 4. nomu, tanoshiku 5. yokere-, ukagai- 6. Renshū sure-, jōzu ni 7. kikanakere-, wakaranai 8. hoshikere-, motteki- 9. Dekire-, todokete- 10. Kangaere-, kangaeru
VI 1. Sakki 2. dekireba 3. sassoku

Lesson 17

I   1. Tanaka-san ikka to soba o tabe ni ikimashita. 2. Nakamura-san desu. 3. Iie, aite imasen deshita. 4. Nihon-jin no dōryō ya tomodachi ya gyōsha kara moraimashita. 5. Hai, utsukushii to omotte imasu.

II First paragraph: zen'in, ita, made
    Second paragraph: kaita, -nikui, ikka, tabe ni
    Third paragraph: -te, shizuka da, na node, yogoreteiru, kimochi ga ii, datta, Ano, itta
    Fourth paragraph: kara, ōi, fude, utsukushii, hotondo

III 1. Nan-ji 2. dō 3. Doko 4. itsu 5. Dare

IV 1. yawarakakute, tabe- 2. fukuzatsu de, wakari- 3. furukute, tsukai- 4. akeru, haitte 5. isogashikute, kaku 6. kirei de

Lesson 18

I   1. (Jonson-san wa) Nihon no shūkan o shiranai node, sōdan shimashita. 2. Tanaka Keiko-san ni okurō to omotte imasu. 3. ¥5000 desu. 4. Yokohama ni sunde imasu.

II 1. hanasō 2. todokeyō 3. aō 4. yameyō 5. noborō 6. arukō 7. wakareyō 8. haraō 9. happyō shiyō 10. matō 11. dēto shiyō 12. mottekoyō

III 1. shite, torō, todokanai 2. kau, kaō 3. ittekoyō, dashite 4. wakareta, awanai, ae- 5. hajimeyō, oshiete

IV A. 2 B. 3 C. 2 D. 1

Lesson 19

I   1. Iie, dare demo riyō dekimasu. 2. Jibun de hon o minagara eraberu toshokan ga suki desu. 3. Hai, hirokute shizuka desu. 4. Tetsuzuki o sureba, kariraremasu.

II 1. demo 2. shika 3. kara, made, de 4. de, o 5. toka, toka

III 1. oyogemasu 2. kakemasen 3. hanasemasu 4. yakusoku dekimasen 5. iemasen 6. neraremasu 7. utaeru 8. aenai 9. wasurerarenai 10. kirareru 11. mottekorareru 12. yasumenai

IV 1. Dono gurai 2. itsu 3. Doko 4. Dōshite

V   1. tomeraremasen 2. arukemasen 3. yasumemasu 4. sotsugyō dekimasu 5. dekakeraremasu 6. tsukuremasu 7. tsukaemasu 8. taberaremasu 9. hairemasen 10. miraremasu

Lesson 20

First paragraph: to iu, koto
Second paragraph: to, -tari, -tari
Third papragraph: Tokorode, kara, e, zuibun, -zutsu, Kono yō ni, saite, no hoka ni, zutto, o, ni, to, Desukara, ichido ni, no desu, hantai ni, to, ikimasu
Fourth paragraph: ni, ni, kisetsu

Lesson 21

I   1. Gakusei no kaisha hōmon ga hajimaru hi desu. 2. Shūshoku shitai kaisha no mensetsu o uke ni kita gakusei desu. 3. Iie, mae wa "konjō no aru hito" o motomete imashita. 4. Kato-san ga itte imasu.

II 1. no, de, ga 2. no, na 3. ni, no 4. ni yoru to, de 5. ni yotte

III 1. dō/ikaga 2. Donna 3. dare/donata 4. Dōshite

IV 1. dokushin no 2. byōki da 3. nigatena 4. nigate da 5. yokunai 6. nai 7. uketa 8. hataraki-

V   A. 1 B. 3

Lesson 22

I   1. Hikōki de dekakeru tsumori deshita. 2. Iie, taifū no tame ni kekkō shimashita. 3. Iie, sono baai wa kyanseru chāji o harawanakute mo ii desu. 4. 4, 5-nichi mae ni uchikin o okutta node, mō todoite iru hazu da to omotte imasu.

II   1. de, o 2. no, ga 3. ni 4. kara, ni

III 1. Dōshite/Naze 2. itsu 3. dono gurai 4. nan-ji

IV 1. tonde inai 2. tsukai-, kaeta 3. kaigi na, isogashii 4. dase-, tsuku 5. arimashita/atta, ikanakatta 6. at-, ikenai

V   1. Kyū ni 2. kanarazu 3. tashika ni

Lesson 23

I   1. Mō ichi-mai kaō to omotte denwa o shimashita. 2. Hai, shitte imashita. 3. 292–3365 ni denwa suru yō ni tanomimashita. 4. Chan-san no dengon o Nakano-san ni tsutaemashita. 5. Zembu de 4-mai kau tsumori desu.

II   1. ga 2. to 3. ka, ka 4. ka 5. ni 6. kara

III 1. mochiron 2. narubeku 3. tonikaku

IV 1. otoshita 2. ki ni iru 3. tabetai 4. yogorete, sōji suru 5. uketotta 6. hima da

V   A. 3 B. 1

Lesson 24

I   1. ¥300,000 desu. 2. 1-mai ¥1,500 gurai no sara ga hoshii to itte imasu. 3. Tanaka-san desu. 4. ¥1,600 ni shimashita.

II   1. de, ni 2. no, ni 3. na, ni

III 1. mō 2. motto 3. mō, motto 4. mō, mō 5. motto

IV 1. isogashi-, taihen 2. yosa- 3. ochi- 4. koronde, shita 5. nai 6. yasukute, oishii

V   A. 3 B. 1

Lesson 25

I   1. Jimusho ga iten shite, Nakamura-san no uchi kara tōku natte shimatta node sagashite imasu. 2. Ima no hoka ni heya ga hitotsu areba ii to itte imasu. 3. Inu o kaitagatte imasu. 4. ¥770,000 ni narimasu. 5. Kariru ka dōka wakarimasen.

II   1. no, ni 2. kara, ka, to 3. toshite 4. de, o

III 1. dono 2. nan 3. Itsu 4. itsu

IV 1. tomatte 2. wasurete 3. tabete 4. kiite 5. haite, ki ni it- 6. norikae- 7. harae-

V   A. 3 B. 1

Lesson 26

I   1. Hai, sō iimashita. 2. 18-nin desu. 3. 20-bu kopī shite arimasu. 4. Hai, shitte imashita. 5. Iie, 4-ji niwa owaranai deshō. (Kōhī no ato de atarashii kikaku no setsumei ga aru hazu desu kara.)

II   1. ni, o 2. de 3. no, o 4. ga, no 5. ni, o

III 1. donna 2. doko 3. dō 4. nan-nin

IV 1. ama-, taberare- 2. keshi-, dekakete 3. wakaranakat-, kii- 4. at-, kiite 5. taisetsuna, shimatte 6. oite 7. hanashite

Lesson 27

I   1. Hokkaidō no keikaku desu. 2. Shomei undō o hajimemashita. 3. Iie, rūto o kaereba takusan ki o kiranakute mo dōro wa tsukuremasu. 4. Kankei-sha ni uttaete koyō to omotte imasu. 5. Hai, sono tsumori desu.

II   1. mo 2. de, mo 3. kara, ga 4. demo

III 1. Doko 2. Dare 3. dō 4. dochira

IV 1. natte, hairi- 2. misete 3. naoshite 4. kaere-, kiranaku- 5. non-, naori- 6. okanaide

Lesson 28

I 1. Edo-jidai no tatemono ga atsumerarete iru tokoro desu. 2. 200-nen gurai maeni taterareta ie desu. 3. Iie, nōmin no ie yori zutto ōkii desu. 4. Daimyō ga toriagemashita. 5. Hai, sō omoimasu./Iie, sō omoimasen.

II 1. ni 2. de, to 3. ni, o 4. o, ni 5. ni, ni/e

III 1. Dōshite 2. Doko 3. itsu 4. dō iu

IV 1. kikareru 2. shōkai sareru 3. tanomareru 4. nakareru 5. kowasareru 6. azukerareru 7. tsurete korareru 8. shiraberareru 9. okonawareru

V 1. mōshikomare- 2. torare- 3. omowarete 4. yamerarete 5. shiraberare- 6. azukerare-

Lesson 29

I 1. Katō-san ga Suzuki-san/-kun ni tsukuraseta mono desu. 2. Iie, Suzuki-san/-kun ni shirabesasemashita. 3. Tsukutta toki no jijō ga fukuzatsuna node, wakarinikui no desu. 4. Yokohama shisha ni itte, keiyaku-sho ni tsuite setsumei shimasu.

II 1. de, ni 2. o 3. no, de 4. o, ni, ni

III 1. sagasaseru 2. kakaseru 3. tabesaseru 4. nomaseru 5. tetsudawaseru 6. todokesaseru 7. yamesaseru 8. mottekosaseru 9. shigoto o saseru

IV 1. sase- 2. ikasenaide 3. matasete 4. kaerase- 5. shirabesase- 6. kangaesasete 7. mottekosasete

V A. 1 B. 2

Lesson 30

I First paragraph: de, hirakare, ni, Sore, Izen, toki, no demo, ijō, kara, hodo, yō ni
Second paragraph: tomonatte, daibu, ga, higaeri, koto
Third paragraph: yotte, hanarete, kanari, naru, kara, ōzei, Hisashiburi, ni
Fourth paragraph: sonogo, soshite, nobi, ni

II 1. hanaseru 2. kiite 3. arukeru 4. notte 5. shukkin shite, shukkin shi- 6. funin suru

Lesson 31

I 1. Iie, Watanabe-san ni dashite moraimashita. 2. Mazu Hayashi-san ga kaite, sore o Jonson-san ga hon'yaku shimashita. 3. Hai, 200-mei yori ōi desu. 4. Hoteru no hito to atte, saishū no uchiawase o shimasu.

II 1. ni/kara, o 2. o, to 3. o 4. kara, ga 5. o, ga

III 1. donata 2. Itsu 3. Donata 4. dō

IV 1. shōtai shite 2. katazukeru, tetsudatte 3. naoshite 4. irete 5. hakonde, tetsudatte 6. todoite

V A. 3 B. 1

Lesson 32

I 1. Suzuki-san no uchi kara denwa o kakete imasu. 2. Terebi ga yoku utsuranakute komatte imasu. 3. 6-kai-date de, fune mitaina katachi desu. 4. Hai, sō omotte imasu.

II 1. ni, to, ni 2. o, ni 3. ni, no, ga 4. ni

III 1. dono 2. Dō 3. nan-ji 4. Dōshite/Naze

IV 1. furanakute 2. kesanai, nete 3. tashikame-, shite 4. migaite 5. mitsukaranakute 6. abinai

Lesson 33

I 1. Katō-san no kazoku ga Sumisu-san no uchi ni manekaremashita. 2. Iie, okurimasen deshita. 3. Katō-san no uchi no niwa de dekita mono desu. 4. 2, 3-nichi tatsu to oishiku naru to itte imasu. 5. Mina-sama ni yoroshiku osshatte kudasai no hō ga teineina iikata desu.

II 1. de 2. no, ga 3. mo, ga 4. -ba, ga, ni

III 1. nani 2. nanji 3. dochira/doko 4. Donata

IV   1. yame 2. meshiagatte 3. mochi- 4. erabi 5. tsuki, tsukare 6. kangae 7. irasshatta 8. itashi-
V   A. 1 B. 3 C. 1

Lesson 34

I   1. 6-ji 10-pun ni machiawaseru yakusoku o shimashita. 2. Jonson-san ga motte imashita. 3.
     Hai, sō omotte imasu. 4. Iie, Keiko-san wa Nakamura-san-tachi to issho ni matte imasen.
     Keiko-san wa kaijō de matte imasu.
II   1. o, to, ni 2. mo, de 3. to, ga 4. ni, ni 5. no 6. te
III 1. ainiku 2. ittai 3. dekiru dake 4. metta ni 5. nakanaka
IV   1. moratta, nakushite 2. tsumetai, oyoide 3. wakaru 4. hetana, utatte 5. shōtai sarete inai 6.
     tabeyō 7. kaerō
V   A. 2 B. 3

Lesson 35

I   1. Hai, atta koto ga arimasu. 2. 4-gatsu kara Tōkyō honsha de hataraku koto ni
     narimashita. 3. Dezain kankei no shigoto o hajimeru koto ni shimashita. 4. Hai, shitte im-
     ashita. 5. Hai. Rondon no jimusho kara Tōkyō ni tenkin shite kimashita.
II   1. ga, o 2. no, o 3. de, ni 4. ni, de
III 1. nani 2. Dare 3. dō
IV   1. sashiageru 2. tōrenai 3. hirakareru 4. ikaseru 5. hon'yaku shite kureru 6. ukeru
V   A. 1 B. 2

Lesson 36

I   1. Hai, dokoka ni itte imashita. 2. Shiryō o soroete oku yō ni iwaremashita. 3. Iie, teineina
     kotoba de hanashite imasen. 4. Oshaberi o shi ni kita to omoimasu.
II   1. ga, no 2. ni, ni 3. o, ni 4. ga, ka, ni 5. kara, ga 6. ni, na, o
III 1. Itsu 2. Donna 3. Doko 4. Dō 5. nan
IV   1. aketa 2. iwareta 3. yasunde iru 4. notta 5. awanai, ōkiku 6. omou
V   1. mottekoi 2. nakusu na 3. mamore 4. mottekite kure
VI   A. 2 B. 1

Lesson 37

I   1. Hai, muzukashii to omotte imasu. 2. Amai mono ga suki de yoku tabemasu kara,
     yasemasen. 2. Futoranai yō ni Nihon ryōri o tabete imasu. 4. Hai, izen mo yama ni nobotte
     imashita.
II   1. kara, made 2. ni, ni 3. no 4. to 5. o, no 6. ni, ni
III 1. zutto 2. tama ni 3. moppara 4. narubeku
IV   1. manabu 2. Kowasanai 3. suwatte, mieru 4. naru 5. nai
V   1. tsukurareta 2. ikaremashita 3. koraremasu 4. azukeraremasu, motteikaremasu 5. set-
     sumei sareru

Lesson 38

I   1. Iie, mada hajimatte imasen deshita. 2. Hai, hito ga ōzei kite imashita. 3. Hai, sō itte im-
     asu. 4. Iie, issho ni ikimasen deshita. 5. Disuko ni ikō to hanashite imasu.
II   1. o 2. ni, no 3. ga 4. ga 5. no
III 1. Nani 2. Itsu 3. Dare 4. Donna
IV   1. yomi-, yonde iru, matte 2. osoku natte, deta 3. me o toshite, dekakeru, oite 4. tsukutte
     iru, tetsudatte
V   1. A: Asoko ni iru no wa Kimura-san dewa arimasen ka?/B. Sō desu ne. Kimura-san desu.
     Issho ni iru no wa Yamada-san ni chigai arimasen./A. Futari o sasotte doko ka ni ikimasen
     ka./B. Demo jama shinai hō ga ii desu yo. Futari wa kekkon suru rashii desu kara.

Lesson 39

I 1. Amerika ya Yōroppa no bijutsu-kan kara hakobarete kita mono desu. 2. Nihon-jin desu. 3. Iie, Tanaka-san wa sō wa omotte imasen. 4. Sono koro no Nihon wa ima hodo okane mo gijutsu mo nakatta kara desu. 5. Hai, sō omotte imasu.

II 1. yori 2. ni 3. o, ni 4. kara, de

III 1. sorede 2. marude 3. soko kara, sore made

IV 1. naranai 2. tsukareru 3. aenakute, zannen ni 4. wakaku 5. shizukana 6. wakaranai

V A. 3 B. 1 C. 3

Lesson 40

First paragraph: mada, shikashi, bakari de naku, de, to

Second paragraph: ya, Ippō, ni, omo ni, ga, sono, naru to, dandan, futsū, na, yō ni natta, yahari, ni, dake demo

Third paragraph: na, no, ga, Genzai, no uchi, natte iru

Fourth paragraph: Kono yō ni, o, ga, nado, okonawarete ita

四十課　江戸時代の教育

　江戸時代にはまだ統一的な学校教育制度は確立していなかった。しかし、各藩では藩の学校を作って、武術ばかりでなく、いろいろな学問を奨励した。十七世紀後半には全国で二百四十校あまりの藩校があったと言われる。

　この藩校では主に武士階級の子供たちに儒学や国学などを教えた。一方、町人の子供たちは寺子屋に通って勉強していた。それまでは主に学校の役割を寺院などがしていた。そして、その場所を寺子屋と呼んだのが、その名の起りである。江戸時代の中ごろになると、町人がだんだん経済力を持ち始め、寺院ばかりでなく、普通の家を使って、「読み書きそろばん」など実用的なことを教えるようになったが、これもやはり寺子屋と呼ばれた。十八世紀の中ごろには、江戸の町だけでも八百くらいの寺子屋があったと言われている。

　江戸時代の有名な学者の本居宣長（一七三〇－一八〇一）には弟子が大勢いた。現在わかっている四百八十人の弟子のうち、町人は百六十六人、農民は百四十四人、神官六十七人、武士五十八人、医者二十七人などとなっている。女性も二十二人いた。

　このように優れた学者を中心とする私塾が発達して、医学や地理学など自然科学の教育も行われていたのである。

中村　シンセサイザーって不思議な音がしますね。

けい子　あら、あそこにいるの、大介君じゃない。

チャン　そうだ、大介君だ。隣にいるのはガールフレンドの
まり子さんに違いない。

けい子　ねえ、コンサートが終わったら、みんなでどっかに
行かない。

ジョンソン　うん、大介君たちも誘って、みんなでディスコに行
こうよ。

みんな　賛成。

三十九課　浮世絵の里帰り

田中夫人　きのう上野の美術館へ行って浮世絵の里帰り展を見
て来ました。

ブラウン　アメリカやヨーロッパの美術館からいい物がたくさ
ん運ばれてきたようですね。

田中夫人　ええ、浮世絵は日本より外国のほうに有名なものが
あるそうです。明治時代の日本人がどんどん売って
しまったらしいです。

ブラウン　そのころの日本人には外国のものはみんなよく見え
て、日本のものはつまらなく見えたんでしょうか。

田中夫人　そうですね。江戸時代の鎖国の反動かもしれません。
でも、外国人の目には浮世絵は新鮮な驚きだったよ
うです。それでたくさんの浮世絵が日本から出てい
ったわけです。

ブラウン　日本のすばらしい伝統美術が外国へ行ってしまって
日本人は残念に思っていませんか。

田中夫人　そう思っている人は多いかもしれませんが、私はそ
うは思いません。きのう展覧会を見て感心しました。
みんなとてもよく保存されているんです。

ブラウン　浮世絵の美しさを認めて、関係者が大事にしてきた
んでしょうね。

田中夫人　そうですね。あのころは日本は今ほどお金も技術も
ありませんでしたから、よい状態で保存できたかど
うかわかりませんしね。

ブラウン　美しいものはすべて大切に保存してほしいですね。

田中夫人　ええ、後世の人のためにもね。

ブラウン　伝統美術はみんなの文化遺産というわけですね。

スミス　ぜんぜん効果が上がりません。私もこのごろかなり太ってきましたから食べ過ぎないように注意しています。

林　妻は甘いものが好きでよく食べますから、ちっともやせません。

スミス　先日、奥さんが作られたケーキをいただきましたが、とてもおいしかったですよ。

林　スミスさんの奥さんの日本料理もすばらしいですね。

スミス　このごろは太らないように、もっぱら日本料理を食べています。林さんは健康のために、何か運動を始められたと伺いましたが。

林　たいしたことではないんです。毎朝十五分くらいなわとびや体操をするようにしています。

スミス　今でも山に登られるんですか。

林　ええ、たまに登ります。運動を始めてから、よく眠れるようになりました。

三十八課　コンサート

チャン　プログラム買ってきますから、ちょっと待っててください。

けい子　ちょうど始まるところです。

中村　コンサートはもう始まっていますか。

けい子　あたしもたった今来たところよ。

ジョンソン　待たせちゃって、ごめん。

チャン　ほんとうにチャンさんのおかげだわ。

けい子　ほんとうにチャンさんのおかげだわ。

中村　よく切符が取れましたね。

チャン　わあ、久しぶりだなあ、こんなすごいコンサート。

ジョンソン　わあ、すごい人だなあ。けい子さん、ここ階段があるから気をつけて。

中村　よく切符が取れましたね。

チャン　わあ、久しぶりだなあ、こんなすごいコンサート。

ジョンソン　けい子さんの好きな歌手はどれ。

けい子　ほら、シンセサイザーの前で歌ってるあの人よ。よく聞いて。

ジョンソン　歌はうまいね。でも、まるで女みたいなかっこうをしてていやだなあ。

398

ジョンソン　こちらこそ、どうぞよろしく。

(2)　辞職

鈴木　山田さんが会社を辞めるんだって。

渡辺　ええ、前から辞めたがっていましたから。三月で辞めることにしたそうです。

鈴木　それで、これからどうするつもりだろう。

渡辺　勤めを辞めて、好きなデザイン関係の仕事を自分で始めるそうです。

三十六課　仕事をさぼるな

加藤　鈴木君、大事な書類を広げたままどこに行ってたんだ。君のいない間に、大阪支社から三度も電話があったよ。

鈴木　すみません。

加藤　もう一度書類に目を通して、メモに書いてある通りに必要な資料をそろえといてくれないか。

鈴木　いつまでにすればよろしいんでしょうか。

加藤　あしたの会議で使うから、今日中に頼むよ。

鈴木　はい、わかりました。

佐藤　鈴木君、ちょっと話があるんだけど。今日はずいぶん忙しそうだね。

鈴木　課長から今日中に資料をそろえろって言われてるので、やってしまわなければならないんだ。

佐藤　それじゃ、邪魔しないほうがいいね。

鈴木　仕事をさぼるなって、さっき言われたし。仕事が終わったら、君のところに行くよ。

佐藤　じゃ、待ってるよ。

三十七課　やせるために

林　スミスさん、ずっとジョギングを続けておられますか。

スミス　毎朝続けるのは、なかなか難しいですね。夜は遅くまで仕事がありますし、日曜日の朝はゴルフに行きますし…。

林　妻もやせるためにジョギングを始めたんですけど、

加藤夫人　二、三日たつと、もっと甘くなりますから、それから召し上がってください。では、どうぞ皆様によろしくおっしゃってください。

スミス夫人　はい。どうもご丁寧にお電話をありがとうございました。

三十四課　約束の時間に遅れる

中村　ジョンソンさん、遅いですね。待ち合わせの時間は六時十分でしょう。

チャン　ええ。もう六時半です。約束の時間を二十分も過ぎているのに、来ませんね。もう会場に行かないと、間に合いませんよ。

中村　そうですね。ほんとうにどうしたんでしょう。先に行きましょうか。けい子さんを待たせると悪いですから。

チャン　そうですね。いっしょに行かなくてもジョンソンさんは場所をよく知っていますし、切符も渡してありますから、大丈夫でしょう。

ジョンソン　どうも遅くなって申し訳ありません。出かけようとした時、電話がかかってきて…。それに来る途中デモに遭ってタクシーがなかなか進まなくて困りました。

チャン　いったいどうしたんだろうって、心配していたんですよ。

ジョンソン　ご心配かけて申し訳ありません。

中村　さあ、急ぎましょう。

三十五課

(1) 転勤

林　ジョンソンさん、こちらは今度東京本社に勤務することになった佐藤さんです。

佐藤　佐藤です。四月からこちらの営業部で働くことになりました。

ジョンソン　京都に出張に行った時、ちょっとお目にかかりましたね。

佐藤　ええ、覚えています。どうぞよろしくお願いします。

加藤　わかりました。
　これがメニューです。

三十二課　テレビの修理を頼む

鈴木夫人　もしもし、あのう、こちら鈴木と言いますが、きのうからうちのテレビがよく写らなくて困っています。ちょっと見に来てもらえませんか。

サービスセンター　場所はどの辺でしょうか。

鈴木夫人　六本木の交差点を渋谷に向かって二百メートルぐらい行くと右側に大きいスーパーマーケットがあります。そのスーパーの先を右に曲がるとすぐ左側に六階建ての白い建物があります。

サービスセンター　ああ、あの船みたいな形のマンションですね。

鈴木夫人　そこの四〇三号室です。今から来れますか。

サービスセンター　午前中はちょっと難しいですね。もう一つ修理の約束がありますから。

鈴木夫人　無理ですか。三時から出かけたいんですが。

サービスセンター　そうですか。じゃ、昼にセンターに戻らないで、直接伺うようにします。

鈴木夫人　大体何時ごろになりますか。

サービスセンター　一時すぎになると思います。

鈴木夫人　じゃ、外出せずに待っていますから、出来るだけ早くお願いします。

三十三課　お礼の電話

加藤夫人　もしもし、スミスさんでいらっしゃいますか。

スミス夫人　はい、スミスでございます。

加藤夫人　加藤でございますが、昨日はお招きいただきまして、ありがとうございました。

スミス夫人　こちらこそ、皆様に来ていただいて、とても楽しかったです。お送りするつもりでしたが、あいにく車の調子が悪くて、失礼いたしました。お疲れになりませんでしたか。

加藤夫人　いいえ。主人も子供たちもとても喜んでいました。ほんとうにありがとうございました。

スミス夫人　こちらこそ柿をたくさんいただきまして、ありがとうございました。お庭で立派なのが出来るんですね。

三十課　新幹線とサラリーマン

一九六四年に東京でオリンピックが開かれ、その年に東海道新幹線が開通しました。それまでは東京から大阪まで特急でも七時間以上かかりましたが、新幹線が出来てから、東京、大阪間を三時間ほどで行けるようになりました。

新幹線の開通に伴って、サラリーマンの出張の様子もだいぶ変りました。以前は東京から関西方面に出張する時は宿泊するのが普通でしたが、今は日帰りで出張することが出来るようになりました。

サラリーマンの中には、転勤を命じられ、事情によって家族と離れて生活している人がかなりいます。週末や休日になると、家族新幹線を利用して、赴任先からうちへ帰る単身赴任の人が大勢乗っています。久しぶりに家族に会えるのを楽しみにしているようです。

新幹線はその後九州方面、東北方面、そして新潟方面にも延び、各地の発展に大いに役立っています。

三十一課　記念パーティーの打ち合わせ

加藤　二十日の創立十周年記念パーティーについて確認をしたいと思います。まず招待状の件ですが、もう全部送ってくれましたか。

鈴木　はい。渡辺さんに出してもらいました。現在出席の返事が二百十名届いています。

加藤　それから、招待したお客様に差し上げる記念品はどうなっていますか。

鈴木　来週早々届くはずです。

加藤　社長のあいさつの原稿は出来ているでしょうね。

鈴木　はい。林部長にまず日本語で書いていただいて、それをジョンソンさんに翻訳してもらいました。最後に社長が目を通してくださいました。これがその原稿です。

加藤　会場の手配は問題ありませんか。

鈴木　出席の人数が決まったら、ホテルの人ともう一度会って、最終の打ち合わせをします。

加藤　料理のメニューは決まりしたか。

鈴木　料理のメニューは決まりました。担当の人を呼んで、林部長が決めてくださいました。

402

ガイド：二百年ぐらい前に作られました。

スミス：中に入ってみてもいいですか。

ガイド：どうぞ。ここは侍が住んでいた家です。

スミス：広くて立派ですね。

ガイド：あちらは農民の家です。

スミス：ええ、侍の家よりずっと小さいですね。

ガイド：大部分の農民は貧乏でした。作った米をほとんど大名に取り上げられて、農民はめったに米のご飯が食べられなかったと言われています。

スミス：この部屋は何に使われていたんですか。

ガイド：ここは居間です。いろりの回りで、ご飯を食べたり、話をしたり、仕事をしたりしていた部屋です。

スミス：冬は寒かったでしょうね。

ガイド：ええ、冬雪に降られると、ほんとうに大変だっただろうと思います。

スミス：今のような便利な時代に生まれてよかったですね。

二十九課　横浜支社からの問い合わせ

横浜支社：先週もらったN社との契約書に誤りがあると思うんですが。

加藤：そうですか。そんなはずはないと思いますが。あれはうちの鈴木に作らせたものです。さっそく本人に調べさせましょう。

加藤：鈴木くん、ちょっと来てください。

鈴木：はい、何でしょうか。

加藤：先週送った契約書の件で、横浜支社から問い合わせがあったんだけど、確かめてくれませんか。

鈴木：はい、わかりました。

加藤：もしもし先程の契約書の件ですが、鈴木に調べさせましたが、間違いはないと言っています。ただ、作った時の事情が複雑なので、わかりにくいかも知れませんね。

横浜支社：じゃ、だれか説明に来てくれませんか。

加藤：そうですね。じゃ、これから鈴木を行かせますが、いかがでしょうか。

渡辺　三時半ごろ持って来るように言いましょうか。

鈴木　三時半は早すぎます。四時ごろでいいでしょう。

渡辺　はい、わかりました。

二十七課　緑の署名運動

林夫人　あのう、お願いがあるんですが。

リンダ　何でしょう。まあ、署名運動ですか。

林夫人　ええ、北海道の山に観光道路を作るので、原生林の木をたくさん切るそうです。何千本も切るらしいんですよ。

リンダ　それはもったいないですねえ。

林夫人　ええ、それでその計画をやめてほしいと思って、署名運動を始めたんです。

リンダ　そうですか。地球上から緑が減っていくのは困りますね。自然保護と開発のバランスは難しいですねえ。

林夫人　ええ、でもルートを変えれば、たくさん木を切らなくても道路は作れるそうです。木を切ってしまったら、後で後悔しても遅すぎます。

リンダ　私もそう思います。

林夫人　関係者の人たちに自然の美しさと大切さをもっと自覚してほしいんです。来週グループの人たちと地元へ行って、関係者に訴えてくるつもりです。

リンダ　そうですか。緑の少ない都会の人のほうが熱心なようですね。私も木を切らないでほしいと思います。

林夫人　あしたうちでパーティーをしますから、友だちに話して、署名してもらいましょう。

リンダ　ええ、ぜひお願いします。

林夫人　でも外国人の署名でもいいんですか。

リンダ　かえっていいと思いますよ。外国人の声には耳を傾けるかもしれませんから。

二十八課　江戸村見物

ガイド　ここには江戸時代の建物が集められています。

スミス　江戸時代というのは何世紀ごろですか。

ガイド　十七世紀の初めから十九世紀の中ごろまでです。

スミス　この家はずいぶん古そうですが、いつごろ建てられたんですか。

スミス夫人（ふじん）
六百円（ろっぴゃくえん）にしましょう。
どうもありがとう。それから、このはし置（お）きもお願（ねが）いします。

店（みせ）の人（ひと）
じゃ、全部（ぜんぶ）で一万二千六百円（いちまんにせんろっぴゃくえん）になります。

二十五課（にじゅうごか）　不動産屋（ふどうさんや）

中村（なかむら）
この辺（へん）でうちを探（さが）しているんですが…。事務所（じむしょ）が移（い）転（てん）して、今（いま）のうちから遠（とお）くなってしまったんです。

不動産屋（ふどうさんや）
広（ひろ）さは、どのくらいのものがよろしいでしょうか。

中村
居間（いま）のほかに部屋（へや）が一（ひと）つあればいいんです。

不動産屋
これなんかいかがですか。ダイニングキッチンとほかに部屋（へや）が二（ふた）つ、一（ひと）つは和室（わしつ）です。

中村
犬（いぬ）を飼（か）ってもいいでしょうか。

不動産屋
大家（おおや）さんに電話（でんわ）して、犬を飼ってもいいかどうか聞（き）いてみましょう。よかったらこれから行（い）ってみませんか。

中村
あの、家賃（やちん）は。

不動産屋
一（いっ）か月（げつ）十一万円（じゅういちまんえん）ですが、初（はじ）めの月（つき）は家賃のほかに敷（しき）金（きん）、礼金（れいきん）として六（ろっ）か月分（げつぶん）必要（ひつよう）です。では、見（み）てから借（か）りるかどうか決（き）めたいと思（おも）います。

中村
そうですか。

二十六課（にじゅうろっか）　会議（かいぎ）の準備（じゅんび）

鈴木（すずき）
会議（かいぎ）は三時（さんじ）からですから、そろそろ机（つくえ）やいすを並（なら）べておいてください。

渡辺（わたなべ）
どんな形（かたち）に並（なら）べましょうか。

鈴木
まずスライドを見（み）てから、新（あたら）しい企画（きかく）の説明（せつめい）をしますから、コの字形（じがた）に並（なら）べてください。

渡辺
出席者（しゅっせきしゃ）は十八人（じゅうはちにん）ですね。

鈴木
はい。いすが足（た）りない時（とき）は隣（となり）の部屋（へや）のを使（つか）ったらどうですか。

渡辺
書類（しょるい）は人数分（にんずうぶん）コピーしてありますか。

鈴木
はい、二十部（にじゅうぶ）コピーしてあります。

渡辺
ところで、スライドの準備（じゅんび）はしてありますか。

鈴木
はい、さっき機械（きかい）を試（ため）して、セットしておきました。

渡辺
スライドを見終（みお）わったころコーヒーを出（だ）しますから、下（した）のコーヒーショップに注文（ちゅうもん）しておいてくれません

スタジオQ　一時すぎに戻るはずです。

チャン　じゃ、言づけをお願いします。六月二十八日の武道館のコンサートの切符三枚の代金をきのうそちらの銀行口座に振り込んだと伝えてください。それから、もう一枚切符がほしいんですが、あるかどうか聞いてください。

スタジオQ　はい、わかりました。

チャン　それから…とにかく店に戻ったら、こちらに電話するように言ってくれませんか。

スタジオQ　はい。そちらのお電話番号をどうぞ。

チャン　二九二ー三三六五にお願いします。これは直通電話です。

スタジオQ　はい、二九二ー三三六五ですね。中野が戻りましたら、すぐお電話するように伝えます。

さっき、チャンさんというお客さんから電話がありました。切符の代金は振り込んだそうですが、もう一枚切符があるかどうか聞いていたそうですが、あなたからの電話を待っていると言っていました。これが電話番号です。

二十四課　焼きものを買う

スミス夫人　あのお皿、いいですね。ほしいけれど高そうですね。

田中夫人　ちょっと待ってください。店の人に聞きますから。

スミス夫人　そうですか。やっぱりいい物は高いそうですね。

田中夫人　もう一枚のお皿はもっと高いそうです。

スミス夫人　三十万円ですって。有名な人の作品らしいです。

田中夫人　そうですか。

スミス　安くなるなら買おうかしら。

スミス夫人　これは千七百円ですが、交渉すれば安くなりそうですよ。一枚千五百円ぐらいのはないんでしょうか。

田中夫人　料理がおいしそうに見えますよ。六枚ほしいんですが、もう少し安くしてくださいませんか。

スミス夫人　すみません、これはいくらですか。

店の人　一枚千七百円です。いい品ですよ。この皿を使うと

スミス夫人　安くなるなら買おうかしら。

店の人　そうですねえ。じゃあ、お安くしましょう。一枚千

二十二課(にじゅうにか) 旅館(りょかん)のキャンセル

スミス　もしもし、東京(とうきょう)のスミスですが、先日(せんじつ)の予約(よやく)を取り消(け)したいんですが。

予約係(よやくがかり)　何日(なんにち)のご予約(よやく)でしょうか。

スミス　あしたです。台風(たいふう)のために飛行機(ひこうき)が欠航(けっこう)して、出発(しゅっぱつ)できないんです。

予約係(よやくがかり)　はあ。申し訳(もうしわけ)ありませんが、前日(ぜんじつ)のお取り消(と)しの場合(ばあい)はキャンセルチャージが五十(ごじゅう)パーセントかかりますが…。

スミス　五十(ごじゅう)パーセントも。私(わたし)の都合(つごう)ではないんですよ。台風(たい)で行けないんです。

予約係(よやくがかり)　はあ。誠(まこと)に申し訳(もうしわけ)ありません。ご事情(じじょう)はよくわかりますが、そういう決(き)まりなので、よろしくお願(ねが)いいたします。

スミス　そうですか。

予約係(よやくがかり)　お客様(きゃくさま)、後日(ごじつ)こちらにお泊(と)まりのご予定(よてい)はありませんか。

スミス　先(さき)に延(の)ばす場合(ばあい)はキャンセルチャージは払(はら)わなくてもいいですか。

予約係(よやくがかり)　はい、結構(けっこう)でございます。来週(らいしゅう)ならお部屋(へや)がござい

ます。

スミス　日本(にほん)にいたら行(い)くんですが、来週(らいしゅう)から海外出張(かいがいしゅっちょう)で、無理(むり)なんです。今(いま)決(き)めなければいけませんか。妻(つま)とも相談(そうだん)したいので…。

予約係(よやくがかり)　いつでも結構(けっこう)でございますので、なるべく早(はや)くご連絡(れんらく)ください。それから内金(うちきん)の一万八千円(いちまんはっせんえん)は届(とど)きましたか。四、五日前(ごにちまえ)に送りましたから、もう届(とど)いているはずですが。

スミス　わかりました。

予約係(よやくがかり)　はい、昨日(きくじつ)確(たし)かに受(う)けとりました。内金(うちきん)はお泊(と)まりの時(とき)の料金(りょうきん)からお引(ひ)きします。では、お電話(でんわ)をお待(ま)ちしています。

二十三課(にじゅうさんか) 伝言(でんごん)

スタジオQ　チケット予約(よやく)のスタジオQでございます。

チャン　あのう、チャンと言(い)いますが、中野(なかの)さんをお願(ねが)いします。

スタジオQ　中野(なかの)は外出中(がいしゅつちゅう)です。

チャン　何時(なんじ)ごろ帰(かえ)るかわかりますか。

度に春の花が見られるのです。これとは反対に、秋になると、紅葉前線は山の木々を赤や黄色に染めながら、北から南へ進んでいきます。

人々は春にはお花見、秋にはもみじ狩りなどをして、季節を楽しみます。

二十一課　会社訪問

ジョンソン　ビルの前にこんの背広を着た人がたくさん並んでいますが、あれは何をしているんですか。

加藤　ああ、今日は九月五日ですね。今日から学生の会社訪問が始まります。

ジョンソン　みんな若くて、大学生のような雰囲気ですが、服装はサラリーマンのようですね。

加藤　あの人たちは来年の春卒業する大学生ですよ。就職したい会社へ面接を受けに来たんですよ。

ジョンソン　今、一般的な傾向として、会社はどんな人物を求めているのですか。

加藤　十年ぐらい前までは「根性のある人」と言っていましたが、今は「個性的な人」を求めているそうですよ。

ジョンソン　そうですか。でも服装は制服のようで、ちっとも個性的じゃありませんね。ところで、学生のほうはどんな会社に入りたがっているんですか。

加藤　給料とか会社の将来性とか、やりがいのある仕事とか、人によって選ぶ基準はいろいろだと思いますよ。

ジョンソン　外資系の会社の評判はどうですか。

加藤　外資系の会社は女性の間で人気があるようです。

ジョンソン　なぜでしょう。われわれ外人男性がハンサムだからですか。あはは…。

加藤　あはは…。外資系の会社では能力があれば男性と平等に仕事のチャンスがあると言っている人もいますよ。

チャン　あれは何ですか。

大介　都立の図書館です。

チャン　都立の図書館ですか。都立の図書館は東京都民しか入れませんか。外国人も利用出来ますか。

大介　ええ、もちろんです。だれでも入れますよ。それにチャンさんは東京都民でしょう。あそこは自分で本を手に取って見られますから、とても利用しやすいですよ。

チャン　それはいいですね。ぼくはカードを見て選ぶのは苦手なんです。

大介　でもチャンさんは漢字が読めるでしょう。

チャン　ええ、意味はわかります。でも、ぼくは自分で本を見ながら選べる図書館が好きなんです。

大介　ちょっと不便な所にあるけど広いし静かだし、いいですよ。

チャン　本を借りたりコピーしたりすることも出来ますか。

大介　ええ、手続きをすれば借りられます。ぼくも今二冊借りています。辞書とか貴重な本とか、借りられないものもあるけれど。

チャン　新聞や雑誌も借りられますか。

大介　借りられないけど、コピーを頼めます。これからいっしょに行きませんか。二、三分で行けますよ。

二十課　桜前線

桜前線という言葉を聞いたことがありますか。日本の春を代表する花は何といっても桜でしょう。人々は春が近づくと、桜の咲く日を予測したり、友達とお花見に行く日を約束したりします。

ところで、日本は南から北へ長く伸びている島国です。九州、四国、本州、北海道ではずいぶん気温の差がありますから、桜の咲く日も少しずつ異なっています。九州の南部では、三月の末頃咲きますが、北海道では五月の初め頃咲きます。このように約四十日もかかって、日本列島を南から北へ花が咲いていく様子を線で表したものが桜前線です。桜前線のほかに梅前線やつつじ前線などの花前線もあります。梅は桜よりずっと早く九州を出発しますが、北海道に着くのは大体桜と同じ頃です。ですから、五月の上旬から中旬にかけて北海道へ旅行すれば、一

今日はきれいで気持ちがいい。近所の店もスーパーもみんな休みだった。あのラッシュアワーのサラリーマンや学生はどこに行ったのだろうか。

日本人の同僚や友達から年賀状が届いた。業者からも来た。やはり美しい。印刷のものが多いが、筆で書いたものもある。もらった年賀状はほとんど全部くじ付きである。

十八課　花を送る

ジョンソン　鈴木さん、ちょっと。

鈴木　何でしょう。

ジョンソン　日本の習慣を知らないので教えてくださいませんか。女の友達の誕生日に花をあげようと思うんですが、おかしくないですか。特別の女友達ではないんですが…。

鈴木　おかしくないですよ。大丈夫。ジョンソンさん、誕生日祝いのデートですか。いいですねえ。

ジョンソン　ううん、まあ。

ジョンソン　友だちに花を送ろうと思うんですが、お願い出来ますか。

花屋　はい。お届けですね。出来ます。何日のお届けでしょうか。

ジョンソン　あした届けてください。

花屋　かしこまりました。

ジョンソン　このばらはいくらですか。

花屋　一本二百五十円です。

ジョンソン　じゃ、これを二十本お願いします。誕生日のプレゼントにするつもりですから、このカードを付けて届けてくれませんか。

花屋　はい。お届け先は都内ですか。

ジョンソン　いいえ、横浜です。

花屋　送料が五百円かかりますが、よろしいですか。

ジョンソン　ええ。

花屋　では、こちらにお客様の、そしてこちらにお届け先のご住所、お電話番号、お名前をお書きください。

山川　何か問題はありませんか。あしたから工事を始めれば、来週中に出来上がります。もし問題がなければ早速始めたいと思います。年末になると業者も忙しくなりますから、早ければ早いほどいいと思うんですが…。

林　そうですねえ。すみませんが、始める前にもう一度会って相談したいんですが。

山林　わかりました。そちらのご都合がよければ、これから伺います。

林　出来ればそうしてください。私は八時ごろまで会社にいます。六時になると表の入口は閉まります。反対側に回ると裏口がありますから、そこから入ってください。裏口は十時まで開いています。

山林　わかりました。

川　じゃ、よろしくお願いします。

十七課　大みそかとお正月

十二月三十一日（水）　晴れのち曇り

今日は大みそかだ。隣の大野さんのうちでは、朝から家族全員で掃除をしていた。みんなで塀や車や、そして犬まで洗っていた。

午後は日本語で年賀状を書いたが、字が下手だから読みにくいだろう。夕方、田中さん一家とそばを食べに行った。夜は普段はあまり見ないテレビを見たが、東京のテレビのチャンネルが七つもあることを初めて知った。チャンネルを次々に変えると、騒がしいショーや侍の時代劇やジョン・ウェインの西部劇をやっていた。衛星中継でパリやホンコンの町を見ることも出来た。三チャンネルではベートーベンの「第九」を演奏していた。先日、中村さんが「毎年、十二月になると日本各地で『第九』を演奏するんですよ。」と言っていたが、おもしろい国だ。

一月一日（木）　晴れ

日本で新年を迎えた。町は人も車も少なくて、たいへん静かだ。工場も会社も休みなので、いつもは汚れている東京の空が、

411

スミス　じゃ、行司はジャッジの権限がないんですか。

田中　ええ、実は決定権はないんです。

スミス　そうですか。ちょっと納得できませんね。

田中　でも発言権はありますよ。

スミス　それを聞いて安心しました。

十五課　預かりもの

ブラウン　きのうスポーツクラブに行ったら山本さんに会いました。

渡辺　おとといここに来た山本さんですか。

ブラウン　ええ。

渡辺　山本さんが傘を忘れて帰りましたが、どうしましょうか。

ブラウン　私がその傘を預かりましょう。来週スポーツクラブへ行く時、持って行きますから。山本さんに会ったら渡します。もし会わなかったら、受付に預けます。

渡辺　お願いします。

受付　お早ようございます。

ブラウン　お早ようございます。山本太郎さんという人はもう来ていますか。ここの会員だと思います。

受付　会員の山本様ですね。山本様は今日は夕方六時にいらっしゃいます。

ブラウン　そうですか。山本さんの傘を預かっているんですが、六時に来るなら、今ここに預けてもいいですか。

受付　はい、どうぞ。

ブラウン　私はABCのブラウンと言います。彼が来たらこれを渡してください。

受付　はい、確かに。

十六課　早ければ早いほどいいです

山川　もしもし、林部長ですか。こちらはM設計事務所の山川ですが、ご依頼のショールームの設計が出来上がりました。さっきファックスで図面を送りましたが、いかがですか。

林　ええ、なかなかいいですね。

ジョンソン　えっ。みんなもらったんですか。

チャン　ギリチョコですよ、ギリチョコ。

ジョンソン　ギリチョコって何ですか。

チャン　義理のチョコレートです。日本のバレンタインデーの習慣です。職場でもよく女性から男性の上司や同僚にチョコレートをプレゼントします。

ジョンソン　「いつもお世話になっています。これからもよろしく。

　　マイケルへ

　　まゆみより」

チャン　残念でした。

ジョンソン　やっぱりギリチョコでした。

チャン　でも、ギリチョコをたくさんもらった人はどうするんでしょうか。

ジョンソン　たぶん奥さんやガールフレンドが食べるんでしょう。

チャン　じゃ、喜ぶ人は女性と菓子屋ですね。

ジョンソン　もらった男性も楽しいですよ。

十四課　行司の権限

スミス　わあ、すごい人ですね。

田中　相撲の初日はいつも満員です。人がたくさんいて、リンダさんや奥さんがよく見えませんね。

スミス　あ、あそこにいました。ほら、相撲を見ながら焼きとりを食べているのが見えますよ。

田中　さあ、私たちもあそこへ行って、ビールでも飲みながら座って見ましょう。

スミス　ええ、でもこの取り組みが終るまでここでいいです。うるさくてアナウンスがよく聞こえませんが、土俵の上にいるのは。

田中　富士嶺と桜龍です。

スミス　派手な着物を着て、土俵の上で動き回っているのはどういう人ですか。

田中　あれは行司です。

スミス　ああ、ジャッジですね。

田中　ええ、でもそれは建前です。黒い着物を着て、土俵の回りに座っているのが審判委員で、本当のジャッジです。あの人たちは力士のOBで、偉いんですよ。

十二課　旅館の予約

予約係り　みやこ旅館でございます。

スミス　もしもし、来月の四日と五日に予約をお願いしたいんですが、部屋は空いていますか。

予約係り　はい、ございます。何名様ですか。

スミス　二人です。いくらですか。

予約係り　一泊二食付きで、お一人一万八千円でございます。税金とサービス料は別でございます。

スミス　はい、じゃ、それでお願いします。

予約係り　お名前とお電話番号をどうぞ。

スミス　スミスと言います。電話番号は東京〇三―四〇五―三六三六です。そちらは京都の駅から近いですか。

予約係り　駅から車で十分ぐらいです。駅に着いた時、電話をしますから、そちらから迎えに来てくれませんか。

スミス　はい、かしこまりました。ご到着は何時ごろですか。

予約係り　四時ごろです。

スミス　はい、わかりました。八時より遅くなる場合は、必ずご連絡ください。

スミス　はい。それで、料金はいつ払いましょうか。

予約係り　恐れ入りますが、内金として一万八千円ご郵送ください。

スミス　わかりました。

十三課　ギリチョコって何ですか

チャン　ジョンソンさん、これ、渡辺さんからジョンソンさんへのプレゼントですよ。昨日ジョンソンさんがいなかったので、僕が預かりました。カードもあります。

ジョンソン　どうもありがとう。渡辺さんからの贈り物、うれしいですね。

チャン　中身はチョコレートでしょう。

ジョンソン　開けたんですか。

チャン　カードはラブレターかもしれませんよ。

ジョンソン　えっ、読んだんですか。

チャン　ははは…。実は僕も同じものをもらったんです。鈴木君も、もらっただろうと思いますよ。

414

十課　九州旅行

田中さん、お元気ですか。

私は今家族といっしょに九州に来ています。きのう、前から行きたかった阿蘇山に行きました。すばらしい眺めでした。

私たちが泊まっている旅館の庭で夕べほたるを見ました。前に東京の料亭でかごの中のほたるを見たことはありますが、自然のほたるは初めてです。農薬の使用をやめてから、川がきれいになって、ほたるが増えたと旅館の主人が言っていました。

あさって、私たちはここを出て、熊本市内を見物した後、長崎へ行きます。長崎は江戸時代の日本のたった一つの貿易港で、そのころは日本の中で一番国際的な町だったと雑誌で読んだことがあります。家内は日本の歴史に興味がありますから、とても楽しみにしています。

南九州にも行きたいと思いますが、来週木曜日にアメリカ本社から社長が来ますから、それまでに東京に帰らなければなりません。

奥様にもどうぞよろしくお伝えください。

七月三十日

ジョン・ブラウン

十一課　面接

林　（履歴書を見ながら）中村さんはおととし大学を卒業したんですか。

中　はい。卒業してから商社に勤めていました。

林　私の専門の仕事が出来ませんでしたから、おもしろくなかったんです。

中　なぜ辞めたんですか。

林　どうしてこの会社を選んだんですか。

中　こちらではコンピューターを使う仕事が多いと聞いたからです。私は大学でコンピューターサイエンスを勉強していました。この会社では私の好きな仕事が出来ると思ったんです。

林　会社に入ってから一か月研修しなければならないことを知っていますか。

中　ええ、知っています。それに外国に出張することも多いですよ。

林　はい、大丈夫です。

中　そうですか。では結果は後で連絡します。

村　そうですか。

415

チャン　日本は人が多いですからね。ラッシュのない所へ行きたいですねえ。

加藤　ラッシュのない所がありますよ。

チャン　どこですか。

加藤　どこだと思いますか。お盆のころの東京ですよ。人も車も少ないし、通勤ラッシュもないし、いいですよ。

チャン　なるほど。

九課　予備校

けい子　あら、ジョンソンさん。

ジョンソン　あ、けい子さん、お出かけですか。

けい子　ええ、これから出かけなければなりません。

ジョンソン　今すぐ出なくてはいけませんか。

けい子　ごめんなさい。今日中に予備校の申し込みをしなければなりませんから。

ジョンソン　けい子さんは大学に合格したと聞きましたが。

けい子　ええ、第二志望の大学には合格しましたが、第一志望の国立大学は不合格でした。来年また受験します。

ジョンソン　そうですか。じゃ、行ってらっしゃい。

けい子　行ってまいります。

けい子　申し込みの書類はこれでいいですか。これ、入学金と三か月分の授業料です。それからサマーコースも申し込みたいと思いますが、よく考えてから後で郵便で申し込んではいけませんか。

窓口の人　ええ、郵便でもいいです。支払いもわざわざここまで来なくてもいいですよ。銀行に振り込んでください。

けい子　現金書留でもいいですか。

窓口の人　はい、どちらでも結構です。

416

七課　空港へ迎えに行く

加藤： あしたはジョンソンさんが日本に来る日ですね。

鈴木： ええ、そうです。

加藤： だれか成田空港まで迎えに行ってくれませんか。

鈴木： 私が行きます。時間がありますから。

加藤： 今朝頼んだ仕事は今日中に終わりますか。

鈴木： はい、出来ます。

加藤： じゃ、お願いします。ところで、ジョンソンさんを知っていますか。

鈴木： ロンドンの事務所にいた人ですね。

加藤： ええ。

鈴木： 写真で見たことがあります。

加藤： 成田空港に着く時間は十四時五十分です。飛行機は早く着くこともありますから、早めに昼食を済ませて出発してください。

鈴木： はい。ジョンソンさんの泊まるホテルはどこですか。

加藤： 渡辺さんが知っていますから、渡辺さんに聞いてください。

鈴木： はい。

八課　お盆

チャン： 八月の十日ごろ仙台へ遊びに行きたいと思いますが、新幹線と飛行機とどちらが便利ですか。

加藤： 新幹線のほうが便利だと思いますよ。でも新幹線の指定券はもうないと思いますよ。飛行機の切符もたぶん売り切れでしょう。

チャン： どうしてですか。

加藤： 八月の中ごろはお盆で、くにへ帰る人が大勢います。十日ごろから、この帰省ラッシュが始まりますから、旅行は止めたほうがいいですよ。鈴木君も十日に仙台の家に帰ると聞きましたが…。彼は一か月前に切符を買ったと言っていました。

チャン： ええ、そうですか。じゃ、仙台まで車でどのぐらいかかりますか。

加藤： お盆のシーズンは十時間以上かかると思いますよ。鈴木君は去年は車で行きましたが、すごい渋滞だったと言っていました。それに、お盆の後は東京へ帰る車で道が込むでしょう。Uターンラッシュですよ。

五課　仕事の進め方

林：ワープロのカタログがたくさんありますね。

チャン：ええ、きのうセールスの人がくれました。来月からうちの課のワープロの機種を変えます。

林：どの機種にしますか。

チャン：A社の45Sが安くなりましたが…。でも、まだ決めていません。

林：システム部の小川さんに相談しましたか。

チャン：いいえ、まだ話していません。

林：ちょっとまずいですね。まず小川さんに話してください。

チャン：わかりました。

林：きっとシステム部の意向もわかりますよ。話がまとまってから、みんなに知らせてください。

チャン：はい、そうします。林さんはいつも関係者と相談してから決めますか。

林：そうですねえ。仕事の進め方に関してはたいてい相談してから決めますが、人事に関しては決めた後で発表します。

六課　早退

加藤：顔色がよくありませんね。風邪ですか。

チャン：ええ、おととい医者に行って薬をもらってきましたが、なかなかよくなりません。今朝は熱が三十八度ありました。

加藤：それじゃ、早くうちに帰って休んだほうがいいですよ。

チャン：でも、このプロジェクトが始まったばかりですから。

加藤：無理をしないほうがいいですよ。来週はもっと忙しくなりますから、今のうちに治したほうがいいですよ。

チャン：それでは申し訳ありませんが、鈴木君か木村君に後をよく頼んでから、帰ります。

加藤：鈴木君にはさっき別の用事を頼んだばかりですから、木村君のほうがいいですよ。

チャン：わかりました。では、お先に失礼します。

加藤：お大事に。

418

ブラウン　あのう、ちょっとお願いします。こちらのクラブに申し込みをする前に、中を見ることができますか。

クラブの人　はい。失礼ですが、どちら様でしょうか。

ブラウン　ブラウンです。

クラブの人　ああ、林さんのご紹介のブラウンさんですね。ご案内しましょう。

ブラウン　とても広くてきれいな所ですね。

クラブの人　こちらのテニスコートにはコーチもいますから、コーチに習うこともできます。こちらは温水プールで、一年中泳ぐことができます。

ブラウン　こちらではみんないろいろなマシーンを使っていますね。

クラブの人　ええ。どれでもお好きなものを使うことができますが、始める前にトレーナーにご相談ください。

クラブの人　いかがでしたか。

ブラウン　とても気に入りました。

クラブの人　では、こちらにお名前とご住所をお書きください。

ブラウン　ええ、そうします。

四課　出張

木村　ブラウンさん、出張ですか。

ブラウン　ええ、あしたから札幌支店に出張です。木村さんは北海道に行ったことがありますか。

木村　ええ、学生のころ一度北海道へ旅行に行ったことがあります。車で北海道を回りました。

ブラウン　札幌はどんな所ですか。

木村　札幌の町はにぎやかで、なかなかおもしろいですよ。ブラウンさんは初めてですか。

ブラウン　ええ、写真を見たことはありますが、行ったことはありません。

木村　一人で出張ですか。

ブラウン　加藤さんもいっしょです。二人で札幌市内の取引先を回ったり、銀行にあいさつに行ったりします。

木村　加藤さんは住んでいたことがありますから、札幌をよく知っていますよ。

ブラウン　そうですか。安心しました。

一課　通勤ラッシュ

チャン　今朝、初めて電車で会社に来ました。とても込んでいました。駅の人が乗客の背中を押して、中に押し込んでいました。すごかったですよ。

スミス　でも、電車の方が車より速いですよ。道も込んでいますから。

チャン　スミスさんは何で通勤していますか。

スミス　私は行きも帰りも地下鉄です。東京の交通機関の中で地下鉄が一番便利ですよ。

チャン　地下鉄は朝も夕方も込んでいますか。

スミス　ええ、でも夕方は朝ほど込んでいません。朝の八時半頃がピークですから、私は毎朝七時にうちを出ます。

チャン　その時間はすいていますか。

スミス　ええ、七時ごろは八時ごろよりすいていますよ。私は毎朝地下鉄の中で日本語を勉強しています。カセットテープを聞きながら、テキストを読んでいます。

チャン　へえ、そうですか。

二課　忘れ物

チャン　すみません。

駅員　はい、何でしょうか。

チャン　忘れ物をしました。

駅員　どの電車ですか。

チャン　二十分ぐらい前の電車で、後ろから二番目の車りょうです。

駅員　何を忘れましたか。

チャン　黒くて大きい紙の袋です。

駅員　中身は何ですか。くわしく説明してください。

チャン　マフラーとセーターです。マフラーはウールで、黒と白のしまの模様です。セーターは赤くて、胸に馬の模様があります。

駅員　今終点の駅に電話をかけて、問い合わせますから、ちょっと待ってください。

チャン　すみません。

駅員　ありました。ウールのマフラーと赤いセーターですね。東京駅の事務室に届いていますから、今日中に取りに行ってください。

HIRAGANA

KATAKANA

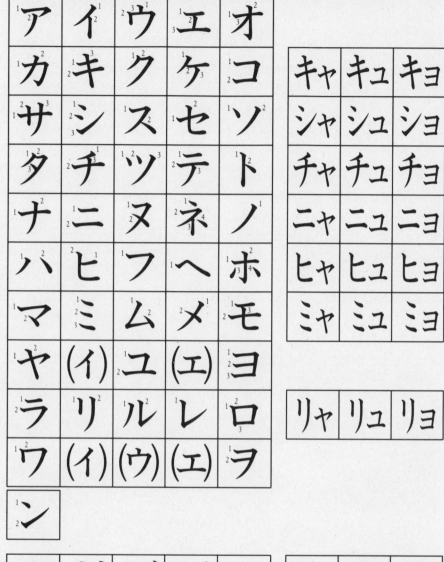

ア	イ	ウ	エ	オ
カ	キ	ク	ケ	コ
サ	シ	ス	セ	ソ
タ	チ	ツ	テ	ト
ナ	ニ	ヌ	ネ	ノ
ハ	ヒ	フ	ヘ	ホ
マ	ミ	ム	メ	モ
ヤ	(イ)	ユ	(エ)	ヨ
ラ	リ	ル	レ	ロ
ワ	(イ)	(ウ)	(エ)	ヲ
ン				

キャ	キュ	キョ
シャ	シュ	ショ
チャ	チュ	チョ
ニャ	ニュ	ニョ
ヒャ	ヒュ	ヒョ
ミャ	ミュ	ミョ

リャ	リュ	リョ

ガ	ギ	グ	ゲ	ゴ
ザ	ジ	ズ	ゼ	ゾ
ダ	ヂ	ヅ	デ	ド
バ	ビ	ブ	ベ	ボ
パ	ピ	プ	ペ	ポ

ギャ	ギュ	ギョ
ジャ	ジュ	ジョ

ビャ	ビュ	ビョ
ピャ	ピュ	ピョ